McCormick

My America

Other Books
by
LOUIS ADAMIC

*

THE HOUSE IN ANTIGUA
A Restoration

CRADLE OF LIFE
The Story of One Man's Beginning

GRANDSONS
A Story of American Lives

THE NATIVE'S RETURN
An American Immigrant Visits Yugoslavia and Discovers His Old Country

LAUGHING IN THE JUNGLE
An Autobiographical Narrative

DYNAMITE
The Story of Class Violence in America (1830–1934)

STRUGGLE
A Story of Terror Under King Alexander's Dictatorship (A Pamphlet)

LUCAS, KING OF BALUCAS
A Short Story (Limited to 300 copies)

YERNEY'S JUSTICE
A Novel Translated from the Slovenian of Ivan Cankar

*

MY
AMERICA

1928 — 1938

BY

LOUIS ADAMIC

Harper & Brothers Publishers

New York   1938   London

TO

John *and* Emily Fearhake

Contents

THE LONG ROAD

One of 130,000,000 Americas

EACH OF US LIVING IN THE UNITED STATES HAS HIS OWN AMERICA, THAT America is the aggregate, the sum-total of people, places, things, traditions, ideas, ideals, trends, institutions, conditions, and diverse other forces and factors in the country which, in one way or another, for this reason or that, have touched or influenced one's life and contributed to one's education—or confusion—as an American and as a person.

This book is an attempt to draw a partial picture of *my* America between 1928 and 1938—or between the twenty-ninth and thirty-ninth years of my life, the period during which I became an American writer—with occasional glimpses or references further back into my past and America's. I wish to emphasize: this is only a partial picture of my America. It is made up—mosaic-like—around a central theme—of things and people, chiefly people, within my experience and observation (from various angles, in various moods) during these last ten years in the United States that seem interesting or significant to me personally as an individual and as an American, and lend themselves to telling at this time. It is, thus, a very personal book.

I wrote this volume, in great part, for my own sake, as a matter of self-orientation in a complex country which is full of promises and dangers . . . and saying this, I want to quote an entry in my Diary in the spring of 1928:

March 24.—Yesterday was my birthday. I celebrated it by forgetting all about it. This morning, as I awoke, I found myself thinking: I am twenty-nine. But the fact didn't seem very important. I was amused it hadn't occurred to me yesterday, for I had seen the date on the calendar and written it several times during the day. I don't think I shall ever worry about getting older, no matter how long I may live. One is, one lives; that is enough, even if but for a while. Of course, one needs to be something, to be doing something, to spend oneself for something, aim toward something, contribute something to the general funds of humanity: more or less to fulfill oneself. So then, lying in bed for a few minutes after awaking, I wondered: was I going to be an American writer? Write books? Go to New York? Was it necessary for one to go to New York to become a writer? . . . Mencken has accepted two of my scripts [for *The American Mercury*], but my English, perhaps, is as yet none too adequate. Will it improve as, or if, I continue to write? Not being born to the English language is a handicap. What other disadvantages have I in becoming an American writer? I may have some advantages.

I want to write; perhaps I *must* write; however, not merely to write, to be a writer, to see my things in print, though egoism or "having something to say" doubtless is an element in my ambition. I want to write partly as a means or, at least, an aid, to my own thinking. For my own sake, mainly as a personal matter, I have much to think about, much to figure out, particularly much concerning America, which fascinates me; and I find that by writing, putting words, sentences, and paragraphs upon paper, I really learn what I think—or perhaps I should say that I learn what I really think—on the subject about which I am writing. Vague, confused, incomplete thoughts, ideas, hunches, bits of knowledge, and feelings become clear, more or less of a piece.

Basically, I suppose, I am a student who is his own teacher, a finder-out, one who is trying to get at the truth about things and making an effort to understand them in their various relations and juxtapositions, and to get a steady feeling about them and about himself among them. In the long run (assuming I develop as a writer), my writings will be, at least in part, self-imposed efforts to approach the truth of this or that for myself; and my readers, if any, will be looking over my shoulder, as it were, while I delve truthward for myself into things and try to understand them and try to acquire or maintain a steady feeling about them and about myself among them. I want to be, to do something, to spend myself for something, more or less to fulfill myself in that way, by being that kind of writer.

Hidden in the last paragraph is a great problem, which I suppose every serious writer must solve, or at least try to solve, for himself: the sooner the better. I have been conscious of it, off and on, for some time. Truth? Understanding? A steady feeling about the world in which one lives? How to achieve or approach them? . . . Of late my inclination is to the following belief or notion: To approach truth and understanding (to say nothing of achieving them) and, through them, to experience a more or less steady feeling, one must be free, intelligent, and essentially sound as a human being; one must possess a wide and deep consciousness, good instincts, intuition, a sense of humor, and a sense of drama. Perhaps even all these are not enough, but they may do as a beginning. I think, however, that the sense of drama is probably the most important. I believe that the drama of things is the truth of things. To say this in other words: the truth of a thing, condition, situation, or whatever it may be, is the essence of the interplay or interaction of all the factors therein, which is the drama thereof. I think that to the extent that one perceives the drama of a thing one perceives the truth of it. . . . To write truthwardly, then, is to write dramatically.

In 1932 I published a semi-autobiographical volume called *Laughing in the Jungle,* in which I tried to put upon paper some of the elements of my relationship with America till about 1927. America appeared to me then a vast socio-economic jungle, and my life in it "an adventure in understanding," as I phrased it; an adventure punctuated with bursts of laugher on my part, evoked by various phenomena in the jungle, and which were not necessarily funny or amusing. The laughter was, to an extent, a device to keep myself—an immigrant from Carniola, a country profoundly unlike the United States—from being scared while exploring the fascinating jungle and trying to understand it. Whistling in the dark. Were I to write that book today, it probably would be a good deal different from what I made it in 1931, when I finished it; for since that time both America and I have changed a bit, and things look somewhat unlike what they seemed to me then. In America more has transpired the last few years than had during the few decades immediately before. As for myself, I think I am a bit freer within myself than I was in the early 1930's. I am more conscious than I was then. My sense of drama possibly is no keener, but because of my greater consciousness the drama—the truth—I perceive has, I hope, more scope, is richer, more inclusive.

Mainly autobiographical, the present book is a sequel to *Laughing*, but independent of it, and rather different from it. It is also meant to be a companion volume to *The Native's Return*, in which I described my old country as I saw it when I visited it during 1932-33.

Here I continue my American adventure in understanding, my education as an American, which will go on, I dare say, as long as I breathe. As I have not attempted in *Laughing*, I do not attempt here to put America into a nutshell, to squeeze America into a tight definition, to hang America on some ism, to tie America to some rigid program. America is a continent, a thing-in-process, elemental, ever changing, calling for further exploration, for constant rethinking, for repeated self-orientation on the part of its citizens. It cannot be caught or imprisoned in words of finality.

I do think, though, that in this book I get a deal deeper and further into the drama, or truth, of America than I got in *Laughing*. I am no longer "scared" of the "jungle," and so I do not need to "laugh" as much as I used to. In fact, hardly at all. As I say, I am a bit freer; a bit less hesitant. As a result of my explorations in recent years, I know my way around a bit more, geographically and spiritually. Since 1931 I have traveled perhaps 100,000 miles in America, by train, by automobile, by plane, as well as afoot, pausing here and there to look and listen, to ask questions, to get "the feel of things"; and I have developed, I think, a fairly steady feeling about the vast place, which I hope the ensuing pages will at least partly convey to the reader.

LOUIS ADAMIC

March 23, 1938

My America

America is a tune. It must be sung together.

—Gerald Stanley Lee, *Crowds.*

America in Action

American life storms about us daily,
and is slow to find a tongue.

—EMERSON, *Letters and Social Aims.*

The Story of My Friend Cantrell

I WANT TO BEGIN WITH THE STORY OF MY FRIEND EDWARD ADAMS CANTRELL, which is not only his life story, but I think also a kind of intimate scenario of America in action, America deeply involved in the drama of her ways, good and evil. It offers, I believe, a close view of the country's basic, essential condition. Directly and indirectly, it has been influencing my view and thoughts of America—and me as an American citizen and writer—ever since he first told it to me, soon after our initial meeting in 1928, which I shall describe in due course.

Its core, as it will appear, is the core of this book.

The first Cantrell in America, one William Cantrell, came over with Captain John Smith, who mentions him in his writings. He was a son of a Huguenot family that had fled religious persecution in France and established itself in England in the sixteenth century. He settled on the James River, in Virginia, at a place still called Cantrell's Point. Seven Cantrells served in Washington's Army. . . . One Joseph Cantrell—Edward's great-great- (seven or eight times)-grandfather—lived in pre-Revolutionary Philadelphia. A branch of his family migrated into North Carolina, whence Cantrells moved West into Tennessee, where my friend's great-grandfather obtained a grant of land on the Collins River, near McMinnville. There his grandfather, Jabin Cantrell, and his father, Pinckney Cantrell, one of eight sons, were born. His paternal grandfather was a Hicks, kin to the founder of the Hicksite Quaker movement, and to the Pinckneys of Revolutionary fame.

Pinckney Cantrell was first married to Jane Rowland, daughter of Benjamin Rowland, owner of a mill near McMinnville, who gave to each of his several daughters a wedding gift of a thousand dollars in cash; and when Jane received hers she and Pinckney set out for Texas, then the Eldorado. There were no railroads in the West in those days. Taking a steamboat at Chattanooga, the young couple went *via* the Tennessee, the Ohio, and the Mississippi to the mouth of Red River, then up Red River to the head of navigation, thence overland to Fort Stockton, Texas. Pinckney Cantrell, a large man of great physical strength, was a blacksmith, and worked at the fort for years, shoeing cavalry horses and repairing wagons and other army equipment. Later he moved to Fort Smith, Arkansas, whence malaria drove him to the uplands of the Ozarks. He was at Fayetteville, Arkansas, at the outbreak of the Civil War.

In politics Pinckney was a Democrat, an admirer of Stephen A. Douglas, but anti-slavery and -secession, and never a man to hide his candle under a bushel. He voted for Lincoln, was mobbed, his house was burned, and he narrowly escaped death. He walked by night to Springfield, Missouri, then a

3

federal post, and sent for his family; but his wife and two daughters died soon after.

At the war's end he married Mrs. Jane Thompson, a war widow, who was of a Scotch-English family named Samuel, well known in Scotland from the twelfth century. To this second wife were born four girls and—in 1870—a boy, Edward.

"I grew up," he told me sixty years later (quoting him freely), "in the hills of South Missouri and North Arkansas, popularly known as the Ozarks. In my time, there were endless forests; in them, deer, wild .turkeys, and many kinds of small animals. I have seen millions of wild pigeons on wing, wave on wave, as far as the eye could see. The sound of their wings was like a strong wind in the trees. In their roosts a man couldn't hear himself shout. They disappeared suddenly, victims of man's lust for killing. I last saw them in 1884. . . . There were wild fruits, berries, nuts; and streams teemed with fish. There was free land for homesteading as late as the 'eighties—one of our last frontiers.

"The early settlers were Tennesseeans and Kentuckians, with a scattering of families from other states. With few and inadequate schools, and scant contacts with the outside world, they were backward folk. Old customs and ways persisted among them. But they were no kin to Gorki's people of 'the lower depths' or Victor Hugo's misérables. Unlike Gorki's and Hugo's characters, who were outcasts, misfits, rejected of society, the Ozark people of my time were— with few exceptions—a positive element, deeply social, honest, hospitable. They were the society, the vanguard of civilization moving into the western wilderness. They had character and values. The man who failed to keep his word, the woman who neglected to keep her house or children or her own person tidy, had no standing. The pioneer spirit of mutual aid prevailed. Quilting-bees among the women and log-rollings and house-raisings among the men were institutions. And no matter how poor they might be, they were 'independent as a hog on ice.' Relations among individuals were essentially on the basis of equality and fair play.

"My parents belonged to the Christian Church, sometimes called Campbellite. In those days there was sharp contention between Campbellites and Methodists—one immersed, while the other sprinkled. In our village was a family of which the man was a Methodist, but his wife a Campbellite. Their daughter wished to be baptized in her mother's faith, but her father threatened personal violence to any preacher who undertook to immerse her. The woman came to my father, crying. He told her to prepare for the baptism. When the time came, he stood with a shotgun on the bank of the creek. The girl was baptized; there was no interference. That was the finest example of 'faith militant' I have ever seen—the old Huguenot spirit on the American frontier.

"My father owned a mill and two hundred acres of land, was well off, and I don't remember a time when he was not helping some family in need or trouble. My mother and sisters were good cooks, Southern style, and our table seldom lacked an abundance of good things to eat—a fact that the neighbors gave frequent evidence of knowing. We often had a dozen or more casual guests for Sunday dinner.

"My mother was typically Scotch, silent, undemonstrative, but withal a woman of deep, intense feeling. Industrious, efficient, resourceful, she wove rag carpets, made hooked rugs and quilts, and turned corn-shucks into mats for various purposes. She extracted dyes from roots, nuts, berries, and tree bark. She embroidered. She scalded, scraped, and bleached the long runners of the buckbush, and wove them into baskets. She steamed, pressed, and plaited rye straw into braids, bleached them with sulphur fumes, and made hats which, with ribbon, bow, and feather, were as presentable as those any milliner could turn out. . . . And with all this, she found time to be a good neighbor. She spent nights serving as midwife, with no thought of compensation.

"There was no idleness in my boyhood. Up before daylight, we worked till dark. I took my place in the field and in the mill. Having access to tools, I developed skill in using them—and my hobby still is wood-carving and making furniture.

"On long winter evenings, father read aloud to us before the open fireplace. He could be interrupted at any time for discussion. Our books were the old pioneer classics: the King James Bible, *Pilgrim's Progress,* histories of the Reformation, American Revolution, and the Indian wars; a few scientific books, a large atlas. We borrowed and lended. From a young teacher, who afterwards became my brother-in-law, I borrowed a copy of Tennyson; from another, who wanted to become my brother-in-law, Byron. A one-volume edition of Shakespeare was the first book I ever bought. I memorized chapters of the Bible, passages from Shakespeare, and numerous poems.

"My father, usually amiable, could at times be stern as a Puritan witch-burner. Sundays I wanted to slip out of church with other boys and go fishing or swimming. But to my father such behavior was sinful, and he was inclined to help God punish the sinner. When I wanted to go to college (before I was of age), my father objected—colleges were hotbeds of infidelity. In our family discussions I had evinced evolutionary views I had picked up studying physical geography, and he declared if I went to college I would go to the devil before I was twenty-one. . . .

"I went to college, as I had gone fishing and swimming on Sunday . . . but determined not to go to the devil, I joined a Campbellite church, and soon began to study for the ministry. The first day in college, in Old Testament history, I was taught that 'before Adam's fall the serpent walked upright.' Later, in Semitics, another professor argued for miracles. I went to the president, an able scholar, and asked for a book that would give me the truth about Old Testament institutions. He looked at me, then said, 'Read W. Robertson Smith.' Smith gave me the anthropological slant on the primitive customs and beliefs which underlie Judaism and Christianity. He strengthened the idea which had occurred to me about then, that everything—life—was a process, a progression from one thing to the next, one change evolving out of the preceding one.

"I discovered Emerson: *Divinity School Address, Essay on Self-Reliance, The American Scholar.* He encouraged my tendency to question and examine everything, especially things about which there was most dogma.

"I became pastor of the largest congregation of my denomination in Chicago, and was considered launched on a 'brilliant career.' But I had trouble with my theology. I tried to make God out as something other than a primitive savage magnified to infinity. My church wouldn't have Him that way. I went to the Unitarian Church, where I enjoyed greater intellectual freedom. I spent a few summer vacations on the Chautauqua platform. But now I began to have trouble over my socio-economic views. I had come to feel that if it were divine to preach of mansions in the sky, it was at least humanly decent and sensible to talk of good homes on earth—especially for those who build them. My congregation wouldn't stand for that. Nor for my questioning the popular belief that private riches were always the result of thrift and sagacious ability. They were uneasy when I was a Populist, and became even more so when, under the influence of my reading and what I saw in industry and the slums, I turned Socialist. So I left the pulpit and accepted the job as national lecturer for the Socialist party."

That was in the late 1900's.

Cantrell was in his late thirties, tall, lean, handsome, with an agile sense of humor, an even temper, a passion for truth, a clear, persuasive voice, a simple social and platform manner, which made him liked wherever he came, whether people agreed with his ideas or not. He was happily married to a charming young woman, who came from the Kentucky branch of the old Massachusetts Adams family. She sympathized with his intellectual problems and decisions, which now abruptly tossed them into the swirl of the Socialist movement. They had a baby girl. But now Cantrell was threatened by a lung affliction, and on his doctor's urging he moved to California with his family. He settled in Los Angeles, but spent a few months yearly in other parts of the country as national lecturer.

Radicalism was then spreading over America. Debs was at his peak as a mass-rouser. There were other nationally prominent Socialists: John Spargo, as yet giving no hint of his subsequent transformation into a rabid reactionary; Morris Hillquit; Jack London, who had lately espoused the Revolution; Upton Sinclair, whose stockyard novel was upsetting the country's stomachs; and, to mention but one more, Job Harriman, of Los Angeles, who had run for Vice-President on the Debs ticket in 1900. Theodore Roosevelt, the trust-buster, was in the White House; and there were such other radical-progressive leaders as Hiram Johnson of California and La Follette of Wisconsin, all borrowing from Socialism. Muckraking was the literary vogue, and Lincoln Steffens, Ida Tarbell, Graham Phillips, and Ray Stannard Baker were estab-

lishing their journalistic reputations, while the magazines printing their exposés
—*Cosmopolitan, McClure's, Munsey's, Everybody's*—built great circulations
mainly on the strength of their radicalism. Gustavus Myers published his
History of the Great American Fortunes. The Socialist weekly, *Appeal to
Reason*, had over 500,000 subscribers. Clarence Darrow's career as "a defender
of the under dog" was at its apex. He had just freed Bill Haywood, who had
no doubt been implicated in the murder of a former governor of Colorado.
There were the I.W.W. and the militant miners in the West. In the East, John
Mitchell's star was rising over the grimy anthracite coal-fields, and Mother
Jones was "raising hell" in endless mine strikes.

Radical audiences were big everywhere, and Cantrell rapidly developed into
a popular lecturer. He did his most effective work, however, in California.

When he got to the Coast, there were a few fairly strong Socialist locals
in California, but in the state as a whole the movement lacked organization
and leadership, and not a few Socialists were deserting it and joining Hiram
Johnson's crusade against the Southern Pacific. In 1909, Cantrell met two other
Socialists as eager to do something about this as he was. They were Francis
Marshall Elliott, of a branch of the family of which Chief Justice Marshall was
the best-known issue, and F. B. Meriam, whose genealogy reached into pre-
Revolutionary times as far as Cantrell's. Both had become Socialists, roughly,
by the same process as Cantrell—not as a result of personal poverty, but
through seeing degradation among the masses and pondering what could be
done about it. Like Cantrell, they were Socialists not because Karl Marx wrote
a book, but because they were Americans, conscious of their American traditions and idealism, and felt that a collectivist order was "the next step" in
American progress. The three of them decided to take over what little Socialist organization there was in California, and encountered no opposition.

Elliott was a lawyer, in his forties, ill and bedfast, but his intellectual energy
and directing force were limitless. A student of sociology and economics, formerly an active Populist and Bryan Democrat, he had had practical experience in party politics. He was a great letter-writer (an admirer of Sam Adams),
did endless propaganda work by correspondence, and was perhaps largely
responsible for the general policy of what shortly became known as the "California Movement" within the Socialist party of America.

Meriam was fifty, a rancher, also a lawyer, with years of executive and
routine office experience in fruit-growers' coöperatives, capable of handling
masses of detail while keeping in mind the general policy. He became state
secretary of the Socialist party of California and, turning his ranch over to
other hands and giving up his law practice almost entirely, took charge of the
state headquarters, which for strategic purposes were transferred from Oakland
to Los Angeles.

Cantrell was state organizer.

These three men—personally congenial, undebauched by the spirit of com-
mercialism, free of individual ambition, and instinctively trusting one another

—were capable of perfect teamwork. Their attitudes and responses were similar. The ideas they shared had been previously advanced by obscure radicals in various parts of the country, but they were the first to try them on a big scale.

A movement, they argued, to be vital in the life of a people, must be a native, organic growth, must derive its inspiration and strength out of the soil and historical continuity of that people. Therefore, in America the Socialist movement could only be democratic, with democratic aims. It should not contemplate at any stage of the process, a "dictatorship of the proletariat," but aggressively—through education, which had been the chief basis for Jefferson's hopes for America—advance its cause with democratic methods.

The basic principles of Socialism—government control of economic activities, coöperation instead of competition, and equitable apportionment of the opportunities of life and the rewards of labor—were the same wherever there were Socialists; however, to make them effective in America, since they had been developed and articulated in Europe under conditions somewhat different from those existing in the United States, it was necessary, said Cantrell, Elliott, and Meriam, to adapt the presentation of them to American psychology, conditions, mass habits, traditions, and folk ideals; to garb them in American terms and idiom understandable to the American mind; to stand them up against the background of American history. How to do that? Socialist agitators needed to realize that the central element of American history was the push toward equality. This push began in the eighteenth century and, *via* the Revolutionary War, led to the penning of the Declaration of Independence and the gradual establishment of a not complete but substantial condition of equality in politics, administration of justice, religion, education, dress, social intercourse. The push continued through the first half of the nineteenth century, climaxing in the Civil War and the winning of at least theoretical equality for the Negro. All through the nineteenth century the push included also the struggle for industrial equality. In 1836, backed by public opinion, workers won the legal right to organize and strike, thus lifting themselves to a theoretically equal footing with the industrialists and financiers. The great economic interests, of course, whose power grew by leaps and bounds, continued to resist labor's aspiration for actual equality and the general public opinion favoring it; none the less, since the 'eighties, various states had enacted laws which clearly or implicitly recognized that labor was not a commodity but a human element, with all the right to claim anything demanded as its due by any other element. There was nothing more consistent in America during the last two centuries than this drive toward equality. The country had almost split over it. All important issues could be traced to it. And Socialist agitators should talk about it, tie Socialism to it, it to Socialism, and show that Socialism was a movement, an effort to equalize opportunity.

Cantrell, Elliott, and Meriam thought it probably was all right for German and Russian Socialists to attack their imperial governments, but had no doubt that it was wrong for American Socialists to attack the American form of government *per se.* They approved of its chief principles, which, having been promulgated by the Revolutionists of 1776, were superior even to the Constitution. True, the Colonies' rebellion against England and the formation of the Republic had not marked the complete break with the past which popular history assumed; but what lived in the American mind was, none the less, not the series of counterchecks Hamilton and Madison inserted into the Constitution, but rather the bold idealistic affirmations of Jefferson, the concepts of liberty, democracy, general welfare, and equality, which held genuine kinship with the spirit of all significant upheavals for human advance. It was upon these ideals the Fathers had sought to build a system of government. Now the thing to do, urged these three men in California, was to attack the current plutocratic laws and administration of the government, and demonstrate how its intrinsic democratic principles honestly and efficiently applied would correct the existing economic and social ills, and operate in harmony with, and influence and vitalize, the fundamental principles of the American Republic; and, in the next breath, to point out that Socialism was really a movement of freedom, equality, genuine democracy, in line with the best, most consistent American traditions.

Big industrialists were called steel, oil, soap "kings"; one was quoted to have said that "every business is a little kingdom"; and Cantrell, Elliott, and Meriam held that Socialist agitators should repeatedly ask the American people: are you in favor of the monarchical principle in industry?—and make it clear that when they opposed it they were carrying on the work of the Revolutionary Fathers who opposed it in politics. There was no point to hissing the word "capitalist" and denouncing capitalists personally; instead, Socialist agitation should make it plain to Americans that as it stood—democratic in politics and absolutist in industry—America was an incongruity. In politics no man could pass his power or influence to his son; if he desired it, the son had to work for it. In economics, however, the dynastic principle did operate, and Socialist agitators should point out that that was basically immoral, was unAmerican and bad all around, for it endowed a few persons with economic, social, and political superiority and imposed inferiority on the masses. It negated the principle of equality. And it was, moreover, contrary to life, which endowed no one with omnipotence from the outset, but merely equipped one with certain potential powers, characteristics, and abilities which the individual had to develop through effort and responsibility. The inheritor of great wealth usually had great power and exercised it effortlessly and irresponsibly. To protect himself against the democratic surge to equality, he corrupted politics; he endowed schools and influenced, usually for the worse, the processes and purposes of education; he joined or built a church and turned God to his support; he controlled the press and hired people who twisted the meanings of American ideals and traditions and obscured the American issues to the advantage of his ends; and, by virtue of his prominent position, he served as an example to many whose lives he touched, and thus, in diverse subtle ways was a factor in distorting human values. However, the thing to do was not to attack this dynastic person as such but to discuss this basic incongruity of the country as a whole, as a civilization; for it was this incongruity that was responsible for most of the evils and perversions in the life of the land. It was the source of all manner of contradictions, hidden conflicts, and violence in the country at large as well as in individuals. The situation must not be blamed on the rich alone, nor even mainly, but on the people of the country as a whole. It was up to them to deal with it, and soon—or they were apt to get caught in the maze of contradictions and distorted ideals and values, and lose their traditional way politically and socio-economically. It was up to Socialist teachers to educate the masses so they would function democratically constantly. . . .

All this, felt Cantrell, Elliott, and Meriam, was to be borne in mind by Socialist agitators and educators; but for the time being they were most emphatic that America was not Europe, certainly not imperial Germany or Russia. And on taking over the Socialist party of California they ignored the tactical code of Socialist fundamentalists, formulated by European psychology and conditions, and worked out tactics of their own, calculated to meet in a practical way American conditions, problems, and mentality. They distinguished between principles and tactics, between the end to be achieved and the procedure to attain it. They believed that the failure of the national movement to do this was one of the serious handicaps of Socialism in America. They insisted on making full use of American traditions and other cultural elements. Where Lincoln and Marx had said the same thing, they quoted Lincoln instead of Marx. Cantrell maintains that every Marxian concept is to be found in Lincoln's speeches, as for instance when Lincoln said:

"No good thing has been or can be enjoyed by us without first having cost labor. And inasmuch as all good things have been produced by labor, it follows that such things of right belong to those whose labor has produced them. But it has so happened in all ages of the world that some have labored and others, without labor, have enjoyed a large portion of the fruits. This is wrong and should not continue. To secure to each laborer the whole product of his labor, or as nearly as possible, is a worthy object of any government."

As secretary, Meriam had to contend with extreme elements in the party, but with tact and persuasion, being a calm, deliberate, objective man, with simple charm and vast reserves of energy and common sense, he managed to pursue his course in matters of agitation and organization. He refused to book in the state speakers who indulged in loose language before an audience, or who would go on a platform drunk. He liked his Scotch as well as anyone, but refused to support any man who, as he said, didn't think enough of the movement to keep himself sober on the job. He angered many Socialists by refusing to route Debs in California, during the campaign of 1910, for the reason that Debs, while a lovable fellow and a passionate Socialist, engaged in wild and whirling words. Most Socialists expected to put Socialism into effect tomorrow morning. Elliott, Cantrell, and Meriam knew that to make it eventually a factor in America meant a long, arduous grind. There were no short-cuts to anything worth while. They urged restraint, hard work, careful thinking, slow and systematic organization and education—education, education.

For the time being, they were eager not to have Socialist candidates elected to administrative offices. What could a Socialist mayor do in a city when the rest of the state and the country as a whole was in the hands of Republican and Democratic officeholders? They were not over-jubilant when, in 1910, J. Stitt Wilson was elected Socialist mayor of Berkeley. During the campaign Wilson had talked of the revolution he would effect in the affairs of the city. In office, his most revolutionary step was to issue an ukase to paint the municipal garbage-cans red.

Elliott, Meriam, and Cantrell saw the need of leadership. They did not consider themselves leaders, or even potential leaders. They were teachers, organizers, preparing the ground which might yield leaders. Cantrell conducted classes in economics all over California. He trained speakers, who were accorded respectful attention wherever Meriam sent them. Local newspapers gave them friendly front-page publicity. Cantrell became a close friend of old man Scripps, who owned nine newspapers in the state and many more elsewhere. Their columns were open to Cantrell and Socialism. Finally, Scripps adopted for his editorial pages a platform which was essentially Socialistic. Ordinary American folk—ranchers, business people, small-town doctors and lawyers—attended Socialist meetings along with workers, and, their former unfavorable impressions of Socialist agitators yet vivid in their minds, wondered if Cantrell, who still looked very much a minister, and his fellow agitators were typical Socialists. They opened their homes to them, placed wagons and horses at their disposal.

In two years—1909 and 1910—the Socialist party of California had 265 locals and branches with 10,000 active members and twenty times that many voting sympathizers. As already mentioned, Berkeley elected a Socialist mayor in the spring of 1910, and Socialist candidates received large votes in Oakland, Fresno, Stockton, San Diego, San Bernardino, and elsewhere. The Socialist political machine promised to become a decisive factor in the state within very few years.

During these two years of uninterrupted work, Meriam, Cantrell, and Elliott demonstrated not only the essential weakness of the national Socialist movement but also how to correct it. They had begun with a small, disgruntled membership. Hiram Johnson competed with them with a quasi-Socialistic platform. The state was preponderantly agricultural, there were no industrial cities to speak of, few railroads, and great distances between centers of population. And yet in two years they made California the fourth state in the union in point of membership. The three states ahead of them—Pennsylvania (pop. 7,665,111), New York (9,133,614), and Ohio (4,767,121)—had populations two, three, and four times greater than that of California (2,377,549). They were ahead of Illinois (5,638,591).

The success of this experiment in Socialist agitation was too sharp, too clear, even if only implied, criticism of the national movement for the national committeemen of the Socialist party and their organs to approve of it, but numerous local and state secretaries, as well as unofficial Socialists, began to evince keen interest in the Cantrell-Meriam-Elliott views and methods when, in the autumn of 1910, the Los Angeles *Times* Building was dynamited and twenty employees of the newspaper were killed.

(Here the story, which runs clear and liquid thus far, abruptly thickens with intense, incredible drama. Big names, fantastic and well-nigh elemental events, business greed, and labor violence leap into it. The fate of entire cities and large rural sections of California are at stake. The future of the American labor and Socialist movements hangs in the balance. The story turns into dynamite; and it is no wonder that for over twenty-five years now writers have permitted it to lie scattered in crumbling newspaper files and in the dimming memories of the aging persons who were involved in it when it occurred, or observed it at close range.

Two writers involved in it, Clarence Darrow and Lincoln Steffens, barely touched upon it in their respective autobiographies, written in recent years. Both suppressed their long-advertised passion for truth-the-whole-truth-and-nothing-but-the-truth when they came to the Los Angeles *Times* dynamiting affair. And I cannot say that my own account of the incident in the book *Dynamite*, published in 1931, is adequate. My publishers' lawyer blue-penciled whole pages of my manuscript before it went to the printer. Nor can I yet tell the full truth as I know it, because for some of the facts and theories pertaining to the episode documentary evidence is lacking or is being withheld, or the people whom they concern are still alive and telling all would harm or discomfit them, to no beneficial purpose. But here I feel impelled to go a bit further with the story than I went in *Dynamite*.)

One day early in 1910, at a class in economics at San Diego, Cantrell was expounding the difference between that which the workers produced and what they received in wages. All rents, interests, and profits, all the extravagant costs of government, the high salaries of executives, the incredible magnitude of certain private fortunes, the fantastic expenditures of the leisure class in what Veblen called its "conspicuous consumption"—all these, he said, represented the surplus product of labor. And that was not all. The organized and institutionalized lies of civilization, the frauds and wars of conquest and exploitation, were, in final analysis, arrangements and efforts to gain possession of this surplus. . . . And as Cantrell lectured thus, into the room strode two husky fellows, slightly drunk. They were San Francisco labor organizers; Cantrell knew one of them, and greeted them with a wave of his hand without interrupting his talk. They leaned against a wall and seemingly listened.

Suddenly one barked out, "Say, Professor, what the hell you think you're doin'?" Cantrell answered, quietly, "We're having a class in economics."— "Jesus H Christ, man," bellowed the San Francisco laborite, "you're wasting your time! What you need in this goddamn' country is courses in chemistry." He meant courses in the use of dynamite, and Cantrell knew it, but asked him, anyhow, "What do you mean?"—"Goddamn it, I mean chemistry. Didn't I say chemistry?" Disgusted and sneering, the two laborites stalked out.

The incident impressed itself on Cantrell's mind. His work brought him into contact with union leaders, from President Gompers of the A.F. of L. down to local union organizers. The best of them, including Gompers, had no comprehensive understanding of the economics of their own movement. Many were dynamic, rash men, fond of drink and big talk. They referred, on the one hand, to employers as the goddamn' so-and-so's; on the other, to workers as "stiffs," and were indifferent or antagonistic to the question of the need for organizing the tens of millions of as yet unorganized workers. The A.F. of L., with its two or three million members, was big enough for them. They couldn't safely manage a bigger organization. It was an organization of and for the favored workers who happened to be in it, and to the devil with everybody else! The A.F. of L. was not opposed to the wage system, which made labor a commodity to be bought and sold in the open market. Indeed, the leaders were for it and existed by it. Many were in the business of selling labor, and profited thereby. They drew fat salaries, wore silk shirts, derbies, gold watch-chains, rings on their fingers, stickpins in their ties. Secretly they received money from employers. Building-trades union officials were silent partners in paint, lumber, hardware, and general building-supply concerns, and the union members who got the best jobs were those who induced their employers to buy the largest quantities of material from those concerns. Labor leaders were go-getters, motivated essentially by the same psychology as the capitalists. They demanded high wages for labor and profit for themselves, and here and there—in San Francisco, for instance—managed to get both.

Cantrell spent some time investigating conditions in San Francisco, a unionist stronghold. Labor had been intrenched there even before the earthquake in 1906; following it, it became the dominant element in the city. Building-trades organizers, taking advantage of the chaotic situation following the quake and fire, had organized so effectively that now they controlled practically every construction job (and many other jobs) in San Francisco. To achieve this control, they had used strong-arm methods, including "chemistry."

Strong economically, San Francisco's organized labor, naturally, developed political potency. The unions were the most powerful element behind the corrupt administration of Mayor Schmitz during the years immediately after the earthquake. Labor leaders shared directly in the proceeds from vice and in the bribes that traction magnates paid the Schmitz gang for franchises. In

1909, after the Schmitz machine was discredited, the laborites put forth a candidate completely their own—P. H. ("Pinhead") McCarthy, president of the San Francisco Building Trades Council, "a blatant bulldozer," the San Francisco *Argonaut* described him, who conducted "the simplest negotiation with the exhibitions of physical and vocal energy adequate to the management of a twenty-mule team." Behind him was a "master mind," O. A. Tveitmoe, a dark Scandinavian of powerful build, who was secretary of the Building Trades Council, boss of the Labor party, and Sam Gompers' good friend and trusted henchman on the Coast. Around Tveitmoe were such fellows as Anton Johannsen, a native of Germany, and Tom Mooney, a young Irishman, blunt, thick-fisted, full-blooded men, trained in the rough school of labor leadership; tyrannical, loud-mouthed, direct, unreflective; not a few frank believers in dynamite. They loved Roosevelt's phrase about "the big stick." The idealistic Socialists called them "gorillas."

The unions were a thorn in the side of San Francisco business. Wages there were higher, and the workday shorter, than anywhere else on the Coast, and San Francisco industrialists found it difficult to compete with Seattle, Portland, San Diego, and particularly Los Angeles. San Francisco was losing especially in shipbuilding; even repair work under the system of competitive bidding went elsewhere. Not only did new capital fear to come to San Francisco, but old capital was drawing out.

On the other hand, Los Angeles was a booming open-shop town, its industrial history closely linked with an energetic personage, General Harrison Gray Otis, a union-hater, the publisher-editor of the Los Angeles *Times*. Son of a famous New England family, Otis had come to Southern California in the early 'eighties and, acquiring control of the *Times*, then a struggling sheet in a town of 12,000, developed "a tremendous and abiding faith in the future of Los Angeles." He was an aggressive man, bound to be noticed in a small city. An ex-soldier of two campaigns, he was full of the martial spirit; when prosperity came his way, he built himself a mansion and called it "The Bivouac," and he required the architect to give the fateful *Times* Building the suggestion of a medieval fortress with battlements and other challenging appurtenances. He became the generalissimo of Los Angeles' open-shop forces, a prophet of the so-called "American Plan" for industry. He often editorialized on "The American Way." During a strike, he mounted a small cannon on the hood of his automobile. In the *Times*, referring to organized workers, he used such terms as "sluggers," "union rowdies," "hired trouble-breeders," "gas-pipe ruffians," "strong-arm gang." He organized a union of business men opposed to labor unions, called the Merchants' and Manufacturers' Association, which employers were compelled to join if they wanted to operate in Los Angeles. He, naturally, acquired numerous enemies, and was personally disliked even by some of his closest business associates. Labor hated the ground he walked on. Union leaders referred to him by unprintable titles. Plain folks, reading his vituperative attacks on labor, wondered audibly why somebody didn't blow him up. Hiram Johnson called him "depraved, corrupt, crooked, putrescent." One generous woman, Mrs. Fremont Older, of San Francisco, said he was merely "an honest man who believes in the sacredness of property above all other things." Due mainly to Otis, the unions were extremely weak in Los Angeles, wages were low, working-hours long.

In San Francisco, when Mayor McCarthy got into office, in January, 1910, business and industry were ebbing away; but the organized employers, though seriously harassed by the unions, were, as yet, far from helpless. The industrial depression, blamed by them on the unions, seriously affected working conditions. Thousands of unionists were unemployed, and their number increased. They could not pay their union fees. So, early in 1910, the big men of San Francisco business and the Trades Union Council got together and concluded it would be mutually beneficial to employers and workers if the labor situation between San Francisco and Los Angeles were "equalized"—that is, if the San Francisco labor leaders went to Los Angeles and organized its workers, compelling employers there to pay labor as high wages as employers in San Francisco were forced to pay.

But how to organize Los Angeles with Otis there? The San Francisco laborites' first idea was to dynamite the Los Angeles *Times*. They "invaded" Los Angeles in May, 1910. The big-shots came—Tveitmoe, Johannsen, Andrew Gallagher, J. A. Kelley, Eric B. Morton, and John S. Nolen. Occasionally two other men, introducing themselves as Edward A. Miller and J. B. Brice, appeared in the same hotels with them. Miller's right name was Schmidt: a local San Francisco dynamiter. J. B. Brice was the *nom de guerre* of James B. McNamara, brother of John J. McNamara, secretary-treasurer of the International Association of Bridge and Structural Iron Workers, a powerful A.F. of L. union, with headquarters at Indianapolis. A Democrat in politics, a friend and admirer of Sam Gompers, and a devout Catholic, he had since 1905 dynamited scores of buildings erected by contractors employing non-union labor, and never been caught. The San Francisco "gorillas" felt the Los Angeles *Times* was an important job and wanted for it the best "chemists" in the movement, so they had asked John J. to "loan" them J. B.

Except when engaged in party field work, too far from Los Angeles to return home for week-ends, Cantrell was in the habit of having to lunch at his house on Saturdays up to a dozen comrades. His purpose was to provide an opportunity for informal discussion of their common problems in a friendly atmosphere.

One of the men who came to these Cantrell lunches rather regularly was the already mentioned one-time Socialist Vice-Presidential candidate, Job Harriman. A Hoosier, but long a resident of California, now in his late forties, he had been a tubercular half his life; was tall, slightly stooped, and emaciated-seeming, but really immensely energetic—a rousing spellbinder, an effective debater and trial lawyer; a quick, shrewd thinker, a born actor, and generally a most curious individual. . . . I met him briefly in California not long before he died, but I cannot say I knew him; however, in the course of my gathering material for *Dynamite* I discussed him with perhaps a score of people who had known him well for long periods of time. He was described to me as everything from a genius and Christlike figure to a crook and so-and-so.

Most of those who met him occasionally, or had only heard him speak, regarded him as one of the rarest men who ever lived. He had a thin, swarthy face under a shock of dark hair, but in moments of great animation, as when preaching Socialism, he was fascinating and handsome even in late middle-age. He had long, slender, eloquent hands and flashing steel-blue eyes, and, as one of his friends put it, "there was something magnetic about him." He was a particular friend of Morris Hillquit's.

Those, on the other hand, who had been most closely associated with him —excepting his wife, who worshiped him, but including his two law partners, both radicals and highly reputable men—had little to say in his favor. Some described him to me as being little short of a scoundrel, and offered me documentary proofs for their statements; others, as a clever schemer and actor who was able to fool all sorts of people for a long time. In their eyes he was possessed by a driving ambition, not wholly conscious perhaps, to become an historic figure of some sort; and was in great haste to realize that ambition. Gamaliel Bradford might have labeled him a "damaged soul."

Harriman no doubt was a sincere Socialist; but unquestionably, too, he used the Socialist movement as a stage on which to exhibit his forensic ability, and regarded it as a medium through which he might realize himself: for it must be remembered that at the turn of the century Socialism appeared to have a tremendous future in America. In this, Harriman was representative of many Socialist politicians. He was a member of the National Committee of the Socialist party, the best-known Socialist in Los Angeles, a frequent candidate for various offices.

Cantrell was "fooled" by him and they were almost friends. Harriman had a standing invitation to the Cantrell lunches, and felt free to bring comrades from other parts of the country who were visiting Los Angeles.

On Saturday, May 30, 1910, however, Harriman came with four men who were not Socialists but prominent San Francisco laborites, including Tveitmoe and Johannsen, who, Cantrell was informed, were here "organizing the campaign to capture Los Angeles for labor." One of the group, slightly intoxicated, voluble and expansive, insisted on making a speech. He told of a "stunt" they were going to "pull" on Otis, that would put that old (unquotable) in his place, unite most of the elements in the city against the open-shop forces, and make Los Angeles closed-shop in no time at all. He ridiculed political action and "this whole Socialist moonshine," and announced himself a believer in force.

Cantrell took the "gorilla's" remarks about the "stunt" as so much loose talk on the part of a man half drunk. He observed that the "gorillas" called

Harriman by his first name as though they were old friends, but—being the sort of man who, accepting an individual as a friend, believed in him thoroughly till he was absolutely forced to alter his opinion—it didn't occur to him that there was anything deep between them. Job, after all, was attorney for the Los Angeles unions and so was obliged to put up with these fellows. Cantrell could not even remotely suspect—as the Burns detectives revealed later—that Harriman had been staying at the Hotel Chapman with them and the professional "chemists"; nor that Harriman was soon to write letters to friends (uncovered years subsequently and still later put before me) in which he discussed the impending events in Los Angeles. Cantrell was glad when Harriman left earlier than was his custom, taking the "gorillas" with him.

The spring and summer passed, with no "stunt" occurring, and Cantrell's memory of the unpleasant lunch receded from his consciousness—till October 10th, when it suddenly came back.

On October 9th, Cantrell went to San Luis Obispo, a town midway between Los Angeles and San Francisco. It was election time in California, and he was the Socialist candidate for Secretary of State, with no chance of winning; scheduled to make a campaign speech that evening before an audience of townspeople and ranchers from the surrounding country, which, as usual, was not to be a campaign speech at all, but an educational lecture on Socialism. Arriving at San Luis Obispo, he met unexpectedly, in the hotel lobby as he was about to register, Job Harriman, the Socialist candidate for the United States Senate, who also had no chance of victory. Cantrell was surprised to see him, for Harriman was not scheduled to be there on that day. He seemed flustered, but gave no explanation of what he was doing in San Luis Obispo, and Cantrell, a tactful man, did not ask him. They took a room together.

In the evening Cantrell delivered his talk. Next morning Harriman rose early and went out. On his way to breakfast, Cantrell met Harriman below. The man was obviously laboring under great excitement. He seized Cantrell's arm and said, "By God! the *Times* Building's been dynamited and twenty people are reported killed!"

They went back to their room. Harriman locked the door and, throwing himself into a rocking-chair, burst into a fit of hysterical laughter. When he stopped laughing, Cantrell said, "What does this mean?" Harriman straightened up, tossed his long hair back from his forehead, and answered, "It means that the boys are on the job."—"Do you mean to say," asked Cantrell, "that some of the labor men have dynamited the *Times* Building?"—"That's what I mean," answered Harriman, adding he had known for some time the boys were on the job. He told Cantrell what lay behind it. A fight for the open shop had started in San Francisco; the Panama Exposition was coming on and the employers of the bay region insisted it be built with non-union labor. The "dynamiting operations" aimed to distract the attention of the capitalist interests from San Francisco, solidify the workers of Los Angeles, and rally them to the union idea.

Cantrell did not realize till much later that this was a deliberately muddled, superficial explanation of the dynamiting. As he listened to Harriman, the event momentarily slipped into the background and the "theory" of it stood out. It had a familiar ring. He recalled the "gorilla" in his San Diego class advocating "chemistry," and the talk at his house during the lunch on May 30th. Not dreaming that Harriman was connected either with the "job" or its theory, Cantrell began an objective argument against such tactics. They were criminal, stupid, suicidal, bound, in the long run, if not immediately, to turn all social classes against the unions. In any resort to individual violence, all power lay on the side of society—the police, the militia, the army and navy. What could a few individuals resorting to strong-arm methods do in the face of this social power? Harriman said, "Well, if the worse comes to worst, they will dynamite the new aqueduct, the water-mains and the gas-mains, and set the city on fire. They will make Los Angeles what San Francisco was after the earthquake and fire."—"Will they do that?" asked Cantrell.—"They will," averred Harriman.

Momentarily, Cantrell could think only of his family. He telegraphed to Mrs. Cantrell: "On the first indication of trouble in the streets take the baby, lock the house, and get out of town."

Why had Harriman come to San Luis Obispo on that day? Knowing the *Times* would be dynamited that night, he apparently wanted an alibi, in case— Also, perhaps, he had become frantic and, in that inner confusion, had jumped on a train and gotten off at San Luis Obispo, where he knew Cantrell was to make a speech.

Los Angeles was beside itself over the outrage. Otis, who had expected the building to be blown up eventually, had built an auxiliary plant two blocks from the now-wrecked structure, and the *Times* appeared with almost no delay. "UNIONIST BOMBS WRECK THE 'TIMES'"—and "O you anarchic scum, you cowardly murderers, you leeches upon honest labor," wrote the General editorially, "you midnight assassins . . ." He announced that laborites had dynamited his building and killed his loyal employees. Who else *could* do such a thing? Anyone daring to doubt him on this point was *ipso facto* a sympathizer of the "criminal unions," an enemy of "the American Plan," a traitor to the future greatness of Los Angeles. In San Francisco, on the other hand, anyone believing Otis was apt to get his face smashed.

Investigations by the police, the grand jury, a mayor's committee, the city council, and various civic bodies unanimously resulted in reports that the building—which had flamed up immediately after the explosion—had been dynamited and the gas set afire by the explosion.

Returning to Los Angeles, Harriman, as the unions' attorney, headed the investigation ordered by the Labor Council, and quickly pronounced that the plant had not been dynamited at all; indeed, all indications pointed to a gas explosion. To accuse union labor of such a crime was a crime in itself! . . .

Finally, the unionists charged Otis with being himself to blame for the tragedy. Was it not well known that there had been something wrong with the gas system? Had not employees been sickened by gas fumes for weeks? Was it not strange that only minor employees had been killed, that all the big officials and editors had been out of the building when the explosion occurred? They intimated that "the old scoundrel" possibly had had the place blown up himself, intending to put the blame on the unions and then to collect insurance on the old plant!

Accusations flew back and forth, but the public began to accept the gas-explosion theory and to blame the twenty deaths on Otis. It was true that for some while past employees in the printing department had been sickened by gas, but the public did not know—as it was later disclosed by detectives—that some three months previously a member of the group which engineered the blow-up had succeeded in getting a job on the *Times* and, during the period of his employment, caused leaks in the gas-pipes. Nor did the public know that Harriman (as he himself later unwittingly admitted under oath) was already spending money—for the purpose of building up the gas theory—out of a fund secretly known as "the McNamara defense fund," which presumably included the sum voted by a recent A.F. of L. convention as "a war fund for use in attacking the Los Angeles *Times*."

The dynamiting, of course, was front-page news the country over. Otis became a hero of the "American Plan" employers' associations. The labor and radical press raised a vast howl. In the *Appeal to Reason*, Debs expressed "my deliberate opinion that the *Times* and its crowd of union-haters are the instigators, if not the actual perpetrators, of that crime and the murder of twenty human beings." Gompers refused to comment on the blow-up. The mere suggestion that labor would do such a thing was absurd.

There is no doubt that the "gorillas" had intended to create a reign of terror in Los Angeles by blowing up sections of the waterworks and the gas-mains, for it was subsequently established that they had surreptitiously obtained from the city engineer's office complete maps of the piping system. Also, two years later, during the so-called dynamite-conspiracy trials in Indianapolis, testimony disclosed that the California terrorists had meant to blow up the new aqueduct and gas and water mains. But after the *Times* "job," only one more explosion occurred in Los Angeles, three months later, when dynamite wrecked the Llewellyn Iron Works, where men were on strike. The theory is that in the *Times* "stunt" the dynamiters had not intended to kill so many people, if any, and that the awfulness of the catastrophe caused them to abandon their other plans.

However, the "gorillas'" original plan to play havoc with the Los Angeles water system was no mere irrelevant hoodlumism or pointless criminality; it had political purpose, to understand which it is necessary to interrupt the tale of the "gorillas'" violent doings, and to look for a moment at the Los Angeles water problem, which interested and perturbed Cantrell from the time he established himself in California.

Early in the 1900's, Los Angeles had a population of 95,000. Its water supply was adequate for a city twice that size; to Otis and other big go-getters, however, that was a mere drop in the bucket. Boosters and patriots, wealth-and-power-eager "men of vision," keenly aware of the great advantage of climate, they were determined to give Los Angeles a push toward becoming the largest city in the world, which they perceived to be its ultimate destiny. They owned vast areas of land in and about the city; the *Times* was their megaphone; and so in 1902 or thereabouts they began to insist that if the city continued to grow at a great rate—and to doubt that was treason—the then available water supply would be insufficient within a decade. Los Angeles *must* think of its future population in millions and immediately increase its water resources.

Some 250 miles away, beneath the Sierras, near the Nevada border, in Inyo County, is an arid region called Owens Valley, and it was thither the Otis men turned their eyes, for through the valley flowed a river of melted snow from the mountains.

In 1903, the National Reclamation Service became suddenly interested in reclaiming the region. The ranchers were agreeably surprised. The Government apparently contemplated storing the flood waters for irrigation and distributing them to promote settlement and development. At last prosperity would come to Owens Valley! Some storage locations had previously been made by ranchers who, however, lacked the means to carry out their projects. These locations were now willingly surrendered at the Government's request, and every cooperation asked by the Reclamation Service was given by the Inyo County folk, some of whom were already deriving water for their land from sources that would be involved in the project. The Reclamation Service went through the motions of making extensive investigations, covering stream measurements, tests of soil, area of farming-lands, the duty of water in that climate, sites of proposed storage dams, and other details. All local circumstances favored the project, and Inyo County, although noting the slowness of definite announcement of action, entertained no doubt of the good faith of the United States Government.

In 1904, ex-Mayor Fred Eaton of Los Angeles, a leading Otis man, realtor, and advocate of the "American Plan," came to Owens Valley, accompanied by William Mulholland, chief engineer of the city water system, also a great and resourceful Otis man, and bought extensive areas of land. Eaton then deeded his purchases to the city of Los Angeles, and after the scheme was revealed the city itself openly and officially purchased some 70,000 acres, thereby gaining full control of the river's flow. And by and by it was also disclosed that an official of the National Reclamation Service in California had been hired by Otis men to manipulate the matter so the city would get the water, and had used his official federal position to defeat the reclamation enterprise after the settlers there had surrendered to the Government their water claims!

Meanwhile the people of Los Angeles were being urged by Otis men to vote for a large water-bond issue, to build a great aqueduct to bring the water to the city. But, unexpectedly, a considerable opposition developed to the bond issue; the people, having been asked to vote for all manner of bonds for years, were growing wary. Besides, influential enemies of the Otis group insisted it was unwise to bring water from Owens Valley; it was to be had much closer to the city.

But Otis men wanted the aqueduct and proposed to take no chances of having the bond issue defeated at the coming election. The City Water Board included Otis schemers; so, to convince the electorate that there was a water crisis, millions of gallons of the precious fluid were secretly released into the sewers, emptying most of the reservoirs in the near-by hills. People were forbidden to sprinkle their lawns and gardens. This artificially created drought lasted throughout the summer, all the lawns in the city turned brown, gardens withered, and the stench from the mud and dead fish drove many families from the vicinity of the empty reservoirs. . . . Thus convinced, the voters sanctioned the water bonds on election day—$22,500,000!

During the "drought" the city secured a temporary injunction, later made permanent, prohibiting the ranchers in San Fernando Valley, a choice section north of Los Angeles, to pump water on their land—and this on the basis of the ancient riparian rights held by the city on the San Fernando Valley watershed under an old Spanish grant. This action ruined the ranchers, who were compelled to sell their properties—to a syndicate of realtors organized for the purpose of acquiring the entire valley.

With the bond issue authorized, Mulholland immediately set out to build the aqueduct, and in less than two years built one as long as England is wide, passing through 142 tunnels and crossing a desert as large as the state of Massachusetts—one of the great engineering feats of that time. Los Angeles—or, rather, the far-seeing Otis men, aided by officials of the United States Government—took the water a naïve God had intended for the use of Owens Valley, and thereby ruined the region for agricultural purposes.

But if the aqueduct ruined Owens Valley, it "made" San Fernando Valley, now owned by the syndicate of forward-looking Otis men; for at the finish Mulholland brought the great new pipe line, not into Los Angeles, but into San Fernando, twenty-seven miles away—thus promptly trebling the values of the lands owned there by the Otis men, who in the next two decades cleared millions on their elegant San Fernando subdivisions.

This became known as the "San Fernando land grab," and Socialist speakers, including Harriman, but especially Cantrell, who had closely observed the whole deal, made it by the end of 1910 into a great political issue in Los Angeles—so great, in fact, that the people began to demand the aqueduct be brought to Los Angeles, and that the San Francisco "gorillas" wanted, until the *Times* horror changed their minds, to tie their cause to it.

The "gorillas" had an elaborate plan. They meant to dynamite the water and gas systems at various points, also to blow a big hole in the aqueduct near San Fernando, and then direct suspicion for these explosions on the outraged ranchers of Owens Valley, who, hating Los Angeles, had periodically been dynamiting the great aqueduct further up along its 250-mile length. This would keep the water and "the land grab" issues alive; people would be frightened; many would quit Los Angeles; tourists would cease coming, and head for San Diego instead; and by and by the Otis forces would be obliged to come to terms with them (the "gorillas") and cease fighting the unions. This, too, would be at least faintly analogous to the post-earthquake period in San Francisco, which had proved so favorable to organized labor in that city. As it was brought out during the so-called "dynamite trials" in Indianapolis two years later, the "gorillas" discussed this plan among themselves through most of 1910. Harriman was their willing tool in Los Angeles. He controlled the powerful central branch of the Socialist party there, which would nominate him for mayor; they (the "gorillas") would support him in the campaign with money, to say nothing of dynamite; he was sure to win; then he would swing to them the now secretly antagonistic Socialists of San Francisco—and then——

They calculated a little too rapidly. After the *Times* horror they did not carry out their entire terror program. Their cause became nevertheless closely linked with the water question and the "land grab"—only differently from what they had expected.

During the months immediately after the *Times* catastrophe, Cantrell kept busy as organizer and lecturer in various parts of California. He was deeply uneasy. Gas? Dynamite? Harriman? What, whom could one believe? He discussed the affair with Meriam, Elliott, and a few others among his close Socialist friends, who were equally disturbed about it; and, having as yet no hint of James B. McNamara, alias J. B. Price, they decided that some San Francisco "gorilla" or "gorillas" had planted the dynamite behind the building, where it exploded, jarred a gas-pipe, ignited the gas, which in turn exploded and wrecked the building and killed a score of people. They did not yet suspect Harriman of even indirect complicity in the outrage. Yet all three were worried. Even as only the unions' attorney, Harriman was too closely connected with the strong-arm element. As such, being a leading Socialist, he was apt to harm the movement; and so Meriam wrote him a letter to the effect that he must not try to make the Socialist party of California "the tail to the A.F. of L. kite." Thereafter Harriman avoided them.

Thus Cantrell and his friends were little prepared for the news of April 23, 1911: detective William J. Burns had arrested the McNamara brothers as being responsible not only for the Los Angeles, which was their worst, but for scores, if not hundreds, of other dynamitings, in which no one had been killed.

The McNamaras were brought to Los Angeles and they became the McNamara Case—the Case of Labor *vs.* Capitalism, of Humanity *vs.* Greed, in which well-nigh the whole country was suddenly involved.

Detective Burns—who, incidentally, was perhaps the most objectively truthful man in the whole drama—hinted that his case against the prisoners was holeproof, and he promptly displaced Otis as No. 1 hero of the "American Plan" forces. Later Theodore Roosevelt hailed him as one deserving the country's gratitude. It was hinted the crime involved many of the top leaders of the A.F. of L., including Gompers. But Gompers dubbed Burns a liar, a servant of corporate wealth. "The whole affair smacks of well-laid prearrangement . . . to strike at the men having the confidence of the working-people." Other radical and labor leaders echoed old Sam: "Frame-up! Fiendish plot!" Debs telegraphed to the *Appeal to Reason*: "Arouse, ye hosts of labor, and swear that the villainous plot shall not be consummated! Be not deceived by the capitalist press!" The executive council of the A.F. of L. issued an official appeal to the workers of America to stand by the McNamaras, innocent victims of industrial greed.

As counsel for the Los Angeles unions, Job Harriman was in charge of the case immediately after "the boys" were brought to California. "We have witnesses living in Los Angeles today," he declared, "who will be called and will prove that they left the *Times* Building early in the evening utterly unable to stand the odor of gas that flooded it."

Later the A.F. of L. engaged Clarence Darrow, the famed friend of the underprivileged, paying him, according to Frank Morrison, secretary of the A.F. of L., $50,000 outright in a lump sum as a retainer, and gave him the assurance of an unlimited defense fund for which he would not be required to render any accounting. Darrow went to Los Angeles in June, and between that time and November, 1911, received from Morrison $200,000 in sums of from $10,000 to $25,000, which were the approximate monthly totals of the donations given by the workers and radicals of America in thousands of union and Socialist halls. What became of this money (which Burns insisted was closer to $2,000,000 than $200,000) remains a mystery.

There is no doubt, however, that Darrow knew from the start "the boys" were guilty; he said so after the case was concluded. Nor can there be much doubt that Gompers and other A.F. of L. panjandrums knew that Burns had dug up enough evidence not only to hang J. B., but to implicate some of them in the blow-up. While dickering with them before accepting the case, Darrow declared that the labor leaders were "panicky."

A month after "the boys" had been apprehended, the Harriman-dominated Los Angeles branch of the Socialist party became the Socialist-Labor party of Los Angeles, which then passed under the direct boss rule of the San Francisco laborites, and nominated Harriman for mayor of Los Angeles. His nomination, as already stated, had been planned a year before as part of the "war" against Otis and the open-shop element. The plan was to capture Los Angeles not only economically through trade unions, but politically by putting their man into the City Hall. John J. McNamara, who was reëlected secretary-treasurer of the Iron Workers while in jail at Los Angeles, sent word from his cell: "There is but one way for the working-class to get justice. Elect its own representatives to office."

Most Los Angeles Socialists, of course, were unaware that Harriman had allied himself with the San Francisco "gorillas." Meriam had no proof of such an alliance. Nearly all would have been outraged, had it been even suggested that Job was implicated in the *Times* plot. The majority were too new in the Socialist movement to know the party's traditional rule against its leaders or locals entering into alliances with non-Socialist elements. The National Committee of the Socialist party itself forgot that rule, approved Harriman's candidacy, and sent to Los Angeles Alexander Irvine, an experienced politician, to manage his campaign.

Most of Los Angeles believed the McNamaras had been framed, and people were outraged—with the result that the case was a source of a powerful emotional undercurrent sweeping the voters to support Harriman, who shrewdly conducted a dignified campaign and, in his speeches, stressed the shame of the Owens Valley "water steal" and the San Fernando Valley "land grab," which he promised to deal with as mayor. He discussed intelligently also other municipal evils: graft, favoritism, inefficiency, low standard of education in public schools.

Cantrell and his friends, convinced that the San Francisco laborites were responsible for the crime, believed that Burns had caught the wrong men. They knew nothing of the previous activities of the McNamaras.

Already in August it appeared highly probable that Harriman would be elected. His leading opponent was Mayor Alexander, an old retired rancher, who ran on the Good Government League ("Goo-Goo") ticket, supported by Otis.

Early in July the McNamaras pleaded not guilty to the charge of having dynamited the *Times* and killed twenty men. District-Attorney Fredericks, a political Otis man, wanted the trial set for an early date, but Darrow objected—the defense could not possibly get the case ready before December. Judge Bordell set it for October 11th.

Darrow knew he had no case legally; but, when considered in relation to the whole situation in California and the United States at large, with the wave of radicalism rolling over the country, the affair was touched by a few rays of hope. The 1912 presidential election was but a year off. A few well-organized mass demonstrations, such as had been staged during the Bill Haywood trial in 1907, would scare the big-party politicians into bringing pressure to bear on the Los Angeles interests and authorities to let up on labor. "The boys" would go free like Haywood. . . . Also, if the McNamara case was a powerful element favoring Harriman in the political campaign, the same was true in a lesser degree the other way around. Should Harriman be elected mayor, he would have Otis arrested and jailed on the charge of having had a defective gas system in the plant, which had caused the death of twenty workingmen. Otis might go free, but his arrest would further confuse the public and thus, in the long run, react in favor of the McNamaras.

All this was discussed in the Socialist-Labor circles during the campaign. There were plans, rumors galore. Many found space in the *Appeal to Reason*, which was "on the inside" of the whole affair, and whose circulation in Los Angeles during those mad months was almost greater than that of the *Times*. The common people of Los Angeles were turning red.

In mid-September, Gompers visited Los Angeles and was photographed with "the boys" in jail, conferred with Darrow, and spoke before a vast audience of workers and plain people, predicting labor's "ultimate triumph" and endorsing Harriman, "candidate of the people." He issued another statement to the working-people of the United States, assuring them "the boys" were innocent and urging them to stand by the case and contribute to the defense fund.

Money poured in. Practically every town and city had a McNamara Defense League, collecting quarters and dollars from the "toiling masses." Much of this money never reached Frank Morrison, who was in charge of the fund. Local labor grafters found use for the huge sums people donated for the defense.

On Labor Day the great anti-Otis public in Los Angeles joined the proletariat, marshaled by Harriman and the San Francisco laborites, in staging an impressive demonstration. Some 20,000 marched through the town. Hundreds rode horseback, carrying banners: "Register Your Protest Against the McNamara Frame-Up!" From his cell, John J. McNamara issued a "Labor Day Message to the Toilers of America," vibrant with optimism: the toiling masses needed but to stand by their leaders. "Elect Harriman!" On the same day, McNamara demonstrations were held also in San Diego, San Francisco, Portland, Seattle, St. Louis, Chicago, Cleveland, Indianapolis, and in numerous cities and towns in the East. Political and social observers became fearful of a great class-struggle upheaval, and two eastern members of the Republican national committee came to Los Angeles to see if there was not some way to dispose gracefully of the whole McNamara mess in a hurry.

The trial began on the appointed day, October 11th.

If Harriman was to win, and as mayor help the case, the election must occur *before* the conclusion of the trial. Fortunately, from this point of view, finding an unprejudiced jury in Los Angeles was like looking for a collar button. Darrow's jury-picking attracted national attention, provoking comment on the jury system in general. In the first eighteen court days only two jurors acceptable to both sides were obtained.

Election day was December 5th. By mid-November the jury-box was only half filled. Harriman campaigned furiously. His energy was amazing, and he was aided by a big staff of speakers, including nationally prominent Socialists from the East.

Otis and his group were in panic. Their vision of a Los Angeles with millions of people was now suddenly blurred red by Harriman. Should he win, what would become of the city, *i.e.*, their valuable subdivisions in San Fernando Valley and their credit in the East? "Can Los Angeles sell $17,000,000 of its bonds in the next year if Harriman is elected mayor?" asked the *Times*, frantically. "In that question is presented the real issue of the campaign. If Los Angeles fails to sell bonds in that sum it cannot carry on the great undertakings on the success of which its continued growth and future prosperity alike depend. Failure in those undertakings means municipal disaster." But how to prevent Harriman's election?

In the primaries on October 30th, with the final election but thirty-six days off, Harriman was the leading man with 15,000 votes against 13,000 cast for Alexander, the next highest candidate. The third candidate was eliminated. On primary night the Harriman supporters staged another demonstration, thousands of people marching and riding in the streets, singing the Marseillaise.

Cantrell stood on the sidelines, wondering. . . .

Early in November District-Attorney Fredericks accused the defense of an attempt to rifle his desk and files. Darrow challenged him to produce proof. Accusations flew back and forth. On November 10th, Darrow and Fredericks, who was under pressure from the "Goo-Goos" to hasten the trial, almost came to blows during the examination of a prospective juror. In mid-November— as Darrow continued to murder time picking jurors, which was driving the Otis men insane—it seemed as if the McNamara trial, still the biggest thing in Harriman's favor, would not start by election day, to say nothing of ending; and even if it should end in a conviction prior to the election, most citizens would still believe the case a frame-up and vote for Harriman.

The "Goo-Goos"—of whom the district attorney was, of course, the key man in the critical situation—had only one more card to play. They had heard rumors that, four years before, Darrow had freed Bill Haywood with the aid of extra-legal methods; so immediately after the primary the prosecution had planted dictographs in his rooms and their agents in his employ—with the result that, according to a statement issued by the prosecution after the conclusion of the case, by November 20th they "knew" that some of the jurors had been tampered with. On November 29th the district attorney's detectives arrested two of Darrow's agents—of whom one, at least, had been planted on him—and charged them with bribing prospective jurors.

The jury-bribing arrests were a sensation. Darrow said, "We told our friends what would come before we went into this trial. I have no knowledge of any attempt at bribery."

The "Goo-Goos" were jubilant. At last they had Darrow where they wanted him, and, having Darrow, they thought they had the McNamaras, and, having the McNamaras, they were sure they had Harriman. The Socialist ticket was now as good as beaten. *Their* Los Angeles was saved! *Their* credit, *their* enormous real-estate properties!

While this was taking place in Los Angeles, plans were under way in New York, Chicago, Philadelphia, Pittsburgh, Cleveland—in all big American cities —for huge demonstrations to be held early in December, whose purpose would be to protest against the "frame-up," as Debs and Gompers continued to call the case; to *force* the "capitalist class" to release the McNamaras. Millions of people throughout the country waited, tense, indignant, getting more radical by the minute. Unaware that the case was about to end in a dreadful fiasco for the American labor and Socialist movements, they gave increasingly large sums for the defense.

On December 1st something seemed to be in the air at the Los Angeles courthouse. When the court convened, the district attorney asked for a post-ponement. "I have certain grave matters to consider between now and the time for convening court this afternoon."

In the afternoon the courtroom was jammed with reporters. The defense withdrew the pleas of "not guilty" in the case. James B. McNamara pleaded guilty to the *Times* dynamiting and the killing of twenty men. "It was my intention to injure the building and scare the owners. I did not intend to take the life of anyone. I sincerely regret these unfortunate men lost their lives." His brother John pleaded guilty as "an accessory" to the dynamiting of the Llewellyn Iron Works in December, 1910.

The judge named December 5th—election day—as the date on which he would pronounce sentence in the case.

The reporters surrounded James B. "Well, if I swing," he spoke incoherently, "I'll swing for a principle."

Darrow seemed on the verge of losing composure. "They had it on us. There was no loophole. . . ." He muttered he was through with law forever, adding: "I want to say one thing. I'm perfectly sure J. B. never meant to kill anyone in that building. He is not a murderer at heart." "Why was this confession made today?" Darrow was asked. "Why not, say, a week from today?" Newspaper-men realized the political significance of the court scene that afternoon. "Well," said Darrow, "you have to take advantage of clemency when it is extended."— "Did the bribery arrests have anything to do with the confession?"—"Not a thing," snapped Darrow. "We knew before that the evidence the prosecution had was dead open and shut."

Darrow made a long statement, in which truth mingled—inevitably—with evasions and half-truths. ". . . I have known for months our fight was hopeless. . . . Then Lincoln Steffens came to us a week ago Monday with the news that prominent men of Los Angeles were anxious that an agreement should be reached that would end the trial and wipe the bitter controversy off the boards. I felt free then . . . to say that we were willing to consider whatever conces-sions they might be able to secure from the prosecution. . . ."

Steffens tells in his autobiography how he converted the prosecution and the capitalist leaders of Los Angeles to the Golden Rule; only his version is extremely inadequate. . . . After the deal was effected and the McNamaras were induced to confess on the grounds that their case was hopeless, that their lives would be spared, and that by confessing they would save the higher-ups in the A.F. of L., both Darrow and Fredericks became frightened by the possible public reaction. They feared that after "the boys" confessed feeling against them would run so high that extreme penalties would be demanded and Fredericks would be unable to carry out his promises. They called Steffens, who had lately arrived in Los Angeles (probably in response to a hurried call from Darrow or on the urging of the big A.F. of L. men in the East), and the three of them decided to play up a story of how the prosecution and the big men of Los Angeles had been touched with pity and were willing to apply the Golden Rule. Steffens thought that sort of thing would go well in Los Angeles. Otis men were consulted. It was as spokesman for Darrow and Fredericks that "Steff" went on his evangelistic tour, and we can well believe his report of how man after man responded to his preaching. The newspapers played up the story: a miracle of grace had been performed. Overnight Otis men became humble Christians. Otis himself was among the converts. Naturally, then, the public was, in the main, satisfied when, in accordance with the deal, John J. was sentenced to only fifteen years in San Quentin and James B. to a life term, instead of the gallows.

Darrow took the sole responsibility for this ending of the case. "Harriman knew nothing of our intentions. I did not want to worry him with the problem. . . ."

The district attorney and the judge were both emphatic in stating that the chief reason behind the confession at this time was that a Darrow agent had been caught bribing jurors. Talk started that the McNamaras had been induced to plead guilty in order to save Darrow from prison. Darrow's partisans, on the other hand, were loud in stating that the bargain had been struck solely for the sake of saving "the boys" from the death penalty.

The effect of the confessions upon the public was terrific. Many would not believe the headlines, thinking it all some sort of political trick. They tore up the newspapers in rage.

Harriman acted surprised, hurt. There was an enraged mob of Socialists in front of his headquarters; he and his manager, alarmed, jumped into an automobile and drove off. The streets of Los Angeles became strewn with discarded "Vote for Harriman!" buttons.

In the country as a whole the reaction was only slightly less intense than in Los Angeles. For months millions had believed the McNamaras innocent; Darrow, Gompers, Debs, and other great men had been assuring them to that effect—now this——

The *Times* was hysterical with joy. "The God that is still in Israel filled the guilty souls with a torment they could not bear. . . . Viewed fundamentally, the stupendous climax of the case is *in essential particulars the most conse-*

quential event that has occurred in this country since the close of the Civil War. . . ."

Burns talked to reporters: "The confessions end the case only so far as the McNamaras are concerned." He hinted others involved in the dynamitings might be arrested any day. Gompers? Burns shrugged his shoulders meaningfully.

Gompers wept. "I have been grossly imposed upon! It won't do the labor movement any good!" Old Sam looked haggard; he had not slept for nights. He was interviewed by the New York *Times,* and beside him during the interview stood O. A. Tveitmoe, Anton Johannsen, and other "laborites" from the Coast. . . . Johannsen, whom I saw during the writing of *Dynamite,* said to me: "Gompers talked and acted all right. I was there with 'im." . . .

Under the circumstances, of course, Gompers could not have acted differently. And, like their chief, trade-union leaders the country over were "shocked," "stunned," "pained" by the confessions. They denounced the McNamaras and "abhorred their crime." John Mitchell was "astounded," and Frank Morrison "simply thunderstruck."

The *Appeal to Reason* was breathless for two issues; then: "The McNamaras were Democrats." The comrades wanted to forget that John J. McNamara, sitting in his cell in Los Angeles, had been Job Harriman's leading campaigner.

On the same day the McNamaras were sentenced, Harriman was badly beaten in the election for mayor of Los Angeles. Socialism was a broken movement in Los Angeles—in California—in America.

The nation-wide publicity that some A.F. of L. unions were dominated by dynamiting groups took nearly all the militant spirit out of Gompers and, through him, out of the Federation, which has been steadily declining ever since—though, of course, the McNamara fiasco has not been the sole factor in that decline.

One day soon after the dénouement, a Socialist woman of his acquaintance—the landlady of a rooming-house where some of the San Francisco "gorillas" had lived in 1910—brought Cantrell a packet of letters she had found in her house. These letters—one from Harriman—left no doubt in his mind as to the complicity of Harriman in the dynamiting plot. The letters clarified the whole complex situation. They dovetailed his recollection of Harriman's remarks to him in San Luis Obispo on October 10, 1910.

Fredericks was the man of the hour in Los Angeles. He had put the dynamiters in prison and secured his "American Plan" friends in the possession of their San Fernando properties. With the aid of Harriman and Darrow, he had smashed the Socialist party and the labor movement in Southern California. Now he held Darrow for trial. Darrow felt he had been double-crossed. Goaded into anger one day by the nagging of the prosecution, he told the court about his understanding with Fredericks, and charged him with having broken his promise in bringing him to trial. The assistant district attorney in charge of prosecuting him admitted there had been an understanding, but said that the "deal" had provided clemency only for the McNamaras, not for Darrow in the matter of bribing the jury. Darrow was tried twice. In one case the jury was hung; in the other, after his two-day-long plea to the jury in which he accused the prosecution of having framed him, he was acquitted. Fredericks himself took no part in the trials. He turned the cases against Darrow over to his assistants and took a vacation. The assistants apparently had instructions to make only a show of prosecuting Darrow. Fredericks finally let him go with a case hanging over his head. In this way, he saved his face with the public and did not wholly break his promise to Darrow.

After the close of the McNamara case there were several "little trials," as they were called, which received no or scant national attention. One of these was Levering vs. Darrow. Levering, a local engineer, claimed the McNamara defense owned him $500 for his aid in preparing "evidence" that the *Times* had been blown up by gas. Too occupied with more serious troubles just then, Darrow evidently did not realize how much damage Levering could do until the case was called in court; whereupon—as the engineer began to talk—Darrow's attorney promptly asked the court for a recess; the matter was settled, and Levering dropped his case.

Soon after the McNamaras confessed, the grand jury reopened the so-called "dynamiting investigations," which then resulted in indictments of a number of minor San Francisco "gorillas" who had been associated with James B. on the *Times* "job." Two of these, Schmidt and Kaplan, were tried and sent to San Quentin. (Schmidt is still there with James B.; both old men now, and never a word of complaint from either of them.) The indictments against the others, including Johannsen, were dismissed. There was talk that Tveitmoe might be indicted, but he wasn't. A big man, he would have caused too much trouble if brought to trial, and Los Angeles, as well as the rest of California, had had enough. The idea of indicting any of the higher-ups was abandoned and investigations ceased.

One day shortly before this, however, Cantrell was subpœnaed to appear before the grand jury. He had been doubly careful in what he told, and to whom, about his meeting with Harriman at San Luis Obispo on the evening of October 9, 1910, and the rest of the inside information he had about the *Times* plot. Meriam, Elliott, and two or three other comrades assured him they had all kept their word not to quote him to anyone else. But now, in the grand jury room, under oath, he was asked to tell what Harriman had said to him at San Luis Obispo. Unequipped for lying, whether under oath or not, he could not deny he had seen Harriman in San Luis Obispo. Besides, he did not know how much the authorities knew. Later he wrote to Fredericks, asking how they had learned of his interview with Harriman on the morning after the explosion. Fredericks replied that the information had come to him from "a very confidential source." Who the "confidential source" was was a mystery to Cantrell. He imagined the Burns detectives had been shadowing the plotters *before* the blow-up; that one or more had been shadowing Harriman in San Luis Obispo and overheard their conversation; and, of course, that Burns had known (as possibly did Otis, through him) who had dynamited the *Times* as soon as the outrage occurred, but did not arrest the plotters and the dynamiters till more than six months later because he wanted first to get all the evidence on the higher-ups in the iron workers' union and the A.F. of L. (Burns was employed not by the *Times* or by Los Angeles, but by the National Erectors Association, who wanted to stop the destruction of buildings erected by non-union workers which, as already mentioned, James B. and his assistants, under the direct supervision of John J. McNamara, had been dynamiting since 1905.)

Anyhow, Cantrell told the truth. Quite apart from his inability to lie, why should he protect a man like Harriman, who had betrayed Socialism and done it endless harm? . . . For several months his testimony remained a secret with him and the grand jury, for immediately after he gave it, as I say, it was decided not to indict and prosecute the higher-ups, and Harriman was still a big man, or at least a well-known man in Los Angeles, in California, and in the United States.

That he was still a big man in the Socialist party despite his defeat in the Los Angeles election became apparent to Cantrell when he went as a delegate to the national convention of the Socialist party at Indianapolis in the spring of 1912. There was a movement to nominate Harriman, instead of Debs, for President of the United States. And Harriman's hat was definitely in the ring. Hillquit seemed inclined to back him. Cantrell thought this "just a little too much." He called a caucus of the California delegation and, looking directly at Harriman, declared that unless he forthwith stopped the movement to make him the party's presidential candidate he (Cantrell) would rise on the convention floor and make a statement which would mean Harriman's political demise. Enraged, Harriman stalked up and down the caucus-room, denouncing Cantrell. Some delegates demanded Cantrell tell what he had against Harriman. Cantrell said he was willing if Harriman wanted it told. Harriman raged; made no acquiescence to the suggestion; the movement to nominate him was stopped. ·

In this connection, something else occurred at the 1912 national convention of the Socialist party which is worth mentioning. The I.W.W., who were a considerable element in the party and some of whom believed in "strong-arm stuff," provoked a fierce debate on "direct action," or violence. One of the Socialists who made an impassioned, well-reasoned, and all-around masterful speech *against* violence in the class struggle was Job Harriman!

The scene in the caucus-room put Cantrell in a difficult position with most of the other California delegates. Some eyed him suspiciously, for, although Harriman had behaved strangely when Cantrell attacked him, they could not believe Job could have done any wrong. Cantrell was eager to explain his action:

but how could he without telling all? He called on J. Stitt Wilson, the Socialist mayor of Berkeley, whom he knew fairly well, and began to explain; but Wilson interrupted him, "What's the itch, Cantrell? What do you want?" Cantrell said he didn't want anything; there was no personal "itch"; he merely wanted to put before him for his consideration certain facts seriously affecting the Socialist party. Wilson said, "I don't know anything and don't want to know anything."

Now, somehow, it became known in the Socialist circles of Los Angeles that Cantrell had made certain statements to the grand jury which were damaging to Harriman—with the prompt result that the central branch of the Socialist party in Los Angeles, still dominated by Harriman, expelled him from its membership; while the national executive committee, of which Harriman was a member, expelled him from the party, and the national office canceled his contract as national lecturer by telegraph.

Cantrell wrote letters and telegraphed demanding an investigation, but received no answer. The party's constitution provided a member should have sixty days in which to answer any formal complaint which might be filed against him. Cantrell's local organization gave him two days. The national committee gave him no time, no hearing. He knew nothing of their actions until he read the minutes of the committee meeting. When an officer of his local brought him a copy of the charges lodged against him, he said: "We don't blame you for going before the grand jury; you had to go when you were subpœnaed, but we blame you for not lying"—oath or no oath—"to protect one of our men when you got there." Cantrell replied, "If that is the way you feel about it, the sooner you throw me out the better."

Soon after Cantrell's expulsion, Meriam and Elliott, and several other locally prominent Socialists who disapproved of Harriman's politics, were also expelled; in most cases, without any charge having been brought against them. When one of them inquired why such action had been taken, Harriman said, "We don't have to tell."

About a year after this "purge," as it might be called today, there was a special election in Los Angeles, and again Harriman was the Socialist candidate for mayor. Officially, his nomination was meant to be a "vindication," though there was no chance of victory; to Cantrell, however, Harriman's candidacy was a challenge to the people driven out of the party and an affront to public decency. He consulted with his friends Meriam and Elliott, who assured him anything he wanted to do about it was all right with them. There was no other paper which would print what he wanted to write, so he went to the *Times*, told the editors what he knew about Harriman, and that, as one who remained a convinced Socialist although he had been tossed out of the party, he wanted to put the man out of circulation as a Socialist politician. Would they give him two columns a day for a week? The *Times* gave him the space and Cantrell wrote a series of carefully documented articles showing that Harriman had been connected with the dynamite plot. He challenged Harriman to sue him or to deny his statements, either in the *Times* (which offered to print the denial) or in the Socialist press. Harriman neither sued him nor denied anything in any public print. On election day he received a handful of votes.

Politically dead, Harriman founded a coöperative colony in southern California, but his methods brought on a revolt among his followers and a considerable number of them went into court, where they told amazing stories about his management of the enterprise. The colony failed, and Harriman moved to Louisiana and founded another. Again there was a revolt and finally he returned to Los Angeles. At the end he turned spiritualist and told his friends that he had been wrong in his philosophy of life. He burned his papers, including the manuscript of a book which was never published, but which, according to those to whom he had read it, was an argument, based on physics and politics, for an extreme philosophy of power.

In October, 1929, shortly after I came to New York, intending to write *Dynamite*, in which I meant to include the full story of the McNamara case, I wrote to Morris Hillquit, national chairman of the Socialist party of America; I was writing a sort of history of the labor struggles in the United States. Would he see me? He invited me to his office and I went. What did I wish to know? I said my book would include the McNamara case and Job Harriman's political campaign. Would he tell me something about Harriman? I understood they had been friends.

HILLQUIT: Just what do you wish to know?

ADAMIC: Your idea of his character.

H. (*smiling*): I'm afraid anything I'll say will be biased. Job Harriman and I were great friends. I always considered him an exceptionally fine man.

A.: There is a group of people in California who were very active in the Socialist party in Harriman's time, who appear to have basis for believing otherwise. Had it ever occurred to you, Mr. Hillquit, that Harriman might have been involved with the gang that blew up the Los Angeles *Times*?

H. (*tense, suspicious*): That's absurd! Job was opposed to all such things! He abhorred the very idea of violence. Absurd!

A.: There is documentary evidence attesting that Harriman entered into a political alliance with the McCarthy-Tveitmoe laborites in San Francisco at the expense of the Socialist party.

H. (*brusquely*): What kind of evidence?

A.: For one thing, a letter written by himself, signed by him, to a friend of his, John Murray, in which he discussed the program. Briefly, he was going to swing the Socialists of San Francisco to McCarthy-Tveitmoe and McCarthy-Tveitmoe were going to throw the Los Angeles labor element to him—practically turn the Socialist political machine over to the laborites.

H. (*tensely*): That's exaggerated. You don't know what you're talking about. Harriman was, of course, in favor of joining the Socialist and the labor movements —but—you're stretching something—you are biased.

A.: I am critical.

H. (*indignant*): Why didn't you tell me so in the beginning? You're writing a criticism, not a history, of labor and the radical movement. Why weren't you honest about it?

A.: I told you I was writing the story of the McNamara case. Could I write it, honestly, without at the same time writing a criticism of the radical movement and the A.F. of L.? I don't want you to question my honesty in this matter. I am sympathetic to radical ideas, but critical of radical and labor movements in the United States.

H. (*rising*): Then, sir, I have nothing more to say to you. Good day.

After his expulsion from the party, Cantrell largely withdrew from public life, but continued to interest himself in many of the things in which he had been active.

He thought for a while that the Socialist agitation, in which he had taken part, to bring the new aqueduct to Los Angeles had not been futile. Late in 1912 it looked as though an aroused public would compel the Otis men, through the courts, to extend it from San Fernando within the city limits. It never was. To silence the annoying demands, the ever-resourceful proponents of the "American Plan" caused, instead, the city limits to be extended by means of a "shoestring" beyond San Fernando Valley, which was annexed to Los Angeles, thus taking the city to the aqueduct—one reason why Los Angeles is so vast in area.

Cantrell had many friends in Owens Valley, and knew the Watterson family, who were prominent pioneers in the region. Two Watterson brothers were bankers in the town of Inyo, and, as such, economic, political, social leaders in the valley. Their business was with the ranchers. And so, after Los Angeles took the Owens River water, the Wattersons naturally led the valley's protest against the "steal." The ranchers sued the city, trying to make it pay them for the land that now lay unproductive because of the lack of water, but they received no satisfaction; for the go-getters in southern California were powerful in the state's politics and courts, whereas the Owens Valley farmers were of no account politically whatever. The cases dragged through many years, costing them a deal of money. Finally, in desperation and contrary to the Wattersons' advice, a group of ranchers, as already suggested, took to dynamiting the aqueduct. Every couple of weeks the giant pipe acquired a hole somewhere along the line. These suits and dynamitings annoyed Los Angeles' leading citizens; so a man in the state banking department was instructed to watch the Wattersons and "not to give 'em an inch." Supporting ranchers to the limit financially, the bankers' legal reserves were depleted. No city bank would tide them over (part of the plot); inspectors "caught" them; they were tried, and each sentenced "from one to ten years" in San Quentin. It was for the state prison board to determine the actual time they would serve, and the board, whose members were in office with the support of the Los Angeles go-getters, gave them the limit—ten years. . . . Thus, ironically, bankers and labor dynamiters served for a decade in the same prison, in order that—as Cantrell saw it—Los Angeles might be a great city in which go-getters, in their drive for profit, might be free to do what they liked under their "American Plan."

One Sunday afternoon in 1925, when I was living in southern California, unaware of the McNamara case and Owens Valley, I paused in front of a small theater on Grand Street in Los Angeles, where a simple hand-lettered placard advertised a lecture on "America Today," by Edward Adams Cantrell. I was a newcomer in California, and the name was new to me. Admission was free; I stepped in.

About a hundred people were scattered through the auditorium which could seat five hundred; and the lecturer—tall, thin, perhaps in his late fifties or early sixties, still handsome, his hair barely beginning to ashen, well dressed, neat— had just begun his talk as I slid into a seat on the aisle in the rear, whence I could easily slip out if I did not like the lecture. But I stayed to the end. Here was a clear, careful, realistic mind. Cantrell spoke slowly in meticulous sentences, was patient, kindly in manner, teacher-like, repeating passages in his well-organized dissertation which he wanted to be sure every one would understand and remember. He gave a picture of America in 1925 which was not pleasant, but, I sensed, accurate and illuminating. He analyzed the social, economic, political, and cultural conditions in the country; explained Coolidge and evoked a few laughs; went into the oil scandals; and outlined what he called the inevitable process whereby the so-called prosperity, then uppermost in the minds of numerous Americans, would in a few years culminate in an economic nose-dive. The lecture lasted an hour and was followed by a question period, which his answers made almost as interesting as the main talk. Finally, some one in the audience went around with a hat and collected, perhaps, ten or fifteen dollars, though the auditorium doubtless cost four or five times that amount for the afternoon. Cantrell announced he would continue to lecture here every Sunday afternoon for the next six weeks. He asked us to come again next Sunday, and bring some one along.

I could not get anyone to come with me, but I attended all the Cantrell lectures that year. The audience was seldom over a hundred. He discussed the American scene, traditions, ideals; the various social philosophies, credos, programs, movements; some book he had just read, or some event or condition that had lately drawn his notice. He never fumed or ranted, seldom raised his voice, yet was invariably forceful, convincing. He frequently quoted Jefferson and Lincoln, Emerson and Wendell Phillips, Thoreau and Whitman, who evidently were his heroes, and some of the more recent American liberal thinkers— John Dewey, Charles A. Beard, Oswald Garrison Villard. He used no notes, often was slyly humorous, and now and then made vague, remote references to his past in Los Angeles, which I did not understand but apparently were meaningful to a few of the older people in the audience. Occasionally, to illustrate how America had changed, he told of his boyhood in the Ozarks, which always fascinated me. . . . Finally, he announced his last lecture for the season, smilingly suggesting that for the time being he could not afford to continue paying most of the rent for the auditorium, but possibly might give another series of lectures next year. If so, he would put an advertisement in the papers.

He gave a series of lectures every year that I continued to live in southern California, which was till 1929. I heard most of them. His audiences ranged from a couple of dozen to a couple of hundred, but he always spoke in a clean, light auditorium or hall; and I am sure that the collections never met his expenses.

In my late twenties I was just beginning to write, reading considerably, trying to sort out and organize in some way the impressions, ideas, feelings, and notions I had experienced and gathered while roaming America. In 1928, I copied in my Diary—because I agreed with them—these lines from an early essay by Van Wyck Brooks entitled "Sargasso Sea":

"America is like a vast Sargasso Sea—a prodigious welter of unconscious life, swept by groundswells of half-conscious emotion. All manner of living things are drifting in it, phosphorescent, gayly colored, gathered into knots and clotted masses, gelatinous, unformed, flimsy, tangled, rising and falling, floating and merging, here an immense distended belly, there a tiny rudimentary brain (the gross devouring the fine)—everything an unchecked, uncharted, unorganized vitality like that of the first chaos. It is a welter of life which has not been worked out into an organism, into which fruitful values and standards of human economy have been introduced, innocent of those laws of social gravitation which, rightly understood and pursued with a keen faith, produce a fine temper in the human animal."[1]

I was looking for a Darwin of this Sargasso Sea; so one day in the early autumn of 1928 I overcame my shyness, which plagued me at the time, and wrote to Cantrell that I would like to meet him. In reply I received a warm, graceful invitation to his house, and he added he had read my stories and articles in the *American Mercury* and elsewhere.

Our acquaintance, which began with long talks on his porch, rapidly developed into friendship. I met Mrs. Cantrell, but she and their daughter were seldom home when I came, and I did not get to know them well at the time. They lived in a modest house on a quiet street. There were books around, and carpenter's and wood-carving tools. The daughter and Mrs. Cantrell had jobs outside; Cantrell worked at home, making furniture, writing, and occasionally was offered a fee for a lecture somewhere.

For two, three months we talked of all manner of things, but I think chiefly of Los Angeles and of America as a whole; he telling me what he knew; I narrating to him my adventures as an immigrant and a migratory worker in the United States, some of which I later put into *Laughing in the Jungle*.

Then one day the late G. D. Eaton, editor of a new liberal "de-bunking" magazine, *Plain Talk*, wrote to me from New York: could I do an article on

[1] Now appearing in *Three Essays on America*, published and copyrighted by E. P. Dutton & Co., Inc., N. Y.

liberals in Los Angeles? It was to be one of a series of pieces by different writers about liberals in various cities of the United States. I went to Cantrell; we discussed the idea for the article and the local liberals and radicals, whose number was extremely meager . . . and suddenly I found myself listening to the most dramatic and fascinating things, for, explaining why there were practically no liberals worth mentioning in Los Angeles, Cantrell launched into the whole long labor struggle on the Coast, ending with the Harriman-McNamara story. I listened to him, returned day after day, and read the documents and newspaper clippings he kept bringing out of an old chest and laying before me.

It occurred to me the story should be written, and he told me to go ahead and see what I could do with it. But at the time I did not yet understand it any too well; also, as I have mentioned, the publishers' lawyers were uneasy about parts of it; and the result, about two years after I first met Cantrell, was *Dynamite*, a somewhat different book from what I had vaguely planned originally. But of this more later.

Cantrell told me of his life since 1912.

In 1914, rather sick at heart, after Elliott had died and Meriam had gone back to ranching, he returned to the Ozarks, bought a little land, and built himself a home. He farmed till the end of the war, when, eager for the platform again, he sold the place and accepted an invitation to become a speaker in behalf of Irish freedom, which took him all over the country and kept him busy until the early 1920's. Then he returned to Los Angeles, where, as I say, I came upon him as a free-lance lecturer. In 1924, he campaigned for "Old Bob" La Follette; in 1928, not so much for Al Smith as against Hoover.

Now, in the spring of 1929, studying the economic trends and the financial page, he was expecting "a panic within the year," and was thinking of selling the real estate he owned in Los Angeles, which he had bought twenty years before, intending eventually to have a home on it. He believed property values would tumble with stocks and bonds when the collapse came, and he might as well "get out from under." He meant to go back to the Ozarks once more, buy a few acres, build a house, or repair an old one, and live on the land. He felt that the next few years, after the panic began, were apt to be "pretty bad."

In the summer of 1929 I left California for New York, and I did not see him for over five years. I heard from him at varying intervals. Family affairs kept him in Los Angeles rather longer than he had expected. Finally, however, in the spring of 1932, he wrote me from the Ozarks:

"One can't make much on the land now, but one can live on it, and I like the sense of security which such a life gives. . . . Have had an interesting experience recently. It is not often that a man can go back to a place, after an absence of more than fifty years, and find old neighbors that he knew in his childhood. I found an old man, Isaac Bray, who was our nearest neighbor, 1873-1879. He still lives on the same old place where he settled in the 'fifties.

His son-in-law told me he had been out of the county but once in his lifetime. That was when he went into another county to join the Union Army during the Civil War. . . . I had a wonderful visit with him."

Cantrell invited me to call on him if I was ever in that part of the world: "the latch-string is always out." But I went to Europe soon after I heard from him and it was more than two years before I saw him. It was midsummer, hot and dry and dusty in the Middle West and in Arkansas and Missouri. The drought was on and duststorms blew every few days. But the Ozark country was lovely even in drought. I found the Cantrells nine miles from Springfield, Missouri, now a city of 60,000 population, probably over half of it on the ragged edge. They had a stone house, in which they could have been fairly comfortable but for the fact that both were ill from exertion, extreme heat and almost endless dust that had been blowing down upon them from the Dust Bowl during the previous fall and spring, and again during 1934. Physically, Cantrell was but a shadow of the man I had left in California five years before, but as alert mentally as ever. His eyes, deep in the sockets and burned almost raw by the sun heat and the hot dust, were still open, as were his ears; in fact, he was keyed up to a pitch of awareness and indignation. He said that after a year upon the land he found little security on it. The country was in worse shape than most people, even these seemingly wide-awake New Dealers in Washington, realized.

"Forests have been cut," he said, "wild life has been destroyed, soils have been washed away, streams have been fouled or choked with sand and gravel or have dried up altogether, farms have been abandoned. I counted fourteen deserted places hereabouts. In an incredibly short time the people have passed from the economy of the frontier to the blight of the industrial age. Once they worked and supplied their needs. Now they are working on worn soils, to produce stuff to sell, to get money, to buy what they need. And when they sell, they don't get the cost of production; and when they buy they pay high prices for almost everything. They are exploited as both producers and consumers. The result is an impoverishment in which many are saved from starvation only by Government relief, which came, I think, in the nick of time. And along with the material impoverishment there has come an impoverishment of character, an erosion of personality, which is much more serious than soil erosion. My grandfather, making a good piece of furniture; my grandmother, weaving a beautiful coverlet or other fabrics; my mother, with her amazing activities and skills—they developed a self-reliance, a pride, in their work and in themselves which gave them dignity and poise. Their work had cultural values. But it is difficult to find cultural values in milking cows, to produce cream to sell, to get money, to buy oleomargarine! . . . It's fantastic; a mess, as you say; but here we are, and what are we going to do about it? Gorki's 'people of the lower depths' and Hugo's *misérables* were what they were, in part, because Russia and France were backward countries and their technique of production was not developed. There was some excuse for them. We have no such excuse for our Tobacco Road, which is longer than Main Street and runs through the rural regions, not only in the South, but throughout the country, as well as throughout cities, and crosses Main Street at many points. We have no such excuse, for our production technique is the most efficient in the world, and we could all live in economic abundance if——"

Discussing that "if," Cantrell and I were both uncertainly sympathetic with, and definitely disturbed by, the New Deal, just then in full swing with its high-soaring Blue Eagle, its sensational Section 7-a, and its fantastic A.A.A. and crop destruction. We thought it had "stirred the people" and might "lead to something eventually"; it seemed a part of America's push for equality, aiming to make it impossible or extremely difficult for employers to refuse to meet labor and discuss grievances and problems on the basis of equal right. Cantrell believed the Administration was apt to restore a semblance of prosperity and thereby achieve nothing basic or permanent, but merely get the country ready for the next crash or war, or both. We agreed there were too many conflicting elements within the New Deal program personnel, and "philosophy," which was no philosophy, but a batch of hunches, good intentions, and expedients, pulling their originators and adherents in various directions, so that with one hand they fed the hungry and with the other destroyed crops. These conflicting elements of the New Deal were an expression or manifestation of the country's fundamental incongruity between its political democracy and its economic royalism, as well as an expression and manifestation of its intention or attempt to make another push toward equality. . . .

In mid-autumn of 1935 I was traveling again in Missouri. But Cantrell had left the farm. I found him living temporarily in Republic, Missouri, getting ready to return to southern California. Neither he nor Mrs. Cantrell was yet fully recovered from their experiences of the past three years. His eyes were still as though burned out with hot irons; he was in his late sixties, but erect and agile, packing Mrs. Cantrell's household articles in cases and barrels. We talked for hours of unemployment, soil erosion, and general waste in America, the confusion of the Socialists and the A.F. of L., Roosevelt——

Packing, he had found among his papers, he said, a kind of prose-poem he had written nearly thirty years ago, shortly before he quit the ministry. Would I care to read it? It was entitled "The Cause," suggested by Whitman's phrase "the great cause." He made no claim for it as poetry, Whitmanesque or any other kind, but it was a sort of credo; it expressed his mood and thoughts at the time—"and, I suppose, even now." It read:

If you accept life, and are willing to exalt it above names, phrases, and things;
If you accept truth, and after the severest tests, are not afraid;
If you accept brotherliness as better than the hates of the jungle;
If you love justice, and hate the very semblance of exploitation;
If you love work as the expression of the Creative Idea,
Then let us work together; we will be comrades!

We will eat our bread by the sweat of our faces;
Our grace at table shall be the consciousness that we have earned what we eat;
We will not ask God for our daily bread, like pious mendicants;
We will ask for the daily tasks, that working together with Him we shall share
    His creations.

And these are the tasks toward which we will set our faces:
Tasks of the seed-time and harvest, tasks of the mills and the mines, tasks of the
    common day, first of all, we accept.
We accept, we will perform, we will transform in the great new way,
For we will bring to them the great soul's love of doing,
And we will bring to them the passionate love of comrades,
And we will give to them a reverent regard for the future.
We will till the fields for our present needs, but we will conserve the fertility of
    the soil as a heritage for the generations yet unborn;
We will fell trees, but we will also plant, and religiously restore the forests;
We will plant flowers, and protect the birds, stopping at once and for all time their
    wanton slaughter;
We will cleanse the lakes and streams and stock them with fishes;
We will drain swamps and reclaim deserts, and build up the City Beautiful.
Throwing our kits over our shoulders, we will go out and build up the New Jerusalem,
The New Chicago, the New New York, the New Every-Other-City under the sun,
The new Heaven and the new Earth wherein may dwell righteousness.

Not that there will be a new astronomy or a new geology. The same old stars will
    be over our heads, and the same old soils beneath our feet,
But the stars will be stars of hope, and the earth will be an earth of promise for all
    the children of man.

And we will ask no man to give up his wealth, but renouncing privilege, we will
    ask every man to work for the Commonwealth,
For we know well that when we work together and do away with waste, there will
    be more than enough for all men.
And we will not ask any man to give up his religion, but we will ask every man
    to live up to the best that is in his religion,
For we know that as life grows, the laws of life will become sacred ordinances,
And as good will grows, our simplest relations will have sacramental values,
And as knowledge grows, work will become worship and love will be the soul of
    all prayer,
And believe me, this love of ours will lift our lives to the light of the skies.

I visited my friend and Mrs. Cantrell again in the spring of 1936 when a
lecture tour took me to California. They were living in a house on the outskirts
of a beach town near Los Angeles. Both of good stock, they had largely recovered their health. They led a quiet life, reading, entertaining an occasional
visitor. He was slowly writing a book.

Cantrell and I

I REMEMBER THAT LISTENING TO CANTRELL I WAS SAYING TO MYSELF: HERE IS A member of a species in the Sargasso Sea who has the power of objective thought, along with the ability to articulate it, and is giving me a close and, I feel, accurate glimpse of things and goings-on in a considerable area beneath the surface.

My admiration for the man, hitherto a matter of my appreciation of his lectures, increased vastly. He was the first old-stock American with whom I had come in close contact, who could tell me about America, not academically or abstractly, second or third hand, but in concrete terms of his own experience and function.

His story made my mind tingle.

I was unconvinced then (as I am still) that Socialism, as represented by the various so-called Marxian parties, was the beginning of all the answers to the important human questions, either in America or elsewhere; and I was not in 1928 or '29 (nor am I now as I write this book) a Socialist in any immediate political sense, which might have caused me then (or cause me now) to sympathize unduly with my friend on the score of his political views, acts, and purposes in 1909-11. But here, it seemed to me, was a man intensely and wonderfully American. His mind and feelings were closely akin to the ideas and ideals, political ways and personal examples of Jefferson, Lincoln, Wendell Phillips, Whitman, and other articulate and active American idealists and popular heroes, whose writings and sayings, actions and ways (with which I had become more or less familiar through reading) unquestionably were at the spiritual core of nearly everything that was best and basic in America. He was linked to the most consistent, albeit often faltering, tendency in American history (which I had been perusing in different versions); the tendency or push toward equality, more democracy. Not that Cantrell believed that all people were equally endowed, but he wanted the scheme of things in America so arranged that everybody would have equal opportunity to develop his powers and talents, and use them in ways that would not impinge upon the effectiveness of others. America as she stood—democratic politically, absolutist industrially, dynastic economically—was to him an incongruity, which he considered worse than outright monarchy and feudalism: for this incongruity was the source of all manner of contradictions, hidden conflicts, social and political perversions, neuroticism, and violence within the country as a whole, within groups and institutions, and within individuals. It put the country out of focus.

Back in 1909-11 Cantrell was an American idealist in action, aiming to abolish eventually the incongruity, to get the country into focus. He joined the Socialist movement, which, although not very American in tactics, was, in his view, closer in line with his idealism than was any other movement at

41

the time. A deeply decent, honorable, reflective, essentially humble, personally unambitious man, who was also magnificently naïve, he shared Jefferson's passionate belief in the urgency of educating the people in the principles and practices of liberty and democracy, and was primarily a teacher in basic Americanism, which was ingrained in his makeup. He believed there were no short cuts to anything worth while. He would have agreed with Van Wyck Brooks, who, some years after Cantrell joined the Socialist party, wrote in the essay from which I have already quoted:

"Issues that make the life of a society do not spring spontaneously out of the mass. They exist in it—a thousand potential currents and cross-currents; but they have to be discovered like principles of science, they have almost to be created like works of art. A people is like a ciphered parchment that has to be held up to the fire before its hidden significances come out. Once the divisions that have ripened in a people have been discerned and articulated, its beliefs and convictions are brought into play, the real evils that have been vaguely surmised spring into the light, the real strength of what is intelligent and sound becomes a measurable entity. To cleanse politics is of the least importance if the real forces of the people cannot be engaged in politics; and they cannot be so engaged while the issues behind politics remain inarticulate."

Cantrell wanted to articulate the issues, rouse the people's democratic responsibility, engage them in politics. But soon after getting into the Socialist movement he came face to face with the vivid confusion of forces and aforementioned contradictions, conflicts, violence, neuroticism, and perversions of American life which flowed, for the most part, out of its basic incongruity, its out-of-focus condition that did not avoid the Socialist party. He bumped up against ways— those of General Otis, of Gompers and the dynamiters, of Harriman and Hillquit, of Darrow, et al.—which were also American, but American in the current, immediate sense; in the sense that they were marked by the tendency to short cuts, by haste, momentary self-interest, rash thoughtlessness, lack of scruples and reflection, by all the evils of America's essential incongruity, even among those who basically, perhaps, were attached to the same American ideals as was he. He began a clean, decent, honorable fight and movement, and was defeated . . . inevitably, it seems, at the time . . . but defeated, let me hasten to say, only in the most immediate sense.

In fact, on second thought, he was not defeated at all.

Soon after Cantrell had finished narrating to me his long, involved story, but before I thoroughly understood all its ramifications and meanings, I discussed it with a friend of his in Los Angeles, who also knew it, and when I remarked to him one day that it was a sad, tragic tale, he replied, "Yes, but I don't think Cantrell is sad. He doesn't feel tragic. The sadness and tragedy are all on the other side."

He was right. Actually, except in the most immediate and momentary sense, defeat never touched Cantrell. Nor Meriam, whom I also met in California in 1929, a hearty old man living upon a ranch near San Diego. But it more than touched, and in terribly personal and vital ways, most of the others who were involved in the Los Angeles drama in 1910 and thereabouts, as well as most of the organizations and movements implicated in it. Under the strain of his schemes, battles, and enterprises, General Otis collapsed as a personality almost immediately following his great "victory." While living in Los Angeles I knew persons who, or whose parents, had become rich on the San Fernando "land grab" and similar schemes and stunts; with but one or two exceptions, they were vacuous, jittery, extremely objectionable persons. Later some were hit by the Depression and, having lost their money, ceased to be anything. . . . I have told what happened to Harriman. His friend Hillquit ended his career as a Socialist leader by acting as attorney for a capitalist firm, in a case against the Union of Soviet Socialist Republics. The Socialist party has virtually ceased to exist as a national organization. *The Appeal to Reason,* which was involved in the McNamara mess, passed out soon after the war. . . . Gompers, as already mentioned, was never the same person following the McNamara confessions; toward the end of his life he was a bitter, bewildered man. As for his organization, in 1935 John L. Lewis declared, "The A.F. of L. has a twenty-five-year record of constant, unbroken failure." . . . Darrow died early in 1938, a bundle of contradictions: an anarchist who played politics, a lawyer who despised law, a pacifist who took the stump for war, a Tolstoyan who was drawn to Nietzsche——

The people "on the other side" were, as already suggested, at once the children and victims of the American civilization's incongruity. They functioned furiously within it, aiming for immediate results. None of them understood what it was all about. *They stalemated, defeated one another.* The incongruous forces of which they were part shattered one another, and the men—their personalities, their movements, their energies—were smashed with them. They were "capitalists" and "radicals," but ultimately and essentially the same kind of people.

When I began to understand the entire drama, Cantrell appeared to me a protagonist in it only as much as a symbol of the force of enlightenment in a dark confused situation could be called a protagonist. Only in that rôle could he be considered as entered in the battle of forces represented by Otis, Harriman, McNamara, *et al.* His function was to illumine the incongruity and dispel it, and lift those involved in it out of it. One might consider his rôle that of the chorus in a Greek play. He was a participant only as a shedder of light. He was a teacher, who was also always ready to learn. Many learned from him what was going on, and he, watching and studying, constantly learned more clearly himself what it was that was happening. None of this was, or can be, lost; no one in such a function can be defeated while he is in it . . . and Cantrell stayed in it after his expulsion from the Socialist movement. He went on teaching. His particular experience in Los Angeles did not separate him from his ideas and ideals. Indeed, it enhanced his light-giving power. I am sure that he was a better teacher in 1928 and '29, when he talked to me, than he had been in 1910. At the same time, too, it cannot be said that Cantrell won. When one talks of a man like him, there is no question of defeat or victory. He just *is*; he goes on. For him there is no victory, immediate or ultimate. He is a factor in education, which goes on and does not cease. It never thinks of itself as victorious, no matter how successful it may be; nor defeated, no matter how it may fail here and there, now and then. It must go on. There is something in humanity that makes it go on. . . .

When I last saw Cantrell, though poor and aging, he stood up as a man, as an American. He was interesting, alive.

The Cantrell story filled a lack in my sense of America which had come to me in the preceding fifteen years of my life in the United States through personal experience, travel, and reading about the country. It vivified and vitalized much of what I had read about America.

It gave me, as already suggested, the idea for my first book; and, with the idea, the immediate impulse to leave California, where I had been living for seven years and had lately written a few magazine pieces, and go to New York and try to become a writer in earnest.

It strengthened my natural scepticism of movements, including (if not, in fact, particularly) the "radical" movements, and their leaders; and was partly responsible for the fact that, during the Depression years when efforts were made in New York to draw me into various political and semi-political "radical" parties and groups, I steered clear of them. The Cantrell story, somehow, helped me to see most of them as a furious lot of nothing, emanations of the country's basic incongruity, doomed to appear eventually just that to all who would see.

It strengthened, too, the idea which had taken hold in me some years before, I think in the early 1920's: that America was a Land Nobody Knew, and that what the country needed more than anything else were a few score of earnest, objective socio-political-cultural Darwins who would get busy in the vast Sargasso Sea that was America.

It gave me the desire to become eventually, in some small way determined by my ability, one of these Darwins.

New York

What else can you expect from a town that's
shut off from the world by the ocean on one
side and New Jersey on the other?
O. HENRY, *The Gentle Grafter, A Tempered Wind.*

Stella

CANTRELL'S STORY, WHICH I WANTED TO PUT INTO A NON-FICTION BOOK ENTITLED *Dynamite*, was the immediate motive for my departure, in 1929, from California for New York. I had, somehow, come to think that being in New York, where most of the books and magazines in America were edited and published, might be advantageous to me as a beginning writer.

But I was drawn there by something else.

Two years prior to this—on the night Lindbergh flew across the Atlantic—I had met a girl, Stella Sanders. Her home was in New York, where she had been born eighteen years before. Now she was visiting her aunt and cousins in Los Angeles.

The meeting occurred at the home of a mutual friend who thought we should know one another. After dinner, we sat on the porch late into the evening, talking. She was lovely, intelligent. She had read a great deal, including something I had written, which she said was "pretty bad."

I think I fell in love that evening.

We met a few more times in Los Angeles, going to a few shows together, taking a few walks. Then Stella was compelled to return East.

During the next two years, while she was finishing college in New York, we kept in touch by correspondence.

In 1931 we were married.

This chapter is the shortest in this book. It is very inadequate. But it is the best I can do. There is a censor within me. There is another too near me to be disregarded.

First Book

BEFORE LEAVING FOR NEW YORK I HAD A LONG TALK WITH UPTON SINCLAIR, WHOM I had first met a year or two previously. He took me to lunch in a cafeteria at Pasadena, where he lived; and I began to tell him the Cantrell story. He personally knew, or had known, most of the persons involved in it, and was very much interested. He was then still a regular Socialist, a member of the party, but not averse to hearing the truth, even if unfavorable, about radicals and their movements and politics. The Cantrell story, as I reeled it off to him, fascinated the novelist in him.

From the cafeteria he took me onto a sunny green lawn in front of the Pasadena public library, where we sat till mid-afternoon, going over the tale again and again. *Dynamite,* thought Upton, was a fine title, but he believed it would be a mistake to write the book as straight non-fiction.

"The blowing-up of the Los Angeles *Times* and the McNamara case," he went on (quoting him freely), "occurred eighteen, nineteen years ago, which means they are ancient history. Few people in America are interested in anything that happened so long ago, or even a year or a month ago, regardless of how important the implications of the event may be. Henry Ford said, 'History is bunk.' That attitude is pretty general. If you write the story as non-fiction, the book will conceivably sell a couple of thousand copies, but probably not a thousand, no matter how well you do it or how important you make it appear. You don't know the American book-reading public. . . . What you should try to do, I think, is write a novel, using the Cantrell tale as your material. Put a love story in it and call it *Dynamite*—something on the order of what I did with the Sacco-Vanzetti story in *Boston.* Then, if you succeed in writing a good novel, you may score a hit. . . ."

But—hoping Upton was wrong in this—as I felt he was in some other things —I continued to see the story as non-fiction.

I had spent four or five months going through Cantrell's documents and clippings, the Los Angeles court records and newspaper files of 1910 and 1911; now, jamming my material into a large suitcase, I took a train for the East.

In New York, I called on Henry L. Mencken at the office of *The American Mercury.* We had had some correspondence regarding the Cantrell story; he had seemed interested; now I told him the entire tale as briefly as I could. Would he consider publishing it serially? Mencken said he was against serials in a monthly magazine; a month was too long between instalments. Also, there was this: He did not doubt what I said about Clarence Darrow; no criminal lawyer could be a saint; but they were friends of long standing, and he would not want to print anything in the *Mercury* that would be damaging to him. Darrow was doing good work fighting Prohibition, in the repeal of which Mencken was then more interested than in anything else. Could I omit mention of Darrow and condense the thing into a single piece of, say, seven or eight thousand words? I was afraid not; I saw the material as a book, and Darrow was part of the story. Mencken then suggested I approach Bruce Bliven, head editor of *The New Republic*.

I did, and Bliven asked me to lunch with the editorial staff. I told them the story . . . but it was not for *The New Republic*. Some of the material in it might be libelous, or else resented by labor and prominent radicals.

I gave up the idea of serial publication.

A few months before, Harry Bloch, a member of the editorial staff of the Knopf publishing house, had written to me: had I a book on the boards? If so, would I give them the first chance at it? So now I saw the Knopf people, including Alfred A. Knopf. They were all very nice, very much interested. *Dynamite,* they agreed, was an excellent title. And the Cantrell story, to be sure, was exciting. It did show certain elements in America in action and explain how the A.F. of L. had lost its militancy. The trouble with it was that it had all happened so long ago and 'way out West, in Los Angeles, where all manner of queer things kept happening all the time, anyhow. Why could I not write a book entitled *Dynamite* which would be a history of violence between capital and labor in the United States from the beginning till the present, with the McNamara case a chapter or a part in that history? They, the Knopf people, thought that that might be a fine idea, and asked me to think it over.

The idea appealed to me. In fact, it had occurred to me (and Cantrell and I had discussed it) a month or two before in Los Angeles while I was digging into the McNamara case, in which connection I came upon masses of rich, stirring material on the strong-arm relations between capital and labor; but at the time it had seemed too big for me to tackle as my first book. Besides, Cantrell had been the focus of my attention. . . . Now, however, after some further discussions with the Knopf people, who continued to be most cordial and genuinely eager to have me write the book, I decided to do this bigger job they suggested, although I felt I would have difficulty in condensing the Los Angeles *Times*-McNamara affair into a mere part or section of a volume. I knew too much about it.

Alfred Knopf promised me an advance when I had completed a certain number of chapters to their satisfaction, and I set out to do research on a hundred years of American capital-labor history. I spent two months in the New York Public Library on Fifth Avenue at Forty-Second Street. The library impressed me as a perfect institution. I found there everything I needed that was available in print. Some of the important material not in print was to be had only in Indianapolis and Chicago; so I went there and spent a week in each place, studying labor dynamiting politics in the former, and the development of labor racketeering and of outright criminal rackets in the latter.

In Chicago I looked up one of the men who figured in the Cantrell story as a co-plotter in the Los Angeles *Times* dynamiting. A squat, thick figure with a massive round head, in his mid-fifties, he was a prominent official of one of the large building trades unions; he met me at its headquarters.

"Gonna write a book on labor!" he exploded in a brass voice, glaring at me. "What labor? . . . What the hell you talkin' about? There ain't no labor in this country! The minds of the workin'-stiffs are capitalized, if you know what I mean. Maybe you don't know what I mean. Maybe you ain't very bright —a goddamn writer who's gonna write about labor! Who ever heard of a writer that had any brains? Lissen: by 'capitalized' I mean that all the so-called workers in this country got the capitalist bug in their beans. They all wanna make dough on the stock market, get ahead, and —— the other guy! And you wanna write a book about labor!" He roared contemptuously. ". . . Oh yeah, things *was* different in them days, back in 1910 and '11, 'specially on the Coast, but everybody's lost interest since. There was a fight on in them days—what I call a *fight*! We had Frisco; we almost had Los. Now, if you ask me, or even if you don't ask me, I'm tellin' you, I don't give a —— what becomes of the workin'-stiffs. I hope they get it in the neck for fair; got it comin' to 'em. You can't do nothin' for 'em. Then why in hell should you worry your head about 'em? Write a book about labor! Christ! I guess you're young and a goddamn idealist—a damn fool, in other words. A writer! . . . Lissen, fellah: all I'm interested in is the fighters, the boys in jail, guys like McNamara and Tom Mooney; see? But, oh, hell, I guess I really shouldn't talk to you. You're liable to queer somethin'. I could tell you lotsa things to write about—interestin' things—make your hair stand on end—but why the hell should I? I don't know who you are. Besides, who d'yuh think is gonna read your goddamn book when you do write it? Think labor's gonna read it? . . ."

By October I had assembled the story of the violent conflicts between labor and capital; then—living in a tiny four-dollar-a-week room in an old brownstone house on Park Avenue near Eighty-sixth Street which had not yet been demolished to make room for a modern apartment building—I plunged into the actual writing of the book. The job fascinated and excited me quite as much as had the original Cantrell story. I was touching an important phase of America. And I worked from twelve to sixteen hours a day. For weeks the only person with whom I spoke more than a few words at a time was Stella. We would walk around the Reservoir in Central Park.

The autumn of that fateful year was lovely in New York.

I was so absorbed in industrial violence that I read the newspapers hastily and irregularly, and I barely noticed the headlines about the stock crash in Wall Street on October 29th. But one day in mid-November, hurrying to my room from somewhere, I heard a woman shriek not far away from me as I turned from Eighty-fourth Street into Park Avenue. I saw a crowd running to a spot in front of a high apartment building. The screaming woman had seen a man leap to his death from one of the upper stories. Theory: he had lost everything in the crash. . . . Later I heard a sort of grim joke, which went about in New York: Park Avenue was not safe to walk on any more, there were too many ruined financiers and speculators jumping from the windows of their ten- and twelve-room apartments. . . .

On arriving in New York early in the summer, I had seven or eight hundred dollars, which traveling and living expenses reduced toward the autumn's end to less than a hundred. But I was not really worried. I did not doubt that soon as I turned in a few finished chapters, with the rest of the script in rough first draft, I would receive the promised substantial advance from Knopf. I think, however, that I hurried so with the work, keeping at it day and night, partly because of my financial situation. I was subconsciously, more than consciously, aware of it. And then, with my exchequer down to about thirty dollars at Christmas time, I took the script—for the same, but now conscious and more urgent, reason—to the publisher's office before it was quite ready to leave my hands.

But when I took it there, I had a sudden feeling that something was wrong. The Knopf office, somehow, was not the same place it had been in the summer. As I waited in the anteroom for the telephone girl to announce me to some one, one of the editorial people, who had been very cordial to me five months before, entered and, seeing me, gave me a perfunctory greeting and accepted the bundle of typescript I offered him with a hasty "Oh yes, yes!" He mumbled something to the effect that I would presently hear from them and went hastily into his office. His manner puzzled, frightened me. Having been busy writing a book, I did not yet know that, in common with other businesses, the bottom was dropping out of the book business; that publishers generally had begun to think of cutting their lists and staffs; that everybody was on edge. The world was not the same place it had been five months before. And I was suddenly conscious of a hundred serious defects in the script I had just turned in.

I was down to the last five dollars when, after I had waited three weeks, a messenger brought me a package—with a letter signed by one of the Knopf people. They were deeply sorry; they had given it long and careful consideration, but the condition of my manuscript was such that they were unable to see a book in it.

It was early January, a cold, sunny, brisk day after a snowfall during the night, and I went for a walk around the Reservoir. The snow squeaked underfoot. I needed a new pair of shoes and a heavier overcoat than the one I had brought from Los Angeles. . . .

Of course, in a way it was a relief to get this decision from Knopf. The waiting for it had been unbearable. I had feared it might be unfavorable: for I realized more and more that, save for the first few chapters, the script was an extremely rough draft of the book I wanted to do, or perhaps even only the raw material for it. But now, at the same time that I knew Knopf was fully justified from his angle in turning it down, I felt terribly low, anyhow. I wished they had given me another chance at it, called me up and talked with me about it. I was sure that that pile of script was potentially a good book, and I did not doubt I could make it good.

Had I not been in love, everything would have been simpler. I had more or less starved during a couple of other periods in my life. Now, when Stella would ask me if I had heard about the book, I would have to tell her and admit a setback. O masculine pride! I was afraid, too, that, although she had said nothing, she had been suspecting for some time that I was in financial straits; that I had been counting on the advance from the publisher, which now was not forthcoming. She had wanted to buy me an overcoat for Christmas! I had given her only a book! These thoughts made me squirm. She had a job, earning thirty a week, and had just recently remarked in a connection—casually but, I did not doubt, very deliberately—that she had some money saved. I squirmed some more when it occurred to me that now she might offer it to me. I realized that to feel as I did was silly, for Stella was the sort of person who would give whatever she had to almost anyone who needed it; but I could not help squirming. . . . So I decided (and hated) to telegraph to a friend in California for a sum I knew he could spare easily and indefinitely, and would not refuse me.

Thus began for me two lean and hectic years—1930-31. It was seven months from the time of the Knopf rejection until *Dynamite* was finally accepted and I received a small royalty advance. Meantime I managed to sell only a story each to the *Mercury* and *Plain Talk*, which yielded me less than two hundred dollars all told. I tried to get a job, but by then the Depression was getting so deep that that was out of the question. Feeling rather confident that eventually I would get out of the woods, I borrowed at various times as need arose from different friends in California who were in position to make me loans. Finally Stella told me I was not fooling her at all . . . and insisted I use what little money she had saved.

On a sudden one day early in this period, when I was feeling especially depressed, trying to work on a story which I hoped would sell to *Mercury*, a large, hulking young man in a vast overcoat stood in my little room, practically filling it. Greeting me, "Hi, Lou!" although I had never seen him before, he handed me a letter of introduction from my friend Joe Jackson, since dead, but then perhaps the most successful screen writer in Hollywood—one of the people from whom I was borrowing.

The young man was Owen Francis, a one-time steel-worker of Clairton, near Pittsburgh; also an ex-soldier of the A.E.F. in France, a former film-writer in Hollywood, and just lately the author of a narrative in the *Mercury* which I had read and rather liked. The narrative dealt with his youth in the steel-mills and how, while in a hospital in France with a wound, he had happened to read a book and, in consequence, abruptly developed the ambition to become a writer. After the war he saw a motion picture which had partly to do with a steel-mill; so he went to Hollywood, where, having no ability in handling money, he earned a thousand dollars one week and was poor the next. He had lately left there . . . and here he was, charged with the ambition to set New York on its ears with his "stuff," as he called it. Accepting his first piece, Mencken had written him that he hoped to publish more of his things.

He was about thirty, over-vital, nervous and restless, with a pronounced talent for describing the color and movement of things, but if the least hint of an idea crept into a conversation, he was lost, confused, inarticulate, miserable. He talked fluently, and with some form, of steel-mills and Hunky steel-workers, for whom he had immense respect and affection. Before he had been with me for five minutes he affectionately called me a "Hunky so-and-so," and wanted to know what I meant by trying to be a writer when, as a Hunky, I should really be working in a mine or a steel-mill, making "lotsa mon." He told me to call him Hal.

An hour following his arrival, Hal was established in a room, which happened to be vacant, on the floor below me . . . and for three or four months thereafter I had my hands full with him. Acting from the very first minute of our meeting as though he and I were lifelong friends and had everything in common, he was a curious mingling of nuisance and fun. On the whole, however, he was very good for me at the time. He kept me from brooding and worrying over *Dynamite*. I enjoyed his steel-mill stories. His idea of the Hunkies was mostly wrong, but amusing; something on the order of Octavus Roy Cohen's idea of the Negroes. His black centerless eyes held a wild, sad, desperate look; diffused through the rest of his abundant person, however, was a tremendous gift of laughter. He roared at the least provocation, often at things which were the opposite of funny.

Hal rented a room three or four times the size of mine, but could not stay in it when awake more than a half-hour at a time. Walls and ceilings oppressed him. He felt and acted like a caged animal. He was at a loss to understand how I endured living and working in so tiny a "hole." He seldom sat still for more than a minute. "Christ, Lou," he would exclaim of a sudden in the middle of a sentence, as we talked, "let's get the hell outa here! Let's get out,"—desperately. "What do you say we take a walk?"

We walked for hours, through all parts of New York, and he told me the stories of the steel industry he was to write "when I settle down a bit and get used to New York. . . ."

Some of his stories were great material; and his oral telling had a touch of the heroic; but, as I soon perceived, he did not have it in him to settle down at a typewriter for more than twenty minutes at a spell, nor to write anything long or greatly. His energy was exploding in all directions, burning up with its own fury. He utterly lacked discipline, calm, concentration. Yet, somehow, he turned out a couple of short manuscripts, which he took to *The American*

Mercury office in person. He did not meet Mencken, who was spending most of his time in Baltimore, but talked with his assistant, Charles Angoff, whom he did not like, though he could not tell me why—perhaps because Angoff, whom I knew slightly, was so clearly an intellectual.

The *Mercury* rejected the stories with a little green slip reading "Thank you," and for an hour Hal was like a kicked dog. He almost whined. Then he raged and fumed. That —— (unquotable) Angoff! Did I think Mencken had seen his stories? Should he write to Mencken and ask him? I did not think it would do much good, for Angoff doubtless had authority to reject scripts. Well, he had a good mind to go and beat up Angoff. I said, "Don't be a fool, Hal." Whereupon he burst out laughing. Tears ran into his mustache. He laughed, too, at the fact that *Dynamite* had been rejected. Whenever he thought of it, he roared, and I had to laugh with him.

One morning Hal burst into my room, his wild eyes ablaze with excitement. "Jeez, Lou, yesterday I met a guy by the name of Tom Wolfe—ever heard of 'im? Neither had I till yesterday. Spent the afternoon with him. Well, he's a writer and, Christ, he writes like a bastard, no kiddin'. He showed me coupla pages. And you should see 'im! A big guy; Christ, I'm a shrimp 'longside of 'im? He must be eight feet, or seven anyhow; and, Jeez, built like a sky-scraper—honest, I'm not kiddin' you. He comes from somewhere down South— North Carolina, wherever that is—and was a college-teacher or somethin' for a while. Imagine, a guy like that a college professor!" He roared. "Now he lives in a warehouse loft in Brooklyn which—I mean the loft—is the size of fifty or a hundred of these rooms you and I live in here. He writes ten thou-sand words a day. Stuff just pours outa him like a goddamn river. I guess the son-of-a-bitch is a genius."

"What is he writing?" I asked.

"I dunno. He don't know himself." Hal went into one of his fits of laughter. "He just writes, and writes, and writes. What the hell! I guess it'll be a novel; two, five, ten novels—nobody knows. Oh yeah, come to think of it, I believe he already published, or is soon to publish, a book called something like *Look Backward* (or *Homeward*), *Angel*. He's got crates and packing-cases full of script in that loft which would fill half-a this room, I'm tellin' you for a fact. When he doesn't write, he walks around in Brooklyn, sometimes all night—alone—from one end of Brooklyn to the other." Hal roared.

In five weeks, Hal had spent the entire considerable amount he had brought from Hollywood. My own situation, as already suggested, was a continuous crisis. We kept sending out our several short manuscripts, which were promptly returned. Few of the better-paying magazines were buying anything.

Since his coming into my life, I had had several fine meals on Hal at Luchow's and Lindy's, at the Algonquin and the Shelton, and in elegant speak-easies in the East lower Fifties; now he ate bean soup and corned-beef hash on me at the Foltis-Fischer cafeteria on Eighty-Sixth Street near Lexington Avenue. He thought this "funny as a bastard," and we laughed.

But then the rent was due, and I was about to wire to California for another loan when Hal and I received on the same day a note apiece from Burton Rascoe, till lately editor of *The Bookman*, now literary editor of *Plain Talk*. He said he liked the two stories we had sent to the magazine a few days before, and meant to use them in an early issue. Since we lived at the same address, he assumed we knew one another. Would we not come together and lunch with him on next Friday? Hal was again on top of the world. He roared; we would yet show New York what was what. I laughed with him. Some time later he sold another piece to *Scribner's*, and I one to the *Mercury*.

Slight of build, not yet forty but already graying, with a thin boyish face and nervous, friendly manner, Burton Rascoe said he was "crazy" about our stories and sorry *Plain Talk* paid so little—only a cent and a half a word, and that on publication. Explaining our situation, Hal and I informed him we needed the money right away, and he promised to try to get the business office to send us our checks at once. If he failed in this, he would advance us the money out of his own pocket.

We ate pigs' knuckles and sauerkraut in an illegal but wide-open beer-place on East Twenty-second Street . . . and, thanks mainly to Hal's informality, we were Burton, Hal, and Louis in no time at all. Burton asked us what we were doing—writing any books? Peppering his narrative with magnificent profanity and obscenity, Hal told him of his contemplated steel saga; then I gave an outline of my rejected *Dynamite*. And Burton—the eager, perennial, endlessly generous, and tireless discoverer of talent, which had been one of his chief functions since his literary editorship on the Chicago *Tribune* before the war—then and there developed the idea that Hal and I were potentially two of the most important American writers and soon after publicly declared so in the New York *World*. He urged Hal to hurry up and write his saga, and asked me to bring him *Dynamite*.

I brought him the inchoate, mountainous manuscript, saying, "This is just rough, Burton—little better than raw material—but, if some one wants to publish it, I'll work on it—rewrite the whole thing. I could do it in six weeks or two months."—"All right," said Burton. A few days later he telephoned me: *Dynamite* was a grand book, and I must not let anybody tell me different. He would place it for me. There would be no trouble. I need not worry about it any more. . . . I reëmphasized that I knew the book needed rewriting, but in his enthusiasm, born of his eagerness as a "discoverer" and an instinctive favorable conclusion about me, he scarcely heard what I said. Later, when I again talked with him about it, I became quite sure he had not read the manuscript, but had merely glanced through it, mostly at the chapter headings. This was all he went on, and on my oral outline of the book, which was much better than the script.

This was in April, 1930 . . . and Burton Rascoe, who had just lost a fortune on the market and had recently had a barrel of other ill luck, threw himself body and soul into the task of finding me a publisher. For three months he vainly wrangled, in succession, with Liveright, McBride, Boni, Vanguard, and other houses. He seemed to insist my book was publishable as it stood; and once or twice, when Burton took me along to the editorial offices, I found myself in the curious position of agreeing with the publishers who were rejecting my script, rather than with my friend and champion.

Burton was one of the judges of the Literary Guild book club; so he decided to try to get Carl Van Doren, the Guild's chief editor, to take it before it had a publisher. He failed in this. Carl Van Doren—a tall, well-built, superbly-tailored man, in his mid-forties, with an unusual haircut, which seemed to frame his sad, heavy face, lighted by a pair of quiet, cool, interested eyes— asked me to come to see him, and he patiently explained to me why *Dynamite* would not do as a Guild selection. It was too controversial. I had to agree with him.

Finally, in July, we took it to the Viking Press. A month or so later I was called to the office, and had a conference with Harold Ginzburg, president of Viking, and two of his editors: all three highly intelligent and well-informed on the subject of capital-labor problems. They wanted the book; we agreed on the revision of the manuscript; and I received a royalty advance of five hundred dollars, which appeared a tremendous sum—till I paid off my most urgent debts.

Thank you, Burton!

Hal did not write his steel saga. He published a few more pieces in *Scribners*, then returned to Hollywood. . . .

Working from twelve to fourteen hours daily, I completed the revision in time for publication early the ensuing spring. But after I turned in the revised script, the Viking editors and attorneys and I wrangled over the McNamara chapters for several weeks. Deciding to make some other use of his story later on, I had kept Cantrell out almost entirely, but dealt rather fully with the Los Angeles events in 1910 and 1911 apart from him—too fully, thought Viking, for a happy balance of the book; and by and by I agreed with them, and we cut entire sections, including the story of the Owens Valley "water steal." The lawyers were worried about this and that; so we cut more . . . till at the end there was left but a substantial skeleton of the Los Angeles *Times*-McNamara story.

Late in 1930, Mary Austin—who had learned from our mutual friend Carey McWilliams, of Los Angeles, what I was doing—came to New York from her home in New Mexico and wrote me to call on her at the National Arts Club in Gramercy Park, where she always stopped. She was in her sixties, a curiously magnificent woman—at once a mystic and a realist, intuitive and intellectually keen, calmly strong, and deeply interested in the West, including (or perhaps, especially) its perennial and epic water problem. There is a chapter about her later in this book.

On the occasion of this our first meeting I gave her the galley-proofs of *Dynamite*, which she read and liked. She asked me to come to see her again, and at our next meeting I told her what I had left out of the book. Having lived in Owens Valley early in the 1900's she had met most of the Los Angeles go-getters who had engineered the "water steal," and hated the whole story but wanted it brought into light of day at this time because she believed that "essentially the same people that pulled the Owens Valley outrage are now behind the Boulder Dam project, using Herbie"—as she called the then President of the United States, who was her personal friend—"to advance their selfish real-estate purposes in southern California, at the expense of the rest of the Southwest and the country as a whole." She was against urbanism and thought all great cities, socially, economically, and culturally unsound, but her feeling about Los Angeles amounted to loathing. She considered herself a prophetess, and told me that on leaving California in 1910, or thereabouts, she had written a prophecy as to the fate of Los Angeles when that city should have attained a population of several million. She did not tell me what that fate would be, but I gathered it would be cataclysmic. She said the written prophecy was in a sealed envelope in her safe-deposit box, and would be opened by her literary executors a certain number of years after her death. Meantime the thing to do was for me to get my story of the "water steal" into some important magazine or newspaper, linking it with the Boulder Dam project. She gave me a letter to Walter Lippmann, then chief of the New York *World* editorial page, which I admired, telling him to drop whatever he might be doing when I came and listen to me.

Walter Lippmann—one of the smoothest-mannered, handsomest men I had ever seen—received me very nicely in his office under the gleaming cupola of the old *World* Building on Park Row, and listened quietly and attentively to my tale of Owens Valley and Mary Austin's and my notion of its current significance in relation to the Boulder Dam; then shook his head, smiling faintly; it was not for the *World*: the story was too old and too locally Western—and, thanking me for coming in, he hoped that eventually I might do something else for the paper. He gave me a note to the feature editor, and some time later, shortly before it passed out of existence, I did write a few special articles for the *World*.

When I reported to her my interview with Lippmann, Mary Austin was "disappointed and disgusted." She was bitter, not particularly about Lippmann, but generally about "these New York editors, most of whom are more in Europe than in America . . . most of whom have not been west of Hoboken since they came to New York from Kokomo, Indiana, or Peoria, Illinois, and who go to Hoboken only to drink beer . . . and to many of whom the American West is as remote as Ethiopia." Somewhile later she published a sizzling letter to that effect in the *Saturday Review of Literature*.

But a few months afterwards I managed to get part of the Owens Valley story into an article on Los Angeles that Henry F. Pringle accepted for *The Outlook*, and Mary Austin sent me a night letter: "My congratulations and gratitude. Am forwarding your article to Herbie." But if Herbert Hoover ever saw it, or what he thought of it, I have no inkling.

By 1931, with the Depression deepening, books by new authors almost ceased selling, and I had no hope of any considerable immediate circulation for *Dynamite*, but felt it was a fairly good book (although I was essentially not entirely satisfied with it) and thought it might get a favorable press, and then, with luck, sell in a small way for a long time.

I was not disappointed. The reviews, in fact, were vastly better than I had expected. All the papers in New York and hundreds of them elsewhere gave it a "big splurge." Most of them praised it for its objectivity. Although mainly history going back anywhere from six months to a hundred years, it was a timely book: for mass unemployment was gradually being recognized as a fact and the country was shot through with vague fears of bloody upheavals.

Sinclair Lewis—just back from Sweden, where he had gone as the first American to receive the Nobel Prize in Literature—gave it an enthusiastic public boost. So far as I know, it was attacked only by the official "Communist" and American Federation of Labor publications. The latter tried to label me a "Communist and I.W.W."; while William Z. Foster, official head of the Communist party of America, published a page-long review of the book in the *New Masses*, ripping into me as a "social fascist"—then a favorite epithet with the regular party "Communists" for all who dared to touch on social, economic, and political questions but disagreed with their rigid "line" established by the Comintern in Moscow.

A few large, ultra-respectable department stores refused to handle the book because of the title, which they felt was too explosive, or else because the volume dealt with labor troubles—and, what with business falling off to nothing and growing rumors of mass unemployment, was there not enough trouble in the world already? Why write and publish such a book? But it sold a bit. It became popular in public libraries, and the American Library Association included it in its list of "fifty notable books of 1931." Even some of the people who called themselves "Communists" read it although Comrade Foster had put it on the Index. Presently college teachers began to use it in sociology, economics, history, and current-events courses. . . . In the summer of 1934 I revised the book, bringing it up to date, and Viking brought it out in a new edition. Again the "Communists" attacked it, now chiefly on the ground that somewhere in the book I referred to a crowd of rioting workmen as a "mob," which was an insult to the proletariat of the United States and stamped me as a contemptible bourgeois writer. Now the book became a mild sort of best seller for a while, then settled down to steady small monthly sales. In 1936 I was told that that year it was used, in one way or another, at some eighty colleges in the United States, including Yale, Harvard, Columbia, and Chicago.

Dynamite has, thus, been a source of some satisfaction to me. It was read, I know, by some workers. It got into the reference libraries of most important newspapers in the country. I received a good many letters from middle-class people all over America who became interested in capital-labor questions from reading it. . . . But it has brought me also some unpleasant moments. In 1935, for instance, when I was in Pittsburgh one day, a newspaper reporter friend of mine told me that the head of a firm called Federal Laboratories, Inc., had been using *Dynamite* to advertise one of its products—tear-gas bombs. He had bought scores of copies of the book, then sent them to open-shop industrialists and police chiefs, with a letter to this effect: Read this book and see what happens—see how many people are killed, etc.—when firearms and dynamite are used in class warfare. Use Federal Laboratories' tear-gas bombs instead, and make strike riots and jobless demonstrations bloodless, painless, civilized! . . .

"Universal Genius"

ONE DAY I RECEIVED A POSTCARD—IN CARE OF *The American Mercury*—FROM A man named James Fuchs. He had read a notice in the papers that I was doing a book which had to do with labor, and he wanted to see me. I sent him my address, and he came—a large, loose man in his sixties, bald, ill clad, obviously very poor, unclean and odorous. During the 1920's he had contributed articles on socio-economic subjects to *The Nation*, which I had probably read when they appeared, but had forgotten his name. An old-time Socialist, he had once been on the staff of the New York *Volkszeitung*. He was an Austrian, but in America for nearly forty years.

On entering my room the first thing he said was that he was hard of hearing: I would have to raise my voice talking to him. Then he announced he was hungry, not having eaten for two days, and before we proceeded to getting acquainted he wanted me to take him somewhere and buy him a meal. I had a few dollars, and said, "All right"; and the old man and I walked in silence to the Foltis-Fischer cafeteria, two blocks away.

Scarcely looking at me, he ate till he decided he had enough. Then, wiping his mouth and glaring at me, he demanded in a sharp voice, "Young man, what business have you, at your age, to be writing about American labor?" He evidently was serious. I did not know what to say. "Are you a Socialist?" he asked.

"No."

"I thought as much from reading your articles in the *Mercury*! And you presume to write about labor! Have you read Marx?"

"Parts of him."

"What?"—cupping a hand around his right ear.

"I've read parts of him"—a little louder.

"Parts of him!" he shouted, staring at me indignantly and contemptuously. People at near-by tables turned to look at us.

I said, "Don't yell so, Mr. Fuchs!"

"What?" cupping his ear again.

I said, "Never mind!" I could not help smiling.

"All right," he said, rising and reaching for his hat and cane. "Pay the check and come with me to my room. I shall tell you a few things that ought to interest you, though, of course, I cannot predict whether they will or not."

Curious, I went with him. He lived somewhere in the East Sixties, in a squalid old brownstone house near the river. We walked there—about twenty-five blocks—without speaking.

His tiny, inadequately lighted and unheated room contained a huge rusty iron bed with bedding that had not been changed for weeks. There was a teakettle which he evidently heated over the gas-jet. All around the bed were piles of books, magazines, and newspapers reaching halfway to the ceiling. The stench in the place was almost unbearable at first. By and by I got used to it, and perched myself on a heap of books.

The old man rummaged about for a while; then, without speaking, he showed me a page in Upton Sinclair's *Boston*, on which the author acknowledged his indebtedness to James Fuchs for his aid to him in the writing of this novel. He showed me similar acknowledgments from Floyd Dell and other well-known writers, and handed me a letter from Mencken.

"Don't read it yet," he said. "Let me explain first. . . . A month or so ago I chanced to read Mencken's last book, *Treatise on the Gods,* and found it full of errors—five, ten, a dozen of them in every chapter. I wrote him a letter citing all his mistakes and giving my corrections—twenty-six pages in all. I told him that, from the point of view of accuracy, his book was no worse than most books published in America. Most writers in this country, I emphasized, are careless with facts, to say nothing of their so-called ideas and conclusions. They get away with murder! And I suggested to Mencken he induce his friend and publisher, Alfred Knopf, to give me a job on his editorial staff and I would read every manuscript for errors before it was sent to the printer. I offered to do that for twenty-five dollars a week, or even less. I requested Mencken to see me and take me to Knopf. . . . Now read the damned fool's reply to me."

"DEAR MR. FUCHS: There is nothing worse in this world than a universal genius. If you come to see me, I shall jump out of the nearest window. . . . Sincerely yours, H. L. MENCKEN—[or something to that effect; I am quoting from memory]."

I smiled.

"Now don't you be a fool *à la* Mencken!" yelled James Fuchs. "I want to see that manuscript of yours and help you make it, if not sound, at least accurate, not because I like your face (for it is unimportant whether I do or not), but because I am interested in labor. Understand? Of course I hope you will pay me for my work, for I am penniless, but not any more than you can and want to. At this moment I need five dollars, and if you have five dollars and you are able to spare it, I want you to give it to me, either in payment or as part-payment for the work I shall do on your manuscript, or as a loan. I need most of the amount for a cable to my attorney in Vienna, where an uncle of mine died eighteen months ago and, from a motive unknown to me, left me in Austrian money the equivalent of three thousand dollars. I'm having some difficulty in getting the money over. A few days ago I received a letter from my lawyer, to which I want to reply by cable."

I gave him five dollars and let him read *Dynamite*, which by then, I thought, was in fairly good shape. He returned it with a list of about a dozen corrections, none of serious errors. His manner was less contemptuous, less indignant; but, having spent, as he said, most of the five for the cable, he was hungry again and unwilling to tell me what he thought of my book until after I had taken him to the cafeteria once more.

"Now listen to me," he said then. "This may be news to you, but you have not written a great book; nor even—from my, or the Marxian, point of view —an especially worthwhile book. Considering, however, that you wrote it—an ignorant young man, a mere youth—I am obliged to say that it is a competent job, of which any *New Republic* editor would be proud, than which, of course, I can give you no lower praise. But that is what I think of it."

His explanation of some of his corrections of my errors revealed to me an astounding detailed knowledge of the history of the American labor and radical movements. He could quote to me the exact words of what one of the four delegates from Toledo, Ohio, had said upon the floor of the Structural Steel and Iron Workers' convention at Philadelphia in 1903. And he had endless information on endless other subjects.

At the same time that he repelled me as a person, I developed great respect for him, and felt more and more that it was a living shame he did not have a secure and steady function somewhere. But I understood, too, why he did not have it. Later I heard that, off and on, he had had jobs in various book-publishing and magazine offices, but seldom for more than a week or two weeks. His fellow employees could not endure having him around. Seldom bathing, he smelled offensively, and he could not avoid behaving contemptuously toward everybody about him.

By-and-by, however, my own respect for his mind and knowledge began to waver. Basically, he was a typical intellectual radical. To him labor was Labor, an abstraction, an entity, complete and whole by itself. In his mind, there was no question of its destiny. The earth was but a wheel of labor, moved by and for the workers. He ignored all forces outside of labor except as they conspired to impede it. These he denounced, and that was that. In short, his outlook was narrow, bitter, perverted. His labor ideas were things made of statistics, passed and rejected resolutions, which were printed in musty books and dog-eared pamphlets. The worker himself, vital and living, was a factor he had lost sight of. . . .

I gave him what little money I could spare. Every once in a while he came to ask me breathlessly for three or four dollars: he must send a cable to his solicitor in Vienna without delay. I never quite believed he had a solicitor or a legacy in Vienna. Eventually I became almost certain he had not. I met people who knew him and laughed at his "cable racket," as one of them called his constant borrowing during the past year and a half of small amounts of money.

I did not hold his "racket" against him and was sorry for him, but was never particularly glad when he came. Every time I saw him he said the legacy, minus the lawyer's fees, might come any day now, whereupon he would pay me. Worrying about him, one day I drafted a letter to Upton Sinclair describing Fuchs' situation, adding I was unable to help him substantially, and suggesting that he (Upton) send him as much as he could, or else get some one else to aid him—but when I showed the draft to Fuchs, he turned furious. Upton had no money; Upton was tens of thousands of dollars in debt; Upton was busy and must not be bothered; I was a damned fool for thinking of writing such a letter to Upton. Besides, the legacy, he said again, was due to reach him any day now; he had just penetrated what seemed the last entanglement of Austrian red tape. . . .

Late in the winter it occurred to me that I had not seen, or heard from, him for a month or longer. When *Dynamite* came off the press I sent him a copy, but the book was returned. The addressee had moved. I met people who had seen him; they smiled about his "legacy"; no one knew where he lived. Once I caught sight of him from a Fifth Avenue bus—a shabby old figure; but when I got off and rushed after him, he had disappeared, I suppose into some building.

I moved to a new address, but thought Fuchs might eventually write me in care of Viking or one of the magazines to which I had contributed; but I never heard from him again. . . . During 1931 he more or less receded from my mind, till one day when I happened to read for the first time George Gissing's *Grub Street*, which contains a character resembling Fuchs.

A few weeks later I chanced to see a story about him in an afternoon paper. He had died in a Bronx Hospital of toxemia, having long lived on scraps he had found in garbage-cans. The newspaper story hinged, O. Henry-like, on his Vienna legacy. He had been waiting nearly three years for it. A draft for $2,200 came the day before he died—after he had lost consciousness and doctors could no longer help him.

Dan

A KNOCK ON MY DOOR . . . AND IN WALKED DAN HENNESSY—AN AGILE, SLIGHT but not frail, dapper young man, twenty-five or -six, with a fine head of curly black hair and a handsome face, at once boyish, cynical, and bitter; French-Irish by blood, but third- or fourth-generation American. His entry was swift, dramatic; his greeting and his explanation that he had procured my address from *The American Mercury* on the strength of a fib, that he was my cousin, held a like excitement.

I had first met Dan in California in 1926, when he, the author of a Haldeman-Julius Little Blue Book entitled *On the Bum*—was still on the bum. By the time he was twenty-two he had been a "road kid" and young tramp half his life. At seventeen he had learned printing and proof reading, and had worked at these trades between "jumps," which often were long and far between jobs. He had been over most of the United States, associating by predilection with the lowest of the lowly; had narrowly escaped death many times, and seen six tramps and hoboes killed hopping freights. "I had a partner once," he told me in California, "who fell asleep while we were riding an oil-car. He rolled off as we went over a trestle." Dan's talk was largely a matter of such episodes, which he narrated with a smirking matter-of-factness.

He had first run away at ten. He told me of his family—a sordid tale. He had no use for any of them, except a little for his father. His favorite relative was Uncle Ed, whose life story he delighted in telling: "Ed started as a precocious boy. He had got through Shakespeare and Dickens before he was sixteen. But he had the wastrel temperament. He failed in the usual first jobs —office boy, clerk, and so on. Later some one got him to go on the stage. He took acting seriously and studiously, and seems to have been very competent. But then his sponsor died and Ed was not sufficiently aggressive to get rôles in plays by himself. Also, he was not disposed to lick anybody's boots. He hung around the house, reading, thinking. One day his father mildly reproached him for not earning a living, and Ed allowed the remark to hurt his feelings and left home for good. He soon degenerated to bumdom, and from that day to this he has been a Bowery derelict. When some one in the family dies, my father digs up Ed and gets him a new suit of clothes so he can attend the funeral. Ed pawns the suit promptly after the ceremony. . . . During the war my father was working in Waterbury, Connecticut. He sent for Ed in the hope he would hold down an elevator operator's job. Ed made the trip to Waterbury by successive trolley cars, taking several days to accomplish it. He worked two days at the elevator job and impressed all with his gentlemanly politeness and smooth speech, which smacked of Shakespeare and the great English novelists. The third day he returned to the Bowery the same way he came. . . ."

Besides printing, proof reading, tramping, and writing the little book, Dan had been also a prize fighter (once, for a moment, within sight of the bantam-weight championship of the world), member of dramatic and circus troupes in various parts of the country, and assistant to Dr. Ben Reitman of Chicago, whose patients came from unusual walks of life. When I saw him in California, his inclination was to be an actor-playwright, more or less à la Shakespeare and Noel Coward.

Now, late in 1930, he turned up in New York, and had apparently arrived not on the rods, but on cushions. He wore a fine belted camel-hair overcoat, an elegant tweed suit, patent-leather shoes, a tip-top fedora, and a silk shirt and necktie, which together comprised an ensemble a trifle flashy but not tasteless. "I made some dough," he explained, "managing a young pug in Chicago who won a couple bouts the last few months. This suit and coat are worth a hundred bucks, but I bought them for ten apiece from a couple of bozos who stopped me on La Salle Street a week ago. The coat was a perfect fit; the suit had to be altered a bit."

He saw me looking at him.

"Naturally, I didn't ask them where they got the clothes. It was none of my business; I am no cop or arbiter between right and wrong. Besides, if you want to look at it on moral grounds, the racketeer-thieves were probably entitled to the clothes as much as was the so-called rightful owner, who, the chances are, had swindled some one in buying the material and then under-paid the people who tailored the garments. . . ."

Since our last meeting, Dan had written a prize-fight play, *We Want Blood,* and a full-length novel as yet untitled. He wanted me to read them and see if there was any chance of "peddling" them. I read both at single sittings.

The play was unconventional in form, undoubtedly "poor theater," but—rich in prize-ring lingo and peppered with superb lines—an effective study of the pugilistic racket and the brutality it evoked in fight fans. Writing from the inside, Dan presented the fighter's life as mean and dull, leading in most cases to disability and degeneration of one kind or another. I knew next to nothing about Broadway, but felt he would not get his play accepted. It was too true, too depressing, lacking utterly in "lift." He took it around for months, in vain.

The novel was obviously autobiography, one of the bitterest things I have read till some years later, when I came upon Louis-Ferdinand Céline's master-piece of sordidness and despair, *Journey to the End of the Night.* It began: "To Mrs. Hara [*i.e.,* Dan's mother] babies were merely the disgusting part of love." The central character of the story was Gene (Dan himself), who, as the story opens, is known among the neighbors as "that Hara baby that's always crying." . . . "His mother responded to his fits of crying by slapping him wherever her hand fell. Not having developed a sense of irony or stoicism, he retaliated by pouring out more tears and noise. Which, of course, meant more slaps. . . . Sometimes his brown eyes gazed at the woman in wonder as they later looked at a punishing, unfathomable world. . . ." He maintained this note through three hundred pages, adding to it obscenity, which was a definite part of the story; and the result—as he convinced himself during the same time that his play traveled from one producer to another—was not publishable as a book for general circulation.

One evening Dan and I sat in a Foltis-Fischer cafeteria, talking after supper. Suddenly, interrupting the conversation, Dan said under his breath, "See that man over there?" He indicated a slight, bald elderly fellow who had just taken a seat at the table nearest ours. His back was to us; his supper consisted of a bowl of soup, a piece of pie, and a cup of coffee. "My old man," said Dan. "I haven't seen him for six years. Funny I should run into him here, isn't it?" By then he had been in New York for a month or longer. He sat, smoking, grinning curiously. I was looking at him. "I suppose you think I should go over and say hello to him," he smiled. I said, "It doesn't matter what I think; you do what you like. If you don't mind, I'll be merely an interested observer."

Dan smiled, looking at me, hesitating; then rose, walked over to the other table, slipped into a chair, and said, "Hello!" They were sufficiently close for me to hear their words. The man looked up from his soup and returned the greeting quietly, "Hello, Dan!" as though they had not seen one another for six days instead of six years. "When did you get to town?"—"This morning," lied Dan. —"Well, ain't that funny. Matter of fact, I been thinkin' of you this afternoon."

Dan came back to me and took his check. "I'm going with the old man if you don't mind," he said, smiling. Next day he told me he had taken his father, who worked as an elevator operator and watchman in a warehouse down on Varick Street, to a movie. Dan did not see him again while he was in New York that trip.

He lived awhile on the money he had made managing the Chicago prize fighter, then found a job as proof reader in the shop where *Liberty* magazine was being printed, and for several months earned forty or fifty a week. He had a room at one of the better hotels on Broadway, patronized mainly by bookies, gamblers, assorted racketeers, and their ladies.

Evenings he associated with fantastic characters on the lowest levels of the theatrical world, and he introduced me to some of them. They had regular hangouts, notably the doorway next to the Palace Theatre's entrance. They were twisted persons, perverts of many kinds, human oddities, a few minor had-beens, the rest would-be's who had not made the grade and never would make it, but who hung onto their frustration, which in most cases was all they had. They lived in impossible holes-in-the-wall. One middle-aged man with the manner of a Shakespearean ham actor lived in a "room" on Forty-second Street three floors below the sidewalk. There were, of course, no windows; no whiff of fresh air ever reached down; and the stench in the place was indescribable. The man had lived there for ten or a dozen years, waiting for his "big chance." He ate irregularly, was clearly disbalanced in his head; and Dan assured me he was typical of thousands on Broadway.

I was sorry for these people, wondered about them, tried to explain them in terms of New York and ambition, but was not drawn to them. In fact, the opposite was true. To Dan, however, they were a sort of sour cream of the earth —*his* people, failures, misfits, victims not of the capitalist system (for he had no social consciousness or anything like that), but of life, which was a brutal institution, a joke perpetrated on humanity by a cruel Power. He believed that New York had probably a million people belonging to this class—would-be actors, would-be writers, would-be musicians, would-be this and that.

But Dan was not really of them, nor essentially like them. They had delusions concerning themselves and coming fame. He was a terrific realist and would not stick to, or starve for, anything if he could help it. He did not admire the would-be's, but was drawn to them like a fly to refuse.

He had a strange, fierce feeling about the city, as though its evil secrets mingled with those in the deep of his own life. He loved to recite passages from James Thomson's *City of the Dreadful Night*, his favorite poem, which he said applied perfectly to New York. In a curious, twisted way Dan suffered for the vast mass of queer, unfortunate people of whom he was sharply and painfully conscious, but, so far as I could ever determine, that suffering resolved itself only into a kind of smirking, negative bitterness, which off and on made me uneasy.

Dan liked what he called "bozos," whom he defined as "tough mugs who don't give a damn and don't slobber all over about Life." He was interested in sports, but not as sports; rather as a department of low life. He read Westbrook Pegler regularly. Pegler, who in those days wrote only sports, was a mug, a bozo, bitter and cynical. He liked also Damon Runyon, whom he met. Among the modern American writers he vastly admired Ring Lardner for being a bozo full of bitterness who could also write.

He read Thomas Hardy's *Jude the Obscure* and relished the story, but especially the scene where the nine-year-old boy, Father Time, so called because of his unchildlike face, kills his half-sister and brother and hangs himself in a closet, leaving a note: "Done because we are too menny."

But it was impossible not to like Dan. He was interesting and had a real charm, which is rather hard to describe. His humor was bitter, but sparkling. He liked me (though it puzzled me why), and we were friends. For a time after he had lost his *Liberty* job I moved to a larger room and we shared it. I had a very clear feeling about him that he was a species of genius who had been savagely hurt early in life, very likely by his mother, who was dead, but whose memory he hated; and I wondered if that genius could not be helped somehow, so it would at least partly emerge and commence to function in some positive way. At this time in his life he was torn between two urges—to act and to write. I could not help him to become an actor; but thought I knew a little about writing; so I egged him on to write, telling him not to let himself be discouraged by the rejections of his play and novel. His mind and feelings held endless material, most of it a by-product of his own experiences as a road-kid and tramp, migratory printer, actor and circus attendant, prize fighter, and lifelong connoisseur of human failure and degeneration. . . . Dan wrote, and some of the stories and sketches he turned out seemed good to me, but the magazine market was well-nigh closed to new writers; and it was a job, as the manuscripts returned, to keep him from curdling up in his smirking, humorous bitterness.

Soon after *Dynamite* appeared, I received a letter from an aspiring writer in Keokuk, Iowa, who contemplated coming to New York. In a recent *Mercury*, which contained a story of mine, he had learned from a notice printed in back of the magazine that I was now living in New York. Would I advise him to come East? He had published a sketch and a poem in *Midland*, and was thinking of writing a book. He was twenty-four and had two hundred dollars; how long did I think that amount would last him in New York? . . . In view of my own recent hardships, I advised him to stay in Keokuk, and showed his and my letters to Dan.

Dan was amused. Then he hit upon the idea that he and I collaborate on a book entitled *Stay in Keokuk!*, written in the form of letters between a young would-be author in Iowa and a writer in New York (himself mostly would-be) who had gone through the mill. The idea interested me awhile, for I was vaguely cognizant of hundreds of thousands of young people in tens of thousands of Keokuks whose ambitions were sensitive to the magnetic attraction of New York. Dan wrote a satiric outline of what he had in mind; together we concocted a preface, then gave up the whole thing—chiefly because it suddenly occurred to me (and probably also to Dan) that we were too unlike to collaborate on anything extensive and complex, and partly because just then Mencken suddenly accepted one of Dan's stories.

The story, *A Little Path of Glory,* was, to my mind, one of the best prizering tales ever written, vastly superior to anything similar by Ring Lardner, Ernest Hemingway, or Jim Tully. It appeared in the August, 1931, *Mercury* under the pseudonym of Robert Jeans. Accepting it, Mencken asked him to send him something else soon; and with this "shot in the arm," as he called it, Dan worked day and night for weeks revising his old manuscript and writing new stories and sketches. He sold two or three more pieces to the *Mercury* in rapid succession, and for a time seemed to feel good about himself.

When I married, Dan went to live by himself again, but the scant *Mercury* honoraria did not last long; I could not loan him anything . . . and suddenly, without letting me know, he returned to Chicago, where he took over the managership of another prize fighter, who, however, was not much good. So Dan drifted to Detroit, whence he sent me a note; whereupon I did not hear from him for a year. I tried to locate him all that time, which included the first few months of Stella's and my visit in Yugoslavia in 1932: for he had left with me the manuscripts of *We Want Blood* and his title-less novel. One of my letters from Yugoslavia reached him, and he answered:

. . . I am a reporter on the Detroit *Times*. The big shot likes my *Merc* stories and invited me to go to work. . . . In order to hold this job, I have revamped my entire personality and acquired a new attitude and viewpoint. Service is my motto. I am 102% for organization harmony and efficiency. I have volunteered to give pep talks to the staff. You've heard of the Voice with the Smile? Nothing to it. My voice bursts right over with cachinnation. . . .

However, your letter from Yugoslavia kicks up such envy in me that my newly acquired habits, etc., are in danger of collapsing. Ships, the sea, Lisbon, the Mediterranean, the Adriatic, Carniola! You fill me with purple melancholy. Too much of the glamour of far places for my Arab constitution. . . . Of course I'm glad you and Stella are having all those wonderful experiences in your native country. You two are unique—about the only people I hear from who are not marooned behind the eight ball.

Before getting this job on the *Times* I had one hell of a time for months—the reason I didn't write to you, as I assumed you were none too flush and didn't want to touch you. But it was nickels and dimes, and few of them. I thought I had been on the umbay before, but you should have seen me this time! . . .

The job is not bad as jobs go, not ill paid; but, though determined to stick on it, I don't really like it. Reporting is a sordid, nasty business. Stinking dead bodies in skunky poverty-blighted places. Tragic children that almost slay you with their eyes. Suicides, sex triangles, morgues, foul courts, ugh and double ugh. . . .

I've been covering a lot of ejection cases. One Polish family was very difficult to kick out. The Communists urged them to resist. Over a hundred cops and nineteen constables threw a cordon around the block in order to get them out. One of the ejectees heaved a brick at me. I ducked okay. . . . Have covered two inquests of cases in which families resisted ejections by shooting the landlord to death. Both were acquitted!

Am covering one now in which a constable killed an ejectee who refused to get out. Looks bad for the constable. . . .

The other day I discovered quite by accident that a man's head had been crushed at Ford's while its owner was engaged in some trivial task. I turned in the story but was told that such stuff is not news. I also learned on good authority that on last July twentieth more than nine hundred men had collapsed in a single department at Ford's—the foundry. All carefully selected huskies, they fainted at the rate of one a minute. This was a particularly hot day, but the one-a-minute schedule for knockouts is not uncommon in that foundry on other days.

Did you know that for work in such departments applicants are examined much as one would examine a horse to be bought? They deliberately feel the applicant's thighs, biceps, etc., as one would feel the fetlocks of an animal. . . .

But don't think I've become "social minded," or that I give a good goddamn what's happening in America or the world. I am telling you these things because I think they probably will interest you. It is all transient, anyway. I mean that the big things—fate, birth, love, hate, greed, stupidity—do not change much. Such events as the American Revolution, the Civil War, etc., have no effect on them——

I'm very glad you'll have *Little Path of Glory* translated into the Yugoslav for the dear people over there. I'll be anxious to see a copy of the magazine when it comes out, and shall always be glad to hear from my public in the Balkans.

No, I'm not writing any more, nor trying to write. Hell with it! Before I got this job I was too hectic to concentrate; now I have no time.

As for the so-called novel and play I left in your possession, don't let them worry you. When you return to the U. S., pitch them into the stove.

Returning to America, I did not burn Dan's manuscripts (as I write I have them still), but communicated with him. He was still on the Detroit *Times*, and remained on that job for a couple of years more—the longest he had ever been in one place. In 1934, after the publication of *The Native's Return*, a lecture tour took me to Detroit, and Dan and I spent several hours together. He publicized me in the paper. We talked. He was rather formally friendly. I met some of his friends—all bozos.

No; he still did no writing of his own. To the devil with writing! It was mostly a racket, like everything else. He mentioned Mencken, who had lately quit the editorship of the *Mercury* and who Dan thought had been exploiting us young writers for years, paying us next to nothing, making his magazine an important publication and himself a great editor. I said that was a little far-fetched—our first disagreement.

I was rather excited about *The Native's Return* selling so well. Dan chided me about my being a "success," and I gathered he was beginning to hold that against me.

There was then, in the larger cities of the United States, a good deal of loose talk about "the revolution." So-called "Communists" were active in Detroit. Dan asked me what I thought of it all. I did not know, but felt that nothing resembling a revolution could occur in the United States in the near future, if ever. I said the "Communists" in America were a fantastic outfit (to which Dan agreed), destined perhaps to be of no serious consequence in the long run, in one way or another. From his demeanor in this discussion, I surmised that Dan was eager that something like a revolution should happen. He admitted I was correct in my supposition. Why did he want a revolution? He did not answer at once. I said, "Where will you be—what will you do should the revolution (whatever you mean by the word) come?"

He answered, "I'm not going to be playing marbles."

"What do you mean?"

He shrugged his shoulders: I could make my own guess.

Suddenly I understood what he meant. He had not changed in the two and a half years since I had last seen him. He was essentially the same Dan I had known in New York—bitter, hating.

"And I'll not be alone, either," he added. "There will be millions to—" He paused.

"—to what?"

"—to take advantage of such a situation if it arises—to get even for all sorts of things; for things 'way back in the beginning of their lives and before that; for things about which they hold the vaguest, and mostly or even wholly unconscious, grudges."

I knew he was right.

"Many, I suppose," he went on, "will join the revolution, if or when it comes, not because they will believe in it, but just to raise hell, murder; just to break out of their own prisons of hate, if you catch on what I mean. Personally, I won't care who wins; all the same to me. I won't join either side, or I'll join both."

I changed the subject. We had dinner together. On parting we looked at one another a long time, shaking hands. Then we said good-by, quickly.

We have not met or communicated with one another since.

I tried to get in touch with him when I was next in Detroit, a year later, but he had quit the *Times*. He had also moved from the hotel where he had been staying when we met last. I was told he was still in Detroit, managing some third-rate pugilists and doing publicity work for various legitimate "rackets," like wrestling and boxing clubs.

I wrote him a letter to his old address. I do not know whether he received it or not; it was not returned, and he did not answer me. In the fall of 1936 when I was again in Detroit, a newspaper man who knew him told me Dan was still around, and I made another vain attempt to get hold of him.

Every once in a while I wonder, worry about him.

Ben Stolberg

DOING RESEARCH FOR *Dynamite*, I CAME, IN NUMEROUS PUBLIC PRINTS OF THE
1920's, but especially in *The Nation*, upon articles by Benjamin Stolberg,
no doubt a leading American writer on labor movements, who was, besides, a
brilliant critic of books dealing with social and economic problems . . . and
some time after I finished proof reading I wrote to him. He replied; "Why
don't we get together some day soon?"

A native of Germany, Ben Stolberg immigrated to the United States in
1908 as a boy of seventeen, after having attended the Gymnasium in Munich
for a number of years. As a greenhorn he worked in a laundry, walked the
streets of New York jobless, slept in parks, served as a waiter in Hotel Astor.
He went to Harvard (class 1918) and did graduate work in sociology at
Chicago; then, for a period, engaged in all manner of activities—teaching
sociology at the Universities of Oklahoma and Kansas, running a vocational
placement bureau for the Chicago public schools, editing the *Journal* of the
Brotherhood of Locomotive Firemen in Cleveland—until, early in the Hard-
ing-Coolidge era, he developed into an interesting free-lance publicist, whose
work was eagerly published by liberal reviews and "quality" magazines and
by the New York *World, Times, Telegram,* and *Herald Tribune.*

So one evening early in 1931 Ben and I got together at his little apartment
on West Thirteenth Street. He was just forty, but younger-looking; a small,
delicately made agile, blond man, with a deep, pleasant voice, a friendly
manner and generally charming personality, illumined every other moment
as he spoke by flashes of his scintillating mind. He had lately been divorced
from Mary Fox, well known as leader of the League for Industrial Democracy.
Several pictures of his four-year-old son David at various ages hung on the
walls.

We went into a tiny Italian basement restaurant near Ben's dwelling for
dinner, and talked late, getting acquainted. Like myself, he was deeply concerned about The Situation—the economic Depression with its growing unemployment problem and the palpable inability of anyone in the country from
President Hoover down to do anything about it. In New York City alone
scores of jobless and bankrupt people committed suicide daily. Men were
turning on the gas, killing themselves and their families. The press reported
but a fraction of such cases.

The worst aspect of The Situation, we agreed, seemed to be that the people
were taking the Depression on the chin. Aside from suicide guns going off,
everything was quiet. Were industrial and white-collar workers physically
and spiritually exhausted? Were they so steeped in individualism and would-
be respectability that now most of them suffered personal shame for being
out of work, and were confused?

I told Ben the Cantrell story, which to me implicitly and almost fully explained the obvious bankruptcy and ineffectiveness of the American radical and labor movements, which I took practically for granted in the present situation . . . but Ben apparently was not impressed by my narration and tried in part to explain the radicals' and labor's current social and political incompetence in terms of the personalities of their "leaders." He had no use for most of them.

Ben and I spoke of such things as that not a few unemployed and bankrupt persons all over the country, while practically starving, drove in Buicks and Pontiacs, vainly seeking work; that in Mississippi and Arkansas white unemployed men were shooting employed Negroes in order to get their jobs!

Russia fascinated us both. We had been reading the books of Maurice Hindus, Louis Fischer's articles in *The Nation*, and Walter Duranty's pro-Soviet dispatches in the *Times*. But both Ben and I had vague misgivings and reservations about the current Russian setup. I had a remote suspicion that the Hindus-Fischer-Duranty picture was not complete. It looked too good to be the whole truth. Ben's remote perturbation issued mainly from the fact that he sided with the exiled Leon Trotsky, whom he considered a great man. He feared Stalin was "just a tough guy" who, power-hungry (although perhaps not that alone), might "turn the party of Lenin into a kind of world Tammany Hall."

Without agreeing with him upon every point or wholly on any point, I liked Ben on that first meeting. He was erudite, but his knowledge crackled with wit. He loved his wit and humor; loved to characterize prominent people in a single phrase or sentence. Coolidge and William Green, for instance, were "men who rose in the world by standing still on the escalator." . . .

Ben always had some idea for a book or an article, which he did not write. On our first evening together he said he wanted to do a satire on American politics. He would take a pair of Siamese twins, one a conservative, the other a liberal, and get one elected to Congress one term and the other the next, then both together; and thus bring out symbolically the essential inner contradictions and absurdities of politics.

Ben had a great sense of fun.

But I felt in him, too, a deep and complex sadness, which was personal, probably linked to his childhood (anything but ideal), but also more than personal—*Weltschmerz* mixed with his own intimate problems as a man and writer, which, as I subsequently realized, were then for many reasons in a chaotic state. He seemed erratic, bitter, at odds within himself and with things about him. For two or three years now he had done very little work.

He was so many things: an immigrant—a European, his keen intellect cast upon European cultural lines—but also an American, who was more American than were many Americans I knew, with a passionate love for the country of his adoption and a sharp intellectual eye for her realities, which disturbed him, partly because they were disturbing, but to no small extent also because he apprehended them fitfully, specifically with his intellect, rather than steadily with his feelings and instincts. I supposed, and I think I was right, that some of the conflicts I sensed inside him were due to that. He saw things, not in a steady glow of light, but in flashes.

He was a warm, lonely human being, honest, confused or unclear about many things, needing friends and affection: which is true of many sensitive immigrants—more so than of sensitive natives—who love America but are not quite at ease here. His face lit up curiously when he spoke of his son David, showing me the pictures on the wall. "You'll have to meet him some day," he said. "He's a real person. A real American. On his mother's side he is one-sixteenth Indian. . . . I wonder what he'll be, what sort of world he'll live in when he grows up."

Through most of 1931 and early 1932 I saw Ben Stolberg perhaps on the average of once a week. Either I visited him or he me. I met a good many of his friends and acquaintances. He seemed to know everybody in New York I had ever heard of, and many others. Not only writers (some of whom occur in the next chapter), but prominent lawyers, professors, doctors, millionaires, social workers, union officials, and just people—workers, small-business folk. Most of his friends—including those who, like myself, were always half annoyed with him—adored him, and he was at somebody's home nearly every night, usually the life of the party, stimulating and entertaining everybody present. His "cracks" were quoted all over Manhattan.

This going out so much, however, and being the life of one party after another took so much of his time and energy that he could do very little writing. Also, speaking his thoughts to all who would hear, he published orally the things he had to say, and thus partly satisfied the inner pressure to say them in print. Occasionally I thought it was rather important he should write rather than talk to friends, for I had no doubt that if he wrote, say, two or three thousand words a week, within a year he could—with his wit, knowledge, on-pushing spirit, and brilliant style—easily become, culturally, in the 1930's what Mencken was in the 1920's, though the comparison, of course, is not fair either to Ben or to Mencken.

My saying this to him one day (and repeating it to him many times after) pleased Ben. But he did not like it when I started to "nag" and "hound" him (his words) to turn out more articles; for not a few magazines, notably *The Nation*, were ready to print well-nigh anything he wrote. He started to call me his "conscience" and "top sergeant," now and then getting really angry at me.

I urged him to get out of New York for a month or two at a time, and establish himself on some farm or in some little town or village, and balance his thoughts and work; but, a confirmed urbanite who felt lost in the country or in a small community, he loved New York with all its noise, cheap excitement, perversions, and insanities. He said he had to be near a big library.

But I knew that—perhaps because of some lack in his early years—he needed his wide circle of intimate friends, who were his audience, more than he needed a big library. He liked, if it was not downright necessary for his happiness, to *see* his wit play upon people, to hear their laughter.

From my Diary:

April 17, 1931.— . . . In the afternoon at Ben's, talking. Ben was recalling things and people from his experiences and observations since he's come to America, analyzing them, diagnosing various social ills and diseases. What material for an autobiography! . . .

November 3, 1934.—Have been seeing much of Ben lately. . . . He is a strange fellow; not very positive, definite, clear, or lastingly creative—not yet, but immensely clever, rigidly honest in his mind, quixotic, mercurial, a stimulating critic (as Mencken was, but entirely different) of the social scene, clearing the stench out of important places, wrecking structures of sham, puncturing inflated personalities. But he is also apt to go off half-cocked. Often he is terribly sound but sometimes, too, a little wild. Emotional. Many things he says are "true, *but.*" In his motives, purposes, and functions he is a curious mixture: a bit of Voltaire, a bit of Mencken, a bit of Marx (both Karl and Groucho, the two about evenly divided), a bit of Proust, and a good bit of an impulsive, ill-disciplined, friendly child and youth (both at the same time) who will never get older. This combination disturbs me; but I think the Proust in him—the intuitive personal and social psychologist, the X-ray diagnostician of the social ills, etc.—interests me most. With the help of the Marxes in him, he could—*if* he could and would—write an extremely worth-while and readable autobiographical study of his time. He sees things uniquely. He is forty-three and I believe in fairly good health. By and by he will (I hope) straighten out his personal affairs and probably begin to work. I told him he ought to write such a book, suggesting that in doing it he could put into play all his powers and talents, and do something positive, clear, and creative which would last; which would not be merely "hot stuff" . . . (although that, too), but would *shed light* and become a help in his self-orientation in this country, of which he is badly in need, as who isn't?

Now and then he implies, or even explicitly insists, that he is a Marxian; and therein lies, I think, one of his chief weaknesses. He is no Marxian; merely knows a good deal (too much) about Marxism with all its historical ramifications. His Marxism now but confuses him, keeps him from being a wholly independent and original thinker, that is, wholly Benjamin Stolberg, which, it seems to me, he will have to become before he becomes really creative, really effective as a writer. Now he is too often merely drastic, merely smart and clever, merely funny or "hot stuff." Now he often exaggerates and is not balanced. He writes too much from the point of labor as he sees it, or as he thinks it ought to be, rather than from the viewpoint of America as a whole, from the viewpoint of civilization. . . . In this he is typical of so many intellectuals.

Stella and Ben became acquainted; he brought David to our home—a quiet, handsome, thoughtful lad, and good company.

In 1932-33, while we were in Yugoslavia, Ben wrote to us frequently, enclosing his published articles, which we had made him promise to send us; keeping us "in touch with home." For some months in 1932 he wrote a weekly column on the literary page of the New York *Post,* then edited by William Soskin. This work, which drew much attention, caused him to feel increasingly better about himself, and helped to make him a delightful correspondent even when he wrote, as he usually did, of the sad and tragic situation in the United States.

May 18, 1932

DEAR LOUIS:

I owe you three or four letters at least. But I am not going to plague my natural predisposition towards a sense of guilt by abjectly begging your forgiveness. I postponed and postponed writing. And the reason, you will be glad to learn, is that I am REALLY—without fooling myself this time—getting back to work. The last four weeks or so I have been turning out at least two thousand words a week. That isn't an enormous amount but, in my case, a real sign of recovery. And I am happy about it. . . . But, to get back even to two thousand words a week, I had to do nothing but work and completely disorganize my life—running Mondays into Thursdays, smoking day and night, drinking coffee cup after cup. That is, I cannot yet work without a tremendous effort of will. My next problem, when I have entirely gotten back to sustained work, is to organize it into some life pattern.

I am sending you my *Post* columns so far, except one on the "American College," which I lost. They have aroused some discussions. There is some other stuff of mine I have clipped for you, a piece on Foster which raised hell, etc. . . . Next week I have a leader coming out in *The Nation* on Owen D. Young. Harry Hazlitt called me up to tell me that it's my best piece—"real literature." And since my long absence from real writing has made me disgustingly receptive to such compliments I, of course, appreciated it.

Now, having spent half the letter telling you what a great guy I am, I'll turn to other topics. The Republican and Democratic campaigns are in full swing. The sheer stupidity is, of course, incredible. And by that I mean that—no matter how well one knows ahead of time just how dumb things are—they do strike one full face as even dumber, beyond all expectation. Hoover has forced the dry side through the convention, and that was the *main* issue. Franklin Roosevelt is just a weak strong man, the kind I love to portray. The press is full of blahhh by the yard, etc. I think it will be Roosevelt.

Now I am leaving the typewriter to call up Stella's mother and receive her report on how she is, etc. . . . Well, I called her up and talked to her for fifteen minutes. I tried to find out how she was, but for twelve minutes it was impossible to get her off that son of mine. He, it seems, is one of the sweetest and loveliest guys ever, has a great future, and is in every way remarkable; with all of which I agreed for the first three minutes. The next nine minutes I was worrying lest she might get him kidnapped. . . .

David is at Martha's Vineyard. If he were here, and I coached him properly to express himself, he would send you two Balkan bums his undying love. He is an eternal delight. I hope he grows up to be a good friend of mine. Just before he went to Martha's Vineyard I was reading a story to him, and when I came across the word "orchard" I asked him whether he knew what it meant. He said, "No. But never mind. Go on!" When you kids get back, I'll have him with me at the dock. . . .

. . . I am sending you some clippings about the Bonus Army battle in Washington. It's all ghastly and appalling, and I do not want to discuss it in a letter. Things are becoming insane and crazy; and yet no historical comparisons about "revolution" hold good. It's characteristic that *Scribner's*, the *Atlantic*, *Harpers*, and *Forum* have in their August issues pieces on the idea that revolution is just around the corner or in the air—pretty bad pieces except George Soule's in *Harpers*. The intelligentsia is all up in arms and in the air. The sociological *speed* in this land of ours alone is confusing to good thinking.

There are many people to talk to and few, fewer all the time in the nature of the case, to think with. Abe [Dr. Abram Harris, professor of economics at Howard University, one of Ben's closest friends] is in Washington. And you, of all places, in Yugoslavia!

Last night I spent with Red Lewis, who in a month is going to Vienna. . . .

Our boy friend [V. F.] Calverton, usual bandwagon style, has a "questionnaire" which he addressed to Granville Hicks & Co. and then entitles, in the current *Modern Quarterly*, "Whither the American Writer?" . . . and it appears that the American Writer is whithering toward "Leninism." Damn fools! All the papers had stories on the questionnaire, which, of course, is what C. wanted.

I wonder if I sent you the *Post* piece of some three weeks ago in which I show how Goethe ruined the Germans as he was ruined by them. I think that I hit the nail on the head in showing the hopeless romanticism of the Germans—Socialism, Fascism, Communism: all romantic. All things in Germany are full of ham poetry and essentially bad. I am betting Hitler will be in power within a year! . . .

. . . Things are getting psychologically worse daily. Our friends drop in on me to laugh as though they were to be hanged, all of us! Hoover has appointed twelve bankers and financiers to run all the finances of these U. S.—just as Stuart [Chase] predicted that evening: remember?

From Union Square to Park Avenue, New York is full of crazy talk about the "coming revolution." The other night some of us made out our own revolutionary cabinets. Here is mine—at this moment:

Chairman of the Soviet Commissars: B. Stolberg (no maybe)
Chairman, Supreme Economic Council: Abe Harris
Commissar of War, Navy and Kites: L. Adamic
Foreign Affairs: Kyle Crichton
Sex and Public Hygiene: V. F. Calverton.

Etc., etc. . . . Some of the names you don't know. But then you'll meet them at the first cabinet meeting when you get back. I haven't decided yet who'll have the OGPU job. I guess we can advertise in the *Times* for somebody. Maybe Red [Lewis] will do.

I am getting silly and so I am closing.

. . . Everybody says, pretty cynical gents at that, that Roosevelt is practically in. The campaign, by the way, is both exciting and uninteresting. It is exciting as a race, otherwise dumb. . . .

Bill Foster has been jerked off the campaign. He is officially "sick." I wrote in the *Tribune* that he sold Liberty bonds during the war, whereupon the press elsewhere picked it up. And his intra-party enemies wired to Moscow, I understand, what to do about it. So Moscow took him off and his worst enemy, Bill Dunne, is electioneering for him. This idea of trying to run things here from Moscow is incredibly stupid, and incidentally incredibly filthy politics.

December 1

. . . Mary D—— stopped in yesterday afternoon. We talked; suddenly she broke into tears. This happened lately with others. Heretofore well-controlled persons are developing "nerves," which seems to me to be all tied up with The Situation. A curious desperation is seizing even people who lack nothing materially.

December 12

Nothing much. Everybody is blue, with a touch of the flu thrown in. Not working one-fiftieth enough, though doing some. And watching the world slowly disintegrate, and men driven ever more by ominous and faked anxieties.

It's eleven A.M. . . . and I am sure I'll feel better later in the day and I should not be imposing this indigo view on you kids. Still, I must get it off my chest.

Our Beloved States are daily becoming more fantastic. The "Communists'" current idea appears to be: Anything to make the front page of the *Times*! It is all just a craze for publicity. The matinée Socialists do the same. Everybody else does the same. Mutual hatreds are called ideologies. And life is just plain nuts: nuts plus publicity, making an awful din—The Racket! . . . And, oh yes, Lewis Mumford is speaking next week on "The Day After the Revolution"! . . .

When we returned in mid-April, 1933, Ben and David were not at the dock. I found Ben in a new, not very cheerful, apartment on East Ninth Street, off Fifth Avenue. He received me rather indifferently, or so it seemed to me. In a low mood, he thought people were developing revulsion for one another. Long-standing friendships were being wrecked on so-called "ideological" rocks. As I subsequently realized, his personal affairs were in none too good a shape. He had given up his *Post* column and was working rather less than he should have been. Hitler was in power in Germany. In the United States, the "bank holiday" was but a month in the past. The confusion was worse than ever. What was Roosevelt going to do about The Whole Situation, which amounted to a social crisis? . . .

I told him that, while my visit in Yugoslavia had been a rich experience, I was untellably glad to be back in America. No matter what was the matter with this country, it was a vastly better place than Europe (for Stella and I had spent some time also in Italy). *Here was liberty*. Here I did not need to glance back every few minutes to see who was following me in the street, nor whisper when I talked to some one. Gloomy Ben did not know how soon America might be like Europe.

But when I saw him next, a few days later, he was in a better mood. He was glad I was back. By and by the New Deal, the "Roosevelt revolution," as it got into action, began to excite him. He went to Washington for *Scribner's* and returned worried, but also amused, exhilarated. Many of his New York friends and acquaintances, former Socialists, I.W.W.'s, Single-Taxers, and what-nots, were in important offices, disbursing millions: which, thought Ben, was "funny as hell." Walking through the new NRA headquarters, he had been greeted "Hello, Ben!" right and left by boys and girls who had lately been clerks in the Amalgamated Clothing Workers' office in Union Square. "The General," as he called Hugh S. Johnson, fascinated him as a personality. Labor seemed to be riding high in New Deal's favor: "but, Lou," he said, "what does it *really mean*?" His mind quivered with questions and misgivings.

In 1935, these questions and misgivings crystallized themselves in the brilliantly written little book, *The Economic Consequences of the New Deal,* done in collaboration with Warren Jay Vinton, and peppered with such Stolbergesque phrases, sentences, and paragraphs as these:

There is nothing the New Deal has so far done that could not have been done better by an earthquake.

The NRA still is, not a whit less than it was under the explosive regime of General Johnson, primarily a scarcity-mongering machine. Its whole purpose is the regulation of competitive greed.

Unlike the farmer who has been so well paid for his sabotage, the small-business man has been unable to persuade his Government to subsidize him for similar destruction, say, by a little well-considered arson under federal control. [In this connection, Ben had the bright idea that the Government should start a sort of AAA for literature, paying authors for "plowing under" their ideas for books, articles and stories! "Boy, wouldn't I be rich quick!"]

The World War was the greatest Public Works project in all history.

The aces dealt by the New Deal have somehow fallen right where they were before.

Economic Consequences (not a very apt title for the contents) was a joy to read for its wit, and I wanted it to succeed as a publication (which it did, mildly), but mainly because I thought its success might add (which it did, mildly) to Ben's urge to write more. I was, in general, pro-New Deal, although in some ways as critical of it as was Ben; and the tiny book, while bright with the flashes of Ben's mind, was marked also by its most serious weakness—its over-intellectualization, its cleverness, which caused his thinking to swing more around words and phrases than around creative instincts, of which, though they were horribly confused, the New Deal Administration at Washington was not devoid.

Traveling through the United States during 1934-37, I was frequently asked by persons in Elizabeth, New Jersey; in Los Angeles, St. Louis, and Pittsburgh; and even in Montgomery, Alabama—if I knew Benjamin Stolberg and was repeatedly amazed that a man who wrote so little commanded so much interest. His articles and book critiques were remembered a year, two years, after they appeared, though almost no one quite agreed with him. He was too European. But, at his best, he was stimulating. Several people wondered why he did not produce more. A man in Chicago inquired if I agreed with Harold Laski, who some time before had allegedly remarked in London that, no matter how bad the situation might be in the United States, "no country that has a Benjamin Stolberg is lost."

But up to 1937 Ben's direct influence was largely in New York. His talk at parties, which often included other writers and editors, inspired or suggested many more articles than he wrote. Himself never too well heeled, he got money from his wealthy friends for his needy ones, so they could go on with their work. And every once in a while Ben became terribly excited about something and a committee came into existence.

In 1933, following a specially gruesome lynching bee in the Deep South, Ben's profound interest in the Negro, along with his passion for decency and fair play, caused him to whip a group of writers, myself included, into a little movement which promptly resulted in the formation of the Writers' League Against Lynching, whose membership roster read—and reads still as I write this—like an index of well-known names in American letters and journalism. Subsequently, by sending at the appropriate moment a telegram to the White House, signed by all the members, the League was responsible for President Roosevelt's inclusion in one of his "fireside talks" of a condemnation of Governor Rolph's approval of the lynching of two men in San José, California; and during 1936-38 became a factor in the increasingly favorable consideration by Congress of the Wagner anti-lynching bill.

Not infrequently Ben telephoned to me, "Come over tonight, and no back talk; we ought to do something about so-and-so. I think we ought to send a telegram; don't you? We'll have a meeting." Or he called me: "Where were you Tuesday? I phoned you; I wanted you to come over. . . . But I knew you'd be for this, so I put your name down as a member of the committee. We sent a telegram of protest. All right?" Usually it was all right, though my feeling generally was to think thrice before joining or signing anything. Once or twice it was not all right, but the thing was unimportant one way or another, and I let it go.

Which brings me to 1937—to the story, from my angle, of the American Committee for the Defense of Leon Trotsky, of which Ben was a moving spirit. The story tells a little about Ben and me, and offers, I think, a few glimpses of certain sections of literary and intellectual New York which during the early and middle 1930's have been commanding national attention.

ANENT THE TROTSKY COMMITTEE

In mid-December 1936—as I shall mention again—I sailed for Guatemala. I did not know whether I would take only a short vacation or stay there for several months and begin to work on this book. My visitor's visa was for the usual two months, but I was assured that if I chose to stay longer there would be no trouble getting an extension. In January I decided to stay till May to write, instead of this book, one on Guatemala, entitled *The House in Antigua*. In the middle of February, however, the Foreign Office of the Republic of Guatemala refused to renew my visa, and declined to explain its refusal. I was, for all practical purposes, booted out of the country. Why, I could not imagine, nor could any one else whom I knew. So far as I could tell, I had been a model visitor or tourist: resting, spending what money I could afford, studying the ruins of Antigua, gazing at the volcanoes, watching the Maya Indians at worship in Chichicastenango, getting a perspective on the U.S.A. . . .

So, puzzled, upset, chagrined, I returned to the United States . . . and immediately on landing found myself caught in the crossfire between the so-called Stalinist and the so-called Trotskyite forces in New York.

I was shown a letterhead of the American Committee for the Defense of Leon Trotsky. On it was a long list of names of the Committee's members: Franz Boas, Lewis Browne, Witter Bynner, V. F. Calverton, John Chamberlain, John Dewey, Emmet Dorsey, John Dos Passos, Max Eastman, James T. Farrell, Harvey Fergusson, Martha Gruening, Louis M. Hacker, Abram L. Harris, Sidney Hook, Sidney Howard, Inez Haynes Irwin, Horace M. Kallen, Joseph Wood Krutch, Ludwig Lore, William Ellery Leonard, Dwight MacDonald, Margaret Marshall, Suzanne La Follette, Burton Rascoe, Professor Ross of Wisconsin, Gaetano Salvemini, Evelyn Scott, Benjamin Stolberg, Norman Thomas, Edmund Wilson, and Helen and W. E. Woodward, all of whom I knew either personally or by reputation. But on top of the alphabetical list was my name!

I could not immediately reach Ben, who I knew had put me on the committee; for who else would? Meantime my telephone rang and rang. A good part of literary New York seemed beside itself over the recent Moscow Trials and executions and over Trotsky (by then in Mexico) who seemingly was really the chief defendant in the Trials but had been given no official or formal opportunity to state his case. Had I joined the Committee? How did my name get on the list? I was urged to resign from it. I was told to remain on it. Some one informed me that two or three weeks before (while I was having my strange difficulties in Guatemala) the Moscow *Pravda* had printed a dispatch from New York saying that I really was not a member. I wondered: why was it so important whether I was or not? . . .

Finally I got hold of Ben. Exhilarated by his activity as a member of the Committee, and happy to see me, he said he had much to tell me. . . . What! I had not received his long letter of three weeks ago? In it he had explained everything to me; told me that he had put my name on the Committee because he was sure that, albeit not a Trotskyite, I was in favor of Trotsky's getting a formal hearing before the world, which might not only help to clear his name of the grave charges in the Moscow indictments but throw a flood of light on the Trials and executions and the whole "Communist business" in Russia and in the rest of the world. I had not received this letter, nor any mail from the Committee's office, which I now learned had been sent me. . . . And so, suddenly, I was fairly certain why I had been virtually expelled from Guatemala. The Trotsky Committee stationery had caused (so I surmised) the postal authorities there to suspect me of being an agent of Trotsky, who was just across the border in Mexico, which was practically a Communist country . . . and so my visa was not renewed.

I was—naturally—angry.

A few months before, in talking with Ben, I had been in favor of Trotsky's finding asylum in Mexico, or in any country willing to receive him. That was a simple issue. I could easily decide upon it. These Moscow Trials and Trotsky, however, were another matter. In common with most people in the United States who read about them, I inclined to the belief that the Trials and executions had been the climax of what was essentially a horrible and stupid frame-up, or, worse, of a deep political disease within Russia; but I was not sure, I had never been there, all my knowledge of Soviet affairs was second-hand; and I did not feel qualified to decide on the current Trotsky-Stalinist issue, nor had I the time to learn immediately more about Russia and Stalin and Trotsky and the Trials. I told Ben I was writing a book on Guatemala, and when I finished it I would start work on a book about the United States, which interested me even more than Guatemala. I was compelled, for the time being, to limit myself to these two interests and jobs. Trotsky, Russia, etc., required full-time study, and just now I simply had to leave them largely out of my orbit. Also, to my view, Trotsky and his conspirational-revolutionary idea, like Stalinism, had no close relation to the United States. If Trotsky came here advocating his idea and method of social progress, I would oppose him, just as I opposed the "Stalinism" of the American "Communist" party. If somebody started a committee for determining the honest-to-God objective truth about the Russian Revolution from 1917 to 1937, I might join it, for it might be important for us in America to know it. It was perfectly agreeable to me if somebody—Ben Stolberg, John Dewey, *et al.*—wanted to give Trotsky a formal opportunity to state his case before the world, but I did not wish to be upon a committee for his "defense." I seriously objected to the *defense* part of the name of the Trotsky Committee. Why did he need anybody's defense? Mine, for instance? Possessor of great literary ability, he was fully capable of writing a defense of himself. And so on.

Ben was angry, too, saying he was sorry he had put me on the Committee; I could go ahead and resign and thereby give comfort to the now dejected "Stalinist" ranks—dejected because people were deserting them. I was a fool! Did I not see that this was an historically important matter—another Dreyfus case, only many times more vicious, more far-reaching?

I saw nothing of the sort. Dreyfus, when Zola, who was convinced of his innocence, took up his cause, was a helpless, inarticulate "little man," rotting on Devil's Island, while Trotsky was an historical figure, a great revolutionary, a formidable political oppositionist who, as such, had to expect all manner of dirty work. Why "defend" him when one was not his partisan?

Could I not see, said Ben (I am paraphrasing him very freely), the anti-Stalinist reaction on account of the Trials everywhere in America, throughout the world? The "Communists" in the United States, to say nothing of the rest of the world, were on the defensive. The thing to do was to keep them there and thus cripple their party apparatus, which was a confusing force in the American scene, serving as a handy red herring, which wily reactionaries dragged—as they did in the 1936 election—over the trail of American progress. That could be done, insisted Ben, by keeping the memory of the Trials and the executions alive as long as possible, and reveal, so far as feasible, the Stalinist motives behind them—by giving Trotsky a world hearing through a Commission, which the Trotsky Committee aimed to bring into existence under the chairmanship of John Dewey. That was why the Soviet Government was fighting the Committee, why Dewey had been visited by an insolent Soviet agent, why *Pravda* had reported that I was not really a member, why efforts were being made to get me off the Committee, just as efforts had been made—a few successful—to get off it many other members.

Ben and I argued for hours, not getting anywhere with one another. He said the "Communists" were to be fought as an apparatus of confusion, and this was the time to fight them. I remarked they were, essentially, an alien factor in America, not important; doomed to peter out, anyhow. Ben agreed they were an alien force; however, in the way that a steel splinter in one's eye is an alien force. They were getting into the C.I.O., and Ben feared they would harm it by creating factionalism. I said that was possible; but why not deal with that directly? Why drag in the Russian Trials? Wasn't that confusion, too? . . .

Ben agreed that the name of the Committee was not fortunate; it was a carry-over from an earlier committee, whose aim it had been to secure Trotsky asylum. The idea was not to defend Trotsky, but to afford him an opportunity to defend himself.

I said there was no need of such an opportunity. Trotsky was accused of high treason, plotting the overthrow of Stalin with the aid of the Fascist powers to which he had allegedly promised Russian territories in payment for their help to him in seizing power. Was it so very important to "prove" that untrue, or "to cast doubt" on such an accusation? Did not every intelligent person already believe or suspect that Stalin was using Trotsky—the existence of Trotsky, which *ipso facto* was treason in Stalin's eyes—to cover up his own weaknesses and get rid of formidable opposition? And why was it wrong for Stalin to do that? Whatever one may think of it, Stalin's Government was a revolutionary government; at least it stemmed from the Revolution; and was not a revolutionary government allowed—and bound—to use any means, no matter how foul or brutal, to hold itself in power, to call any opposition treason? Was not that in the very nature of the conspirational-revolutionary business? Was not "treason" and calling the opposition "traitors" in the very nature of Revolution? Was it not true that Revolution justified anything? That it believed in, and tolerated, no ordinary morals? Had not Lenin used Imperial Germany in 1917? Had not Lenin been a "traitor" then? Was it not possible—was it not almost *certain*—that if Stalin's and Trotsky's position were to be reversed, Trotsky would use, perhaps more refined, but essentially the same tactics against Stalin? . . . Was it the aim of this "defense" Committee to clear Trotsky's name for the annals of history? If so, I was not interested. I would be interested in forming a committee for the hard, skeptical study of Revolution as a method of human progress. And this because there was so much crazy, half-baked, reckless, confusing talk about the "Revolution" in the United States. . . .

It may be that I did not say all this to Ben in that heated argument on the day of my arrival from Guatemala, but this was approximately what was going on in my head. Our points of view did not meet anywhere. Our friendship was seriously strained for the first time in more than six years.

Reaching home, I jotted a few lines in my Diary:

February 25, 1937— . . . Oh, Ben is terribly sincere in this Trotsky matter. I don't deny he knows a great deal about it, including all sorts of things that aren't quite so. Nor do I deny that there is some basis for his passionate interest in the extraordinary Trotsky, and for his hate of Stalin and "Stalinists." But I think the initial reason why Ben is in this Committee neck-deep is this—there is in him a compelling personal need to get into action every once in a while, into something big and important, and feel himself function. He is the scholar, the student, the intellectual, who every now and then must *do* something, preferably something "important"; for way down in him he knows that as a mere writing and talking intellectual he is not very effectual, but does not know yet that that is so in great part because he still is not a well-rounded-out Benjamin Stolberg, but a messed-up "Marxian," cluttered up with big, fascinating ideas not intimately his own. I think I understand him, and in a day or two I will have cooled off about his putting me on the Committee. . . .

I wrote a letter to the American Committee for the Defense of Leon Trotsky, asking my name be removed from its roster. But before I mailed it, diverse "Stalinists" and anti-Trotskyites and professional, neurotically loyal, and well-meaning friends of the Soviet Union pounced on me. Resign! Resign! If I did not resign I might eventually be sorry. It was all right for John Dewey to get mixed up in a thing like this; he was past seventy, while I was young. His name was so well established that it could not readily be unfavorably affected in the long run. It was hinted to me that should I ever want to go to the U.S.S.R. I might be unable to get a visa. My books might never be translated into the Russian. People who refused to give their names called me up: was I or was I not a member of the Committee? I was told to answer Yes or No.

Finally, a man named Kenneth Durante—a member of a wealthy Philadelphia family who had gone "proletarian" and now served as correspondent of

Tass, the Soviet news agency, in the United States—got me on the telephone, demanding to know: was I or was I not? Yes or No? . . . This was a little too much. Was this U.S.A. or wasn't it? One thing I have never been able to stand is pressure tactics. The conversation with Durante ended abruptly. Next day I received a letter from him, which in tone and obvious purpose was offensive to me.

Resenting all this, I did not withdraw from the American Committee for the Defense of Leon Trotsky. Indeed, as a reaction to this near-intimidation, I became briefly interested in the Committee of which I was a member, although I continued to be deeply uneasy about being on it. Two or three times I went to the Committee's headquarters and talked with the people who, all very serious and sincere, were actually running the Committee.

I discovered that only a few people on the Committee were more or less clear as to what it was all about and why. I went to a general meeting, which was attended by probably one-eighth of the total membership, and found that most of this one-eighth was obviously more ignorant about the facts and issues involved than was I, who had just been kicked out of a foreign country on account of them. Their remarks and questions indicated they had not thought the thing out. There was no clarity, no solid understanding. Many were on the Committee possibly for the same reason I was—because some friend had put them on, or urged them to join. Yet, having come to the meeting, these few people evidently possessed more interest in the matter than the majority of the members who did not attend but merely allowed people whom they probably did not know to use their names for what they saw fit. This seemed to me all wrong. I had, at least, the extenuation of having never really joined, but having been caught in a situation from which, not wanting to yield to pressure as a matter of principle and personal resentment, I could not extricate myself.

The Committee was run by a few deeply interested and intensely motivated persons who were obviously Trotskyites, that is, who believed in Trotsky's conspirational-revolutionary ideas. The idea to clear Trotsky as a matter of principle of justice was probably clear and paramount only in John Dewey's mind; I admired him for it. A few people of the Committee's inner group, as well as most of the Dewey Commission, were more or less pro-Trotsky personally. They admired some part of his mind or past, without agreeing entirely with his basic philosophy and future aims. Politically they were "anti-Stalinist" without being Trotskyite. They were outraged by the Trials and executions. I think that Ben Stolberg, Suzanne La Follette, and John Chamberlain were of this group. Otherwise the idea among the Committee leaders was, for the most part, politically pro-Trotsky (*i.e.,* pro-conspiracy, pro-Revolution) in purpose. Having, in the past two or three years, given Revolution what thought I could give it, and having decided that the conspirational-revolutionary method of progress was not for the U.S.A., I was against it; and yet, due to a complexity of things, there I was—a member of the Committee, which was a great many things, but which in the final analysis was an expression or manifestation of the intense confusion within a section of America's (mostly New York's) intellectual world, affected by the country's basic incongruity and the insane and dangerous international situation, of which the Trotskyist-Stalinist feud was an important phase.

I tell the story of my connection with the Trotsky Committee (for brevity's sake somewhat simplified) as a matter of record. The entire history of the fantastic Trotskyist-Stalinist furor in America during 1937, which continues as I write into 1938, would require many pages which I cannot and don't wish to give it. I find myself here too far ahead of the story about my America, as it is. I want to say, however, that in retrospect—despite my near-expulsion from Guatemala, my words with Ben, and my long discomfort as an involuntary "defender" of Trotsky—I am almost glad I was drawn into it. I watched the whole mess more closely than I might have had I been outside of it; and I witnessed something that may be very important in the long run. In fact, it may be so important that some day I am likely to boast of my having been, even if unwillingly, involved in it. In 1937 a considerable number of American liberal intellectuals, contemplating the political developments in Russia, painfully extricated themselves from under the long and strong influence of the Russian Revolution and began a reëxamination of revolution as a method of progress. I had been more or less under that influence myself till about 1935, when I had begun gradually to break away from it; and now in 1937, free from it, I could watch rather objectively the violent inner torments of others.

Ben's case, in this respect, interested me. As already suggested, he had strong misgivings about the Soviet régime already in 1931, but it was not till early in 1937 that he gave up the Marxist-Leninist-Trotskyist revolutionary idea as unfeasible. This freed him of some inhibitions in writing. Till then he had hesitated to tell the truth about the "Communists" in America as he saw it, for fear some one might accuse him of attacking Russia or consider him a red-baiter. Early in 1938, however, he went the whole hog and published in the Scripps-Howard newspapers a series of articles on the "Communist" activities in the American labor movement, which, immediately on their appearance, created a sensation and much confused and bitter resentment among the radicals and liberals, and especially in the Communist Party and among its sympathizers.

But, as I say, I am ahead of my story. To Ben Stolberg there are numerous references scattered through the rest of this book, which will tend to complete his portrait begun here and generally to touch on the problem of the contemporary intellectual in America.

Literary Rotary

EARLY IN 1931, SOON AFTER I HAD MET BEN STOLBERG, HE AND HENRY HAZLITT originated the idea of starting a small discussion group, which would consist entirely of writers and editors. They did nothing about it, except tell V. F. Calverton about it; and Calverton—characteristically—took hold of it and turned it into what I subsequently labeled in my mind as the "Literary Rotary." The original members were Hazlitt, Calverton, and Ben, who asked me to join.

Born in Baltimore thirty-odd years before, Calverton was a large, convex, bustling young man who, off and on, seemed in danger of bursting with energy and ambition. His personality rode like a circus performer on two steeds: egoism and idealism. His goal was a better world, in which he would be a sort of Lenin-Casanova-Pericles. A radical intellectual, a go-getter, an opportunist, he was editor-publisher of *The Modern Quarterly*, which he had founded while he was still in his early twenties and managed to keep going (for a time as *The Modern Monthly*), with the aid of various "angels," ever since. Calverton was a Modern with a capital M, in touch with Moderns the world over. He knew everybody; made it a point to meet people who were, or might become, Somebodies. He had his feelers and traps out for them. The range of his interests was wide; in fact, it included nearly all phases of human life and, geographically, it reached to the Orient and Latin America; but at this time—1931-32—he specialized in, or emphasized, Sex, which was the great Motive Force of Everything. Ben called him "one of the sex boys." The other important sex boy was Samuel D. Schmalhausen, with whom Calverton collaborated in getting out such symposia as *Sex in Civilization*, *The New Generation,* and *Woman's Coming of Age*, which included approximately as much ultra-modern pseudo-radical nonsense as sound science and philosophy. Ben had scant respect for Calverton as a writer, considered him little more than a "plagiarist of the current intellectual atmosphere," and Calverton did not mind this. Ben liked him personally. Calverton was so obvious that he had about him almost an air of honesty. He was a great mixer, back-slapper, believer in the old American institution of house-raising and log-rolling. The house, periodically in semi-collapse, was his magazine, for which he needed contributors whom he could not pay. So he called meetings, sent out questionnaires, drafted manifestoes, organized groups, started "movements." When one group broke up or petered out, he started another. Literary Rotary was his latest.

Henry Hazlitt was then on the staff of the left-wing-liberal *Nation*, but the most conservative and probably the best informed member of the group—a Philadelphian in his mid-thirties, quiet, studious, serious. He had been a writer on the *Wall Street Journal* and financial editor of the New York *Evening Post*, then a conservative newspaper. In 1933 he took over the editorship of *The American Mercury* after Mencken, but presently quit it; then went as an editorial writer to the New York *Times*, where I have ever since imagined him as entirely at home.

One of the early joiners was Carleton Beals, well-known as a writer on Latin America, particularly for his interview with the idealistic insurgent leader of Nicaragua, Sandino, in 1928 for *The Nation*. He had a short, stocky, aggressive body, with a rather curious, not unattractive face—unsymmetrical, tough features; small mouth, pug nose, high brow, heavy cheeks, sandy hair and lashes, and an almost sleepy colorless expression in his eyes. His soft, mild voice surprised one coming out of the "toughie" personality. He was a kind of subdued, held-in Hotspur, with hard words for sentiments and an inclination for "quick-conceiving discontents." A native of Kansas, where he had spent part of his childhood in the ample lap of Carrie Nation, who was a friend or relative of the Beals family; educated in California, Mexico, and Italy; and speaking fluent Spanish, he was then in his late thirties. He had been in Rome when Mussolini came into power. His best-known book then was *Mexico—An Interpretation*. He had just been awarded a Guggenheim fellowship, and was still to write *The Crime of Cuba* and *America South*. He was one of the two or three best friends of Ben Stolberg, who liked him immensely as a man and a writer. I met Beals with Ben shortly before the Literary Rotary got going. The three of us had dinner somewhere and talked half the night—or, rather, Beals narrated, on our urging, his adventures as a journalist, giving trenchant word portraits of prominent people in Mexico and Central and South America, while Ben and I listened. Afterwards Ben said to me, "Isn't Carl a great fellow?" Beals' picture hung in Ben's apartment, and one day as we happened to be looking at it he exclaimed, "Now, isn't that an honest mug for you!" . . . Five years following that first meeting, after I had been with him perhaps a dozen or more times, I tried to characterize Carleton Beals in my Diary:

Beals is one of the most traveled and hardest-working men I know. He publishes a book a year, and many magazine articles. He is nearly always interesting; venturesome, full-blooded, temperamentally given to quick, reckless action. He changes his plans suddenly. He is in New York today; enroute to Peru or Mexico tomorrow. . . . He seems to love danger, or likes to think he loves it. Or is he naturally fearless? I doubt it; such men are rare. He is intensely self-conscious in the matter of his love of danger, his independence, his freedom, etc. His Sandino articles told as much about his independence and the dangers he encountered to reach Sandino as about Sandino. Is he naturally independent, or is it an effort to be so? His independence has a hasty, assertive quality, though he tries to disguise it in matter-of-factness. It can be reckless and rash; one better not offend it! And it may be quick to perceive or interpret offense where none is intended, or where there is an omission of recognition of it. Beals reminds me of A—— [a prize-fight referee I knew in Los Angeles who was apt to swing at anyone questioning his honesty or wisdom, his ability in rendering decisions]. Incidentally Beals and A—— greatly resemble one another physically and in manner. Beals seldom engages in discussion; he is good at telling one something, making a statement. He knows! I doubt if he gets along well with very many people at close quarters for any length of time. He likes (probably needs) to stand out in situations in which he finds himself. It is possible that he and Ben are such good friends because Beals is so seldom in New York and they see one another briefly only two or three times a year. . . .

In 1937 Ben induced Beals to serve on the Dewey Commission which gave Trotsky a hearing in Mexico City. Beals resigned in the middle of the hearing, throwing a bombshell into the proceedings, and making the front page of the New York *Times.* To Ben this was a severe blow. Beals made matters worse by publishing in *The Saturday Evening Post* a rather one-sided article about the inside goings-on during the hearings, and the Trotskyite circles in New York buzzed with the careless rumor that Carleton Beals had "gone Stalinist." I saw Beals immediately after he came from Mexico. He seemed very anxious to explain the whole thing. The Commission, he said in effect, had been so pro-Trotsky he could not stand it. I saw also Ben, who, too pained, refused to say anything about Beals; and Suzanne La Follette, also a member of the Commission, who was "simply puzzled" about his resignation. For a while I did not know what to think. In time, however, I tentatively decided that the sensational resignation had been at least partly a result of Beals' independence, which the setup of the Commission had, somehow, offended. He resigned amid a confusion of superficial motives, which became less convincing the more he explained them.

The others who joined the Literary Rotary were:

Harry Hansen, book critic of the New York *World,* later of the *World-Telegram*—a tall man in his mid-forties, Iowa-born, educated at Chicago. He began his journalistic career as a European war correspondent (and was later the literary editor) of the Chicago *Daily News.* When I first saw him he seemed cold and distant. This initial impression vanished, however, as soon as he spoke.

Lewis Gannett, lately of *The Nation,* now literary columnist ("Books and Things") on the *Herald Tribune*—born in upstate New York, just forty, handsome, direct, natural, even tempered, tolerant, a moderate-liberal, and very sociable and friendly.

George Britt, book critic of the New York Scripps-Howard paper, the *Telegram,* before it became the *World-Telegram*—a Kentuckian in his mid-thirties, slow-talking, slow moving. When Harry Hansen took over the literary column on the *World-Telegram,* George returned to reporting; then became an editorial writer and published a book on the Jewish problem and one on Frank Munsey.

Jacob ("Jake") Baker, a member of the Vanguard Press publishing house— a humorous fellow in his early forties, formerly of California, where he had been close to the labor movement, including the I.W.W. In 1934 he became an important New Dealer, assistant to Harry Hopkins, dealing out relief billions. He was, I think, partly responsible for the art, theater, and writers' relief projects. He originated the idea for the "American Guide" series of books. In 1937 he joined John Lewis' Committee for Industrial Organization as head of the Federal Employees' Union.

Kyle Crichton, associate editor of *Scribner's*—very tall, loose-limbed, awkward, forty-four or -five, originally from Bethlehem, in Pennsylvania, where he had worked in the steel mills before and after attending Lehigh University. It never occurred to me to ask him how he had happened to stray into writing and editing. He considered himself a humorist, and now and then really was funny. In 1931-32, he was one of my favorite characters in literary New York. He had a nice family, of which he was very proud. We remained rather good friends till early in 1935, when his "Communism" began to annoy me. It seemed to make him an incongruous figure. From *Scribner's* he went as a staff writer to *Collier's* at the same time that, under the pseudonym of Robert Forsythe, he contributed regularly to the *New Masses* and engaged in other activities under the auspices of the regular Communist party, including calling by ill-considered names all who did not toe the current "line" drawn by the Comintern.

Claud Cockburn, New York correspondent of the London *Times*—a tall, thin young Englishman, intelligent and well-informed. He lived at the Lafayette Hotel, where I saw him a few times in addition to the Literary Rotary meetings. Later he returned to England and started the famous mimeographed "dope-sheet" on international and internal English affairs, *The Week*.

Among the early "Rotarians" were, I think, also Sterling Spero, co-author with Abram Harris of a book on Negro labor; Louis Hacker, the young historian, teaching at Columbia; Lewis Titterton, of The Macmillan Company's editorial staff; Maxim Lieber, formerly of Brentano's, now a literary agent; and Walter White, Negro writer (*Rope and Faggot,* a study of lynching) and secretary of the National Association for Advancement of Colored People.

Calverton's idea, to which everybody agreed, was that the group meet once a month for supper at Scheffel Hall on Third Avenue near Seventeenth Street, a wide-open German place serving real beer (for this was before Repeal), and thence go to the apartment of a different member each month, and talk. Members were allowed to bring along as guest anyone they thought the rest of us ought to know. Ben once brought Sinclair Lewis. Other guests brought by different members were Malcolm Cowley, of *The New Republic*; John Chamberlain, of the *Times*; Stuart Chase and Matthew Josephson; Harry Elmer Barnes, the Scripps-Howard columnist; Sidney Hook, Jay Lovestone, Waldo Frank, Granville Hicks, and Robert Briffault, the elderly English anthropologist who later turned novelist (*Europa*). Knowing very few people in New York, I never brought anyone. Not all the members came every time; I think I went only to about every other meeting; and, with guests, the attendance was usually between twelve and twenty.

The group was typically New York in that, I think, only one or two members were native New Yorkers. Several of us were foreign-born. I was the most recent arrival in the great city, and—although my inclination generally was (still is) to avoid big company—I was glad of this opportunity to meet and gradually get to know these men whose names, in most cases, had been known to me for some while before.

During supper there was much joking, joshing, kidding—all very friendly and pleasant, with an occasional dig at somebody from one or another, which was not resented. We were all Harry, Ben, Lewis, Louis, Kyle, etc. Funny stories were told. There was too much and over-hearty laughter. The only way in which we superficially differed from a Rotary or Kiwanis luncheon or supper was that we did not sing. There was much gossip—at first all interesting to me, as I knew very little about the inside of book-publishing and magazine-editing. I kept still most of the time, partly by preference, but mainly because I was ignorant about the majority of the things under discussion.

The joking, kidding, story-telling, and gossiping occasionally continued after we came to the apartment. I think the first time we went to Ben's place, the second time to Calverton's; then to Lewis Gannett's, to Lewis Titterton's, and so on. Married members, when the party was to be held in their apartments, sent their wives to stay with friends for the night, as sometimes it was long past midnight before we disbanded. I had no apartment or room large enough to hold so many people; and when my turn came, the party was held at Ben's. I only paid for drinks, sandwiches, and pretzels.

Now and then the party was very worth while. Harry Hansen told of his experiences as war correspondent. Walter White spoke of the latest lynching. Someone came from Europe and had things to tell. Or the question of the Depression, the Crisis, the Revolution, came up.

The group, which included two or three men who momentarily considered themselves Communists, had leftward, pro-collectivist or economic-planning leanings and was sharply, sarcastically critical of President Hoover and his "rugged individualism." It more or less believed (Henry Hazlitt strongly but quietly dissenting) that we were "at the end of an epoch," meaning that this was no ordinary Depression, no usual dip in the business cycle, but a definite break-up of the entire American idea of prosperity, mass production, and high wages within the capitalist system. What next? Revolution? Several believed it probable or possible. The two or three out-and-out "Communists" desired it. Gradual changes or reform? Was economic planning possible within the capitalist system? . . . Actually, the group as a whole and nearly all the individual members tossed upon a sea of uncertainty. Most of the talk that went on was excited, big, incongruous and empty, and I recall very few specific discussions. One of the calmest men was Henry Hazlitt, who knew the inner workings of the capitalist system and thought it would go on for a good while yet. It could—and, if necessary, would—spend ten or fifteen billion dollars a year to keep people from starving and revolting, and the people were willing to be thus "bribed."

Perhaps half of us sat silent when the Depression, the Crisis, and the Revolution were discussed. Now and then Kyle Crichton, not yet a "Communist," came off with a good "gag," which reduced the Depression to absurdity and caused everybody to roar. But of Kyle more in a moment. Those talking took a gloomy view of current America. Several eyes flashed, however, when Russia was mentioned. At one or two meetings, it was nothing but Russia, Russia, Russia, the Five-year Plan, Stalin and Trotsky. The talk was full of excitement, pro and con, mostly pro-Soviet. I was generally sympathetic to Russia, and what was being said about the great experiment was interesting enough, but— "How about this country?" I once put in, feeling at a disadvantage. I meant: was not there something in America from which we could draw a little inspiration? A few of my fellow members smiled to me, then the talk went on about the Soviet Union, the Five-year Plan, Stalin and Trotsky.

Occasionally, listening, I was rather disturbed. Revolution? Now, what did Calverton or Robert Briffault mean when he used that word? Did he mean that the people would suddenly go into the streets, put up barricades, and seize the White House and the Capitol in Washington, and the House of Morgan and a few other buildings in Wall and Broad Streets in New York? Which people? The masses? What did they mean by that? The workers, the proletariat? Did they mean that the workers would seize the factories? Which workers? Which factories? How many workers did he—Calverton, for instance —really know? Did he mean that the people—the workers—would have a great leader? Where would the workers' leaders come from? Did he think that the America of 1931 was the Russia of 1917? That a Lenin and a Trotsky were about to appear here? That capturing the White House would be like capturing the Winter Palace in Petrograd? Suppose "the people," "the workers," did seize the White House and the House of Morgan and fifty or even five hundred factories—what did he suppose the Army and all those interested, for one reason and another, in the preservation of the *status quo* would do? I decided that Calverton and those who talked as he did had not thought the thing out, were careless with words, and talking nonsense. And now and then it occurred to me that they knew their words were largely nonsense. Their consciousness of the deepening Depression seemed to push individuals down into themselves, from which depth they emerged with things they had read in Marx, with personal desires, ill-thought-out "solutions," and diverse absurdities which were uttered excitedly as profound statements.

One evening three or four of the most radical, the most collectivist members and guests held a long discussion—only "discussion" is not the word to describe what went on. I noticed that they scarcely listened to one another. They held little speeches, which were not meant to persuade anyone, to engage the others in their thoughts, but merely to present their views and get them unquestioningly accepted, to impress everybody with their brilliance, the amazing erudition and cleverness of their minds. It was one of the clearest exhibitions of rivalry, extreme individualism, dogmatism, lack of democratic spirit, and intellectual non-coöperativeness I had ever seen. The Hoover individualism was mild compared to theirs. There was no light; there were only flashes of brilliance. . . .

I could not help thinking of my friend Cantrell.

In 1935 and later I found it interesting and amusing to recall some of my fellow "literary Rotarians" as they were in 1931-32. Kyle Crichton, for instance, before he became Robert Forsythe and "redder than the rose," once opened his humorous vein with the following plan to balance the national budget: to put in effect a hundred-percent inheritance tax, then hire Al Capone to bump off all the rich. When serious, Kyle was then not even a liberal, but a sound and sane conventional conservative. One evening, as a guest of the Rotary, Stuart Chase, economist and statistician and generally well informed and careful with his words, expressed fear that, unless the Administration took quick measures, hundreds or even thousands of banks, including some of the largest, were liable to be forced to close their doors during 1931. He remarked that, to his view of the national monetary situation, no one's bank deposits were safe. Whereupon, deeply indignant, Kyle turned on the alarmist Chase, "What the hell are you talking about! This country is essentially sound. What we need is faith. Our big men have the situation well in hand; don't you fool yourself!" It developed that Owen D. Young was Kyle's ideal among the big men of America in whom we were to have faith.

Kyle was an Elk who had read Mencken and then heard of Marx.

I forget, if I ever knew, who brought Granville Hicks to the January, 1932, Literary Rotary party . . . but there he was: a slight young fellow, whose smooth boyish face made him appear even younger than he was. He looked about nineteen, but was probably in his mid- or late twenties, an instructor of English at the Rensselaer Polytechnic Institute in Troy, New York; also, an occasional book-reviewer and a reader and "scout" for The Macmillan Company. Sometime before, he had written to me: had I a book to be published?—and, if so, would I not let him see it as a possible title for the Macmillan list? Tonight, however, I noticed him glancing askance at me every now and then while we were still at Scheffel Hall. From Scheffel's the group went to Calverton's apartment, where Hicks suddenly lit into me like a witch-burner out of his New England ancestry.

A few days before, *Scribner's* had come out with an article of mine on "hunger demonstrations" and riots as a means of publicity for the under dog. I held that prior to the Communist-staged unemployment demonstrations in

March, 1930, which had resulted in riots, no newspaper or person of any importance in the United States had manifested the slightest awareness of the national unemployment situation. The demonstrations had become sensational front-page news—not, to be sure, because they were demonstrations or because the Communists had organized them, but because they had produced bleeding heads; and I gave the Communist party a sort of left-handed credit for starting the country toward unemployment-consciousness, which finally—in the autumn of 1930—forced even President Hoover to draw his ostrich head out of the sand-pile and admit the existence of a social emergency. I quoted a labor-union official: "Often there is nothing that throws as bright a spotlight on the sufferings and unrest of the workingman as a flare-up of violence. The worker is not news when he quietly starves. The papers pay no attention to him except when he gets rough or his head is bloody." I hinted that the leaders of the Communist party had conducted the demonstration so as to prompt the police, seldom reluctant to swing a club and crack a head, into violence; and that they had desired riots not only for domestic publicity but to impress the Communists abroad, especially in Russia, with their work to hasten the revolution in the United States.

Granville Hicks took fierce objection to this. What did I mean by writing such a thing? And in a bourgeoise magazine like *Scribner's*! I was playing straight into the hands of anti-revolutionary forces! And I was supposed to be a former workingman and even now a friend of labor! . . . Hicks' smooth boyish face was purple; his eyes blazed behind the spectacles. He reached for the magazine, a copy of which happened to be in the apartment, and read the offending passages from my article.

He took me by surprise and I hardly knew what to say. I asked, "Do you dispute the truth of what I say?" But my question seemed irrelevant. Hicks ignored it. He had just become converted to Communism, much in the way one becomes converted to religion, and he had all the zeal of a new adherent to a great cause. As I discovered that same evening, he was as yet poorly oriented in his new ideology and politics, but appeared to believe that the Revolution in the United States, which would result in Soviet America, was a matter of no remote future, perhaps only a year distant, possibly less; hence writing such an article as I wrote for *Scribner's* was giving intelligence to the enemy, and he could not refrain from speaking out against me in the presence of all these other writers.

Harry Elmer Barnes, who was a fellow guest of the Literary Rotary on that occasion, spoke up quietly to the effect that I was probably correct in stating that unemployment riots and demonstrations were effective publicity for the under dog. He said that a wealthy man on the Gifford Emergency Relief Committee had remarked to him the other day that he wished there would be some riots, so the rich would contribute to the charity funds.

Another guest that evening was Jay Lovestone, once upon a time the leader of the American Communist party, but recently relieved from that position by orders from the Comintern and kicked out of the organization because his analysis of the American situation had disagreed with Moscow's. Now he was the leader of a small opposition to the regular Communist party. But, to all seeming, Hicks knew only that Lovestone was a Communist; and so, exhausted from his attack upon me, he sank upon the floor at Lovestone's feet and, looking up at him, inquired what he as a Communist should do. Lovestone, who considered himself a Communist despite the Moscow disapproval, smiled at the flushed boyish face with the blazing eyes and said there probably was not much he (Hicks) could do right away, but he might study Marx, keep informed on world and domestic affairs, and speak to likely people on Communism. He implied the Revolution was a long way off, and there was no use getting excited about such trifles as my article. Besides, what I said was true, even if it did appear in *Scribner's*—the present leaders of the American Communist party *were* engineering unemployment riots to impress Moscow with "the rapidly ripening revolutionary situation in the United States" which they were hastily bringing to a head.

In the ensuing years, when Granville Hicks became the high priest of Marxian criticism and the midwife of "proletarian literature" in the United States, writing his critiques in the *New Masses*, assassinating established "bourgeoise" writers with spitballs, I sometimes recalled him sitting on the floor of V. F. Calverton's apartment at the feet of Jay Lovestone, than whom few were lower in the eyes of the regular members of the Moscow-recognized Communist party of the United States.

I remember that evening better than any other Literary Rotary evening except one—on which Ben Stolberg, as I have mentioned, brought Sinclair Lewis to Scheffel Hall to be a guest of the group.

"Red" Lewis

ASIDE FROM CANTRELL, THERE WAS NO ONE—DURING THE 1920's—WHO HAD CONtributed more to my sense of America than Sinclair Lewis. I had read him avidly while I was still in California. *Main Street* and *Babbitt* were powerful books, invaluable as stimuli to critical thinking about the United States, while *Arrowsmith* seemed to me a great novel. It contrasted the go-getting materialism with, setting it in action against, an intense and high idealism, which Gottlieb expressed in his incomparable speech to Martin Arrowsmith on the religion of science, that ended "I will try to protect you from Success. . . . May Koch bless you!"—and that Martin himself then echoed in the prayer of the scientist: "God give me unclouded eyes and freedom from haste. God give me a quiet and relentless anger against all pretense and all pretentious work and all work left slack and unfinished. God give me a restlessness whereby I may neither sleep nor accept praise till my observed results equal my calculated results or in pious glee I discover and assault my error. God give me strength not to trust to God!" *Arrowsmith* contained also Leora, Martin's wife, one of the finest woman characters in world fiction.

Early in 1928, shortly after I had read *Arrowsmith* for the second or third time, my friend Carey McWilliams, of Los Angeles—who had an uncanny talent for finding good books of which almost no one had ever heard—brought me a novel called *Weeds*, by Edith Sumner Kelley, urging me to read it. It had been published by Harcourt, Brace in 1922 and, receiving almost no critical attention, sold but three or four hundred copies. It was a powerful, dramatic, beautifully written story—evidently autobiographical—of the Kentucky tobacco country. The central character was a young woman named Judy, who strongly reminded me of Leora Arrowsmith. Some time later Carey McWilliams located the author, who, married, mother of three or four children, and fighting blindness, lived at Point Loma, near San Diego. He corresponded with her, then visited her; and finally, on Carey's suggestion, I wrote to her, saying how much I liked her novel, and mentioning the similarity between Sinclair Lewis' Leora and her Judy.

In reply, she complimented me for noticing beneath all the superficial differences the fundamental resemblance between Judy and Leora, and explained that she was an early friend of Sinclair Lewis' and was his model for Leora. "I put a good deal of myself into Judy, and so you see the two girls are sisters."

Later I visited Mrs. Kelley, who told me Sinclair Lewis and she had met in 1907 at Upton Sinclair's Helicon Home Colony in Englewood, New Jersey, where Sinclair Lewis, just out of Yale, had come to take care of the furnace.

I was thrilled when, late in 1930, Lewis became the first American writer to receive the Nobel Prize . . . then delighted by his fine, challenging speech at Stockholm when the Prize was officially conferred upon him. . . .

Ben Stolberg, a close friend of his, brought Sinclair Lewis—"Red," as everybody called him—to the first Literary Rotary evening after his return from Sweden. The date was April 1, 1931. I think it was only our second party, and the group happened to be small that evening—about a dozen. We were all sitting about the vast round table in the corner, and had given our orders, when neat, round little Ben and tall, reedy, gangling Red entered.

Red had had cocktails somewhere else, and his eyes seemed to stick out of the narrow red face like a beetle's. He was forty-eight, and his red hair was graying above the large ears. His hands were long, slender, beautiful; the hands of an artist. His manner was intensely self-conscious, uncomfortable.

Ben introduced him around the table. Red knew Harry Hansen, Lewis Gannett, Henry Hazlitt, and Walter White and had heard of some of the others. His eyes stabbed into Hansen and Calverton.

I scarcely knew most of my fellow Rotarians, and was embarrassed when, as I was introduced to him, Red exclaimed, "Christ, Louis, you wrote a grand book!—*Dynamite*—just read it—jeez, a grand book!" He kept this up for half a minute or longer, holding my hand. I said, "Thank you," and saw the others smile at my embarrassment.

Red sat next to Ben, across the table from me. He ordered a wiener-schnitzel, which he hardly touched. He drank a seidel of beer.

The meal lasted about half an hour and everybody was uncomfortable. Red talked only to Ben and Lewis Gannett, and was almost antagonistic to all the rest, except me. There was very little conversation at the table, no joking or kidding, no telling of funny stories. Most of the men tried—vainly—to ignore Red. They did not dislike him, but were self-conscious before Ultimate Success in Literature in person.

Red kept looking at me; and when our eyes met, he winked. To Ben, who told me later, he mumbled, "I don't like this bunch. Louis is the only proletarian here. All the rest of you are highbrows."

He tried to talk to me, but it was next to impossible across the wide table. Scheffel Hall was a large, dinful place, with a small German orchestra playing a piece every five or ten minutes.

Embarrassed at being singled out by Lewis like this, I said, "Why don't you eat? Your schnitzel will be cold."

Red's face went into a grimace; he shook his head. "Say, Louis," he raised his voice when the orchestra stopped, "what do you say we go to Detroit and Chicago, you and I. We'll tour the industrial Middle West."

"What for?" I asked.

"A trip," said Red. "I asked Ben to come with me, but he's a highbrow—doesn't want to come. What do you say?"

I said, "It's hard to talk here. Let's wait till we get out."

He nodded and, folding and unfolding his long arms and clasping and unclasping his long hands, he continued to mumble to Ben about not liking this bunch, to stare and wink at me, and to look the picture of self-conscious discomfort.

Red's gaze suddenly fixed itself on Calverton, who had lately written an article, "Sinclair Lewis—Babbitt," for *The Literary Review*, published in Paris. He looked at him for several minutes, then said sharply, "So I am Babbitt, am I?"

Calverton tried to laugh it off, unsuccessfully. He said something I could not hear. Red's eyes burned holes into him.

Thereupon Red turned to Harry Hansen, who was still on the *World*. "And you, Harry, what do you mean by printing in your 'Book Marks'—and on the day I return from Sweden, as if to greet me with it—that piece of gossip as to why I left Harcourt, Brace and went over to Doubleday, Doran?" He was referring to a brief item Hansen had published about a week before, explaining why America's first Nobel Prize winner in literature had changed publishers. The item had seemed harmless enough when I read it, but had evidently been salt on some raw spot in Red's makeup. He ripped into Hansen, who replied calmly, trying to reason with him. Ben had his arm around Red's shoulder, saying, "Now, don't be a damn fool, Red." Lewis Gannett—typically of him—poured oil on the waters, saying to Red that now he was big news and all sorts of things would get into papers—even into his friends' columns; and by and by the storm subsided.

As we were all leaving, Red took me by the arm. "I don't like this bunch. Do you? Highbrows!"

"Most of them," I said, "I met just recently, and I really know only Ben, but some seem very nice fellows."

"Highbrows!" he repeated. "You come with me."

"Where?"

"We'll go somewhere."

I said: "I'm supposed to go with the group. We're having a sort of party. It's a monthly affair. Why don't you come with us?"

"No, no. . . . Highbrows! They think they know so much. Nothing worse than a highbrow. You come with me. I want to talk to you about taking a trip to Detroit and Chicago, Gary, Indiana, and places like that, and look at industrial conditions—workers, proletarians—not highbrows!" As I learned later, he had been thinking for some time of writing a labor novel and was working himself into a mood for the task. Hence his constant reference to "proletarians."

I spoke to Ben, who thought it would be all right with the group if I went with Red. I said I would rejoin them at Calverton's after Red got through with me.

Red wore a marvelous English overcoat and a fine hat, which made me sharply conscious of my shabby coat and cap. Third Avenue "L" trains rumbled above us.

"What do you say we go to Detroit tomorrow?"

"I don't know," I said, "this is a little sudden."

Red stopped in front of a tobacco store. "Wait a minute"—and went in to buy a package of cigarettes. He came out, smoking, and I found myself in a strange situation. Sometime between his saying "Wait a minute" and his coming out of the cigar-store he had lost all interest in me and nearly ceased to be aware of my existence, although there I was, facing him, walking by his side.

I said something; he made no answer. We crossed the street and—still on Third Avenue—walked another block, at the end of which he became interested in a black tomcat perched atop a garbage-can that stood against the wall of a closed butcher shop. He stroked the animal, saying, "Kitty-kitty-kitty!"

I stood beside him and, disturbed by his manner during the last five minutes, I asked, "Do you like cats?" So far as I know he did not hear me.

The cat stretched himself, jumped off the can, and walked away, whereupon Red continued down Third Avenue, and I beside him, feeling more uncomfortable with every step. What had happened to him? Had I said or done something to offend him? Did he mind because I had hesitated to leave my party to come with him, or because I had not eagerly seized on his invitation to join him on his trip to Detroit? . . . I accompanied him for several more blocks, wondering what to do. He might never miss me if I suddenly stopped or turned about and let him go on alone. Should I ask him if anything was wrong? . . .

Then he noticed me by his side and, stopping, looked at me. He stuck out his slim, limp hand, which I took, and he said, "Well, good night."

"Good night!" I said.

We parted. I was confused, worried, amused. Rejoining the group at Calverton's, I told Ben what had happened. Ben thought I need not worry; Red was apt to do anything.

Two days later I learned from Ben and other sources that Lewis was going about in New York, boosting *Dynamite*. He called up the Viking Press, "raising hell" because my book was not advertised more extensively.

Stella and I were married that spring; early in the autumn a family emergency obliged her to go to California for two months, while I, writing *Laughing in the Jungle,* accepted an invitation to Yaddo, the writers' and artists' place near Saratoga Springs.

While at Yaddo, I applied for a Guggenheim fellowship and wrote to Sinclair Lewis: might I give him as reference? "Sure," he answered, "I'd be delighted . . . and I'll do whatever I can."

A few days later I was called to the telephone. Long distance. Waiting for the connection, I feared bad news from California. But the call was from somewhere in Vermont.

"This is Dorothy Thompson."

"Who?" I said. The fear of bad news from California had confused me and for an instant, though the name was very familiar (she was not as well known then as she became later), I did not know who she was. I had never met her.

"Dorothy Thompson," she repeated. "I am talking for Hal."

"What?"

"I am talking for Hal—for my husband, Sinclair Lewis."

"Oh yes, yes."

"Hal is going to Vienna in about two weeks to write a novel on labor, and would like to have you join him there after New Year's, to help him with information he might need—as Dr. de Kruif helped him with *Arrowsmith*. . . . Do you hear me?"

"Yes," I said. "It sounds wonderful, but I don't know. You see, I'm writing a book of my own . . . my wife is in California. . . . This is a bit sudden. . . . Can I think about it awhile?"

"Could you come to Vermont for a couple of days? It's very nice here now, and probably not very far from where you are. You and Hal could talk about it and come to some agreement. . . ." Dorothy Thompson had a beautiful, clear voice.

I went to Vermont and spent two days at the Sinclair Lewis-Dorothy Thompson Twin Farms near the village of Barnard . . . then wrote to Stella in California:

September 19, 1931

. . . Vermont is perfectly lovely this time of the year . . . and Red and Dorothy have a marvelous place in the hills, 350 acres, largely wild, 'way off any main highway. There are two houses, the main one with a superb long view down a little valley between two rows of hills. I like Dorothy; she is very good-looking, perhaps in her late thirties, intellectual, brilliant. Red was charming, nothing like the first time I met him in New York. It was sheer pleasure to be with him, and I had a feeling he was really a big man and, as Ben says, a *fine* human being, though apt to shoot off any moment at some impossible tangent—just like America. Perhaps more than anyone else, he personifies, encloses, contains America, many of her virtues, her dynamic qualities, her spontaneity, and many of her faults. . . .

We had a long talk last night. Lewis seems to be on the verge of beginning to write an important book, from what he told me of it—the story of three generations of American idealists. His modern protagonist will be a character resembling Gene Debs, an honest, idealistic labor leader. . . . He wants me to come to Vienna in January, when he expects to begin working on the more or less current labor part of the book.

Dorothy apparently did not hear me over the phone when I told her I was married, and Red had thought I was single, but it phased him only a little when I told him otherwise. He proposed to pay your and my fare to Austria and back, and pay me $50 a week for two or three months, possibly longer, just to be near him in Vienna, so he can refer to me if he gets stuck with something. If I get the Guggenheim fellowship and we stay in Europe, he will not pay our return passage to America. Dorothy is an old resident of Vienna, has many friends there, and she will see that we get established in decent, not too expensive, quarters. She said that on $50 a week two can live excellently in Vienna. I shall have all the time in the world to do my own work. . . . I believe the thing will work out all right. Some details will probably have to be ironed out. We shall have a chance to visit my people in Carniola, which is just south of present-day Austria.

I am sure you will like Lewis. He was really charming and very amusing; so American. Dorothy is joining him in Austria in December. She has a very vivid mind, but quite different from Red's. She is more an intellectual than he. His intelligence is not only in his brains, but distributed, I felt, through his entire being. I like him very much, and I feel it will be a privilege to help him on this book, which, if he manages to do it anywhere near according to the idea and plan he revealed to me, will be his best novel, better than *Arrowsmith*, more important than anything he has written heretofore. I hope I am really qualified to help him. He has apparently been reading on American idealism and labor, on the "dream" of American democracy, for a number of years; he showed me a large shelf of books on the subject. . . .

. . . So plan on going to Europe in January; it does not even occur to me you may not want to go!

I had written to Ben Stolberg, before leaving for Vermont; returning to Yaddo, I found a letter from him:

. . . Why, certainly—go! That, at least, is my immediate reaction. The change of scene and culture will do you no end of good, both personally and for a better comparative understanding of what America is all about. We all should have such changes. . . . Of course, if you go, you'll have your hands full, for Red is *ein verrücktes Genie*. But that will have its compensations; he is enormously interesting and, as I have said to you before, a *very* lovable human being. . . .

I was back at Yaddo two days when I received a telegram:

PLANS CHANGED PROBABLY WON'T GO TO EUROPE DO NOTHING TILL YOU HEAR FROM ME AGAIN.—SINCLAIR LEWIS.

Then a letter from the same source:

September 24, 1931

DEAR LOUIS:

I decided quite suddenly that it would be dangerous to try to do the book so far away from America as Austria. I had been worrying about it for some time—the desire to go abroad warring with a sneaking suspicion that I ought not to. Dorothy will go for six weeks, then return.

I hope to God this won't have inconvenienced you any. And I hope that you will be able to come and work with me in New York, where I'll have a flat, some time say in December or January, when you're between books. Let me keep in touch with you; if I forget to send you my New York address, Ben Stolberg will know it. Dorothy is going down today to look for a flat, and I'll probably go down about October 15.

If we do work together in New York, I'd be glad to pay you fifty dollars a week, and it wouldn't take more than about four hours a day of your time, I should think, so that you could be writing at the same time. Meanwhile, I'd like to pay

you your expenses from Yaddo here and back, as you came really on business and
as I don't imagine you're very flush, just finishing a book. Please let me know how
much it cost you. Otherwise I'll feel rather guilty.

I replied:

September 27, 1931

DEAR SINCLAIR LEWIS:

Thanks for your letter of the twenty-fourth. . . . I am glad you have decided to
do your book here. You did not inconvenience me; only excited me a little.

I am eager to work with you, beginning—as you suggest in your letter—some
time next December or January. I assume the work will last the same length of
time as you had thought it would last in Vienna—between two and three months.
Fifty dollars a week is agreeable to me. (I would not accept this amount but for
the fact, as you have guessed, that I am not very flush.) I wonder, however, if
you would be willing to make this definite between us. This may not be a fair
request and I hesitate making it. I suppose the reason I ask for a definite arrangement is that it would help my wife and me in making our plans for the coming
year, getting an apartment, etc. Also, my immediate past has been so chaotic and
uncertain that I long for a whiff of certainty.

If you decide to take me on, I shall do my best to be of help to you. I am mindful
of the honor your offer gives me, and grateful for your confidence. I shall be
prepared to tell you anything I know in conversation and look up things at the
library and get information for you from other sources.

I don't know the exact amount I spent going from Yaddo to your place and back.
Anyhow, I got my money's worth and I should hate to submit a bill to you.

From Lewis again:

October 1st—and maybe it's the 2nd—1931

DEAR LOUIS:

I don't see how I can make a definite arrangement with you, as long as I shall
remain in America. If I were going to Vienna, as I had planned, I should have
chucked all else to be ready for you when you came. But as I remain here, I may
go West, I may go to Harlan, I may twist my plans in all sorts of ways. Therefore,
all I can do is later to ask for your help if you do remain within striking distance
of New York and if you do happen to be free for some time—or sufficiently free
so that you would be willing to recoup financially by helping me. So don't make any
arrangements, with your wife or otherwise, dependent on me. But I do think we
shall be able to get together for a certain length of time.

I wish I *were* going to Vienna. I rather dread the impact of New York after this
secluded quiet. But I must stay.

Meanwhile, I have received the query from the Guggenheim Foundation, and I
am glad to be able to give you a—let's follow Rotary diction and say a 100% boost.

My reply:

October 4, 1931

DEAR SINCLAIR LEWIS:

I understand your position. The chances are that I'll be in or near New York,
anyhow, and available to help you.

Thank you so much for your 100% boost to the Guggenheim Foundation. I am sort of hopeful about it. . . .

Next thing I heard—some time in November: I think from Ben—was that Lewis had abandoned his idea and plan for a novel on American idealism and labor. He was working on a story about a feminist, which subsequently received the title *Ann Vickers*. The news upset me a bit—not so much because it meant I would not have a chance to help him (for I realized more and more that that might involve all manner of unpleasant possibilities), as because I had felt that Red might very likely have produced a great novel upon a theme of immediate and long-range importance to America. I wished for a chance to ask him why he had given it up, but, although I saw him two or three times during the winter of 1931-32, an opportunity did not offer itself.

So far as I know, he never explained why he had decided not to do the book for which, apparently, he had been preparing himself for two years or longer. I have often wondered about it. Did the theme suddenly frighten him? Did it abruptly occur to him that labor and idealism were not popular enough among the regular book-reading public to assure a novel dealing with them a wide success even if its author was a Nobel Prize man? I suspected there was some justification for asking this latter—nasty—question. Talking with him in Vermont, I had gathered that he wanted to continue to be "successful." He was so American, so contemporaneously American! When I saw him in Vermont in September, he had seemed to be bothered by a feeling of insecurity about himself (which was also typically American, of all classes, including the uppermost). I had suggested that, in view of his Nobel Prize, that feeling was unjustified. His reply to that remark had startled me: Doubleday, Doran were happy to have him, but they were strictly business; one "flop" and ——! He had alimony worries; the Vermont farm took a good deal to keep up; he liked to travel. Also, he was a male, and Dorothy Thompson was rapidly forging ahead as an important, "successful" journalist. . . . Oh, there probably were all sorts of motives and forces in his decision. Had Dorothy, once an active feminist, had a hand (a wholly unconscious, undeliberate hand) in diverting him from idealism and labor to feminism? . . .

I hoped that some time in the future he might return to the idealism-labor novel. He continued to be friendly to me, to boost *Dynamite*. When the Guggenheim fellowship was awarded to me, he sent me a message: "I am simply tickled to death—" During the following year we exchanged several letters and notes. He seemed to want to keep in touch with me; I thought he might have some sort of unconscious idea of wanting to use me sometime. I was willing to be used. But ——

I rather liked parts of *Ann Vickers*. Then came *Work of Art*, which I could not read; then *It Can't Happen Here*, which disturbed me. The character of Doremus Jessup, the American idealist, was all right, but, to me, only a suggestion of the idealists he had roughly sketched for me in September,

1931, that he was to have in the novel he was then planning. On finishing the reading of *It Can't Happen Here*, I wrote in my Diary: "I wonder if this is all he is going to do with that marvelous material—with that feeling he had then about American idealism? That feeling was positive, and it could have led him to do a positive book; a book, that is, which would have been *for* something fine—while *It Can't Happen* is largely a negative, defensive job, *against* fascism (the danger of which, I think, is very questionable in America). There is altogether too much of this sort of defensive writing. . . ."

From My Diary

November 5.—I've been overworking and eating irregularly and too hastily. . . .
About eleven o'clock last night I went for a walk, heading up Fifth Avenue
on the Park side. Passing Ninetieth Street, or thereabouts, I suddenly felt a
little faint. I tried to shake off the feeling and walked on, till I staggered into
an iron bench put there for waiting bus passengers. I took hold of the back
of the bench, while everything about me—lights, traffic, noise, buildings, people
—became a ball of motion.

My legs folded up under me, and I went down beside the bench. How long
I was out I don't know; probably no more than a minute, possibly less. The
next thing I knew I was sitting uncomfortably on the bench, a man's voice
asking me if I was all right. I managed to say I was. "I guess you fainted,"
said the man. "Yes," I agreed; "I'm all right now, though. Thank you." I saw
him in a kind of dancing mist as he walked away from me. A bus passed—a
thundering immensity. The stream of after-theater taxies ran now uphill, then
down; the world appeared a rocking device. . . .

The man had picked me up and placed me on the bench—and taken $17
from me, all I had in my trousers pocket! I had a remote recollection of having
been frisked, of a hand going into my pocket. Fortunately, he did not find the
little money I carry pinned in my vest. . . . A sweet town!

December 7.—I couldn't work well today, so I walked around. Lunched with
S. . . . In the afternoon, I had a rather nice little experience. At Fifty-ninth
Street and Madison Avenue a very old Jewish man with a long white beard,
which has been growing all his life as it wanted to grow, addressed me in
Yiddish. I didn't understand him. He must have been eighty and looked like
a character out of Zangwill; no doubt he lives somewhere in the Bronx or
down around Canal or Delancey Street, and came to midtown on some business, or maybe to see his son's or grandson's office, who may be a lawyer or
business man. Finally I guessed that he wanted me to take him across the
street; he was afraid of the traffic. When I got him across, he spoke to me
solemnly for at least two minutes, doubtless asking God to bless me for my
good deed. Then he went on. I suppose some one else helped him across Park
Avenue. . . .

December 25.— . . . Last night, after seeing S. home, I walked around till
'way past midnight, with an acute attack of *Heimweh*. Christmas in America
is different from Christmas in Carniola. I vividly recalled walking as a boy,
with my mother and several other people, the four or five kilometers from

Blato [my native village] to the parish church in Shmaryé for the midnight mass. The road went through the village of Gatina, over a hill, through a wood. Walking ahead, a young man carried a torch high over his head. Our shadows fluttered on the snow. The trees in the wood stood naked and still. We were all garbed in heavy clothes; the women with heavy shawls over their heads. There was little talk; the dry snow, glistening in the light of the torch, spoke underfoot. . . .

Within an hour, last night, as I walked on Lexington and Madison Avenues and in the Forties, three men stopped me. Could I help them get something to eat? One was young, not a professional bum. . . . .

Going back to my room at about two o'clock, I came upon a tall gent in a high hat, with a white silk scarf and a cane, trying to attract the attention of an indifferent yellow cat sitting in the window of a grocery-store on Madison Avenue. Pleasantly mellow, he rapped on the pane, saying, "Aw, come on, Cat, give a fellow a break; it's Christmas—aw, what the hell, come on——"

1930

Under various dates.—Not quite in the dumps, but almost, on account of *Dynamite* [having been rejected] and my financial situation, and I don't feel like writing regularly these Diary notes. I don't think I'll want to remember the details of this period, anyhow. . . .

Last week I wrote Joe J. for a loan; he wired me the money this afternoon— just in time. The rent was due yesterday; this morning, when I met her, the landlady gazed at me significantly. . . .

Tried to work; suddenly I had a terrible what's-the-use feeling. I may never get the book accepted. The publishing world (books and magazines) is in a chaos. Some of the older, respectable houses are having a row with a few of the newer firms which are trying to introduce price-cutting into the book business. . . .

As I walked around today, four panhandlers stopped me. To three I gave a nickel apiece, which I thought was very funny: for my exchequer is down to less than three dollars. When the fourth one asked me if I could help him get a cup of coffee, I laughed and said he had taken the words out of my mouth. He was a young man and laughed, too. We had a little talk. He had come to New York from Passaic, N. J., but was unable to get anything to do. He asked me: had I read in the papers that President Hoover had said good times were just around the corner?

Says Vice-President Curtis: "There is just as much money in the United States as ever before." I have a hunch Hoover and that whole bunch in Washington have no idea what it is all about.

Says General Evangeline Booth, of the Salvation Army: "Cruel as it is, poverty has its uses." I wish she'd elaborate.

Witnessed a "Communist" demonstration on Union Square during the lunch hour. Big crowd. But I think most people there were stenos and clerks from near-by office buildings. Perhaps a hundred policemen, many on horseback. Three orators spoke simultaneously and very excitedly. Many of the persons in the crowd just stared. Here and there some one yelled out. Two of the speakers, holding forth with great intensity, had their left thumbs hooked in their left vest armholes while chopping the air with their right hands by way of emphasizing their words, which I could not understand. This oratorical manner seemed familiar. Where had I seen it? Then I remembered—Lenin, of course! I had seen Lenin in a news film years ago talking like that. The American "Communists" are imitating him! . . . Yet, absurd as they are on the surface, the "Communists" are the only group interested in the unemployment situation. . . .

May 18.—Lovely day. Walked from Eighty-sixth Street to the Battery, then back as far as Fourteenth. . . . Near the docks on West Street I came upon a group of longshoremen who were Croatians. Somehow, hearing their speech as I approached them gave me a deep thrill. Passing them, I said, *"Dobar dan!"* [Good day!] They fell silent and looked at me. I stopped, feeling strangely happy and amused.

One man was quite old, but powerful. *"Ko si?"* [Who are you?] he asked. I smiled. *"Jeli si nash?"* [Are you "ours"? *i.e.,* of our nationality?] was the next question. Then a younger man said, "Of course he's ours, didn't he say *'Dobar dan' po nashki* [in our language]?" I said, *"Slovenets sem"* [I am a Slovenian]. "Eh," said the old man, "but that's all the same."

I talked with them awhile. They said there wasn't much work. Times no good. What was my work? I said I was trying to become a writer. A writer, eh? Was I going to work for the Slovenian paper in New York? I said no, I was writing in English. In English! *Boga ti!* Write for American papers, eh? Purty goot! What was my name? I told them. They had not heard of me. Had I succeeded in getting anything printed yet? Yes, in the *American Mercury,* etc. They had not heard of any of the magazines I mentioned. I said the *Mercury* came in green covers. "Oh yes, *boga ti!*" exclaimed one of the younger men, half in English, half in his own tongue. "I seen it! Yeah! But that's a high-class book—no?"—"I guess he must be smart," remarked the old man in Croatian. The younger man said, "It's one way to make a living."—"Little *you* know!" I cried. Suddenly I became embarrassed and said, *"Zbogom!"* [Good-by!] and left them, feeling very good. . . .

July 2.—Things are looking up. Sold an article on labor and racketeers to *Harpers.* The chief editor, an elderly man named Wells, who is also head of the entire Harper house, is easy to talk with. He said he wanted something else from me soon. He asked whether I was doing a book; I told him Viking had accepted *Dynamite.*

October 10.—S. told me about the mother of her friend Nora R——, whom we visited the other day. . . . Years ago the woman's husband was pushed off an "L" platform before an on-rushing train by a pressing crowd of tired people hurrying home. Mrs. R—— was left with two daughters: Nora, fourteen, named after the heroine of *Doll's House*, and Gertrude, nine. No money. Gertrude was in the fifth grade, Nora attended the same high school as S. With a friend, who was also a widow with two children, Mrs. R—— started a tobacco and candy store. All six of them lived in the same apartment. S. says that Nora always hurried from school to relieve her mother in the store. Mrs. R—— recently sold her share in the store and, having always been successful in making clothes for the girls, became a dressmaker; and she and Nora, now a public-school teacher, and Gertrude, holding an office position, have an apartment of their own.

Mrs. R—— never commiserated her lot, though the store hours were from five in the morning till midnight seven days a week. She and her partner and their children worked in shifts. Each person in this two-in-one family got one day off a week. Nora and the other children did their home work in the store between serving customers. . . . Mrs. R—— was always cheerful, often buoyed to the point of exuberance by one thing or another. S. says she had a great zest for life, was healthy and strong. She loved to read when time permitted, and sought the best books, then discussed them with her friends and daughters. When S. was reading *The Rise and Fall of Susan Lennox* and asked Mrs. R—— if she had read it, she answered: "Oh yes, when it was coming out in the *Cosmopolitan* magazine in 1907 or 1908. My husband and I could hardly wait for the next instalment. At first we used to fight over who would read it first, then we read it aloud." She always had something to rejoice over, be excited about—a new dress for one of the girls; somebody's new boy friend; a new recipe; a suggestion on how to set the table; the cover on this week's *New Yorker*; a postcard with Michelangelo's *Adam* some one had sent her from Rome; some dishes bought in Woolworth's. Her store and home were always full of Nora's and Gertrude's friends, who liked to come in because they liked Mrs. R——. They called her Aunt Dora. They slept there, in close quarters, in preference to going home, although some of them lived in spacious houses and apartments. They dropped in to chat with her even when the girls weren't home.

But I needn't write of her in the past tense. She is now an elderly woman, intensely but quietly alive. An immigrant from Russia, she is in constant wonderment at the greatness and dynamics of things in America, and is gently, carefully critical of the evil conditions in this country. She was outraged by the Sacco-Vanzetti case, thinks keeping Tom Mooney in prison is a crime, and is sensitively aware of the millions of people suffering in the United States because of the Depression. But so far as she is concerned— never a complaint. She probably hasn't five hundred dollars to her name, yet seemingly has everything she wants. She is without envy of anyone, but full of a hunger, a yearning, for things like knowledge, understanding, tolerance, culture. Her face holds an expression which she must have had when, reaching America, she first saw the Statue of Liberty. She seems to carry within her a Dream with a capital D. She never was good-looking, yet she impresses one as though she thought she had been specially singled out for the world's beneficences and that life in itself—just life, the good and the bad of it—is rich, exciting, colorful, fine.

Some day I should like to write a portrait of her.

November 13.—I watched a breadline on Third Avenue near Thirty-sixth Street, conducted by some kind of gospel mission. In the line I saw a man wearing a topcoat that must have cost seventy or eighty dollars when it was new.

1931

Under various dates.—The "big men" of the country spout endless nonsense. "These really are good times," says Henry Ford, "but only a few know it. There is plenty of work to do if people would do it." . . . Calvin Coolidge thinks "the final solution of unemployment is work." . . . George Horace Lorimer, announces: "It is good to have money and the things money can buy." . . . "What the hell!" suggests Al Capone.

January 5.—I rose early and went out to breakfast. It was still dark and it felt like snow in the air. In front of the cafeteria were a lot of cans waiting to be dumped into the garbage-truck when it should come. A woman was digging into one can with both hands, a boy of ten or eleven into another. Spread on the sidewalk between them was a newspaper, onto which they were putting the scraps of food they found in the cans. I asked them a stupid question, "Why are you doing this?" The woman hid her face, did not answer. The boy looked up defiantly. "Whyn't yuh mind your own business!"

I went into the cafeteria, took a check, picked up a tray, knife, fork, and spoon; and went to the counter—then suddenly changed my mind about having breakfast. I went out, but the woman and boy were gone. . . .

With daylight snow began to fall in heavy flakes.

February 16.—Had a talk with [the editor of one of the better magazines]. He said, "No, I don't believe it does any good to print true, intelligent articles, appealing to decent, intelligent people. The country is at the mercy of mass actions, mob behavior. All the newspapers in New York are intelligently opposed to Tammany, but they can't keep it from winning elections. In fact, Tammany majorities increase. . . . The country is on the toboggan, going down at a terrific rate. The collapse of this civilization is not far, in spite of anything we might print. . . ."

Undated note.—Theodore Dreiser called a meeting of writers, artists, and generally "intellectuals" in his apartment at the Ansonia. He sent me an invitation, and I went, not knowing what it would be about. . . . Marvelous apartment: a duplex with great windows to the north. It must be very pleasant in the daytime. . . .

There were about a dozen people in the high, large room when I came. A servant asked me to put my coat and cap upon a pile of other coats and hats in the rear. I recognized Dreiser from the pictures I had seen of him: a large, loose-faced, gray man. He was talking with somebody, seemingly noticed me, but just let me be. I didn't know anybody else in the room; so made myself at home; looked at the pictures on the walls, which included a lovely nude and a portrait of Dreiser; at the bookcases, and the copper things distributed about.

More people came every few minutes. I knew no one, but some of the faces appeared familiar; I had seen them in the New York *Times* book section. Finally Burton Rascoe arrived and introduced me to Dreiser, who was very uncomfortable; then to Edmund Wilson, of *The New Republic*, and to C. Hartley Grattan. Ben Stolberg came. One of the last people to arrive was a short, elderly man with a little beard, whom some one greeted, "Hello, Steff!" Later I realized he was Lincoln Steffens.

There were about fifty people present, when Dreiser took a handkerchief out of his pocket, rapped on a table with his knuckles, and while folding and unfolding the handkerchief, opened the meeting with remarks to the effect that things were in a terrible state! what are we, what is America, going to do about it? He said fellows like Hoover, Mellon, [Secretary of Commerce] Lamont, [Secretary of Labor] Davis and Charlie Schwab and Julius Barnes, etc., didn't know what was going on. There was misery. There were bread-lines in America. Nobody knew how many people were unemployed, starving, hiding in their holes. Perhaps millions. Dreiser spoke for twenty minutes, folding, unfolding the handkerchief. The situation in Harlan County, down in Kentucky, was a disgrace. And so on. What are we, what is America, going to do about it? Then he declared he was through speaking; we were now to have a discussion. It was suggested that a group of writers go to Harlan to investigate and throw the light of publicity on the conditions there. But nothing definite came out of this. Dreiser's own great honesty and bewilderment had engulfed everybody. Lincoln Steffens got up and spoke; what about I don't know. He rambled around in his own past and tried to be sage. By-and-by the meeting closed and people began to leave. . . .

November 17.—Lunched with Paul Gallico of the *Daily News* [whose father, the great music-teacher, I had met in California] and Westbrook Pegler. They took me to a place somewhere in the Forties. Gallico is a large, slouchy fellow; Pegler, neat and trim. Gallico wants to become a magazine writer: sports and short 'stories. Pegler seems shy, taciturn; was pleased when I said I had liked a column of his some time ago, which was a story about a Singalese prize fighter. From the restaurant we went back to the *News* Building; Gallico wanted to show me the plant, which is supposed to be one of the most up-to-date newspaper plants in the world, especially the great press; and enroute, on Forty-Second Street, we ran into Gene Tunney, who was very affable. Quite irrelevantly he began to tell us that a few days previously he had gone to a concert in Carnegie Hall and asked if we preferred Beethoven to Bach. A handsome brute, he wears marvelous clothes. . . .

Undated (*probably November or December*).—S. took me to see "1931," the play by Paul Sifton about the current unemployment situation. Good in spots. The lead was excellently played by a young man named Franchot Tone, who is said to be a millionaire's son and a radical, feeling in real life much as he acts in his rôle of a jobless worker. The sets by Mordecai Gorelik were interesting. . . . Between acts I ran into Maxim Lieber, who introduced me to the fellow he was with—Albert Halper.

November 9.—Walking in the Park this afternoon, I got to talking with a man who addressed me, saying it was a nice day. Middle-aged, he had a washed-up air about him; obviously was lonely and wanted to talk. I learned he had been out of work since before the stock crash, but had a daughter who was married and had a job. He did not live with her, but she sent him ten dollars weekly. He roomed with another man who was in about the same position as he. Yes, he agreed, things weren't so good. "Now, for instance," he said, "look at all these great apartment-houses here around the Park. They tell me that some of them are hardly one-third occupied. Evenings the janitors turn on the lights in the empty apartments so the buildings don't look dark and empty. I don't see how the landlords get along. Do you? And paying for all that extra electricity in the vacant rooms . . . !"

1932

Under various dates.—Blind lead the blind. Says Herbert Hoover: "The march of prosperity has been retarded." He has just found out!
Says Henry Ford: "The Depression is a wholesome thing in general."
Says Mrs. Hoover: "If all who just happened not to suffer this year would just be friendly and neighborly with all those who just happened to have bad luck, we'll all get along better."
Says O. O. McIntyre: "This Depression has taught me never to worry."
"I am a reputable citizen"—Al Capone.

January 20.—Ben called. Dorothy Thompson is having a few people at her apartment tonight. Could S. and I come? S. couldn't go. . . . Nice apartment on Ninetieth Street between Park and Madison Avenues. Dorothy looked very handsome in evening gown. Red was not there; is snowbound in Vermont, writing (said Dorothy) from four to six thousand words a day on his feminist novel. Besides Ben and me, Lewis and Ruth Gannett were there, and a few others, whose names did not register with me. One was a journalist from Berlin, who spoke English. Talk was about Hitler, Germany, Russia, "revolution in the United States." Some of the things said were pretty wild. . . . Dorothy said that, having lived in Europe through most of the past decade, she did not know much about the United States, and was anxious to learn, get a feeling about the country.

February 11.—Dinner at the Sinclair Lewises. Red was in New York; he is finishing *Ann Vickers*. He left the rest of us after the meal. W. E. Woodward, John Farrar, Ben, and I were there to discuss with Dorothy the idea of starting a new magazine. Dorothy wants one somewhat on the style of *Time*, the news magazine, only radical; not affiliated with any left wing movement, but generally radical, hard-headed, truthful. We wrangled back and forth. There is some one (I don't know who) who wants to finance the venture to the extent of fifty or a hundred thousand dollars. I wasn't greatly interested in becoming an editor of a weekly like that, although it might become a success, for it would take all my time and energy, and I want to write rather than edit. I told them, though, that I would be very much for a quarterly magazine, which would not aim for a circulation much above a thousand copies, but would publish solid, carefully thought-out, authentic, analytical articles with a hard outlook upon things and forces in the United States, written by people—socio-politico-economic-cultural Darwins—who knew what they were talking about. Ben was for such a quarterly, too. But I don't suppose anything is going to come of it, either quarterly or weekly. We really are not the people for any such venture.

Toward eleven o'clock, after we had been discussing the thing for two hours, Red, who had been working or taking a nap in another room, joined us and suggested we all go out. John Farrar had to go home; the rest of us went to a chop-suey place on Eighty-sixth Street. Bill Woodward is an amusing fellow.

January 14.—Lots of evictions in the Bronx [where S. and I lived then] and eviction riots, led by "Communists." At the same time, I hear, racketeers are "muscling" into the landlord business, posing as Communists, organizing rent strikes, complicating evictions both for the apartment owners, the tenants, and the "Communists." . . .

Numerous small business failures. Last week the little tobacco-and-candy store in the next block, where I used to buy the morning papers, closed. . . .

Theodore Dreiser is getting out a book called *Tragic America*. He seems to have given up fatalism and mechanistic determinism and is 'way over to the left, not far from Communism.

February 6.—I do hope I get the Guggenheim [fellowship]! I should know in about three weeks.

I should like terribly to get away from America—certainly from New York—for a while. One needs a perspective upon things and goings-on in this country. One needs to check up on one's sense of proportion. Living in New York, it is next to impossible to think clearly, to be calm, to see the woods for the trees. There are 120,000 destitute families in Greater New York; how many single persons is anybody's guess. Many are actually starving. Children ringing doorbells and asking for food! Unemployed stenographers living on a banana a day! And excited voices are yelling, "Are you for us or against us? There are only two sides! Revolution begins, if not tomorrow, day after tomorrow! On which side of the barricades will you be? Decide!" Which sounds all crazy to me; yet——

If I don't get the Guggenheim and go to Europe for a year, I shall try to persuade S. to leave New York for a time—perhaps for this coming spring and summer—and we'll go to some village or small town or farm in Pennsylvania or New England.

March 3.—This morning at seven a special-delivery letter from Henry Allen Moe [secretary of the Guggenheim Foundation]: I have been awarded a fellowship! S. is very happy. We are going to Europe in about six weeks. . . . Moe suggests I come to see him.

This *awful* Lindbergh kidnapping! . . .

March 6.—Called on Moe. He is in his early forties, and one feels in him a wonderful person. Almost made me think it was an honor for the Guggenheim Foundation that I received the fellowship! There are no strings to the award. I am required to make no reports. I am free to do anything I like, or nothing. The only thing I must do is go abroad. When ready to sail, I shall receive three hundred dollars in cash; the rest in a letter of credit. It's all pretty incredible.

March 17.—S. and I went down to the Battery to apply for passports and get some steamship literature. We haven't decided yet how we'll go, but I believe it will be the *Saturnia*, of the Italian-Cosulich Line, on April 29th. She takes two weeks to Trieste, stopping at Lisbon, Gibraltar, Cannes, Naples, Palermo, Dubrovnik——

Notes aboard the M/S "Saturnia" (*April 29-May 13*).—We bought second-class tickets, but on our agent's recommendation in New York they transferred us to a spacious first-class cabin immediately on leaving the dock. There are only about 150 passengers in first class, the capacity of which is 360.

It is fine to be comfortable, etc., and I would have been foolish to decline first-class accommodations for the price of second-class, but in a way I am uneasy up here. A great ocean liner is a miniature of society with its inequalities. One hundred and fifty of us in first class occupy more than half—the best half

—of the ship. The second-class quarters are tight; in third class people can barely move around; while most of the crew, numbering two or three hundred, work and sleep in ill-ventilated, poorly and only artificially lighted holes 'way down below. . . .

I hate flunkeyism. Every move I make, there is somebody bowing to me, trying to do something for me. I am shocked by the waste in the dining-room. The food is superb, abundant, too abundant. Eight, ten courses at lunch and dinner. The menus are examples of fine printing. Each table has a waiter and a bus boy. The head waiter or maître d'hôtel bows one in and out. Every piece of cake is served from a whole cake. Once cut, the cake is spirited out of the dining-room. It probably goes to second class.

The passengers interest me. Twenty or thirty of them are Italians, including several Metropolitan Opera singers, with whom we have no contact. The rest are Americans. Five or six of these are radio technicians, experimenting with broadcasting from the ship. . . . There is a New York divorcée, who told S. her entire unhappy story the first day out, though we had never met, or heard of her, before. . . . There is a New York importer who thinks he has Socialistic leanings, likes Norman Thomas, reads *The Nation*, and is quite sure Hoover is to America in 1932 what Tsar Nicholas was to Russia in 1917. . . .

There is Mr. X——, a big man in the radio industry with international connections, who lost eight million dollars in the stock crash and doesn't care; he still has about fifty thousand left. Tall, gangling fellow, frank, direct, genuine; reminds me of Sinclair Lewis. He told me he didn't know he had eight million when he had them. He lived in a three-room apartment in New York and owned a small country home near Montclair, New Jersey. He doesn't "give a hoot" if the United States remains capitalistic or goes Communist, so long as he can work at radio, which fascinates him. Television will be the next "big thing." He is going to Italy for a conference with Marconi. . . .

There are a couple of dozen old American ladies, some traveling alone, others with their nieces or in pairs, still others with private physicians or nurse-companions. According to a rumor aboard, some one has figured out that amongst them they control or own, I forget which, one or two billions of dollars in various forms of wealth. They are the widows of rich men. Or spinsters whose fathers had been great manufacturers or what-nots. I talked with one of them, a Mrs. —— of Cincinnati, who is worth about five million dollars. She takes two or three trips a year. She has a grandson, who is some sort of Tolstoyan, refusing to accept her money, living on what he earns painting pictures, roaming all over the country, mending his own clothes. . . . "Imagine!" she said.

Mr. M——, a Mid-Western manufacturer, started a conversation with me the first day out. He is in his late fifties, well preserved, with a gold service-club emblem on his gold watch-chain, and an Elk pin in his coat lapel. Almost the first thing he said to me was, "My son—that's him over there, in the second deck chair: he likes to sit in the sun—he and I got tired of the Depression, of hearing all the talk about it, of answering 'phone calls from people in need of help which we couldn't render, of seeing our well-to-do friends go broke, of feeling our own purse-strings tighten in the face of it all—so we decided, he and I, to take a little vacation and make a trip on a comfortable nice boat and forget all about business and troubles for a while. You know the old song, 'Pack up your troubles in your old kit-bag'? Well, sir, we, my son and I, packed up our troubles"—he laughed a little, palpably pleased with his clever-ness—"and we left the old kit-bag back home with my brother-in-law (my wife's been dead now for ten years) and put him in charge of the plant and office. There's nothing doing to speak of, anyhow. In good times we employed as many as 280 people; now all we have is 27 on the payroll."

In the ensuing days he told several people on the ship about the old kit-bag. Forgetting he had already told it to me, he repeated it to me the third day out. I asked him what he thought was the answer to the current situation in the United States. "Well, sir," he replied, "I'm not worried about it. We've hit a snag; we're in a Depression, but we had 'em before. I remember a couple of them myself. Depressions come and go. Economic cycle, you know. This one came and it'll go—sure as day follows night. The country is sound at the core. Sound as a bell. . . . We need to have only faith in ourselves, in our country. Our traditions, our institutions are sound. Sound as a bell," he repeated. He didn't know where he and his son would go after landing. They had their car with them. They probably would just drive around for two or three months and see Old Yurrup. Maybe they would stop somewhere in Switzer-land awhile, because they heard a lot of people there spoke English. They would return to the United States early in the Fall. By then things probably would begin to pick up.

I spoke with his son, who looked very much like his dad. He wore the same style of clothes. From his gold watch-chain dangled a gold Kiwanis emblem; on his coat lapel was an Elk pin. He was less inclined to talk than the old man, perhaps out of deference to him. . . . "All we need," he said, "is faith in ourselves, in the country. The country is all right, sound at the core. Sound as a bell. . . ."

With Mr. J——, a young New York stockbroker, I became acquainted to-ward the end of the voyage. He is twenty-nine, he told me, but looks thirty-nine. Nervous. His lips often twitch in an uncertain smile. Apropos of nothing in particular, he said, "Life in the United States, in New York especially, is crazy, nuts, haywire. When you're in business, you're almost bound to develop a bunch of business and personal friends; some are personal and business at the same time. Then you get to be a slave to your friends. There's the social life. You have a hot time while you can hold up under it. Out every night. Dinners—theaters—midnight suppers—night clubs. Women. They have nothing to do all day, or rather all night, but chase around, and as a gentleman you can't turn 'em down. There are week-ends, which last from Friday till Monday, even till Tuesday. You gotta spend money and when you spend money in New York you gotta spend a lot of it. To spend a lot of it, you gotta have a lot—it's the only way to be happy in New York; anyhow, what is called happy. And to have lots of money nowadays you gotta be lucky and hustle like hell—you gotta rush around, make new contacts, make more friends, and so on, and so on, till you don't know where you're at and what it's all about. And when you're going on thirty, as I am, you're played out; or damnear to it. You have a hell of a good time, sure, while it lasts—then blooie!" He said he was making this trip all by himself To Get Away From It All, and he smiled. He didn't know how long he would stay in Europe; maybe six months, maybe longer. "What the hell!"

In the Mediterranean.—S. and I liked best a young geologist from Texas, Bob Manes, who got off at Lisbon, whence he takes another ship to Angola, a Portuguese dependency in western Africa, where he will prospect for oil for the Sinclair Oil Company.

His deck chair was next to ours. One day I noticed him reading a book by Norman Thomas. S. asked him for a match; then I remarked about the book on his lap. No, he smiled, he was not a Socialist; apart from being an American, he didn't know what the devil he was; but was interested in social and economic conditions, in the Depression, etc., and wanted to get different viewpoints. He had bought this book by Norman Thomas in New York just before sailing. He said he was terribly ignorant, but wanted to "know things." Too many people liked to look at the bright side of things—one reason, perhaps, the world was in such a mess. . . .

S. and I liked him instinctively, and invited him to share our table in the dining-room. He is young (only twenty-four), but definitely a man. There is something more solid about him than about any of the other people aboard we have come to know. He is welded together, integrated, with a simple inner strength that is anything but exhibitionistic; in fact, just the opposite. Talking with him, looking at him, one felt he would meet any situation simply, inquiringly, without prejudice; look at a thing for what it was rather than what he might want or prefer it to be. He reminded me of a boy I once knew who had been ill for two years and had somehow become a man during that period of aloneness and dependence upon his own resources. He had gone into himself and emerged humble and unafraid of himself or of anyone or anything else. Bob Manes—we called him Bob right off; then Red, for his hair —has that kind of modesty and shyness and sociability. This is his second trip to Africa. He was there for a year when he was barely twenty, and has been on his own before and since then. He likes to be alone, and he likes to be with people. He did not tell us this; we gathered it from his manner and what little he said that was indirectly autobiographical. He is pliable, flexible, but both intuitively and deliberately discriminating. He can read people, but is kindly in his judgments. There are reserves in him, power for continuous growth; and a resistance, natural and thoughtful, to the worthless, frivolous, petty, and bad. The best, the soundest people liked him. Mr. X [the radio man who had lost eight million dollars in the crash] became very fond of him and said to me, "Listen: when America turns out people like our young friend, she is O.K."

Bob is thin, strong and healthy; not good-looking, but attractive; honest, unassuming, and matter-of-fact. He wears a bracelet on his left wrist, which is really an identification disk. When S. asked him why he wore it, he told of a friend of his who had died of a sudden illness in Africa along with several other men. They had found their skeletons, but could not identify them. Now the company required all its employees in Africa to wear these identification bracelets.

He promised to write to us.

[He did write a few times to Yugoslavia. He enclosed snapshots of his camps, of strange jungle trees and beasts, of a buffalo he or his native "boys" had killed. Then we ceased hearing from him. Late in 1934 he suddenly announced himself in New York. Something dreadful had happened to him; he begged us not to insist upon his telling us what. He evidently had barely escaped death. He was ill; one of his legs, apparently, was of scant use to him. He was returning to the Southwest, hoping eventually to return to geological work. He expected to recover. . . .]

1933

Various dates in April.—S. and I returned three days ago [the 13th]. The impact of New York is rather harsh, but I am glad to be back, as is S. This still is the best country under the sun that I know anything about. *Here is freedom!* . . . Radio City looks lovely: so clean, such simple lines. . . . Went to a literary tea. The intelligentsia appear to be drinking less. I hear there are fewer and smaller parties. . . . Had lunch with Kyle Crichton and Erskine Caldwell. Kyle has turned 100 per cent "Communist"; seems strange, unconvincing. Caldwell has an interesting, calm face; doesn't say much. His novel *Tobacco Road* has been dramatized, is now on Broadway; apparently a hit. . . . Everybody I meet is depressed by things here and the events in Germany. . . . Everybody's horizons appear lost in a fog, which is getting redder and redder. . . . Riots. . . . What will Roosevelt do? . . . The other night Stella's mother was afraid to open the door when a Western Union boy rang the bell about one o'clock. She thought revolution had broken out and there was a mob outside. This is not so ridiculous. Her mind was prepared for it. Her neighbors are talking of it. She had been reading the papers, which are full of portentous news. . . . I am told that last fall and winter numerous people everywhere had stocked up with food supplies to last them a year. They had expected chaos to seize the country. . . . What will Roosevelt do? . . .

August 11.—Trying to finish my book on Yugoslavia by November 1st, as required by contract, I have been too busy, too tired to write anything in this Diary since April. I have been trying to shut my mind to everything not connected with Yugoslavia, but can't help knowing that important things are going on in Washington, all over the country. It is all very sudden, but something may come out of this "New Deal." . . .

August 15.—I wish I had this Yugoslav book off my hands so I could pay more attention to the NRA, etc.

November 4.—Turned in the completed MS of my new book, *Home Again* or *The Native's Return*, whatever it will be called in the end. Harpers prefer the latter title. . . . I am tired.

S. and I have very little money—and I owe [various people] nearly twelve hundred dollars! There is a chance that a few more chapters of my new book will sell to magazines as articles, but I don't know. One of the best chapters, on King Alexander, nobody wants; so far nine magazines have turned it down. The other day I met [the editor of one of the better magazines] and asked him why he had rejected it. I said Alexander was a unique, important figure in European politics; he might be assassinated one of these days, which conceivably might precipitate a crisis, even a war. He looked at me as though he thought I was a little foolish. We spoke awhile, and he said, "But who cares about your Yugoslavia and King What's-his-name? Yugoslavia—Syria—all the same? Has Syria a king? I don't know!" . . .

I'll probably be lucky if the new book sells enough to earn the advance Harpers have given me.

November 10.—Well, it's been decided: the title will be *The Native's Return.* I don't know if anyone at Harpers likes the book or not; no one has yet said so. S. thinks it's not bad as a whole and parts of it are first-rate. She believes it may "go." I don't know. I feel the book is inadequate. Too short. To keep it down to normal length, and to finish it by November, I have left out so much—writing only a sentence or a page where I should have written a chapter. But what is, is! I am tired and restless. I don't sleep. New York is so noisy. Whenever I look at a newspaper, something hits me. The world is popping, exploding with important events. The mood of the United States, however, seems vastly better than it was in April. Roosevelt is giving the people what they wanted—action.

November 13.—Received the first batch of galley proofs of *The N.R.* The thing reads pretty well . . . but I am afraid just now America is too absorbed in her own doings to be interested in what I have to tell about Yugoslavia. Parts of the book are rather well written, but that is not enough to put a book across. Besides, I am told the book business is nothing to boast of.

December 2.—Harpers have submitted *The N.R.* to the Book-of-the-Month

Club and the Literary Guild. It probably hasn't the ghost of a chance. But I guess I'll be on pins and needles. . . .

December 16.—Last night I learned *The N.R.* is the Book-of-the-Month selection for February! In one month some fifty thousand copies will be distributed. . . . S. terribly happy. . . . I guess my financial worries are over—for a while, anyhow. Suddenly I feel very calm. . . .

December 19.—Yesterday I received my check from the Book-of-the-Month. More money than I had ever thought I would ever have. . . . Today I mailed out nine checks, paying all my debts! Lord! it feels wonderful! . . .

After "The Native's Return"

There was a touch of spring in the air. The birds were flying back from the south. Carniola looked very lovely. . . . Near the track, as our train sped Trieste-ward, we saw a peasant plowing. He looked like my brother Stan, tall, husky, bent over the plow-handles. There was a great dignity in his task. . . . As we passed him he reached the end of a furrow. He glanced up and waved. . . . I had an enormous lump in my throat.

—The Native's Return.

On Being of Two Worlds

FOLLOWING THE PUBLICATION OF *The Native's Return*, LEWIS GANNETT REmarked to me on several occasions that he had difficulty in believing any place could be quite so nice as I described my native Carniola to be; and in the summer of 1935 he and his wife, Ruth, also a sceptic, took a trip there to "check up" on me. When they returned to New York their criticism swung the other way: I had understated the scenic loveliness of Carniola and the charm of the people, the Slovenians, who inhabit it! . . . Be that as it may, I believe that what I told of my old country was the truth; but, of course, not the whole truth in all its aspects and details. The book dealt with my impressions of Carniola only during the first four weeks immediately after my homecoming, from mid-May to mid-June, a season when most lands are at their best, not only scenically but psychologically and spiritually—humanly. I did not tell what happened to me, or in connection with me, afterwards.

Among other things, I mentioned how in the little city of Lublyana, the capital of Carniola, I met a number of Slovenian writers, the parties they gave for Stella and me, and that they came to my parents' place in the country and joined in the celebration of the "prodigal's return," as some of the folks in the village referred to my homecoming. All those writers—poets, novelists, editors, critics, playwrights, essayists: about a dozen of them—seemed such splendid human beings; their friendliness toward me appeared so genuine, their interest in America was so eager and deep, and Stella and I liked and enjoyed them. I had a vague idea from the beginning that most of these new friends of mine were liberals, progressives: people who thought and felt more or less as I did. It was natural that I met them first. But I did not realize then, that, having met them first and gone to their parties and invited them to my birthplace, I was automatically all but excluding myself from contact with writers labeled *klerikaltsi*, who adhered to the Clerical party, dominated by political leaders who were priests in the Catholic Church, and some of whom were economic radicals or progressives but conservatives or reactionaries in religious, moral, and cultural matters. Slovenia's literature, as all other phases of her culture, is closely linked with, and affected by, Slovenian and general Yugoslav (as it formerly was affected by Austrian) politics; and there is almost as fierce partisanship among writers as there is among politicians. This leads to an occasional burst of vitality in writing, but also to the formation of ingrown coteries, usually around some journal or review; then to the splitting of old coteries into new groups and cliques, and the starting of new journals and reviews; and, of course, involving no end of pettiness in this process.

I had a distant taste of this when I heard—I think from one of my brothers—that the Clericals were reproaching me for having taken up with the liberals

123

and progressives. They felt, it seemed, that I should really have taken up with them, for had not *Dom in svet* (*Home and World*), their leading magazine, been the first periodical in Carniola to review my book, *Dynamite,* immediately after it had appeared in America? I did not know what to say to this. In the United States, I felt, and was expected to feel, no obligation to anyone who wrote a review of a book of mine, nor to any paper or magazine printing such a review; and if the New York *Sun* published a favorable notice of my work that did not make me a Republican. So I was amused, but also a little disturbed; not so much from my personal angle as because this gave me a glimpse of a phase of Slovenian life which probably was inevitable in tiny, narrow Carniola but, nevertheless, which I did not like.

One of my new friends was Fran Albrecht, the editor of the old and traditionally liberal and progressive literary monthly *Ljubljanski Zvon* (*Lublyana Bell*). He had printed a translation of a story of mine shortly before I arrived in Carniola; now he asked me if I would help him get out an "American number" of his magazine. I procured for him stories, poems, and articles by American writers which were then translated, and, heeding his request, I wrote a piece on the United States in general, specially for the issue, which on its appearance, late in the summer, created a deal of interest throughout the province, as well as in Croatia and parts of Serbia—and caused a reaction in the Clerical camp not unrelated to envy, which, as I got wind of it, also jarred me a bit.

Some time prior to this another liberal literary friend of mine, seeing the folly and pointlessness of my getting further involved in the literary politics of the country, approached unbeknown to me the editor of a Clerical publication, with whom he was personally on speaking terms, suggesting he print the translation of a story of mine. Now, as I had become so closely and obviously associated with the liberal *Zvon*, this proposal was rejected, for—unlike in America, where one could simultaneously contribute to the *Cosmopolitan* and the *New Masses*, as did Ernest Hemingway, and to *The Nation* and *The Saturday Evening Post*, as did Sinclair Lewis—in Carniola one could normally write only for the publication of his party or coterie, if he knew what it was.

In America, rejections were matter-of-fact, impersonal, decided—as a rule—upon unpolitical, mainly editorial and business grounds, seldom on the basis of the author's political affiliations, and at one time or another in the preceding few years my work had been turned down by dozens of New York editors or their assistants; so that this rejection in Lublyana, when I heard of it, was no great blow to me. But it caused no little talk in Lublyana, for there it had all sorts of political implications. It most definitely established me as an un-Clerical, if not an anti-Clerical, person. It was followed by little attacks on me in the Clerical press, which, however, soon ceased: for the Clericals—evidently—decided it was best to leave me alone. They knew I would return to America before long: and good riddance.

However, these were but mild hints of what was to follow.

Among my new literary friends to whom I was most closely drawn was Oton Zupanchich, a man in his mid-fifties, Slovenia's foremost living poet and essentially a great man and a beautiful human being, beloved by the people in general for his poems, although the Clerical critics, the academicians, pedants, and politicians took digs at him for his tendency to be a free spirit, responsible to no one and nothing but the principles of truth and beauty as they appeared to him as a man, a poet, a creative artist, and a Slovenian living in the twentieth century in the country he loved. He is the author of numerous volumes of poetry, done in exquisite, mainly untranslatable Slovenian, and the translator of several Shakespeare plays, parts of which, to me, are well-nigh better in his Slovenian than in the original. We got along beautifully. He was keenly interested in my circumstances and problems as a writer in America. Did I have difficulties getting published because I was not a native of the United States? I told him no; on the contrary, at least one important editor, Henry Mencken, of whom he knew slightly, had encouraged me to write when I first began sending him my things from California. Later, in New York, another well-known literary man, Burton Rascoe, had spent no end of his time and energy pestering the publishers till one of them accepted my first book. . . . Did I manage to live and get married on what I earned writing? Was I giving all my time to writing? And so on.

Shortly before, *Laughing in the Jungle* had come out in New York, and one day I received a bundle of clippings of reviews that had appeared in newspapers and magazines in New York and Los Angeles, Boston and Chicago, Detroit and New Orleans, Seattle and Miami; Kokomo, Indiana, and Keokuk, Iowa; Ventura, California, and Gloucester, Massachusetts; Washington, D. C., and Dayton, Ohio; Phœnix, Arizona, and Scranton, Pennsylvania; Walla-Walla, Washington, and Rutland, Vermont; Cherokee, Oklahoma, and Montgomery, Alabama: which I showed to Zupanchich when he asked me how the book was being received. He looked through them; then, a curious expression on his fine poet's face, he said (quoting him freely):

"You are living and functioning, or beginning to function, in a big, big world, quite different from our little world here in Slovenia. These reviews . . . from cities thousands of miles distant from each other. . . . But, you know, when I was a boy, my father and mother almost went to America, too, and I with them. In fact, it is due to the merest chance that we did not go. . . .

"I am from Bela Krayina, a region not distant from your own home-place; and from Bela Krayina people began to emigrate to America as far back as 1850. In my boyhood, which is to say something like forty years ago, the outer walls of the winehouses in our village were covered with Red Star, White Star, Hamburg-Amerika, Bremen-New York, and Lloyd-Triestino posters with pictures of great ships: and, lured by these advertisements, our people went over 'the big pond' in droves. A house where the head of the family was at home was rare in Bela Krayina. The man went first, then, often, the wife followed with the children. As eight- or ten-year-old boys and girls, we dreamed of Bremen, Hamburg, Trieste, and great steamers; while New York, Chicago, Cleveland, Montana, Minnesota, Pennsylvania, Pittsburgh, Dakota, Nebraska, and California were familiar names to most of us. Our fathers were there, and our older brothers, uncles, cousins, and neighbors, working in mines and factories, earning money which they sent home. There, too, were our aunts and sisters, running boarding-houses or working in millinery and garment factories, or as waitresses in saloons. Instead of arguing among themselves whose father or elder brother was stronger or taller, or whose *pipets* (penny pocketknife) was sharper, or whose willow-bark whistle blew loudest, boys were wont to boast, 'My father went to America in a ship with two smokestacks and now lives in New York, where houses are taller than our church steeple,'—or, 'My father went over in a ship with one smoke-stack, but he got there as quickly as yours, and he is now in Arizona, where they have gold-mines, and which is as far from New York as New York is from here.' . . . I was unusual in that I had no close male relatives in America, but my mother had five sisters 'beyond the sea,' scattered between Pittsburgh and Chicago, and her heart pulled her there. She urged father to sell out, but then a chance circumstance intervened—which is another story—and we did not go to America; we remained in Carniola. But, had we gone, what would have happened to me? Would I have been Americanized? Would I have become an *Amerikanets*, like you—an American writer, a poet writing in the language of Keats and Shelley and Whitman? . . ."

The curious, wistful expression on his face as he talked to me crystallized itself into a poignant mingling of wonder, happiness, and sadness. He contemplated me kindly, pondering. During the previous sixteen years in America, associating almost exclusively with native Americans, I had not spoken sixteen words in my native tongue, with the result that now my Slovenian was unskilled, broken, awkward; and Oton Zupanchich guardedly asked me how I had lost the fluency of my mother tongue. I answered I did not know; I had merely lost it, without giving it any thought. "But tell me," he asked, hesitantly, fumbling for the core of the truth about me, for a method to get at me, "do you consider yourself an American or a Slovenian? In other words, do you hold yourself to be entirely of that great world beyond the Atlantic which we over here can scarcely imagine, or do you still belong to us in this tiny world of ours?"

"Well," I replied, thinking aloud, "I am an American citizen and as such, of course, an American at least legally or technically. But I believe and hope I am an American not only legally and technically but actually. Watching other Americans in the United States who were born there, I sometimes think I am more American than a great many of them. Certainly America interests me more than it does a good many native Americans I know who happen to be there simply because they were born there. And I really like America, with all her faults (perhaps partly for her faults); and her future fascinates and intrigues me. In fact, I think I love the place. Writing, I use the American language, which is also part of my means of thinking. Once I was overheard saying something in my sleep; I spoke English. I guess I am an American, all right. And I feel I belong there. But, of course, I was born a Slovenian, here in Slovenia or Carniola; there is no denying that; and, if I may judge by the feelings I have experienced since my homecoming, I am also a Slovenian. There is my mother—she is a Slovenian woman; I am her son. . . . I have never thought of this before, for in America I have been too occupied with immediate problems, too busy discovering America, wondering about her, going from place to place, earning my living, trying to become a writer; now that you ask me, I would say that I am an American of Slovenian birth; but, if you like it better, you can consider me a Slovenian who went to America when he was not quite fifteen and became Americanized, became an American. It is all the same to me; personally, so far as I am aware, I have no problem on this point. There is no conflict in me between my original Slovenian blood or background and my being an American."

From the look on his face, I knew that Zupanchich understood what I was saying, and I felt he was also thinking about himself. Had he gone to America as a boy, would he have remained a Slovenian, even if he had "lost" the fluency of the Slovenian tongue? Would he have become a writer, a poet in America, writing in one of the major tongues of the world, understood by, perhaps, two or three hundred millions of people, instead of in the language used by one of the smallest civilized nations (1,300,000) in the world? He seemed to me one of the finest persons I had ever encountered, but deep in him I sensed much bitterness, which he tried not to show—the bitterness of the exceptional man who was the son of a tiny nation and trying to function within that nation's narrow confines.

Stella and I left for Dalmatia, where word reached me that Oton Zupanchich was writing an essay apropos my homecoming for the *Ljubljanski Zvon*, and that among the intelligentsia in Lublyana there was much expectant, speculative talk about it—not so much because it was to concern me as because it was to be by the great poet, who, having been occupied as director of the National Theatre in the provincial capital, had not written a line of either verse or prose for years. I was myself, naturally, curious as to what he would say and waited eagerly for the magazine.

When it appeared, the Zupanchich essay was, of course, the leading piece, entitled "Adamic and *slovenstvo*"—an imperfect translation of the last word being "Slovenianism": everything that pertains to, or concerns, being a Slovenian. The entire meaning of the word is richer, more varied, complex, and many-sided than, say, the corresponding meaning of "Americanism." To a great many Slovenians, *slovenstvo* is intense nationalism, inextricably tied up with every bit of Slovenian tradition and history, cultural and otherwise; with every word of the Slovenian language and all its problems; and with every inch of Slovenian soil. It involves quick, strong emotions, which Americans, whose nationalism is not so complex and intense, would find difficult to understand and appreciate, even if I succeeded in fully explaining it.

The essay was beautiful prose, poetic and general, very friendly and kind to me, too kind; and permeated with the wistful tragedy of a great poet writing for a tiny nation. I shall not tell here everything it contained, for that would require me to explain a hundred and one things not generally understood by members of a great nation, and *that* would require a book by itself. But—at the risk of oversimplifying the thing—one of the main ideas and arguments running through the article was that, although I had gone to America as a boy and become Americanized and had lost the fluency of my mother tongue and taken to writing in English or American, *slovenstvo* was an important, if not the dominant, factor in my life and my function. Basically, maintained the poet, I was an offspring of Slovenia, "the true inner Slovenia"; and the spirit of "inner *slovenstvo*" lived in me. I had received it from my peasant mother, from the very air of rural Slovenia, and America did not kill it, nor harm it. America took nothing from me, nothing good, vital, new, fresh, vivid, generous, and important, and gave me much, because America was big, and had much to give. In America, I had room; there I could develop, grow, find for the essential *slovenstvo* in me wider, fuller expression than I could probably ever have found had I remained at home. He insisted that, although I had—regrettably—become more or less separated from my native language, and even if I myself inclined to emphasize my *amerikanstvo*, I was still a Slovenian; and that my work had certain virtues stemming from the virtues inherent in the sound mass of the Slovenian people.

I had no quarrel with this idea; on the contrary, I found it pleasant to hope that it possibly contained some truth. A short while before, *Harpers Magazine* had printed my article "Home Again From America," describing my homecoming, which later became the opening chapter of *The Native's Return*; and one day I received a packet of "fan letters" including one from a, to me, unknown Slovenian immigrant living in Cleveland, who said that, reading the piece, he had not been conscious it was written in English. "When I finished it, I was surprised to realize that what I had been reading was not in Slovenian." So, I thought to myself, Zupanchich probably was right in saying that *slovenstvo* was strong in me, though just then I tried to close the matter in my mind with the hundred-per-cent American phrase, "O.K. by me!"

But I did not succeed in closing the matter. I kept thinking to myself, "I *am* originally a Slovenian," and began gradually to understand things about myself that had puzzled me in America, and that I now remembered. . . . While serving in the United States Army during the War, for instance, I had almost suffered when, doing kitchen-police duty, I was ordered by the cook or mess sergeant to dump perfectly good food which had been left over into slop-cans. Now, checking up on my background, I knew why I had suffered. The reason was the same that compelled me always to clear up my plate, whether I was hungry or not. I was my mother's son, and she was a woman of Carniola, where food was not abundant, and thus by necessity no waste was permitted. To throw away a piece of crust, no matter how dry, was a sin in Carniola. In our home, although we were comparatively well-to-do, the rule, seldom spoken, was that nobody must leave anything on his plate. No waste. Nothing was ever thrown away that could be of any conceivable use—not only food, but anything. The Slovenians had a proverb, *"V sedmih letih vsé prav pridé*—In seven years everything comes handy." While at home for a few days immediately after my return from America, I had noticed that my sisters picked up every scrap of paper I threw away (for in America I had acquired a few such wasteful habits). When I changed the ribbon in my type-writer, my mother picked up the little tin box that had contained it, and that I had carelessly discarded. Only God knows to what use that little box would eventually be turned. . . . In my native village and elsewhere in Carniola I had seen people pick up little twigs as they fell off trees, and tie them up into *butartsé*, bundles of kindling-wood, which were then either used at home or sold on the market-place in the city; and now I knew why occasionally while walking in the country in America I had been almost unable to refrain from picking up little twigs under the trees! . . . Carniola was probably one of the cleanest, most orderly little lands in the world; in a way, a work of art. No rubbish allowed anywhere; in fact, there was no rubbish, or practically so, for, as I say, nearly everything was used. Hence, in part at least, my uneasiness as I traveled about in America and saw rubbish dumps, piles of tin cans, old rubber tires, or discarded machinery. . . .

Late in the autumn we traveled a good deal in Dalmatia, Montenegro, Bosnia, and Herzegovina. I did not see any Slovenian papers for weeks and allowed my mail to accumulate at the post-office in Dubrovnik. When I finally called for it, there were numerous clippings from Lublyana papers sent to me by my brothers and my new friends, all about the Zupanchich article, most of them attacking Zupanchich. But this was only the beginning. A fierce contro-versy developed. What was *slovenstvo*? Was *slovenstvo* possible apart from the Slovenian soil and language? Was I, who had lost the fluency of my mother tongue, really a true representative of *slovenstvo*? These questions were not only what they seemed to be on the surface, but were tied in devious ways with the current political and socio-economic situation in Slovenia, with Slo-venia's opposition to the Belgrade regime under the dictatorship of King Alexander, and with Slovenia's suspicion that the dominant group in Yugo-slavia, consisting mostly of Serbs, meant to Serbianize the entire country. Behind these questions were also the strained, jittery nerves of the sensitive, more or less neurotic intelligentsia, disconnected from the masses and reality, uneasy under the censorship, and perturbed by the situation in Yugoslavia and in Europe as a whole. (The intelligentsia is more or less neurotic the world over, but perhaps especially in a small nation.)

Writers, well-known in Slovenia and obscure, sent Editor Albrecht of the *Zvon* articles in reply to Zupanchich. Not wholly sympathetic to Zupanchich's views, but a passionate believer in the principle of the freedom of the press, he was willing to print them; the publisher, however, was unwilling to have the pages of the magazine opened to what threatened to become a long polemic, either because he agreed with Zupanchich or because he feared the controversy, full of nationalistic, politico-cultural dynamite, might get the publication in trouble with the Belgrade censor, whose function was unfriendly to *slovenstvo*. So, balked, Editor Albrecht resigned; there was no one ready to take his place; and the magazine, till then seemingly the best established periodical in the country, suspended publication, which was not resumed till after my return to the United States.

Meantime the ex-editor and some of his former contributors issued a pamphlet, which was almost a book, telling their part in the incident in all its details, which to members of a big nation would be amusing or ludicrous; a new magazine was started in direct consequence of this fight for *slovenstvo*; while numerous other monthly publications published long articles, most of them taking Zupanchich "for a ride" (as I put it in my Americanized mind), and some of them not sparing me, although I had stumbled into the controversy quite innocently. The critics of Zupanchich's concept of *slovenstvo* maintained, or hinted, either that the virtues he had discovered in my work or in me as a person really were not so noteworthy, or that, if I possessed them, they had no special or clear ties with *slovenstvo*. Certainly they had no bearing upon the current problems of *slovenstvo*, which were such and such, page upon page.

This went on for months, throughout the rest of my stay in Yugoslavia and after I left. The clerical monthly *Dom in svet* was gleeful about the suspension of *Zvon* and printed an endless essay by one of its leading writers, commenting on the matter with all its ramifications. It was all *Zvon's* own fault! Why had *Zvon* and the other so-called liberal and progressive publications taken me up with such unrestrained enthusiasm and thus made me into a sensation, a fad? They had built me up into so great a man that they themselves believed that I was a person and a writer of consequence. It served them right! And, with philistine righteousness, *Dom in svet* congratulated itself and the Clerical coterie for the wisdom and foresight they had manifested in taking no hand in building me up.

All this was funny to my American, or Americanized, eyes and mind; the Slovenian in me, however, was no little distressed; while both the American and the Slovenian in me were sorry for my fine friend Zupanchich, who had gotten himself into a predicament on my account, or at least in connection with me. The whole thing was so petty, so provincial, so Main-Streety, and, in a way, so unavoidable, so interesting, even fascinating, so closely linked to bigger things, to things that were wrong in Europe at large. I was returning to America in a few months and could smile at *Dom in svet* and at the entire affair, but Oton Zupanchich—a big man, a great poet and artist—had to remain here and take the consequences of his words. To him it might not be funny; he might not be amused; he could not leave; Slovenia was his life. Driven by motives linked to current politico-social movements and problems in their country, and to the entire deep neurosis of the European civilization, his petty critics did not realize that if he did make a mistake, or even half a mistake (and I do not know that he did so far as *slovenstvo* apart from me was concerned), it was because—or mainly because—he was a great artist and poet caught in a provincial-intellectual, small-nation trap, living through me, momentarily projecting himself into the big world through the speculation of his own fate had he emigrated to America as a boy, and at the same time not taking anything away from his tiny, narrow, lonely, beloved Slovenia; indeed, giving me, "the prodigal," back to her and endowing me with virtues which, if at all, I possessed only in embryonic stages.

I worried: was Zupanchich sorry he had published the piece?—for I did not hear from him, and, uncertain about his feelings, I did not know how to write to him. But when we met again, during the winter—unexpectedly, in a driving blizzard in front of the Royal Palace in Belgrade, where he happened to be on business as director of the National Theatre—he gripped my hand heartily, after he had studied my face and manner for a second, to see how I felt; then drew me into a coffee-house. He said he had worried about how I felt about it, and had hesitated writing to me, fearing I might be offended by the things his article—which, apart from this, he did not regret—had provoked other writers to say about me. We had a good laugh. He remarked that he, himself, was inured to this sort of thing, or almost so; but, of course, it was sad and unpleasant, too. One could not do anything about it. . . . We discussed *slovenstvo* and his late good friend, the great Ivan Cankar.

In my early 'teens, between 1910 and 1913, just before I came to America, while a student in Lublyana, Ivan Cankar was my favorite author (and in some ways he is to this day). He was then at his apex as a creative writer; an authentic genius; a novelist, poet, dramatist, essayist, social critic, polemicist, and—with Oton Zupanchich—an important factor in the development of the Slovenian language as a means of communicating the subtlest and deepest feelings and most complex thoughts. Writing, he practically created a new language, fluid, limitless in its possibilities of expression, and profoundly intimate (which, unfortunately, makes it difficult to translate him adequately into another language), yet completely understandable to everyone who knew the words or the materials out of which he made them. In the entire history of Slovenian literature (which, for a nation of slightly over a million has a surprising number of interesting figures), Cankar was the one writer who made his living—a very meager one, of course—solely with his pen throughout his literary career. He was, perhaps, as successful as he possibly could have been writing in the language of the smallest national unit in Europe, but his life and function as a son of such a tiny nation was a constant and painful problem to him, which influenced all his work and drove him to drink and, soon after the war, to an untimely death.

Since Zupanchich and I discussed Cankar on that wintry day in Belgrade in 1933, Janko Lavrin, who is a Slovenian by birth, a member of the faculty of the Nottingham University in England, and a noteworthy literary critic and essayist writing in English, published an essay on Cankar in his book, *Aspects of Modernism,* from which I quote:

The dilemma Ivan Cankar had to face was a double one: first of all, the fate of a tiny nation in the chaos of the contemporary political and economic struggle; and secondly, his personal fate within the frame of that nation—the fate of a great creative artist, working in the pettiest provincial atmosphere which seemed to exclude beforehand any kind of greatness.

Trying to solve this dilemma, Cankar produced a picture of his nation which (unlike mine of the same nation in *The Native's Return*)

is often gloomy past belief. What makes it so is not only the heavy struggle for existence, but the general aimlessness, the lack of any hope, of any wider perspective for the future or even for today. The smallness of the national body itself seems to be a drag upon its courage and vitality. It saps the will, and demoralizes sooner or later even potentially strong men, who are compelled to witness the farcical party struggle on the one hand and rancorous servility, backbiting, envy and intrigue on the other.

Much of his best work, which is almost invariably bitterly satiric or Gogo-lesquely ironic, concerned the exceptional individual—himself—in a nation too small and poor to be in position to afford anything big or exceptional.

Able [says Lavrin] but unwanted talents, homeless originals, frustrated active men—such were the characters into whom he projected his own ego. All of them are depicted against the background of a small nation, as its conscience and living reproach. Some of his heroes give up the fight altogether, because in the conditions in which they are compelled to live there is nothing even worth fighting for: one's struggle becomes a ludicrous caricature. Those, however, who take up the fight, usually succumb; and Cankar is careful to show that their failure is in itself a proof of inner superiority.

This morbid attitude of Cankar's, however, was only a superficial characteristic. It was strong and apparent in nearly everything he wrote, but that, I think, chiefly because, as an exceptional son of a small nation, he was caught in the complexity of his personal problem and had to work his way out of it; and, working his way out of it, he stirred endless antagonism on the part of people about him who were unable to understand his personal conflict and aim —including the antagonism of the Bishop of Lublyana who, early in Cankar's career, bought an entire edition of a book of his poems and burned it in public! Deep in him, as a genius, he was a profoundly positive man who was motivated not only by hatred but by a great love for his tiny, lovely, civilized country; who found no long-range satisfaction in mere protesting against aggression, oppression, and brutality, but who wanted to build and create. He was beginning to emerge into this positive rôle when I became old enough to read and (more or less) to understand him. Love of his country, to quote Lavrin again,

helped him to see many things in a different light. . . . The *via crucis* through which he himself, his characters, and his nation had to pass, was now viewed by him as a necessary trial at the end of which there was not death but a new life.

But his intense early struggles—both within himself and with his tight environment—had so weakened his physical and spiritual makeup by the time he attained his early forties that the war struck him as a great blow from which he never recovered, and he died.

As Oton Zupanchich and I sat in that Belgrade coffee-house, and he, on my prompting, talked to me of Ivan Cankar, I knew he was, indirectly, talking of himself. His story was, in many details, unlike Cankar's but essentially the same. He, too, now—after twenty years of intense inner agony and petty bickering with his environment—found his positive strength in his love of Slovenia, in a lyric sort of nationalism, in his hope for a better future for his country, somehow, somewhen; but, evidently, too, he was not substantially or completely happy either as a man or a poet. I felt that to love Slovenia and to extol her lyric virtues was not enough for him. True, "inner *slovenstvo*" was made of fine elements, some of which were factors in the better side of other nations; yet it restricted and circumscribed him too much. I felt that, perhaps without his clearly realizing it, the inner stature of him had originally demanded, if it did not now demand, a scope—at least a potential scope—much greater than he had in Slovenia. But what could he do?

His essential greatness had helped him to rise above the bitter, petty, momentary squabbles of the sensitive, neurotic, quixotic, mercurial intelligentsia—at least publicly, or when he spoke to me, for he suspected I might write about him; but deep in him their pettiness and narrowness rankled.

I could not help thinking—then and since then—of the various Slovenian writers who had attacked Zupanchich, and of other intellectuals more or less like them, some physically half-starved, many (and no wonder!) spiritually mediocre or warped. Some, perhaps, were mediocre only as they appeared to function as writers; originally they might have been only a notch or two below Zupanchich or Cankar. But that was enough to keep them incapable of rising above the neurotic intellectual mess, enough to warp them. In a wider, freer world, they might have been, perhaps not great, but big, effective men.

Since coming to Yugoslavia—not so much in Slovenia as in Croatia and Serbia, but where the intellectual-literary situation was virtually the same as in Slovenia—I had met numerous young writers, artists, and diverse intellectuals, most of them clearly above-the-average, some even superior, but ill functioning, who were Communists or called themselves Marxists or "leftists," and were intense fanatics, suffering prison for their views and enduring indescribable tortures at the hands of the Belgrade political police; and I wondered how many of them were Communists or "leftists" merely or largely because their spirits and their creativeness rebelled against non-function or ill-function in narrow, warping provincial environments, and conceived Communism or Marxism as a possible way of escape from spiritual and creative frustration. Of the mediocre or essentially non-great intellectuals, they seemed to me the best. Communism gave them hope of a better future; perhaps erroneously, but hope, which filled them, made them stand up as men, enabled them to endure prison, hunger, and torture. It gave them character and personality, a staunch integrity. Before I left the country I asked a few of these if their "leftism" perhaps did not have some such motivation, and two or three—after pondering a bit—admitted that it had. One said, "Oh yes, all these boundaries, geographic, spiritual, and linguistic; all these restrictions, political and cultural, that frustrate millions while but one or only a few can be full men—they must all be shattered; and, so far as I can see, only Communism, only a new social order, a United States of Europe, of the World, can shatter them. . . ." What this young man said seemed to me significant. I could not doubt that many intellectuals of several other small countries, which together comprised half of Europe, were "leftist" for the same reason; nor that, in a lesser degree, this was true also of the big countries. A young Serbian writer, who was not a Communist but inclined leftward, said to me, "We will, somehow, sooner or later, have to break through mere *serbiyanstvo* and pour ourselves into the creative pools of the entire humanity."

Before I returned to America, I made it a point to have a close look at the Clerical intellectuals in Slovenia, and several of them compared rather well, as persons, with the non-Clericals. They were stronger, more solid; their work was mediocre but healthy or wholesome, and was more popular among the healthy, simple peasant folk than was that of the liberals; for the Clericals were Catholics, some passionate Catholics, and Catholicism, which, like Communism, is an international idea and cause, gave them scope. In a way, it shattered for them the geographic, political, and spiritual boundaries of Slovenia.

And, in this connection, I could not avoid speculating about myself. At thirteen, two years before I went to America, I had written something that was published in a juvenile magazine in Lublyana; and had I remained in Slovenia, I might very likely have become a Slovenian writer. But what kind? My inner qualities probably were no kin to Cankar's and Zupanchich's inner greatness; so I might possibly have turned out some sort of warped, bitter intellectual, or a mediocre Catholic scribbler, or a Communist or "leftist" propagandist. . . . It is fine to be a native of lovely Slovenia, my mother's son, a fellow countryman of Cankar and Zupanchich; but, well, I was deeply glad, too, I had gone to America and become an American writer, and could return there. America was vast and free, comparatively unnationalistic, young, a universal melting-pot, as yet not settled or fixed in her ways, unformed, chaotic, a country admittedly in process of becoming something or other, with all manner of possibilities in her future, both immediate and distant.

Of course there was much to be said in favor of being a writer in a small country. Zupanchich, for instance, could hear himself in the everyday language of the Slovenian people. The same had been true of Cankar; while in America Sinclair Lewis was a great success partly because he gave new meaning to "Main Street" and invented "Babbitt"—two expressions that have found their way into the speech of the country in his lifetime. Shortly after my homecoming, walking on a country road in Upper Carniola, I had heard a group of homebound school children late in the afternoon, declaiming in unison one of Zupanchich's poems. Such a thing could not have happened in America with any poem by, say, Robert Frost, Robinson Jeffers, Edna St. Vincent Millay, or even Whitman. Equally impossible in America was what I had witnessed one day in front of the university in Lublyana, where a student read, through a megaphone to a great crowd of several hundreds of his fellows, a passage from Cankar, originally written as a protest against injustice under Austria, but now voiced as a protest against the tyranny of the Belgrade regime. . . . But in America, writing in the American language, I had scope, spiritual and physical elbow room, a potential audience of many millions of people, an opportunity to develop ——

A year after my talk with Oton Zupanchich in Belgrade, *The Native's Return* was published in New York; and, as already suggested, the Book-of-the-Month Club distributed something like 50,000 copies of it the first month, and it was a so-called best-seller for nearly two years. And some of the thoughts occurring to me, off and on, ever since have been: I could not have written the book, had I not come to America and become an American writer. . . . No book that I, or anyone else, could possibly have turned out in Slovenia could have achieved such circulation. . . . Had I remained in Slovenia and become a Slovenian writer, I could not possibly have published a book that would have infuriated King Alexander, thrown the Belgrade Foreign Office into panic, and generally had the effect of a blow at tyranny. . . .

Soon after publication all manner of things began to happen to me in connection with *The Native's Return*. For months I received from twenty to fifty letters a day, most of them so-called "fan letters," but also not a few critical and abusive ones. I enjoyed reading the former, but the latter interested me more. They were, almost exclusively, from my Yugoslav fellow-countrymen in the United States. Serbians were upset and outraged because, in the last part of the book, I criticized the Belgrade dictatorship and predicted the assassination of King Alexander, whom I had met just before returning to America. They sent me clippings from Serbian-language newspapers published in the United States, denouncing me as a traitor, liar, an agent at once of Stalin and Mussolini. During 1934 and 1935 I received from Serbian sources about a dozen threatening letters, which I considered mostly hysterical bluff; but as a precaution I lived through the greater part of these two years on the twenty-fourth floor of a New York hotel, where no one could possibly take a pot-shot at me through a window, and where no one could reach me without first calling me on the telephone. A number of New York Serbians stayed up nights to ring me at two or three o'clock in the morning, to have the satisfaction of interrupting my sleep and calling me some unprintable name. Such calls were frequent during the day. Finally I was compelled to make a special arrangement with the switchboard operators which put an end to these annoyances.

At least two Slovenian-language newspapers, but particularly one published in Cleveland, along with possibly a couple of hundred letter-writers who were Slovenian immigrants living in various larger cities of America, denounced me for the first part of my book, in which I described Slovenia and told of my family, my cousin's wedding, and my uncle's death. In their opinion, these chapters did the good name of Slovenia and the Slovenian immigrants' in America incalculable harm, for, in their opinion, I presented the country as being inhabited by a superstitious, semi-pagan race. The priest of a Slovenian church in Cleveland all but called the wrath of God on me. When I came to Cleveland, which is the biggest Slovenian colony in the United States, a lady got me on the telephone at my hotel to tell me I ought to be ashamed of myself for writing as I did about the old country. . . .

But all this bothered me very little. The book was so successful that every once in a while I had to pinch myself and rub my eyes. While the Serbian nationalists attacked me, I knew that what I said about the Belgrade regime and King Alexander was true. When the Slovenian paper in Cleveland ranted against me week after week for a whole year, chiefly because of the chapter on my uncle's death, I received some letter such as the following one, which came from a, to me, unknown woman living in a Western university town, who probably was a teacher or the wife of one:

"On last Sunday my father died, miles across the Continent from me. Since receiving the telegram, I have struggled with what I had believed to be long-put-away superstitions, fears and false, exhibitionistic grief over the idea of death. But in spite of myself, my reactions to his death (it is the first in my family) have proved to be not an entirely intellectual experience.

"Last night, just to read something, I picked up your book, *The Native's Return,* which a friend had asked me to look through a week or more ago. . . . Your story of how your uncle died gave me a strange peace. My father's funeral is to be this afternoon, and I feel that I have attended it—minus the barbarousness and pomp of our American ceremony.

"Thank you for the help you have given me."

By and by I realized, too, that those attacking me were mostly the self-styled intellectuals and "leaders" of Yugoslav immigrant colonies in the larger cities, petty, narrow, spiteful, never missing an opportunity to raise a howl—crude copies of old country intellectuals, lacking in the cultural refinements of the originals in Slovenia, and possessing many of the worst qualities of American go-getters, pushers, and peanut politicians. The majority of my fellow-countrymen in the United States who had heard of me and my book had nothing against me. They were simple workers living in industrial towns. A few read the book, others heard about it. Their American-born children came home from school with happy faces, saying that the teacher had told them of a book about their parents' Old Country, which, from the author's description, must be a lovely, interesting place. So far as the parents were concerned, the teacher had never said anything nicer to their children, and I was responsible for that; so in a great many colonies, from New York to Montana, they met in their fraternal lodges and passed awkwardly worded but deeply sincere resolutions thanking me for presenting the old country to the Americans as I had presented it, and inviting me to come to visit their colony and speak to them.

Moved and curious, I went on a tour, which took me as far west as Minnesota, visiting forty or fifty towns, speaking in lodge halls, and having the time of my life, although at the end of the trip I was practically dead. The people all but killed me with hospitality. They were distressed because I seemed unable to be guest at more than one house a night, to eat more than a half-dozen meals a day, and to drink more wine and homebrew than I did. In effect, and sometimes almost in these very words, they said to me, "For decades now few Americans knew who we were. Some called us Hunkies. Others thought we were Austrians. But now you told them who we are and where we come from. Now they know what our old country is like. Now the whole of America knows."

The Slovenian and Croatian iron-miners around Eveleth, in Minnesota, organized a big meeting and reception for me. They invited their Finnish and Swedish fellow-immigrants, some of whom had read or heard of my book. It was late in April, but a couple of hours before the meeting a terrific blizzard swept the Iron Range; yet about a thousand people—most of them, I was told, from a twenty-mile radius around Eveleth—gathered in a barn-like hall, which had no facilities for heating. When they rented it, they had not expected a blizzard. I talked to them, shivering throughout the speech; then shook hands with all of them. Or, rather, they shook my hand, which is only medium-sized, with their vast miners' hands, squeezing it, holding it as in a vice while expressing their appreciation, and pumping my arm like a handle on a cistern. The next morning I woke up in somebody's house with a bruised and swollen hand and a half-numb arm, which I was then compelled to carry in a sling for several days.

This tour will always remain a highlight of my life in America. I would not have missed it for anything. It was an experience on a par with my trip to Yugoslavia.

What did it all mean? . . . Clearly, I was an American from Slovenia, or a Slovenian who came to America and became an American. By coming to the

United States and becoming an American writer, I had jumped the boundaries and restrictions, the profound and elaborate pettiness, of the Old World. I was of two worlds, which met in that blizzard on the Iron Range in Minnesota, in Cleveland and elsewhere—not perfectly, but still, they met: America and Slovenia.

My Friend in Herzegovina

ONE EVENING IN THE EARLY SPRING OF 1934 I WAS SCHEDULED TO LECTURE ON Yugoslavia in the high-school auditorium in the iron city of Hibbing, Minnesota. In the afternoon, the program chairman, an old-stock American, who was also the head of the local county unemployment relief organization, drove me around, showing me the immense iron-pits and other interesting sights.

A few miles out of the town we came to a cluster of shabby workingmen's dwellings huddled against a broad bare hill, which protected the tiny settlement from the fierce Iron Range winds on that side. Said my program chairman, a bit hesitantly, "Some of your countrymen live here."

"Is that so?" I said.

"We don't quite understand them," continued the program chairman. "In fact, people on our relief committee consider them not quite sound in their heads. Some of them have been out of work now for two years, a few even longer. They live on next to nothing. In fact, they practically starve. And yet they refuse to go on relief. We have sent our investigators around to talk to them, but they—four or five families and perhaps a half-dozen single men, or men whose wives and children are in the old country—were insulted. We were offering them charity! In their eyes, to offer them relief was almost equivalent to calling them a bad name."

I asked the program chairman to stop the car, and went into one of the houses. As I had expected, the people of the settlement were all Herzegovinians.

In the evening, instead of delivering my usual talk on Yugoslavia, I told the following story:

Leaning against a wall on the sun-flooded main street in Dubrovnik, in southern Dalmatia, early in the summer of 1932, I was glancing over a newspaper when I heard myself addressed in a deep resonant male voice. "Excuse me, please: may I speak with you?" The words were in Serbian as it is spoken by peasants in the high mountains along the western rim of the Balkans.

I looked up from my paper—way up, for the man was six feet six if he was a foot, straight as a rod and as thin, all skin, bone, and sinew. His face was very Slavic: square and compact, with a blunt broad-nostriled nose, a strong round chin, firm lips, very high cheek bones, a dark mustache, and several days' growth of beard, and wide-apart gray eyes which, though half hidden under the shaggy jutting brows, were intensely alive and alert. Not a handsome face, but a striking vivid one, at once hard and gentle, simple and complex. Character was impressed upon it all over; with networks of tiny wrinkles around the eyes and heavy lines at the mouth and across the full width of the slowly sloping forehead. The deep-brown leathery skin was the result of a long collaboration between the high-mountain summer sun and the fierce *bora*, or north wind, which in the winter roars over the Dalmatian Highlands, Montenegro, and Herzegovina, sometimes at a hundred kilometers an hour, much as the winter winds roar over Minnesota's Iron Range.

The man was in his late forties or early fifties.

His hair was short, bristly, dark, and dusty, with a light sprinkling of gray at the temples and above the large ears, out of which grew tufts of curled hair. A great Adam's apple moved up and down the long, veiny throat.

A soiled shirt of unbleached homespun linen was open in front, revealing a hairy, fleshless chest and two powerful collar bones. From the broad, bony shoulders hung a pair of long, skinny arms, the longest I had ever seen, and probably also the strongest. The hands were huge, big-veined, knotted, bruised, and cracked. The shirt sleeves were rolled above the sharp elbows and the hair on the dusty long forearms and the back of the hands was bleached to a dull gold.

The man's costume (for in Yugoslavia, as elsewhere in the Balkans, many peasants still wear homemade national garb which indicates whence they hail) told me that he was a peasant from Herzegovina, the barren limestone country dominated by the awesome Dinaric Alps, immediately to the east of the Dalmatian coast.

On top of the medium-sized globose head, a little to one side, he wore a tiny round cap of red cloth with black embroideries and a black fringe in back, rather dirty and frazzled from years of steady wear. His long lean torso was encased in a tight-fitting jacket of crude dark wool which reached midway between the shoulders and the waist, with no buttons, no sleeves, no pockets, and patches in many places. His breeches, also mended in several spots and held up by a cord drawn tightly above his sharp hip bones, were of similar material and vast in the seat, which hung loosely down below his knees. His *opanké*, or sandals, were of the most primitive kind and (as I correctly suspected) worn out on the bottom.

He stood still before me on his slim long legs, but I could see that his body was agility itself. There was something very dynamic in that still, straight posture. Much later it occurred to me that he could have become a great dancer.

A real mountain man, a Balkan Slav of the so-called Dinaric type, he had great natural dignity, an innate wholly unconscious pride, more animal than human, in being what he was. He had in him the Slavic peasants' so-called "heart culture," which is deeper, more vital and dependable than culture acquired in schools. There was a profound politeness in his words. His rich voice rang pleasantly in my ears for moments after he had spoken to me.

Although I had seen several other Herzegovinians in Dubrovnik and elsewhere in Yugoslavia who in looks, bearing, and attire greatly resembled this man, he none the less startled me, and I looked at him for perhaps a quarter of a minute without answering his question. At the end I almost forgot what he had asked me; so pretending I had not understood him I said, "What was it you wanted?"

A faint smile enlivened his face still more and he said, "I begged you to excuse me for addressing you; I wish to talk with you."

"Certainly," I said, quickly. "What is it——"

"I want to ask you if you know where I could get something to do—some work—anything—so I might earn a few coins."

"I am sorry," I replied, "but I am a stranger here, only recently arrived, and as yet very little acquainted with anything in Dubrovnik or in Dalmatia; certainly I cannot say where you might find work. Do you understand me?"—for my Serbian was rather lame.

"I understand you," he said. "I asked you because, as I saw you standing here, I thought you were a native of this city." He hesitated an instant, looking at me intently, then asked, "But, if you will permit me to inquire, you are *nash*"—ours: of our nationality: a Yugoslav, "are you not?"

"Yes and no," I answered. "I was born in Slovenia, but during the last nineteen years, more than half my life, I have lived in America, and am a citizen of the United States."

"Ah . . . you are from America!" he cried and an eager expression flashed on his face.

I nodded. "I lately returned to my old country. I shall stay in Yugoslavia about a year."

"Then you will go back to America?"

"Yes."

He offered me his hand, we shook; and he told me his name—Yovan Vukomanovitch. I told him mine.

He said, "Perhaps you know my uncle, or have heard of him. He is also in America. His last name, like mine, is Vukomanovitch, but his first name is Dushan. He must now be an old man—my uncle Dushan."

I smiled. "America is big, you know."

"To be sure," said Yovan Vukomanovitch, "and I should have explained to you that when he arrived in America—back some thirty-five years ago—he went to a region known as Arizona and to a city called Bisbee. I remembered the names, because 'Arizona' has a beautiful sound, and gold is mined there; and when I was much younger than I am now I used to dream of some day going there. Do you know the place?"

"I have been to Arizona."

"And you have not seen my uncle Dushan? . . . Well, I should have thought so, for he doubtless is dead. We back here heard of him for a few years; he was mining gold and sent money home to his wife and his brother, who was my father; then—then, for over thirty years now, no news from him. His widow said, 'America swallowed him.' What do you imagine has happened to him?"

"I don't know, Yovan Vukomanovitch," said I.

To change the subject, but also because I wanted to know, I asked him from what part of Herzegovina he came.

"From the village of Sirilovitch," he answered, "about seventy kilometers or two days' walking from here."

"You walked the whole way?"

"Of course," he smiled.

"And how are things in your village?" I asked.

"Not good. All summer the sun was unusually strong; it burned nearly everything we had planted in our fields. There will be almost no corn, very little tobacco, if any; and the grass on the ridges is so scant that our sheep and cattle are dying for the lack of it. The last two months more than half of my own sheep have died."

I had not yet been to Herzegovina. When I went there later, I found that what Yovan Vukomanovitch called "fields" were tiny spots—seldom over a hundred square feet—of fertile soil hidden away in gullies, gorges and ravines. The sheep and cattle were small and spindling; the tough, wiry grass on the mountains, when the sun did not burn it altogether, was their sole food.

Yovan Vukomanovitch spoke with a profound calm, and amazing dignity. The situation in his country was not at all a unique one. Herzegovina is a land of perennial economic crisis. During the five centuries, since the Turks had driven a part of the Serbian nation into the Dinaric Alps, the people have become inured to hardships such as persons in prosperous fertile countries are unable to endure; and in the historic process their physical and spiritual fiber has been toughened to an incredible degree.

I wasn't any too well aware of all this then, so I said, "But what are you going to do about it? Have you a family?"

"A wife and three children," answered Yovan Vukomanovitch. "I came here to Dubrovnik"—which in the summer and early autumn is a lively tourist town—"hoping to find some work and earn enough money to buy two or three hundred kilos of corn and a few other things. If I manage to do that my family will not starve during the winter. Most of the other Herzegovinians you see in Dubrovnik probably have come for the same purpose."

"When did you come?" I asked.

"Four days ago."

"And no luck yet?" I smiled.

"No," and he smiled, too.

I looked at him in silence a long moment and was more and more impressed. There he stood, gaunt and lank, a head taller than I, bony and angular, but with a quiet dignity that I cannot over-emphasize or mention too often. It was a reflection, a glow of his physical and spiritual strength; also, a characteristic of the country that one recognizes only if one looks long and close. Unlike in America, poverty is no shame in Yugoslavia.

I noticed again the extreme leanness of his body and became a little uneasy about him, suspecting that he probably wasn't eating regularly. I said, "You've been here four days. How do you manage? Have you any money?"

He laughed briefly. "No, I have no money. In the whole village of Sirilovitch, which has about one hundred and fifty souls, there is at this moment not a hundred dinars in cash"—the equivalent of two dollars.

Later I learned that in hundreds of such villages as Sirilovitch, not only in Herzegovina, but in other so-called "passive" or unfertile Balkan regions, as, for instance, in Montenegro, Dalmatian Highlands, and parts of Albania, most families, lacking the necessary money to buy anything, used no matches, no salt, no petroleum in their lamps (in fact they had no lamps), while sugar and coffee were undreamed-of luxuries.

"But listen here, Yovan Vukomanovitch," I said again, "how do you manage?"

He laughed, shrugged his shoulders, and cut a short, swift gesture with his long, thin arms as if to say, "How do you suppose!" But his laughter and the expression of his face were not mirthful; rather, they were sad, which is true of most laughter and of most peasant faces in the Balkans, especially in Yugoslavia, where centuries of social, economic, and political agony have left their impress upon the people's personal character and looks. Their faces are maps and mirrors of those lands.

"Don't you know anyone in Dubrovnik?" I asked.

"No."

"Where do you stay? Where do you sleep nights?"

"Anywhere," he replied. "Last night I slept on the beach, on the sand." He smiled. "Toward morning the Adriatic reached up—or, as they say, the tide came in—and when I awoke I was wet all over. It took the sun all forenoon to dry me." He smiled again.

I laughed. I liked his humor. We were beginning to understand each other.

"But, seriously," I said, "when did you eat last?"

"When I left home," he answered, simply.

"That was—let's see: two days coming, four days here—six days ago. No?"

"Yes."

There could be no doubt that he was telling the truth. To me six days was a long time to go without food; in America I had known people who became panicky and whose characters were on the verge of collapse after not eating for two days. But nothing seemed wrong with this man, Yovan Vukomanovitch. He was straight, proud, good-humored; his voice was virile, beautiful.

I did not know then, as I learned subsequently, that in the Dinaric regions it is not unusual for people, especially men, to go foodless for a week and even ten days; that there one does not become really worried till one has not eaten for, say, two weeks; that during the World War Montenegrins, of the same general makeup as Herzegovinians, had often fought for ten days, even two weeks at a stretch, without food and very little water and tobacco. So, vaguely disturbed, I reached into my pocket and brought out all the change

I had with me—eight dinars, or twelve cents—and said, "Here take this and go buy yourself some bread—anything you want."

Yovan Vukomanovitch looked at me, startled. The rich brown color of his face deepened a shade. He put his hands behind him.

"Go on, take it," I urged.

"No, no!" he cried, stepping back. "You are shaming me. You are offering me charity. It would be *sramota* [shame] for me to take it."

For a moment I hardly knew what to do. I saw that I had blundered. I should have casually invited him to come eat with me. Now it was too late; he would refuse.

So after a while, rather annoyed with myself, I said, "Shame, nothing! Don't be foolish: I am not offering you charity. I think it is a shame that you have no money while I have more than necessary for my immediate needs."

He still looked hurt, bewildered, holding his hands desperately behind him.

"These few dinars," I went on, trying to be casual and funny, "mean nothing to me. As I have told you, I am from America and I am rich. I could give you a hundred dinars and never miss them. Here, now, take this and go buy yourself some bread."

"No, no," Yovan Vukomanovitch cried again. "No charity. I cannot—I cannot take it—unless you let me do something for you—some honorable work ——"

I said there was nothing he could do for me.

"Then I cannot take it." He looked miserable, humiliated, but spoke in a well-controlled voice, which now sounded even more beautiful and dramatic than at first. "No charity," he repeated.

"But listen," I said to the Herzegovinian, "this is not charity."

He seemed on the verge of walking away from me.

The situation was a mutually painful one.

I said, "Very well, then, I'll let you do something for me," though at the moment I didn't know just what I could find for him to do.

Then I asked him to come with me to the market-place near by, where I bought a fifty-kilo sack of firewood and kindling, in order that I could have him carry it home for me so that he would finally accept the eight dinars.

Despite the long fast, he carried the heavy bag on his back and shoulders up a considerable incline for nearly a mile without resting. In his step and movements were a dynamic grace and litheness found only in Balkan mountaineers. Where the road turned downward for a few hundred yards, he started to run in a free, easy, bounding lope; and when he finally deposited the load in the courtyard of the house where I lived, only a few drops of perspiration were sliding down his face.

When I placed the eight dinars in his hand, he protested that it was too much for so trifling a job. He was still afraid I was giving him charity. I believe it never occurred to him that I did not need the kindling and firewood; such a thought was too fantastic for his mind. Before he finally accepted the payment I had to argue that for a similar service in America I would have to pay twice or three times the sum.

During the next two months I saw Yovan Vukomanovitch every few days; some weeks almost daily. I came upon him on the main street or the quay, in front of the post-office, at the bus depot, or near one of the tourist hotels, where he was ceaselessly vigilant for a chance to earn a dinar or two. My respect for him deepened. I liked to see him, talk with him. Knowing that he spent as little money as possible for food, I frequently drew him into some eating-place, or Stella, who had met him soon after my first encounter with him and grew to respect and like him, offered him food when he came to our lodging.

"Well," I would ask him, "how are you making out?"

Then he would tell me that yesterday he had had poor luck; the day before yesterday, however, when a ship came in, he had made six dinars by carrying a lot of baggage from the quay to a hotel; while today, so far, he had helped to unload a wagon of grapes and figs, for which he had received two dinars, a big cluster of grapes and a capful of figs. Wouldn't I have some figs? They were very good; he had saved some for me. "You must take some home," he said, "to your American wife—may God bless her!"

Sitting in the eating-house or standing outside, where he could watch for opportunities to get work, he and I had long conversations about the United States and Herzegovina.

I was interested in Yovan Vukomanovitch and his mountain country, and prompted him to tell me about his and other peasants' circumstances in the village of Sirilovitch. He described his house in Sirilovitch: a primitive one-room stone affair, chimneyless and without windows. The food (mostly corn meal) was cooked in the center of the room and the smoke found its way out through the cracks. In the winter time he herded in his ten or fifteen sheep, and their body heat helped to keep his family warm.

Life in Herzegovina, he admitted, was a rigorous proposition. In winter the *bora* sometimes blew for days at a spell and stabbed one's lungs till they bled. Food was scarce. Corn and tobacco grew best, but tobacco was a state monopoly and the government agents paid little for the crops. Last year, for instance, he had received only ninety dinars—a little over one dollar and a half—for his whole crop.

Many children, he said, died in infancy; only the strong, the tough-fibered, survived, and those were apt to attain to a ripe old age. And for women also, life in Herzegovina was anything but easy. He told me about his wife, Dushana. So far she had borne him five children, but two had died. He palpably had a high regard for his wife; she was a good woman who did her best; but he seemed to think she might not live long. Since the birth of her last child she was not the same Dushana. All this he told me calmly, with a profound fatalism.

One day I said to him, "But, Yovan Vukomanovitch, why don't you—why don't most of you people in Herzegovina move elsewhere? There are regions in Yugoslavia where you probably could do much better."

He looked at me a long time before answering; then he smiled and said: "Maybe we could move, at least some of us, but we don't; most of us stay in Herzegovina, in our gray barren mountains—because . . . well, because we are Herzegovinians. We were born in Herzegovina and our race has lived and suffered there for centuries and fought for liberty against the Turks. It is our country."

I tried to make him elaborate on this, but did not succeed. There was nothing more to say. Herzegovinians were rooted in Herzegovina. They loved their country in a way that for a non-Yugoslav it is hard to understand. Herzegovinians who leave their homeland eventually return even from America, if only just in time to die there.

Not long after my first meeting with Yovan Vukomanovitch I became acquainted with a number of well-to-do people in Dubrovnik whom I asked to find some work for him, and they did, with the result that in two weeks he accumulated about eighty or a hundred dinars—enough to buy a fifty-kilo sack of corn meal and a few other urgent necessities, including a new pair of *opanké* for himself. Then he burdened himself with these purchases and *carried* them seventy kilometers up the steep rocky mountain roads and trails to his wife and children in the village of Sirilovitch.

In less than a week he was back in Dubrovnik again. He told me it had taken him three days to get up there with the load; that his wife had been glad to see him, but that she was not well. He said, "I told her about you, that you came from America, and she sends you greetings, and my children send you greetings, and to your American wife, of whom I have also told them."

In another two weeks he got together another hundred dinars, purchased another sack of corn and a few other things, and, strapping everything on his great back, made his second hike to his mountain village. It took him three days again. He stayed home a day, then made the trip back in two days, bringing Stella and me once more the greetings of his wife and children. When I asked him how his wife's health was, he said, "No better."

Soon after his second return to Dubrovnik, Yovan Vukomanovitch found out that some of the people who were giving him work were doing so on my suggestion or urging; whereupon he became devoted to me in a way that only a man from that part of the Balkans can become devoted to another man. It was not merely gratitude; in fact it was not gratitude at all. It was a passionate appreciation of, a powerful respect for, the impulse which had prompted me to speak to my well-off acquaintances in his behalf.

When we met for the first time after he had made this discovery, he was full of a strong emotion. He took my hand and said, "You are my friend and I am your friend—*za uviek* (forever)," he added, simply.

The word "friend," as I vaguely knew then and more fully realized later, is no light casual word in Herzegovina. It is in fact one of the most serious and precise, one of the strongest, words in the vocabulary. It has a deep, powerful meaning intimately connected with the Herzegovinians' long racial background, full of hardships, danger, and suffering, in which unswerving personal loyalty and readiness to sacrifice for another were of the highest and constant importance.

"I hope," said Yovan Vukomanovitch, "that some day I shall be able to do something for you. If you ever need me, you must call on me, any time, from anywhere, and if at all possible, I shall come." These were no mere words. I felt he was ready to die for me.

"*Dobro* (very good)," I said; "and should I ever need you, I shall let you know; and should you ever need me and think I can help you, you must call on me—any time, from anywhere."

But my words, although I meant what I was saying, did not have quite the same significance, sincerity, and naturalness and strength as his. He had impressed me so, he seemed so dramatic to me, that by now, being a writer, I had already begun to think of him as possible "material" for a story; and as I spoke the above words I was uneasily conscious that I was saying something which I perhaps later would quote.

Yovan Vukomanovitch and I shook hands, then I took his post-office address, which was in a town some distance from his village, and gave him my mail address in Dubrovnik, in Slovenia, and in several other places in Yugoslavia where I was planning to stop, and in New York. He said he knew how to write, though not very well.

Then he began to worry that our friendship would be too one-sided; that in all likelihood he never would be able to do anything big for me. "You are rich and do not need anything that I can give you or do for you, and you are going back to America. That is far away, but"—he smiled—"should I hear that you are in trouble and you want me to come, I shall swim the great ocean to America."

"*Dobro*," said I and laughed.

He laughed, too.

Some time before I had mentioned to him that I was a writer, which seemed to impress him only mildly. Now I told him that I was thinking of putting him into a story which might appear in some American publication and be read by many people.

He was surprised, puzzled, interested. "I am a poor man. What can you write about me?" he asked.

I said that was my business, and added that if my story was published I would send him a sum of money which he might consider big but which really would be only a small part of the amount I should receive for it.

"No, no," he began again. "Why should you send me money from America? You are trying to give me money again—charity—and we have just become friends!" He was offended.

It took me days to convince him that, in case I wrote the tale, he would have a definite and important hand in it, and would therefore be entitled to some payment. "I could not possibly write about you," I said, "if I had not met you, if you had not told me about yourself and Herzegovina."

All this was very strange to him and my idea of putting him into a story in America baffled him so that for a few days he seemed to avoid me. I believe he wanted to have time to think the matter over. Finally we got together again and he said that he was beginning to see my point, and he would take what I would send him; only I must swear by our friendship that I would not fool him and send him money without first selling the story.

I laughed and swore.

Meantime, working at odd jobs here and there, he earned another hundred dinars or so, and before starting off with the usual load of corn meal and other purchases on his second trip to Herzegovina, bade me, as was his wont, *"Do vidjenya!* (So long!)"—and said he would return again in six days or a week.

But I did not see him again in Dubrovnik.

On the fifth day after his departure I received a telegram signed by the public magistrate in the town of Riksitch, a county seat in Herzegovina:

"Peasant Yovan Vukomanovitch, arrested yesterday on serious charges, is in prison here. Claims you are his friend and implores me to inform you of his predicament. Am compelled to send this telegram collect, as Vukomanovitch is without means."

I could not imagine what the man had done. I thought it probably was a mistake or the result of some unusual combination of circumstances over which he had had no control. But whatever it was, the wire was a test of our friendship, which I knew Yovan Vukomanovitch, with his background, took very seriously. I had to go to Riksitch to see what I could do for him. Besides, everything in me impelled me to go. He *was* my friend, and I his. This suddenly became a vital urgent fact in my mind.

I immediately hired an automobile with a chauffeur who knew Herzegovina and in about five hours of rather perilous motoring over narrow, rocky, winding roads amid gray, barren mountains we covered the eighty-odd kilometers to Riksitch. Such desolation I had never seen before, yet every few kilometers there was a village or hamlet. On the road here and there we came upon men and women, men like Yovan Vukomanovitch, tall, thin, and poor, some of them carrying great burdens, most of them too startled by the sudden appearance of an automobile in their country to raise their hands in greeting. It was mid-autumn and the cold north wind already was stirring over the mountains, swooping down into the ravines, whistling through the gorges. For long distances there was almost no vegetation of any sort. Upon a ridge, below which we slowly rounded a dangerous curve, I saw several scrawny, small sheep standing still a few feet apart, their heads down—a melancholy sight. With peculiar Slavic humor, the chauffeur remarked, "Those sheep probably stand there waiting for a few blades of grass to grow so that they may snatch them up as soon as they appear. But they are too optimistic; there will be no more grass this year."

Both the chauffeur and I laughed at this. Slavs often laugh at sad things.

Riksitch I found, by contrast with the rest of Herzegovina I had seen, a surprisingly prosperous town, situated in a long and narrow fertile valley enlivened by a curious little river, a subterranean stream, which tumbles out of a hole in another mountain: for, as I have said, most of Herzegovina is limestone country, and has many such fantastic natural phenomena.

I hastened to the public magistrate's office and inquired what were the charges against Yovan Vukomanovitch.

"He was caught digging up a grave," answered the official.

"Digging up whose grave?"

"It seems his wife's," said the magistrate. "The man was arrested night before last, but we have not had time yet to investigate the case fully, and I can't tell you much about it."

"May I see him?" I asked.

"Yes,"—and the magistrate ordered a gendarme to take me to the prison, next to the magistracy.

I found Yovan Vukomanovitch in a tiny low-ceilinged cell with a barred window less than a foot square. It was late afternoon and a few pale sun rays formed a narrow rungless ladder of light between the rusty iron bars and the dirty brick floor.

Folded up like an immense jackknife, his sharp knees under his chin, his thin long arms around his thin long legs, my peasant friend sat upon a wide straw-strewn wooden bench, which was also his bed. At the sight of me he leaped up, bumping his head against the ceiling, emitted a cry in which pain and joy were about equally mingled, and seized both my hands.

"My good friend!" he cried. "I am sorry—sorry—" He looked older, tired. The lines on his face were deeper. His eyes had receded still farther into their sockets.

I thought it would be best to appear casual; so, extricating my hands from his, I forced a laugh and said, "What are you sorry about, Yovan?"

"I am sorry," he said, "that I had to call you to come here. I had no one else who I thought could help me."

I laughed. "But that was our agreement, wasn't it? Didn't we say 'any time, anywhere'? Didn't you say that if I needed you in America and called you, you would swim the great ocean to come to help me?"

"I would, I swear I would!" he said, fervently, and a couple of tears suddenly welled out of his eyes and began to slide down his face. "Only—only you never will call me, from America or anywhere else. You are rich and no doubt have many friends in America, as you have them here; you never will need any help from a poor man like me, here in Herzegovina."

His face was a picture of misery.

"Oh, never mind, Yovan Vukomanovitch," I said, laughing. "Stop that nonsense and sit down, will you, or you'll bump your head again and bring the ceiling down."

I sat on the bench and pulled him down beside me. "Now tell me all about it," I said.

But it was several minutes before he could talk. Then, fully regaining the dynamic composure which was so characteristic of him, he began to tell me—slowly, simply, straightforwardly—what had happened.

"Walking home from Dubrovnik," he said, "I had a heavy feeling, a premonition or whatever you would call it, that everything was not well in my house in Sirilovitch. I walked as fast as I could with my load of corn meal and other things I had bought. Where the road turned downward, I ran. I walked and ran almost night and day, stopping here and there for a little rest, and arrived home quicker than on the two previous trips—in less than three days.

"And when I came home I learned that my wife, my good Dushana, was dead. I found my children without their mother. One of the neighbor women had taken the youngest one to herself; the other two were managing by themselves. They had been alone for several days.

"Well, it seems that a week before I returned, a sudden sharp blow of *bora* sprang up in our mountain while Dushana was on the ridges looking for a stray sheep, and the wind inflamed her lungs. Pneumonia, they call it. Our neighbors put her into a basket between two donkeys and brought her to the government health station here in Riksitch. But it was too late. As I have told you, she had not been well for some time. . . . Anyhow, two days after they brought her to Riksitch my poor Dushana died.

"The doctor at the health station sent word to my house that she was dead and asked for instructions as to what to do with the body, but I was still in Dubrovnik, readying myself, as you know, for my trip home.

"When I reached home four days after Dushana's death and was told the news, I was weary from nearly three days' steady trudging, but I had to find out what they had done with her body; so I told the neighbors to watch my children and walked here to Riksitch—twelve kilometers, if one knows the short cuts.

"I came in the middle of the afternoon and found that Dushana had been buried that morning in the local churchyard. The doctor at the health station and the authorities had waited to hear from me, and when they got no word, they buried her.

"'But how did you bury her?' I asked them. 'How was my Dushana dressed when you put her into the earth?' And they said, 'She was not dressed at all, your Dushana. We had nothing to dress her in. We just wrapped her dead body in a big clean linen sheet, placed her in a coffin (for which, by the way, you owe us two hundred and twenty dinars), then took the coffin to the churchyard, and the priest prayed over it and we lowered it into the grave and shoveled dirt on it.'

"Now the doctor and most of the other people who are in authority here in Riksitch are fine people, but, without meaning to say anything bad about them, many of them are not natives of Herzegovina. They come from Serbia and Slovenia and Croatia . . . good people in their own different ways, educated in schools, readers of books and newspapers who know many things that are right and true, but some of them do not understand our ways and customs here in Herzegovina. Just think! they buried my Dushana, who was a good woman, a good wife to me, a good mother to my children—they buried her wrapped in a sheet!

"Only bad women, those who never marry or are faithless to their husbands, are buried any old way, like wrapped in a sheet. A good woman like Dushana must be buried in her wedding dress, if she had one, and my wife did have one. When we were married, seventeen years ago, her father, who once upon a time had worked as a sawyer and ax-man in the Bosnian forests, provided her with a beautiful costume and she had saved it.

"And they buried her in a sheet!

"I talked with the young doctor at the health station and he is a nice young man, clever about many things, but a Croatian; and he smiled at me and said, 'But, my dear man, what difference does it make whether your wife is buried in a plain sheet or a beautiful costume? She is dead, isn't she?' 'Yes, Doctor,' I said, 'she is dead, my Dushana, but she was a good woman and she should have been dressed in the clothes she wore at her marriage. That is the custom here among us common peasant people. What will my neighbors say when they find out that Dushana, whom they all knew as a good woman, was buried in a plain sheet?' And the doctor said, 'Well, I am sorry, but it is too late now. Too bad you did not come this morning before we buried her. And now I am very busy. Please go.'

"Since the doctor was busy with people who needed his attention, what could I do but go? I thought of going to some one else in authority in Riksitch, but was afraid they were all alike—fine people, you understand, in their own way, educated, kind, and helpful (at least some of them), but not acquainted with our customs.

"So from the doctor's office I went to Dushana's grave, which was marked by a pile of brown dirt mixed with gray gravel, and I was very sad. I wept, for a better woman than Dushana never lived—and here she was under this mound of earth and rock, wrapped in a sheet!

"What could I do? I walked home to my village, and on the way I thought and thought, and was much upset in my soul. My good Dushana buried as if she had been a bad woman! I worried, 'What will the neighbors say? What will my children say to me when they grow up?'

"I was very tired; so when I got home well after nightfall and found my poor children sleeping, I lay down too and fell asleep.

"But in the middle of the night I suddenly woke up. I looked in the darkness and heard my two children breathing—the baby was at the neighbors'—and thought to myself, 'Poor things!' Then I realized that I had been dreaming of Dushana, and that in the dream she had said to me, 'I was a good woman, Yovan, my husband, and you must dress me up in my wedding garb.'

"I rose right away, raised the lid of the old chest where she had kept her wedding dress, and groped for it with my hands in the darkness till I found it; then took my shovel and walked back to Riksitch.

"The moon was up, and I was no longer tired. I felt good, thinking, 'I shall do what is right by Dushana.'

"Here in Riksitch, when I came, everything was dark and still. I guess it was around four o'clock, a good two hours before dawn. Everybody was asleep, or so I thought; only a dog barked at the moon. I went straight to the churchyard, to Dushana's grave, and began to shovel the dirt heaped on her coffin.

"I shoveled and talked gentle words to my dead Dushana, for she had been a good wife to me, a good mother to my children and in my own way I had loved her. I told her that I still loved her, and wept while I shoveled, and scolded her, 'Oh, Dushana, why, oh, why, did you go looking for that poor lost sheep on the ridges? Didn't you know *bora* was going to blow? And did I not tell you, Dushana, not once, but ten times, that, since your last child has weakened you so, you must mind your health?'

"I shoveled and talked with Dushana, and was halfway down to the coffin when a gendarme suddenly stepped before me. He was the night patrol, and had heard my shovel striking gravel and had come to see what was going on.

"'In the name of the law,' he yelled, and stuck the bayonet on his gun against my breast, 'you are under arrest!'

"I dropped the shovel and told him I was peasant Yovan Vukomanovitch, husband of Dushana who was buried there, and all I wanted was to dig her up and dress her in her wedding clothes, for now she was wrapped in only a sheet. I said that after dressing her I would bury her again, and everything would be right once more.

"But the gendarme would not listen to me. He picked up my shovel and Dushana's dress, and marched me to this prison.

"Morning came and I was in this cell and didn't know what to do. Then I thought of you, my friend from Slovenia and America, and pondered a long time, and hesitated. I felt bad about it all, but at the end, worrying about my children in Sirilovitch who didn't know where I was, I begged the prison guard to take me to some big official in authority.

"That was yesterday and I had to wait long before they took me to the building across the courtyard, where they led me before a gentleman"—the public magistrate—"whom I asked to please send word to you in Dubrovnik that I was in trouble, for you were my friend, the only one who could help me. I had spent every dinar I had earned in Dubrovnik, as I intended to go back and earn more, and so I had no money to telegraph; and the gentleman said that if you were my friend you would pay for the message ——"

Tears welled from his eyes and he clutched his big hands and banged them on his hard knees.

Knowing nothing about law and legal procedure in Yugoslavia, I was not sure how much I should be able to do for Yovan Vukomanovitch, but he was—in my eyes—so obviously innocent of any crime or criminal intent that I told him not to worry, I would fix up his trouble and everything would be right, and left the cell.

The public magistrate, with whom I had a long talk, was mildly amused by my presentation of the whole affair, and said that the peasant, to all seeming, was innocent before the spirit of the law. "But technically," he added, "he is guilty of digging up a grave, and I cannot free him without trial. However, if you desire, we shall try the case tomorrow; meantime, if you wish to see him released so that he can go home overnight to see his children, I shall allow you to put up bail for him—three thousand dinars."

Luckily I had brought several thousand dinars with me.

Out of jail, Yovan Vukomanovitch was so full of gratitude—not mere gratitude, but friendship and misery; misery because there was nothing that he, who would not hesitate to die for me if necessary, could do for me in return—that he embarrassed me and I did not enjoy being with him. I suggested to him that he hurry home and return to Riksitch in the morning for trial.

I stayed in Herzegovina overnight. The young doctor, with whom I became acquainted, put me up at the health station.

In the morning Yovan Vukomanovitch was given a nominal sentence, which was suspended, and I got back the bail money.

All this was very easy to arrange; and for all I know, the man would have been cleared eventually without my aid.

I had some difficulty, however, in inducing the magistrate to give my friend permission to dig up his dead wife and dress her in the wedding costume.

"That would be much too irregular," said the official.

Then I placed before him a thousand-dinar note and suggested that he use it for some good cause, and after a time he said that, if the priest in the church had no objection, the peasant could go ahead and dig up the grave. He detailed a gendarme to go with Vukomanovitch to supervise the digging, the dressing of the corpse, and finally the reburial.

The priest had no objection, and by noontime everything was straightened out.

I thought of going with Yovan Vukomanovitch to his village to see his and his neighbors' circumstances at first hand, but then decided against the idea. It was impossible to go by automobile, while there and back on foot would have taken too long. I was supposed to be in Dubrovnik the next morning on a personal matter.

Besides, as I have said, the man's gratitude and friendship were deeply embarrassing to me. Also, I felt rather guilty about my relationship with him, for two reasons. One was that he was story material to me, and the other was that all I had done (and, for that matter, ever would do) for him was nothing alongside what he was ready to do for me, should he get a chance.

All this made me feel so low that I did not want him to return to Dubrovnik while I was there; and so, after he had finished his task in the graveyard, I handed him an envelope which contained money but which he accepted before he realized what it was.

When he did realize, he started to cry, "No, no!" again and tried to stick the envelope into my coat pocket, but I evaded him.

I mimicked him, laughing: "No, no! No, no!"—then seized his arms and held him fast and said, seriously: "Now, you listen here, Yovan Vukomano-vitch, and don't be a fool! Don't say again that I am trying to give you charity. I am not! This envelope contains what is yours. I shall be paid for the story I am going to write about you and this is your share. Remember, you agreed to accept it. I am giving you this money now because you need it now and I don't. Another thing: don't go back to Dubrovnik any more this year. The tourist season is over and you will find very little to do. Stay home and watch your children so they will not catch pneumonia when *bora* blows, and feed them—and pay for the coffin."

I released him.

Clutching the envelope in both hands, he made a helpless gesture full of agony, then looked past me at the gray mountains above the town, pondering. Finally he turned to me again and said, "You are certain you will sell the story?"

I wasn't, but I said I was.

"Very well, then," he said, "and do not forget to let me know if you ever need me—anytime, anywhere."

I said: "That is our agreement. Now good-by, Yovan Vukomanovitch, and good luck always!"

"Good-by, my friend!" Then his voice choked.

We shook hands. I quickly parted from him and he turned toward his village.

A half-hour later, driving back to Dubrovnik with the top of the car down, I suddenly caught sight of him, tall and lank, upon a great cliff by the road-side, his figure silhouetted against the gray mountain behind him.

He waved to me. I waved back and tears came to my eyes. He seemed to me at once infinitely tragic and infinitely heroic—a big human being—one of the finest I had ever experienced.

For a minute something—perhaps a condition in the atmosphere, perhaps the tears in my eyes—made him appear at least twenty feet tall, a colossal gallant figure, still, calm and firm, with a tremendous dynamic power, like a statue done by a great sculptor.

The car turned sharply on a curve and that was the last I saw of my Herzegovinian friend.

My Friend Maxo Vanka

IN YUGOSLAVIA I MET A NUMBER OF INTERESTING OR IMPORTANT PEOPLE, WHOM I then put into *The Native's Return*. To the subsequently assassinated King Alexander I gave a chapter, the same to the sculptor Ivan Mestrovich . . . and to Maxo Vanka, the painter, two or three paragraphs, telling a few simple surface facts: how we—Stella and I—met him and his American wife, Margaret, and spent part of the summer with them at their seaside villa on the island of Korchula, in Dalmatia; and how the four of us, without knowing very much about one another, quickly became good friends, and in the winter met again many times at their apartment in Zagreb, Croatia. Which was about all I knew and understood about him that lent itself to brief telling. I did not mention the curious feeling I had about him from our initial meeting. He was a most extraordinary person—one of the strangest I have ever come upon anywhere.

Maxo was then—in 1932-33—in his early forties, a small, slim man with a soft golden-brown Vandyke beard, thinning brown hair, and mild gray-blue eyes, which illumined and enlivened a thin, smooth face, faintly Semitic-seeming and strangely handsome, suggesting that this was approximately how Jesus might have looked at forty-two. Twenty years earlier, in Brussels, Maxo's fellow art students had nicknamed him Inri, after "INRI," the inscription on the Cross. He was not Jewish; had been baptized and raised a Catholic, but was now a species of mystic who swung gracefully between intellectual agnosticism and a profound peasant-like faith in God, the Virgin, and all the saints and angels in Heaven. He was born in Zagreb, but, I gathered, was not a Croat. He spoke excellent German, French, and Croatian, some English, Hungarian, Italian, and Slovenian, and evidently had wandered more than casually in several fields of knowledge and speculation: philosophy, psychology, ethics, history (especially the history of art), sociology, botany, birdlore, metaphysics, comparative religion.

What first impressed me about him was his physical strength and stamina. He was slightly over five feet, frail-, delicate-appearing, but able to walk all day, as he and I did, over the hot stony roads on the island of Korchula and, unlike myself, not be tired in the evening. He swam for hours in the Adriatic, and I marveled how that bony, almost emaciated-looking body could contain so much energy and power of endurance, and be so agile, vivid, precise, and graceful in its movements. He was a superb cook, concocting all manner of delicacies out of the simplest materials, but he himself ate little more than a sparrow.

He had been for years professor of painting at the Zagreb Academy of Art, one of the best institutions of its kind in Europe, then under the directorship of Ivan Mestrovich, who had high regard for him as a stimulating, sophisticated teacher; and was also a recognized painter of oils and watercolors in the styles of numerous schools: a veritable virtuoso. He had annual shows at the Art Pavilion in Zagreb, and had exhibited also in Belgrade, Prague, Vienna, Munich, Brussels, and Amsterdam. His pictures were in museums and galleries all over the Continent, and in numerous private homes. In Zagreb, I saw scores of them and I liked several, including the humorous, unpretentious murals in Gradski Podrum, a popular café; but he interested me less as an artist than as a person. However, while in Yugoslavia, though I wondered much about him, I made no serious effort to delve into his makeup or learn his story. I was too busy watching and investigating other things, personalities, and conditions which momentarily seemed more important than Maxo. Then, too, I felt he was an extremely subtle, indirect fellow, whom it would take time to know. Perhaps Margaret would succeed in getting him to America eventually, where I might see him and he might more or less reveal himself to me.

Meantime, in Yugoslavia, I was not greatly startled when, as we talked, he repeatedly guessed or anticipated my thoughts or words, and began to respond to my remarks or questions before I completely uttered them. Nor when I saw his little canary Muri fly to him from the open cage and alight on his head, hand, or shoulders, or "play dead" at his command in his palm, or be perfectly content to squat on the bottom of his coat pocket. This sort of thing, somehow, appeared normal for Maxo. When he played with the tiny green-yellow bird, the two were sheer delight to watch. Both comedians, Maxo called Muri bad names in several languages, and Muri responded mock-angrily in his canary language, flying off, teasing his master, hiding, eluding him, jabbering away, then abruptly sailing back to him again, and song rolling out of his tiny throat the moment he landed on his head, hand, or shoulder.

Nor was I greatly surprised when I came upon Maxo in an olive grove near his house on Korchula and saw perhaps ten or a dozen sparrows, siskins, and wild canaries circling about him, cheeping and crying, swooping down between his legs, the while he laughed at them, scattering bread crumbs, some of which they caught in the air; calling them scoundrels, blackguards, unquotable names, and reaching out at them as if trying to catch them. He explained he had a "touch" of what was known as "the gift of sympathy," which he himself could not define. Very few people had it. He attracted wild birds and other wild creatures, and said that if he came to this grove regularly every day for a couple of weeks, and brought them food, the sparrows, siskins, and wild canaries would get used to him and land on his head and shoulders à la Muri, and let him touch and hold them in his hands. I had no difficulty in believing this.

Nor did it seem unnatural when, one day, as we passed a stone fence near his villa, a tiny gray lizard suddenly scurried up Maxo's trousers leg and dived into his pocket in search of crumbs, and in a few moments emerged again and, while Maxo called him a thief and scavenger, sped around the small of his back, dived into the other pocket, came out once more, then sped down the other trousers leg and vanished in the roadside rubble. Maxo said he had "made friends" with the creature a few days before; now it seemed to be waiting for him every time he came by this spot.

Nor did Stella and I doubt him when he told us that, off and on, especially after he had not used soap for a while, butterflies were attracted to his beard. He did not know how to explain this, either, but thought there probably was something in the odor of his body that drew them to him. "Sometimes," he said, "they're really a nuisance. They get me into trouble. Once an old peasant woman in Turopolyé, where I was spending a holiday, saw me with several butterflies on my beard, and she concluded I was a saint or miracle-worker; and I had to leave there, lest I became an object of pilgrimages and a subject of superstition and endless controversy among the peasants. . . ."

He possessed a unique, delightful sense of humor, to which he gave free exercise in connection with his "gift of sympathy." One day he observed a black-and-blue butterfly flying awkwardly from stem to stem, a few feet from where we sat. One of its wings was broken. So Maxo picked up the poor, delicate little thing, which then rested on his palm; and he went in back of the house, where a few minutes before he had seen lying amid grape leaves a lately deceased yellow butterfly, whose wings—one undamaged—were about the same size as the black-and-blue one's. Then he got scissors and mucilage, neatly clipped off most of the injured wing of the live butterfly, and pasted in its place the yellow wing of the dead butterfly; and, thus mended, the live one flew off, half black-and-blue and half yellow—one of the funniest, weirdest sights imaginable. Perfectly still while Maxo was working on it with his deft, light fingers, the butterfly had seemed to know he was trying to help it. Then it flew around the house for a few hours, amusing us all, and finally disappeared.

Margaret entertained Stella and me with the story of their marriage. She was the former Margaret Stetten, daughter of the well-known Park Avenue physician and surgeon, Dr. DeWitt Stetten. In several respects the exact opposite of her husband, she was a buxom young woman in her late twenties: frank, simple, direct. A former art student, she had touches of culture in other fields, speaking French and German besides English, and some Croatian. Her face, with its clear big eyes, was lovely, and she impressed me as "just woman," patient, generous, without ambition for herself; immensely healthy and natural, deeply and quietly purposeful.

In the summer, 1931, Margaret was motoring with her father and his wife Alice through Central Europe and the Balkans, and one day, nearing Zagreb and seeking water for their car, they halted at a small château off the highway. The people of the little castle, who were somewhat run-down but proud Croatian nobility, asked them in and, proceeding further along the lines of their traditional hospitality, served them refreshments.

A week-end guest at the place, Maxo Vanka was introduced to the Americans; then, following his wont, he made sketches of all of them, presented the drawings to them, and was generally very charming—one of the easiest things he can do. His hosts owned a few of his paintings, which they showed to the Americans, who liked them. And to keep a short story short, Margaret fell in love with him, but managed not to tell him so then and there.

Basically a highly sensible person, she had lately realized she possessed no artistic talent herself and, attached to art, determined to marry an artist, preferably a poor, unrecognized one, and help him. She had a monthly income, which she wanted to put to some use. She had been looking around for some time. Now, suddenly, here in this strange country of Croatia, was this wisp of a Jesus-like man who looked every inch an artist, was evidently not rich and but faintly famous in Yugoslavia, Belgium, France, and Central Europe; and whose career, her instinct told her, had scarcely begun. She asked for his Zagreb address and said he would hear from her.

Maxo's ability to guess people's thoughts did not work in this instance. He imagined the young lady would send him a card from somewhere, or perhaps some art books he had discussed with her, for Americans were reputedly generous. In the next few weeks, when no card nor anything else came, he all but forgot her.

Then, of a sudden, a telegram from Athens: she was Zagreb-bound, and would he please promptly resign his professorship at the Academy; she wanted to marry him and they would go to live in Paris or New York, where he would really realize himself as the fine artist he was. Since their first meeting she had looked up his work scattered through the Balkans and Central Europe, and shed all doubt as to the extent of his talent.

Maxo laughed, for of course it was all a joke. These American women!— An ascetic, an æsthete, a celibate, happy with his art, living in a tiny studio, he had never given marriage a thought. His professor's salary was meager, but adequate for his modest requirements. He owned the little house on Korchula, where he spent the summers. His fame, true, was nothing like Mestrovich's, but not a few people here and there appreciated him as an artist. His students responded to his teaching. His colleagues at the Academy respected him. He had valued friends and was invited to their houses. Besides, he had his little Muri; and when weary of Zagreb and human contacts, he could always go into the country week-ends and have a gay time in the woods and fields, all by himself, with the birds, butterflies, squirrels, and lizards.

But the next thought turned Maxo's mirth into panic. The young American person might be crazy and really come and want to marry him! He decided to hide. Not finding him, if she came, she would soon depart. And, acquainting one of his Academy colleagues with the ludicrous situation, and instructing him to tell her he had unexpectedly journeyed to Siam and Java, Maxo shuttered his studio-dwelling and disappeared.

This would have been all very well but for the fact that Margaret Stetten, a most untrifling person, had never been more serious about anything in her life than she was now in her idea to make Maxo her husband. She came and upset the Academy, demanding they produce Professor Vanka, then turned over half of the capital of Croatia, frankly stating her purpose; and, hearing of this in his near-by hiding place, poor, chagrined Maxo was obliged to emerge. He begged her, politely, to go away. He was an artist, a teacher of art, a confirmed bachelor, an eccentric, completely content to live alone, and, begging her to forgive his bluntness, he queried, "And, anyhow, Miss Stetten, who are you to invade my life in this manner?" She answered she loved him; in fact, if he would pardon her using American slang, she was "nuts about him," and declared her determination not to depart from Zagreb till he came with her— now what did he think of *that*?

Trying another tack, and being genuinely humble, Maxo asked, "But who am I that you should honor me with your love?"—"Never mind about that," returned Margaret. "I know what I'm doing." He pointed out he was fifteen years older than she, funny-looking and skinny; all to no avail. She replied she had eyes to see and knew all about that.

Staying at the Hotel Esplanade, she insisted on seeing him daily. She argued: didn't he realize he was wasting himself in a provincial city like Zagreb, in a small country like Yugoslavia? Here were no opportunities for real work, unless one was a Mestrovich; and there was room for but one Mestrovich, and he had made his name not in his native land, but in Austria, Italy, France, England, and America. . . . "I want to help you," declared Margaret, simply. "In France, in America, especially in America, oh, in America, you will have opportunities galore to *really* show what you have in you."

Maxo saw her daily, for otherwise she would have resumed upsetting the city, and he hinted he was in truth a most difficult person, a woman-hater, and what not. Beneath his seeming mildness he was really cruel. Like all artists, he was temperamental. His Jesus-like aspect was but a disguise for the devil in him. As a Balkanite, if they married, he might beat her. Margaret laughed. He told her he was an illegitimate child, in fine, a bastard, and she averred, "What do I care!" She was utterly uninterested in his origin; it was all-sufficient to her that he lived and painted. He asked her to pardon his frankness and remarked that he thought she was crazy, and she laughed again, saying she did not care if she was. Too many sane people in the world, anyhow.

Maxo perceived "crazy" did not dispose of the young woman. She was something elemental, genuine. Although the exact opposite of her on this point, he began to respect her directness and frankness. Then, with no slight inner perturbance, he realized he was growing generally fond of her as a person and a woman. Those tremendous, honest eyes of hers! Her whole generous personality. . . . By and by he began to look forward to their meetings, following his classes at the Academy. Somewhere deep inside him, he was flattered that this girl had picked him out of possibly dozens of men she knew in New York and elsewhere who probably wanted to marry her.

This went on for weeks; the affair was the talk of Zagreb. Finally, with the amused approval of all of Maxo's friends, he succumbed and they were married.

Margaret's victory, however, while great (everybody admitted that), was only partial. Consenting to the marriage, Maxo had stipulated they would not go to France or America, but stay in Zagreb, where he had his friends and his position, which gave him a standing and an income, which, however slight in her American eyes, was enough for his expenses. In New York or Paris he would have to live off her—something he was unwilling to do. Margaret said he was silly, for what money she had was not good for anything else than to support him; but she gave in to him temporarily, and they rented an apartment that was bigger than Maxo's old dwelling.

They had been married a little over a year when Stella and I met them. Talking with Margaret, I saw that, aside from the facts that he was an illegitimate son of high Austrian nobility, and a fantastically nice human being, she knew nothing—yet, in another sense, everything—about him. His illegitimacy did not interest her. She loved and accepted him.

Two months after we met the Vankas, Margaret gave birth to a girl— Peggy, from the start a remarkably vivid, enjoyable child, amazingly vital and and healthy, a blend or fusion of her parents. When Stella and I visited them during the winter, the four of us wontedly spent most of the time around the crib admiring the baby, then four or five months old.

Margaret was happy in Zagreb, but her mind remained set on getting Maxo to France or America, preferably America; and, quite frankly and directly, she enlisted me in her cause, which I served willingly, urging Maxo to quit his professorship, come to New York, and take a chance at making a place for himself in American art, the modern trends of which greatly interested him. I kept telling him that his scruples about living on Margaret's income were really silly. She, herself, was not earning what she had, but was receiving it from a trust fund; and he half admitted my reasoning was sound, then expressed his fear he might have difficulty in getting himself oriented in New York. He was no longer young, there was a depression in America, and —silly or not—he had been making his own living now for so many years that he would not be comfortable there if he failed to earn some money. We argued back and forth nearly every time we got together, and when Stella and I returned to New York in the spring, 1933, Maxo did not know if he would follow us or not; I had a feeling, however, that he would, and said so to Margaret.

But Maxo hesitated for another year and a half. Then—in the autumn, 1934— he, Margaret, and little Peggy, now two years old and palpably a prodigy, arrived in New York, and I got a mighty triumphal hug from Margaret, who believed I had helped her in getting him to decide to come to America. What had, I think, really decided him just then was his thought that he had no right to keep his wife and child in Europe, where the dangers of war seemed to be increasing by leaps and bounds.

I enjoyed showing Maxo New York. Every few minutes, as we walked in midtown, or in the financial district, or through the Rockefeller Center, he exclaimed, "*Ovo yé kolosalno!* (This is colossal!) *Kolosalno!*" Or, "There is something here! . . . power, energy, the future. . . . *Kolosalno!*" The city exhilarated him, and for two or three weeks after he came he scarcely slept. Worn out from eight or ten hours' tramping with him on hard pavement, I left him somewhere late in the evening, then he wandered alone for eight or ten hours more before he finally went home. And the next day Margaret told me he had been exclaiming "*Kolosalno!*" in his brief sleep, and he recounted to me what he had seen and experienced.

Because of his beard and Jesus-like appearance, or for some other reason that does not occur to me, experiences came to him thick and fast in New York, whether he was with me or alone. People gazed at him; many smiled to him; others paused to talk with him. Jews asked him was he a Jew; others, was he French or what was he. An actor? An artist? A Greek Orthodox priest? To Maxo's amusement, urchin's shouted "Whiskers!" and ran. Somewhere on the East Side I left him on the sidewalk as I entered a drug store to telephone, and on coming out found him surrounded by a mob of little boys, arguing whether he was Santa Claus; and Maxo had a great time, talking with them in his picturesquely broken English, blessing them and clowning before them. Negroes came up to him, smiled, and shook his hand. An obvious prostitute stopped him to inquire if he would let her touch him "for good luck."

Almost immediately on their arrival in New York, the over-eager Margaret arranged for an exhibition of her husband's pictures in a gallery on Fifty-seventh Street, but it was ill-managed; the paintings shown were not his best; much of his finest work remained in Europe, owned by private persons and public museums; and the New York art world did not get excited. Later the Yugoslav consul in Pittsburgh arranged an exhibition of his work there, which also set nothing on fire.

Margaret found an apartment near Peggy's kindergarten, while Maxo made his studio in an empty loft of a building owned by the Stettens in the warehouse section off the Bowery, and began to work. He drew and painted mostly bums, white and Negro workers, prostitutes who stopped him in the street or with whom he otherwise became acquainted. On warm days he went outdoors and sketched or painted warehouse-district and river-front scenes, which fascinated him. Or, clad in a pair of corduroy pants and a leather windbreaker, he just "bummed around" with his sketch-book; then came to me with vivid word-pictures, accompanied by pencil drawings, of the unemployed living in fantastic "Hoovervilles" on both ends of Williamsburg Bridge, of diverse Bowery degenerates and unfortunates, of prostitutes on the lowest rung of their profession, of drunkards imbibing shoe polish and "canned heat," and of other characters from the substrata of American society. I saw that, somehow, his sympathies and proclivities drew him in that direction more than to Park Avenue, although he was deeply fond of his in-laws and many of their friends.

He continued to be excited about New York; and, hypersensitive to line and form, he pointed out to me beauty or ugliness where I had not seen it before, so that by and by he was showing me the city as much as I was showing it to him. We visited the art museums and galleries, and he was impressed by the power and technical skills and innovations of the recent and current American artists. But, essentially a child of the Old World, he was often also deeply confused by the New World, and, brooding, came to me with tremendous questions. What was this civilization, with these sharp contrasts? What was its center, core, motivating force? Had it a "soul"? Was it all materialism? There were so many incongruities. The "lower depths" here were frightfully deep. . . . He witnessed a "Communist" demonstration on Union Square, and wondered if a Red revolution was not a part of America's immediate future. I assured him no. His impression was that deep in them, many Americans were unhappy people, hungry for something, with which I more or less agreed; and he wished, laughing, he really were Jesus and able to perform in America the miracle of loaves and fishes on the spiritual and cultural plane. . . . I hardly knew how to explain the country to him; I tried merely to assure him that New York was not America.

In autumn and early winter I had to give some lectures in New England, upstate New York, Philadelphia, and Washington, while magazine assignments took me as far as Pittsburgh; and, if I happened to drive, I took Maxo with me. We had a great time; his reactions to places were nearly always interesting, and I was afforded new glimpses of certain phases of his character and attractiveness which I had but dimly noticed before. For one thing, it became clear to me that he was perhaps the most intensely conscious and observant person I have ever known. Nothing escaped him.

He liked rural New England; it was "so chaste, so austere," a bit bleak and cold—and this not only physically that time of the year (late November), but spiritually. New England faces fascinated him; some, he said, were like "ghosts of Puritanism, but strong, strong; so competent, held-in, and reserved." Unlike the people of New York, where Jews, Irish, and other "foreigners" predominate, no Yankee smiled to him, or came up to speak to him, though many looked at him, curious. Those who did smile, or who paused to talk to him, in New England were invariably Irish, Jews, or Polish or Canadian immigrants or Negroes. . . . As we stopped in such towns as Concord, Salem, Lynn, and Lenox, Massachusetts, or Brattleboro, Vermont, he quickly sensed—somehow, in rough outline—these communities' past, though he had never read the history of New England. He was really uncanny.

Lecturing, I was usually obliged to put up at fairly good hotels; but Maxo always went to some fourth- or fifth-rate place, often no better than flop houses— this partly because he was naturally frugal, partly because he did not want to spend any more of the money he had not earned than he had to (he wouldn't hear of my paying his bill), but perhaps largely because, as I say, he seemed inevitably to gravitate toward the lowly, dirty, degenerate, and neglected.

In Washington, for instance, where I had to be for a week, he established himself in a "hotel" within a few blocks of the White House, where he paid a dollar a day, and the furniture, what there was of it, seemed on the verge of moving under the impulse of the vermin that must have inhabited it. . . . Busy, seeing people, I left Maxo to his own devices during the day. Evenings, he usually had many things to tell me. He had discovered that his "hotel" was really a brothel, but that did not disturb him. In the Negro district, an old black woman had invited him to her house and served him coffee with molasses, which she had stirred in his cup with her finger; and he had drawn a sketch of her. . . .

He made friends with a young policeman who in his spare time was trying to become a writer, and who had stopped him to talk with him. He did not know why he had stopped Maxo, unless it was that he looked like an artist who might sympathize with a would-be author, or because he had a mouthful of aching teeth he could not afford to have pulled or treated, for he had a family and other responsibilities and expenses. He had not yet succeeded in getting anything published, but had manuscripts constantly in the mails or in the editorial offices. Maxo duly sympathized with him, and the cop visited him in uniform at his "hotel," which threw its owner or manager into panic, thinking the place was being raided. Maxo showed the policeman the sketches he had done since leaving New York, and mentioned he was traveling with me, and that from Washington we were going to Pittsburgh, where a gallery was having a show of his pictures.

Pittsburgh—with its great, smoking, flaming steel mills and its ugliness which is so honest and intense it almost becomes beauty—excited Maxo even more than New York, where we returned a week or so later, and where Maxo received a long letter from the Washington policeman, written on the Pittsburgher Hotel stationery: which I want to quote, in part, because it is an amusing self-portrait, indicative of the sort of people Maxo attracts, and why:

DEAR MAXO:

I have a long story to tell, and much time in which to tell it. I am in Pittsburgh. Two things brought me here: my interest in you and your art, and my toothache.

The toothache, itself, is a long story. I was unable to do anything about it, as I have told you, because of "economic conditions over which I have no control." The other day, however, my sister came to Washington for post-graduate work in nurse-training; she met a dentist at a Government hospital and arranged for me to meet him. He offered to pull my teeth without charge. He pulled seven of 'em, oh boy! . . . and I sold a bit of gold bridgework for $2.90 and got a three-day sick leave; so, having now both time and money, I bought a bus ticket to Pittsburgh.

At twelve midnight, with a hundred aspirin tablets, which I was supposed to take one every hour, I boarded an old wreck of a bus. First stop Baltimore, with a half-hour lay-over, giving me a chance to get a cup of coffee. An aspirin. Then, for two hours, to a one-horse town called Emmitsburg. The restaurant there is usually closed at 3:30 a.m., but this time it was open, waiting for some runaway boys to be brought home by the east-bound bus. Another aspirin. When the four fifteen-year-old boys arrived, I could sympathize with them; I had done the same thing at that age. At five o'clock the west-bound bus picked us up, to take us over the mountains. It, too, was light and rickety, and the road humped in the middle, rolling like a ground-swell, as well as having many turnings, going up and around mountains. Fog reduced visibility to zero, but the driver was a good one; we got to Pittsburgh at eleven, as per schedule.

I walked to the gallery, hoping to surprise you, but learned you had left the day before. I looked at your pictures through pain- and sleep-weary eyes, and could not see them till I stood well back. . . . They are wonderful; that's all I can say. . . .

While I was there, two poorly-but-neatly clad men of swarthy complexion came in. I guess they were your countrymen from Yugoslavia, for they exclaimed delightedly to each other, pointing at pictures that seemed to represent scenes from near their home region in the Old Country.

Leaving the gallery, I wanted only to get into a horizontal position on an innerspring mattress, but I couldn't afford a hotel room; so I walked the streets. I wanted to talk to a policeman about his pay, working-hours, and equipment, but every cop I saw was busy as could be. I went into a dentist's office to ask a simple question— were my gums healing properly? He tried to high-pressure me into letting him make me a plate. I told him I was returning to Washington in a few hours; then he used high-pressure trying to sell me a thirty-five-cent bottle of mouth-wash.

I like a cup of coffee at such a time in a cheap restaurant, where I can sit at the counter and nudge the guy next to me, and ask him, "What do you think Roosevelt is trying to do?" and get some kind of answer. But here I, somehow, walked into a drug store with a fountain, all stainless steel and marble and mirrors, which chilled me, and I almost turned around, but went in, anyhow. I ordered coffee and, because of the atmosphere in the place, I spoke to the clerk instead of my neighbor on the next stool. "Well, what do you know?" said I. "Not much," said he. "How's your razor blades?" I thought this was some kind of Pittsburgh gag, and made a gesture which might mean anything. And, presto! he dropped a milkshake on the stainless steel and brought forth from each vest pocket a package of Gillette razor blades. "We're having a 'special' on these: two packs for forty-three cents." I said I was a stranger in a strange city and had only enough money to get home. He whisked the blades out of sight and left me to my coffee. Conversation comes high in Pittsburgh.

I thought to myself: "I'll write to my friend Vanka and I'll feel as though I talked to him." So here I'm writing to you in the lobby of the Pittsburgher, hoping a bell-hop will not stop me as I go out, and charge me for the stationery. . . .

Driving about the country, Maxo and I talked, and he gradually told me his story.

His illegitimate parents were a son and a daughter of two of the foremost families in the Hapsburg Empire. His mother's home was in Moravia; and when her condition became apparent her conventional, scandalized mother and elder sisters sent her to distant Zagreb, in Croatia, where no one knew her; and she lived there incognito, in charge of a midwife who specialized in such cases, till the child was born and baptized. Supplied with a sum of money for the purpose, the midwife then turned the infant over to a poverty-ridden peasant woman named Dora Yug from the near-by village of Pustcha Kuplenovo; and Dora, receiving periodically a small sum of money from the midwife for his keep, fell deeply in love with the child as though he were her own, and raised him till he was about eight years old. Though she never knew anything but poverty, Dora was a large, buxom woman of extremely rich, open, generous nature . . . and it is possible that, decades afterward, Maxo succumbed to Margaret Stetten because, albeit a daughter of Park Avenue, she physically and otherwise recalled to him Dora, who—as I have tried to show in my novel, *Cradle of Life,* which is based on Maxo's life-story —was more his mother than was the noblewoman who had borne him.

When Maxo was eight, his maternal grandfather, one of the wealthiest Austrian noblemen, suddenly learned of the lad's existence and came in person to Pustcha Kuplenovo, took him away from Dora and, through his confidential agents, established him in a castle in Croatia, where the boy thereupon lived for some years in charge of professional tutors, not knowing who he was. His surname "Vanka" had been given him in Putscha Kuplenovo, when he started going to school and was required to have a second name.

Following his removal to the castle, Maxo never again saw his grandfather, who died soon after; but there always was ample money for his needs throughout his youth. Having an extraordinarily acute mind, and being generally very sensitive, he puzzled endlessly about himself; and puzzling, enhanced his natural acuteness and intuition, and developed an intense consciousness of himself and everything about him. Already in his 'teens, if not even earlier while he was still with Dora, nothing escaped his eyes, ears, and mind. His paid tutors and other persons with whom he came into contact, and none of whom knew who he was, were consistently kind to him; but even so a subtle insecurity or uncertainty was the principal note of his early life, and he instinctively felt it urgent for him to get along with everybody, and he learned— somehow—to anticipate everyone's thoughts and desires. Which probably is important to know in order to be able to theorize about some of his experiences in America, which I shall narrate.

In his mid-'teens, he determined to become an artist and went to an art school in Zagreb. At eighteen he had a profoundly unsatisfactory interview with his real mother, who—now a highly respected married noblewoman with several legitimate children—came to see him in Zagreb. This was his first meeting with her since birth, and his last. And about this time, through channels too complex to trace here, he also learned the entire story of his origin, including the name of his father, which he was sworn to keep forever secret. And soon after this, at once vaguely and deeply unhappy as he brooded about himself, he decided to leave Croatia, to leave Austria-Hungary, and study art in Brussels, Belgium.

He lived in Brussels during the six years immediately preceding the war, and for some months during the war. There he began to grow a beard and acquired the already-mentioned nickname "Inri." He became acquainted with Queen Elizabeth, formerly a Bavarian princess, who, Maxo suspected, knew whose son he was. She was extremely kind to him, sending him weekly bouquets of flowers from the royal gardens, inviting him frequently to musicales at the Court, and bestowing upon him other favors as though they were his due; while her husband, the late King Albert, was also graciously attentive to him whenever they met.

At the war's outbreak in 1914, Maxo was twenty-five, officially an Austrian, and, as such, internable in Belgium as an enemy; but with Queen Elizabeth's great influence he was made an officer in the Belgian Red Cross, in which capacity he witnessed the German conquest of Belgium.

As Queen of the Belgians, Elizabeth went into exile to England; but as an erstwhile Bavarian princess and a niece of the late Empress Elizabeth of Austria, she gave Maxo a letter addressed to the German High Command, requesting he be given every possible consideration without being subjected to humiliating examinations or questioning. The German military authorities did not know what to make of Maxo, but respected Elizabeth's wish.

Feeling a sudden need to go to his beginnings, to see Dora Yug in Pustcha Kuplenovo, Maxo wanted to return to Croatia, and was allowed to do so, in charge of a trainful of Croatian miners, whom war had caught working in Belgian mines, and who had been interned until the German occupation.

In Croatia, being of military age, he was subject to serve in the Austro-Hungarian army; but, unwilling to be a soldier because opposed to killing under any pretext, he communicated with some one in high authority in the Hapsburg Empire who knew of his secret parentage and procured for him an exemption from military service and immunity from molestation on the part of any Austro-Hungarian official.

He lived in Zagreb all through the rest of the war, devoting himself to art and the amelioration of war's horrors in Croatia. He had considerable money, which had been sent him, through devious channels, by his mother; also, he sold the estate on which his maternal grandfather had established him; and he frequently visited Dora, his "real mother," helping her financially, and generally giving full play to his inclination to favor the lowly. He spent much time living in poverty-stricken Croatian villages.

Puzzled by, and deeply unhappy, about the whole mess of things, feeling now like a Hamlet, then like a Van Gogh or a character out of Dostoievski, he studied various religions and philosophies, including those of the Orient, and upon the base of his Catholic youth he built a structure of mystical concepts in an atmosphere of speculative freedom, which (and this is also important to remember if one wishes to be able to theorize about his subsequent adventures in America) kept his psychological makeup open to anything and, I think, helped to make him unusually attractive to a vast lot of different people.

After the war, when Croatia became a part of the new Yugoslav state, there was a great, Europe-wide currency confusion, in which Maxo lost most of his money, but he did not care greatly about that—he had enough left to build himself the little seaside villa on the island of Korchula which I have mentioned; he became professor of painting at the Academy . . . and thereupon led for many years a quiet, industrious life in Zagreb, till Margaret Stetten invaded it.

In the spring, 1935, the Vankas took several weeks to drive from New York to California, stayed West most of the summer, and returned to New York early in the fall. Maxo brought back a load of paintings and sketches he had done during the trip, and he told me of encounters with people which were monotonously strange. An old man in Johnstown, Pennsylvania, who probably was an unemployed immigrant steel-worker, and whom he asked to pose for him for a quick sketch as he sat in a park, burst into tears when Maxo showed him the picture, and exclaimed "Oh, you think I am good!" A middle-aged Indian in Oklahoma came up to him at a filling-station and reaching for his hand, said, "How!" and passed on. In Los Angeles, a man made him a proposition to start a new religion, "because you have the personality for a religious leader," and spoke of being willing to guarantee him a huge annual sum in profits therefrom. . . .

During the rest of 1935 and through the winter months of 1936, my own work took me out of New York and I saw little of the Vankas, while the following spring they went to Yugoslavia, to attend to some of their affairs there, and they did not return till late in the autumn. I saw Maxo briefly soon after. He had just taken out his first naturalization papers, and was glad he finally was in America to stay, for in Europe a new war seemed almost a certainty. But he still felt uneasy about himself in this vast, strenuous New World. Did I really believe he would make a place for himself here as an artist? He was forty-six; happy with Margaret and Peggy, both of whom he adored, and they him; but he would hate to live off his wife for the rest of his life. Should he not open an art school? . . . Hardly knowing what to advise him to do, I chided him about his masculine pride. I had overworked the past year and was tired; Stella and I were going on a trip to Guatemala, and rest.

Months later, early in 1937, when we returned, Maxo met us at the dock. He seemed dejected. He had worked hard all winter, had painted several pictures that he considered better than anything he had done in Europe, but . . . there was the old "but": he was not earning anything. "Don't be silly, Maxo," I said, repeating what I had said to him many times before, "you're doing Margaret a favor by living on her money." He was seriously thinking of starting a school of painting; he had several prospective pupils.

He accompanied us from the pier to our apartment, where I found a basketful of mail that had accumulated in our absence . . . and one of the first letters I opened was from a Croatian priest of whom I had not heard before—the

Rev. Albert Zagar, pastor of the Croatian Catholic Church of St. Nicholas at Millvale, an industrial suburb of Pittsburgh. He inquired if I knew the whereabouts of Mr. Vanka, explaining that his parishioners and he were thinking of "decorating" their church with murals, and would like to know as soon as possible if Mr. Vanka painted murals and was interested, for they hoped to have the job completed by mid-June, the time of one of their celebrations.

"Maxo," I said, handing him the letter, "your future in America seems about to begin. This looks like the opportunity you've been hoping for."

Maxo hastened to Pittsburgh to see the priest and the church, returning in a few days ablaze with creative enthusiasm. Father Zagar, he bubbled, was a grand fellow, a Franciscan and, in many respects, a true follower of Saint Francis of Assisi; instinctively intelligent, simple, direct, well-intentioned, and much beloved by his people, who were exclusively Croatian immigrants and their American-born children, most of whom were for letting him do what he liked with the church. He had been twelve years in America, and parish priest of St. Nicholas for half that time. The murals were his idea, and he was giving him (Maxo) entire freedom to paint what he liked on the walls, so long as, at least, some of the pictures were to be of a religious character.

Maxo told me further that, along with the parish house and the parochial school, which was in charge of nuns, the church stood atop a knoll, overlooking a vast industrial area, which included a street-car barn, an extensive railroad yard, and several factories and mills, with rows of workers' houses. It was not a very large church, nor an architectural masterpiece. "But," said Maxo, "I think I can do something with it. In fact, the walls, although mostly concave, curving in all directions, are well-nigh ideal for murals. It is a marvelous opportunity, and I would be willing to paint the whole place for nothing." But the priest— a thoughtful, generous man who momentarily had a considerable sum of money at his disposal—had insisted on giving him a substantial advance on the amount he had himself suggested in payment for the work, and to which Maxo had agreed.

While the church in Pittsburgh was being readied for him, according to the instructions he had given to a contractor, Maxo worked in New York on his sketches for the murals; then, early in April, he returned to Pittsburgh, whence I received a note from him: "I begin tomorrow. I'm not going to write to you till I finish, which must be by June tenth. I shall have to work day and night. Meantime, please don't come here, and don't let Margaret come. I hope to surprise you all with the completed work."

During the next two months nearly all the news I had of Maxo were a couple of Pittsburgh newspaper clippings describing his work-in-progress at Millvale. The photos accompanying the stories showed him doing immense and lovely figures on the church walls and ceiling.

Finally, exactly two months from the day on which he had begun, I—along with Margaret and the Stettens—received word from him: "Finished! Dedication on Sunday; please come; am eager for you to see what I have done." And so we all journeyed to Pittsburgh, to dismal Millvale . . . and I was never more amazed by anything in my life. Here was work single-handedly and superbly accomplished in two months that would doubtless have taken most artists a year, except that very few could have achieved a corresponding artistic excellence even in that time.

Over the main altar was a five-times-life-size Madonna with the Child, both in costumes decorated with Croatian peasant designs; and beneath the Madonna, on either side of the main altar, two pictures, each with several life-size figures: one depicting religion among Croatian peasants in the old country; the other, religion among Croatian immigrants in America. Over one of the side altars was a picture of the Crucifixion; over the other, of Mater Dolorosa. Upon the arched ceiling were the strikingly beautiful figures of John, Mark, Luke, and Matthew; and on the two straight walls beneath the choir, probably the two best pictures of the lot—one showing Croatian mothers in the old country sorrowing for their sons fallen in wars; the other, Croatian immigrant mothers in America weeping over the body of one of their sons killed in an industrial accident. Executed in indescribably vivid colors, all the murals and other elements of the interior were—with sheer artistic power and with the aid of ornamental strips of Croatian peasant designs, which occurred also in the garments of many of the figures in the pictures—closely integrated into an exquisitely blended whole, a superb composition whose quality was the sum total of all its parts which, in turn, enhanced the quality of the parts.

Had I not known when he had begun, I would have had difficulty in believing that my little friend Maxo had done all this in eight weeks, which had allowed him only four or five days to a mural; and as I remarked to him to this effect, he said that he himself could scarcely believe the calendar and his own eyes. I learned that he had not only done every bit of painting himself, but had mixed most of his paints; only Father Zagar—whom I found a remarkable, intense, marvelously genuine, spontaneous, and delightful man, a few years younger than Maxo, and also small and baldish—had helped him occasionally at night. He had used almost no models, painting nearly everything from his imagination.

To my question "How did you do it?" Maxo answered, seriously, "I don't know." Father Zagar smilingly advanced the explanation that God, the Madonna, and St. Nicholas had helped him. I noticed—as had Stella, Margaret, and the Stettens—that Maxo was terribly thin, but he insisted he was not tired. He felt better at the finish than at the start, which was evident in his work. We were informed that, except on Sundays, he had worked every day, under great creative tension, from nine in the forenoon till two or three the next morning, and had slept very little when not painting, and eaten rather less than a sparrow, but drunk much coffee.

The church was packed for the dedication ceremony, during which Father Zagar delivered an impassioned address, thanking Maxo for his art and bringing tears to most eyes. In the afternoon, there was a picnic in a near-by wood, attended by thousands of Croatian immigrants and their children who, on several spits, roasted scores of lambs; and people, mostly steel-workers and their wives, crowded around Maxo to take his hand, congratulate him on the completion of his work, and express their gratitude to him. Many exclaimed, *"Vi sté nashé suntsé, vi sté nasha zviezda!* (You are our sun, you are our star!")—moving Maxo to the brink of tears and open hysteria. The praise and gratitude of these people meant more to him than the subsequent favorable articles about his murals in the magazines and newspapers.

In the ensuing weeks strangers by the dozens, by the score, Catholics, Jews, Protestants, people of no definite religion, began to come to the little, externally unattractive Croatian church in Millvale, to ask the happy, proud, bustling Father Zagar to let them see the paintings. This stream of visitors continues as I write, and the majority are deeply impressed, especially when the priest tells them that the artist had done all this in two months. But they are unaware—as I was, when I first saw the murals—of the extraordinary, really fantastic circumstances under which Maxo had worked.

From Pittsburgh, Maxo returned East in my car; we were alone and he seemed to me half hysterical most of the way, talking incessantly about what a marvelous man Father Zagar was; how he loved him; how fortunate he was to have received his first big job in America from a man like him, and been free to paint what he liked; how fine it was to have earned so large a sum of money in a couple of months; how glad he was he had come to America . . . and often about nothing in particular, or at least I could not make out what he was driving at. He was repeating himself, just talking, talking, till it became a strain to be with him. At first I ascribed this to his weariness; then, somehow, it occurred to me that he simultaneously wanted desperately to tell me something and was trying just as desperately not to tell me. But I let him be, thinking if it was anything important he was sure to tell me by and by.

During the next two months I saw him once a week or so; he looked better, enjoying the publicity his murals were receiving throughout the United States and Europe. One critic had called them "the best church murals in America." But Maxo had continued a bit hysterical or uneasy . . . till one day late in August he suddenly said, "I must tell you something that happened in the church while I worked there. Terribly strange. I would have told you long ago, but Father Zagar and I had promised one another we would not tell anyone for a while. We were afraid it might result in some crazy, inappropriate publicity. Now I want to know what you will think of it, and I hope you will have Zagar tell you his version of the thing. I know he is nervous about it, for a few other persons connected with the church know or suspect what happened; and, with visitors coming daily to see the pictures, it is possible the story will eventually reach the ears of some newspaper man or writer and get into print—in all likelihood, I fear, superficially, inaccurately, to the possible damage of the reputation of the murals. . . .

"Well, when I got to Millvale, on April fifth, I was obliged to wait four days before I could start work, because the scaffolding—although it already hid the entire ceiling and most of the wall space—and other preparations were not yet completed. This was all right; for I could spend the next few days procuring my paints and other supplies.

"I had a meeting with the church committee, under the chairmanship of Father Zagar, and I promised them—without knowing how I would do it—to complete the job by about June tenth, in time for their celebration in the middle of that month.

"I asked Father Zagar to request everybody around the place please to remain out of the church while I was working inside. I did not want curious people to come climbing up the scaffolding to watch and distract me, and possibly fall. I knew that if I was to complete the job in two months, I would need every minute I could get; and, therefore, I also suggested to Father Zagar that, so far as possible, he, too, stay out. I feared that, if he came in too often, I might spend too much time talking with him, for I found him from the start very charming, intelligent, and entertaining. He said, 'O.K.,' which is one of his favorite expressions; and proposed to have all the church doors locked every weekday from nine o'clock on, after the last mass—for, as you know, there are two priests in the parish—Zagar, and his assistant, the Rev. Nezich. I was given a key to a small side door, entering under the choir, which enabled me to go in and out as I pleased.

"On April ninth the church was ready for me, and I locked myself in; and, with all my materials on the scaffold, I began the Madonna and Child, which, because of the curvature of the wall above the main altar and the size of the figures, was very difficult to do. Also, I had never done anything like it. To save time, I had decided not to draw even an outline of the figures before I started to paint, but to work directly with paint, as I would upon canvas; and as the paint I used dried very quickly, I had to work extremely fast and carefully. But I felt fine and—except for the few minutes I took out for lunch, and the few minutes for supper—I worked from nine in the forenoon till two-thirty the next morning. Or, rather, I discovered that it was two-thirty when I came into the parish house, where I had my room, for I had determined to have no watch with me on the job. My reason for this was that if I had the watch where I could look at it and see how late it was getting I might feel tired before I was really exhausted for the day, and quit earlier. Throughout the two months I never took my watch with me into the church.

"By way of further introduction to what I have to tell you, let me add that everytime I came from the church to the parish house after quitting for the night, which was always between one-thirty and three-thirty after midnight, I found Father Zagar waiting for me with a pot of coffee on the stove and cake and fruit on the table. This annoyed me, and I told him not to stay up for me; I could take my own coffee if I wanted it. But he said, 'Never mind, *gospodiné profesor*'—he called me professor at first. He assured me that he seldom slept more than three or four hours, anyhow. . . . So every night I had coffee and a bite, and chatted with Father Zagar for a while; then we both went upstairs and to sleep.

"At night while I worked the church was dark except for the powerful moveable lamp on the scaffold, whence a few sharp sheafs of light reached down, illumining parts of the altar or the communion table, depending on where I had the lamp. Mixing the paints, I turned the lamp down, so I could see what I was doing; and at such times most of the altar below me was doused with light—but I scarcely had time to look down.

"Now, too, before I come to the story that I want to narrate to you, I should probably help you to imagine the atmosphere of the church at night and, so far as I can tell you, how I felt working in it. The scaffolding, of course, creaked all the while, all over the church; but that did not bother me. It rained a good deal, and it was cold and damp, and on some nights I wore two shirts and two sweaters and a windbreaker; which kept me warm enough in my body, but my hands frequently were none too warm to be efficient in holding the brush.

"For an instant, now and then, it felt a bit strange to be alone in the church; but only for an instant—I had no time for feeling strange or otherwise. Outside I could hear the whir of automobile traffic on the road below-hill, and the clanging of locomotives and the clattering of trains in the railyard. Every once in a while the church—the whole hill—shook when a heavy truck passed, or when the trainmen were joining cars, making up their trains. . . . Occasionally, the two dogs that belonged to the parish house—a police she-dog and a nondescript hound—barked, squealed, howled violently outside. . . . On the second or third night, a sudden long sound came out of the organ in back of the church, which startled me; but then I thought it was due to the vibrations from the motor traffic or from the railyard. . . .

"On the fourth night, as I say, while mixing paint and feeling rather cold and tired, but not exhausted, I glanced at the altar beneath me, which was rather fully illumined by my lamp's downward flood of light . . . and there was a figure, a man in black, moving this way and that way in front of it, raising his arms and making gestures in the air.

"I thought, of course, that the man was Father Zagar, and, in my frenzy of work, I did not take a very good look at him. I was slightly annoyed for a moment. He had agreed to stay out like everybody else; now here he was! But then I said to myself I had no right, really, to require him to keep out. I went on mixing the paint, then began to put it quickly on the wall, and could not help wondering why he should be going through all those motions in front of the altar at this time of night, for—having no watch, remember— I judged by my weariness and by the work accomplished since nightfall that it was around midnight. Thinking about it, it occurred to me he might be a perfectionist and was practicing ritualistic gestures; and I said to myself, 'To the devil with him! I'm busy!' But then another question popped into my head, 'Why didn't he say something to me as he came in?' This seemed strange, for

Zagar is a very talkative, almost effusive, man. After a while, however, I decided that he had kept silent in order not to disturb or distract me; and, the Madonna being one of the hardest jobs I had ever attempted to paint, I finally dismissed him from my mind. It never occurred to me that the man could be the other priest, Father Nezich, who, I knew, always went to bed early in the evening.

"That night I quit shortly after two o'clock. As I got out of the church, the dogs, which had been barking violently during the past several hours, dashed up to me, terribly excited. They rose on their hind legs and pawed me and licked my hands. But I thought nothing of this. As I entered the parish house, there was Father Zagar, as usual, full of talk and concern for my welfare. Was I cold? Would I have a brandy? He hurried into the kitchen to fetch me coffee and cake and a dish of canned peaches; whereupon we chatted, perhaps till three o'clock. But he said nothing about having been in the church. I thought this was strange, and almost asked him about it, but did not; I was tired and wanted to get to bed as soon as possible, and did not care to start any sort of long conversation, which, I feared, might be the case if he began to explain to me why he practiced those ritualistic gestures. Besides, *shta mé briga!*—none of my business!

"The fifth night, working till past two o'clock, I saw nothing out of the ordinary; and I noticed, by comparison with the previous night, that the dogs were quiet. When I quit, again coffee, cake, fruit—talk with Father Zagar—and so to bed.

"The sixth and seventh nights, the same.

"On the eighth night, skipping Sunday, which is to say on April nineteenth, I happened, about midnight, to look down from the scaffold while mixing paint, and there was the figure again, the man in black who I assumed once more—without looking carefully—was Rev. Zagar. His gestures were a bit fantastic, but I thought this was due to the fact that I saw them from above, and there were shadows; and I was annoyed again—why was he coming in like this? Was he, perhaps, a little crazy? The explanation that he might be a perfectionist practicing ritualistic gestures, which had satisfied me four nights before, now suddenly impressed me as improbable. I felt weird, cold; and, trying not to think of him, I worked furiously on the Madonna, who was practically finished. . . .

"Awhile later I heard him walking slowly down the main aisle of the church, mumbling rhythmically. 'Well,' I thought, 'he's praying. To the devil with him!' But, vaguely vexed and feeling very unpleasant, I determined to have a talk with him tonight. I would ask him, as a sort of joke, what he thought he was doing in front of the altar so late at night? Didn't he do enough praying in the daytime? . . . He paced the aisle, mumbling, for half an hour or an hour. Glancing down, I saw him momentarily as he cut the light, here and there, that poured down through the scaffolding. Then—all quiet; only the dogs were barking outside, the cars honking and, way off, a locomotive bell clanging.

"I assumed Father Zagar had gone out; and after a time, still feeling strangely cold and uneasy, I decided to quit, though I sensed it was still early—perhaps only twelve-thirty. I used up what paint I had made, cleaned my brushes; then climbed down, extinguished the lights, and went out, and into the parish house.

"Entering, what do I see but Father Zagar asleep on the couch in the living-room. Waking with a start, he jumped up and said, 'Hello, *gospodiné pro-fesor!*' Then, looking up at a clock he cried, 'Oh my, it's past one o'clock! Why didn't that woman wake me?' He meant his cook and housekeeper, Mrs. Dolinar, an elderly widow, also known as Dolinarka. He was angry, explaining he had lain down at about nine, having instructed Dolinarka to wake him at eleven; but she had apparently gone upstairs and also fallen asleep.

"Now, this was strange! I said to Father Zagar, 'Do you mean to say that you have lain asleep here since nine o'clock?'—'Why do you ask?' said Father Zagar. I smiled and asked him to answer me, and he said, 'I believe I fell asleep soon after I lay down; by nine-thirty, anyhow.'—'And,' I asked, 'you've been asleep ever since?'—'Yes.'—'Are you sure?'—'Sure!'

"'Well,' I thought, smiling to myself, 'all this is easily explained now: he is a sleepwalker.' Father Zagar asked, 'Why do you smile?' I told him; then he laughed and lighted a cigarette, pacing about the room. I sat down. 'You saw something?' he asked then. —'I saw *you* in front of the altar, making gestures like this' (illustrating). 'Sure you saw me?' asked Father Zagar, very serious. I said I had not looked very carefully, but had assumed it was he; now, if he insisted that he had been asleep ever since nine-thirty, I was impelled to think he was a somnambulist. We laughed.

"Smoking nervously, Zagar said, 'Believe me, *gospodiné profesor,* I am not a sleepwalker. I was really on that couch from about nine till you awakened me.' He hesitated, then asked, 'Tell me: have you, since coming here, heard there is a tradition that this church is occasionally visited by a ghost or some strange phenomenon?' I answered, 'No.'—'Are you sure?'—'Yes.'—'Well,' Zagar went on, 'there is a fifteen-year-old tradition to that effect, dating nine or ten years back before I came here. I have never seen, or had any experience with him, or it, but not a few people say they have. Before I came, there were quarrels and arguments among the Croatians hereabouts pertaining to this ghost, or what-ever it is. I am a sceptic as to ghosts and apparitions, and never believed the tradition, not really, but sometimes, listening to people speak of it, I admitted there might be something to it—some phenomenon which we do not under-stand. . . . Do you know why I asked Dolinarka to wake me at eleven?'—I said, 'No'—'Do you know why you always found me here so late, when you came out of the church?'—'No.'—'Because,' said Zagar, 'ever since you decided to work late, I was half afraid that, alone in the church, you would have some "experience" and get frightened and possibly fall off the scaffold; and every night since you began to work, except today, I have stood watch outside the door between eleven and one. You never saw me, for I was outside, behind the door, looking in, keeping still, listening. My purpose was to rush in, in case you cried out, or started hastily to climb down.'

"I said, 'Father Zagar, you aren't crazy, are you?' He answered, 'I don't know, but I don't think I am!' We laughed again, then had some coffee and cake and canned peaches; and, discussing the thing, decided that hereafter Father Zagar would come into the church at about eleven or before every night I worked, and stay with me till quitting-time.

"So the following night he came in, announcing it was quarter to eleven, standard time; then, by way of horseplay, he called out, 'Come on, ghost, show yourself and see if the *gospodiné profesor* and I are afraid of you.' I laughed, and went on working. Father Zagar climbed up, bringing me a pot of coffee; helped me with paint-mixing—something he did regularly thereafter; then went down again, lest he distract me, for I had started on the new mural, *Religion in the Old Country*, on the left side of the main altar . . . and suddenly there was a strange click or knock in back of the church, beneath the choir. It sent a chill through me. 'Hear that, Father?'—'What?'—'That strange knock back there?'—'Yes; but wasn't it a creak in the scaffolding?'—'I don't know,' I said; 'I don't think so.' It sounded terribly strange. I kept working as we talked.

"Then—another click or knock, the same as the first, but in another part of the church. I turned around and looked down at Father Zagar, who stood on the other side of the communion table. He turned, to face the rear of the church, and in a tense, sharp voice challenged, 'Come on, show yourself, if you are a ghost, or whatever you are; or speak, if you can. We're busy here, the *gospodiné profesor* and I, decorating the church, making it beautiful, and we should like to be let alone. If you are a ghost; if you are a dead man, go with God,—peace to you: I shall pray for you. Only please don't bother us.——'

"I interrupted him with a yell, for just then I saw him—the ghost—or at least let me call him that—sitting in the fourth pew. I saw him very clearly: a man in black, an old man with a strange angular face, wrinkled and dark, with a bluish tinge. He leaned on the front part of the pew, looking up—not so much at me as at everything in general: a sad, miserable gaze. I saw him for just a moment, then—nothing. He vanished. But I felt cold all over, at the same time that sweat broke out of every pore of my body. I got off the scaffold, which was not high for that mural, and barely managed not to fall off the ladder, I was so frightened—only the sensation I had was more than fear: something indescribable, but related to the milder, more remote sensations I had experienced on the two previous evenings when I saw him gesticulate in front of the altar.

"Rushing to me, Father Zagar put his arms about me and asked what was the matter, but I had no time to talk with him. I pushed him aside and rushed out of the church as fast as I could. Outside, the dogs were barking. They rushed to me, yelping and whining.

"Father Zagar, who followed me out, had not seen the ghost; and, taking the attitude of the sceptic again, he said I had probably only imagined I saw him. 'But,' I insisted, 'I *really saw* him, Father—with these eyes, as I see you now.'—'You imagined it!' Zagar repeated, and I became angry and went to my room and made a sketch in my notebook of the man—the ghost, whatever he was—as I clearly recalled him sitting in the pew.

"I calmed down, went into the bathroom, and changed my sweat-soaked underclothes. Father Zagar came up and I went down with him. We begged one another's pardon, I had coffee and cake; we talked, speculating, Father Zagar telling me what the tradition had to say; and shortly after one, when I felt perfectly quiet again, we returned to the church, where also everything was entirely normal, and I resumed work. Zagar stayed with me till I quit, then I had more coffee and he went to his room, and I to mine. Exhausted, I fell asleep at once.

"In the morning Father Zagar told me of the following occurrence: A few minutes after he had turned out the light over his bed, there were three clear and distinct clicks or knocks in the closest proximity of his bed. The knocks were not as if some one struck a piece of wood or metal or a wall, but something different and strange, as though one snapped one's fingers, yet not quite that, either . . . as though they came out of infinity—the same that we had heard in the church. 'They touched my heart, and everything in me with a long chill feeling,' he said, 'and, though I could not see him, I knew there was a dead man in my room. I blessed myself and began to say an Ave Maria, and switched on the light and saw nothing. The chill feeling in me persisted. I was frightened and angry, and said: "Who are you? Why don't you show yourself to me, when you do show yourself to Mr. Vanka? I am the boss here. I am the pastor. Talk to me if you can. Let's settle this once for all. Have some consideration for us. I work hard all day and I am tired, and I want to sleep. Poor Mr. Vanka has a task on his hands; you should let him alone. But now talk to me and tell me what the trouble is. I shall pray for you." I waited, but there was no reply, so I turned out the light, said a paternoster and an Ave Maria for the peace of his soul, and the cold feeling left me and, I think, I soon fell asleep.'

"The next night, and for two or three nights after, we were left in peace, and I worked right through, finishing *Religion in the Old Country* and beginning *Immigrants' Religion in America*, in which I included a portrait of Father Zagar. He posed for me in the daytime, then came in late in the evening. He was beginning to credit himself with sending the ghost away. It took a fellow like him, by golly, to deal with ghosts and spirits and such strange phenomena. He had given the ghost a piece of his mind the other night; now he stayed away. Ghosts, apparitions, and things of that sort, he said, were like people. If you talk to them as though you mean it, they listen to you. . . .

"Father Zagar came in shortly before eleven, unlocking and locking the door, and cracking his usual jokes, boasting he had sent the ghost packing . . . when the whole *komedia* started all over again. There was again that strange, awful knock or click in one corner under the choir, then another in the other corner. 'O-ho!' cried Zagar, scratching his head. I used up what paint I had in the pail, then laid everything aside and got off, intent on fleeing: for I was abruptly all cold inside and beginning to drip with perspiration. But the Father detained me, seizing my arm, suggesting we face the situation. 'Not I,' said I, and made for the door, Zagar after me, seizing me again.

"There was another knock, I could not tell just where, but it cut into me like a knife. Then I saw him—the old man in black—moving down the aisle altarward. Terrified, horror-stricken, panicky are faint words to describe my sensation. 'Look, Father,' I yelled, 'there he goes—to the altar—he's at the altar—*he's blown out the light!*' The last few words I shrieked out with more lung power than I ever thought I possessed, and simultaneously lost sight of the figure, and began to feel a trifle better.

"This—his putting out the light—is, perhaps, the most important point in the story. The light was the sanctuary lamp. It usually hangs in a special fixture depending from the ceiling above the altar. It burns all the time; the nuns next door see to it; the tallow and wick inside the bulb need to be changed only about once a year; and the sisters assured us afterwards that as long as any of them had been there—for eight years, at any rate—it had never been out. The glass bulbs around the flame are so arranged that it is almost impossible to blow it out. No wind or draught can touch it; besides, all the doors and windows were closed. . . . The light usually hangs, as I say; but now, because of the scaffolding, the fixture had been pulled up and the lamp stood like a huge red cup on the altar, where the ghost, or whatever it was, now blew it out with a puff of breath.

"When I yelled that he had put out the light, Father Zagar demanded, 'What light?' I said, 'The sanctuary lamp! There! Can't you see it's out?'—'*Bomé,* by golly!' he exclaimed and rushed to the altar, where he saw that the wick in the lamp was still smoking. He touched the lamp; it was hot. The flame had, obviously, just been extinguished.

"Meantime, I had left the church. The dogs were yelping and squealing outside. Father Zagar followed me out. 'Till now,' he said, 'I still had a glimmer of doubt. I thought, possibly, it was your fantasy. I thought, possibly, I had imagined the knocks in the church and by my bed the other night. But now I believe. *Bomé,* now I believe. There is something here. That light was blown out just when you said it was.'"

"At one o'clock we returned to work again, and everything was normal. Whereupon we had two or three 'good' nights, as we began to call those when nothing happened. Then 'he'—we called him 'he'—came two or three nights in succession. I had no watch, but when 'he' came I knew it was somewhere between eleven and twelve, standard time. 'He' paid no attention to the fact that meanwhile Pittsburgh had gone to daylight-saving. One night Father Zagar tried to fool me when he came in, apologizing he had fallen asleep—it was nearly one-thirty; wasn't I quitting yet? I might readily have believed this under ordinary circumstances for I was weary enough for it to be one-thirty; but not this time. He no sooner spoke than the chill feeling pierced me, which was always the signal, and I said, 'Father, you're a fibber; it's somewhere between eleven and twelve, standard time. I must go.'

"Almost always I left the church immediately I got 'the signal,' as I called the chill feeling. I tried to ignore it a few times, and worked furiously. I put blinders, made out of newspapers, on either side of my face, like a horse, so I would see nothing but the spot on the wall where I worked. I stuffed cotton in my ears. No use! At the end I had to go; the sensation and the situation were intolerable. I saw 'him' on each of these occasions when I stayed after getting 'the signal.' He looked perfectly mild, pensive-like, sitting in the pew or moving up and down the aisle; yet he filled me with indescribable horror, with something higher and stronger than fear; what, I cannot tell you. Father Zagar, who also got 'the signal,' though usually later than I, and not as terribly, wanted me to stay and 'face the ghost and the whole business' with him, but I could not. Twice, when he tried physically to detain me, I pushed him violently away, bashing him once against a wall, the second time against a door, and he suffered bruises. He had locked the door and I was so crazy with that fear which was more than fear that I told him I would kill him unless he forthwith let me out.

"This went on throughout the job—for two months. When 'he' came, 'he' came always between eleven and twelve, standard, except once, early in June. On that occasion, he came earlier in the evening, perhaps at nine or nine-thirty, but gave me no 'signal.' The feeling I had was unpleasant, but not intolerable; I put on my newspaper blinders, stopped up my ears, and worked. 'He' burned candles on the chandelier in front of the little altar on the right from the time 'he' came till Father Zagar entered the church at eleven. 'What's this smell?' demanded Father Zagar, entering. I said, 'He's been burning candles all evening.' Then Mrs. Dolinar, the housekeeper, came in, too, in the wake of the priest, who told her what I had said. The two of them inspected the chandelier; it was full of molten tallow, while one wick, burned almost to the bottom, still flamed. Mrs. Dolinar put it out.

". . . This is my story," concluded Maxo, "absolutely true, as I know it. I think I am not crazy. Nothing so intense, so terrific has ever happened to me. A ghost! I think so—something, some one, that is not substantial with flesh and bones and blood. An astral body, if you like—*something*: call it what you like. I know that I had a most terrific experience. . . ."

Listening to him, I was thinking, "This is too weird even for Maxo." Not that I questioned his statement about having had an intense and terrific experience. Nor did I doubt that Father Zagar would substantially corroborate his story, and I knew both of them well enough to feel they were genuine, beyond any charlatanry or trickery. But the "ghost," to me, was a ghost in quotation marks. I had long since become settled in my belief that once we died we were dead; that our personalities disintegrated into atoms, molecules and other such basic life-units, which then became available as material in the construction of other life forms.

The matter of the sanctuary light going out, I realized, was hard to explain, save as a coincidence; but I inclined to believe that Maxo's experience was largely, if not entirely, of his own creation. I did not doubt his saying that no one had told him of the fifteen-year-old "ghost" tradition, which was the creation of a few superstitious persons, the like of whom might be found in any group; or the result or manifestation of a collective psychosis or illusion; but I thought that, since the tradition existed, it was not beyond Maxo to get wind of it, somehow, *via* his acute, penetrating intuition, which was a matter of his whole strange background. After being a few days in the church, he could have sensed it. He was somewhat like D. H. Lawrence, who had the ability to sit down immediately on arriving in a city he had never visited before and write an article about it. I, myself, who was not nearly as acute and intuitive as Maxo, had lately lived in a three-hundred-year-old house in the city of Antigua, in Guatemala, and dimly sensed some of the things that I later learned had happened there long ago. Before that, in Yugoslavia, while interviewing King Alexander, I had had a feeling, which had amounted almost to knowledge, that he would be killed before long, and then had predicted his assassination in print in America a year before it occurred. . . .

Of course, Maxo's conscious mind, with which he told me the story, had had, I figured, no part in creating the "ghost" and the whole terrific drama he had narrated to me. The "ghost," I theorized, was a creature of his subconscious. But why did his subconscious create him? Perhaps to keep himself constantly stirred up so he could carry out the great task before him. Perhaps, way down in him he doubted that he could complete the job on time, and his subconscious, getting wind in one way or another of the ghost tradition, had created the "ghost" to have him there as an excuse in case of failure. Other such thoughts occurred to me. I expressed them to Maxo. He smiled, complimenting me on my resources as a psychologist, but shook his head; I was all wrong.

We let Margaret and Stella in on the story, but, both sceptics, they joined my party against Maxo.

He was asked, "Why didn't you quit when these dreadful things began to happen?" He answered, "I thought of quitting, but how could I return to New York and face all of you? How could I have explained it to you? You would all think I had gone crazy. Besides, how could I leave Father Zagar with a partly painted church? I thought of painting only in the daytime, but then I could not possibly have finished in two months as I had agreed. I took that agreement very seriously, for I had entered into it, not only with Father Zagar, but the whole church committee. The parishioners generally were very much interested in what I was doing. There was much talk. Everybody was expecting me to finish by about June tenth. Also, when I started the job, the big Pittsburgh newspapers printed stories about me and my project; and now, if I quit, the thing might get into the papers in some way that might make me look ridiculous and be ruinous to my future in America. . . ."

Maxo showed us the sketch of the ghost in his notebook. This was no proof to us. We did not dispute that he had "seen" "him" after his subconscious had created him. We asked him: did anyone have any theory who the ghost was?

"The popular belief is," said Maxo, "that 'he' is a dead priest who, while alive, took money from parishioners for masses which he never read, and who had not read his breviary daily and had neglected his other priestly duties; and is

now coming to the church to make up for his sinful negligence during his life. Father Zagar inclines to this theory; so does the other priest there, the Rev. Nezich, who has never had any 'experience' and, not wanting any, never enters the church after dark. Mrs. Dolinar accepts the ghost as a permanent institution, and has no fear of 'him.' The same is true of the parishioners, who believe that 'he' comes. They say the thing to do is to stay out of the church late at night, and let 'him' have the place to 'himself.'

"The nuns, who live over the parochial schoolhouse, next door, do not disbelieve in 'his' existence; none enter the church at night. The dogs seem to feel 'him,' for they barked violently nearly every time I saw 'him' or heard the knocks or felt the 'signal.' On the night that 'he' burned candles in the church, Mrs. Dolinar felt a chill pass by, or over, her in the church.

"There are persons in Pittsburgh, all Croatians, who have had 'experiences' with 'him'—have heard the knocks or clicks; have heard the organ play, which is electrically operated and, therefore, not subject to vibrations from the traffic either on the road below-hill or in the railroad yard. There seem to be people who claim to have seen 'him.' Before Father Zagar's time, there have been arguments in the parish between those who believed in the ghost and those who considered the whole thing a superstition, a collective illusion, or simple nonsense. One of the priests before Zagar, a certain Rev. Sorich, quit the parish on account of it. He claimed 'he' frequently knocked in his room, and that he had had other experiences with 'him.' Many people did not believe Sorich. He almost came to blows over the matter. He is still alive, living somewhere in Chicago. . . ."

Maxo paused, then said, "I don't know what it is, but I *saw* a figure who looked as I have drawn him in my sketchbook. I am certain there is *something*."

Whether *"something"* or a psychological quirk on Maxo's part which involved the priest and the housekeeper in his "experiences," the thing was interesting . . . so in mid-August, asking Maxo to join me, I drove to Pittsburgh and we spent two days with Father Zagar at Millvale. We had long talks, back and forth, from all angles we could think of. The priest and Mrs. Dolinar, both of whom impressed me as utterly incapable of any charlatanry, corroborated Maxo's story to me in every respect, adding a few insignificant details. Father Zagar repeated to me Maxo's account of the incident with the sanctuary lamp. He could not think of it as a coincidence. Both he and the housekeeper insisted that on the occasion when "he" had burned candles all evening, no living persons could possibly have got in to burn them, for all the doors had been locked and the keys—except Maxo's—were in the parish house. Joking, I accused Maxo of burning the candles himself. He laughed; he had too much to do to bother lighting candles. . . .

I looked up a number of other persons who had had "experiences." Much of what they told me was confused and confusing. Some believed, with Father Zagar, that "he" was a dead priest trying to make good what he had neglected in his duties while living. Some thought "he" might be a parish priest who had served at St. Nicholas about twenty years ago. There appeared to be a number of people who had heard the strange knocks, both in the church and in the parish house, and had felt the chill that Maxo, Father Zagar, and Mrs. Dolinar had experienced. None with whom I talked had seen "him," but some had heard of persons who claimed they had seen "him," and that "he" looked like a priest. Certain it is that a number of people accepted the tradition. None of these were afraid to enter the church in the daytime, but they shunned it at night, especially between eleven and twelve, standard time.

The majority of parishioners, however, seemed to be sceptics in this regard; a few were emphatic there was no such thing as a ghost. They held that those who believed in "this nonsense" were superstitiously inclined, not very bright, apt to be influenced by "this crazy talk which was started God knows how or by whom, long ago." None of these knew of Maxo's and Father Zagar's recent "experiences," and thought the less said of the so-called "ghost" the better.

They were afraid that, now that Mr. Vanka had made the church famous, the thing might get into American newspapers and thus act as a reflection on the Croatian people in the United States. They all thought Mr. Vanka's paintings were wonderful, and that he must be a great man to have done all that work in such a short time.

Father Zagar and I went into the church at eleven, standard time, on Tuesday, August 17th—and stayed there about an hour. I was, I think, perfectly prepared to have an "experience"; but there were no knocks or clicks, we felt no chills and saw nothing unusual. Maxo did not want to come into the church with us. I was told that sometimes, apparently, "he" did not come for weeks or possibly months at a time. The dogs had been very quiet at night now for many weeks.

I left Pittsburgh, not as definite a sceptic or scoffer as I had come there, but certainly an agnostic. There seems to be *something* in that church, but what it is, I don't know. The thing intrigues me both by itself and in connection with Maxo, whom—frankly—I do not understand any more than, apparently, he understands himself, but whom I like and whom I instinctively trust a good deal further than I can see him. I can say this: if there was *something* to see and experience, Maxo Vanka, if anyone, would see and experience it.

Ellis Island and Plymouth Rock

Here is not merely a nation but a teeming nation of nations.
WALT WHITMAN, Preface to 1855 Edition of *Leaves of Grass.*

There is here a great melting pot in which we must compound a precious metal. That metal is the metal of nationality.
WOODROW WILSON, in an address delivered
at Washington, April 19, 1915.

America! half brother of the world!
With something good and bad of every land.
P. J. BAILEY, *Festus: The Surface.*

My Interest in the Immigrants

B EING MYSELF AN IMMIGRANT, I WAS NATURALLY AND RATHER STEADILY INTER-
ested in immigrants and their problems while—as I tell in *Laughing in
the Jungle*—I was still roaming America in the rôle of a migratory laborer in
the early 1920's. Many of the men on the jobs on which I worked were immigrants from various lands. They, as myself, were distinguished as such by our
native fellow workers and the bosses. I learned the stories of some of them:
why they had come to America—what America had done to them—and what
they thought of America.

This interest on my part continued through the middle and late 1920's, after
I had more or less settled down in southern California and begun to experiment with writing. My earliest stories and articles in *The American Mercury*
—some of which subsequently became chapters in *Laughing*—dealt with immigrants and their American-born children and grandchildren. In 1928, or
thereabouts, I became conscious of a germ of an idea in my mind that in the
ensuing seven years developed sufficiently to resolve itself into my first novel,
Grandsons, a story of the lives of three young Americans whose grandfather
had emigrated from Carniola to America in the 1880's.

When the Depression followed the 1929 stock-market crash, I became aware
of the fact that as industrial production fell off immigrant workers were
losing jobs before other employees who were native Americans. In New York,
during 1930-32, I was stopped innumerable times by destitute men who turned
out to be immigrants. In some cases I learned their sad stories and scribbled
them in my Diary for possible future use or reference.

Always, too, I was reaching for books about immigrants, about "the land
of promise" and the Melting Pot; and for such autobiographies as those by Edward Bok and Michael Pupin. Nearly all interested me; none, however, were
deeply satisfying (I scarcely knew why), except three novels: Willa Cather's
My Ántoniá, O. E. Rölvaag's *Giants in the Earth*, and Abraham Cahan's *The
Rise of David Levinsky* . . . and I had a notion even before I came to New
York that if I developed as a writer I would eventually devote some part of
my time and energy to the immigrants.

Cantrell's story, as I pondered it while writing *Dynamite*, and later, gradually
turned the above notion into determination. Cantrell's roots in America reached
into the Virginia of Captain John Smith; in 1909-12, however, he had collided
with forces and tendencies which centered partly in a few other old-stock
Americans (Otis, Harriman, Darrow), but also in immigrants or sons of immigrants (the McNamaras, Tveitmoe, Johannsen, Gompers, Debs, Hillquit).
This fact made me deeply uneasy.

The McNamaras, Tveitmoe, Johannsen, Gompers, and Hillquit had secretly
believed in violence or political intrigue and plots, or in both; that is to say,

in quick, superficial, short-cut solutions of American problems. I realized, of course, that the recent immigrants or "foreigners" had no monopoly upon short-cuts in contemporary American life, and that in America everybody was more or less in a rush about one thing or another; the get-rich-quick artist and the radical were brothers under the skin. But I knew, too, that the immigrants' very coming to the United States was itself a short-cut solution of their problem in Europe, and I suspected that after they became "Americanized" and took on various American ways the natural preference of many was for the simplest and easiest, the short-cut variety. Violence à la McNamara was one of these.

I felt, also, that the vast new-immigrant element might be more exposed to the confusion of forces, the contradictions, conflicts, neuroticisms, and per-versions of American life that issued out of its fundamental incongruity, its out-of-focus condition, than were the old-stock Americans; and that, for Amer-ica's sake, an awareness of the presence in the United States of tens of millions of immigrants and their American-born children would be increasingly neces-sary in any intelligent contemplation or consideration of America.

But I did not get really close to, or become emotionally involved in, the subject of immigrants and America till I went to Yugoslavia in 1932 and then returned to the United States and published *The Native's Return*.

Traveling in Yugoslavia, I encountered numerous returned *Amerikantsi*, who were different from other natives of the villages and towns in which they lived. Some were wasteful, others more efficient, because they had lived in America; some more interesting, others less charming than the general run of people in their communities. In the larger cities, journalists and other edu-cated persons asked me eager questions about the situation of the Yugoslav and other immigrants in America.

Finally, at Split, in central Dalmatia, I met Ivo (John) F. Lupis-Vukich, whom I have mentioned in *The Native's Return*. A highly intelligent man, he had published and edited a Croatian-language newspaper in Chicago for twenty-odd years and in that capacity had gained an insight into America's immigrant problems. He believed, and I agreed with him, that the United States had as yet no idea of what those problems were, or even that they existed. What the American people did know about them was swathed in sentimen-tality and linked to unsound, impossible "Americanization" drives and pro-grams which were typically short-cut, un-thought-out stunts; or twisted by racial prejudice and blind fear of strangers in their midst whom they did not understand.

Lupis-Vukich told me of speeches he had delivered before civic bodies in Chicago and elsewhere on how America might utilize the racial, national, and cultural traits, urges and qualities of the diverse new-immigrant groups. Those speeches had been applauded but ill understood, and went unheeded. He was sorry about this, but did not blame America. "It was just one of those things," he said; "it could not be helped. America was too busy with her industrial revolution, too excited about other things, to be able really to think and do anything intelligent about her non-Anglo-Saxon population. But one of these days she is apt to become wise all of a sudden; for, as you know, that is how things happen in America—all of a sudden. If she does not become wise about her immigrant problems, it is liable to be just too bad all around." He urged me on my return to the United States to go further into the important subject than I had gone in *Laughing*.

In the preceding section of this book I have suggested what happened among my fellow Yugoslav nationals living in various parts of America after *The Native's Return* had suddenly become a popular book. Simultaneously I began to hear from immigrants of other nationalities. It seemed that I had returned vicariously to the old country for no end of immigrants, regardless of where they were from. Some came to see me, and we talked. I was naïvely urged to go next to Poland, to Czechoslovakia, to Hungary and to write books about those countries, so that America would get some idea and feeling of who the Poles, the Czechs and Slovaks, and the Hungarians were. It was necessary for me to explain to these new friends of mine that in all probability I would be unable to write as effectively about their old countries as I did about my own. But I was very much impressed by their keen realization of the need of finding some way of getting America acquainted with themselves.

The Native's Return, as it got about, brought me in contact also with old-stock Americans everywhere; and, touching with some of those whom I met on the immigrant problems, I became acutely cognizant of what seemed to me a serious socio-pathological situation among them, due to the presence of the large new-immigrant elements in the country and their (the old-stock Americans') immense ignorance about them. Here—even in such towns as Salem or Cambridge, Massachusetts—were all these foreigners, people not of their stock, with customs, tendencies, and appearances different from their own; people with unpronounceable names, who were not really part of America and perhaps never could be in the same way that they (the old-stock Americans) were. Here were these foreigners and their children, who, although born here, also were not Americans, certainly not *their* kind of Americans: and the question was, What did it all mean? Was America no longer America? . . . And so not a few old-stock Americans, including many whom I met, were deeply, in many cases, unconsciously or secretly, uneasy, living in their country, or even afraid, alarmed: which, I thought, was a subtle (though, of course, not the only) factor in making some of them hectic, jittery persons, afflicted with hidden inferiority feelings. They were less charming, and less effective than they might have been otherwise, for their uneasiness and fear often blazed into hate of these foreigners; and the fear and hate affected their personality and manner. They were ready material to be exploited by sincere, fear-driven patriotic leaders of anti-alien movements, as well as by unscrupulous racketeers-in-patriotism, whose function was to drive the "foreigners" deeper and deeper within themselves and away from the spiritual-cultural centers of America, thus making matters worse and worse; for the worse they were the better it was for them. . . .

Thus, briefly (and much simplified), I became emotionally and intellectually involved in the immigrant problems. Up until *The Native's Return* I looked upon them from the point of view of the immigrant; then I decided that was the wrong point of view. Since about 1934 I have been groping toward an approach to the immigrant questions purely from the standpoint of America, of her cultural, spiritual, social, and political future, which I feel will inevitably be affected by them; and the next few chapters are a kind of record of that groping.

A Letter I Did Not Mail

ONE DAY LATE IN THE AUTUMN, 1933, I PICKED UP A BACK NUMBER OF THE *Saturday Evening Post*, which contained a lengthy leading editorial, probably written by the late editor, George Horace Lorimer,[1] on the subject of immigration or, more exactly, "the hordes from southern and eastern Europe" that had entered the country since the 1880's. Most of these foreigners, it appeared, were evil, lawless individuals of "unassimilable blood strains," who made it necessary for good old-stock Americans to maintain ever larger police organizations and no end of jails. Worse yet, these aliens (and apparently from Mr. Lorimer's point of view, they were "aliens" whether naturalized or not) had the tendency to procreate at a terrific rate, and decent, well-to-do native citizens were forced to pay ever higher taxes for schools and other institutions in which the otherwise respectable communities had to "feed, wash, and disinfect" the immigrants' nasty, unsound progeny, lest it contaminate the clean, healthy children of more fortunate origin.

The point of the article was that immigrants, especially those from eastern and southern Europe, were a very bad thing for America. During the current Depression they cost the country more than they had benefitted it in good times.

The editorial irked me a little when I first read it, then I dismissed it from my mind as something too stupid and un-American to be taken seriously by any considerable number of the American people. In the next few weeks, however, my attention was drawn to other pieces of propaganda clearly designed to create prejudice against the immigrant and his American-born children, who were also discussed as aliens or foreigners. In fact, a growing movement appeared to be on foot to "save America for *real* Americans" and to send or drive as many of the immigrants as possible "back where they came from."

There was a circular distributed by a "patriotic" organization in Chicago urging old-stock Americans to bring pressure upon Congress and the Administration in Washington to put a heavy tax upon certain classes of immigrants. From other leaflets, "confidential" letters, and newspaper and magazine clippings it was evident that in a number of states agitation was in progress to compel every foreigner, citizen or not, to be fingerprinted; and that dozens of small fascist organizations scattered the country over were stirring intolerance against foreign groups in the United States. I saw a copy of an anonymous chain letter then being circulated in several states with the injunction "Send this on to six other patriotic, eagle-eyed Americans; don't break the chain!"—and the "never-to-be-forgotten message" of the letter was that "*real* Americans" must wake up and join in the "war against tolerance of foreigners residing in their communities or in *our* country."

[1] Died 1937.

The phraseology of one or two of the circulars and the chain letter resembled in spots the *Satevepost* editorial, while one "strictly confidential" letter quoted from it; so I started a letter to Editor Lorimer, intending to send it to him attached to his editorial:

I am writing this to you as an immigrant, one of the thirteen or fourteen million people now living in America who were not born here. I claim a right to speak for several million Slavic immigrants and their American-born children; particularly for those who call themselves Yugoslavs.

I am a Yugoslav by origin. I have been here more than twenty years. But men of my race were sailors on Columbus' ships when he bumped into this continent. Yugoslavs from Dalmatia were in California decades before the Yankees. They were pioneers in the now important California industry of fruit-growing. If you wish to know more of these early Californians, I refer you to Jack London's *Valley of the Moon*.

In the 1880's the Yugoslavs, like the Poles, Czechs, Slovaks, Finns, Lithuanians, Russians, Rumanians, Italians, Jews, and other peoples from the Balkans and eastern Europe, commenced to come over in "hordes," to work in America's mines, forests, and steel-mills. In many cases they came largely because American industry pleaded for workers. For sixty years my people have been digging no end of coal and ore, felling and sawing no end of timber, and making no end of steel the country over. Ask any steel-mill superintendent or boss and he will tell you that without the Slavic immigrants steel-making in this country would not be what it is—and steel is the most important item in American industry today. Some steel men go so far as to say that, in very large part, America is the foremost steel country in the world because Slavs have been working in her steel mills these several decades.

Now, when the *Satevepost* chooses to insult us editorially, there is not a single steel building, a single steel bridge, a single mile of railroad anywhere in this country in which some of my fellow immigrants' energy is not frozen. You, Mr. Lorimer, can dismiss this contribution to America's present-day greatness only if your sense of values is such that you have nothing but contempt for hard and dangerous manual labor.

But my immigrant group's contribution to this country's current magnificence is not only on the side of brawn and hard manual labor. If mining and steel production in America is more efficient in 1934 than it was in 1884, it is partly because "Hunkie" workers and foremen in the mines and mills have invented thousands of devices now employed in our mining and steel centers. It might be instructive to you, Mr. Lorimer, to scan the United States Government patent records and note the numerous Slavic names under which the inventions are registered.

Michael Pupin, without whose inventions radio and long-distance telephony would be far less efficient, is a Yugoslav immigrant. So is Nikola Tesla, who from the viewpoint of individual achievement doubtless is the most important man alive in America today. His motors run practically everything that moves in this country, from sewing machines to battleships, from gramophones to the presses that turn out your magazines. Thomas Edison referred to Tesla as an inventor and scientist of genius.

In the field of education our "unassimilable blood strain" gave to America Dr. Henry Suzzallo, until his recent death president of the Carnegie Foundation for the Advancement of Teaching, who was born in California of Yugoslav (not Italian, as erroneously assumed by the American press) parents, whose name in the old country had been Zucalo, which is common in Herzegovina.

The *Satevepost*, I assume, regards America's participation in the World War highly. Well, hundreds of thousands of us immigrants from southern and eastern Europe were in that war on the side of America. The only man who received two Congressional Medals of Honor for his part in it was a Yugoslav, Captain Louis Cukela of the Marines, a native of Dalmatia. Two other Yugoslavs, Alex Mandusich and Jacob Mestrovich, also received the Congressional Medal of Honor; the latter posthumously.

But enough of this. . . .

Mr. Lorimer, with your peculiar sense of values, you may succeed temporarily in making some of my people feel unwanted in America, inferior in the face of American social realities; you and others like you may distress them to the extent that they will return to the old country or commit suicide (as not a few of the immigrants are doing these days); but more and more of us are beginning to feel that, by virtue of our creative achievements here, to which we can point wherever we look, we have earned the right to belong here, that America is our country perhaps as much as anyone else's; that we are the New Americans—and as such we are becoming increasingly cognizant of both our duties and privileges here.

It is true, Mr. Lorimer, that some of my fellow immigrants and their American-born children, turn to crime; but in many cases that is due to the feeling of inferiority which such intolerance as that of the *Satevepost* imposes upon them. As a natural reaction to intolerance toward us on the part of native Americans some of us become anti-social or refuse to be "assimilated." But let me add that, if one is to believe the official crime and delinquency statistics, proportionately fewer immigrants and immigrants' children serve jail and penitentiary terms than do old-stock citizens.

It is true that some of the immigrants' children have to be "washed, fed and disinfected" in schools and other public institutions, but in most cases that is because they have been born in poverty, although their parents have worked hard whenever they had a chance to work—and that poverty is not their fault. On the other hand, I am personally and intimately familiar with foreign settlements which include dwellings that are as pleasant to the eye, nose, and mind as any in this country among people on the lower economic levels. I think that even you would be entirely comfortable, if you gave yourself a chance, in the home of my fellow countryman John Troha, a steel worker in Strabane, Pennsylvania, whose guest I was recently.

I believe that you know nothing about the "hordes from eastern and southern Europe"—not really. So far as it may be judged from the contents of your magazine, you don't want to know anything. Off and on you print a "Hunkie" novelette in which the characters and situations have no relation to the life of actual Slavic immigrants in the mill and mining towns. Your purpose, obviously, is to present the immigrant here as a curious animal and put him in an even more inferior position than he already is in.

Why do you do that? ——

I never finished the letter and, of course, I did not send it to Mr. Lorimer. I was too angry and, writing, I suddenly realized the great man might never see it, anyhow; and if he did see it, it would do no good, for he doubtless was fully convinced and sincere. Instead, I wrote a short article for a magazine called *Common Sense*, which was later reprinted on the English pages of a number of foreign-language newspapers, and I received several resolutions of various immigrant fraternal lodges expressing their appreciation, which pleased me deeply.

At the same time, however, I was uneasy both about the letter I had meant to write and the article I published. They were part of my groping toward an approach to the immigrant question, and, I felt, all wrong. They were defensive. I had written them mainly as an immigrant, not purely as an American. In this I had made the mistake common to immigrants who replied to alien-baiters (and I publish my unfinished letter in this book as an example of how this problem ought not to be dealt with). But what to do about alien-baiting? What was alien-baiting?

These questions, which were really one question, disturbed me throughout the Depression. By-and-by it became clear to me that alien-baiting was a complicated business. Perhaps its most important motivating element was the already-mentioned fear, conscious and unconscious, on the part of numerous old-stock Americans that their America was changing in ways undesirable to them; and being involved in alien-baiting was, of course, also an example of what I called the country's basic incongruity, of which this Depression was a symptom or manifestation, and which created the need of scapegoats.

A man like George Horace Lorimer was at once a product and a victim of America's fundamental incongruity, as well as its unconscious servant. He was afraid not only that the country was changing racially, but even more of the Depression and what it might lead to. It was full of dangers; anything might happen. The situation must be quickly confused, blamed on something or somebody. So, consciously or semi-unconsciously, he chose the helpless "hordes from southern and eastern Europe" to be the scapegoat.

It occurred to me that what was needed was not a reply to the alien-baiters, but an analysis of the alien as a scapegoat. I felt that through such an analysis one might find an approach to the problem of the immigrant and America as a whole.

The Peril of the Alien as a Scapegoat

> *Give me your tired, your poor,*
> *Your huddled masses yearning to breathe free,*
> *The wretched refuse of your teeming shore,*
> *Send these, the homeless, the tempest-tost, to me:*
> *I lift my lamp beside the golden door.*

THESE WORDS BY EMMA LAZARUS ON THE BASE OF THE STATUE OF LIBERTY ONCE had vital meaning in America. Immediately behind the great goddess, Ellis Island was one of the liveliest, most colorful places in the world. In 1910 immigrants were pouring through it at the rate of seventy thousand a *month* and Americans proudly spoke of their country as The Melting Pot. Of course many foreigners returned to their native lands after being here for a few years, and some (mostly criminals) were deported; but by the side of the in-rushing flood the emigrant and deportee totals were negligible before the War and for a while even after it.

Beginning in 1924, however, the quota system reduced Ellis Island's importance as a receiving depot. Most immigrants, having been "passed" by American consuls abroad before starting over, plunged into Coolidge Prosperity right off the boat. The famous island commenced to slip into reverse. More and more, thanks to the postwar anti-alien hysteria and the deportation laws enacted during and soon after the War, its business became the expulsion of foreigners.

Already in 1925 more than 9,000 were sent at Uncle Sam's expense back to "where they came from," while about an equal number of aliens "deported" themselves after having been told they were subject to deportation and would be deported unless they went "voluntarily." The business got into full swing while "Puddler Jim" Davis, himself an immigrant, and William Doak, a rabid xenophobe, were Secretaries of Labor under Coolidge and Hoover, respectively. Doak took personal charge of deportations and devoted most of his time and energy to them. In 1929 the total number of expulsions and "voluntary departures" was 39,000, while during 1930-33 it averaged 29,000 a year. Under the New Deal the annual totals have been about 17,000.

Now, as I write this book, almost no immigrants go through Ellis Island in person; only their records are filed there. The island is America's chief deportation depot. At frequent intervals trainloads of deportees from points west roll to the edge of New Jersey, whence they are ferried to the island, and thence returned to the lands of their origin; while smaller groups of deportees come also from New England and up-state New York, and the ferryboat *Ellis Island* brings them from New York City and environs.

Not only Ellis Island but the whole trend of migration has been in reverse throughout the Depression. During 1931-36 immigration has been exceeded

195

by aliens' departures from America almost two-to-one. During this entire period (in round figures) only 159,000 immigrants came in as against 300,000 going out!

Other causes too are helping to reduce the country's alien population. (I write in the present tense, for the process is bound to continue for several years after this book appears.) Each year in the last half-decade an average of 120,000 persons have been naturalized, thus ceasing to be aliens. This number is destined to increase; for of the aliens now here about 1,500,000 have applied for citizenship. Also nearly half of our aliens are over fifty years old, and death takes no holiday. Just how many unnaturalized foreigners have died since the 1930 census is not easy to estimate, but this is certain—their number was high and, say, during 1938-50 alien mortality will increase at an ever-rising rate.

Nor is there any doubt that we have in America today only about 4,300,000 aliens (slightly over three per cent of our total population) as against approximately six million five years ago; and that, at this rate, in another decade the number will have reduced itself under a million, or below one-half of one per cent of our population.

In short, the so-called alien problem is in the main solving itself. No one of any influence in America today seems to want to raise again the old "Welcome!" sign; reports of our unemployment situation have greatly reduced the number of people in Europe who want to come here; and resumption of mass immigration is out of the question for a long time to come, probably forever.

In itself the alien question—as distinguished from the bigger problem of national integration (to be discussed in the next chapter)—has thus become one of the minor problems now before America. Furthermore, the alien himself is no menace to anything sound in the land. There are elements connected with the alien problem, however, that constitute an extremely ugly situation, which is perilous to America through no direct fault of the aliens themselves.

This peril is due to the fact that Americans, by and large, including many of the legislators—plagued by greater, more obvious problems and, in common with other peoples, guilty of insufficient, too casual interest in their country—are uninformed or misinformed about the alien question; while professional patriots, some disbalanced into fear-driven fascistic fanatics, are exploiting it to their strange ends. In this the patriots are aided by racketeers trading in patriotism; by bombastic, narrow labor-union lobbyists; by reactionary, obscurantist newspaper and magazine publishers and editors; by hack journalists eager to put their names to anything that sells; by would-be politicians using the American Legion and kindred organizations to promote their personal aspirations; and by a few members of Congress seeking national publicity.

Together, these individuals bedevil Congress as a whole with their flag-waving and their exaggerations and inaccuracies about the alien problem and obscure it and make it worse. They impede the intelligent efforts of experienced public servants whose job it is to deal with it, and they obstruct those working for sensible legislation needed to cope with recently developed immigration and deportation situations. They are generally doing their best to spread alien-hatred and, through it, the mutual distrust of American citizens of diverse racial and national strains, thus retarding the process toward a desirable homogeneity of our population; and to induce the Government to violate America's traditions of fairness, decency, humanity, and tolerance in dealing with all the people living within her borders, thereby increasing the complexity of her social, cultural, and spiritual condition in the near and distant future, lessening her ability to deal with it democratically, and threatening to inflict upon her certain characteristics of European fascist states.

To jam my point into a nutshell: it is these people who are the menace, not the alien. Or to put it in another way: it is not the alien who is the menace, but his being made into a scapegoat.

All through the Depression, deportations—which, under existing laws, constitute probably one of the most difficult administrative matters the government in Washington has to face—were the core of the alien situation.

In the last half of the Hoover regime the Department of Labor, which includes the Immigration and Naturalization Service, might well have been called the department of immigration and deportation. Infected by the anti-alien virus, Secretary Doak drew a strange satisfaction out of hounding aliens; raiding homes, wedding parties, and other gatherings in which it was suspected that a foreigner illegally in the country might be present; arresting aliens and others without warrant, requiring them to prove they were here legally, keeping people in detention or under heavy bail for months, putting them through cross-examination; tearing husbands from wives and fathers from children who were either American citizens or legal residents, and deporting them. In many cases the deportations were marked by a cruel disregard of human values which, one may assume, few members of Congress had intended when they enacted the expulsion laws; and some of Doak's agents used these laws to develop lucrative rackets, extorting money from ignorant immigrants whom they threatened to deport even when their status here was perfectly legal. Doak and the Immigration Service were sharply criticized, especially by social workers who came in contact with families left destitute because their bread-winners, many of them people of good character, had been deported, often for technical irregularities in entry which were not their fault but the United States Government's.

When the Franklin Roosevelt Administration came in and Frances Perkins took over the Department of Labor, her first move was to induce Colonel Daniel W. MacCormack of New York to become Commissioner of Immigration and Naturalization, and she wisely gave him a free hand in reorganizing and rehumanizing the Service. Early in 1937 he died in office.

A native of Scotland, in his mid-fifties, with a record of varied administrative, business, and military experiences in many parts of the world, including the Philippines and Panama Canal before the War, France during the War, and Persia and New York after the War, Colonel MacCormack was, as it turned out, the man for the job. Innately a decent human being, resourceful, shrewd, simple, efficient, unexcitable, never dictatorial but always direct and definite in whatever he attempted, he was a conservative by temperament, but not without strong liberal tendencies, which, when accused of them, he called merely "common sense." Adroit even in situations with which he was not intimate, he knew how to handle men by tactful persuasion and enjoyed seeing their good qualities come out. Doing a good job at anything he tackled seemed to be one of his passions. The others were liberty, democracy, human decency, and law, which he believed to be the principles and mainstays of Americanism. In short, a very unusual man—though I felt on our first encounter as if I had known him all my life.

Soon after taking office MacCormack communicated his character, ideas, wishes, and sense of law to the personnel of the Immigration Service. Extra-legal alien-hounding ceased, while effective steps were taken to reduce to a minimum alien-smuggling and individual illegal entries. Deportations continued; for the laws demand them for certain criminals, dope-peddlers, illegal entrants, immoral classes, the insane, those likely to become public charges, or those who have previously been deported, or are without proper visa, or have remained longer than their permit allows them to remain, and so on. But deportations were made as humane as a nasty business of that sort can be, and their number fell appreciably.

The xenophobes, or alien-haters—who had previously been cheering and aiding Doak's illegal raiders, and whom I shall presently introduce—immediately raised a howl. Why this decline in deportations? The jingoist press screamed: Why was the alien scum allowed to remain here while our citizens were jobless?

MacCormack and his assistants explained that, in conjunction with other agencies and forces operating in the world of migration, they had succeeded in drastically reducing illegal entries, which of course reduced the number of deportable aliens. In 1933, under the old regime, the Government spent $247,958 to deport 2,125 Chinese who had illegally entered from Mexico; since then these entries have nearly ceased. Owing to the Immigration Service's greater vigilance, there had been a falling-off in illegal entries of deserting foreign seamen—another reason for fewer expulsions. Also, the Depression had lately begun to remove the incentive not only to lawful immigration but to illegal entries as well: this circumstance had produced a decrease in deportation figures already toward the end of Doak's administration.

The same devotion to law that caused MacCormack to stop illegal raids, searches, and arrests without warrant, made him strongly prejudiced against those who broke laws; and late in 1933 and early in 1934, Congressmen and others interested in deportations were shown that under him the Immigration Service had entered into more systematic co-operation with law-enforcement agencies and prison officials the country over, with the result that the deportation totals include a higher percentage of criminals than ever before. This pleased Congressmen as well as the alien-baiting lobbyists.

Still more pleased were they when MacCormack indicated, with obvious sincerity, that he desired legislation authorizing the expulsion of some 20,000 habitual alien criminals, alien-smugglers, and gangsters known to the Immigration Service but not deportable under existing laws.

The next bit of information, however, that MacCormack gave out explaining why expulsions had fallen off caused the xenophobes to hit the ceiling. He said that the Immigration Service had recently accumulated a number of so-called "hardship cases," in which he had stayed deportation warrants, though the laws required these people to be deported. In staying these expulsions he was disobeying none of the several deportation laws, for they did not say *when* an alien must be deported. He explained that, like most other deportable aliens, these people had been reported to the immigration authorities anonymously by persons who wanted them removed from the communities, in most cases perhaps to get their jobs or because they had had a personal disagreement with them; but that, in the opinion of the Immigration Service, they (these "hardship cases") were people of good character, with nothing against them except that (in the majority of instances) their status in this country was technically irregular. They were people—to quote from one of his statements during a Congressional hearing—"who have been here for many years, and whose wives and families are here, and who have sunk their roots so deeply in the country that to deport them would impose an infinitely greater hardship and punishment upon their wives and children (most of them American citizens), and, as a matter of fact, a punishment on the United States, than upon themselves."

MacCormack made it clear that, in common with the rest of the Immigration Service as it now stood, he did not care to be in the business of uprooting people of good character and breaking up decent families. It was cruel, futile, expensive, stupid. In 1934 there were about 1,200 of these "hardship cases." If deported they would leave here about 1,500 American-born or otherwise legally resident wives and children to become public charges on the United States. "Let us look at this in terms of dollars—1,200 such deportations, at an average rate of $75, cost the Government $90,000 annually. The maintenance of dependents, at an average rate of $8.33 per month per person, would cost the Government $147,800 a year." Besides, many of these people, if deported, would immediately become eligible under existing laws to return on a nonquota visa issued at the instance of their citizen or legally resident kinspeople.

Moreover, some were deportable through little or no fault of their own. Years ago, for example, a woman had entered legally but ignorantly neglected to register her baby; now the child, having a technically illegal status, was deportable. . . . An immigrant here since 1924, father of American-born children, took a trip from a point in Michigan to Rochester, New York, not realizing the train went through a corner of Canada during the night; arriving in Rochester the next morning, he was deportable. . . . An immigrant deserted his wife in Canada, leaving her with two Canadian-born babies, and entered the United States illegally. Determined to find him and make him do the right thing by her, she followed him here with the children, all entering illegally. She found the man, fell ill, and died. He was caught as an illegal entrant and deported. Under the law the children were deportable to Canada, but there was no one there to receive them, except perhaps some orphanage, while in the United States a legally resident sister of their mother was eager to adopt them. . . . Not a few aliens, fathers or mothers of American-born children, thinking they were in America legally, applied for citizenship and, in that connection, discovered their status had some technical flaw, which may not have been their fault at all; and they not only failed to become citizens but were deportable.

In all such instances, if the deportable person was not a criminal or prostitute or dope-peddler, but of proven good character, Colonel MacCormack "stayed" the deportation pending further study of the matter. He said that on the basis of this study, Congress would be asked to pass a bill giving the known "hardship cases" legal immigrant status, and giving the Secretary of Labor, or an interdepartmental commission, limited discretionary power to deport or not in cases to be discovered after the law's enactment.

The xenophobes, as I say, blew up on learning this and began a campaign against MacCormack and his proposals. Though he was an ex-Army officer of high rank and splendid war record, and had been a citizen and public servant most of his life, and his father and grandfather had spent most of their lives in this country and Cuba, while his grand-uncle had fought in the Mexican War, he was denounced as a foreigner, a sentimentalist, an alien-coddler, a communist. What business had he to consider what he called "the human aspects" of these cases? The deportation laws were mandatory. Suppose families *were* separated, what of it? Out with these aliens, regardless of circumstances! The gall of MacCormack and that woman Perkins to want discretionary power in such cases! It was, cried the xenophobes, all a deep-laid un-American plot of the subversive elements—reds, Jews, and so on—to re-open America to mass immigration!

But this first blast of xenophobe wrath was as nothing compared to the bitter struggle that began when, late in 1934, Representative Kerr of North Carolina introduced the new deportation bill prepared by immigration experts in the Department of Labor. As I write, this struggle is still going on. For nearly five years now the battle has been waged in congressional committees, at hearings, on the floors of Congress, behind scenes; over the radio, in public prints, from platforms. . . The full story would require a book by itself.

As leader of the Government forces in this fight, Colonel MacCormack

scored a slight victory in August, 1935, when—after rejecting the Kerr bill—
the House passed a resolution authorizing the stays of the known 2,862 "hardship cases" till March 1, 1936, by which time it hoped to get a bill it could
pass. Congress, however, was extremely busy all spring and when a much-
amended, badly messed-up bill finally came out of the Senate immigration
committee at the very end of the 1936 session, its active opponents, taking
advantage of the congressional eagerness to adjourn, kept it from being voted
upon by threatening a filibuster. Meantime, by July 1936, the number of "hardship cases" reached 3,620. As this book goes to press, nothing has yet been done
about the situation, and the number early in 1938 was probably around seven
thousand, involving some fifteen thousand relatives, most of them American
citizens.

The new Commissioner of Immigration, James L. Houghteling, formerly
an Army captain and Chicago banker and newspaper executive, and also a
highly decent and humane man, who took over the difficult job during the
writing of this book, was expected to follow Colonel MacCormack's policy—
of not deporting "hardship cases" as soon as they are discovered, but taking
temporary advantage of the law's silence as to *when* he must deport them, and
hoping for some sort of act, eventually, from Congress which would cover at
least this phase of the alien situation.

Who, precisely, as I write this, is fighting the Immigration Service's efforts
to humanize the deportation laws? What are the opponents' means and
methods? How much backing have they really among the American people?
Why have they been so effective with Congress thus far?

The first on the list of xenophobes is a Wall Street lawyer, Captain John
B. Trevor, than whom, if a man's love for his country is measurable by his
detestation of all who had the bad taste to be born elsewhere, there probably
is no greater patriot in America to-day. During the late War he was in the
Army intelligence service in New York City, where he did not come in contact with many, if any, of the tens of thousands of foreign-born officers and
soldiers in the American Army, but combated spies and other aliens whose
atrocities were part of one of the dirtiest sideshows of the dirty business of
war. They were probably the first foreigners he had had occasion to study,
and he was not favorably impressed. Another man might have concluded that
war releases the worst in human nature, without respect to race or nationality,
but Trevor charged up everything to the innate depravity of aliens. He discovered the alien problem and resolved on leaving the Army to devote himself to it.

There were others who at the War's end decided that there was an alien
problem demanding attention. That idea was widespread and movements and
rackets grew out of it. "Patriots" made names and fortunes for themselves, but
after immigration was restricted many dropped out of the fight. Trevor remained in it and now—still influenced by war phobias, still believing that

every alien is essentially an enemy alien—is America's alien-baiter No. 1, the most irreconcilable opponent of any attempt on the part of the Government to be humane with the "hardship cases." He apparently believes it is better that a thousand American women and children should suffer than that one alien should escape.

To obtain serious consideration for his views, Trevor, who did not practice law in Wall Street in vain, made use of a group of societies through the familiar device of a holding company, floated, according to holding-company precedent, with a minimum of trouble and cost. He called his holding company the American Coalition and made its object "to co-ordinate the efforts of patriotic, civic, and fraternal societies to keep America American."

Any society eager to keep America American may join, and, according to the Coalition's letterhead, over a hundred were members in 1936 (when I last investigated Captain Trevor's outfit) on the apparent understanding that the expenses of this high effort shall be paid by some person or persons unknown: for there is not a word in the organization's printed constitution concerning dues, assessments, or contributions. The membership is curious and catholic. It includes well-known national societies, and, seemingly with no other object than to make a more impressive showing, local chapters of the same organizations. One of the members is another holding company very like the Coalition itself. This is Allied Patriotic Societies, Inc., of which more in a moment. Other groups listed are either local or obscure. In 1936 I found among them the Aztec Club of 1847, the Betsy Ross Corps, the Chicago Women's Ideal Club, Inc., the Immigration Study Commission, the Rhode Island Association of Patriots, the Ridgewood Unit of Republican Women, Inc., the Westchester Security League, the Wheel of Progress, and the Old Glory Club of Flatbush, Inc., Beacon No. 1. A specialist in patriotism might be able to explain the aims and activities of these organizations; my own erudition—like that, I wager, of the average Congressman—does not extend so far.

The Coalition's organization, albeit scarcely logical or democratic, is simplicity itself. Its affairs are managed nominally by a board of directors consisting of the executive officer and one other delegate representing each of the member societies. Under this system the National Sojourners have only the same number of votes as the Chicago Women's Ideal Club, and the Old Glory Club of Flatbush, Inc., Beacon No. 1, is as influential as the Veterans of Foreign Wars. Not only that, but the three local chapters of the National Sojourners listed as members, with a total of six delegates, can outvote their own national organization which has only two. Would this system of representation be tolerated in an organization transacting serious business in which the constituent societies were deeply interested? The fact that it is continued without objection is evidence, I think, that the Coalition is not considered important by its own members, or that its operations are more or less entrusted to the discretion of the leader.

The board thus constituted is convened once a year in a meeting which may or may not be attended by delegates from all the societies. It elects a president, four vice-presidents, and an executive committee of not less than ten, or more than fifteen members. The president and vice-presidents are ex-officio members of this committee, which meets "upon the call of the president" and "conducts the affairs of the Coalition with full powers of the board of directors between meetings of the board." For all effective purposes the thing boils down to this executive committee of not more than fifteen members, dominated by the president, who, annually re-elected without opposition, is Captain Trevor.

Detailed information concerning the Coalition's finances, if available, would be interesting. The member societies, apparently, contribute only their moral support. The Coalition at one time solicited, and perhaps still solicits, money from individuals. One might become a contributing member, without vote or any voice in the management, by paying annual dues of $10. An associate membership, also without voting privileges, costs $25 a year. To become a patron costs $100 per annum. For $250 one might be listed as a life member; for $500, an associate benefactor; for $1,000, a benefactor. In the absence of any published information, we can assume that the bulk of the Coalition's expenses are paid by the great patriot himself or such of his friends as approve of his methods for keeping America from going Albanian.

But whoever pays the bills, and whatever may be said of the scheme of organization and control of this patriotic holding company, it serves the purpose for which it was designed. It enables Captain Trevor to appear before Committees of Congress and before the public in the rôle of spokesman for scores of societies, all with some claim to consideration, many of them important numerically and by reason of the character of their members; while his contacts with these groups also afford him opportunities for propaganda in support of his personal views on aliens and immigration.

When a bill is introduced in Congress to which Trevor objects he sends to his member societies a brief, usually incomplete summary, with the assurance that it undermines the principle of keeping America American, and with the suggestion that letters and telegrams denouncing it be promptly addressed to members of Congress: which too is standard holding-company practice, though perhaps not so effective today as it once was. He then appears at committee hearings and expresses the same views on behalf of the Coalition.

Next on the roster of America's xenophobes is Francis H. Kinnicutt, who is as gifted as Trevor in the application of the methods of high finance to the field of patriotic endeavor. He is president of Allied Patriotic Societies, Inc., a holding company similar to the Coalition, but by no means its rival. Collaboration of the two is so intimate that some organizations listed on the Coalition's letterhead appear also on Kinnicutt's as members of his merger, which, as already mentioned, itself is named on the Coalition's.

Major General Amos A. Fries (Retired), personally delightful, honest, sincere, distinguished on the military side as an expert on poison gas and politically as an unrelenting foe of communism, is another valuable side-kick (to use an old Army expression) of Captain Trevor's. Representing now the American Coalition, then the National Sojourners or the Sons of the American Revolution, he is one of the nervous patriots who are determined to save the country from Communism and protect its liberties if they have to register, index and cross-index, fingerprint, gag, blindfold, and handcuff every man, woman, and child in the United States, to do it.

For many years one of the leading anti-aliens in Washington was William C. Hushing, lobbyist of the American Federation of Labor, who strongly attacked all efforts to humanize deportation laws.

The American Legion has xenophobic tendencies. In 1935-36 H. L. Chaillaux, director of its National Americanism Commission, was an aggressive anti-alien operating nationally, but he by no means succeeded in forcing his interpretation of Americanism on all—or nearly all—Legionnaires, as witness the splendid pamphlet *Americanism: What Is It?* by Cyrus LeRoy Baldridge, of the Americanism Committee of the New York County American Legion, which Chaillaux tried vainly to suppress because it endorsed democracy, equality of opportunity and before the law, freedom of speech and press, and other such old American idealistic standbys. But at his height as a xenophobe Chaillaux had alien-baiting Legionnaires active in many parts of the country, who used the alien as a pretext for patriotic utterances which got them into papers, to the attention of political bosses, and onto the limelit road to public office.

I have mentioned George Horace Lorimer in the preceding chapter. He died during the writing of this book, but his *Satevepost*—under the new editor, Wesley Winans Stout—goes bravely, patriotically on its alien-baiting way. During 1934-37 the Hearst newspapers were notoriously xenophobe. Ditto Bernarr Macfadden's *Liberty* magazine. In 1937 the Scripps-Howard columnist, General Hugh Johnson, was bitten by the anti-alien bug.

All through the Depression scores of publications printed editorials and articles on the alien situation which were full of exaggeration and inaccuracies. Here are a few "facts" and "ideas" that, thanks to these publications, have been drifting through the country between 1930 and 1938:

The number of aliens in the United States is from six to twenty million, of whom from three to ten million are here illegally and subject to deportation. I already have given the actual number of aliens—which, to repeat, is being rapidly reduced. There, naturally, are no statistics covering aliens without legal status, but immigration experts believe that their total probably is below 100,000.

One million alien seamen enter American ports annually and fifty per cent of them remain here illegally. The truth is that less than 250,000 enter annually and only some 250 stay.

Nearly all aliens are criminally inclined and our prisons are full of them. The number of alien criminals and gangsters (as this word is loosely used in various localities) is considerable. Professor Kenneth Colegrove of Northwestern University informs me that some 2,800 alien criminals and gangsters who are not deportable under present laws are operating in the Chicago area alone. But, to repeat, the truth is also that the percentage of criminality is *lower* among aliens and foreign-born generally than among native Americans. For details see the well-known Wickersham Report and the figures of the United States Department of Justice.

Most of the reds or Communists in this country are aliens. Actually, America's two outstanding "Communist" leaders, Foster and Browder, are natives, with long backgrounds in New England and Kansas, respectively; while most of the party membership is also native. Our three leading "Marxist" literary critics, Granville Hicks, Malcolm Cowley, and Newton Arvin, are also of old New England stock. Besides, Communism is not an alien philosophy; it was practiced in numerous "communities" in America long before anyone gave it serious thought in Europe.

From three to five million aliens are in jobs which rightfully belong to citizens now out of work because of them. Of the 4,300,000 aliens in America at this writing about half are women, who are preponderantly housewives, and thus outside the competition for industrial jobs, as are at least 150,000 of their children who are listed as aliens. Nearly half of the male aliens are over fifty, most of them probably unemployable and supported by their American-born children, or on relief. In other words, there are perhaps less than a million aliens holding or competing for jobs. Which automatically disposes of the next xenophobe "fact":

Millions of aliens are on relief. Formerly when a Depression came hundreds of thousands of imigrant workers promptly returned to their old countries for the period of its duration, because it was cheaper to pay passage, live at home for a while, and then re-migrate when the "panic" passed, than to stay in the United States. When the 1930-37 Depression began rather fewer aliens left, because many of them had married during the prosperous years and acquired homes, steamship rates had increased, there was danger of war and other unfavorable political conditions in the Old World, and—most important of all—the new immigration laws would not permit them to return to America. Result: not a few aliens *are* or *were* on relief. Just how many nobody knows. The relief administrators properly paid no heed to whether a person needing relief was an alien or not: for aliens too have a stake in this country. Did they not in recent decades (as suggested in the preceding chapter) do much of the heavy and dirty work in the building of America as she stands today? Are they and their fellow-aliens not subject to the same taxes as the native-born? Are they not entitled to aid in continuing their mere existence when the country has stumbled into a crisis, which is probably due in part to the fact that immigrant workers had worked too hard, for too low wages, in the past?

The best way to end the Depression would be to deport all the foreigners. This is the most fantastic of xenophobe ideas. In September 1936, as reported in the New York *Times*, the United Spanish War Veterans adopted a resolution recommending the deportation of ten million aliens, or nearly six million

more than the actual number. Such mass deportations would dislocate the life
of scores of American cities and towns where the aliens now live; break up
over a million families, which include four or five million American citizens;
involve a transportation problem unprecedented in the history of mankind, and
create international complications that stagger imagination. . . .

But enough of this nonsense. Our xenophobes get hack journalists to write
articles on the subject, supplying them with their curious material, and thus
the ground is prepared for racketeers-in-patriotism, who start fake societies
and leagues for the deportation and suppression of aliens and the salvation of
America. There are scores of such rackets operating in various parts of the
country, mulcting uninformed, well-meaning patriots, and of course not really
doing anything to suppress or deport the aliens or save America. In 1936 one
of these outfits, run by four men with previous police records, was uncovered
in Philadelphia, after considerable sums had been extracted from prominent
people in that city.

And, finally, we have the xenophobe Congressmen, who are few but not
unimportant; almost all of them Southerners—doubtless because in the South
there are very few foreign-born voters and native voters of recent-immigrant
stock who might resent alien-baiting. A few hate the alien honestly, sincerely,
stupidly; others use him cunningly to emphasize their patriotism and make
themselves, through publicity in the xenophobe press, into statesmen of national
caliber.

Of course the overwhelming majority of members of Congress—truly re-
flecting in this the majority of the American people—are not alien-baiters, but
are hard-pressed, over-busy men and women, all too apt to be influenced by
well-directed propaganda, especially when accompanied by flag-waving on the
part of people who claim to speak for more than a hundred societies, or for the
American Legion, or for organized labor. Some Congressmen too—although
they were bestowing new powers on the President and other Government officials right along—resented the fact (which Trevor & Co. had pointed out to
them) that the new bills aimed to give the Secretary of Labor discretionary
power in the "hardship cases," and rose to denounce this attempt to take away
from Congress its direct authority in immigration matters. The result was that
during 1934-37 Congress as a whole was considerably confused and rather
angry about the deportation and immigration bills; and, in the face of greater
questions, was also somewhat indifferent to them. And thus the alien mess,
so far as needed legislation is concerned, was in 1937 where it was in 1934—
with thousands of people of good character, including thousands of American
citizens, involved in the "hardship cases" dangling in uncertainty, and the
Immigration Service badly handicapped in dealing with alien matters; while
the strange "patriots" and their camp-followers were busy trying to turn the
alien problem (even if unconsciously) into a wedge to open the way to methods
of government now in effect under European dictatorships.

The alien-baiting in America immediately after the War was an aftermath of the war madness, a symptom of general postwar uneasiness and disorientation. The 1933-37 xenophobia was, as already hinted, a product of the socio-economic crisis of this decade, and of the various fears among the dominant economic and cultural groups in the country. These fears led them to think and act in ways wholly out of line with traditional Americanism. They had to have a scapegoat. The alien situation, as we have seen, lends itself readily to "patriotic" exploitation. Out of it were evolved such "facts" and "ideas" as I have quoted, and were used to obscure and confuse the bigger problems and situations.

Therein—at the risk of overemphasizing the purpose of this chapter—lies the menace, not of the alien, but of the alien problem, which now, as I have already suggested, is in itself of relatively minor and declining importance.

I am an ex-alien who became an American citizen while in the United States Army during the late War, and the views expressed here are only my own. I represent no one and nothing—except, I hope, a certain emotion for this land of my adoption which is an amalgam of love and hope, and on which I have no monopoly. In a way perhaps this emotion is a logical extension and revision of the feeling and thought expressed in the inscription on the Statue of Liberty. It has to do with the America of to-day, which—as I shall say again and elaborate in the next chapter—is an extension not only of the British Isles and the Netherlands but of other parts of Europe, to say nothing of Africa and of Asia; and whose potentialities as such are immense, exciting, and inspiring.

I am deeply mindful of the fact that one-third of our population is of recent, largely non-Anglo-Saxon immigrant stock, the beginning of whose background in this country is Ellis Island rather than Plymouth Rock. I belong to this numerous new element; but I am not for it as it is, as against the old American stock as *it* is, nor the other way about. I am for the whole of present-day America, not as something that is finished and satisfactory, for I have been stressing the country's deep incongruity and its manifestations—but as material out of which the future has to be wrought, as something in the process of becoming. And I am against those who blindly and ignorantly or selfishly and cunningly try to harm or destroy that material, impede that process.

America is only beginning, and every beginning is somewhat of a mess. As I have tried to show in my novel *Grandsons*, human America is chopped up into numerous racial, class, and cultural islands surrounded by vague seas, with scant connection and communication among them. The old Melting Pot or Crucible idea has not been carried out any too well. Human America is poorly integrated, and I am for integration and homogeneity, for the disappearance of the now sharply defined, islandlike groups, and the gradual, organic merging of all the groups into a nation that culturally and spiritually will be a fusion of all the races and nations now in the United States on the general politico-cultural pattern laid out by the earliest immigrants to this continent and their descendants. Hence my entrance into this quarrel with the alien-baiters.

Their doings are directed not only at the helpless unnaturalized alien, but also at the naturalized foreign-born and the tens of millions of native children and grandchildren of immigrants—as witness Captain Trevor's contemptuous remark during a congressional hearing, "New York is a foreign city." Consciously or otherwise, the xenophobes oppose the Melting Pot process toward integration and homogeneity, now painfully continuing or commencing in various parts of the country. They aim to keep the population chopped up into racial-cultural islands and to whip the seas of vague distrust surrounding them into active antagonism.

I did not exaggerate when I said early in this chapter that the xenophobes were trying to induce the Government to violate officially the country's traditions of fairness and decency; nor when, later, I remarked that they were trying to make the alien problem a wedge for the opening of the way to fascism. They are the boys who are aware of the country's basic incongruity and don't like it any more than I do, but they—stupidly, un-American fashion—want to abolish it by abolishing what democracy there is. They heil-ed Doak when his agents raided immigrants' wedding parties, and now lead or support local and national movements to register and fingerprint all aliens and require them to carry identification cards and report personally every so often to the local police or postmaster. Several bills with these provisions were introduced in Congress during 1933-37. Once aliens are required to carry cards and report periodically, it may not be long before the rest of the population will have to do the same, and each of us will have a dossier filed somewhere without knowing what it contains and be in the general predicament of people now living in fascistic countries or in Russia.

Fascists and reactionaries the world over incline to be careless with facts; our xenophobes are no exception. They yelled that MacCormack was leading a fight to open the gates to mass immigration. Actually, he was in favor not only of restricted but of selective immigration and, as I have shown, was seeking authority for the deportation of 20,000 alien criminals, gangsters, and professional alien-smugglers undeportable under present laws. Actually too, as I have also said, no one else of any influence wants mass immigration resumed.

Personally, I am against mass immigration, not because we already have millions of people unemployed, but for two other, I think more important, reasons. First: America needs to give herself a chance, to take time to merge and integrate her population, study herself and determine what she really is, and gain some control over her cultural destiny. Second: America has been too long a vent for European discontent. Let the European masses for the time stay where they are, without chance of escape; and let them bring their socio-economic-political-cultural crisis, which is at least a hundred years old, to a head and solve their problems while we work out our own. I believe that by adopting this policy we shall, in the long run, be doing the best we can for the future of Europe and America and all humanity. I agree with Struthers Burt who says—in his book *Escape from America*—that "the only possible hope for an intelligent internationalism in the future is an intelligent nationalism in the present."

During 1934-36 Colonel MacCormack was criticized by people in his own camp on the score that to win support for his "hardship cases" he was putting too much emphasis on the alien criminal, and thereby perhaps helped to enhance the impression in certain quarters that *alien* and *criminal* are practically synonyms. There was some ground for this criticism; in fairness to his memory it must be said, however, that he wanted to deport as many alien criminals as possible not merely because they were criminals, but because as such they gave a bad name to the foreign-born at large and thus helped the xenophobes, and were—with native gangsters and such people as I have described in the chapter on Dan Hennessy—material for fascistic terrorist organizations.

But, be that as it may, I hope that before this book is very long in print, Congress will be able to bring itself to ignore the xenophobes, who probably do not represent five per cent of the American people, and do something humane and intelligent about the "hardship cases." If a popular vote were taken on the issue, I wager that after hearing the truth the overwhelming majority of citizenry would be in favor of—in fact, would insist on—turning the "hardship cases" into legal immigrants (charging them against the respective quotas), with opportunity to become citizens. Here and there in America the foreign-born *are* looked at askance, but less so, I am convinced, than in other countries. By and large, there is here little active antagonism to them. On the whole the American masses are friendly and tolerant.

The professional alien-baiters oppose touching any of the existing immigration, exclusion and deportation laws. Their fear is that some one, somehow, will pull a trick on them and open the gates to mass immigration. The fact of the matter, however, is that the legal scheme under which the United States Immigration Service operates is fantastically complicated, full of contradictions; so that only an expert can see that it was not devised by a madman. And, speaking for myself, I suggest that the President eventually appoint a commission— consisting of intelligent and humane patriots, with a sense for present-day America and for her future—to study the whole complex subject of alien and immigration questions, with the purpose of recommending to Congress a measure which would replace the numerous immigration laws, good and bad, now scattered through the statute books; officially recognize the inadvisability of a resumption of mass immigration; provide asylum for certain political refugees; simplify naturalization; put Ellis Island, not out of reverse, but largely out of business, by reducing—through prevention—to the absolute minimum illegal entries and thereby necessary deportation; hasten the disappearance of the alien problem and, so far as possible, the dangerous alien-baiters I have introduced here; and get the Melting Pot really going.

Thirty Million New Americans

WITHIN ITS POPULATION OF SLIGHTLY LESS THAN ONE HUNDRED AND THIRTY million, the United States has today over thirty million citizens—the overwhelming majority of them young citizens—who are the American-born children of immigrant parents of various nationalities: German, Italian, Polish, Czech, Slovak, Serbian, Croatian, Slovenian, Bulgarian, Jewish, Russian, Carpatho-Russian, Ukrainian, Lithuanian, Finnish, Hungarian, Norwegian, Swedish, Danish, Dutch, French, Flemish, Spanish, Portugese, Rumanian, Armenian, Syrian, Lett, Albanian, Greek, Turkish, and, of course, English, Scotch, and Irish. The country as a whole is but dimly cognizant of this fact and its implications which, in my opinion, are of fundamental and urgent importance in America's contemporary social and cultural scene. It should perhaps particularly interest those Americans who consider themselves of the old Anglo-Saxon stock: for here is a tremendous new element—what will it do to the old stock?—to the country?—how will it affect the development of civilization and culture, of racial types on this continent?

These questions had vaguely interested and perturbed me already in the late 1920's and the earliest 1930's, but I did not really go into them till 1934. I have told that in the spring of that year I went on a lecture tour. It took me to the great industrial centers of New York State, New Jersey, Pennsylvania, Ohio, Michigan, Illinois, Indiana, Wisconsin, and Minnesota, where the population is preponderantly "foreign." Actually, however, my trip was not so much a series of speaking engagements as an attempt—a device—to get some clear idea, if possible, of this immense mass of so-called "second-generation" citizens, numerically predominant in some of the most important cities and towns, whom I choose to designate the New Americans. I spoke, or rather tried to speak, more or less on the subject of this chapter, to about fifty audiences of anywhere from one hundred to twenty-five hundred men and women and young people, in big towns like Pittsburgh, Cleveland, Akron, Detroit, Chicago, South Bend, Milwaukee, St. Paul, and Duluth, and smaller communities like McKeesport, Canonsburg, Ambridge, Farrell, Sharon, and Strabane, Pennsylvania; Lorain, Ohio; Flint, Michigan; and Hibbing and Eveleth, Minnesota. Some of my audiences were almost wholly "foreign," others mixed "foreign" and old-stock American. At the time I knew very little about the subject; I merely sensed its importance; and, to keep going for an hour or so, I discussed things more or less akin to it and at the end, admitting my ignorance, invited my listeners to get up and say anything they liked in relation to my remarks. Those who were too diffident to talk in a crowd, I asked to speak to me after the lecture or to call me at the hotel or write me a letter. Many of them, both old-stock Americans and New Americans, responded to this invitation. Some of them then asked me to their homes. Others wrote me long letters. And the result was that before my tour was half over I began to think that these New Americans—twenty-six million of them in 1930 and increasing at the rate of perhaps more than a million a year—constituted one of the greatest and most basic problems in this country; in some respects, greater and more basic perhaps than, say, the problem of unemployment, and almost as urgent.

This problem has existed, in nearly the same proportions that it exists today, for a long time, but few people have shown eagerness and ability to deal with it in a broad, fundamental way, or even to discuss it. Much attention—most of it, as already suggested, ill-focused—has been paid to the problem of the foreign-born; but not to that of their children, the American-born second generation. There is no acute or intelligent appreciation of it. Very little is being done about it; and the longer it is neglected the worse it will become, both for the New Americans and in the long run for America as a whole.

In this chapter it is not my ambition to present the problem in all its details, ramifications, significances, for it is a vastly complicated one and different in every locality and in every racial group; and, frankly, I still have a great deal to learn about it. My purpose here is merely to give as strong and broad a general suggestion as I can of its character and what I think might be done concerning it.

The chief and most important fact (the only one I shall stress here) about the New Americans is that all too many of them are oppressed by feelings of inferiority in relation to their fellow-citizens of older stock, to the main stream of American life, and to the problem of life as a whole; which, of course, is bad for them as individuals, but, since there are so many of them and their number is still rapidly increasing, even worse for the country.

These feelings of inferiority are to some degree extensions of their parents' feelings of inferiority as immigrants in a country so drastically different from their native lands. The fathers and mothers of these millions of New Americans were naturally at a disadvantage even in the most friendly surroundings, and the surroundings were seldom wholly and continually friendly. As foreigners, in many cases not speaking the English language, they occupied inferior positions in the country's social, economic, and political life. Most of them were workers, performing, by and large, the meanest tasks and receiving meager wages. All too often in one form or another, they bumped up against racial or general anti-immigrant prejudice. Old-stock American workers looked askance at them. When work slackened, they were laid off, as I suggest in the first chapter of this section, before the native employees. Many of them lived in the worst districts of their cities and towns, and were called Hunkies or Bohunks, Squareheads, Dagoes or Wops, Polacks or Litvaks, Sheenies or Kikes. They were frequently—and unavoidably—discriminated against. And, in the face of all this, they inevitably felt, as individuals and as members of their immigrant groups, somewhat inferior in their relation to America and to other people here, and their tendency was to segregate themselves and mingle as much as possible only with their own nationals. And, just as inevitably, that feeling and that tendency were extended to the children, these New Americans, who shared their parents' lives and experiences, and who too were (and still are) called Hunkies or Dagoes by children of Anglo-Saxon origin, and whose names—names like Zamblaoskas, Krmpotich, and Wojiezkowski—were (and are) subjects for jokes on the part of ignorant teachers, at which the whole school laughed.

But in this respect the majority of New Americans, as individuals, are in an even more unfortunate and uncomfortable position than were (or still are) their immigrant parents. The latter, even if they were uneducated peasants or laborers, living here on the lowest social-economic levels, had in them a consciousness, or at least a powerful instinctive feeling, of some kind of racial or cultural background. They knew who they were. They remembered their native lands. They were Italians or Croatians, Finns or Slovenians; and that meant something to them. Many came from countries which culturally and perhaps in some other respects were superior to the United States, which as a new country had not yet had time to develop along those lines; and when oppressed by feelings of inferiority induced by their circumstances in America, could take partial refuge in their racial and cultural backgrounds. Some of the better educated ones, who did not have merely instinctive feelings about the culture and history of their old countries, but were also intellectually conscious of their heritage, could even look down upon America and consider themselves superior to old-time Americans, thus counterbalancing or compensating themselves as persons from time to time for the unpleasant feelings about their immigrant status in the New World. This was unhealthy socially in the long run, for it was not reaching out toward an understanding with America, real or basic, but it did help individual immigrants to stand up as men and women.

Unlike their parents, who are (or were) aware not only of their European background but of having made the transition from Europe to America and gained a foothold here, most New Americans have no consciousness or instinctive feeling of any racial or cultural background, of their being part of any sort of continuity in human or historic experience. Some of them seem almost as if they had just dropped off Mars and, during the drop, forgotten all about Mars. I know this to be so; I talked to scores and scores of them in more than a dozen different cities and towns, not only during that tour in 1934, but on several occasions and in various connections since then. In the majority of cases, the immigrant parents—uneducated working people or peasants from the various European countries—were too inarticulate to tell their sons and daughters who they (the parents) really were, and thus transmit to them some feeling or knowledge of their background.

The average Slavic peasant, for instance, who came to this country during the last twenty or thirty years in nine chances out of ten is unable to inform his children adequately who he is, what his old country is like, what his background (which, *ipso facto,* is his children's background) consists of. He tells his numerous sons and daughters that he is a Pole, a Croatian, a Slovak, a Slovenian; but that is about all. The children do not know what that really means. The man acts as if he were proud of being what he is, at least in the privacy of his home; for his instincts and his memories of the old country occasionally make him act that way. To his children, however, who are growing up under anything but the best influences of American life and who do not know that behind their father's pride is a rich and vital past, he very often seems not a little ridiculous, certainly not worthy of their respect. To them he is just a Hunky or Polack, a "working stiff," a poor, pathetic creature constantly at somebody's mercy and repeatedly stepped upon, and as such not much according to American standards—standards which they pick up in the movies and from other powerful agencies in American life. Often they are half ashamed of him. The immigrant mother frequently finds herself in the same situation. There is a mutual lack of understanding; the children as they grow older have begun to grasp at superficial and obvious American realities, and sink themselves in America as far as they can by adopting the easiest, most obvious ways of the country of their birth. And the results are unsatisfactory family life, personal tragedies of all sorts, maladjustments, social perversities.

It is not unusual for boys and girls in their late or even their middle teens to break away from the homes of their immigrant parents, and eventually to repudiate entirely their origin and to Anglicize their Polish, Croatian, Finnish, or Lithuanian names, which old-time Americans find so difficult to pronounce and so amusing. But that, of course, does not solve their problem. In most instances it only makes it worse, though as a rule they do not realize that. I met New Americans of this type; they were invariably hollow, absurd, objectionable persons.

However, the situation of many of those who do not break with their parents, change their "foreign" names, and wholly repudiate their origin is but little better than of those who do. They were born here and legally, technically, are citizens of the United States; but few—even in the most fortunate homes—have any strong feeling that they really belong here and are part of this country. For, by and large, the education which is inflicted on them in public schools and high schools and in parochial schools, or in colleges, fails to make them Anglo-Saxon Americans or to give them any vital and lasting appreciation of the American heritage, while their Anglo-Saxon schoolmates, purposefully-by-accident stumbling over their feet and calling them Hunkies and Dagoes, and their teachers, making fun of their names, increase their feeling that they are not indigenous Americans, but outsiders who are more or less tolerated. Their instincts, if they have any, are at cross-purposes. They are bewildered persons, constantly oppressed, as I have said, by feelings of inferiority. Their personalities are faint, lopsided, out of focus.

These feelings of inferiority manifest themselves variously. Some of the New Americans turn them inside out and become chauvinistically patriotic; only their chauvinism has no basis in any vital feeling. It is insincere, empty, mere lip-service, intended only to impress the dominant Anglo-Saxon element, with which they have to cope; and hence worse—for the development of their own characters—than chauvinism that has some basis in conviction or feeling in racial or national background. And where there is any sincerity in this sort of "patriotism," it is based solely on shallow materialistic concepts, which they have picked up in school and elsewhere. "This is the greatest country . . . we have the biggest buildings . . . the best ice-cream . . . more automobiles, more bathtubs than all the rest of the world," etc. Without realizing it, these New Americans are ready for almost any sort of shallow, ignorant nationalist or fascist movement which will not directly attack the new racial strains in America's population; and thousands of them perhaps would have no great trouble in bringing themselves to deny their parents, pose as old-stock Americans, and serve even a movement which would terrorize the immigrants and their children as the Hitler movement in Germany terrorized the Jews.

Other New Americans turn their inferiority inside out in another way. They become loud and tough, sometimes actively anti-social. But let me hasten to repeat that this last group is not so numerous as is generally imagined by those who occasionally glance at crime and juvenile-delinquency statistics, or who read the headlines. The surprising thing to me is that there is not more delinquency and crime among the New Americans. And I should add too that the chauvinists mentioned above are not very numerous either. These categories together include perhaps less than five per cent of the New Americans.

The majority of the grown-up New Americans just hang back from the main stream of life in this country, forming a tremendous mass of neutral, politically lifeless citizenry; while their younger fellow New Americans, boys and girls in their teens (about twelve million of them), now—in 1938—attending public and parochial schools and high schools, show dangerous signs of becoming the same kind of neutral, unstirring citizens, unless something is done about it. There is among them little aggressiveness, little spirit of any sort. Most of them merely hope to get along, to get by, somehow. Without a vital sense of background, perennially oppressed by the feeling that they are outsiders and thus inferior, they will live outside the main stream of America's national life. This is especially true of groups which linguistically and culturally are farthest removed from the Anglo-Saxon, and still more of groups which, besides being unrelated to the Anglo-Saxon, are (or till lately have been) suppressed or subject nationalities in Europe.

And these widespread personal inferiority feelings are producing in large sections of this New American element *actual* inferiority in character, mind, and physique. There is no doubt that, by and large, in bodily and other personal qualities many of the immigrants' children do not favorably compare with their parents. They cannot look one in the eye. They are shy. They stutter and stammer. If an old-stock American, or anyone of some standing, is due to come to their house, they fuss and fret with their parents. They force their peasant mothers to go to the hair-dressers, to put on American ladies' dresses and high-heeled shoes which often make the mothers incongruous figures. Then, when the visitor arrives, they tremble at what the old lady or the old man might say, or that he might mispronounce English words even worse than usually. Their limp handshakes gave me creepy feelings all the way from New York to the Iron Range in Minnesota. Those handshakes symbolized for me the distressing tendency on the part of this vast and growing section of America's population toward characterlessness, lack of force and spirit, and other inferior personal qualities.

From whatever angle one looks at it, this is a serious matter for the New Americans as individuals and for America. Thirty million—or even fifteen or twenty million, a probable number to which most or all of my generalizations here are directly applicable—are a lot of people, and this "second generation" will be (many already are) the fathers and mothers of the third generation, and it is not impossible that in two or three decades half of the population of the United States will be of these new cultural and national strains.

What then should be done—what can be done about it?

In going about the country in 1934 and subsequently I met several New Americans of whom most of the things I say above are not true. None of them was totally free of personal inferiority feelings (in fact, I find that even very few old-stock Americans are entirely free of them), but they were, nevertheless, fine-looking young men and women, boys and girls, keen and alert, articulate, ambitious, personally charming. Some were still in high school, one or two in college, and doing well as students; in fact, rather better than old-stock American students. Three or four of the boys were locally prominent football and baseball players.* Their handshakes were firm and they looked me in the eye. A few had a lively sense of humor which they could apply to themselves. Their laughter had a healthy ring. They knew something of what was going on in the country, in the world. Some of them, although still very young, seemed to know what they wanted from life. Two or three had literary ambitions. One told me he would try to get into politics "in a big way," by which I understood that the United States Senate was not beyond his gaze; and his name was Wojciezkowski. Another, attending the University of Pittsburgh, thought he would get a job in a steel-mill and become a labor leader. In a bleak iron town in Minnesota I met a pretty girl of Slovenian parentage who was the best student in her school, had a vivid personality, and seemed entirely normal in all her attitudes. And so on, and so on. They impressed me as real, solid persons who would be an asset to any country.

Nearly all of them, in their childhood and later, had been unpleasantly affected by their parents' humiliating experiences as immigrants and industrial workers, and had had disagreeable experiences of their own which touched them vitally. They had been called Hunkies, Polacks, Litvaks, Dagoes. Many

* Athletes with "foreign" names, as generally known, are not unusual. But most of them, in high schools and colleges as well as in more or less professional sports, are New Americans who are exceptional in the sense as stated in this and the ensuing few paragraphs.

of them had had (and were still having) difficulties with their names. A young man of Lithuanian parentage in Pittsburgh, and attending the university there, who was attractive, "clean cut" in the best American sense, but whose surname was Lamblagoskas, told me that when he was a young boy in McKeesport the teacher had been too lazy or too indifferent to take the trouble to pronounce his name, so she had called him only Johnnie, while all the other children in class had both a first name and a surname. Then the two-name children had begun to call him "Just Johnnie" or "Johnnie the Litvak," which annoyed him very much. As in hundreds of thousands of similar instances, this, in conjunction with other experiences of that nature, produced in him an acute inferiority complex which oppressed him for years—"until," as he put it, "I sort of worked myself out of it."

A young man of Slavic origin, whose surname also was difficult for Anglo-Saxon tongues, told me that in his boyhood he had suffered a great deal because old-stock American boys called him "Sneeze-it," because in school one day the teacher had said that his name could not be pronounced but thought that perhaps she could maybe sneeze it. "But now," he said to me, "things like that don't bother me very much."

Others in this category with whom I came in contact had had and were still having—inevitably, let me repeat—other troubles on account of being immigrants' children; but these troubles were not seriously affecting them, were not preventing them from developing into balanced, strong and healthy, charming human beings.

Why? There are at least two explanations. One is that most of them lived, during at least part of their lives, in comparatively favorable economic circumstances, and their parents managed to give them some schooling in addition to the legal requirement, which helped them more or less to work themselves out of their various second-generation complexes. The other explanation (probably not unrelated to, but I think more important than, the first) is that, in all cases without exception which came to my attention, their fathers and mothers were wise and articulate enough to convey to them something of their backgrounds in the old countries; tell them what it meant to be a Finn, a Slovenian, a Serbian, a Croatian, a Slovak, a Czech, a Pole, or a Lithuanian, and inspire in them some respect for that meaning; make them conscious of their backgrounds and heritage, give them some sense of continuity, some feeling of their being part of America, in which immigrants like themselves played an important rôle—part of something bigger and better than the bleak, utterly depressing existence led by them and their neighbors in the grimy steel-mill and iron- and coal-mining towns where they lived.

During my 1934 trip and later I met, as I say, scores of these New Americans. Among them were some of the most attractive people I have encountered anywhere. Some of these I already have mentioned. Another was a girl born and still living in Cleveland whose father and mother were Slovenians; and there is no doubt in my mind that much of her charm issued from the fact that she was keenly conscious of her parents' native land and culture. Two years before they had taken her on a visit to Slovenia, and she had discovered a tiny country which is physically as lovely as anything she had seen in America, with an old, mellow culture, a rich folklore, a considerable modern literature, and interesting folkways behind which there are centuries of wisdom and a long, unbroken chain of experience on the part of a quiet, peace-loving little nation that has lived there for a thousand years.

Still another of these exceptional New Americans was a young six-footer of Finnish parentage on the Iron Range in Minnesota. He had never been to Finland, but knew a good deal about the basic cultural qualities of that country from his mother's word-pictures of it. He also had a fluent command of the Finnish language which did not interfere with (indeed, enriched) his English. He knew dozens of Finnish folk ballads and lyrics and sang them well, and had read and re-read in the original the great Finnish epic-poem "The Kalevala." He was quietly proud of his people's achievements on the Iron Range both in the mines and on the land, and thought that Minnesota was his country. Despite the bleakness of the region, and the hard life led there by most of the people, especially the Finns, he loved the Iron Range. His people had worked and suffered there for decades and converted great parts of it into farming country, although before they came nobody had thought it could ever be made suitable for anything.

In short, he was conscious of his background; he had a sense of continuity, of being part of a great human experience, which was part of the still greater American adventure. Largely, I think, in consequence of this, a strength of character was discernible in his every move and utterance.

I could give several more such cases of exceptional New Americans, but that would be, in the main, repeating what I tell of the girl in Cleveland and the boy in Minnesota. All of them—representing, however, but a small minority— were conscious and, in a greater or lesser degree, proud of their racial groups' background in the old countries, and some also of their racial groups' background and history in this country. They had a sense of continuity, a feeling of being a part of something. And they, I think, are the answer to the question: What should be done about the problem sketched in this chapter?

The answer is that the New Americans, whose inarticulate and otherwise inadequate (through no fault of their own) parents have been unable to give them much along these lines, should be helped to acquire a knowledge of, and pride in, their own heritage and makeup; and this help should come, in very large part, from already established and functioning social and cultural institutions and agencies—schools, libraries, settlement and community houses, newspapers, lecture forums, and so on—in co-operation with a central organization which should be formed for the purpose of devising ways to disseminate information about the several racial or national groups represented among the thirty million "second generation" citizens, of studying the problem and working out programs of action for its gradual solution or amelioration, from the point of view of honest, intelligent concern for the country's future.

By now it is obvious to many people interested in the problem that it is impossible and, what is more, *undesirable* to make the offspring of Lithuanians or Serbians into Anglo-Saxons; that the aim should be rather to help them become real men and women on the pattern of their own natural cultures. There should be a recognition of the fact that America is not purely an Anglo-Saxon country, if only by virtue of numbers, it is also something else. *A new conception of America is necessary.* There is no doubt that in the few places where no attempts have been made by "patriotic" old-time Americans to force immigrants' children into the old-stock American mold— as, for instance, in the Bohemian communities in Nebraska and Texas, where Bohemians already are in the fourth generation; in the little city of Hamtramck near Detroit, where the public school system consistently encourages the large Polish group there to keep its individuality; in O. E. Rölvaag's Norwegian settlements in the northwest; in some of the foreign "colonies" in New York City, notably the Ukrainian one on the Lower East-side; or in several small Polish, Italian, and Finnish rural communities in New England, upstate New York, and elsewhere—the development of character, mentality, and physique in the New American element has been vastly more felicitous than where such attempts have been made.

Social and cultural institutions and agencies in various cities and towns where the problem stares them all in the face wherever they turn already are beginning to do things to help New Americans develop more or less on the pattern of their backgrounds. To give a few examples: in Cleveland the excellent public library organization, with its scores of branch libraries, has begun to help the New Americans to learn something about themselves, their parents' native lands and their national groups' history in this country, particularly in Cleveland. All three of the big newspapers there have special reporters covering the "foreign sections" of the city, and print feature articles about the various foreign groups' contribution to the growth and development of Cleveland (of this more in the ensuing chapter). Public-school and high-school teachers in Cleveland, as in one or two other cities, whose classes are anywhere from forty to eighty per cent "foreign," are becoming eagerly interested in "second-generation problems" which face them in the form of numerous neurotic and backward or "problem" children who, for no apparent reason, burst out crying in the middle of a lesson. Of late teachers nearly everywhere, I am told, have advanced so far that they take the trouble to learn the correct pronunciation of difficult Polish, Yugoslav, Lithuanian, Czech, Finnish, and Slovak names, and to caution the old-stock American boys and girls not to call the New American children Hunkies, Wops, and other such names of derision.

In more than half of the cities and towns which I visited in 1934 and since I found the so-called International Institutes, some of them part of the Y.W.C.A., which—with their club-rooms, reading-rooms, lectures, social affairs, exhibits of European peasant arts, and printed matter—are beginning to attempt to do something for the second generation, especially the girls. In Flint, Michigan, in Toledo, Ohio, and in one or two other places, I came upon purely local organizations, some of them officered and run by such exceptional New Americans as I have described above, aiming to help the general run of New Americans to fight their feelings of inferiority.

I came upon professional social workers who were doing research in certain phases of the problem and knew a great deal about the local departments thereof. The directors of most of the settlement-houses in Pittsburgh, Detroit, Chicago, and Milwaukee were more or less awake to the situation as it existed locally and—in most cases, however, without having any real understanding of it—were also trying to do something about it. The same could be said of various settlement-house workers, teachers, a few ministers, and other agencies elsewhere.

All these efforts or, rather beginnings of efforts are local, however; usually honest enough but very restricted in scope. The International Institutes, for instance, appeal largely to girls. There is no central or national organization interested in the thing as a countrywide problem, which it undoubtedly is, and, as I have tried to show here, a tremendous and important one—important to old-stock Americans and to Americans of the third and fourth generation no less than to these New Americans, and to America as a whole.

The organization I have in mind, which let us designate here as XYZ, would have, during the next twenty or thirty years, a vast and complicated task to perform—namely, to give these millions of New Americans a knowledge of, and pride in, their own heritage, an understanding of their own makeup, which, to some extent, would operate to counteract their feelings of inferiority about themselves in relation to the rest of the country; and, simultaneously, to create a sympathetic understanding toward them on the part of older Americans, so that the latter's anti-"foreign" prejudice, which is partly to blame for inferiority feelings in the new racial groups, would tend to lessen and ultimately be reduced to a minimum.

It would be a great educational-cultural work, the basic aim of which would be (1) to reach, in one way or another, almost everybody in this country with the fact that socially and culturally the United States, as it stands to-day, is an extension not only of the British Isles and the Netherlands but, more or less, of all Europe; and (2), with constant reiteration and intelligent elaboration of that fact, to try to harmonize and integrate, so far as possible, the various racial and cultural strains in our population without suppressing or destroying any good cultural qualities in any of them, but using and directing these qualities toward a possible enhancement of the color and quality of our national life in America.

Probably the first group to be reached by XYZ are the public-school and high-school teachers in communities with large "foreign" populations. They should be helped to find out who these youngsters filling their classrooms and responding to such names as Adamovicz, Kotchka, Zamblaoskas, Hurja, Balkovec, and Pavelka really are. They should be informed that the children of Yugoslav (Serbian, Croatian, and Slovenian) parents, for instance, have, by virtue of their birth, a great heritage which reaches a thousand years into European history and almost five hundred years into American history—that (to repeat some of the things I mentioned in the letter which I did not send to George Horace Lorimer) there is good reason for believing that Yugoslavs were on Columbus' ships when he discovered this continent—that Yugoslav marines touched this continent in their own ships only a few years after Columbus—that Yugoslavs were in California before the Yankees arrived there, and were pioneers in two of California's now most important industries, fruit-growing and fishing—that in the last fifty years Yugoslavs, hundreds of thousands of them, have been among the competent workers in America's most important industries, mining and steel-making, and as such have contributed enormously to the upbuilding of this country—that Nikola Tesla and Michael Pupin came from Yugoslavia—that Henry Suzzallo, one of America's most important educators, was a second-generation American, born in California, of Yugoslav parents—that Ivan Mestrovich, the sculptor, whose works are to be seen in Chicago, Detroit, Minneapolis, New York, and elsewhere, is a Yugoslav; and so on. I mention here what the teachers should be helped to find out about the Yugoslav strain, because I know more about it than any other; but they should be informed also about the Polish, Czech, Slovak, Lithuanian, Hungarian, and the other strains—so that occasionally, preferably at some dramatic moment, as, for instance, after a clash between an Anglo-Saxon boy and a "Hunky" boy, they could talk about them in class.

The XYZ might develop a special literature on the subject of New Americans, addressed to teachers; it might have competent speakers able to address teachers' conventions, college student bodies and faculties, women's clubs, and other groups.

It might start a campaign for the revision of history text-books, giving recognition to recent immigrant groups from Eastern Europe, the Balkans, and elsewhere for their contributions to the upbuilding of America as she stands to-day. Such revisions should mention, perhaps, that in this upbuilding of modern America at least as many "Hunkies" and "Dagoes" died or were injured as early American colonists were killed in subduing the wilderness and in the War for Independence. The part played by the newer groups should be fitted into the history of the American adventure as a whole. This revision of text-books might, indeed, be among its first and most important tasks.

It might start a press service for English-language newspapers published in cities and towns whose population includes a large proportion of "foreigners" and for English pages of foreign-language newspapers. This service should include vividly written, authentic material on the backgrounds, history, culture, and contributions of the different "foreign" groups to the up-building of America, and stories of individual and group achievement.

It might publish pamphlets in English dealing with various phases of the problem; start a library of all available literature and material on the subject; make special efforts to stimulate interest and participation in the folk arts.

It might utilize the radio for this work, with special programs including, let us say, music and folk-songs of the various nations. It might try to draw the motion picture industry into its enterprise. Eventually it might arrange essay contests dealing with the history and contribution of the different "foreign" groups and other appropriate topics, open to New Americans in high-schools and colleges, with suitable prizes such as scholarships or trips to the native countries of the contestants' parents. It might organize group tours to European countries on which New Americans could discover their parents' old countries.

But enough of these suggestions. I make them largely to elucidate the problem further. Perhaps, if the national XYZ organization is not formed in the near future—though I feel certain that eventually something like it will be formed—local groups already interested in the matter possibly will find them helpful.

I realize, of course, that the problem I sketch here is closely tied up with the socio-economic system under which we live; that, next to their being more or less strangers here, the worst factors behind the inferiority feelings of these millions of New Americans are poverty and its sister-evil, ignorance, both of them brought over by the immigrants and then fostered by conditions here; and that the cure for most of the second-generation ills lies, ultimately, in the solution of our socio-economic problem. I doubt, however, whether the latter problem will be quickly and satisfactorily solved in this country if we permit to develop in our population a vast element, running into tens of millions, which is oppressed by acute feelings of inferiority and, largely as a result of those feelings, is becoming actually inferior human material—bewildered, politically neutral, economically unaggressive, culturally nowhere. If this element is left alone in the face of its growing economic difficulties, and in the face of the organized and unorganized prejudice against it on the part of "patriotic" older Americans, there might eventually be no help for it. I imagine that hundreds of thousands of New Americans already are hopeless as potential constructive elements in any sort of vital, progressive civilization and culture; and if their number is permitted to increase, they will—let me repeat—profoundly affect the future of this country in a way that no one would want to see it affected.

On the other hand, if something is done about the problem in the spirit of the above general suggestions, I believe that the majority of the New Americans and the generation that they will produce will have an opportunity to become a great body of self-respecting, constructive citizenry; and that, with the diverse racial and cultural backgrounds they inherited from their immigrant parents, they will enrich the civilization and deepen the culture of this New World.

Up to this point this chapter is, for the greater part, what I published as an article in the November, 1934, issue of *Harpers*. The article caused a considerable stir in many parts of the United States. It was editorially commented upon by scores of newspapers the country over. It brought the editors of the magazine and me several hundred letters, both from old-stock Americans and New Americans; from social workers, including Miss Lillian Wald; from numerous public- and high-school principals and teachers and general educators, including Richard J. Purcell, secretary of the Catholic University of America at Washington, whose students are preponderantly second-generation; from Miss Rachel Davis DuBois, of the Service Bureau for Education in Human Relations, which has since become the Commission on Intercultural Education of the Progressive Education Association; and from directors of International Institute. The letters were informative and suggestive, most of them agreeing that the article touched upon a problem whose importance it was impossible to exaggerate. Here and there young New Americans started to discuss my views of them in their high-school newspapers, not a few of them—naturally enough—resenting the fact that I brought their problem into the light of day. Many denied they were inferior or oppressed by any kind of inferiority feelings in relation to America, and they denounced me; but in most cases these denials and denunciations were unconscious documentations of my thesis. Traveling through the country during 1935-37, I was approached by young New Americans who more or less agreed with me, and who told me that the debate about their predicament in America, as I had stated it, was still going on—this, no doubt, partly because Miss DuBois' organization had reprinted the article in pamphlet form and distributed thousands of copies to high schools.

I want to quote from some of the letters.

The director of the International Relations Project, University of Minnesota:— I had a good friend, now dead, who used to express your idea of what should be done about the new-immigrant groups somewhat differently than you do. He objected to the use of the "Melting Pot" phrase for the United States, saying that "Symphony Orchestra" would be more desirable. By this, of course, he meant that our finest results would come from a recognition and harmonizing of the various cultural contributions of our New Americans. It is especially important to recognize this in Minnesota because the 1930 census shows nearly four hundred thousand foreign born in our state and a millon more of second-generation Americans. These two make about fifty-five percent of our total population.

Franklin F. Hopper, chief of the circulation department of the New York Public Library:—. . . As time goes on, we in the New York Public Library realize more and more that the service which we have attempted to build up for foreign groups must be modified to meet the needs of the "second generation" who are rapidly growing in numbers. In some of the neighborhood libraries in New York we have been quietly developing for a good many years a specialized service for the foreign groups of the locality. Perhaps the outstanding one is at the Webster Library on York Avenue near Seventy-eighth Street, where the leading collection of Czechoslovak books in this country, or, I believe, anywhere outside of Czechoslovakia, now exists. . . .

Norman M. Hunter, high-school principal, Oakdale, Pennsylvania:—. . . The problem of these New Americans, as you call them, has troubled me for a long time. More than half of our children are of Yugoslav, Polish, and Russian descent. They are prey to all the ills you describe. During the eight years I have been here we have done what we could in an unorganized manner to maintain in the children a proper pride in their own heritage, but it has been insufficient. In an effort to overcome this, our history classes have put some emphasis on those European nations with which our pupils are most closely connected by ties of blood—but this, too, does not begin to take care of the problem. Working alone, fumbling for a method, is difficult when the urgent task stares one in the face. . . .

George Latsko, Jr., of Lamberton, Pennsylvania:—. . . I am proud to say that my father does not belong to the class of immigrants who, as you describe them, came to this country during the last twenty or thirty years and are unable to adequately inform their American-born children who they are, what their old countries are like, and what their background consists of. . . . I am now twenty years of age and I never get tired of hearing my father tell us different stories and tales of his native Czechoslovakia. He may tell the same story many times (which he usually does), but each time makes it more interesting. When a discussion arises at the breakfast table, you may be sure that Dad will draw a comparison with conditions in his native land. . . . Much as he would like to, I don't suppose Dad will ever go back to Czechoslovakia. But I have resolved that at the very first opportunity I will go there and see the birthplace of my father, whose word-pictures of the customs, superstitions, and religious views of a hardworking and proud race I shall always retain in my memory. . . .

A young New American of Lithuanian parentage, Pittsburgh:— . . . I come of a poor family. My father died when I was ten. I am an only child. My mother worked continually for the past fifteen years with but one purpose: to give me a college education and, if possible, send me to law school. I received a B.A. in Education, but was unable to go to law school—lack of funds.

I have led an ordinary life. While in high school I recall I was treated rather aloof, not because of appearance, but because of my foreign name. There were few other foreign boys or girls in that school.

In high school I made my first contacts with girls. My first girl was one of good American-born parents. I was looked down upon by them because of my name. I hope you won't think me egotistical, but I believe I was as well-mannered as any youngster. I also noticed while at some affair or party, that, after making friends with some one and then being introduced formally to others, a certain aloofness or coolness set in. My name —— The young lady and I ceased keeping company after a time. A year or so later, at college, she made some effort to revive the friendship, but it was no go, though I liked her. My going with her led to too many embarrassments all around.

. . . It is hard. I suppose we New Americans, as you call us, are a sort of "lost" group. We are nowhere, really. The American employer tolerates us, is nice during the interview until he learns our names and nationality; then he says he's sorry, he can't use us. After all, we are capable, and all we ask for is a chance. If we changed our names, perhaps we would have an easier time of it, but why——?

I believe in Americanizing the foreigner, but I also believe in allowing him to retain what culture he has from the old land. I am proud of Lithuania; I have read her history. But I know American-born Lithuanians who are ashamed of the country where their parents came from.

P.S.: I just remembered while at college I was rushed for a social fraternity. I think I was almost taken in—almost. Later I was told confidentially that several members objected to my being inducted because this was an American club and they oughtn't to have any foreign-sounding names on their list of members. . . .

Joseph Zarzyski, a Polish immigrant in Cohoes, New York:— . . . Perhaps you are aware that it is not only the Anglo-Saxon who is looking down upon the second generation of east- and south-European extraction, but also the second and third generation of the Irish and French, who are high-hatting the American-born Slav or Lithuanian. The true Yankee, being more cultured, more sure of himself, and better mannered, shows his superiority more gracefully, while the Irish and the French tend to become chauvinistic and hysterical in professing Americanism. . . . The young American-born Slav is probably better treated in the shop and factory than was his foreign father; socially, however, he is still in a sort of no man's land. He is not good enough. At best, he is only tolerated. . . . Of course it is partly our fault that we have not won for ourselves better respect from others. The educational and cultural background in our homes was rather poor, both from the European and American standpoints. Our fathers worked liked slaves and drank and prayed when idle; our mothers, overburdened with large families, had no time for spiritual and cultural development. No wonder we suffer from an inferiority complex. . . .

A teacher in the Boys' Technical High School of Milwaukee, whose student body is overwhelmingly Polish-American, protested my suggestion that teachers generally in such cities where immigrants and their American-born children are numerous equip themselves to deal with the problem of New Americans. He said my suggestion was impractical; teachers generally were overworked as it was. He went on, "My idea"—which, I think, is excellent—"would be that educational systems of the various cities with large foreign populations engage or develop *special* teachers who would be attached to the various public schools and high schools and teach along the lines you recommend, say, an hour or two a week in each class and occasionally talk to the whole school. . . ."

An editorial writer of the New York *Times* agreed that the problem I took up in *Harpers* was important, but remarked that what I was saying applied only to about ten million, instead of thirty million, New Americans. It applied, he said, only to the children of the recent immigrants from eastern and southern Europe, but not to the New Americans of Scandinavian, German, German-Austrian, Swiss, and French groups, which had no inferiority feelings. On the day that this editorial appeared I received the following letter which is more or less typical of at least thirty others written to me by Scandinavians:

I am myself a second-generation Swede now in my middle thirties. My father came to this country when he was twenty, my mother when she was eight. My father died when I, the youngest of the family, was three, leaving my mother with four young children and about two thousand dollars in property, which did not include a home. My mother moved from Salem, Oregon, to a small town located not far from her sister, a farmer's wife, and by sewing, mostly for a tailor who paid her nine dollars a week, put us all through public school, and what is still a miracle of financing to me, bought a house and furnished it comfortably! One of my sisters died at the age of eighteen, but the two surviving sisters and I earned our way through college. Just prior to my finishing in 1919, my mother contracted influenza and died. Since that time one of my sisters has married, the other has taken graduate work and is teaching in ——, and I have taken graduate work and am teaching at the university here in ——. This is the background of essential facts. Now for the question: what has it meant to be a second-generation Swede?

First of all, the inferiority complex which you mention I confess at once that I have. It was developed I think by my early intimate acquaintance with poverty, by the feeling that to be a Swede was not quite normal, and by certain temperamental qualities. Poverty forces the children of a family to wear "coo-coo" clothes, to do odd jobs for pay while other children have leisure hours, and to refrain from giving "parties" to other children because of the time and expense involved. It also prevents a child's boasting of the affluence of his parent, an American child's common means of expanding his own ego. If he were to boast on false grounds he could be routed in a hurry by his inability to show a new bicycle, a new pony, or any of the insignias of wealth in a child's eyes. Some children with a kind of precocious fortitude can overcome this last attack on their equanimity, but not many.

The racial angle is harder to analyze in my case. Very early, I am sure, I learned what the great tough world thought of Swedes. They had square heads, they were slow-witted, they ate raw fish, they had crazy ideas, and they scrubbed their floors but not their feet. On Fourth of Julys I learned from orators at local celebrations that they made good solid citizens, and that they were honest. Presentations of these two points of view have persisted in my own experiences to this day. Persons who have wished to throw obstacles in my path have leaned heavily on more or less subtle exploitations of the first estimates. Persons who have wished to flatter me have used the second. On the other hand, my close old-stock American friends, I think, have never seriously thought of my nationality in connection with my character. But there you have it. One's nationality in this country passes at face value until one begins struggling to get his chin over the ledge. Everything is fair in love and war, and the competition to "get on" in the world. The police don't do a more thorough job of digging up your ancestry and past than does your competitor in the race for advancement. I will say this, in the academic world, unless you are a

Jew or an Irish Catholic (and in all regions this exception does not apply) your chances are fairly well equalized. At that, however, in H. L. Mencken's humorous phrase, one's "Anglo-Saxon" colleagues regard the second-generation American as "an assistant-American." He can hand up the spices and the spoons but the old-stock American will do the cooking.

In the matter of my own temperamental deficiencies, I feel this: they are in part induced by my "second-generationism." I have an unholy hatred of "go-getterism," of hypocrisy, and of smugness. I see these qualities in a great many old-stock Americans, but I suspect that at times my inner vision is bad. For a true view in many cases I should translate go-getterism to energy, hypocrisy to tact, and smugness to an inner composure, which I lack. There are excellent qualities in the true American character and I suspect that the "New American," since from now on he is committed to being an American, should strive to develop in himself these qualities. On the other hand, when he sees character correctly and knows that he is dealing with a smug, hypocritical go-getter he ought to speak out. That I think is what a great many of us second-generation Americans do not do. We weakly applaud the shallow-brained man with the loud voice whether he be state senator, college president, football coach, or more often our own particular boss. We are trying to emulate the chameleon and become in the eyes of the people around us "true Americans." I find myself on occasion trying to simulate an interest in an old-stock American's collection of antiques, his family tree, or his "old Southern mansion owned by the family since 1700." I know that he is an ignorant collector, a liar, and innocent of the knowledge of what a Southern mansion really looks like, but I am inclined to show him respect—in his presence. Two things are at work—my second-generation lip-veneration for the "Americanistic" and a defect in character.

Last of all, I would like to say that I have never hid my nationality, been ashamed of my origin, nor failed to acquaint myself with Swedish culture. I worked my way to Sweden in 1923 and spent four months there. I am thoroughly proud of many things that Sweden has done in literature, art, and science. Where my inferiority complex starts working is at that point where Swedish character in itself is called in question. That is my Achilles' heel, and just as the American farmer has been given an inferiority complex a yard wide by the publication over the years of rube jokes and rube cartoons so I, together with many members of other nationalities of recent foreign origin, have been made to feel myself ridiculous as a Swede, but all right as an "assistant-American." Bringing up to par one's ego is in a measure dependent on the possibility of teaching Americans the dignity, the special values, and excellence of Bohemian, Swedish, Jewish, and other cultures. As you have indicated, that can be done by teaching these cultures to the New Americans themselves first, but there is still the task of buttonholing the "type American" and holding him down long enough to let him know that there is such a thing as a culture outside his own. And after that is done it should be a fairly easy task to win back those second-generationers who have gone old-American in name and temper and get them to cease their chauvinism and, by no means incidentally, their rabid rantings against "foreigners." I have heard Swedes of this latter class approach the insane bitterness of Hitler in denouncing Jews, and one of my own most ardent defamers (on the grounds that I am a Swede) in the town where I live is a Jewess, the wife of a faculty member. . . .

A Jewish New American wrote to me:—

There are some immigrant parents who took on American standards and ways of living with a vengeance. They are chauvinistically pro-American. They harp on how wonderful things are in the United States. As their children grow up, they [the children] suddenly become aware that their parents' patriotism contains an element of falsity, is forced and exaggerated, unnatural. Without knowing why, they hate it; sometimes they hate the parents. Many of these young people become Reds.

From a New American of Rumanian parentage:

. . . The trouble with the second-generation is that we are (many of us) merely spectators, but spectators who have no particular or vital interest in the scene or show before us. It is like going to a ball-game in which you have no interset. We sit in the bleachers, hoping some one may hit a ball in our direction which we could take home for a souvenir. We are held up by this hope. In a way, it is like waiting for a fortuitous accident. This is partly a development or extension of our parents' attitude. But our parents were spectators as a *group*. They isolated themselves in little "colonies," communities of fraternity. And the members of these groups more or less understood one another. They had the same problems. They were content to play in a smaller league. They made a living, a humble one in most cases, and were satisfied. It was better than in the old country. They were happy within the colony, took part in its society, affairs, etc., and thus were comfortable within their own group. We of the second generation are no such compact group. We are all in the same boat, troubled by the same uncertainties, but do not know how to discuss them, or are even ashamed to acknowledge our uneasiness. The parents now and then laughed at America; they were outsiders; they knew it clearly. In a way, it helped to orient them. At least they knew what they were not. We, their children, have no such clearness. We were born here, should be of America, and yet somehow are not. This cannot readily be talked about. So most of us feel that it is our own fault, this not being of America, and are ashamed of it. The feeling finds no vent. We withdraw into ourselves. We belong neither in the big leagues nor in the small leagues. Now and then, when we begin to grow a bit more sure of ourselves, the "foreign" background exerts another bit of unexpected influence, and there we are again, all mixed up, lost emotionally. Thus the softest rôle for us in the end is that of the onlooker. There we have no responsibilities. If we make a mistake it is lost in the anonymity of the crowd. Now and then we think we will play ball ourselves, but we don't know enough about the game, so we go back to being bleacher fans. . . .

An interesting critical letter came to me from a young college man whose parents were Slavic immigrants:

My first reading of your article in *Harpers* upset me for days. I thought it was horribly true. When I re-read it, however, I became critical. I thought about it a good deal, and I hope you will not mind when I say that your XYZ idea is too pat, almost glib. I believe that this is because your solution poses to settle the problem almost entirely through an outside agency, to be still created; that is, by getting us New Americans acquainted with our background. . . . No matter how full you attempt to pump us with this background, it will *be only a part* of our rehabilitation—if it comes about. Before we are New Americans, we are human beings, and as such bundles of individual problems. No matter what solution you suggest in the end its merit will be determined by its effect on one person. No solution is worth anything unless it is brought down to ground, unless it comes out of the experience of the person.

You must forgive me for what I say. In fact, I scarcely know what I am talking about. I guess I am only groping around in this letter, trying to articulate my dissatisfaction. Your remedy would apply to me. When I first read your article, you convinced me intellectually; now I am, somehow, unconvinced emotionally. I suppose this is because I don't believe the second-generation problem is the Big Problem, but only the result or a phase of some other problem, which is bigger than the second-generation one. As I say, I scarcely know what I am trying to say, but here is a thought which may interest you:

Most people can stand only so much misery or unhappiness. All of a sudden they want to leave all that is and has been behind and make a new start with no obligations to the past. In short, they run away. This was true of most immigrants. I know that this is, essentially, why my father came to America. A few years ago I found it impossible to be my parents' son and live in their home, so I ran away. I bummed around for a year. But the hell of it is that you can't leave all those things behind, and not suffer for it. . . . The average Slavic immigrant (my father, for instance) did not run away only from Europe. When he came to America, he also ran away from being a low-down peasant; then practically turned a traitor to his peasant class, and became a pusher and climber. In some cases he became so full of the American go-getting spirit that he lost sight of his background and *wanted* to lose it. Thus he turned a traitor also to himself as a man, a human being; and way down in him he felt guilty about it. He was dissatisfied with his old self, so he rushed about trying to "succeed," starting an insurance business, a store, building a house for his children, etc.—anything *outside* of himself. Physical, mental labor allayed his spiritual or psychological unrest that was caused by his feelings of guilt. . . . Now we, his children, we New Americans, yanked first this way and then that way by the old country and by America in his home and outside it, are trying to do the same thing. Some of us run away and change our names. Some of us pretend to ignore our discomfort and function outside of ourselves. Some of us (I just now) try to face our problem in relation to America and life generally, and the problem of America in relation to us, and we don't know what it is all about. . . . Your article only deepens my perplexity. . . .

Not unrelated to the above letter was one from another educated young New American, who was trying to reach deep into the problem:

In many instances, the second-generation kids really don't know *how* to be American. They are ignorant of the real meaning of the word. Sometimes it means nothing to them except as a geographical term, the place in which they live. This is the result of faulty education, where history is tossed out at them, and from which they are supposed to absorb enough to enable them to pass examinations. The spirit of America is not there. How intensely some of them want to be American! But how? What *is* American? Who even tries to answer that question? So they do what they can do—grab only at the superficialities of America which they can see and understand, or think they understand. They reach for success. They are impressed, as you say in your article, by bigness, by material things in America. And, reaching or even achieving success, they are miserable, jittery, hectic, as you describe them. Inside they are hollow. They don't really understand anything. If they understood the whole situation in which they find themselves, they might become comfortable in it; they could adjust themselves because they would then know their limits and shortcomings. As it is, they exist only in a desperate confusion, which in most cases never comes out clearly in their daily lives, yet rules everything they do or say or think. The whole problem in which they find themselves is so vast-seeming and complicated that they can select nothing from it, nor get a true picture of themselves. The failures do not see themselves as such; the potentially successful ones do not get a glimpse of their potentialities. There is a lack of sense of reality on the part of those involved in the situation most acutely. . . .

XYZ may be all right as a beginning, but what is needed, I think, is a new interpretation of America in big lines—a poetic interpretation, if you will; one which will not treat America as a mass of historical compendium, but a living process, into whose acceleration have gone many kinds of people, things, events. Let's have the human side of America. Show that human beings are more or less the same, no matter what their names. In a way I think that here I am making a plea for universality, or universality within the nationalist confines of America, if you know what I mean; I am not sure that I know myself, exactly. Let me put it in another way: I believe that the "brotherhood of man" principle will always hold good, whether you call it Christianity or Americanism. The question is not—should not be—that people of foreign-sounding names like mine have a *right* to be here and to function normally, but that they *are* here and have been here for some time, and that they are to be accepted as part of the natural course of events in America. It may be that some day, merely through the passage of time, this will come about, and the name Zambloaskas will be accepted as authentically American a name as Hamilton or Perkins; but this could be hastened and inculcated more deeply if we would try—and, *as a beginning,* to say again, your XYZ may be the thing to hasten the solution.

To me America has such a wonderful future *largely* because of this chance for universality among the people. America accepts the names Beethoven, Einstein, Toscanini, forgets their nationality and uses them and their gifts. But America does not use the immigrants here; not really. She just uses their hands and muscles. They are tolerated, and tolerance in itself is a negative business; often it is implied hostility. In fact, most of the psychological forces in America today function negatively. We New Americans are negative, because we are, consciously or unconsciously, on the defensive. We want equality with the old-stock Americans, but get nowhere because we are ignorant of America and ourselves, our urges are neurotic, and we use wrong tactics. Oh, if all of us could become intelligent, if our urges toward equality and real Americanism would become sound and joined—then we would have a new America, a new culture, a country that would be a poem written upon a great reality.

I suppose we don't really disagree. I hope some sort of XYZ does appear. I should like to help. . . .

In 1934, mainly in consequence of my interest in the problem of the New Americans, I became associated with the Foreign Language Information Service, a national organization with headquarters in New York City, directed by Read Lewis, an old-stock American, native of Illinois and educated at the

University of Wisconsin and Columbia. In 1915 he started in law practice in New York, but was almost immediately after appointed a special assistant to the American ambassador in Russia, in which capacity he administered relief funds in Kursk and Voronezh in 1916-17. During the next two years he directed American publicity in Moscow and Archangel. Returning to the United States in 1920, he became interested in the problems of the foreign-born, and in 1922 took over the Foreign Language Information Service, or FLIS.

FLIS had come into existence during the War as a branch of George Creel's propaganda organization created by President Wilson under the title of Committee on Public Information. At the end of the War FLIS was in charge of Miss Josephine Roche, of Colorado, who, seeing the long-range peace-time worth of such an organization, determined to continue it. For two years, till Read Lewis came along, she directed it as a non-government organization.

When I got into it as a member of its board of trustees, FLIS was trying— with a terribly limited financial energy—to deal with the problem of assimilation, adjustment, and mutual appreciation, resulting from a century of mass immigration. It was working toward (1) an understanding of the American language and institutions on the part of the immigrant and his children; (2) equal rights and opportunities for the immigrant and his family and an attitude of friendly understanding and tolerance toward the newcomer on the part of the older Americans; (3) the full and free participation by men and women of foreign birth and parentage in all the activities of the American community and national life; and (4) a recognition of what our foreign-born peoples have contributed to America and the encouragement of those contributions which, because of their different heritage, they could make to the enrichment of life and culture in the United States. In pursuing these objectives, FLIS was carrying on the following activities:

(1) It was sending to about nine hundred of the 1,076 foreign-language newspapers in America weekly articles, in nineteen languages, on American life and institutions, history and government, on citizenship, employment, and economic problems, schools and education, health, the care of children, etc. Through these articles it was reaching several million foreign-born citizens and aliens, and thus accomplishing a worth-while job of adult education and assimilation.

(2) It assisted annually about four thousand individual immigrants who came to the office or wrote from various parts of the country for information and advice in straightening out some difficulty. It published a naturalization guide.

(3) It issued special articles, reports and legislative bulletins giving authoritative and up-to-date information on immigration and naturalization matters, sending them to about three hundred welfare and civic organizations, public libraries, universities, and government agencies which subscribed to them.

(4) It was active in urging legislation to promote assimilation, unite sepa-

rated families and humanize the deportation laws. Read Lewis frequently appeared before Congressional immigration committees.

Its work, in brief, was up my alley; and I liked Read Lewis, a thin, tall, pleasant, even-tempered man in his mid-forties. With his long experience and profound interest in immigration questions, he unquestionably was a key figure in the whole complex situation from the viewpoint of the present and the future. I liked his attitude, which he expressed one day when I practically forced him to become autobiographical. "I have never had any special interest in the matter," he said, "but I believe my Lewis forebears landed in Massachusetts about 1630. I have a sister who is a member of the D.A.R., so I must have had some ancestors who fought in the American Revolution. My maternal grandfather, a Read, crossed the Isthmus in 1850 and spent five years prospecting on the Pacific Coast, especially in Oregon when that was still a part of the frontier. My father fought in the Civil War and later moved from New England to the Middle West." He added, "I like to think sometimes that in my FLIS work the family is still on the American frontier, and one quite as significant as the older geographical frontiers of the West."

I liked, too, those of my fellow board members whom I met at the meetings which I attended: the prominent New York lawyer and civic leader, Nicholas Kelley, who was our chairman; Sigurd Arnesen, editor of a Norwegian newspaper in Brooklyn; Mrs. Thomas Capek, a leader among the Czechs in New York; Mrs. James A. Kennedy, of Detroit; Eliot D. Pratt, Mrs. George Backer, and Mrs. Jacob A. Riis, of New York; and the well-known writers, Ida M. Tarbell and Will Irwin.

But, in the face of the problems of which I was aware, FLIS was most inadequate. By necessity, partly due to the Depression which had caused many of its regular contributors to cease their donations, it operated on a ridiculously low budget. Many of the people in its office, including writers and translators, received next to nothing for their work. Read Lewis, I suspected, drew no regular salary. And I did not like the name "Foreign Language Information Service," which stuck to it from the war days, although its function now was entirely different from what it had been then. The name helped to focus the organization on the immigrants, rather than on America: which, I felt, tended to limit its outlook. It was all very fine to help the immigrants, to send releases to their newspapers about the Constitution, democracy, and Social Security; but how about the second generation? The number of immigrants was being gradually reduced by death and by virtue of immigration restrictions. In themselves (as I have shown), they were no serious problem. The second generation, however, would go on into the third generation, and so on. That meant the future of America. I was not in favor of giving up the immigrant problems as such, but thought most of them might very well be handled by tackling the problem of their children. I was for taking steps, which might eventually, pending the raising of necessary funds, lead FLIS to become the starting-point of the development of some such XYZ organization as I suggested in *Harpers*.

I was aware of at least a half-dozen other societies and committees, scattered through America, which were interesting themselves in immigration problems and not getting anywhere; why couldn't we in FLIS make an attempt of bringing some of them in time around to the XYZ idea?

Read Lewis was very sympathetic to all these suggestions as were most of our board members. We approached some of the other groups trying to work in the field of immigration problems, but there were personal and other difficulties. Read Lewis and I sweated trying to think of a name for the XYZ organization; none that occurred to us seemed to cover all that we thought XYZ ought to do. But the most serious problem in this idea was financial. We might need, as a beginning, two or three hundred thousand dollars a year. And here was this Depression.

So we more or less dropped the thing, for the time being. As I write, FLIS is still merely FLIS, having a hard time financially to remain even that. But I have a notion, which may not be entirely a wish-notion, that by and by something will yet come of the XYZ suggestion.

Of course I meant from the start that XYZ would be only a beginning in tackling the problem I outlined.

"Foreigners" Are News in Cleveland

I HAVE MENTIONED THAT IN CLEVELAND THE IMMIGRANTS AND THE SECOND GEN-
eration receive a good deal of space in the three large local newspapers:
the *Press*, the *Plain Dealer*, and the *News*. And therein lies a story.

One day early in 1927 a young Rumanian immigrant, Theodore Andrica, who
had had some education in the old country, appeared in the editorial department of the Cleveland *Press*. He said, in his broken English, that he had an
idea he desired to discuss with the editor. The editor saw the young immigrant,
who proceeded to say, in effect, that Cleveland newspapers were missing a bet
when they paid so little—almost no—attention to the foreign-born and their
American-born children in the city.

After all, he went on, about sixty percent of Cleveland's population consisted
of immigrants of approximately forty different nationalities, and their children,
who, although American citizens regardless of whether their parents were
naturalized or not, were still often referred to as "foreigners." Their existence
was almost never recognized by the press, except, of course, when some Slovak,
Pole, Czech, or Slovene got in trouble with the law. This, maintained Andrica,
was an all-around mistake, with the result that the big English-language papers
were not read as widely in the foreign quarters as they would be if they gave
the various national groups some representation in their columns. A paper like
the *Press*, he hinted, was losing money by neglecting the foreign sections. Also,
this neglect was good neither for the city nor the foreigners. There was too
much unhealthy segregation by nationalities and, in consequence, assimilation
or Americanization, or whatever one wished to call it, was slow. Foreigners
had the feeling that no one of any importance in Cleveland was really interested in them; that most persons in the socially and economically dominant
group—the so-called old-time Americans—inclined to look down upon them.
The foreigners' general tendency, as well as that of their American-born
children, was to hang back from things, not to take part in the affairs of
Cleveland, although, said Andrica, they—both as individuals and as groups, or
some of them, anyhow—had a good deal in them which might be useful in the
long run. One way to help bring out that good was to recognize their existence,
to write of them as though the paper considered them part of the city, and thus
make them feel good about themselves and the fact that they lived in Cleveland.

Andrica pulled out of his pocket a batch of scribblings about recent affairs
in the Bohemian, Finnish, German, Jewish, Hungarian, Italian, Lithuanian,
Polish, Rumanian, Russian, South Slavic, Slovak, Scandinavian, Ukrainian
and one or two other foreign groups, and said that he thought these affairs
were news of some importance to Cleveland. He believed that not a few of the
old-time American readers of the *Press* would be interested to know about
them, while the others, perhaps should be made interested.

But what the young Rumanian stressed, of course, was that, if the paper opened its columns to "foreign" news, its circulation would go up—perhaps immediately; if not immediately, in a few months surely. Seeing that the editor was interested, he offered himself for the job of reporting immigrants' doings and affairs and their numerous communities-within-the-city in general, hastening to add that he wrote English a little better than he spoke it and believed he would improve. He said, too, that he already had connections in several foreign groups and thought he would have no difficulty in establishing them in others.

The editor promptly hired Andrica with the understanding that it was to be considered an experiment. But the experiment was almost an immediate success.

Andrica became acquainted with the leaders of the thirty largest nationality groups in the city and brought daily to the office bits of news about the coming meeting of the Slovak Women's Society of Cleveland, the play in rehearsal by a Slovenian dramatic club, the colorful marriage of a Polish couple, the lecture before a Swedish or Jewish group, the death of a worker who had settled in Cleveland in 1901 and in consequence had been the oldest Lithuanian in town, and so on.

These meetings, dramatics, marriages, lectures, deaths, etc., received as much space in the *Press* as similar events in the life of the old-time American citizens of Cleveland and were written up as respectfully. And the circulation of the paper in the foreign quarters went up at once and continued to increase.

Andrica then suggested that the *Press* sponsor a great public festival which would bring together national groups having a background of more than a quarter of a century of life and activity in Cleveland and give them an opportunity to demonstrate before each other and the city at large some phase of their artistic and cultural potentialities. At first there was considerable skepticism in the *Press* office as to the results of such a festival, for many of the groups nursed century-old grudges against one another. However, it was decided to organize an affair called the Dance of the Nations, as dancing was something in which all groups were interested and there was no danger of conflict.

"We began to publish many articles about the characteristics of each nationality's folk dances, and also many pictures," Andrica told me in 1934. "It was the first time that a metropolitan paper of our size had given column after column to the details of folk dances and other features characteristic of these nationalities, and I believe we accomplished a two-fold purpose. We made the nationalities feel that they have something worth while to give, and gave opportunity to non-foreign-born readers to know something about the qualities and accomplishments of the foreign-born."

On the night of November 12, 1927, over eight hundred Swedish, Slovak, Greek, Czech, Ukrainian, Lithuanian, Serbian, Italian, Polish, Irish, Jewish, Hungarian, Slovenian, American Negro, Croatian, "old-fashioned" American,

Scotch, Tyrolian, and Rumanian dancers, male and female, performed in the vast Public Hall. All but three of the groups had orchestras of their own to play for them. "I expected a crowd," Andrica told me, "but even I was surprised when we packed in 14,000 people and turned away 2,000 others for lack of room. The performers, all amateur, did their best and succeeded in showing to the large audience that each country's dances were beautiful and interesting and worthy of being perpetuated in America. Purely on the financial plane, the affair paid for itself."

Encouraged by the success of this venture, the *Press*, in co-operation with the City Recreation Commission, repeated the Dance upon a still larger scale on Labor Day the following year. More than a thousand dancers, again in their picturesque costumes, performed before a crowd estimated at 100,000 in the natural amphitheatre in Brookside Park.

In 1929 the All Nations Council was formed with Recreation Commissioner John H. Gourley as chairman and Andrica as secretary for the purpose of staging an All Nations Exposition in 1930. The Council consisted of three representatives from each participating group and each group was given complete freedom to work out its individual plans. Commissioner Gourley and Andrica were there merely to co-ordinate things, give information and advice. The exhibition occurred in mid-March in the Public Hall, lasted a week, and consisted of twenty-nine full-size reproductions of old-country homes. Nothing was left undone to make the picture as realistic as possible. Most nationalities chose replicas of garden-enclosed peasant houses in their native countries as models for the exhibition, and into these buildings were placed over 50,000 hand-made articles—tapestries, rugs, pottery, goblets, embroideries, lace, scarfs, wood carvings, paintings, etc.; some imported from Europe for this purpose, but most of them loaned by nationals living in Cleveland. In the huge hall were over twenty kitchens in which one could buy typical foreign foods prepared on the spot according to ancient recipes brought over from the old countries by the housewives of the various language groups. Evenings there were folk-dancing and singing programs. During the week more than 100,000 persons visited the exhibition, paying a small admission fee. The fee was charged to cover the expenses of $24,000, advanced by the *Press*, but at the end there was a surplus of $7,300, which was distributed among the participating groups. Several afternoons, schools were closed to enable teachers and children to see the exposition.

The exposition was not marred by a single incident of old-country animosity, and it proved to the *Press* (which not only got back its investment in the affair, but saw its circulation figure go higher and higher) and to the city as a whole that the so-called foreign groups in Cleveland really had more things to contribute to the general culture of the community than even the enthusiastic Andrica had imagined.

The whole idea of giving the immigrant a break was so successful that the *Plain Dealer* and the *News* took it up. The *Plain Dealer* sponsored the so-called

Theater of the Nations project, which included twenty-two productions by the various foreign-language dramatic and singing clubs. The performances were of the same type regularly given in neighborhood and lodge halls in the foreign sections, and the purpose was to show the Anglo-Saxon element that immigrants and their children had much to contribute to the city's life.

Ever since, all three newspapers have continued to give space to the affairs of the foreign-born. When I was in Cleveland in February 1935, one of the papers had in a single issue stories with pictures under the following heads: "Slovaks Stage Mock Wedding—900 Crowd Hall to Witness Reproduction of Old Country Rites"; "Scandinavian Triad Plans Dinner-Dance in Cleveland Club"; and "Association of Polish Women Grows to Membership of 9,000 Here in 22 Years."

In 1932 Andrica hit on another idea in this connection. He knew many immigrants idolized their native villages in Europe, but that few had been able to visit them for many years. Why not "go home" for them collectively, photograph what was new in their villages, talk with their relatives and former neighbors, and write about it in the *Press*? "The idea was a sure-fire one," Andrica told me. "In the summer I was sent to Europe, east and south of Vienna, because that is where most of our Cleveland immigrants came from. I went to the villages and made the stories personal. I met John S——, whose uncle lives at 5598 East 5th Street in Cleveland, and he said . . . etc. I took pictures of the main street, the church, the new priest and mayor, and the stories were a success in Cleveland. In the summer of 1933 and 1934 we repeated it. Now I'm known as 'the man from the *Press* who goes to our village.' Hundreds of persons come to the office or stop me on the street and say, 'Say, next time you go to Poland (or Hungary or Yugoslavia), go to my home town, will you?'"

In 1935 and 1936 Andrica, with an assistant, went again to the old country for about one-fourth of Cleveland, and on these two trips took colored motion pictures of the colorful life in the villages, towns, and cities of Bohemia, Slovakia, Poland, Austria, Hungary, Yugoslavia, Rumania, and two or three other countries. Returning from abroad, he showed his films all over Cleveland. During the fall and winter of those two years he was one of the busiest men in Ohio, also one of the most popular. He presented his films and told of his trip as often as three or four times a day, and this not only before numerous "foreign" groups, to which the scenes shown were intimately interesting, but before endless American clubs and in public and high schools—advertising the *Press* and getting Cleveland acquainted with itself.

In 1937 the "foreign" department of the *Press*, with Andrica in charge, collected enormous masses of historical material about the various immigrant groups in Cleveland, publishing some of it and filing all of it away for the eventual use of future historians of the city.

The *Press* and its two rivals, of course, are doing all this because it is good for circulation, but there are, I think, some excellent by-products of it all. The immigrants and their children in Cleveland appear to me to feel much better about themselves than do immigrants and second-generation people in most other towns where I have been, and this fact, I believe, is due largely to the recognition they are receiving from the big English-language papers in that city. They have a much stronger feeling than immigrants and their off-spring elsewhere that they belong and are part of the place. The old-stock Americans in Cleveland are inclined to accept their fellow citizens of foreign birth or foreign parentage with fewer misgivings. There is less stupid anti-immigrant prejudice in Cleveland than elsewhere. In consequence, there is less unhealthy inversion in the foreign groups than in other sections and, it seems to me, a stronger tendency to the kind of Americanization or assimilation which does not involve suppression of a great many good qualities and potentialities inherent in recent immigrant strains.

What I tell here makes, to my mind, the Cleveland *Press* one of the most remarkable newspapers, and Theodore Andrica one of the most important journalists, in the country.

The Immigrant Press

RIDING IN STREET CARS, SUBWAYS, AND ELEVATED TRAINS, OLD-STOCK AMERICANS, as well as Americans whose background in the United States is a matter of but three or four generations, are wont to feel vaguely uneasy when they see the person next to them reading *Eco d' Italia, Hair[onik]* (Armenian), *Zayednichar* (Croatian), *Svornost* (Czech), *Eteenpain* (Finnish), *Nowy Swiat* (Polish), or any of the other 1,076 foreign-language newspapers and magazines which, as I write this, are published in the country in thirty-eight different languages. They are wont to give the reader of such a publication a suspicious glance. And every once in a while professional alien-haters and patriotic alarmists emit a yell against the immigrant press, which causes well-meaning but ill-informed organizations to pass resolutions and telegraph to Washington.

Actually, the immigrant press is a logical American phenomenon.

Well-nigh every nationality represented in American immigration has, or has had at some time in the past, more and larger newspapers in the United States than in the old country. The reasons for this are several; the most important is that events which vitally affect the people's lives transpire in America with greater frequency than back in Italy, Croatia or Latvia. There life was fixed and settled; hardly anything ever happened, and custom and tradition provided for all the exigencies of daily life. In America, on the other hand, the immigrants found themselves in an utterly changed environment, in a vast, dynamic new country still in the process of formation where conditions changed overnight and without warning. Conduct in Chicago was not based on neighborly gossip. In nine cases out of ten, peasants, on arrival in the United States, became laborers and as such suddenly realized that they were part of the tumultuous life of a modern industrial city or town in a country of vast distances and, so far as they could perceive, without traditions and stability. The peasants were compelled to discard their old-country habits, acquire a few notions about America, and adjust themselves. And the foreign-language newspapers, whether issued by a fraternal organization, the parish priest, or a business man for profit, played (still plays) no small rôle in this process.

For twenty, thirty years before the war the majority of immigrants came from the lower strata of European society and millions of them experienced national consciousness for the first time after arriving in America. The greenhorn was bewildered, then lonely, and in this plight his thoughts naturally turned to his native land and his fellow immigrants. The strangeness of the new surroundings emphasized his kinship with the people and things he had left behind. Soon he discovered that the church, the national fraternal societies, and the foreign-language papers gave him the strongest feeling of home ties, and his life began to revolve around these institutions, which at once helped him to adjust himself in a measure to American conditions and, for their own preservation, naturally enough, saw that he did not become too quickly and too well "Americanized."

Then, also, in many cases the foreigners received their first insight into the political affairs of their old countries only after coming to America. Before the war a number of nationalities heavily represented in the American immigration—the Slovaks, Poles, Czechs, Slovenes, Croats, Finns, Letts, Lithuanians, Syrians, and Armenians—were still under foreign rules, which were inimical to the free dissemination of political news through the vernacular press and, indeed, took drastic measures to extirpate it. In America many foreign editors were political exiles and as such naturally continued to work for the cause among the immigrants to whom the newspaper was addressed and who not infrequently became passionately nationalistic and began to keep in close touch with the political doings at home, sometimes even taking active part in them—all of which, as may be easily seen, also tended against rapid assimilation: and the complaints against the immigrant press of those interested (however unintelligently) in assimilation were somewhat justified—if we forget that this situation was for the most part inevitable.

The World War altered the political status of nearly all the peoples I mentioned. The European nationalist movements, most of them materially aided by immigrants in America, achieved their aim—independence; and, of course, the motive of the nationalist editors to save the immigrants from the influences working for "Americanization" were largely gone. A good many of those nationalist papers passed out soon after the Peace Conference, or became entirely different journals.

During 1917-18 vast numbers of aliens were pulled into the military service, where they were naturalized *en masse*, whether they had lived in the United States ten years or ten weeks. Living forcedly in close daily contact with Americans for a year or more, they learned English and became more or less "Americanized." Many of those who were not drafted worked in shipyards, munitions plants, and steel mills, where it was also best for them to speak English and show as few evidences of their foreign origin as possible, particularly if they came from Central Europe, even if they were Slovaks, Czechs, Slovenians, or Croatians.

This decline of extreme nationalism included the Italian and German immigrants. Some of the Italians, however, worked themselves up again after Mussolini established himself in power and sent over his fascist agents in the mid-1920's; while not a few Germans have done the same since 1933 under the leadership of Hitler's agents. (This is touched upon again in the next chapter.)

Due to the above-mentioned post-war developments in the general immigrant situation, plus the fact that immigration was drastically restricted beginning with 1924, about three hundred foreign-language newspapers and magazines went out of existence in the 1920's. This number included some of the worst examples of journalism. During the Depression of the 1930's about a hundred more passed out. Few new ones were started. Scores cease publication every year or consolidate with others. Some of the best remain. Several of these are financially and otherwise well established, but many barely manage.

In short, the great immigrant press is on the decline. However, it is bound to be an important factor in the life of the United States for some time to come, as it has been heretofore; and it is fitting to glance briefly over its recent history and consider its present rôle and its probable future.

To repeat: the immigrant press is an American product. But it is wholly unlike anything in the English-language journalism, except to some extent in technical makeup. Few foreign-language publishers and editors had any training in the newspaper field in the old country. Most of them stumbled into publishing and editing. Few were well educated in Europe, but some are nevertheless exceptionally intelligent men. Many are self-educated former mill-workers. They edit the large non-profit organs of the fraternal societies. A salary of fifty dollars weekly is exceptional. Some exist on fifteen, twenty a week. Numerous papers they edit are shabby affairs, written down to the most ignorant subscriber. On the other hand, three or four hundred of them, or probably one-third of them, are issuing fairly good publications for what they are intended to be. A dozen or two of them publish occasional original poems, stories, and articles about immigrant life. A Slovenian paper, *Glas Naroda* (*People's Voice*), has now had a humorist-columnist for twenty-odd years, whose comments on the trend of things often are extraordinarily penetrating. The Croatian *Svijet* (*World*), publishes some of the best editorials in America in any language. The quality of the Jewish *Daily Forward*—whose editor-in-chief, Abraham Cahan, is the author of *The Rise of David Levinsky*—is well known. . . . By and large, however, the columns of foreign-language newspapers are filled with American and world news culled from the large English-language newspapers, fiction reprinted from old-country publications, jokes, lodge announcements, news of working conditions in the various sections of the country sent in by worker-correspondents from mining towns and manufacturing centers, personal notices, and items about events in the homeland, the latter also cut out of old-country papers. In many foreign-language editorial offices, scissors are called the first assistant editor.

The workers' reports of labor conditions in the various places are important. They are to be found in most papers. They cause people to move where work is said to be more plentiful or better paid.

In the 1900's and 1910's, the most interesting characters among the foreign-language journalists were the "Americanized" go-getters, who published their newspapers as part of their business and boob-baiting schemes. One of these fellows, operating largely among the Slavs, was at the height of his success about 1910. At various times he published successful papers in four different languages. They were written to appeal to the most gullible immigrants. He flattered them and did his best to convince them that he was a great man and their God-given friend in a strange country. He printed fake photographs of himself shaking hands with the President of the United States, Teddy Roosevelt or Taft, or some cardinal, governor, ambassador, or justice of the Supreme Court. Tens of thousands of immigrants eagerly ate up the ding-dong filling his columns and swore by him—even after thousands of them had lost several million dollars in a private bank scheme of his, which, somehow, had failed to work out. He engaged clever lawyers, evaded the law, and convinced not a few of his victims that he was really the victim of a plot on the part of forces preying on all immigrants; which, in a measure was true, for the most important part of his "Americanization" was a passion to get rich quick.

The story of the foreign-language press as a factor in the political life of the United States should interest the student of the American scene. Its climax centers around an uneducated but extraordinary immigrant from Poland, Louis N. Hammerling, who back in the 1900's and 1910's made a monkey of the Republican elephant and became a millionaire.

The dawn of this century found Louis Hammerling, then in his early thirties, advertising manager of an obscure Polish sheet in Wilkes-Barre, Pennsylvania. In his spare time he solicited ads for the *United Mine Workers' Journal* and studied the American laws of success. The political game fascinated him, and, getting next to the local Republican organization, he took an active part in a gubernatorial campaign. He was noticed by the mighty Penrose and in the fall of 1904 was in New York taking charge of the immigrant press for the Grand Old Party. Four years later, although not legally a citizen of the United States, he was a delegate to the Republican national convention from Pennsylvania and not long after, having learned all there was to know about success, he decided to make New York his permanent headquarters, in order to "milk the fat cow of the Republican party and bully the simple calves of the foreign-language press in a more efficient way." With money which presumably he secured from the Republicans he purchased an unsuccessful Italo-American advertising agency and relabeled it the American Association of Foreign-Language Newspapers. There was little doing politically till 1912 and meanwhile Hammerling began to function as a commercial advertising agency. A go-getter of great acumen, he secured large advertising contracts from such concerns as the Standard Oil Company and the American Tobacco Company for hundreds of immigrant newspapers which had subscribed to his service. In 1911 he had the jovial idea of giving a great banquet for the customers on both ends of his business, among them some of the most prominent business men in America. His guests of honor included many of the leading Republican politicians, including four members of the Taft Cabinet. These men, Hammerling later boasted, "were glad to come. . . . I had all the standing I wanted among them." And, of course, these contacts with the high and mighty Hammerling immediately capitalized with the publishers of the foreign-language newspapers all over the country.

In the 1912 Presidential campaign, according to his own testimony on December 3, 1918, before the Senate committee investigating various alien agencies in the United States, Hammerling handled 70,000 lines of Republican advertising, for which he received "over $100,000," about half of which was supposed to go to the publishers, but which he paid mainly in stock issued by his company—for, as he was wont to insist, in all his political and business transactions he conformed strictly to the American political and business methods and customs "as I found them."

Hammerling became a big man. His banquets were attended by the "cream of the country." In the 1916 Presidential election he again handled a great sum of Republican money and kept most of it. In addition, during 1915 and 1916 he received over $200,000 from the Brewers' Association for his so-called "personal liberty" campaign, which consisted of a monthly 1,000-word article in several hundred immigrant papers. These articles, written for the most part by unknown American press agents, were perhaps the best thing that ever appeared in many of the foreign-language papers. They really went into the problem of personal liberty. Few of the editors and none of the readers knew at the time that they were inspired by the brewers, who were afraid of Prohibition.

Hammerling had his fingers in other luscious pies. He mixed in and settled labor troubles. He was friendly with the employers and devoted to the workmen. Through his connection with foreign-language editors he could influence the workers and then advise the bosses accordingly. As a rule he managed to get the entire credit for the settlement. This placed him in confidential relations with big-business men, increased his prestige all around and enabled him to secure ads for the immigrant papers almost on his own terms, for no one knew the value of advertising in the foreign-language press outside of the German and Scandinavian papers; with the result that he acquired a monopoly and had the publishers at his mercy.

But his greatest coup was the "Appeal to the American People" to stop, "in the name of humanity," the manufacture and shipment to Europe of munitions, published as an advertisement in all the important American dailies on April 5, 1915, for which he received from Dr. Heinrich Albert, the German agent in the United States, as it was subsequently revealed at a Senatorial investigation and printed in Senate Document No. 62, $204,900 in cash, out of which he paid the advertising agency which had placed the advertisements $48,138. The appeal was signed "The American Association of Foreign-Language Newspapers," purported to represent 450 publishers. The next day the New York *Times* quoted Hammerling as having said that he had engineered the entire thing out of humanitarian motives, but three and a half years later he admitted to the Senate committee that "times were hard and I thought it good business to get the advertisements."

In fine, Hammerling was an *allrightnik*, a successful immigrant according to American standards; one who "got away with it." He considered himself one of the most thoroughly "Americanized" foreigners. Before the Senate committee he said that he was simply doing what he had "learned in this country from the American newspaper people in the way they are doing it." His "association" was a fake, yes—what of it? he said in effect. He saw the opportunity for much "honest graft" and exploited it. He made no conscientious effort to do anything but enrich himself. He acted as middleman between the immigrant press and the advertiser, but neither knew at any time what he was doing on the other end. He rose on his ability to capitalize and sell to each his influence, real and pretended, with the other. In the political field most of his influence with the foreign-language publishers was a myth, and the Republicans might as well have hired a Zulu to herd them in into their camp. After he forsook his naïve political friends, he said: "I had about as much political control over the foreign-language paper as the Pope has in a synagogue, if you will permit the expression."

As a result of his German propaganda work in the United States and certain irregularities in his naturalization papers, he was shortly after the war forced to leave the country. He returned to Poland, a millionaire several times. He started a paper in Cracow, became a Senator during the Pilsudski regime, and in 1934 returned to New York for a visit and was killed in a fall from a hotel window—probably a suicide.

The Hammerling organization was the first and last large-scale attempt on the part of a great American party to get control of the foreign-language press. The cunning immigrant from Poland had taught them a lesson. Now, during election campaigns, they hire contact men of various nationalities who are supposed to know the public prints of their respective groups, and thus place their political advertisements more discreetly.

Since the war great sections of the immigrant population (Czech, Slovak, Polish, and South Slavic) have been overwhelmingly Democratic, partly because they believe that Woodrow Wilson was largely instrumental in freeing their old countries from foreign oppression, but—during the 1930's—mainly because they are preponderantly working-people and the New Deal has been good to them as such. Their press supports them in this belief. In 1936, perhaps, ninety-five per cent of foreign-language newspapers were for Roosevelt and the Democratic candidates generally.

When the alien-baiters let out their yells against the foreign-language press, they mean particularly the radical or Red newspapers, which their fear-ridden minds imagine are, unbeknown to the country at large, successfully hacking away at the American foundations. In point of fact, most of the leftist immigrant journals barely exist, for the majority of the foreign-born are, if anything, rather more conservative than the general run of old-stock Americans. Not being entirely at home here, many are afraid to be, or to appear, radical. A few of the foreign radicals are extreme, but their chief—unwitting—effect is that they impel most of their fellow countrymen farther to the right than they would be otherwise.

Some of the foreign-language papers have become English-language. Others have merged with regular American papers. Several hundred have English columns, or sections. This is especially true of the organs of fraternal societies, which are practically coöperative insurance companies and, as such, eager to draw to themselves the immigrants' American-born children who know only English. In a few (too few) instances, these English pages and sections are well written and edited, and help New Americans to acquire some sense of their background. None, however, have as yet begun to sink their teeth into the second-generation problem.

The Native's Return put me in touch with a few Croatian and Slovenian editors in New York, Cleveland, Pittsburgh, and Chicago, who are probably representative of the better sort of foreign-language editors of other nationalities.

Don Niko Grskovich, who edits the already-mentioned Croatian daily *Svijet* in New York, is probably the dean of South Slavic editors in America. As I write, he is in his mid-seventies, a giant of nearly six and a half feet, straight as a rod (both physically and morally); with a classic Dalmatian face (he comes from the island of Krk), a thick thatch of iron-gray hair, every tooth in his mouth, no glasses, and a deep, persuasive voice, which he wontedly uses to say something worthwhile. His interest in America is as profound, intelligent, and perturbed as it is in the old country; and the contents of his paper are a graceful balance between the Old and the New Worlds.

I know little of the background of Milan Petrak, chief editor of the weekly *Zayednichar* (*Unifier*), organ of the great Croatian Fraternal Union, or "Zayednitsa," which has eighty thousand members, with headquarters in Pittsburgh. Through the newspaper, Petrak's office distributed several hundred copies of *The Native's Return*. But he was distressed by my novel, *Cradle of Life*, which is laid in Croatia before the war, and which rather more than hints that everything was not sweet and perfect there at the time. He bitterly attacked me in the paper; and when I visited Pittsburgh late in 1936 we engaged—Balkan fashion—in a long, heated, and futile argument. While the papers in Croatia praised the novel in extravagant terms, Petrak insisted that I had put Croatia in a bad light before the eyes of America. I countered that either he completely misunderstood the book or was one of those immigrants I have mentioned before who fear and tremble lest the American public learn something unpleasant about them or their old country, which might then react unfavorably upon them.

Due mainly to its editor, Ivan Molek, the daily *Prosveta* (*Enlightenment*), published in Chicago as the organ of the Slovenian National Benefit Society, doubtless is one of the best balanced, most effective immigrant publications; and Molek's personal story is probably not unlike that of hundreds of foreign-language editors. He was eighteen when he emigrated from Carniola in 1900, and for years worked as a common laborer in the steel-mills of Pennsylvania, earning from $1.20 to $1.50 for a ten- or twelve-hour day. Then he headed West and located some relatives in Calumet, Michigan, which is one of the oldest Slovenian colonies. There he obtained work in a copper-mine and all but lost his life in an accident. He became a citizen, learned English, and occasionally sent a piece to a Slovenian paper in Chicago, describing working conditions in Calumet as they affected the immigrants. By and by the publisher invited him to come to Chicago and become the editor. . . . In the *Prosveta* he publishes original novels and one-act plays about Slovenian immigrants, many of which he writes himself. The paper has an English section and a special correspondent in Carniola, who happens to be one of its better younger poets. . . . The fraternal union that issues *Prosveta* publishes also a juvenile magazine, *Mladinski List*, which prints folk-tales in the original Slovenian and in English translation.

In Cleveland, Vatro Grill, the young publisher-editor of the daily *Enakopravnost* (*Equality*), had been exceedingly kind and friendly to me in print even before I realized he knew of me. In 1934, throwing the whole force of his paper behind the book, his office distributed six or seven hundred copies of *The Native's Return*, because he believed it would be a good thing if the New Americans of Slovenian origin in Cleveland would read it and learn something of their parents' homeland. Meeting, we discovered that as boys in our early teens we had attended the same school in Carniola (only in different classes) and had come to America the same year. Gifted with a quick intelligence, speaking fluent English, and possessing a deep concern for America, he uses his paper to encourage sound, gradual assimilation without unnecessary suppression of old-country cultural backgrounds, and urges the thirty thousand Slovenian nationals in Cleveland to take active part in the city's civic and political life. He intends to publish *Enakopravnost* as long as there is need for it; when that need passes, he will be glad.

And finally there is Anton Terbovec, editor of *Nova Doba* (*New Era*), organ of one of the smaller Slovenian fraternal unions and one of the most delightful persons I know. He came to America in 1906, in his mid-twenties, and worked at various ill-paid, unsatisfying jobs in Pennsylvania, Ohio, and Utah till 1911, when he became a citizen and a pack-peddler, going about the United States with an assortment of watches, watch chains and fobs, rings, tie-pins, ear-rings, brooches, and other jewelry, which he sold to his fellow countrymen in out-of-the-way mining towns and labor camps, mostly in the West. He was one of several such peddlers among the Slovenians, but not because he had the soul of a business man, rather in consequence of a powerful desire to see the country—for he had fallen in love with the immense place almost immediately on his arrival. With brief intervals between trips, which yielded him just enough to live, he traveled all over America till 1924; and, traveling, wrote little pieces for Slovenian-language newspapers—reports of working conditions in Jenny Lind, Arkansas, or Butte, Montana; accounts of social and lodge life among Slovenian immigrants in various settlements, as he saw it, usually with a humorous touch; and poetry and brief travel stories and articles most of which were also funny or gay: for he is that sort of fellow. Even now, in his late fifties, his face is a perpetual grin, which is typical of many Slovenians, though more so in the old country than in America.

In 1924 Terbovec was asked to take over the editorship of *Nova Doba*. The organization of which it is the organ is a non-partisan, non-political group. Its name is South Slavic Catholic Union, but it is not really very Catholic, nor anti-Catholic. And the paper's editorial policy, which was explained to him when he accepted the job, was for the most part a. negative one. He could report politics, but not comment on anything political. There must be no religious discussion. No propaganda, no bias, in any shape or form. All of which pleased Terbovec no end, for, as he told me, "I don't like squabbles and arguments, least of all political and religious ones." The paper is a six-page weekly. The society's affairs take about four pages; there is a half-page of advertisements, and the rest he fills with things that interest and please him.

Before coming to America, Terbovec served as a gardener on a great estate in Styria; so now he often writes about flowers and seeds and spring and the gayeties and follies and wonders of nature in general, and this as likely on page one as anywhere else. Also on page one he runs his regular column *"Vsak po svoyé"* ("Each in His Own Way"), wherein he humorously and objectively comments on events, conditions, and personalities:

An undeclared war between the Chinese and the Japanese is going on in which thousands of soldiers and civilians already have lost their lives. Yet the Japanese insist it is not war. What it is, if not war, is hard to say. It is not a picnic.

Our soldiers in America, however, can make a picnic, if not out of war, certainly out of military manoeuvers. Somewhere in Massachusetts, an infantry unit of the State National Guard recently failed to carry out an attack as ordered because, while crawling through a wood, the boys came upon a lot of ripe blueberries and forgot about the enemy.

In every number he writes an autobiographical article about his travels in the United States. He never repeats himself; he has enough material for the rest of his life, regardless of how long he continues as editor of *Nova Doba*. He urges his readers to move about and see the country; "when you see it, you will be sure to love it."

During 1934-37 I called on him, or he came to my hotel, every time I visited Cleveland. Once he said to me, "You know, in my own funny way I am proud I am a Slovenian and glad I am in America. . . . Traveling, I would come to some dismal mining or mill town in Michigan, Montana, or Utah; and, turning a corner, there would be two or three little houses with gardens and hedges around them, and potted flowers along the window-sills, and I would know they were inhabited by Slovenian families. Another sure way to spot a Slovenian home in America is to look for wash drying on the fence instead of a rope. . . . And these Americans! I mean the old-stock kind—say what you like about them or the country: everything is true; but to me, especially those in the West, Americans are a wonderful breed. There is *something* here!

Look what happened in two hundred years. These cities and roads and railways. There was vision. . . ."

Traveling, he had spent most of his time among Slovenians, stopping in their homes and *bordingauses* (boarding-houses). I asked him what they talked about.

"Oh, of all sorts of things—of work and working conditions, wages and hours, and of hunting and fishing. Our people who went West became great hunters and fishermen, because in the old country poor people could not fish or hunt, as the large estate proprietors owned all the forests and fishing rights. . . . What else did they talk about? Well, of their fraternal lodges, which greatly contributed to their feeling of security here, and of picnics and singing societies. Always there was much singing and drinking—here and there rather too much of the latter, if one asked the women. . . . And occasionally they talked of the old country; however, mostly when there seemed to be something wrong here. When there were strikes and violence, women dreamed of the quiet villages of their birth in Carniola. . . ."

"Oh, yes," Terbovec said on another occasion, "I had lots of fun in the West. . . . In Colorado and Utah, in those days, the mining companies owned the towns or camps where the workers lived. The companies feared union organizers, and no stranger was allowed to come in, certainly not to stay any length of time. Frequently I was shipped out of town by sheriffs, who were really company guards. My business was always only selling jewelry or visiting some countryman, but I had to slip into town as though I were a criminal just escaped from prison who wanted to see his dear old mother before she died. If I wanted to stay overnight, I had to hide in somebody's house; and even there I wasn't safe. Several times I was caught at night and sent on my way.

"There were whole counties owned by the companies. Once I decided to have a little fun with the county sheriff in Castle Gate, Utah, who was a very strict company man. He had thrown me out of Castle Gate the year before. So now I approached the gate, smoking a long stogie, my hat cocked to one side. What did I want? I said I was going to Castle Gate. Was I looking for work? No, I replied. Then, he said, nothing doing; the company allowed no strangers in Castle Gate. I said I wasn't worried about the company; I was going to Castle Gate. Oh no, I wasn't! I asked if there was a United States post-office at Castle Gate? Of course there was, said the sheriff. I made sure he realized it was a United States and not a company post-office, then said that that was where I was going—to the United States post-office in Castle Gate, and I would like to see the man who was going to stop me. He let me go through the gate, then accompanied me all the way to the post-office, several miles away. I knew there was no mail for me there, but I asked at the general-delivery window, anyhow. I bought fifteen postcards and spent a couple of hours slowly writing to my friends all over America, for I had more time than anything else; and the sheriff waited for me. He escorted me back to the gate, where I thanked him for his company. He thought I was a funny fellow. Just some crazy foreigner! . . ."

From My Diary

January 10, 1934.—Some day I hope to write a short story or novel which will show the profound tragedy of immigrant parents in America in relation to their American-born children. But perhaps I scarcely need to do it. Read Lewis just sent me the translation of a letter that a Lithuanian immigrant wrote to FLIS, which I think is a little masterpiece:

I am now a broken old man, physically. The best years of my life were spent in the steel blast furnaces of Pennsylvania. There I helped with my muscle to complete the work which nature started.

My wife has gone to her just reward these many years past. Her grave lies amongst these hills. Flowers will barely grow upon it. The dust that is in my lungs, and which gives me and my friends no peace, also covers her grave.

My children have grown up. They are educated, and the education given them by America has taken them from me. I speak English only as an untaught alien can speak it. But my children know all the slang phrases. They speak differently, they act differently, and when they come to visit me they come alone. They do not explain why they do not bring their friends, but I instinctively sense the reason. They should not fear. I would not cause them any embarrassment. But they too look upon their old father as an inferior, an alien, a bohunk.

So my only consolation is my memory. And strange as it may seem to you, my experiences in America are not the ones that crowd my thoughts. No, it is the memory of my childhood days, spent in far away Lithuania. I remember the folklore and the great green forests.

Once I asked my mother to explain the noises that we heard coming from the heart of the forest after sundown. And my mother said the sounds were the songs of joy uttered by the spirits of departed animals that had lived freely. The heart of the forest, she said, was their heaven. After I learned that story the heart of the forest and all natural fastnesses were always holy places to me.

So now these simple memories are with me, not the thought of America's greatness. Maybe it is because I was so strong in body when I left Lithuania, and am now a broken old man. And the forest did not take my health and my children away from me.

COMPLEXITY OF THE PROBLEM

March 26, 1934, in Pittsburgh.—Three days ago I spoke here before The Hungry Club, a luncheon group of liberal business and professional men. My subject was the second generation, what I know of it. The audience was interested, for Pittsburgh and vicinity are more than half "foreign." In my talk I used the phrase "New American," but now I find that I am not the first to use it. After the meeting I was introduced to a man in his early forties, Edward O. Tabor, a local lawyer, also active in politics; a Czech by origin, who then sent me a printed copy of a speech of his, entitled "The University and the New American," which he had delivered a couple of years ago before the faculty and trustees of the University of Pittsburgh, and wherein he urged that educators become interested in the immigrants and their American-born children.

Last night I visited at the Tabors' home. Mrs. Tabor is a lovely American-born Irishwoman from Boston, in love with the Slavs, especially with their songs and music. She sang for me several Carniolan songs, and sang them well. I was very much moved.

We talked of the immigrant and second-generation situation in Pittsburgh. There is much discrimination. Many firms, owned or managed by old-stock Americans, which hereabouts usually means Scotch-Irish, refuse to employ anyone whose name ends in *ski* or *ich*. Persons with such names are said to be discriminated against even when they apply for municipal or state civil service jobs. Generally speaking, the socio-economically dominant Scotch-Irish element looks down upon and resents the new immigrants, except in so far as they serve its interests, which, in a way, is amusing, for not so long ago the Scotch-Irish themselves were newcomers here and were held in low esteem by the snooty English. Tabor told me that among the old Pittsburghiana at the public library there is the original letter of an English lord, who passed through what is now the Pittsburgh region, then wrote home that the Scotch-Irish settlers were a low, disgusting lot, expectorating in their homes, lacking utterly in the refinements of life. . . .

Of course I realize that if some of the present-day new immigrants ever became socio-economically dominant, they will probably look down on, or discriminate against, somebody else. The trouble in Pittsburgh, for instance, is not really only with the Scotch-Irish; the trouble is all around. Nearly every group hates, or is contemptuous of, some other group. Not a few of the Slovenians don't think very much of some of the Croatians, and *vice versa*. Many of the Czechs don't like the Slovaks. Few Germans think anything of the Slavs. Most of the non-Jewish immigrant groups are more or less anti-Semitic. The Jews scorn the Hunkies, but have this in common with them: they both stick up their noses at the Negro. (There is a Slovenian paper in Cleveland, controlled by the local Democratic machine, which once called upon the naturalized Slovenians to vote Democratic because the Republican party had freed the Negro!) . . . All of which, to a very great extent, is due to the fact that each of the groups knows no more of the others than the old-stock Americans know about immigrants as a whole. . . . It's an immense problem; but, clearly, a problem of education.

NATIONALITY ROOMS IN THE CATHEDRAL OF LEARNING

March 27, 1934, in Pittsburgh.—I don't like the looks of the University of Pittsburgh's new building, the Cathedral of Learning. Its forty-odd Gothic stories loom irrelevantly. Frank Lloyd Wright called it "the biggest 'Keep-off the Grass' sign in the world." But it is there to stay; if for no other reason, because it is worth several tens of millions of dollars! . . . However, there is one good thing about it, so far as I am concerned. On the main floor are the so-called Nationality Rooms, as yet unfinished, which will be used as class-rooms during the day, and evenings as meeting-halls on special occasions for the various nationality groups. The designs and plans are more or less worked out.

The Polish Room, for instance, is a copy of a room in the fourteenth-century Jagiellonian Library at the University of Cracow, where Copernicus once studied. The Czechoslovak Room was designed by a leading Prague architect. The Italian Room will be Renaissance. The Yugoslav Room will be done in Slavonian oak. And so on. The rooms are being paid for by the various national-ities. If nothing else, the project is a recognition of the existence of these several nationalities within the life of Pittsburgh.

ONE IMMIGRANT'S CONTRIBUTION

August 3, 1934.—Two weeks ago I started to write *Grandsons*. . . . I wish I were ten people so I could write about ten books a year and, say, a hundred magazines pieces. . . . Some day I simply must do a book on the immigrants' contributions to America. I know, more or less, only what the South Slavs have contributed. . . . Last night I came on the following story in one of the FLIS publications, translated from the German paper, the *New Yorker Herold*.

Wendlin Grimm, a German immigrant from Kuehlsheim in southern Ger-many, emigrated to Carver, Minnesota, at the age of thirty-nine. In his old home he had known the value of lucerne as a means of loosening the soil and as a good feed for dairy and work animals. He therefore took with him to America a small bag of lucerne seed. Soon after his arrival in the month of September, 1857, he bought a small hilly farm, and in the following spring sowed his precious grains. In his home they called the plant "everlasting clover," because it shoots up every year without fresh planting. Today, after sixty-seven years, the same lucerne plants are found on the hills of the little farm where Grimm had sowed them.

His first crop was almost a total failure. But, believing in the plant, he was not disheartened. As the seed had come from the temperate lowlands of Baden and Wuerttemberg, the much more severe climate of Minnesota killed most of the plants. However, Grimm was persistent. He collected the seed of the plants that had withstood the fierce cold, made new trials in other fields and found that his lucerne crop became finer and more luxuriant year by year. The plants gradually hardened to the climate, and the new seed showed a high degree of germinative capacity, so that as time went on the gaps in the field filled up.

Without knowing it, Grimm had carried out a successful experiment in natural selection. Every year he saved the seeds selected by nature and was thus able to sow ever increasing areas with plants that were able to stand the severe winters of Minnesota.

In 1891, Grimm bought another farm and gave the old one to his son.

Grimm's everlasting clover was soon found in every part of the region where all the other kinds of clover were killed by the cold weather. People in distant parts of the country heard of it and thought that the soil of Carver County was chiefly responsible for the results. A young teacher drew the attention of the St. Anthony Park Agricultural Station to the plant. It was tested and found of great value. Then someone sent a packet of the seed to the United States Bureau of Plant Industry. All the experimenters found that Grimm's lucerne surpassed all other varieties in yield and in resistance to cold.

The results of the last thirty years corroborate these findings. Grimm's variety is now sowed in all the northwestern States as well as in Canada. Today there are large lucerne seed farms which send their products as far as Montana, Kansas, New England States and Canada. In 1924 the farmers and business men of the Northwest expressed their appreciation of Grimm's gift to the country by erecting a monument to him on the exact spot where he sowed his first bag of everlasting clover in 1858.

LETTER FROM META

May 27, 1934.—I am thinking of doing a piece, perhaps for *Harpers*, on the immigrants' children, or the second generation: a most complicated and delicate subject, about which almost nothing has been written. I am fumbling about for material; almost no one I know has any idea about it. . . . Two weeks ago I wrote to Meta [the eighteen-year-old, exceptionally intelligent daughter of a friend of mine in Hollywood, who is economically successful and partial to Gibbon's *Fall of the Roman Empire*], asking her what it meant to be the child of immigrants and how things looked to her. Today I received her reply:

. . . I *am* the child of immigrant parents. My father didn't come to this country until he was twenty-one. He left Poland to escape Russian militarism. They would have put him in the army and marched him across Russia to Siberia. Imagine Daddy, with his flat feet and that inertia which comes from a good knowledge of Roman history, marching to Siberia! Mother came to this country when she was twelve. Her father had left his wife and four girls in Hungary and had gone off to America, and that was practically the last they heard of him, except that he made a lot of money in something. So Mother, at that age, went to work making ties in New York.

Both my parents became quickly Americanized, despite their deep traditional background in Europe. Neither of them associated much with foreigners in this country. Daddy learned English during his first year here—as you know, by re-reading Tom Paine's *Appeal to Reason* till he understood every word in the book. . . . Therefore my upbringing has less of the immigrant trace than many whose parents constantly spoke their old language, lived among their own people, and in the case of Jews, kept strictly to their old religion. Nevertheless, I shall always have a certain flavor in me that is distinctly not American. The almost inherited familiarity, for instance, with some aspects of European village life. All this, of course, is very early childhood association, stories my parents told me, and their reactions here to what was familiar to them in Europe. I cannot tell you what the sound of the Hungarian language means to me, although I do not understand it. Or how deeply I love Hungarian gypsy music, its tremendous gaiety and passion.

You ask me what it means to me to be an American. Why, almost nothing. Except that I am glad I was born in America because it is more comfortable here for me than it probably would be in Europe. Then, too, the country itself gives me a shiver; it is magnificent. Although its arms and legs are falling off from disuse and its sex is slightly frustrated from cheap evasion, still it has the possibilities of the gods, and one day it may be a decent place. That is, if the world ever will be a decent place.

You ask me if I belong. I belong perfectly. Sometimes it frightens me, because I sing the song and dance the dance and am very definitely a product of super-mechanism and standard grapenuts. I went through the public schools, and although I rebelled constantly I still belonged there. I think, however, that my tendency to decry the hokum of what everything "constitutional" stood for had something to do with a background of parents who didn't exactly know what constitutional meant.

You ask me what I think my future here is and the future of young people in general. I think the future is terribly vague, quite hopeless-seeming on the whole, and chaotic. It lies, in each case, entirely with the individual and his luck in cir-cumstances. It is tragic, I believe, that we of the younger generation cannot see a future for ourselves in which we all take part toward an honest social progress. I suppose those young people who are Communists do see that sort of thing, but although my sympathies are very much with them, to me that too is uncertain. The shreds of individualism are still somewhat with us and we step out of child-hood into our separate rackets and creeds.

NATURALIZATION

January 5, 1935.—I read that Congressman Taylor of Tennessee has intro-duced a bill "to deport any alien who has been eligible for citizenship for five years or more and does not take the necessary steps to become naturalized within twelve months from the passage of this act"—which is a good example of thoughtlessness connected with immigrant problems. This bill, which, of course, has no chance of passing, is a gesture in the dark. If enacted, its effect would be to cause many aliens to apply for citizenship who would not other-wise do so, and many undesirable aliens would become citizens. . . . Natu-ralization must remain entirely voluntary.

A POEM

March 15, 1935.—A week ago I received a letter from a lady in New York, Mrs. Julia Glasgow, telling me of her experience when she first registered as a voter. "Native born or naturalized?" she was asked. Her answer, "Natural-ized," seemed to cast a reflection on her. Then she wrote a poem, which was published in the New York *Evening Post* "in that year when so many aliens had but lately shed their blood for the country of their adoption." I liked the poem and wrote to Mrs. Glasgow for her permission to reprint it somewhere eventually. Today I received her permission:

Is he the only true American
Whom chance so favored that his cradle stood
Beneath the flag, that others, not so blessed,
Yearned for in distant lands, and made their own
Through ruthless sundering of every tie
That bound them to the land that gave them birth?
He's not the truer son who lightly says
"I am thy child, begotten of thy flesh
And 'tis my duty that I honor thee,"
Than he who came, craved nurture at thy breast,
Saying: "I am aweary and athirst;
I will requite thee later with my strength,
My manhood give to make thy days secure.
I will cleave unto thee as flesh to flesh,
Receive upon my breast blows aimed at thine."
Nor is he the better citizen who says:
"I'm an American; my fathers won
This title for me," which he lightly holds—
Many there are such—than the foreign born,
Who sought the citizenship as the Grail,
Who feels it as one feels the holy chrism,
Who counts it as a buckler and a shield.

THE JEWS

Undated Notes.—The Jews, I think, fascinate me more than any other racial or national group. I hope some day to be able to make a study of them in America. They are probably the most important group here, next to the Anglo-Saxon. Probably not quite so important economically as generally supposed, but very important intellectually and culturally. [During a lecture tour early in 1936] I spoke at several forums in various parts of the country. Invariably, it was a Jew, either foreign born or native, who kept the forum going, though usually he kept discreetly in the background. . . .

Anti-Semitism, which I encounter everywhere, is a complex, stupid business, and full of dangers also for others than Jews. It only makes the delicate Jewish Question worse for the Jews and non-Jews. But not all Jews know how to deal with it; many, in fact, are as unwise about it as the anti-Semites and make it worse. These are some of the public-character or professional Jews who act like modern versions of the prophets of Israel and usually provoke resentment. . . . [Late in 1936] I became acquainted with some of the people running the American-Jewish Committee in New York, of which I had not heard before —for the reason that they work quietly and do not seek publicity for themselves. They are Jews, but also Americans. They do not fight merely anti-Semitism, isolated from other manifestations of intolerance, but rather intolerance and prejudice generally. But "fight" is not the word. What they are doing is really education. They are as much against alien-baiting directed against the

Slavs or Italians as they are against anti-Semitism, for they know that the two
are closely akin. . . .

THE FASCISTS AND THE NAZIS IN AMERICA

January 6, 1937.—Lately I received two newspaper clippings. One is from
Milwaukee showing German immigrants and American-born Germans parad-
ing in Nazi uniforms, giving the Nazi hand salute. The other is from Philadelphia, showing a similar Italian-fascist parade. On the Milwaukee clipping,
the anonymous sender wrote: "What do you think of *this* sort of thing?"

Answer: I don't like it; I am against it; my first impulse is to suppress the
Nazi German immigrant groups, as well as the fascist Italian immigrant
groups, inspired from Berlin and Rome, respectively—but it is the wrong
impulse. The thing to do is not to make them illegal, but to show them up as
un-American, expose them in public prints and elsewhere with criticism, which
is based on American ideas of liberty and democracy.

On the other hand, these Nazi and fascist groups in this country are not
really as numerous as they may appear. One hears of them because they are
so obvious, dramatic, or fantastic, which gets them into papers. But one does
not hear of the majority of Italians and Germans in the United States who
are not Nazis or fascists, but, for the most part, merely human beings.

A BOOK ABOUT IMMIGRANTS

Undated Note (1935).—On the suggestion of Miss DuBois [of the Service
Bureau for Education in Human Relations] I have been reading a volume
called *Our Foreigners,* by Samuel P. Orth, which is said to be one of the books
much used in the sociology and American-history classes of colleges and universities in the United States ever since it was published early in the 1920's.[1]

On page 162 I read of "fetid tenements swarming with immigrants," and
how Henry James, on revisiting Boston after a long absence, "was shocked at
the 'gross little foreigners' who infested its streets, and he said it seemed as if
the fine old city had been wiped with 'a sponge saturated with the foreign mixture and passed over almost everything I remembered and might have still
recovered.' "

On page 163 I am told that in consequence of "the new immigration," which
began in the 1880's, "the larger cities of the United States are congeries of
foreign quarters, whose alarming fecundity fills the streets with progeny and
whose polyglot chatter on pay night turns even many a demure New England
town into a veritable babel."

On page 167 "the recent Polish immigrant is very circumscribed in his
mental horizon" and on page 168 the spirit of American democracy makes no
"headway against his lethal stolidity" until the second or third generation is
reached. Still the Pole is "more independent and progressive" than the Slovak,

---

[1] All quotations on this and the ensuing two pages are from *Our Foreigners* by S. P. Orth, Volume 35, The Chronicles of America, Copyright Yale University Press.

who, on page 168, keeps "aloof from things American" and "only too often" prefers "to live in squalor and ignorance."

On page 169 the Ukrainians "are birds of passage, working in the mines and steel-mills for the coveted wages that shall free them from debt" back in Ukraine. "Such respite as they take from their labors is spent in the saloon, in the clubrooms over the saloon, or in church, where they hear no English speech and learn nothing of American ways."

The Slavs generally, on pages 173-174, are children of ignorance and feudal oppression, "bound in superstition by a reactionary ecclesiasticism. The brutality with which they treat their women, their disregard for sanitary measures, and their love for strong drink are evidences of the survival of medievalism in the midst of modern life, as are their notions of class prerogative and their concept of the state." Their "fecundity is amazing," as "is the indifference of the Government and of Americans generally to the menace involved in the increasing numbers of these inveterate aliens to institutions that are fundamentally American."

On page 175 "the one mercantile ambition" of the Lithuanians and Magyars "is to keep a saloon. Drinking is their national vice; and they measure the social success of every wedding, christening, picnic, and jollification by its salvage of empty beer kegs." On the next page, "Drinking and carousing are responsible for their [the Magyars'] many crimes of personal violence."

The Jews, on page 179, are "the intellectuals of the new immigration . . . and one wonders how many Trotskys and Lenins are being bred in the stagnant air of their reeking ghettos." They "have a tendency to commercialize everything they touch."

On page 180, the Italian quarters of America's great cities swarm with "vast hordes of children." Nearly every other Italian is illiterate. The Sicilians are "swarthy criminals" slinking through "the dark alleys."

And so on, and so on, till page 214, where "from manufacturing centers like Chicopee, Worcester, Ware, Westfield, and Fitchburg, areas of Polish settlements radiate in every direction, alien spokes from American hubs. Here are little farming villages ready-made in attractive settings whose vacant houses invite the alien peasant. A Polish family moves into a sedate colonial house; often a second family shares the place, sometimes a third or fourth, each with a brood of children and often a boarder or two. The American families left in the neighborhood are scandalized by this promiscuity, by the bare feet and bare heads, by the unspeakable fare, the superstition and credulity, and illiteracy and disregard for sanitary measures, and by the ant-like industry from starlight to starlight. Old Hadley has become a prototype of what may become general if this racial infiltration is not soon checked. In 1906 the Poles numbered one-fifth of the population in that town, owned one-twentieth of the land, and produced two-thirds of the babies. Dignified old streets that formerly echoed with the tread of patriots now resound to the din of Polish weddings and christenings, and the town that sheltered William Goffe, one of the judges before whom Charles I was tried, now houses Polish transients at twenty-five cents a bed weekly."

On page 39 I read that in *1891* [my italics] Henry Cabot Lodge published an essay on *The Distribution of Ability in the United States,* based upon the 15,514 names in Appleton's *Cyclopædia of American Biography,* which came out in *1887.* He found that of this number 14,243 were "Americans" and 1,271 "immigrants" or non-Americans, who came to the United States after the adoption of the Constitution. This is offered as proof that "leadership . . . is the gift of but few races." The figures of fifty years ago are thus used to prove the inferiority of immigrants who had not yet left their own shores, nor (most of them) even been born!

If this was a textbook or required reading in American colleges during the 1920's, the wonder is that there is not more alien-baiting; that the New Americans are not in a worse psychological plight than they are; that the editorials in the *Satevepost* are not even more offensive——

A Suggestion for an Encyclopædia

IN WRITING THIS SECTION UPON THE IMMIGRANT SITUATION, I MAKE NO CLAIM to being exhaustive or one-hundred-per-cent correct or consistent in every detail. These chapters are, in fact, but a few suggestions on how certain phases of the situation looked to me during 1928-38. America's problem due to her new immigration is an immense field, which has barely been touched; about which almost nothing is really known.

Early in 1935, after much mulling over the whole thing and after my XYZ suggestion in *Harpers* proved to be full of the difficulties I have mentioned, there occurred to me another idea. Congress had just appropriated $4,800,000,000 for relief purposes. I heard that, along with numerous road- and bridge-building projects, the Government was to organize also writers' and artists' and theater projects. And so, wondering what sort of writers' projects could possibly be initiated, I thought that the Government perhaps could take a few million dollars and start a project for the preparation of a great Encyclopædia of the Population of the United States, from the Indians down to the latest immigrant group.

I was not looking for a job, for *The Native's Return* was making me all the money I needed . . . but I wanted the Federal Emergency Relief Administration (FERA), as it was currently known, to organize a central staff of executives, editors, researchers, and writers, which would be given between three and six years to prepare such an encyclopædia consisting of anywhere from five to twenty-five volumes: for, of course, I could not imagine the exact size of the task. This central staff—headed by some one like Henry Allen Moe, who would be sympathetic to the idea and would know his way about—would be responsible for carrying out the project. It would create hundreds of sub-staffs according to regions and/or nationalities, which would function for one or two years, as long as it might take them to get the material together. And these sub-staffs, under the general supervision of the central staff, would, so far as possible, engage in this preliminary work the entire populations within their respective regions and/or groups. This could be accomplished, I thought, by intelligent, well-directed publicity through various media, stressing such facts, ideas, and urgencies as—

(1) That in America today Ellis Island is rapidly becoming as important historically as is Plymouth Rock.

(2) That America is the result of effort not only on the part of the early Anglo-Saxon immigrants to this continent, but also of recent-immigrant groups.

(3) That about two-fifths of the population of the United States today is of non-Anglo-Saxon stock, and that this constitutes for the country an opportunity for creating a civilization and culture that is unique in history.

(4) That America must soon and deeply realize the above facts [for I was sure they *were* facts]; or she is apt to develop serious internal ills—political, social, cultural, and spiritual—which may eventually bring her to a pass within herself which will incapacitate her to do anything about them.

(5) That Ellis Island is now in reverse and mass immigration is ended, and this is the time to determine, in as great detail as possible, of what sort of human stuff America is made; what her potentialities are; which group has contributed what to this civilization, what it can still contribute, etc.

And (6) that the Encyclopædia of the Population of the United States is a step to achieve the above.

My idea was to exploit the educational value of the gathering of the material for the Encyclopædia; to draw into the task thousands of schools, colleges, and universities, newspapers and magazines, libraries and churches, immigrant fraternal societies and old-stock American clubs, etc., and millions of individual old-stock Americans, New Americans, and immigrants, whether they had anything specific to contribute to the great book or not. Most of them would not have to be dealt with personally, but would merely write their ideas and suggestions to the regional and/or group sub-staffs. This, I believed, would excite all America about herself.

The material thus assembled would then be sifted and articles prepared about the various groups: their background in the Old World, their history in the New World, and so on. There would be, for instance, a long article about the Poles in America in general; and there would be also more detailed articles about the Poles in Buffalo, Toledo, New York, Chicago, Detroit, Cleveland, etc. All this would appear in the huge Encyclopædia; but, in addition, the entire Polish material would appear in a special volume, and there would be, too, small separate publications dealing only with the Poles in Buffalo, in Toledo, etc., for local circulation. This would be done for each of the twoscore groups which were now vital factors in America's population. The Encyclopædia and its hundreds of separate parts might be published under Government subsidy by a private publisher. . . .

I thought that such a work would be invaluable Americana. It might very well revolutionize American writing and affect all thinking about the United States. It would be Education with a capital E even before the Encyclopædia was written and compiled. Once written, it would be invaluable to thousands of such school principals and teachers as the man who wrote to me from Oakdale, Pennsylvania, and to librarians and social workers. It would appeal not only to New Americans and their immigrant parents, and more or less generally to the people of such cities as Pittsburgh or Cleveland where these new elements predominated and the second-generation problem was obvious on every hand, but to America as a whole. It would lead old-stock Americans to get to know the New Americans, and help the latter to get a sound feeling and idea about America, her history, her "Dream," her greatness and old Anglo-Saxon culture. It would tend to lessen the unsoundness of various manifestations of America's

basic incongruity and would help to spread and deepen the country's democratic mood.

I went to Washington—to the FERA office, and there had a long talk with
Jacob Baker, who, as one of Harry Hopkins' closest assistants, was then an
important man in the capital. Jake was interested in my idea. He called in a
few of his assistants, and we discussed the thing back and forth. But there were
all manner of difficulties. Who would organize and manage such a project?
Would I? No; I was afraid I could not; if desired, I would be able to serve
only in an advisory capacity. I realized this was a job no one man could work
out in all its details. But I thought somebody could be found to head the project.
I suggested Moe. Then: where would we get the people to do the preliminary
and final work? Among the unemployed? Hardly. This was the biggest stum-
bling-block, for the $4,800,000,000 had been appropriated specifically for jobless
relief. There was no way of getting around it.

I met Henry Wallace, Secretary of Agriculture, and told him my idea. We
discussed it. Wallace thought it was a good idea, but did not see how it could
be handled at that time.

During 1935-37 Read Lewis and I and some of the others in FLIS frequently
discussed the "Encyclopædia idea," as we began to refer to it. Could we not
get some foundation interested in it? We tried. One or two of the foundations
were interested. How much money would it take? We did not know. Perhaps
a million or two. We tried to get a few hundred thousand dollars to make a
general survey of the job and do some preliminary work on it. No luck.

But eventually, I think, this job will have to be done—somehow.

The Depression

This country is not in good condition.

CALVIN COOLIDGE, January 20, 1931.

Tragic Towns of New England: 1930

I HAVE ALREADY SUGGESTED HERE AND THERE IN THE SECTION ON MY EXPERIENCES in New York during 1929-34 how the Depression touched me, and I was rather well aware, of course, that—while the number of the wealthy and well-to-do had been increasing during the fabulous Coolidge period—perhaps one-third of the American people, distributed through tens of thousands of communities, large and small, had been living in poverty. But I did not realize till the autumn of 1930 that entire cities and towns in the United States had been in dire socio-economic circumstances long before the Crash.

One day, scanning the recently published 1930 Census Report which I happened to see on a table while I was in the New York Public Library, I noticed that, while nearly all communities had increased in population during the 1920's, a number of considerable New England towns had decreased. These were all textile and shoe centers.

I was then still busy with *Dynamite*; but, curious, I decided to visit those towns as soon as I finished the book. But before I went I chanced to meet in New York, Thomas F. McMahon, then president of the United Textile Workers of America. He had just returned from a visit to several textile towns in the New England States, and when I told him that I was planning soon to go there, too, he said to me:

"The conditions in many parts of New England are nothing short of tragic, not only from the textile workers' point of view, with which I am most familiar and sympathetic, but also from the point of view of entire cities and towns where textile mills exist, to say nothing of the mill owners, who are badly hit, too, though in my opinion a few of them—not all nor even most of them— are quite undeserving of sympathetic consideration in the New England textile crisis.

"Lowell, Lawrence, New Bedford, Maynard, and Fall River, in Massachusetts, and most of the mill towns in the Blackstone Valley of Rhode Island, as well as Manchester, New Hampshire, are sad, sad places. The bulk of the population of those cities and towns are mill workers who even in the best of times have lived practically from hand to mouth, and whose plight today it is almost impossible to exaggerate.

"There is, perhaps, more destitution and misery and degradation in the mill towns of New England today, because of bad working conditions, than anywhere else in the United States; for the textile workers' situation at the moment is due not only nor even mainly to the current business depression, but is for the most part a result of immensely complicated and chaotic forces and circumstances within the textile industry itself which have worked against them in a cruel conspiracy, and over which they as individuals or even we as a union have no control.

263

"There are approximately 280,000 organized and unorganized—mostly unorganized—textile workers of various classes, native and foreign born, in New England. Of these, we estimate that about 120,000 or forty per cent, are unemployed and most of them are likely to remain 'out' throughout the winter. Indeed, many have been jobless for months, some for years, and large numbers of those who have jobs work only one or two days a week, earning on the average less than ten dollars a week. Can you imagine how a man or a woman can support a family, or even himself or herself alone, on less than ten dollars a week in wintertime?"

A week later, in Boston, I spoke with D. M. FitzGerald, secretary of the Shoe Workers' Protective Union, and John J. Mara, president of the Boot and Shoe Workers' Union, both conservative trade organizations. Their separate statements to me agreed that in all likelihood close to two-thirds of the 100,000 or more shoe workers in New England, organized and unorganized, native and immigrant, were jobless or employed only one or two days a week, earning extremely meager wages. They also agreed in saying that such communities as South Boston, the Chelsea district of Boston, Lynn, Brockton, Stoneham, Haverhill, Newburyport, and Georgetown, in Massachusetts; Manchester and Derry, in New Hampshire, and certain smaller shoe towns in Rhode Island, Connecticut, and Maine were, from the shoe workers' point of view and otherwise, distressing places—"cursed by the awful chaos within the shoe-manufacturing racket," as another labor official in Boston bluntly characterized it.

From Boston I went to Lowell, which but a decade ago was one of the most important cotton-textile centers in the United States. On the train which took me there I aimed my journalistic curiosity at a man who sat near me, carrying a copy of a New York liberal weekly in his overcoat pocket. He turned out to be a traveling salesman. At first his replies and remarks were reticent, but after a while he became more outspoken. He told me that six years ago he had worked in the office of a cotton mill in Lowell; now he lived in Chelsea.

"Things are pretty low in Lowell," he said. "That's a gag among us salesmen who cover this territory, but 'low in Lowell' is putting it mildly. The 1930 census figures show the population of the city has gone down from nearly 113,000 to 100,300, or eleven per cent. And most of this decrease in population has occurred since 1927. People, of course, are still moving out—those who can—and unless a miracle happens and the go-getters in Lowell manage quickly to build up new industries to take the place of cotton, in 1940 Lowell is likely to be a very small town.

"Till recently no one dared to say out loud that things were on the decline. It was merely a sort of public secret for years that everything was not as it should be. The unemployed—thousands of them—walked around like ghosts (they still do; you'll see them) or were hiding away in their shacks and hall rooms. Then, a few months ago, Herbert Hoover himself announced that there was danger of widespread distress, with winter just around the corner, and so the city officials and the Chamber of Commerce in Lowell, as in other places which find themselves in Lowell's predicament, began to talk openly about distress, too. Now everybody in Lowell and Lawrence admits that things are bad, and I don't suppose it's disloyal even for me, a former Lowellite, to talk to a stranger about the fact. . . ."

Until the mid-'twenties Lowell was a comparatively prosperous town. Not a few people there had a great deal of money, lived in fine houses, wore nice clothes, drove good cars. They were mostly business and professional folk and the better-paid mill employees. The general run of mill operatives, male and female, who formed numerically the largest group in town, the under-dog class, earned less than twenty-five dollars a week when they worked full-time, which barely enabled them to lead decent lives. By pinching they saved a little, but very little; a small percentage of them managed to acquire homes of their own.

Then, about five years ago, the mills began to shut down in Lowell. King Cotton was sick. With Coolidge Prosperity in full swing throughout the land, the people began to wear silk, imported from Japan, and other fine materials instead of cotton. There was still some demand for cotton goods, but only for the cheaper kind. Mill owners were starting new mills in the South, where raw cotton was produced; and, what was still more important to them, "the pore white trash" of Tennessee, Alabama, and South Carolina was even cheaper labor than were the Italian, Lithuanian, and French-Canadian immigrants in New England, who since 1912—the year of the Lawrence strike— had developed unruly tendencies to unionism and demands for higher wages and, when the latter were not granted, to sabotage. Also, there were no laws in the South, such as there were in New England, regulating the number of working hours and female and child labor.

In 1927 and 1928 Lowell practically ceased as a cotton-textile center. I found there eight enormous mills, all idle for years, dominating the town, each six or seven stories high and covering several blocks, with tall, unsmoking chimneys. Only here and there upon the lower floors a few hundred square feet were occupied by tiny industries, such as radio assembly shops, which the desperate community, working through the Chamber of Commerce, had recently managed to lure to Lowell in an effort to create jobs for the thousands and thousands of former textile operatives who, caught by the circumstances of their lives, had not yet moved away. But these new industries in Lowell, lost in the immensities of the former cotton mills, were, of course, only a drop in the bucket so far as the local unemployment situation was concerned.

How many jobless people there were in Lowell who needed work desperately or urgently, nobody knew exactly. Labor officials told me that perhaps two-thirds of the town's working population were idle or employed only part time. Not only textile workers were "out," but nearly two-thirds of the organized building trades craftsmen had had nothing to do for nearly two and a half years. Except for the new post-office, there had been practically no building in Lowell for more than three years.

The mayor and the other city officials had somewhat lower estimates of the extent of idleness in Lowell. Chester M. Runels, executive secretary of the Lowell Chamber of Commerce, said to me that he knew exactly how many jobless people there were in the city—"too damned many." All the responsible public and semi-public officials admitted that, as the salesman had remarked to me on the train, "things are low in Lowell," but nobody seemed to know what to do about the situation.

Bewilderment, perhaps, was the outstanding characteristic of the Lowell psychology. Mr. Runels confessed that he was spending sleepless nights trying to think of something—anything—that would put the city back on its feet industrially, but, in common with other leading Lowellites, remained only deeply perplexed. He was starting emergency measures to relieve "immediate distress," encouraging charity, trying to induce the better-to-do people in the community to renovate their homes before Christmas and otherwise "create" jobs for needy family men during the winter months. He realized, as he told me, that what Lowell needed was industries, for it was essentially an industrial city; it had started as a mill town and could continue only as an industrial community. But, obviously a very decent person, he was loath to try to lure manufacturers—with low rentals for floor space and cheap labor—from other towns and thus create unemployment elsewhere. Instead, he strove to "create" more new industries by urging local people with money to organize companies for the production of novelties and new commodities. But so far his success in this respect was meager. Several shoe companies had established themselves in Lowell since 1928, but civic and business leaders were frank in saying that they were "afraid of the shoe industry," because, with its cruelty to workers and its utter lack of organization, self-discipline, and public conscience, the shoe industry (of which more later) was seldom, if ever, an asset to a community.

Charity, as one citizen remarked to me, was "the biggest industry in Lowell" and it promised to continue big for some time to come. I was told that the priest in charge of the Catholic charity organization and his two assistants were busy from twelve to fourteen hours daily investigating cases of poverty, collecting funds from the well-to-do, who still formed a rather numerous class in Lowell, and distributing what they collected. I was assured that the donations were spontaneous and liberal. There were other charitable agencies in the city, including a municipal welfare bureau, trying to eliminate so far as possible extreme hunger and suffering for want of clothing and fuel.

Business, obviously, was poor in Lowell. Every third or fourth store in the main streets was vacant. There were few "For Rent" signs in the windows, the proprietors figuring, I suppose, that it was no use putting them up. One sign read: "For Rent at Your Own Price."

I had a desolate feeling as I walked through some of the streets. There were rows of old wooden houses, unoccupied, uncared-for, their window panes broken. Many of the tenanted houses in the working people's districts, evidently, had not been painted for years. I saw broken window panes pasted over with paper, the residents, apparently, being too poor to replace them.

In the main business section, the five-and-ten-cent-store seemed to be the only really busy place. A butcher told me that he sold few steaks and chops; most of the customers bought tripe, soup bones, and the cheaper cuts of meat. He had ordered but few turkeys for Thanksgiving. Grocery and dry-goods prices were at least one-third lower in Lowell than in New York or Boston, but even so the stores were doing little business. Two merchants confessed they were operating at a loss; they were "caught"; people owed them money for years back, and they were hoping "things would pick up soon." Said one shopkeeper, "But I don't know how much longer I can hold out on hope."

A barber told me that people obviously were cutting their hair at home; several barber-shops had gone out of business. A second barber, when I asked if many of his customers took hair tonic, said, "Hell, no!"—and proceeded to elaborate upon the tragedy of the barbering trade in Lowell.

I spoke with physicians. One admitted that he, like the other doctors in town, had difficulties in collecting his fees; perhaps more than half of his patients were "charity." A dentist informed me that the number of extractions, in proportion to other dental work that he performed, was increasing rapidly. "I suppose people haven't the money," he said, "to come for treatment before it's too late and the tooth has to be removed. Also, I imagine that improper or insufficient food the poorer people have been eating the last few years hastens the decay of teeth."

A neighborhood druggist, having nothing better to do, spoke to me for several hours. "Oh, quite a few working people in Lowell still have money," he said; "at least the number of bank accounts shows that, but they're holding onto it as if it was all there was in the world. Even some of the mill workers seem to have money saved up. How they managed to save anything is more than I know. Now, with the Depression at its worst, they hold onto it. They're scared. They spend only for absolute necessities. They say, God knows how long the panic will last in Lowell. They're stuck in Lowell. They probably own a little property or have old parents who can't be moved. Some of those who were foot-loose back in 1928 and had a little money cleared out soon after the mills closed down for good. Some stayed, thinking the mills would open up again soon. They waited. Then it was too late for them to clear out. Now they're stuck. Their little savings, maybe, are all gone; and if not, since Wall Street went smash the rest of the country is not much better off than Lowell, and there's no use going elsewhere. . . . Of course, I'd like nothing better than to sell out, even at a loss. In the last few years I've been making less than two and a half per cent on my investment. Next year I probably shan't make that much unless things pick up. But who's fool enough to buy me out? Besides, I'm married, kids are going to school, and people in the neighborhood owe me money; so what can I do but stick? If I were single, I'd probably just take my week's receipts, close up, and go."

In Lowell I saw shabby men leaning against walls and lamp-posts, and standing on street corners singly or in twos or threes; pathetic, silent, middle-aged men in torn, frayed overcoats or even without overcoats, broken shoes on their feet (in a town manufacturing shoes!), slumped in postures of hopeless discontent, their faces sunken and their eyes shifty and bewildered—men who winced and jerked queerly when they noticed me looking at them, and shuffled off uncertainly, wringing their hands in a mingling of vague desperation and of resentment at my gaze. I spoke or tried to speak with some of them, and I went into a few of the unemployed's homes in Lowell and heard and saw things which, if I described them, would make very melancholy reading.

But even so I was scarcely prepared for the painfully awry conditions that I found in Lawrence, once the leading wool and worsted city in the United States, a half hour's trolley ride from Lowell. According to the census, since 1920, or more exactly since 1927 or thereabouts, the population of Lawrence decreased from 94,270 to 84,949, or nearly ten per cent.

The situation was different from that in Lowell, where, as I have stated, the cotton-textile industry had almost completely deserted the community and gone South. Most of the mills at Lawrence had not yet shut down. However, since 1936 they had operated very irregularly, giving for brief periods only part-time employment, and gradually decreasing the number of even part-time workers, for during the 1920's the wool, worsted, and carpet industries had also been moving out of Massachusetts, where the law provided a maximum forty-eight-hour week for workers, and were starting mills in near-by Maine, New Hampshire, and Rhode Island, where employers might work their people fifty-four hours a week, and in Connecticut, where they had a fifty-five-hour law. Another motive in the tendency of the textile interests to start new mills outside of Massachusetts was that in such old centers as Lowell, Lawrence, New Bedford, and Maynard labor unions had become powerful, forcing up the wage scale. The mill owners in Massachusetts realized that they had made a mistake in getting so many mills into a few towns close together. The labor agitators' work was easy when twenty or thirty thousand operatives were concentrated in one city. And the tendency now was not to build more than one small mill in any one town in Rhode Island, Connecticut, Maine, or New Hampshire. The mill owners figured that this diffusion would prevent "labor troubles."

Lawrence, with its tremendous mills, was a "mistake" which the mill owners had been trying to rectify by operating the mills only a little more than was necessary to pay the overhead on the old mills, and thus killing the unions; for when jobless or working only part-time, workers cannot pay their union fees. The process of rectifying this "mistake" was still going on when I came. And it was a painful process to the people—especially the working people—of the city of Lawrence.

I happened to arrive before daybreak on a Monday morning and, walking about, saw hundreds of shabby, silent, hollow-eyed men and women, native and foreign born, going toward the immense, dark mills. I discovered later that very few of them were going to work; most were seeking work. On Mondays they usually went to the mills to learn from the employment managers if any help would be needed during the week. Many of them had been making these Monday-morning pilgrimages for months, some of them for years, getting only a day's or two days' work now and then.

By eight o'clock the great majority of them were returning from the mills. Some had been told to come to work on Wednesday or Thursday or Friday; others, perhaps a majority of them, were told there was no work for them this week. Perhaps next week.

Women hurried home. Men stood on curbs, wretchedness inherent in their every action and aspect; penniless men, most of them without any intelligent, objective idea of what was happening to them, what was going on in Lawrence or in the textile industry. One of them said to me, "I don't know nothing, only that I have no job. No job—no job," he repeated in a shrill, half-hysterical voice.

I saw men standing on the sidewalks clapping their hands in a queer way, obviously just to be doing something. I saw men talking to themselves, walking around, stopping, looking into shop windows, walking again.

For several minutes I watched an elderly man who stood on a deserted corner near the enormous and idle Everett Mills in the posture of an undotted question mark. He did not see me. Every now and then he swung his arms, not because it was cold, but no doubt because he wanted activity other than walking around, which he probably had been doing for years, in a vain effort to get a job. He mumbled to himself. Then, suddenly, he stepped off the curb and picked up a long piece of string from a pile of rubbish, and his big, work-eager hands began to work with it, tying and untying it feverishly. He worked with the string for several minutes. Then he looked around and, seeing me, dropped the string, his haggard, hollow face coloring a little as though from a sense of guilt, or intense embarrassment. He was shaken and confused and stood there for several seconds, looking down at the rubbish heap, then up at me. His hands finally dropped to his sides. Then his arms swung in a sort of idle reflex motion and he turned, hesitated a while as if he did not know where to go, and finally shuffled off, flapping his arms. I noticed that his overcoat was split in the back and that his heels were worn off completely.

The general aspect of Lawrence was not unlike that of Lowell: empty stores —rows of shabby, unpainted, untenanted old houses—broken window panes— no new buildings going up—people still moving out when they could—and so on and on. In Lawrence, too, charity was one of the main industries.

The Lithuanian priest, Father Juras, spoke to me for a couple of hours, evidently glad of the chance to get things off his chest. "Yes, conditions are bad," he said. "I don't know, I don't know. I can do so little. Many of my people work only one or two days a week. They earn so little. I hear that some workers in order to get and hold jobs must give a part of their small earnings to unscrupulous mill bosses who have the power to hire and fire them. . . . Mothers come to me and cry and say they have no money to buy shoes for the children, and winter is here. We make collections in the church, and I give them money for their children's shoes. Not only for shoes, but for clothing, food, and gas bills. Some of my people don't work at all. For months and months—for years—no work. Some have gone out of Lawrence, to the farms near-by, where they work just for food and lodging. It is better than nothing. . . . No, very few become Communists; almost none. Lithuanians are good, patient people. They suffer, but they don't know what is going to become of them. They come to me and cry: What is going to happen to our children? One family I know has lived on lentils, nothing but lentils, all this year. They can't afford to buy bread. No work for them. The young people are restless. They want money. They want to go to picture shows and dances. . . ."

He shook his head.

"Many of my people pay very little rent," he continued. "Some pay no rent. The house owners don't throw them out. The tenants at least take care of the houses. . . . Yes, some of the men drink. They're desperate. It helps them to forget. But their characters degenerate. That is bad. They feel helpless: what's the use! I try to help. But ——"

Again he shook his head.

The rector of one of the two French-Canadian parishes spoke to me similarly. "Oh, yes, we, too, have to buy shoes for children," he said. "We have a Catholic school here and we watch the children. If they need clothing, we give it to them. Many parents have nothing—no money, no work, or very little work. I have six priests in this parish assisting me. All day long they go around, from house to house, where we hear there is distress, and we help as much as we can. Our well-to-do parishioners are generous. Last Sunday we received three hundred dollars for the poor." He was unwilling to fix the blame upon the mills or any other factor in Lawrence. "I have come here only recently," he said. "I don't know whose fault this condition is. All I know is that things are terrible—no work for the people."

Speaking with the jobless, I noticed acute desperation. One man said to me, "You're from New York? Say, do you think there'll be a war soon? A fellow I heard the other day, a Communist, said that the United States might attack Russia because this country is capitalistic and Russia is communistic." I said I didn't know about that. "I wish there would be a war again," he said. "There was lots of work and high wages during the last war: remember? Mills were going day and night."

Few of the unemployed in Lawrence—and elsewhere, for that matter—impressed me as competent people. They were willing, eager to work, but there was something dead in them, as from exhaustion or perhaps too much idleness; they lacked personal winsomeness or any power of demand. Lost, bewildered souls, victims in the pinch of the machine, victims of the 1920's industrial-financial processes, of "rationalization" and speeding-up in the textile industry, victims of the greed for higher and higher profits on the parts of the industrialists; victims of the country's incongruity. . . . The situation was infinitely pathetic, not to say appalling.

The Census Report showed that in the 1920's the population decline of New Bedford and Fall River, both cities with populations of over 100,000, was only 6.9 and 4.3 per cent, respectively; but the conditions in these towns were perhaps no better than in Lowell or Lawrence.

Fall River, one of the oldest mill towns in New England, was also practically dead as a textile center. Were I to describe its plight from the human point of view I should be only repeating, with slight changes, what I have said about the plight of Lowell and Lawrence. The immediate reason for Fall River's decline, however, was somewhat different. A former labor leader in Fall River said to me, without any attempt at hiding his bitterness, "The trouble with this place is that the machinery in all these big mills which you see is archaic. In some of them the equipment has not been replaced since the mills were built, thirty and forty years ago. Of course, they cannot compete in production efficiency with mills equipped with modern machines, each of which produces with the aid of a single worker more than twenty machines here used to produce with ten workers. But years ago most mills were tremendous money-makers. They paid dividends of as high as two and three hundred per cent. At the same time the wages were slavery wages. They employed children in their early teens and women, pregnant and otherwise. They worked them night and day, twelve and fourteen hours at a stretch. That was before Massachusetts legislated against such things. The mill managers gave as little as possible to the employees. The community of Fall River was something for them to exploit. They put as little into the community in the form of wages as they could help. And not only that. They put as little as possible—almost nothing—back into their industry. Instead of buying new machinery from time to time and keeping up-to-date, instead of building for the future of their business and of Fall River, the mill managers paid out the enormous profits in dividends to the investors, many of whom had scarcely ever heard of Fall River and had no interest in the working people or the community. All they cared for was immediate high profits. It was a high-pressure 'racket,' cruel to the workers, cruel to the city of Fall River, suicidal for the mills. . . . McMahon was correct in calling Fall River a tragic city."

New Bedford was a victim of a combination of circumstances. There was archaic machinery in some of the mills. New Bedford, too, was a "mistake"— like Lawrence—which was being rectified; the companies whose mills dominated New Bedford had also new mills in the neighboring States and in the South where laws allowed longer working hours and there were no labor unions. But the outstanding feature of the New Bedford situation was a deep antagonism between the managements of some mills and the unions, which were comparatively strong there in spite of the long slump. In 1928 New Bedford had been the scene of a bitter strike, and the war was not ended yet. Thousands of mill workers were totally unemployed; some worked part-time, earning from $6 to $12 a week—with dire social consequences not unsimilar to those I saw in Lowell and Lawrence.

In New Bedford I took to a lunchroom a jobless worker who told me he had not eaten a decent meal for months—"or maybe it's years. I'm losing track of time." He had a family of four. A brother of his in New Jersey, he told me, had recently killed his wife and child and committed suicide. "I don't blame 'im," he said. "I'd do the same; only I ain't got the guts. I'd have to kill four of 'em. And I couldn't . . . I couldn't. Christ, ain't it awful! . . . And suppose I do get a job soon. I am in debt hundreds of dollars and it'll take me years to pay it back. There's nobody I know in town who's ever had any money that I don't owe him some. We owe to the grocery-man, butcher—everybody. You don't know what it means to have a wife and kids and no work and no money, and be in debt."

In Maynard, Massachusetts, the conditions were extremely chaotic, too, though—quantitatively, at least—not as tragic as in the larger towns. There is but one considerable mill in Maynard. Once it had employed 1,500 people; when I was there, two-thirds were completely "out" and the rest worked only part-time, earning from $8 to $9 a week. Approximately the same was true of Housatonic, another small mill town in Massachusetts which I visited.

I spent a few days in the Rhode Island mill towns—Manville, Woonsocket, Ashton, Berkley, and Lawnsdale, not far from Providence; most of which have but one good-sized mill working part-time. But those who worked there, while they worked, worked long hours for lower wages than similar workers received in Massachusetts. Some of these towns were the result of the mill owners' early efforts at rectification of such "mistakes" as Lawrence and New Bedford. The same was true of such towns as Dover and Somersworth, in New Hampshire, and Waterville, Lewiston, and Biddeford, in Maine. In some of these latter towns the mills worked full-time, here and there overtime, but practically everywhere I saw bad working conditions—men and women and even boys and girls in their 'teens working fifty-four hours a week. I saw "speeding-up" and "stretching-out." I saw girls in one town, for instance, running thirty wide looms from before sunup till after sundown. In most Massachusetts towns where the unions had some power, operatives ran on the average of only twenty looms eight hours a day, and even that was considered a great strain upon a person's energy and nerves.

And the average shoe-manufacturing town was no better than the average textile town in New England. Indeed, here and there—as, for instance, in Lowell and Lawrence and in Manchester, New Hampshire—the shoe industry had been adding its chaos and cruelty to that of the textile industry, and the workers and entire communities with tens of thousands of people found themselves in dire circumstances.

Haverhill, Massachusetts, one of the largest shoe centers in the country, was a tragic city whose population in the 1920's decreased from 53,000 to 48,000. When I passed through Haverhill, the mayor of the town sent a communication to Col. Arthur Woods, generalissimo of President Hoover's Unemployment Relief, declaring the situation in the city to be "serious," with over 4,500 of its 8,000 shoe workers entirely idle, while most of the others worked only part-time, earning insufficient wages. Shoe-factory employees comprised four-fifths of Haverhill's laboring men and women, and from the human point of view the situation was as appalling as in the textile towns. Things were further aggravated by a dispute between shoe manufacturers and the Shoe Workers' Protective Union, which included about half of the shoe people in town. Threats to remove their plants from Haverhill had been made by eight firms as the result of union opposition to contemplated wage cuts. The whole city was beside itself. People with whom I talked, including responsible public and semi-public officials, seemed unable to discuss the situation objectively. They talked incoherently, emotionally about emergency measures to prevent suffering during the winter. The people of Haverhill seemed to be agreed upon one thing alone: that the shoe industry was an evil they wished they could get along without.

A public official who asked me not to quote him by name said to me, "You say the textile industry is stupid and chaotic. Well, it has nothing on the shoe industry. Here in Haverhill we have over thirty shoe factories. Most of them have been started by selfish little fellows with a few thousand dollars at their command. They rented a little floor space and then had the United Shoe Machinery Company lease to them machines which turn out shoes hand over fist. The manufacturers don't own the machinery; they pay royalties to the U.S.M. on every pair of shoes made. They get a shoe model that they think will sell and then they work day and night producing that model. When they think they have enough shoes manufactured they quit, and to hell with the workers, and to hell with Haverhill. Their most pressing problem then becomes to sell the shoes. And this goes on all over the country. The U.S.M. installs machinery almost anywhere. There are hundreds and hundreds of shoe manufacturers in New England and more elsewhere. The U.S.M. machinery has been working overtime; now there is overproduction. Now there's no work. And the workers who made millions of pairs of shoes did not make enough to have decent shoes on their own feet!"

Shoe manufacturers were organized in associations, but not for self-disciplinary purposes, to put intelligence and order into their business; merely or largely to fight the unions and the attempts of unorganized workers to organize, to improve their conditions. Their main concern was not the appalling cost to them as individual manufacturers of the chaotic unintelligence within the industry; their chief worry seemed to be the cost of labor, and they did everything to keep it down. Not a few shoe manufacturers in New England had no previous experience in or knowledge of the shoe industry when they started in the business during the late 1920's, when shoe manufacturing suddenly appeared to be a way to quick money. Their wastefulness, I was told, was colossal. A labor leader who impressed me as a very intelligent and competent man said to me, "We have in many of our factories supervisors who, I assure you, have no real knowledge of the right way to fit shoes or how to handle help. We, as union officials, have tried to put efficiency into the shops, not because we love the bosses, but for our own sake, to decrease costs which are being blamed upon us; but the factory owners have scorned us. They don't care for long-range efficiency and lower profits extended over a long period; all they want is high immediate profits—and to hell with labor, the public, and everything else!".

But Haverhill, perhaps, was not the worst hit town because of this chaotic overproduction and underpayment of workers in the shoe industry. In Lynn, Massachusetts, only about two thousand of the six thousand shoe workers were employed, full- and part-time. In Brockton and South Boston the production of working and jobless shoe people was approximately the same. In Manchester, New Hampshire (which city was in a general crisis because of the subsequently famous Amoskeag mess), most of its 3,500 shoe workers were out about the time I was there, with no prospect of new employment till late in the winter, perhaps not until spring. Among those laid off were men who had worked in the Manchester shoe factories for from eighteen to twenty-five years. I spoke with one of these old-timers, obviously a sober, work-eager man, who told me—half ashamed, half angry—that he had practically nothing on which to fall back during this lay-off. Another Manchester worker, long out of a job, told me how, a month before, he had gone to New Haven, Connecticut, in search of work; how a policeman there arrested him for vagrancy, and how a judge threatened to jail him unless he left the city within thirty minutes.

Everywhere chaos and suffering because of stupid greed—because of no vision, no sense of social responsibility on the part of industry.

I describe the social-economic-industrial situation in these New England shoe and textile towns in such detail because what was true of them in 1928-30 became largely true by 1932 or 1933 of the entire United States—and for essentially the same reasons!

In my eleven days of traveling through New England I found but one busy, happy, prosperous town—Salem, Massachusetts, which impressed me as almost a complete antithesis of such places as Lowell, Lawrence, Fall River, Haverhill, and Manchester. In comparison with these, Salem was a veritable boom town. In a population of about 40,000 only 600 were unemployed, most of them shoe workers. The stores and hotels in Salem were attractive, busy places. The homes were painted and the whole community had an aspect of well-being.

The reason for this happy status of Salem was mainly that the city had a great textile mill—the Pequot—whose management was intelligent and humane, trying with no small success to run its business not solely for its own immediate, narrow profit, but also for the benefit of its two thousand operatives and, through them, of Salem. The Pequot Mill workers' average weekly wage was around $34 for forty-eight hours—an amazing stipend for the textile industry. Their employment was steady; at least no one was laid off at a moment's notice, irrespective of his or her circumstances; for the Pequot management had tried in the past, and continued in its efforts, to stabilize production as much as possible and plan ahead. The sanitary and safety appliances in the mill were the most modern. I inspected the mill and spoke with the workers and their union's leaders. Nowhere within the realm of the textile industry—and in very few other industries—were employees treated half so well as at Salem. The result was that the relations between the management and the workers, all of whom were organized, were excellent, and that Pequot had a force of contented, healthy, efficient operatives who, individually and through their union, did everything possible to help the firm decrease the production costs. The textile workers' union at Salem was recognized by the Pequot people; indeed, the mill management and the union, headed by an intelligent labor leader, maintained a joint research bureau under the direction of an efficiency engineer, with the purpose of further decreasing the production costs, stabilizing production, and increasing the profits and wages as the operating costs were lowered in the mill.

In Pequot was a strong touch of industrial democracy. The employees did not live in constant fear of losing their jobs. When I was in Salem everybody there knew that the mills had enough work to run full-time until the spring, and the workers were fairly sure that there would be work after that. In consequence, the people did not hesitate to spend their money. I saw mill girls come to work in the morning clad in raccoon coats, and in the evening I saw a group of them in evening gowns dining with boy friends at the Hawthorne Hotel. Naturally, then, Salem—in sharp distinction with Lowell, Lawrence, New Bedford, and Fall River—was a pleasant, thriving town.

I CAUSE AN UPROAR IN NEW ENGLAND

Before taking the above trip I saw Editor Wells of *Harpers* and expressed to him my idea that the new census figures on those New England towns probably held an important story. He agreed to pay my travel expenses, and for the story if I found one.

Harpers published my story in its May, 1931, issue, and the article promptly caused a terrific uproar in all the towns I described or mentioned, but particularly in Lawrence and Lowell. The piece became front-page news and the subject of scores of editorials, all roundly denouncing the magazine and me, especially the magazine, for the weight of the article came, of course, from its prestige, not from me. I was, if not a liar, an unbalanced, tragic-minded person, hard to say which; while the editors had shown poor judgment in printing what I had written. Libel suits were threatened.

The city councils of some of the communities I mentioned passed resolutions against the article. Particularly condemnatory was the official action of the city council of Lowell, which inspired the cartoonist of the Lowell *Sunday Telegram* to cartoon me as a wailing little boy lying across the lap of "Mother Lowell," who vigorously pounded my middle. The city clerk was instructed to convey the outraged feelings of Lowell to the editor.

I was, frankly, very uneasy for a few days. . . . Finally, under the date of May 8, 1931, Editor Wells, who retired soon after, sent the city clerk of Lowell a letter (and similar letters to other official protesters), for which I shall be ever grateful to him:

Dear Sir: . . . It seems to me it is always a mistake to become over-excited in matters of this sort and to attempt to refute what an author has stated by comments on him and his position and by imputations that he is lacking in integrity. Mr. Adamic is a well known writer and is the author of various articles which we have printed and also of articles which have been printed in other magazines of the highest class. A book by him dealing with labor matters was recently published by the Viking Press—one of the first-class houses of New York. In addition to this, Mr. Adamic was brought to us by a well known literary agent here in New York who vouches for him in every way, and we ourselves have been greatly impressed by his sincerity and honesty. In no case heretofore have his statements been questioned.

The fact that Lowell is "a city of over one hundred thousand population and rich in tradition of over one hundred years" does not seem to me to enter into the argument. I may venture to call to your attention that New York is a city of considerably more than one hundred thousand population, which is also rich in tradition for a considerably longer period. Yet I failed to discern any great excitement when, just before the present scandalous condition of affairs was revealed by the Seabury committee of investigation, we published a scathing attack on the political system here and those responsible for the present conditions. Nor did the city of Boston exhibit any signs of disturbance when one of our leading writers recently ventured to comment somewhat caustically on conditions in that seat of culture. Pittsburgh, which was the subject of a very critical article recently published in our pages, protested mildly but in no such outpouring of wrath as we have received from the industrial cities in your neighborhood. Chicago was apparently somewhat irritated but made no protest to us in regard to an article dealing with conditions in that city which have since been revealed to be far worse than our correspondent depicted them. Los Angeles saw that a good many editorials were printed in the pages of its newspapers but made no protest to us. In fact, the only home culture from which we have received any protest which is comparable to that which comes from your city, was Tulsa, Oklahoma. This is quite natural. The Tulsa mind may be assumed to be a provincial mind. I had hardly supposed that the minds of the city of Lowell and other cities of Massachusetts could be characterized as provincial. Yet the violence of your protests leads me inevitably to that belief.

I have no doubt whatever but that "the men and women of Lowell are as good, as honorable, as clean and decent as any people within the limits of any similar city" in America, or in any country in the world, and that their thrift, industry and self-respect are all that they should be. But all this has nothing to do with the case. I have no sympathy with any attempt to censor honest, fair-minded criticism, and such I believe Mr. Adamic's article to be and shall continue so to believe until it is proved to the contrary. And I regret to say that I cannot accept as proof the statements of Chambers of Commerce of various cities and other bodies that have written us rather over-eloquently on the subject.

I cannot see that the figures that you quote in the last page of your letter have anything to do with the case. Certainly they have no bearing on conditions such as Mr. Adamic describes. The banks of New York are more powerful than ever before, but that does not prevent a deplorable condition of unemployment prevailing throughout the entire city.

Let me say again that I regret very greatly that you and your associates have been disturbed by Mr. Adamic's article. Perhaps if your city council had employed some outside investigator to look into conditions in the city of Lowell he would have brought to your attention the same situation as Mr. Adamic has discovered. It is quite natural that you yourselves, going about your business of governing the city, have little time for a thorough study of its people and their lives.

With all good wishes and many thanks for your letter, etc.

The next day the Lowell *Sun* carried this headline across the entire page:

MAGAZINE REFUSES TO RETRACT
STATEMENTS CONCERNING CITY

Two columns removed from the story dealing with this failure to retract, was another headline:

3,690 VACANT TENEMENTS HERE

—the story beneath which suggested that, in that respect at least, the situation in Lowell was much worse than I had described it.

During the fracas I received a good many letters from New England, most of them thanking me for the article. Then such letters-to-the-editor, as the following one in the Haverhill *Gazette*, began to appear in the New England press:

I must confess that I am not in complete sympathy with the attitude taken by our local Chamber of Commerce toward the article . . .

Conditions in Haverhill are bad. The present nation-wide business depression has aggravated the situation. Neither now nor in the past ten years has the local situation shown symptoms of improving. In fact, without resort to statistics, it can safely be said that the number of factories here has been on a steady decline.

The matter in point is not who is to blame for the predicament, nor the possible cures (these are matters of economic controversy), but whether the chamber's attitude is justifiable. The article may be distasteful in its viewpoint, it may be in a degree impressionistic, but its main points in regard to Haverhill are true. . . .

Finally, the powerful New England Council, in its official publication, counseled my "tragic towns" to cease their indignation, which but advertised my article and did not make their situation any better.

Subsequently I learned that much of the heat I had provoked was due to the fact that just as the article appeared some of the towns affected, especially Lowell and Lawrence, had been trying to obtain loans from Boston and New York bankers, and to induce certain new industries to come there. In their difficult, bewildering situation, they had feared that my publicity might anything but help them.

This *Harpers* article brought me many letters from outside of New England. Several people asked me for addresses of needy people in the "tragic towns" to whom they might send money. I referred them to a labor leader and a priest, both of whom were close to the unemployed.

In the spring of 1936 during a two-day train-ride from Los Angeles to Chicago I engaged in conversation with a pleasant-looking man who turned out to be from Lowell, Massachusetts, and was apparently prominent in that city's civic and business affairs. As is usual in such casual train acquaintanceships, we did not exchange names. I asked how things were in Lowell and in those other towns around there: Lawrence, New Bedford, etc. I mentioned that some years ago I had read an article—wasn't it in *Harpers*?

"Yes," said my fellow traveler, "but that's ancient history. We didn't like the article at the time, and I can't say we do now. It was radical and unconstructive, and made us angry. The author was a Communist."

I said I once knew the author—Adamic—who, so far as I knew, was not a Communist.

"Yes, that's his name," nodded the man from Lowell. "Seems he published a book some time back which was read rather widely. My wife had it. As I say, he got us angry, but didn't really do us any harm. Perhaps he helped to snap us out of it, put us on our toes."

I said, "Adamic might like to hear that. If I remember right, he was a bit upset when the article was attacked."

"He might well have been," said the man from Lowell, his eyes narrowing in a close, shrewd look. He suspected I was the culprit. I kept a straight face, wondering if I should admit that I was. I didn't. The train stopped at a station, which offered me an excuse to rise and terminate the conversation.

In 1937 I drove through Lowell: it unquestionably did look a more cheerful city than it had six years before.

The Doorbell Rang: 1932

S TELLA AND I WERE LIVING AT HER MOTHER'S.
    At about a quarter to eight one cold morning in mid-January 1932, while we were at breakfast, the doorbell rang. Thinking it was the postman, I did not press the button which would open the outside door, but, as usual, went out to get the mail.

Instead of the postman, however, I was confronted by two children: a girl, as we learned afterward, of ten and a boy of eight. Not very adequate for the season and weather, their clothing was patched but clean. They carried school books.

"Excuse me, Mister," said the girl in a voice that sounded older than she looked, "but we have no eats in our house and my mother she said I should take my brother before we go to school and ring a doorbell in some house"—she swallowed heavily and took a deep breath—"and ask you to give us something to eat."

"Come in," I said, with a strange feeling. I had previously heard of children ringing doorbells in the Bronx, in Harlem, and in Brooklyn, but had scarcely believed it, though one part of my mind knew it was true.

The children were given food. The girl ate slowly; the boy quickly, greedily. He looked at no one and made no reply even when Stella or her mother asked him if he wanted more. When he got more food, he bolted it down rapidly.

The girl, however, answered every question directly, thoroughly, thoughtfully. Some of the information she volunteered. In fact, she was almost loquacious, as though eager to explain everything, to be understood, or eager just to talk. There was an unnatural, almost unreal, air about her. Her personality was vivid but, somehow, askew. Her curious un-childlike stare remained fixed on the face of the person to whom she spoke.

When her brother did not answer, she explained his silence, "He ate a banana yesterday afternoon, but it wasn't ripe enough or somethin', and it made him sick and he didn't eat anything since. He's always like this when he's hungry and we gotta ring doorbells."

Twisting angrily in his chair, the boy gave a little grunt.

"Do you often ring doorbells?" the girl was asked.

"When we have no eats at home." She drank her milk slowly.

"What made you ring our bell?"

"I don't know; I just did."

After a while I asked her, "What is your name?"

"Mary S——." She spelled her last name. "My brother is Jimmie S——."

The boy twisted in his chair again, self-consciously.

I studied the girl. She was tiny for her age, no doubt underweight, but appeared more an adult who had shrunk than a growing child. She was keen

279

and knew more of the immediate world in which she found herself than people four times her age had known of the world they were living in before 1930. She told us where they—her mother, her brother, and she lived: in a poor neighborhood five blocks from us. "We used to live on the fourth floor upstairs and we had three rooms and a kitchen and bath, now we have only one room downstairs, in back."

"Why did you move downstairs?"

The boy winced.

"My father," answered his sister simply, "he lost his job when the panic came. That was two years ago. I was eight and Jimmie was six. My father he tried to get work, but he couldn't, the Depression was so bad. But he called it the panic."

We were all startled by her vocabulary—"panic," "depression." She was entirely at ease.

"What kind of work did your father do?" I asked.

"Painter and paperhanger. Before things got so bad, he always had jobs when his work was in season, and he was good to us—my mother says so, too. Then, after he couldn't get any more jobs, he got mean and he yelled at my mother. He couldn't sleep nights and he walked up and down and talked, sometimes he hollered, and we couldn't sleep, either."

"Was he a union man?"

"No, he didn't belong to no union. He said unions was rackets."

Shocked, curious, fascinated, I could not help asking her further questions—especially since she did not mind them.

"What did your father holler about?"

"He called my mother bad names." The girl hesitated a moment. Her brother winced again. "He was angry because my mother, before she married him, she was in love with another man and almost married him. But my mother she says it wasn't my father's fault he acted mean like he did. He was mean because he had no job and we had no money."

"Where is your father now?"

"We don't know. He went away four months ago, right after Labor Day, and he never came back, so we had to move downstairs. The landlord didn't want to throw us out, so he told my mother to move in downstairs."

Between sips from her milk glass, Mary talked on. Her mother did housework when she found some to do; however, earned very little that way. A charity organization had been giving her $2.85 a week, but lately it had stopped—Mary did not know why. Her mother had applied to the Home Relief, but had not yet received anything from that source.

The boy, who had stopped eating, suddenly turned to his sister and muttered: "You talk too much! I told you not to talk."

The girl said nothing. She sat quietly. There was an awkward pause.

I said, "It's really our fault, Jimmie; we're asking too many questions."

"Yeah," he agreed.

My mother-in-law had wrapped up a lunch for them.

"Well, you better go to school, now," said Stella, "or you may be late."

"I think we're late already," said the girl, "but we was late one time before when we had to get breakfast outside like this, but I told Jimmie's teacher and mine why, and the teachers they sent us down to the principal and the principal he didn't say anything."

"Come again," said my mother-in-law, on the verge of tears.

I asked what school they attended and for their teachers' names and their mother's house number. She promptly gave me all the information and thanked us for the breakfast and the lunch. The boy said nothing. And they went.

I went to the school and learned from the girl's teacher that, while such cases were not yet numerous in that neighborhood, they were increasing. Some children rang doorbells, others brought slips of paper from their mothers, asking teachers to please "get the school" to provide shoes for them; they were unable to do so themselves. The school had no funds for such emergencies; so some of the teachers bought shoes for these pupils out of their own pockets.

I visited Mrs. S—— in her crowded single-room dwelling. She was evidently American-born of immigrant parents, but I hesitated asking her of what nationality; it did not matter, anyhow. She was about thirty, neat, a white iciness on her face. She wept when I gave her a few dollars. I found it hard to talk with her, especially after I learned that she believed in the imminent Second Coming. She gave me a leaflet entitled *The Kingdom of Heaven Is At Hand*. The cult of which she was a member expected the millennium in 1933.

I went to the local Home Relief office, where one of the social workers knew my name. She took up "the case" at once and two or three days later, when I telephoned, I was informed that Mrs. S—— had received a food order.

Little Mary fascinated me more and more, as I thought of her. She was, apparently, a child of the Depression. The last two years had done a great deal to her, physically and otherwise. Why did she talk so much? Did she, too, believe in the Second Coming? Whenever the bell rang early in the morning, I went out, hoping it might be she and her sullen brother, but they never came again.

About ten days later Stella and I were out walking in the afternoon, and we decided to visit Mrs. S——, to see how she and the children were getting along. But we were informed that they had moved two days ago. Our informant was the landlord, who thought that Mrs. S—— had thrown in her lot with the Second Coming cult, who were banding together in close quarters, living on relief, waiting for the Kingdom of Heaven to include the earth.

This is all I can tell of the S——es.

But our brief contact with them led me to hire myself out for a month to the

Home Relief as an assistant case worker, visiting the homes of the jobless, studying the Depression's effects on family life. I thought I might publish an article on the subject, but did not. My experiences and observations during that month—February, 1932—had affected me so that I could not write of them objectively at the time; then I received the Guggenheim award and went to Europe.

The ensuing chapter is an attempt to make use of a mass of notes that I took during that month.

Family Life and the Depression: 1930-32

THE DEPRESSION'S EFFECTS UPON THE HOME OR FAMILY LIFE IN THE UNITED States were as varied as they were profound; but they can be put into two general categories: On the one hand, thousands of families were broken up, some permanently, others temporarily, or were seriously disorganized. On the other hand, thousands of other families became more closely integrated than they had been before the Depression.

The reason for these different effects due to the same cause was that the economic crisis, which came upon many families in all sections of the country with the force and suddenness of a cyclone, in most cases intensified the various antagonistic and affectional attitudes or reactions of one to the other among the individuals within the family groups. Sudden economic adversity made family life more dynamic. In some cases, the so-called "hostility reactions" among the members of the family became more explosive, more damaging to the stability and harmony of the group. In other cases, conversely, the bonds of mutual affection, coöperation, and sacrifice were greatly strengthened, or even brought into full play for the first time.

These general statements apply, in greater or lesser degree, to all classes of society, except, of course, the uppermost class, in which the Depression was not felt acutely, at least not so far as family life was concerned. They apply most of all to the classes hit by unemployment.

In many working-class or white-collar homes, the man—the father and husband—was, by virtue of the dynamics of his position as bread-winner and conventional head of the family, the first to feel the impact of the unemployment situation. It was he who lost the job; in most cases, suddenly and unexpectedly. In the preceding years, what with children, illness, high-pressure salesmanship, and keeping up with the neighbors, he had been unable to save any substantial sum of money from his pay. Morally and legally he was responsible for the support of his wife and children. As soon as he lost his employment the atmosphere in his home changed. He noticed that his wife and children looked at him "funny," or at least differently. Sometimes, of course, he merely imagined that their looks were "funny" or different, but the effect upon him was the same. He became self-conscious, uneasy, resentful. This was the first hostility reaction, which often led to other sharply discordant reactions.

At the same time he began to have serious doubts about his own worth and abilities. Why had he lost his job while Bill Jones and Steve Komonski remained working? Why hadn't the boss kept him on at least upon a part-time basis? In many cases, to hide these doubts and feelings of inferiority, which usually were not new but merely intensified, he assumed a gruff, hard, or even violent manner toward everybody, including (or especially) his family. He grumbled, growled, barked back at his wife. He issued sharp commands to his children, while two or three weeks before he had never or seldom bothered them. Such behavior, of course, produced open hostility reactions on their part toward him.

This happened especially after he had come to realize that job-hunting, somehow, was a hopeless proposition and his bewilderment deepened and he was being seized by a sense of frustration. Consciously or unconsciously, he commenced to feel that forces utterly beyond his control were operating to take from him the important rôle of provider for the family. This was a serious thing in his life, for, as Dr. Thorndike points out in his book, *The Original Nature of Man,* "the truly original tendency of the human male" is "to offer a little child scraps of food and to see it eat." Also, in America, more than elsewhere, the father holds the head position in the family chiefly by virtue of "bringing home the bacon."

The father was the first to realize the seriousness of the growing unemployment situation in relation to himself and his home. To the rest of the family, at the beginning, unemployment was half a myth. In many cases, the mother and the children blamed the father for losing his job. In her ignorance of the conditions, the woman, half hysterical because income had stopped, nagged him. Why didn't he get busy and get a new job rightaway? Why was he staying home so much? Did he expect somebody would come and offer him a job? What did he think this was, anyhow? She knew that Mrs. So-and-so's husband still had a job. She had heard that some one else in the next block, after losing his job, picked up another position three weeks later. Why had her husband lost his? Why couldn't he get another one? Knowing many of his faults, she imagined all sorts of reasons. Now and then she dropped meaningful hints, infuriating him.

Something similar was true of the children's attitude toward the father, especially if they happened to be adolescent boys. Until lately they had more or less looked up to him. One of the reasons for this was that he had been passably successful in his line of work; at any rate, in one way or another he had managed to maintain an air of competence and superiority which had impressed them. He had been making enough money for all of them to live on in comparative decency and comfort. By virtue of his position as the sole or chief breadwinner, even if he was not a particularly inspiring specimen of manhood, he had been a vital factor in the development of his sons' ego ideals. Consciously or unconsciously, they had aspired to be like their father when they grew up: get a job, work, and earn money. They had boasted of their father to other boys. Now, of a sudden, he was out of work, while some of the other boys' fathers—early in the Depression—still had jobs and wages. Immediately, because economically inadequate, he became less of a hero in their eyes. Very often he was right when he thought that they were looking at him "funny." Naturally, he did not like this and often he could not control himself.

During the 1931-32 winter, when the schools and social agencies began to interest themselves in the material welfare of the children apart from their parents, there was a tendency among numerous depression-stricken youngsters to look to their teachers and to social workers and even to policemen—*i.e.,* to the community—for their necessities.

I talked to an American-born Italian boy who, I had been told, had asked a policeman to get him a pair of shoes. He had received the shoes, and I asked him where he supposed the policeman had gotten the shoes or the money to buy them. The boy's first answer was that he did not know; then he said, "I guess at the police station or the City Hall or in the bank." It did not greatly interest him where.

But some of the most serious intra-family reactions developed in cases where one or more of the boys had little jobs after school, or shined shoes or sold newspapers. In such cases the sons soon commenced to assume superior attitudes, thus infringing on the father's position in the family; which, as a rule, simply burned him up. In some cases young boys earning money allied themselves with the mother against the father in the belief that, since he was jobless, he was inferior. Then there was trouble, of course; especially if the man was just beginning to develop his gruff or violent manner as a defense mechanism.

When the Depression was still young and unemployment was not yet so general as it became later, it often was months before the man succeeded in imparting to his family a sense of reality about the situation. In some cases he clipped out of the newspapers the items and articles dealing with the situation and left them on the kitchen table for his wife and children to read. In other cases, he asked employment agents and social workers to call on his wife and tell her, the poor, ignorant ninny, that there was no work to be had, for when he himself told her she did not believe him.

Nagging on the part of the mother, who was unaware of the general unemployment situation, or for some other reason could not look at the problem from the man's angle and sympathize with him, was one of the worst things that the suddenly disemployed *paterfamilias* had to contend with in the early stages of the Depression. In some cases, the children—girls more frequently than boys—on realizing that the jobless father was a victim of circumstances, allied themselves with him against the mother on the grounds that she was unreasonable and unfair. Such a development inevitably caused new hostility reactions of the most damaging and complex sort—damaging to the family as a group as well as to individuals as characters and personalities.

There were cases where the father, on losing employment in his line, took a job in a grade of work lower than that in which he had earned his living before the slump, and in consequence also lost considerable standing in the eyes of his children—to say nothing of his wife. This was natural enough.

Indeed, it seems that the fear of losing their families' and friends' respect was one of the main reasons why a majority of jobless men—particularly in the early months of the Depression—refused to take or seek employment in lower grades of work than those in which they had earned their living before.

But no matter how much he resented his plight, in numerous cases, as the Depression went from bad to worse, the father was compelled in the end, in one way or another, to give up his position of authority and prestige in the family. He became a back number. The position of authority sometimes passed to the mother, who had become the provider. Sometimes he retained but vestiges of his old standing. In many instances authority and discipline entirely disappeared from the home.

Often the man was finally overwhelmed by the feeling of being rejected, not only by the social-economic system, which he had heard praised so much by great men like Arthur Brisbane and President Hoover, but even by his own family. His gruff or violent attitude toward his wife and family began to falter. His reactions toward them were still hostile, but gradually they were less deliberate, less a part of his defense mechanism. They became real, spontaneous. Now and then he was seized by blind punitive impulses. I came upon cases where, a few months after losing his job, the man—like Mary and Jimmie S——'s father, in the preceding chapter—had walked up and down the room all night, talked, shouted, wept, cursed, and finally beat his wife and children. One man I met almost beat his wife to death upon learning that she had accepted food from a neighbor. His explanation was, "I couldn't see straight."

If the wife, after realizing that the man could not get another job, went out and herself found employment in spite of the Depression, that fact frequently was the cause of an explosion in the home. In good times, largely to keep up his sense of adequacy, the man had forbidden her to seek outside employment. Now, all at once, she became the breadwinner and, consciously or unconsciously, began to usurp his natural position in the house. In his hurt pride he developed new hostile reactions. Time hung on his hands. In the morning before she left for work his wife told him to make the beds. The children, seeing him in this new rôle, sometimes laughed at him. I came upon a man who, making the beds one day, was so enraged by his son's laughter that he had nearly killed the child.

Gradually, with all this discordance and bickering in the home, the man began to seek "escapes" from the situation. If he had liked to drink before, he now took to alcoholism, drinking, of course, only the cheapest stuff, including "canned heat," which undermined his whole makeup. If he had the gambling instinct, he began to gamble. Sometimes he took to both drinking and gambling. Or, as Mary S——'s father, he deserted the family. Or, as suggested earlier in this book, he committed suicide or turned on the gas at night and wiped out the whole family.

In a good many cases, too, the woman, on becoming the sole or principal breadwinner, responded to the man's hostility attitude or "escape" tendencies by so conducting herself and manipulating the affairs of the home, or what was still left of it, that ultimately the man was compelled to leave. In some cases employed women took their children and literally deserted their husbands.

Of course, these latter cases, although numerous, were extreme. In most instances where hostility reactions were intense for months immediately after unemployment first hit the family, the relations of individuals within the home more or less adjusted themselves; very gradually and very painfully, of course; and the family stuck together in a loose, desperate way, fighting the battle against inimical economic forces.

So much, for the time being, of the first category of Depression-smitten families as they were affected by their economic misfortunes early in the crisis.

On the other hand, as I have suggested, almost the exact opposite was true of families in whose cases economic adversity operated to preserve the spiritual and economic unity of the home or even brought the individuals within the family closer together than they had been before the Depression. Indeed, some of the social workers with whom I discussed the matter inclined to the belief that this category was more numerous than the one I have just described, while others—apparently just as competent to express their views on the matter—maintained that the Depression had caused more destructive havoc than consolidation, integration, or reintegration in American family life. Which of the two opinions is correct will, perhaps, never be known.

At any rate, in no end of instances, as soon as unemployment struck a family, the individual members thereof immediately pooled their resources and were welded closer together by mutual sympathy and willingness to sacrifice and coöperate. In such cases, of course, harmony rather than discord and a sense of humor rather than bitterness and nagging had been the rule before the Depression, just as in the other category the opposite was true prior to the slump. In this category, when the crisis came, everybody became more appreciative of one another and of whatever comforts they jointly possessed. This inevitably deepened the spiritual quality of home life; it made the group more compact than it had been before, and helped individuals to bear their plight with more fortitude. The family discipline was preserved. There was much good-natured joking in the home. The father, although out of work, usually retained the headship of the family without any struggle.

Of course, in this category I found also a great many men and women who suppressed their various emotional difficulties when the panic came, and stayed together mainly or merely for economic reasons, figuring that apart they probably would be even worse off than they were together.

Also, the crisis suddenly brought out the fine characteristics of a great many people which in good times had not been apparent to other members of the family. There were cases, for instance, where husbands or wives who commanded some resources were seized by the spirit of sacrifice and helped their in-laws or their spouse's friends, although but a short while before the couple had been on the verge of separation or divorce; and later, when their own affairs were anything but looking up, the desire for breaking up the marital or family ties on the part of one or the other, or both, was less strong, with the result that they stuck it out.

The Depression also had some curious beneficial effects upon families not directly affected by it in an economic way through unemployment or otherwise. There were instances where the wife had been hostile to the husband before the crisis because she considered him economically inferior. His job was low-grade and his income was small in comparison with incomes of their friends, neighbors, and acquaintances. The family's social standing was low. They had no car, no radio, which made her unhappy. She nagged him. There were emotional storms. Then, when the Depression came and *he kept his job* at a time when everybody else seemed to be losing theirs, all this suddenly changed. The woman's opinion of the man, including his economic standing, immediately improved. Her disparagement of him diminished. She ceased to nag him. He was all right. He had a job. People who formerly used to look down upon them as economically inferior now envied them; the man had work while they had none. The family's social standing improved immensely. Now the home that once was full of discord, thanks to the Depression, became a happy one.

A great many families of "the better classes," of course, were also affected almost as soon as the Depression began. They were the business and professional people. They had played the stock market and enjoyed annual incomes running into five figures. In the fall of 1929 many of them, desperately trying to save their stakes in the Wall Street débâcle, mortgaged their homes and other properties to the limit, and in the course of the next year or two were deprived of everything, anyhow. During 1930 they lost their positions or failed in business, and it was not long before many of them were not far above the level of the unemployed men's families. Some of the formerly opulent people who once had supported charity organizations became charity cases themselves. I found a man whose fortune in 1928 was figured in millions. In 1925 he had donated a million dollars to an Eastern college, his alma mater. In 1931, lest he and his family starve, he was forced to appeal to the college authorities to put him on the payroll.

This, of course, was an extreme case. But I became aware of many families who had been compelled to give up their suburban homes, motors, motor-boats, along with their several servants. In these families the same sort of antagonistic and affectional tendencies that I have described as true among the working-people had been at work since 1929. Some of them now were closer together than ever before. Women went back to housekeeping in narrow quarters without servants. Some joked about their plight from the start. Many of them, however, had had no previous experience in managing a home; such things had previously been left to their housekeepers. Not a few women in such changed circumstances were anything but happy. They were rather helpless and absurd.

They could not prepare a decent meal. This led to words with the husband, and so on. There is no doubt that some of these women—to say nothing of the men—suffered as much on account of economic reverses as most of the unemployed men's wives whose plight actually was much worse than theirs. They wept for days at a spell and suffered nervous breakdowns.

In times of prosperity, many marriages among the well-to-do were endurable only by virtue of the money. These couples had large houses or apartments, where they did not see one another for days. The woman could have a lover, the man a mistress. When they found it impossible to stay in the same town, one or the other took a trip. . . . Now, with not enough money left to pay for a divorce, life was simply hell. There were divorces or separations—more of the latter than the former, for the reason that divorces were more expensive than separations.

One of the biggest problems of those people who were no longer rich—in 1930 and through most of 1931—were their children. In good times the children had been raised by governesses and in private schools. Some of them had been spoiled or problem children, but wealth had worked to smooth things over. The parents actually had had little to do with them. In the summer they sent them to camps while they themselves went on a cruise around the world. Now governesses, private schools, and summer camps were out of the question. The children were more difficult than ever before and the parents did not know what to do with them.

Early in the Crisis, as I have suggested, the father and husband bore the brunt of the family difficulties. For a while—especially in the lower-class homes in which there was little harmony—the Depression was in many cases almost purely his personal problem. Later, however, when the Depression was recognized even by the Hoover administration as the paramount fact in America's national life, the difficulties were accepted by all members of the family. There followed a painful process of mutual readjustment. Hostility reactions drowned in common misery. Standards of living were consciously lowered—in millions of cases to rock bottom. There were evictions, foreclosures, actual starvation, crime, deep social agony.

A case history:

Jim F—— had worked as a truck-driver for the same concern for five years, making forty-five dollars a week. He and Mrs. F—— were a happy, respectable couple. They had four children, all of them fairly normal. In April, 1930, when he was thirty-six years old, Jim lost his job when the firm went bankrupt. For six months he had no work at all. In September he drove a truck for another concern for two weeks, making only twenty-three dollars a week. It was his last job. In December he lost all his savings—$350—in a bank failure. Then two of the children became ill. He had a hard time in borrowing money to pay the doctor and the druggist. They began to pawn things; finally, Mrs. F—— was forced to pawn her wedding ring. In September, 1931, the rent was three months in arrears. The landlord threatened eviction. Then Jim "got out of his mind," as Mrs. F—— put it to me, and joined two other men (also married men and fathers of children, living in the same apartment-house) in a robbery. They got thirty-three dollars and were arrested almost at once. The family situation was explained to the district attorney and reputable persons testified as to Jim's pre-Depression character, but in vain. Jim was sentenced to five years in Sing Sing. In October, when Jim was being tried, Mrs. F——, not knowing what else to do, appealed to organized charity for the first time and now, living in a single-room flat with her children, she managed to keep them and herself alive on the few dollars she received as relief. She felt disgraced. None of her relatives and former friends knew where she was. Jim himself was a hopeless man in Sing Sing. He felt that when he got out of prison, even should the conditions improve, his chances of employment would be slim because of his criminal record. Mrs. F—— visited him in prison just before Christmas (the fare was paid by the charity organization). His forehead, when she saw him, was scarred and blue, because every now and then he went "crazy" and banged his head against the walls of his cell. But the worst phase of the situation was that the children were being seriously affected. Unable to restrain herself, Mrs. F—— wept a great deal, and the children bawled with her. There were nights when all five of them cried for hours. They all slept in the same room, except the oldest boy, whose bed was the tub in the windowless bathroom. All four children, two of them of school age, were underweight, suffering with frequent ailments due to poor resistance. When I visited the family one child was in bed with a cold; two other children were in the same bed—the only one—"to keep warm." There was no heat in the dwelling. Mrs. F—— said to me, "We'd all be better off dead."

In some cases which came to my notice whole families had developed antisocial, criminal tendencies. In extreme cases entire families whose heads formerly were respectable and successful workingmen now coöperated in making their living expenses by thieving.

One of the worst problems in connection with family life during the Depression, especially on the lower economic levels, was the problem of shelter. During 1931 there were nearly 200,000 evictions in New York City alone, a majority of them during the second half of the year. In Chicago there were almost as many. New York had more than 60,000 eviction cases in the first three weeks of January, 1932. Dr. John Lovejoy Elliott, headworker of the Hudson Guild, said in a public address early in January: "I was told the other day of a judge who had 425 eviction cases in one day! The situation for the rent-payer, as well as the landlord, is a terrible one."

Alone or in company with professional social workers, I visited 107 depression-stricken families in Greater New York; practically all of them were threatened with eviction. Four of them had been evicted twice and eleven once before since 1930. In the Williamsburg-Greenpoint slum districts of Brooklyn I visited thirty-one families. In every case the rent had not been paid for from two months to a year. In many cases the landlords "hadn't the heart" to evict them. In one instance the landlord was even paying the family's gas bill. Most landlords, however, pressed eviction actions. With their buildings one-third or half vacant, they themselves were desperate. If they let one family stay without paying, other families in the same house learned of it and stopped rent payments, too.

Things were little better in the "nice sections." Thousands of families which in 1930 still could afford eighty- and ninety-dollars-a-month apartments were evicted in 1931. These evictions continued at an increasing rate in 1932.

When families were evicted, they sometimes moved into one-room flats in the cellars, or into cheap furnished-room houses. I came upon families of seven, eight, and even ten living in one-room flats. They slept on chairs and on the floor, in bathtubs (if they had them) and over sinks.

Other evicted families "doubled up" with other families, sometimes in the same apartment-house. The families often were comparative strangers. The better-off people took pity on the evicted ones. In some cases the families were related, or of the same nationality or religious faith. I saw or heard of cases where two, three, and even four evicted families pooled their resources and moved into one flat or apartment. In one two-room flat I saw eleven persons; in another flat with the same number of rooms, twelve persons, eight of them children. In one three-room apartment I came upon four families, which included two deserted wives, two wives and their husbands, and thirteen children. Two of the latter were ill in bed. Most of the others were clearly undernourished.

In a basement flat of two rooms in Harlem I found three white families, which included nine children and four adults. One of the men was an unemployed carpenter—out of work since 1930—who had "picked up" some lumber somewhere and built about a dozen bunks along the walls, one above the other, three deep, like berths on a steerage steamer or in a trench dugout.

Most of these people were charity cases to begin with; others became charity cases later. In one way or another they "chiseled along." But, of course, there was a great deal of bickering and intriguing in such establishments. Mothers hid food from one another, in order to feed their children. Men came to blows. They got on each other's nerves. They stole from one another. Some dwellings sheltered two or three different nationalities, and the diverse temperaments clashed. But they stuck together because that was all they could do.

A great many young couples, married in the years just before the Depression, were forced to give up independent apartments, store their furnishings, and move in with the old folks, if the latter happened to live in the city where the young husband, perhaps, still had a part-time job. If the parents, who still had a home, lived elsewhere, the couple separated. The young wife and the baby went home to her people, while the young man remained in the city, to fight things out alone.

During 1930-31 numerous families lost their furniture because unable to continue payments on the instalment plan. Instalment-furniture houses were crammed with "junk," as they called furniture recovered from Depression-stricken families. The collector of a Bronx firm told me that many families, on moving to smaller and cheaper quarters, simply abandoned their partially paid-for furniture in the old, more expensive apartments.

In 1931 tens of thousands of families in New York and vicinity lost their homes through foreclosures, which was true also in other cities. Most of these luckless families, of course, were working-people, but a great many of them also were families who, not so very long ago, belonged among the "better classes"—business and professional people, some of whom considered themselves wealthy in 1929. One such case was brought to my attention:

In 1929 Mr. D—— was worth over $200,000. He was a retired business man, playing the market "a little." He had a fine home in a New York suburb. His oldest son was at Harvard. Two daughters were in private schools. Mr. and Mrs. D—— had just booked a 'round-the-world passage when the Crash came. Of a sudden the world tumbled down about their heads. Hoping to save at least a part of his fortune, Mr. D—— mortgaged his home, but he no sooner got the mortgage money than it was "swallowed up by Wall Street." He was too proud to appeal to people he knew who were still wealthy. For two years the whole family struggled to save the home. During 1931 they actually starved. They sold their expensive furniture, piece by piece. The girls had to be recalled from their schools. The son quit Harvard. But it was no use. Gradually the family broke up even before the foreclosure on the home, late in 1931. The children now were scattered all over the country. One of the girls sang in a night club in Chicago. The son was a Communist who swore he would never marry or have children under the "present system." After the foreclosure Mr. and Mrs. D—— moved into a furnished room in New York City. He could get nothing to do. His mind was being affected by his plight. Finally, Mrs. D—— appealed to the charity organization they had supported in a small way for years before the Crash.

The above, again, was an extreme case. In a great many cases, of course, Depression-stricken families still hung on to their homes, which, since they had to fight to keep them, were all the more precious to them.

The Depression was having several other general effects on the home or family life of the country, and on the individuals in the home.

The number of marriages fell off during 1930 and still more during 1931. It was hard for a young man to get or keep a job. They, too, boys and girls saw the economic agony and frustration of their elders and they figured—girls more frequently than boys—that it would be sheer madness to marry. I heard boys and girls still in high school state their decision never to marry. They appeared to have an instinctive feeling that they were living in a period of uncertainty and insecurity which was apt to last a long time. They were developing so-called "balked dispositions."

There was this tendency among children of Depression-smitten parents, especially among adolescent girls: they saw the agony of their fathers and mothers, and responded to them with intense love, an overdevelopment of filial affection, which precluded normal interest in contemporaries of the opposite sex, laying the basis for various neuroses.

As a result of financial and related difficulties, men in their prime became

victims of psychic and physiological disorders, which led to sexual impotence.
Physicians, whom I met in Home Relief work, informed me that Depression-
induced impotence was common in men under forty. This was true not only
of jobless workers, but of business men whose fortunes had been affected by
the slump. One doctor in close touch with the situation maintained that many
separations and not a few suicides and wife-murders during 1930-31 had been
due in part to the fact that economic frustration made men sexually inadequate.
On the other hand, this was true, too—since the men were home so much,
many more children were produced than there would have been normally.

The Depression tended to cramp social intercourse among families. Fewer
invitations were extended, fewer parties given. Those most seriously affected
by the crisis and most in need of a good meal did not accept invitations, if they
received them, because they were unable to invite anyone in return.

The hard times cooled many friendships among families, especially on the
lower levels. Groups and individuals kept more to themselves. Endless instances of homely pleasures and contentment were curtailed and forbidden by
narrow means.

Many learned and elaborate studies of the great Depression will be written
from various angles, for it had many angles. As I work on this book I learn
that Charles and Mary Beard are preparing a history of it, which will surely
be more than worthwhile. . . . But it was such facts, conditions, and tendencies as the above-mentioned that interested me most. For me they were a
part of the essential picture, the human drama, the human truth, of the complex, painful, deep and far-reaching situation, for which, I inclined to think, no
one and everyone was to blame. It was a product of America's basic incongruity.

Bread Lines

During the first two depression years, but especially in wintertime, I gave a good deal of attention to bread lines in New York—to the men who stood in them and the people and organizations who operated them. This chapter is mostly about the latter; throwing, I think, a peculiar light on the American scene in the early days of the great crisis.

According to the Welfare Council of New York City, early in January, 1931, there were eighty-two bread lines in the city, serving at an average of eighty-five thousand meals a day. These bread lines were operated by churches, hospitals, the Salvation Army and other rescue missions and societies, the Seaman's Institute, veterans' organizations, fraternal and religious orders, convents, the Y.M.C.A., Tammany Hall, newspapers, private individuals and groups of people specially banded together for the purpose, which included racketeers. One line was operated by the City of New York in connection with the Municipal Lodging House which, in midwinter, served an average of twelve thousand meals a day. The Salvation Army bread lines in Manhattan, the Bronx, and Brooklyn—over a dozen in number—averaged more than fifteen thousand meals a day. The others were small lines, some of them serving less than a hundred meals daily. I tried some of them; most put out meager "feeds": bread, soup, and coffee; stew and bread; cheese or meat sandwiches and coffee; beans, bread, and coffee; oatmeal, bread, and coffee (for breakfast), or rolls and coffee. At some places dimes or nickels were given out.

Late in the fall of 1930 and early in the following winter there was no coordination whatever in the New York bread lines. A new line was started almost every day—as a rule, a hastily organized affair of the poorest makeshift. The Salvation Army was a sort of pioneer in the field, but, according to one of its officers with whom I talked, it soon found itself "rubbing shoulders with many other organizations and individuals operating bread lines."

Weeks before the winter began in earnest, there was in New York an overabundance of feeding-places for what the social workers termed the "destitute homeless," while to quote from a report of the Welfare Council's Coördinating Committee on Unemployment, of which Alfred E. Smith was chairman, "there was much silent suffering of an acute nature on the part of the hitherto self-supporting young girls and older single women alone in New York, 'white collar' workers, as well as among families not reached by any social agency." Most of the bread lines were out-of-doors; many of them on busy thoroughfares. The men were not only required, before being served, to stand in line in the open for long periods of time in all kinds of weather, but to eat outside, in view of passers-by.

A confidential investigation made in December, 1930, for one of the bread line sponsors revealed that "some needy and worthy individuals" were being served by bread lines. They were men who never before had been dependent and were not in bread lines by choice, but who lacked experience and probably the courage and initiative to arrive at a better solution of their plight. However, the general sympathy extended to these was capitalized by large numbers of men who never had a job to lose and probably would not have taken one had it been possible to provide it for them. They were the "unemployables," to whom the economic Depression brought on a season of veritable prosperity. Some of them did nothing all day but go from bread line to bread line, eating as many as ten or twelve meals a day. People who made a careful study of the situation were unanimous in their belief that "never before was the Bowery such a free-for-all happy hunting-ground for bums and professional hobos as in these sad months of Depression."

And this was true not only of the Bowery, where rival lines situated on opposite sides of the same block often met end to end. In certain other sections of New York—and this, I am informed, was true also of Chicago, St. Louis, Detroit, and other great cities with bread line booms—one could not walk five blocks without coming upon a bread line. There were dozens of bread lines on the East Side, and in Harlem, the Bronx and Brooklyn. There was even a line at each end of the Great White Way—one at Times Square and the other at Columbus Circle.

Professional racketeers took advantage of the much-publicized unemployment conditions by starting bread lines and soup kitchens on prominent streets, usually near some high-class apartment-house district. They served scant meals to a few hundred men a day—most of them bums and hobos—the while collecting big sums of money from philanthropic emotionalists and persons eager to see their names on the sign over the entrance to the kitchen. At one time there were as many as a dozen of these bread lines in New York, some of them running only for a few days, just long enough for the racketeers to collect everything in sight—although, of course, a majority of the lines were conducted and supported by fairly well-intentioned, if misguided, persons and institutions. One of the racketeer-sponsors of a bread line said to the workers of the Welfare Council when they called at his place on a mission of inquiry: "Sure this is a racket!" He laughed. "Youse guys ain't workin' for your health, are youse?"

But, to my notion, worse than any racketeer bread line were the two lines, already mentioned, at Times Square and Columbus Circle. They were operated by a Hearst newspaper, between eight o'clock in the evening and midnight, serving ham and cheese sandwiches from huge army trucks.

I often watched the bread line at Times Square. The wretched men, many without overcoats or decent shoes, usually began to line up soon after six o'clock—in good weather or bad, rain or snow. The big truck, accompanied by a screeching motor-cycle police escort which made all Broadway pause and look, usually came on the spot long before eight o'clock. There were huge signs on the truck informing the public that the food was provided by the munificence of this newspaper.

As a rule the men in charge did not begin to distribute the sandwiches till half past eight, and sometimes later. They worked very slowly; to all seeming, deliberately stretching out the serving and keeping the men in cold rain or snow or wind, their wretchedness exposed to the gaze of the theater crowds. Thus they advertised the high-mindedness and generosity of one paper directly in front of the building which houses the main offices of another. They fed on an average of only 960 men an evening; and part, if not most, of the expenses—about $600 a day—were contributed by the readers of the newspaper. In fairness to Hearst, it must be added that these two bread lines were not his idea, but that of one of his executives.

Early in February 1931, the Welfare Council's Coördinating Committee on Unemployment induced several of the sponsors of bread lines to close their kitchens, and the Salvation Army closed some of them on its own accord, until the number of lines was reduced from eighty-two to fifty-four. But in all probability even these were far too many.

To repeat: many of the bread lines in New York, as well as in other large cities, were necessary, and not a few were run by individuals and organizations of high motives, although perhaps only two or three were operated in a manner beyond criticism. But on the whole, bread lines did more—much more—harm than good to the unemployed. By unemployed I mean people who were without work through no fault of their own, because of great economic forces and local circumstances over which they had no control, as distinguished from the chronically destitute and homeless men, the bums and hobos, who refused to work or were utterly unemployable.

Perhaps eighty per cent of the bread-line customers in the winter of 1930-31 were men of the latter category. The other twenty per cent were for the most part single migratory workers of the lowest class, perhaps mainly immigrants. Very few of them were of the skilled type of workers, or family men. This last class of men, who lost their jobs because of the slump, did not go into the bread lines even after their savings were gone. They were too proud. They had lived independently, on their own resources for ten or twenty years; now they would have been ashamed or mortified to be seen in an outdoor bread line. In preference, many of them suffered extreme want and let their families suffer with them. Some of them, as already told, committed suicide. Not a few appealed to charity or family-aid societies, but——

And here we come upon the chief evil that the over-abundance of bread lines caused in the winter of 1930-31.

As the winter wore on, most family-aid organizations in New York—and elsewhere—began to receive more calls for help than ever before. Many of them were fresh cases, and all were unusually acute. And these societies were experiencing increasing difficulties in getting money to take care of their growing number of cases. The reason for this was not necessarily that the rich were less charitable than in the past.—At least part of the reason was in the entire bread line situation.

When winter started in earnest, many of the wealthy already were contributing regularly to the maintenance of one or more bread lines. Others, seeing new bread lines frequently formed, and reading about them in the newspapers, believed that, with all this food being handed out, the needy were receiving adequate relief. Thereupon they packed up and went to Florida or the South of France.

In January, 1931, I could not help overhearing a shrill-voiced lady who did not go South say to her friend between acts in a theater: "My dear, it's an outrage the way this so-called unemployment situation is being played up in the newspapers, isn't it? I get appeals for charity in every mail. So-called public-welfare organizations call me on the telephone, asking me for donations. But you won't catch me giving them anything any more! . . . You don't know what is going on in these bread lines. Well, I'll tell you what Mrs. Carter told me. She said that some one told her that the men in the bread lines were overfed. Mind you, overfed! They go from place to place and eat till they get ill." The lady, of course, did not know that most of the bread-line customers were not the unemployed, who were too proud to line up for a bowl of soup, a slice of bread, or a nickel, and yet were desperately in need of help.

In February another wealthy woman refusing to contribute to the Prosser Committee for Emergency Unemployment Relief in New York, said to one of its representatives: "Frankly, I think that the suffering of the unemployed is greatly exaggerated both by the newspapers and you people who come around collecting money. I am reliably informed, sir, that during the Christmas week whole families—man, wife and two or three children—lined up in front of free food stations run by various emergency organizations where large baskets of food were being given away; and then, after each of them got a basket, they went around the block and drove off in their own automobiles or in taxicabs!"

Many Christmas food-basket lines were operated in the same fashion as the bread lines, by emotional, publicity-hungry people or by groups or organizations which expected to get more out of the distribution of baskets than the food cost them. At some of the food stations baskets were handed out to all comers amid the clicking of newspaper cameras. Other stations were operated during the Christmas week by Tammany Hall politicians and policemen who allowed their friends to "get in on" the baskets. These were not all the destitute unemployed. The above-quoted lady did not know that the Prosser Committee, which was raising money to create emergency jobs and wages for unemployed heads of families, offered perhaps a better solution of their immediate problem than anyone else.

I think the next winter the bread-line situation was somewhat better.

But it was more and more apparent to me that—since the Depression grew worse and worse, increasing the general social agony—before long the Federal Government would be compelled to take over the handling of unemployed relief.

From My Diary

December 15, 1931.—Economically the most severely affected by this crisis—which, however, is *much* more than an economic crisis—are, of course, the ordinary, most numerous folk: the factory workers, the many kinds of unskilled laborers, and petty clerks: the anonymous mass, which some of our current "revolutionary intellectuals" think Marx had in mind when he wrote the words "proletariat" and "revolution." But I believe that if Marx saw this "proletariat" in America today he would see precious few who might encourage him in his idea (if I understand him aright) that the impetus for the great change toward a new collectivist social order would come directly from this class.

A good many American "proletarians" have been living from hand to mouth in so-called good times; now that they have lost their jobs millions of them are completely down—and I think that is where, alas! many or even most of them are going to stay. Many, I believe, are mainly done for as positive human material. No movement, no "revolution," can save them. I think I know workers as men, as functioning organisms [I have long been one of them], and I have seen hundreds of them lately, talked with scores of them, watched their gait and movements, observed the postures of those few who got into the bread lines; and I have a definite feeling that millions of them, now that they are unemployed, are licked as men, as "proletarians," or whatever positive they ever have or could have been. They are licked by the chaos of America, by the machine, by industrialism; by regimentation on the one hand and by their futile, frustrated individualist psychology on the other. It is horrible to say this, but it is true—millions now unemployed are mainly or completely paralyzed, impotent, "washed up," doomed never again to be part of the vital, constructive economic processes of the country. They are caught in the Depression, which is grinding them down, destroying whatever spirit they may still have possessed before they lost their last job, and—for complex reasons—they cannot rise above it, see beyond it, fight it.

These people—not all, of course, but many, perhaps most of them, millions of them—seem to me the residue, the unsuccessful leftovers from the struggle in America on the part of the working-people during the last few decades to become middle-class, to get on socially and economically. Essentially, they are as individualistic as those who have more or less succeeded in the struggle. Or maybe even more so: for they, it seems to me, are much more hopeless, because, failing so drastically as individualists, they have lost something from their makeup as men, as co-operative human beings.

They have been unwilling "proletarians" all their lives—industrial slaves,

298

wage slaves. And here I want to make this point: Wage slavery has had a dire effect on their characters as men, on their manhood, especially on those who are, say, forty or over. For ten, fifteen, twenty years these proletarian individualists of America, possessed by the prevalent psychology of the country, have been competing with one another in the labor market. Always they have been looking for immediate advantages, no matter at whose immediate or long-range expense. There was little or no class-consciousness. No *social* consciousness whatever. 'Rah for Number One! To the devil with labor unions, which were mostly graft schemes on the part of the leaders, who, also looking out for Number One, had frequently betrayed the workers. The thing to do was to earn money, to work, hold one's nose above the water, watch for a chance to improve one's individual lot—and, to keep one's little job, one had to compromise right and left; compromise with one's manhood and human dignity, betray one's class, act against one's own best feelings and instincts. As a worker, a man had to go around and humiliate himself, peddle his brawn, his hands, as though they were not a part of him, but articles he had picked up somewhere. Always he—this factory hand, this common laborer, this petty clerk—was afraid he might lose his job, and then his wife and kids would suffer and reproach him. Always he feared somebody was going to step on him; and often somebody did step on him, and he had to take it, for he was without say-so or comeback. Always he looked for a chance to escape from the low-down working-class and get on, get up in the world, become a foreman, a boss, a business man, an insurance agent, an exploiter of others, and do to others what had been done to him; but there was always some one else trying at the same time to squeeze himself through the same hole through which he had been aiming to escape, and so he stayed where he was—a worker, a balked individualist, his ego a pathetic affair which he kept from collapse by puffing himself up in various artificial ways, but in his essential being really a victim of the profound and complex basic socio-economic-political incongruity and chaos of American life, which became vividly apparent to me in connection with the story of Cantrell.

And all this wanting, but being unable, to become something better had an evil, degenerating effect on the worker's character, on his manhood, his mind. This was true of many a native, as well as foreign-born, "proletarian" now unemployed. He had little, if any, self-respect even when he worked: how could he when he usually had no idea when he might get the boot? He lacked pride in his job, because it involved, or called for, no skill. Now caught in the Depression, jobless, his family wanting, he is in many cases bewildered to the point of all-around ineffectiveness. In many cases, when one talks with him, there appears a faint symptom of disbalance in his mind, a faint nervous jerkiness in his movements and manner. No wonder. He cannot make head or tail of the situation in which he painfully finds himself; in fact, is afraid to really think of it, lest he be overwhelmed entirely. He squirms a bit, but lacks the spunk and character of a muskrat, which, caught in a trap, will gnaw off his leg to remain a muskrat and be free.

If one of the new Union Square "revolutionaries" were now looking over my shoulder and reading the above, he would indignantly exclaim, "You're contemptuous of labor!" . . . But I think I am not really contemptuous. For a long time I have been close, not to Labor (the sociological-political abstraction) but to laborers in several parts of the country, and I think I know them and see through them in their present plight; and I believe I have a right, as one of them, to say what I feel about them. Certainly I have a right to react with a squirm or a yell to anything in them that makes me suffer.

Occasionally I am unable to watch for any length of time unemployed men as, standing one in back of the other, mixed with professional bums, they quietly stand in bread lines against long, bare gray walls. Watching them, every now and then I want to go up to them and pull them out of the line and hit them and call them names, which would get them angry and make them look like men again, instead of slumped shadows leaning against walls. I want to say to them that they are not equal to muskrats; and that if they stand there they are not even deserving of the bowl of soup which somebody is willing to give them at the end of the line, but are doomed to nothing better than their present predicament—except the dole eventually, and death, for most of them are in their thirties and forties, and by now the Depression has gone so far, partly because of them, because they are not even muskrats, that no fundamental change, no reform, no "revolution," nothing can be effected that will really help them to become men or muskrats again. I want to say to them that no new social system can be fixed up in time to take care of them, to save them. Even should prosperity return within a year or two, industry will not take most of them back and use them, for meantime two or four million youngsters will have grown up to the age where they will want jobs. . . .

This is a terrible way to feel about millions of people. It is terrible for one to feel so. Of course my feeling about them is not continually so strong. Usually, in fact, I feel quite different—sorry, wanting to help them individually and collectively: but I believe that when I feel sorry I am less right about the situation than otherwise. . . .

Sometimes—when I am in a detached mood—the Depression-hit American individualist-"proletarian," 1931 model, makes me think of Tantalus, who stood in a pool, his chin level with the water, yet was parched with thirst and had nothing to assuage it. When he bowed his head, eager to quaff, the water sank and fled away, leaving the ground at his feet dry. Tall trees laden with fruits stooped their branches to him, but when he tried to reach up and seize the pears, figs, and pomegranates, winds whirled the boughs beyond his grasp— and finally, worn out, he died. . . .

Again, were one of the Union Square "revolutionaries" to look over my shoulder and read what I have written, he would say, "You're all confused!"

in a tone which would suggest that I am a "defeatist" or "social fascist," fit but to be a target for a revolutionary bullet. . . . I *am* confused, for The Situation I am contemplating is immense, complex, confused, and confusing, and I am trying to see it and understand it, be honest about it—honest, at least with myself: for what I am writing here in the Diary I would hesitate to say in print at this time. I *am* confused, and I believe that one who is not confused is either an intellectual superman who sees things far beyond the present (and the chances are he is no such thing) or a damn fool kidding himself with some convenient formula like Marxism or some other simplification which he has just inhaled, along with an idealization of the working-class, and the hope that tomorrow "the Revolution" will occur and resolve everything into Utopia in a jiffy. I believe that the present situation cannot be resolved into anything in a jiffy. It is something that will be, if at all, taken care of only by a long process, which will be also confused and confusing and humanly awful—a matter, perhaps, of the next several decades or centuries.

Oh, I know that what I am writing here—as things occur to me—is not the complete psychological picture of American workers, jobless and employed, caught in the Depression. What I say is true, for the main part, only of *most* of the unemployed, the six or seven million, whatever the staggering number may be, who are the heart of the immediate, pressing situation, and many of whom are older men. I know that some twenty million people are still employed or working part time. They are the steel men, miners, railroad men, skilled mechanics, building-trades men, printers, etc., who are not defeated, at least not hopelessly so; who have gotten on a little in the past couple of decades or in the few years immediately before the Crash and some of whom still hold onto their winnings. They have some notion of their importance in the economic and industrial life of the country, along with a little pride in their work. Some of them once received good wages and get now but ten or twelve dollars a week on part-time jobs. Others once had homes of their own, or still have them but may lose them. When "prosperity" was at its height, these people thought they were getting somewhere; now they are discovering that perhaps it was all an illusion. . . . This class of workers, *which is the majority*, is not characterless or seriously unbalanced in their minds or nervous makeups, but is also preponderantly individualistic, each tending—now, man as in the past—to take care mostly of his own skin and ego, congratulating himself that he is not quite as badly off as some others he knows, and distrusting collective action if it is suggested to him. Still, if labor does anything about The Situation, it will be this element of workers that will do it. But, as it seems to me, it cannot possibly sufficiently crystallize itself to do anything for some time to come—for years. Maybe not until some while after conditions improve; when they do, however, the workers will not be "revolutionary" in any current Union Square "Communist" sense, but, in all probability, merely tough, aggressive, violent, starting strikes, demanding more wages, and so on, which will not be anything fundamental, of course . . . and things will go on to the next depression.

December 16, 1931.—The notes on Depression psychology that I wrote yesterday are, I think, more or less true, but—of course—not the whole truth, which probably is too complex to be determined while we are still in the midst of this situation, whose existence is just beginning to be recognized.

. . . In addition to those I have mentioned, there are other reasons why the unemployed are taking the Depression so quietly and why the "Communists" find it necessary to organize artificial, unspontaneous demonstrations and riots. One is that many unemployed are foreign born, or children of foreign born, and as such, not feeling entirely at home here and afraid of the consequences of calling attention to themselves and their plight, hesitate to join in any sort of action. Another reason is that the American jobless man, even if he is foreign born, is an American, not a Russian or Balkan peasant who can subsist and even thrive on a little corn, a piece of hog fat or an onion, or starve for weeks without being much the worse for it. Centuries of meager but natural living have trained the Russian or Balkanite for a scant diet, even starvation. In America it is different. This is a land of plenty in so-called good times, when most of us, including some of the lowest-paid laborers, have been used to a variety of foods and a complex, elaborate manner of life, which have softened the people; so that now, when extreme want suddenly hits the individual, it practically knocks him over. He has not .the power of resistance to withstand adversity. In many cases, he just folds up and hides away in shame. . . .

But I suppose these additional reasons do not bring me very much closer to the whole truth than I was yesterday.

AMERICA—A SENSITIVE COUNTRY

December 28, 1931.— . . . Still, with all the dumb and hidden agony going on, and with things generally in a dreadful mess, America is a marvelous country. I *feel* this, rather than know it. Or perhaps I should say: I feel this in spite, as well as because, of what I know about the place. . . . People like [an acquaintance of mine] who endlessly rave about Russia and are but pained by U. S. A. annoy me more and more, though I am deeply interested in Russia, too.

February 9, 1932.—The Depression is hell, no doubt; however, without justifying the Depression or anything of that sort, and although hundreds of thousands and millions of persons are palpably in a hopeless psychological-economic state, the present situation seems to me *essentially* no worse than was the Prosperity era, which, to my way of looking at things, was in fact more destructive of the human, on-pushing spirit of the American people than is this so-called crisis. Indeed, with its diverse agonies, the Depression has begun to restore that spirit in the people who had lost it, and to augment it in those who still had it in 1930.

Socially, America is a most sensitive country: and this is a fact whose importance cannot be exaggerated. During the last half of 1931, but especially since New Year's, I have been noticing everywhere a profound perturbation. Except on the very lowest levels, where a sort of paralysis continues to prevail, the country is alive again—painfully so, but alive; which to me, as I remember the deadly prosperity period, is wonderful. The middle and upper-middle classes are no longer stagnant, slothful, but acutely aware that the country is in the grip of a far-reaching wrong or incongruity, which, the more intelligent of them realize, is nothing new; the Depression is but the reverse side of the pre-1930 prosperity.

Well-to-do and wealthy people are afraid and ashamed; not all, of course, but many of them. They are afraid partly because they are ignorant of their country and of the immediate situation. Tens of thousands of them seem actually to believe that the unemployed and the "proletariat" generally are about to heave up and annihilate them. They do not know that the unemployed and the "proletariat" generally are incapable of heaving up against them at this time; nor, I think, ever in any drastic, fundamental way. The riots on Union Square frighten them; to read the morning papers brings well-to-do people to the verge of nervous collapse; for they do not know that the occurrences on Union Square are not spontaneous mass-revolutionary demonstrations, but only organized "revolutionary" theatricalism—which the ignorance of the wealthy and well-to-do thus makes effective and desirable. . . .

There is much viewing-with-alarm all over the land. Solemn and hysterical voices are uttering pleas and warnings to industrial and financial leaders. People are writing letters to the press about the unemployment situation. Lectures on economic and social topics are popular. Editorials, in progressive and conservative newspapers alike, are pointing to the degenerating effects of unemployment and kindred industrial evils on the national character. Business and industry, one hears on every side, will have to "stabilize" and become "humanized." Professor What's-his-name of Yale wants industrial managers to make periodic "human audits" of their industries as well as financial audits and inventories, for, in his belief, they owe consideration to the human element in their businesses. . . . Preachers have become social agitators. . . .

The country, unquestionably, is *alive* again: and that is something!

HOOVER'S FACE

February 11, 1932.—The old rugged-individualist idea is on the chute. . . .
Apropos of this, and also to supplement what I have written the other day upon the social sensitiveness of America, I think that Herbert Hoover's face probably is one of the most noteworthy phenomena in the country today. I saw Hoover in 1928 in Los Angeles. He was then campaigning for the Presidency on the platform of rugged individualism, which he proclaimed would put a chicken in every pot, two cars in every garage, and silk stockings on the legs of every woman in America; and his round face with its square jaw was

smooth, chubby, aglow with confidence. Now, when I see him on the screen, his face is lined with care; it is loose, bewildered, worried, afraid: a *helpless* face—though in many respects Hoover doubtless is a clever, competent man. His face seems to me a composite portrait of the "clever, competent," well-to-do class of the American people today.

The other day I heard E—— [who considered himself a "Communist" and expected a "revolution" any day] say that Hoover in the United States of 1932 will go down in history as the American analogue of the Tsar in Russia of 1917: which struck me as far fetched. When in the history of Russia had the face of a Tsar changed so quickly and profoundly as has Hoover's because of a national crisis? I am sure never, for the Russian ruling class was insensitive, while the top-dogs of America are not. The Tsar—mistakenly (as proven in 1917), but firmly and constantly—believed that his power was permanent and invincible, although Russia was in a revolutionary crisis for fifty years. Hoover, 'way down in him, did not know where he stood six months after the Wall Street crash. His ignorance of what is going on is an entirely different matter from the Tsar's ignorance. Hoover's ignorance, paradoxically, is something active, dynamic, almost positive. The Tsar's encased him in a false armor, which he thought made him secure; Hoover's strips him . . . and there he stands: the temporary center of America's incongruity and confusion; a tortured, desperate, pitiful person, torn by inner conflicts, brooding, very unlike the Tsar.

The average radical or liberal considers Hoover an evil so-and-so, and my own day-to-day opinion of him, as I watch his squirming and read his statements, is nothing he would like to hear. In his fear, he is apt to do anything desperate and stupid [including the calling out of the troops as he did against the ragged Bonus Army a few months later]. And yet I think that, deep down in his confused makeup, he has a dreadful time not to yield to every prick of his conscience, to every criticism, to every wail of a hungry child: for, despite his "success" and wealth, he is an American in America, where nothing is permanent and everything changes, where nobody is secure, least of all people in high places; where the powers-that-be fight furiously against change, but always yield immediately after—if not all, then part, of the way. They must yield right along, for this is America, with its Declaration of Independence, its democratic "Dream"; not Tsarist Russia. This is a sensitive democracy, not an insensitive absolutist country. This is America, and the name America is synonymous with revolution, process. Revolution goes on here all the time. America is changing, revolutionizing her ways and institutions, her status, all the time. America is a continent, a world, elemental, chaotic, unpredictable on the whole. And Hoover, the plutocrats, the rugged individualists, will have to yield . . . are already yielding.

Americans are sensitive to misfortune in the lives of their neighbors and fellow citizens; that is part of their pioneer traditions. In the old days they helped—had to help—one another: for life in the wilderness was insecure. The tradition goes on.

Americans, too, are pragmatists, which is also part of the country's pioneer tradition. It is part of the American way never to worry too much about anything more than a day or so ahead; for, in the insecure, dynamic pioneer era, it was almost impossible to foresee what shape the problem would really take when it appeared—so why worry! When the problem did arise they worried like the devil and dealt with it on the spot. If one thing did not work, they worried again and tried another. Occasionally merely trying to deal with it was. satisfying. . . . So now pragmatic America is beginning to see the problem, and presently she will deal with it in one way or another. If one way fails to work, she will try another; and trying the various ways will keep her from going extreme, and thus in the long run perhaps (I am almost sure) not far off from the direction of true progress.

BUSINESS IS BUSINESS

April 2, 1932.—One of the questions agitating the country these days is: can business acquire social conscience and function for the benefit of humanity not only now and then, but steadily?—and the intellectual air buzzes with nonsense. . . .

There is the old saying, business is business. Its aim is profits, the higher the better, and all else, to business, is irrelevant. . . . Business corporations, as we have them nowadays, are not social or humane institutions—not even human. They are, for the most part, impersonal, unsocial, powerful, outside the control of society. To be a successful business manager, a man must be or become dehumanized, almost inhuman, at least in his capacity as a business man. Indeed, it can scarcely be said that corporations are managed by men in any real, vital sense of the word. They are operated almost purely by policy, which in the course of years and decades—since the beginning of Big Business —has jelled into tradition, and which has scant, if any, consideration for the human element in business. Profits, profits—that is the thing!

I don't mean to say that business men are evil people. They are not personally to blame for the lack of business' social sense. No one is to blame. The lack is inherent in the business structure as it stands. Inevitably. In its very nature, business, as we find it today, can by itself have or develop no social philosophy or social intelligence. It can, by and large, have no statesmanship or long-range foresight. It is essentially opportunistic, anarchic, fatalistic. A Depression is not its fault; it is an act of God. So ——

Business today, to be sure, has certain ethical rules, but they have nothing to do with the wider social morality. There is, for instance, considerable honesty in business, that is, in transactions between firms, but not because honesty is a social virtue conducive to higher civilization and human nobility; only because, quite apart from every other consideration, it is essential to the con-

duct of business. Business honesty has nothing to do with honor; it is, as Garet
Garrett once put it, merely "formal honesty."

Society, of course, derives great and many benefits from modern business,
which is full of little progressive tendencies; but these benefits are largely
incidental to the main and original purpose of profit-making. Take the
tendency of putting on the market dependable goods, which has become noticeable in American industry and commerce in the last two decades. The motive
behind it is ethical in a purely narrow, formal business sense, not in any large
social way. It is, like the practice of honesty by firms, simply good business
policy, for in the long run, as a rule, the buying public supports the manufacturer of reliable articles, enriching him not only by its purchases, but by
automatically increasing the capital value of his trade-mark and his credit,
which enables him to sell more shares and expand his business.

In fine, although here and there we find an enterprise like the Pequot mills
in Salem, or the Richman Brothers clothing factory in Cleveland, to look for
social-mindedness, social idealism in business generally, as we have it today, is
to appear rather naïve. And to call upon business—Big Business—to fulfill its
"social duty" to labor, to the community, is to appear worse than naïve. One
may as well yell at a speeding train to have a heart and not crush the ants and
caterpillars on the rails.

Business being what it is, then, its attitude toward labor and toward
society is what I have seen in the New England textile towns—cruel, haphazard, irresponsible. Business concentrates solely on making money. Since one
of the simplest ways to cut down expenses is to slash salary and wage rolls,
it of course lays off men right and left as its production efficiency increases
or its market wanes. The most valuable executive is he who can produce
the most with the least labor—the smallest number of workers and the smallest
payroll. . . . What happens to the hordes of workers it releases is not its
concern. Business is much too engrossed in increasing profits to give thought
to what happens to individuals, to the country, or even to itself, because of
its reducing the number of workers. Its traditional and natural duty is to
exercise every ounce of ingenuity to do away with jobs, not to create them—
this in times of prosperity, and of course even more so in bad times. . . .

Immediacy is the big thing; quarterly dividends and the annual balance are
what matters. One must scheme and hustle. There is no time for vision, for
social consideration. The process is charted from day to day.

Now I don't mean to say that some of the Big Business men who get
themselves in the papers for advocating high wages and steady employment
are insincere. Some really believe in high wages and steady employment—for
the other firms, the other corporations. Not long ago the New York *Sun* ran a
leading editorial urging that payrolls be kept up everywhere, for the paper
believed that conditions could be kept from growing worse only if the purchasing power of the masses was to be maintained. And last week, I am told,
that same newspaper, which is of course a large capitalistic corporation of

stockholders, discharged forty-two of its employees and reduced the wages of those it retained ten percent. . . . And that is how it goes!

The other day I read an editorial in another New York newspaper which called upon business leaders to "do something about it"—about unemployment —or prove themselves morons. Now, to my mind, business leaders are no more morons than are practically any other group of average men. They, too, are victims of the immense, chaotic, impersonal, tortuous economic structure within which they function, though, of course, their worst plight is seldom as acute and tragic as that of the workers they throw out of employment. Since the Crash, proportionately, perhaps as many capitalists and industrialists have committed suicide on account of the Depression as jobless men, and it is possible that, as I write now, proportionately, more rich men are dying of melancholia, caused by the uncontrollable chaos in their business, than idle workers of starvation.

I don't deny that some business men are morons, but that is unimportant. It is merely that the average business executive, so called, moron or not, does not run his business, but that, conversely, his business runs him. He is in the grip of a Frankenstein. He acts according to the policy or tradition of his corporation; and essentially, as I have hinted, most corporations are alike. His social conscience, if he happens to be burdened with one, is often uneasy, but—such is human nature—he seldom suffers severe remorse, for he neatly and conveniently rationalizes and blames all evils on the corporation. He passes the buck to the great organization, which, with its impersonal character, readily serves as a hide-out for his conscience. As a manager or director of the corporation, he says, "Well, if this were my own business, believe me, I'd deal differently with labor. But, hell, it isn't mine—not really. I'm but an instrument of our corporation's policy. Don't forget, I'm responsible to our ten thousand shareholders, who, regardless of everything, want their dividends." And each of the thousand shareholders comes back with, "Well, what can I do? Am I running the business? I am *not*. I'm only one of ten thousand people, none of whom has anything to say personally about how things ought to be run."

In a word, no one in corporate business, as it functions today, is personally or directly responsible to society or civilization.

Whenever attempt is made to curb business, business fights on the theory that any curbing is bad for it as a profit-making scheme; however, if the attempt succeeds and the curbing turns out to its own advantage, business accepts the new conditions, but fights again—reflexly—the next attempt to curb it, never asking if such additional curbing might not be good for it, too. It knocks down wages where and whenever it can, thereby reducing its customers' purchasing power. In fine, brilliant as it may be off and on in making profits, business is—essentially, generally, in the long run—stupid, even from the viewpoint of self-interest. And it can't help being stupid. . . .

The humanistic or social interests and intelligence have been fighting a feud with business' stupidity for decades, but have not gotten very far. Aided by the general confusion, which issues from America's basic disharmony, it has been too powerful for them. In 1928 it triumphed and in 1929 put its man, a great apostle of business anarchy or rugged individualism, in the White House, where he—now that his rugged individualism has landed the economic machine in the ditch, and the country is in agony—is completely out of place, a miserable man, and the country will have to wait till next fall for a chance to gain some control over the most important factor in its life.

The problem is what to do about it—not only this coming fall, but generally. I don't believe the American people want to abolish private capitalism and go communist or entirely state-socialist or state-capitalist—not yet. I think that in the next several years, if this current excitement about making business social means anything, effort will be exerted to make business behave and act consistently for the benefit of the people. Such effort will probably result in a terrible fight, which will shake the United States to its depths. Business will oppose it. The people are liable to have a hard time deciding on just how to turn business the master into business the servant. They are apt to have extreme difficulty in doing that chiefly by political means, through laws, etc.; for business has the power to pervert politics and laws, and much experience in such perverting. Labor ——?

Labor is a big question mark, for the workers are not purely, entirely labor in any definition of that abstract politico-sociological term one wishes to make which will hold good for any length of time. The workers are also Americans, with all the glory and confusion of that fact in their souls. . . . But, anyhow, what will labor—the workers—do? What can they do? I am not sure; in fact, I don't know. I am writing this in an attempt to think about the industrial [or capital-labor] problem, which is one of the central, most disturbing realities of contemporary America.

Just now [spring 1932] the idea of violence is in the air, at least in the intellectual circles in New York. Labor must organize and become revolutionary! So say the extreme radicals. The less extreme say: Workers must organize and develop the power and intelligence to *force* (they emphasize) the conversion of business the master and disrupter into business the servant of our civilization, for such dehumanized, impersonal, and arrogant stupidity as characterizes business responds but to force, sustained pressure. . . . Now and then I agree with this, perhaps mainly because I live in this atmosphere of intellectual New York; but when I do agree, I think I do so only superficially. In back of my mind, there seems always a doubt. Somehow, instinctively, I feel that "revolution" and "force" just *won't work* in America. Not at all; not really; not in the 1930's or 1940's, not any more than they worked in Los Angeles in 1910. "Revolution" and "force," if they get started again, are bound to go wrong and culminate in a smash-up essentially, and perhaps in many particulars, very like the Harriman-Debs-Gompers-McNamara fiasco; only, of course, upon a larger scale.

We who are interested in a better future, in civilization and culture, in progress, will have to begin to think, really think, not merely accept Marx or anyone else who once had an idea . . . and seek new concepts of civilization and new methods of social advance which will be in accord with the American temperament and the American historical experience so far. . . .

[As indicated, this was written in 1932. I return to the subject later in this book.]

AMERICA ON THE VERGE

April 28, 1932.—We are sailing tomorrow. To be gone a year! In a way, I hate to go. I shall miss America. I have a strange feeling that the country is on the verge of something or other. While I am away almost anything is apt to happen. Hoover, I think, is finished, although I can't see how the Republicans can avoid renominating him, which party tradition and his natural egoism require them to do; and when I get back in the spring of 1933 there will be a new President. Who? Franklin Roosevelt seems to have the best chance for the Democratic nomination.

Things are livening up. . . . Fred [a newspaper friend of mine] tells me that for several weeks now, in and around New York and no doubt elsewhere, groups of men—thirty, forty of them—have been entering chain grocery-stores and asking for credit. When the clerk tells them business is for cash only, they bid him stand aside: they don't want to harm him, but they must have things to eat. They load up and depart. The police are not called, for that would mean a big fuss, which would get into the papers; and the chain-store companies do not want the thing publicized, for they figure that the less anybody hears of it the better. Many more unemployed might get the same idea. . . .

The New Deal Calls Me

ON MY RETURN FROM YUGOSLAVIA TO NEW YORK IN THE SPRING OF 1933, AS I have told, wanting to finish *The Native's Return* as quickly as possible, I tried—with but partial success—not to be interested in the immense socio-economic-political developments in America which began and went on under the general title of "The New Deal" or "The Roosevelt Revolution."

The Native's Return was out about a month, early in 1934, and I was clearing up my affairs in New York preparatory to starting on the already-mentioned lecture tour which was to take me mostly to immigrant "colonies" as far west as Minnesota, when I received an excited—and exciting—telephone call from my publishers' office. Somebody at the White House in Washington was trying to reach me, and I should stay home. A few minutes later Washington was calling. However, it was not the White House, but some one in the Federal Emergency Relief Administration speaking for the assistant administrator, Colonel Westbrook, who, it seemed, wished to see me and consult with me on the condition of immigrants in the hard-hit industrial towns. Could I come to Washington at once—or within the next few days?

I said yes; but just what did Colonel Westbrook (of whom I had not heard before) desire to know? Well, he was in charge of the transfer of the surplus labor in industrial cities and towns to model rural communities, which were to be built by the Government. The plans for these communities were as yet vague; they were just being worked out; but I gathered that the general idea was at least remotely related to the Russian farm collectives, of which I had been reading.

I promised to be in Washington in two days. When I put down the receiver, my head reeled. Was this possible? Was the New Deal really incipient revolution? . . . On the face of it, the idea of model rural communities interested me very much. But was it possible to carry it out? It, apparently, was still more or less a secret; when it became known, would it not forthwith evoke terrific opposition on the grounds that it was Communistic and what not?

Oh, this fantastic, wonderful America! . . .

But first of all: what did I know—*really* know—of the Depression problem among the immigrants? How did their situation differ from that of the native unemployed workers? I supposed that I would be asked how destitute immigrants and their families might be transferred, along with old-stock natives in the same situation, from grimy coal and steel towns to ideal farm villages. I did not know how, but thought I might be able to give a few suggestions. I wrote air-mail letters to three or four Slovenian- and Croatian-language newspaper editors and two or three presidents of South Slavic fraternal organizations in Cleveland, Pittsburgh, and Chicago, with whom I was more or less familiar. I thought that, if anyone, the foreign-language editors and fraternal-organization presidents were competent to advise the Government; I explained the idea to them, and asked them to wire me their reactions and suggestions to the hotel in Washington where I was to stop.

The telegrams I received were long, thorough, and intelligent . . . and when I finally sat down with Colonel Westbrook I was, I think, prepared to talk with him: for what was true of the South Slavic groups, I had no doubt, was largely true of all the others.

Colonel Westbrook was a Southern landowner, a World War army officer with some engineering experience. He and two or three of his assistants and I talked in a dinful office, amid endless interruptions of telephone calls from Atlanta, San Francisco, and Chicago: which was typical of the New Deal in those days. Twice as I talked to him, it occurred to Westbrook to call the Coast and he talked ten or fifteen minutes each time while I figured that the Government, even with special rates, must have quite a telephone bill. Then:

"Now where were we? ——"

I never found out who had suggested me to the Colonel, but learned that the idea for these farm communities was mainly Mrs. Roosevelt's, or rather that it was an extension or elaboration of her original subsistence-homestead idea. This elaboration had her approval and the President's, and the FERA had twenty-five or two hundred and fifty (I forget which) million dollars "as a start" to work with on the idea. I was told that "if the thing works out," by and by there would be billions for carrying out the plans now in preparation. I met pleasant, eager young men, who were in charge of the various phases of the plans.

It was all rather amusing. The project, it seemed, was only a couple of weeks old, but the Government already owned, or had options upon, vast tracts of land on which these new communities were to be started, while two or three state governments and numerous private owners were offering the FERA great areas free of charge for this purpose. I was shown drawings, representing tracts of ten thousand acres, in the center of which were model towns for about one hundred families, with churches, schools, libraries, and other public buildings and one-acre gardens around the lovely little dwellings. Each house and garden would belong to a family, either by lease or gradual purchase; while the land surrounding the town would be owned by the Government and worked collectively by the inhabitants of the town under the direction and management of an agricultural expert, who would be a Government official and, "till local democracy got going," head of the community.

As a start, the Government would give each family entering such a community a certain sum of money—I think twenty-five hundred dollars—as a loan to be repaid in small instalments within twenty years. The net profits from the collectively worked farmland would be divided among the inhabitants. In addition, various industries—perhaps mostly hand industries: furniture, weaving, notions, garment-making, woodwork, and ironwork, which would not compete with regular industries—were to be started for the purpose of keeping the people occupied and bringing some money into the community.

And now, where did the immigrants and their families figure in this idea? My mind bristled with misgivings. The initial trouble with the idea was that it was too good to be carried out to any great extent at this time. It was sure to hit gigantic snags. As I had imagined on first hearing of it over the telephone, it was bound to raise the cry of Communism on the part of the most vocal and articulate in the country. Besides, it meant to put under cultivation great new areas of land, which seemed to me in conflict with the Department of Agriculture's sensational new program of crop reduction and crop destruction, that was being put into effect on the seeming theory that too much land already was under plow. But I said nothing of my misgivings and, showing Westbrook and his young assistants the telegrams from the foreign-language newspaper editors and the presidents of fraternal organizations, made my suggestions along these lines:

(1) The foreign born now economically stranded in the Depression-hit industrial cities and towns were perhaps ideal material for such collective communities as the Government contemplated starting. Speaking for such groups as the Poles, Czechs, Slovaks, the South Slavs, the Finns, Lithuanians, Hungarians, and Italians, most of them were peasants in the old country, people of the soil, in good times, many of them had been working in mines and mills with but one thought: to save enough money to buy a farm. Tens of thousands of them (I could not say how many) were now down and out, and if the Government invited them to come into such collectives as had been described to me, they—or most of them—would be untellably grateful and, I had no doubt, would strive with everything in them to help the new towns succeed as communities. The Government would probably have far less difficulty in handling these people than the native born.

(2) The Government, I felt, could reach the immigrants it desired to aid most effectively through the fraternal organizations and the foreign-language press. If the Government was really serious in the matter (I emphasized the if), it should call a conference of the important fraternal-organization presidents and foreign-language editors in some such centrally located city as Cleveland or Chicago. The people who would actually handle the problem of transferring the people for the various national groups might in all likelihood be found among them.

(3) Just then, as already told, I was becoming intensely interested in the immigrants and their children as part of America's cultural problem; so I urged that, if such rural collectives were to be actually started, the Government should create largely Polish, largely Slovenian, largely Croatian, largely Swedish, largely Finnish (etc.) communities within which these nationals would be free to bring out their cultural and artistic talents, as was the case with the so-called Pennsylvania Dutch, or the Scandinavians of the Northwest, or the

Czechs in Nebraska. By "largely" Polish (etc.) I meant about two-thirds; the other third to be old-stock Americans who might volunteer to live in such towns. If the Government decided to help these immigrants start handicraft industries, it probably could do no better than to have them return to their old-country peasant arts and crafts.——

The thing excited my imagination as an idea; at the same time, because of my misgivings, I felt no little foolish talking as I did to Colonel Westbrook and his assistants. Every once in a while I was sure he was not listening to me. He was so full of other business. I felt certain he was not really interested in the destitute immigrant workers, nor in the idea as a whole for its sake.

I was asked if I would accept a position with the FERA and take charge of the immigrant part of this great project, or some phase of that part, if or when—— I replied that I hardly thought so, for I was not sure what sort of politician-executive I would make. *If* the idea was carried out, I might like to serve in some advisory capacity. *If* ——

I stayed in Washington for four days and hung around the FERA offices. I had an interesting time. The place was full of eager messianic people. It was wonderful and a little crazy.

One day I stood in the lobby near the desk of the receptionist, who was a young girl. People were lined up in front of her, seeking information: where would they find Mr. So-and-so?—was Mr. Hopkins in?—whom would they have to see to get five million dollars for this or that? Some of the questions were really amazing to me, as I had lately returned from poor tiny Carniola, where fifty dollars was a lot of money; but the young lady answered them with a loquacious, chatty matter-of-factness, never flinching an eye.

One man who looked to be a Texan or Oklahoman, was out for some petty amount like a quarter of a million dollars for his county, which he said had gone nearly eighty-nine per cent for President Roosevelt in the election. "Oh," said the young lady, "that really is not important—we are not at all partisan, really. But, aside from that, I don't know if there is much chance of your getting anything just now. We did have an awful lot of money awhile back; I think, however, that the other day we had to borrow something like forty million—or a hundred and forty—from Mr. Ickes. We are waiting for new appropriations from Congress, or a new allocation of funds from the President—I don't know which, but I *do* know we are not as rich as we were."

I could hardly keep from bursting into a guffaw. The man from Texas or Oklahoma, however, accepted the information very calmly, without even the twitch of a smile; then reckoned that maybe he would like to see Mr. Hopkins or one of his assistants, anyhow.

Two or three weeks later, soon after I had started on my tour of the immigrant "colonies," I found myself in a difficult position. Some of the Yugoslav-language papers had published long reports of my having been called to

Washington, and what about; and now—in Pittsburgh, McKeesport, Farrell, and Sharon, Pennsylvania; in Youngstown, Cleveland, and Lorain, Ohio; in Chicago, Milwaukee, and St. Paul—I was approached by people long unemployed who begged me to make sure they would get a chance to go to one of those wonderful farm communities that Uncle Sam was going to start for all who could no longer find work in industry. I was asked to put in a special word for them. "Oh, to work on the soil again! . . . I will build my own house. . . ."

I realized how marvelously constructive such communities could really be, if—*if* —

Nothing came of the idea. God knows how many millions were spent on the plans for it; then it was dropped—partly, I think, in consequence of a certain Dr. Wirt of Indiana repeating, in the spring of 1934, some radical remarks made at a private dinner by a few irresponsible New Dealers, which resulted in a country-wide cry of "Communism" against the Roosevelt administration; but chiefly, perhaps, because it contradicted the AAA. . . . Only a few subsistence-homestead projects were started on a very small scale.

THE NEW DEAL IN GENERAL

It is, of course, not my purpose in this book to write a history of the New Deal, but merely to touch on it here and there, as it caught my attention. I might say at this point, however, that I was generally for it, and that I thought it an inevitable development.

Following the above initial contact with the New Deal, I made several more trips to Washington, some of which are referred to elsewhere in this book; and every time I was impressed by this—that the Roosevelt administration, while it unquestionably brought into (and to the peripheries of) the Government several obvious crooks, quacks, and crackpots, it also brought to the national capital thousands of sound, decent, intelligent American men and women whose minds and emotions were definitely hooked to Progress. Many of these were very young in 1933 or 1934, some just out of college, and they made bad starts and mistakes. Many, as I don't doubt was the case with some of the young men who in March, 1934, were working with Colonel Westbrook on the plans for collective farm communities, suffered disillusionment. And many did excellent work under the inspiration of President Roosevelt and such clearly superior people as Frances Perkins and Henry Wallace, for whose coming to Washington the President was directly responsible. But the probability is that the experiences of most of them will be of great value to the country for the next two or three decades. Partly because of them, America can never again completely return to the pre-New Deal era.

To give another generalization, the New Deal was many things, but fundamentally it was American—gloriously, preposterously American—well-intentioned, experimental, not thought-out blundering, successful in spots to a degree, scandalously wasteful (I wince whenever I think of the billions of dollars scattered out with the recklessness of wind with autumn leaves), and instinctively liberal and progressive. Its political-social background was definitely that of the Progressive movement of the first three decades of the twentieth century, which had been headed in the 1920's by the late "Old Bob" La Follette of Wisconsin and by George Norris of Nebraska. Probably its greatest achievement was that it was politically educational to the wide masses of the American people.

The Great "Bootleg Coal" Industry

ONE DAY IN DECEMBER 1934 PEGGY MARSHALL, EDITOR OF THE "LABOR AND IN-dustry" section in *The Nation*, called me: had I heard of the "bootleg coal" industry which had developed in recent years in Pennsylvania's anthracite country? I had not. She told me what little she knew of it, which sounded like an important and exciting story; then suggested I go to Pennsylvania and get a "scoop," for till then almost nothing had been written about "bootleg coal" in any national publication.

A few days later I put up for the night at a roadside hotel in the town of Mount Carmel, in the southern part of the hard-coal region, and, although tired, slept hardly a wink all night. My windows faced on the crossing of two state highways, and every three or four minutes a truck roared by. A coal truck. Now and then four, five trucks thundered or sputtered past in a row, shaking the ground under the hotel. I could not help rising every once in a while and going to the window to watch the procession. Through the night there passed that spot hundreds of trucks, large and small, new and old—some loaded with coal to the rim, others empty. The loaded ones, as I learned in the ensuing days, were headed for New York City, Brooklyn, various New Jersey towns, Philadelphia, Chester, Wilmington, Baltimore. The "empties" were returning from these places. The two-way stream of heavy traffic moved thunderingly all night and continued, a bit thinned out, in the daytime. But this was nothing new. It had been going on at this rate for over a year, practically without interruption. And similar streams of coal trucks had been moving all that time on other highways connecting the south-ern section of the anthracite region with the great population centers on the Atlantic seaboard and in upstate New York.

They were part of one of the most interesting, not to say exciting, socio-economic phenomena developed in the United States during the years of the Depression—coal illegally mined by the unemployed in the anthracite mining towns from company-owned lands, for the most part in open daylight, by the most primitive methods imaginable, in complete disregard of private property rights and successful defiance of company police, and in most places with the full approval of the constituted authorities and of the overwhelming majority of the other inhabitants of the community; and sold in the open market to the tune of nearly a half-million tons a month in competition with the legitimately mined coal—a fact which was beginning to cause anthracite operators and regular coal dealers in numerous Eastern cities and towns no end of per-turbation.

Bootleg coal has a long, complicated history. Here, for brevity's sake, I shall summarize its innocent beginnings and, lest I strain some reader's credulity, somewhat simplify the fantastic situation as it existed at the end of 1934.

Ever since anyone in the Pennsylvania anthracite field can remember, it has been customary for miners and their families to go with sacks or pails to the culm dumps surrounding their bleak towns and pick coal from among the rock and slate thrown out in the breaking and cleaning processes at the big collieries. The pickers usually were the poorer families. Most of the companies permitted this, and the "pickings," as a rule, were used for fuel in miners' homes. Occasionally some miner paid his church dues or a small grocery bill with a few bags of coal he had picked up on the dumps. No one ever sold it for cash.

An old miner in the town of Shenandoah told me that during the great 1902 strike, when many families experienced serious difficulties in keeping body and soul together, so many pickers invaded the culm heaps that after a while hardly a lump of coal was to be found; so he and several other family men went "in the woods up on the hill over there," where they knew coal was near the surface, and "sunk a few holes," and dug what coal they needed for their own use. They worked at night. They had an uneasy feeling that this was not unrelated to thievery, "but what could a man do, I ask you, with winter here and not a dollar to his name to buy fuel with?" This, so far as I can determine, was the first time that miners started "holes" on company property without authority from the owners.

Early in the 1920's equipment in the collieries became so efficient that not only were thousands put out of work, but practically no coal was thrown upon the culm dumps; free pickings became scarcer and scarcer, and finally almost a matter of history. The result was that when hard times hit them, the miners resorted to illegal mining in increasing numbers, but still only for their own use and mostly at night. During the winter months of the stubborn 1925 strike several hundred holes were opened throughout the anthracite region. The strike ended, but conditions went from bad to worse because the companies, finding labor more and more difficult to deal with, began to install still more efficient machinery, which threw additional thousands out of work and permitted other thousands but part-time employment; so some of the holes opened during the walkout continued to be operated, and from time to time others were started. By and by, under the stress of extreme economic necessity, miners began to dig coal illegally for their neighbors for cash, and in 1928 and 1929 there probably were from seven to nine hundred men in the six anthracite counties whose income came solely or mainly from "bootleg" coal— as they and their customers commenced jokingly to call it, because it was, in most cases, mined and delivered secretly at night.

In 1930, when the Depression engulfed the country, coal bootlegging probably doubled. In the town of Centralia, where nearly all legitimate coal production had ceased even in 1929, the number of illegal miners at least trebled. In the winter of 1930-31, when growing numbers of people appeared before township and county poor boards with requests for fuel, the board in not a few cases told them to get their own fuel. Where? How? The board members sometimes shrugged their shoulders or suggested that the nearby hills were full of coal. That winter coal bootlegging again doubled or trebled in most towns. In Centralia it became the main industry. It kept the stores open, the people from moving out. The bootleggers, as they actually called themselves, started to work their holes and haul their loot in the daytime. When the coal companies had some of them arrested, the poor boards promptly effected their release if they proved they had dug the coal for their own use; and in most cases the bootlegger's say-so was sufficient proof to satisfy the poor-board members, most of whom were ordinary townspeople and, for reasons of their own, more or less anti-company. Then, too, the local courts were strongly disinclined to sentence these offenders; and when they sent them to jail, the wardens soon turned them loose. Here and there the companies blew up the bootleggers' holes, but, as the Depression continued, for every hole they blew up three or four new ones immediately appeared. Also, town and county officials cautioned the representatives of the various companies that unless they allowed the jobless to operate their holes, taxes would have to be increased to pay for more relief, and some of these higher taxes would be levied on the coal mines. Thus the companies were forced or induced to "tolerate" the bootleggers, and boot-legging—not only digging, but selling as well—came into the full light of day (as in Centralia a year before) in Shamokin, Mount Carmel, Ashland, Trever-ton, Kulpmont, Shenandoah, Girardville, Mahanoy City, Tamaqua, Lansford, Coaldale, Pottsville, Lykens, Tower City, Reinerton, Valley View, Hegins, Donaldson, Tremont, Branchdale, Minersville, Heckscherville, Brackville, Gil-berton, Middleport, Port Carbon, Williamstown, William Penn, Big Mine Run, Lost Creek, and other towns and villages in the southern section of the hard-coal region.

In 1931 most of the coal distributed by the bootleggers was sold within twenty-five miles of where they had dug it. Much of it was delivered in sacks in the back of the bootleggers' flivvers or in small trucks hired for the purpose. That year the whole illegal output probably did not amount to more than half a million tons. In 1932, with unemployment reaching a new high, the number of bootleggers at least doubled once more and their output and business probably trebled. In the same year about a thousand men, mostly young men and boys just out of high school, sons of bootleg miners, acquired second-hand or new trucks on the instalment plan by paying one, two, three hundred dollars down, and bootleg coal began to be sold as far as fifty, seventy, ninety miles distant from the holes.

Since bootleg coal was peddled at a price of anywhere from one to three dollars cheaper than regularly mined coal, there was great demand for it, and after a high pick-up in the last half of 1932 the business got into full stride in '33, and late in '34, as the fifth year of the Depression was about to amble off, there were in the anthracite region about five thousand holes or tiny coal mines in places where coal was near the surface of the earth, operated six days a week, each by from two to five men who, in most instances, had no other equipment than picks, shovels, dynamite, a lamp, a pail, and a hoisting rope; while ten thousand or more such holes already had been "robbed out." In a single town, Shamokin, about thirty-five hundred men and boys were busy every day of the week but Sunday illegally digging and transporting coal. In Mount Carmel their number was close to twenty-three hundred, in Shenandoah approximately the same, and so on. In the entire region of five hundred square miles which stretched from Forest City in the northeast to Shamokin in the southwest there were between fifteen and twenty thousand men and boys thus occupied, more than two-thirds of them being in the southern field, where bootleg mining was favored by geological conditions too complicated to be explained here. The total number of trucks hauling bootleg coal from the holes to the consumers was between thirty-five hundred and five thousand, from two to three men earning their living on each vehicle.

Most of the miners and truckers were heads or members of families; so it is safe to estimate that one hundred thousand men, women, and children were directly dependent for their livelihood, solely or mainly, on bootleg coal, while indirectly nearly everybody in the above-listed and several other towns and villages benefited from bootleg coal. Bootleg coal, in fact, was the chief basis of economic life not only in Centralia, which I have mentioned, but to a lesser extent also in Shamokin, Mount Carmel, Shenandoah, Girardville, Mahanoy City, Tremont, and at least a dozen other communities. Even Pottsville and Hazleton would not have been the lively cities they were without bootleg coal. The amount involved in the bootleg coal business in 1933 was estimated to have been between $30,000,000 and $35,000,000, while during 1934 the illegal miners and truckers "stole" from the anthracite companies' lands from four and a half to five and a half million tons of coal, involving between $40,000,000 and $45,000,000; and most of this money stayed right in the communities where the miners and truckers resided, and was spent and respent there.

In other words, bootleg coal was big business; only no one engaged in it made big money. Through the year few bootleg miners and truckers averaged more than $2.50 a day. The huge total sum involved in the bootleg industry was spread out very thin. It benefited enormously, not privileged individuals, as did the so-called legitimately mined coal, but the communities and the region as a whole. It kept stores, banks, movies, restaurants, drinking places, gas stations open. It enabled business people to employ help and buy advertising space in local newspapers. And so on.

Naturally, then, nearly everybody in the towns where bootleg coal had become an established industry was very much in favor of it. I interviewed hundreds of persons, and practically no one free of connection with a coal company had anything to say against it. I spoke with scores of bootleg miners and truckers, and the following were some of their statements: "We gotta

live, don't we? . . . There's no work for us in the collieries with their new
machines and new ways of doing things. We must do something! . . . In
this town seventy-five per cent of the mine workers are unemployed. The
relief we're supposed to get isn't half enough even for food; how about rent,
light, gas, and water, clothes and tobacco? And we're entitled to a glass of
beer once in a while, ain't we? Our kids and women want to take in a movie
now and then. Also we gotta pay our union, lodge, and church dues. . . . As
for the 'stealing' part of it, how did the different companies get their coal
lands? In some cases they paid six dollars an acre; was that a fair price?
In other cases they stole it from the Indians. Was that a nice thing to do?
Well [laughing], we're the new Indians, taking what coal we can back from
the companies. . . . We 'steal' coal in order to keep from becoming thieves
and hold-up men, which, to keep alive, we probably would be forced to
become if we didn't have these holes."

The storekeepers with whom I talked were unanimous in saying that, as
far as their businesses were concerned, bootleg coal was a lifesaver. Most
of them burned illegal coal in their homes and stores. The chief of police
and a city councilman of Mount Carmel were unreservedly in favor of bootleg
coal. An editor of the Mount Carmel *Item* remarked that while the paper
was neutral in the matter, he had no hesitation in saying that but for bootleg
coal he might not have a job. Other newspapermen expressed themselves
similarly. An officer of the state police, when I asked him what his force was
doing to protect the company's property rights, smiled and shrugged his
shoulders; for Governor Pinchot's administration in Harrisburg was decidedly
friendly to the bootleggers—as was, later, Governor Earle's.

The bootleg towns are preponderantly Catholic; so, feigning concern for
the Eighth Commandment, I approached several parish priests, some of whom,
I had heard, were accepting church dues in the form of bootleg coal and were
using it to heat their churches, parochial schools, and parish houses. All declared that the Eighth Commandment had no bearing on coal bootlegging.
The so-called bootleggers, they said, had as much right to the coal they were
digging as the companies. Besides, most of the bootleg holes were in places
where the companies would never have bothered to take the coal out anyhow—
which was true. Father Weaver, the rector of a parish in Mount Carmel, said
that should the companies employ armed force to clear their lands of illegal
miners, and should the men in such a case decide to fight, he would be unable
to restrain himself from getting into the battle on their side. "Some of them,"
he went on, "are my parishioners; honest, upstanding working people. I'm
proud to be their priest. It is absolutely untrue that this bootleg coal situation
is having a bad effect on the bootleggers' characters or that, as the companies
say, there have developed in this town 'other rackets' in connection with, or
as a result of, bootleg coal. Coal bootlegging has no bad moral effect on the
people. It keeps them from starving and turning into criminals. . . . Let the
companies give the men work in the collieries and illegal mining will cease

at once. The men are not bootlegging because they like it. They risk their lives every minute they work in those holes, and deserve everyone's respect and admiration. They have mine."

They had mine, too. In fact, after I saw them work in and around their holes, my respect for the human race in general went up several notches. The sheer "guts" and stamina necessary to sink and work a bootleg coal hole were all but incredible. Imagine a hole in the ground, barely wide enough for a man to let himself down in, usually vertical, sometimes cut into living rock, anywhere from twenty to a hundred feet deep, with just sufficient room at the bottom for the miner to sit or kneel and work his pick and shovel and sticks of dynamite. Personally, I would rather have done anything than start and operate such a hole; but then, of course, I was not a miner in extreme economic circumstances, nor a miner's son with mining in his blood and no chance of regular employment. It took two, three, or four men from two weeks to two months to sink a hole and reach the outcrop, after which they usually struck coal. Working mainly on hunches, they very often found no coal, and all the terrific labor was in vain. When they found it, two, three, or four men produced about as many tons a day, hoisting the stuff to the top of the hole with rope and buckets, then breaking it, often by hand with hammers or chunk against chunk, and cleaning and sorting it also by hand, unless they had a primitive breaker and shaker either at the hole or behind their houses in town. The work was back-breaking and extremely hazardous. Most holes were inadequately timbered and cave-ins were frequent, trapping or crushing the men below. Sometimes the ground at the bottom of the hole, where the man was knocking out the coal, sank away from under him and he tumbled into the flooded cavern of some worked-out mine, and that, of course, was the last of him.

Everybody who knew anything about the conditions under which bootleg coal was produced respected and admired the bootleggers, and often considered them heroes; and this—together with the fact that the whole thing was so typical of this resourceful, highly individualistic, anarchic, and fantastic America of ours—operated to create public sentiment strongly in favor of the illegal miners, quite apart from the economic benefits that this curious industry brought to the communities. Even a company official said to me: "Those fellows take such gosh-awful chances that in a way they're entitled to that coal."

The coal was sold to truckers who came to the holes at from $4.50 to $5.75 a ton, depending on the quality and on whether it was stove or nut. The truckers had either direct customers of their own in Philadelphia, New York, Baltimore, or wherever they took it, or agents who got the orders for them from housewives and landlords. Delivered, say, in Philadelphia, Newark, or New York, the coal sold from $8.50 to $11, or a dollar or two cheaper than regular coal. The agent got from twenty-five to seventy-five cents a ton commission. The bootleg coal usually was not as clean-looking as regular anthracite, but actually most of it was quite as good. Demand for it exceeded production, and everywhere in the southern section of the region I saw trucks waiting for loads at the holes. Production, however, rose steadily and, despite sporadic efforts to suppress it, the industry continued through 1935-37.

Most of the coal "stolen" from the bootleg holes, as already suggested, would never have been touched by the companies who legally own the lands. It would have been too uneconomical for them to mine it. Much of it was left over by regular mining operations. Only in a few places—Shamokin, for one— were the bootleggers tapping big veins, which the owners eventually would strip and get out with giant steam shovels. So in most cases the regular operators did not object so much to the coal being "stolen" as to its being sold so successfully in such large quantities; for between five and ten per cent of all anthracite sold in the United States during the mid-Depression years was bootleg. That was serious competition, cutting deeply into the profits of the operators and distributors. In view of the fact that the whole law and order apparatus, the moral forces, and most of the general public opinion favored the bootleggers, the operators could do little about it at the sources of bootleg coal, after the thing had been allowed to develop as I have described it. In Shamokin, early in December 1934, the Stevens Coal Company tried to start stripping operations on the so-called Edgewood Bootleggers' Tract, where seventeen hundred illegal miners eked out their livelihood, but the men promptly dynamited the steam shovel and told the company employees who brought it up to "beat it." No one was arrested for the deed. At Tremont, during the autumn 1934, more than a thousand bootleggers faced about fifty company police, and a battle was averted only by the withdrawal of the police. At Gilberton a while later the automobile of a coal-and-iron cop was dynamited after he had blown up several holes. The Philadelphia and Reading Coal and Iron Company's private police blew up, between the first of January and the last of November of 1934, 1,196 holes, but in that time at least four thousand new ones were started on their properties. During the same period the same company caused the arrest of seventy-seven bootleggers, but in vain. No jury in any anthracite county was ready to convict anyone for "stealing" or trucking coal.

So about the time I visited the region the desperate operators and distributors began spending vast sums of money and no end of energy and legal and public-relations talent to ruin the bootleg coal business in Philadelphia, Newark, and elsewhere by telling the public, through the newspapers and otherwise, that bootleg coal was a heartless racket run by a few wise guys who exploited thousands of men, women, and children; that bootleg coal was dirty and otherwise inferior; that bootleg truckers delivered short weights, and so on. In Philadelphia the authorities were induced to invoke against the bootleg coal truckers old ordinances regulating weights and truck traffic which had not been enforced against the regular coal dealers and truckers for years.

Upon the highways in New Jersey the state police were induced to arrest bootleg truckers for transporting stolen goods, and there were instances of heavy fines and jail sentences. But up to late 1937, so far as I know, all these efforts of the companies had no serious effect on the virility of the bootleg-coal industry.

The bootleggers organized to protect what they called their interests. In Shamokin I attended a meeting of the Independent Coal Producers at which I was given to understand that, while eager for peace, they were ready to fight "for their right to live." The same was true of organizations in the Tremont district and in Mahanoy City, where, not long before I came there, a Congressman spoke at a meeting of four hundred bootleggers called to protest against the dynamiting of a number of holes by the companies. The Congressman, who was a Coaldale man and a New Deal Democrat, declared he was with the bootleggers. They had been instrumental in electing him. Several illegal miners said to me: "If they close our holes, we'll gang up on their collieries and close *them*."

As I am finishing this book, early in 1938, bootleg coal is still a thriving industry in the Keystone State, despite several half-hearted efforts since I was there to do away with it. It is the cause of many an official headache in the gold-domed capitol at Harrisburg. Whenever the Governor or the legislature attempts to tackle it in some way that seems detrimental to the bootleggers, the latter and their fellow-townspeople stage a "march" to the capitol in two or three hundred bootleg-coal trucks and effectively demonstrate against any such action.

I think, however, that by and by this curious industry will peter out, as do most such makeshift things in America. Already when I was there, small groups of bootleggers were coming to terms with the companies and were beginning to pay them royalties on every ton of coal they dug. I met company officials who felt that eventually the Federal Government might come to their aid. The idea (which I have described in the preceding chapter) of trans-ferring the surplus populations in such towns as Shamokin or Mount Carmel to the land had died by then, but they believed that in the course of years the Government might be compelled to do something like that.

Meantime, I think, bootleg coal is a most suggestive and significant bit of the American scene. Some of the wishful-thinking "Communists" on Union Square in New York thought at various times that it was part of the "revolu-tion" they were about to lead. Actually there was—is—no revolution in coal bootlegging. When I was there, most of the bootleggers (for reasons to appear in the next chapter) were rabidly anti-Communist, and the few, very few articulate free-lance radicals I met among them told me that bootlegging was partly responsible for the fact that there was no real radicalism, no leftist movement of any size, in the southern anthracite region. Coal bootlegging, to repeat, was and is nothing more or less than a Depression industry. Its motives and purpose were, I think, closely akin to the motives and purpose of the unemployed men in New York City and elsewhere who formed into groups and raided the neighborhood chain stores.

The story of bootleg coal reveals, however, this extremely noteworthy fact: that American workers when in need are apt to disregard the principle of private property, which is so important in the Constitution of the United States, as generally interpreted; and, disregarding it, are apt to "get away with it" before public opinion and even constituted authority. This does not mean that American workers, the American public, and the American authorities are anti-property or against the Constitution. It means simply that, off and on, the American people in general—having, in this, the backing of the Declaration of Independence, which is older than the Constitution—tend to take things in their own human, blundering, effective hands.

Notes on the "Communists" and Some American Fundamentals

AT SHAMOKIN, IN PENNSYLVANIA, AS I SAY, I ATTENDED A MEETING OF THE LOCAL coal bootleggers' union called the Independent Coal Producers. I asked the group if they were affiliated with similar associations in near-by Mount Carmel, Shenandoah, Mahanoy City, and other towns in the region, where coal bootlegging went on. The answer, which came in unison from several men, was a loud, explosive *No!*—"You won't catch us affiliating with anything!" declared the president of the Independent Coal Producers. "Never again, no sir!" Having thought that an affiliation might be advantageous, I inquired why this emphatic objection to it. The meeting was rather informal, and three or four men were going to answer me, when the president as chairman suddenly rapped on the table and said: "Never mind, men. Our friend the writer will excuse us if we don't answer his last question. There is no use going over all that again. Let bygones be bygones." The assembled coal bootleggers agreed that that was really best; and, curious, I was compelled to get the following information from other sources:

In the autumn of 1932, the Communist party of the United States sent its representatives to the southern anthracite region of Pennsylvania to organize the unemployed. Most of these organizers, describing themselves as "Marxists" or "Communists" and talking "revolution," were New Yorkers and Philadelphians, recently converted to the cause of Marx and Engels, Lenin and Stalin. The "revolution" in the United States they believed imminent. They were for the immediate and complete overthrow of capitalism and everything it stood for. They were passionate champions of the proletariat and the dictatorship thereof, which would "liquidate" all non-proletarians; and of Soviet Russia and Soviet China, which (especially the former) they appeared to consider the sole immediate sources of all hope for humankind. They read the *New Masses* and the *Daily Worker* which recognized "revolution" in every strike threat and in every grumble against a wage cut, and *The Communist,* their party's official organ, wherein such leaders of the masses as Bill Foster and Earl Browder, imitating the literary style of Lenin in the *Iskra* period, wrote elaborate analyses and diagnoses of the rapidly disintegrating socio-economic structure of the United States, which within very few months the revolutionary working-class would be able to push over. Most of these "revolutionaries" were native-born and of old stock, but in their new state of mind, if one could judge by their talk and publications, they hated nearly everything in the United States, but especially the leadership of the American Federation of Labor, which included John L. Lewis, head of the United Mine

Workers of America, whom they considered "the corrupt, unsavory tool of the vicious, despicable mine barons" and a "betrayer" of the working-class who employed sluggers to maintain himself in power.

In groups of various sizes, and under orders of their party leadership, they "invaded" various industrial regions. The "invasion" of the southern Pennsylvania anthracite region was described to me by one of the coal bootleggers, an intelligent man who was politically a Socialist but uncertain as such, and somewhat of a satirist. "When they first came," he said, "they discovered that we unemployed miners already had our organizations, which to their eyes had all the earmarks of being revolutionary soviets. We were called, and called ourselves, bootleggers; which, thought the newcomers, was odd, but probably some sort of joke or—on second thought—revolutionary disguise. Then they found out why we called ourselves bootleggers. In short, they discovered coal bootlegging, which impressed them right off as a form of revolutionary activity; and they got busy to perfect our organizations, for while we were 'rich in instinctive revolutionary leanings,' many of us had never heard of Marx and, they insisted, we needed the leadership of the party whose cause was sweeping the world.

"But before I go any further, I must say that, personally, when you got them alone and talked to them about something else besides the revolution, most of them were pretty nice people, mostly kids; in fact, most of them were idealists, no doubt about it. Way down in them, good people; and maybe I shouldn't be talking about them as I do, because they meant well and all that. When you got to talking with them about the Depression, though, or the United Mine Workers and capitalism and the Socialist party, something happened and you wondered if they were crazy or you. I couldn't make out for some time what it was, then decided that the trouble was this—they looked at things in too large a way and, because of that, saw things cockeyed and talked and acted accordingly, trying to press everything they saw into their 'line.'. . ."

To shorten a long tale, which easily turns into farce without much effort on the teller's part, the "Marxists" from New York and Philadelphia affiliated—somehow—the several little local bootlegger organizations into a central association. "Then," to continue quoting my informant two years later, whose statements largely agreed with other versions of the same story, "there was hell to pay around here. These Communists thought that Shamokin, Mount Carmel, and Shenandoah were just like Union Square. They organized demonstrations and parades, in which some of the local unemployed people took part the first couple of times. In these demonstrations they carried signs, demanding more relief, which was all right, but some of the signs also read: 'Protect Soviet Russia!'—'Stand by Soviet China!'—'Free Tom Mooney!' They pulled a parade early in 1933, after Hitler got into power and jailed the German Communist leaders; so the signs now read: 'Free Thaelmann!'—'Fight Fascism! Save the First Workers' Republic!'

"Well, people around here are O. K., 's far's that goes, but when it comes to Soviet Russia and China and fascism and Thaelmann, they just don't know their elbow from a knothole in a fence-post; and there is nothing you, I, or anyone else can do about it, at least not in a hurry. Folks in little towns like this are just dumb that way—so what! So, naturally, all of them said, 'What *is* this?' I read the papers regular and go to the library in Pottsville and read *The Nation*, sometimes I even get ahold of a *New Masses* and *New Republic* and once when I was a kid Gene Debs patted me on the head; so I tried to explain things to a few of them, but that only made matters worse. 'What's it to us what happens in China or Germany!' said everybody—which you and I know is the wrong attitude, but there it is! The question is how to overcome it. But these people from Union Square didn't even know this attitude existed, or didn't care if it existed or not.

"Another thing they did was this. Passing the collieries and company offices as they demonstrated, they yelled, 'Down with capitalism!' and sang the 'Internationale,' which didn't make much difference with the folks here, because they are all more or less against the company and the 'Internationale' is not bad on the ear. But then, passing the little city hall in Mount Carmel, a few of the boys and girls from New York and Philly yelled out at the mayor, who stood in the doorway with the chief of police, calling him a company tool, a stool-pigeon, a crook, and I don't know what else. This was a cockeyed thing to do because the mayor is one of the people, a former miner, elected by the miners, including bootleggers, and is disliked by the company. His son-in-law is a bootlegger. Everybody calls him by his first name; he's no crook nor anybody's stool-pigeon. So calling him bad names, of course, didn't go so hot with him, nor with the folks of Mount Carmel. They wanted to know, 'Who are these crazy people? Where do they come from? Who asked them here? Who sent them?'

"On Sunday the priests told the parishioners that these loud, bad-mannered trouble-makers were Communists from New York, which was the same thing as the Bolsheviks in Russia. They did not believe in God and wanted to destroy the Government of the United States and the Stars and Stripes, family and home life, and the Church.

"This made the Communists very unwelcome. But they seemed to like the outcry against them; it proved to them they were right. They retaliated by distributing leaflets saying that the priests were stooges of capitalism, and things like that. They repeated that the mayor was a stool-pigeon; and so on.

"Well, this sort of thing went on for seven or eight months. By the end of that period there was nothing left, not only of the affiliation which they brought about, but of the different coal bootleggers' unions of which it had been made. Everything was wrecked. The bootleggers blamed the heads of their unions for letting these people come in. There were terrible fights among the men. Some thought that the agitators were not really Communists but company agents and spies who came in to destroy the bootleggers' unions. If they had been company agents, they could not have done a better job for the companies.

"A couple of the Communists were finally beaten up—not by the company guards, as the *Daily Worker* reported, but by the bootleggers . . . and then the whole bunch of them left, and they haven't been back since.

"For four months the disorganized bootleggers were up against it. The company dicks were blowing up our holes, and as individuals we were helpless to do anything about it. It was four or five months before the bootleggers gathered their scattered forces and began to form new associations. Lots of them still refuse to join. . . . Now, as you heard at the meeting, the idea is: no affiliation ever again with anybody!

"But, no kidding," concluded my narrator, "some of those people who messed up things around here weren't half bad personally; you'd like them, as I did one or two of them. It was just that they were all hepped up on an idea that made them see things crazy and cockeyed."

MY INTEREST IN THE "COMMUNISTS"

I met several American "Communists" early in the Depression. I observed their movement through the binoculars of the press, both their own and "capitalist." I watched their demonstrations in Union Square and elsewhere. In my Diary I began to refer to them in quotation marks already in 1931. I felt that, as it stood, the Communist party of the United States, which was a branch of the Third International, would in all probability have precious little to do with bringing about Communism in America if it ever came, say, sometime between the years 2000 and 3000. It seemed to me an inorganic, unindigenous organization, too full of shallow, momentary excitement. It received most of its idealistic inspiration from outside the United States, notably from Moscow; and, disregarding American material and psychological realities, tactically it was fantastic. The *Daily Worker* and some of its other publications were yellow journalism gone red. In all these respects, the Communist party was worse than had been the Socialist party early in the twentieth century, when Cantrell was a member of it.

But it seemed to me that no matter what one thought of it, specifically or as a whole, one could not dismiss it. Here it *was*, part of the American scene, making the front page of the New York *Times*. The Cantrell story helped me to feel that in a sense, which I shall try to explain, it was, in fact, a typical American phenomenon, a manifestation or symptom of the country's basic incongruity; and if one studied it closely, it told one a great deal about America. So the Communist party, its membership and leaders, its motives and doings, interested me no end all through the early and middle 1930's.

As I say, I met not a few "Communists," at first mostly the literary kind, and liked some personally and disliked others. I have mentioned my encounter with Granville Hicks; also, that some of the members of the Literary Rotary were more or less "communistic" in what they were saying orally or in print,

but actually more individualistic than Hoover in the basic makeup of their
beings. Off and on Ben Stolberg insisted to me that he was a Communist—of
course without the quotation marks; but, somehow, I always thought different.
Deep in him, he was an individualist. Everything he said or did was individualistic.

I met some whom I did not put in quotation marks. One of these was
Grace Lumpkin, the author of the finely felt novel *To Make My Bread*, whom
I met at Yaddo, in Saratoga Springs. . . . Essentially made as a person for
collective living, devoid of malice, she appeared to me a deeply humble and,
at the same time, marvelously positive human being. Her struggle, immediate
and long-range, was not *against* people who probably differed with her, or
who were involved in things of which she disapproved, but *for* her ideal, which
was a sound social order. This positiveness was ingrained in her makeup.
(I speak of her in the past tense because I have not seen her or heard of her since
1932.) She was fundamentally unlike a rather well-known "Communist," who
tore into me at a private house party a few months after the appearance of *The
Native's Return*. A native American, he demanded what I meant by saying
that I loved the United States. "How can you love a goddamn country like this,
that has eleven million unemployed, that elects Hoovers and Roosevelts to
the Presidency, and so on? What the hell are you, anyhow: just a lousy
bourgeois patriot?" . . .

I met "Communists," party members, and so-called "fellow travelers," who
were at least remote kin to Dan Hennessy's people described in an early chapter
of this book, or what the European Marxists once upon a time had in mind
when they spoke of the *lumpenproletariat*. I came upon them in New York and
on my travels. They came to me to quarrel over something I had written or
said from the platform, and when I continued to disagree with them there was
clearly, almost literally, murder in their eyes. I met others who were primarily
and unmistakably neurotics of various kinds, or whose immediate (though, of
course, seldom conscious) motives in becoming "Communists" stemmed out of
momentarily neurotic or unhealthy conditions or developments in their personal lives.

Having said this, however, I hasten to make as plain as I can that during
the 1930's thousands of actually or potentially superb people, mostly unformed,
uncrystallized youngsters, went into, or came close to, the so-called regular
(Moscow-controlled) Communist party because they were idealists and social
dreamers; because they loved America or something in America, or saw misery
about them; because they sensed the country's basic incongruity, though most
of them did not call it that, or even consciously recognize it as such. They
were against injustice, want, frustration; in short, they were human beings
and Americans, mostly negative, but wanting to be positive. And, what is also
important, they were innocent, naïve, impressionable, easily swayed and exploited. The Communist party was aggressively active; deriving its inspiration,
as I have said, chiefly from outside the Depression-smitten and groggy America,

it was doing things, building organizations, starting this and that, "raising hell," agitating, demonstrating, starting a new school in literature, getting the unemployment problem on the front page, while everybody else in the United States (before the New Deal) was paralyzed. For one who wanted to do something, who wanted to see something done or happen, there was early in the Depression no other party to which to turn, seemingly no other vent by which he could release his pent-up, incoherent sense of rebellion against the forces that had taken away his employment, reduced life to a series of petty bickerings within his family, and threatened to make him in his late 'teens or early twenties an empty, despairing creature. The Communist party linked its cause at times to various vital issues and dramatic conditions in the country, and staged stirring, emotional meetings at which the young person was afforded an opportunity to escape his own personal misery at least for a while. One evening in 1934 I met in a street in Cleveland a young man whom I had known for some time as an impressionable and impulsive but essentially splendid chap; he was coming from a "Communist"-sponsored meeting held in behalf of the Scottsboro Boys, and he had tears in his eyes and could not talk. He became a "Communist" for a while; or, at least, he so called himself (but of course without quotation marks), though he never joined the party.

One must not underestimate, or fail to respect, the sincerity of these thousands of young people, who were drawn to "Communism" also by the glory of the Soviet idea and its rapid realization in Russia, as reported by Maurice Hindus in his popular books and by Walter Duranty in the New York *Times* and other newspapers (neither of whom was a Communist or "Communist"), and by party writers in the *New Masses, New Republic,* and elsewhere.

Then, too, some of the "Communists" whom I met were obviously inferiority-ridden New Americans or second-generation youngsters, though I think they were not proportionately numerous. A few of them I studied rather closely—and here, again, we come upon a group which, albeit small, is significant and calls for thoughtful consideration and respect. From my close contact with the few whom I examined and studied, I am convinced that the motives of many of these in becoming "Communists" for a short or longer period were, although outwardly very different, not unrelated to those of the young intellectuals in the Balkans I have mentioned in the chapter "On Being of Two Worlds." As New Americans, they were hedged in by all sorts of racial, cultural, spiritual, social, and economic "boundaries" which they wanted to jump or remove. They were confronted by frustration. The "boundaries" were intangible, undefined, ill understood; and therefore worse, more maddening, and tending to lopsidedness in the individual than were the obvious, tangible geographical and national boundaries of Europe.

Another thing: Some of the New American "Communists" were obviously the true children of their immigrant parents, as well as true children of America, in that they were what I call "short-cut people," as discussed in earlier chapters in this book. The Marxist "revolution," as described by the official

"Communists" between 1930 and 1936, was instinctively and emotionally recognized by some of the New Americans as a short-cut idea, which would—or might—solve their profound and complex second-generation problems as Americans, as human beings in America, as their parents' children; or at least change them, break them into pieces, or transform them into more tangible problems.

Studying the second-generation "Communists," I had the feeling, too, that Marxism appealed to some of them also because it emphasized class consciousness. They were children of immigrant workers and by identifying themselves in an intense class-conscious way with the proletariat they automatically acquired a background, the lack of which had hitherto caused them vague misery.

I want to emphasize that for many reasons, some of which must be respected regardless of what one may think of the Communist party's record in the United States so far, or of Communism as a method of progress, thousands of very fine persons became "Communists" or near-"Communists" during the Depression, and for a while found some function and satisfaction in the movement. But, in common with other kinds of "Communists," which were not so respect-worthy, most of these people sooner or later quit the party or its peripheries. Their sudden "revolutionary" fervor wore off, or dissipated itself in confusion far worse than that which had driven them into the movement; some regained their basic integrity, balance, and sense of realism, and they withdrew from the imaginary barricades for that reason. This is attested by the fact that the turnover in the rank and file of the Communist party was often over one hundred per cent a year, while the fellow-traveler personnel changed even more rapidly. Only the leaders of the party and its various auxiliary organizations remained pretty much the same, year after year.

To stress again, there *were* (still are) excellent people in, or close to, the Communist party of the United States; indeed, now and then its membership and its supporters included some of the essentially best, that is, most idealistic individuals in the country . . . but their qualities as persons never had much chance to project themselves into the movement of which they were a part. One reason for that was that the movement included too many people unlike them. Other reasons were that, as I see it, the movement was pretty much all wrong philosophically, in outlook, in tactics, in basic character; that its national leadership was (and is) largely mediocre, crackpot, exhibitionistic; that it actually was not a growth from American roots, but an extension into America of an international movement deeply involved in the entire insane world situation that has developed since the first World War; and, finally, that it was not democratic, that is, not influenced from below, but run arbitrarily by a small inner group in compliance with orders from the Comintern.

FURTHER CONSIDERATION OF THE "COMMUNIST" MOVEMENT

In the pages preceding this chapter there is, I think, but one favorable or uncritical reference to the "Communists." I credit the leaders of the Communist

party for the demonstrations and riots of 1930 which, although they had (as I
have explained) other purposes, dramatized the unemployment situation so that
Washington, the great newspapers, and the general public could no longer
ignore it; and helped to make the better-to-do classes of the American people
acutely (even if, for the most part, none too intelligently) sensitive of the widespread social agony caused by the Depression.

But before I proceed with my adverse report on the "Communist" movement, I must enumerate a few other things that must definitely be chalked up
to its credit.

Through the period of 1930-35 the "Communists" were definitely a factor
in stirring the country to politico-social consciousness and thus, in preparing—
unwittingly—the way for the New Deal. Threatening "revolution," they—unwittingly—frightened great numbers of the naturally conservative but uninformed middle-class people into supporting, however half-heartedly, the New
Deal reforms and the immense relief expenditures during 1934-37. In this the
"Communists" played the same rôle that had been played, in the first fifteen
years of the twentieth century, by the Socialist party, which was then also
"Marxist," "revolutionary," and basically crackpot and worse (as shown in
connection with Cantrell), and whose only real achievement was that it gave
certain social ideas to such realistic and practical Progressive politicians as
Hiram Johnson, "Old Bob" La Follette, William Borah, and George Norris,
who received much of their following from ex- and quasi-Socialists and from
conservatives who had been scared by Socialist agitation. For such, on their
good side, is the function of so-called "radical" movements in America; and
in the long run, as a rule, *only* such. They are socio-politically effective only
indirectly, and only in part the way they want to be effective. This function
conspires with that of the conservatives and reactionaries, and helps to provide
that area defined by the extremists within which the pendulum of organic
growth or progress comes to rest and thence gets under way. . . . I am, therefore, let me say here, not against extreme political movements, but sometimes
I feel they could be of greater value if they were less productive of fuss and
fury and confusion. . . .

But to return to the "Communists," one must credit them with a few other
specific accomplishments during the Depression. Here and there they organized groups of the unemployed, partly in order to use them in demonstrations.
This was all to the good; to be in any organization was, as a rule, better for
the morale of the individual jobless than to be in no organization.

The "Communists" made themselves a nuisance to the federal government
and the state and the local authorities, which in consequence doled out greater
relief sums than they might have otherwise.

The best among the "Communists" and their "fellow travelers" were partly
responsible for the fact that after the New Deal got going the WPA writers',
artists', musicians', and theatrical projects—all excellent in purpose and, to an
extent, in results—were continued from year to year.

The so-called American Committee for the Protection of Foreign Born was an organization created and conducted under the auspices of, and mainly financed by, the Communist party or its supporters. The Committee's office in New York was in charge of a couple of men who I think were members of the party and who unquestionably did valuable work which was directly in line with American tradition by fighting deportations of aliens illegally in the United States who were refugees from persecution in Hitler's Germany, in Yugoslavia and Italy. Occasionally the methods of this Committee were "Communistic" in the worst sense, in that they were sensational and hysterical, and that they publicly directed unjustified epithets against Secretary of Labor Perkins, Colonel MacCormack, and the Immigration Service as a whole. But, although I was never entirely comfortable in being associated with these people, I took part in their work when I could, because so far as I knew they were the only outfit in the country fighting for the old American principle of political asylum.

The Communist party developed a chain of workers' bookshops, selling mostly "Communistic" propaganda, Russian and American, much of which had no deep relation to truth or to desirable ends in the United States; on the other hand, numerous books which were worth while and might not otherwise have been read, got into circulation through them.

And there might have been other things that should be credited to the "Communists" during the Depression years, when they were extremely active in all kinds of fields.

By and large, however, as well as in important specific respects, the "Communists" endowed Theodore Roosevelt's phrase "lunatic fringe" with new meanings; and their doings in various parts of the country, where I traveled during the Depression, were characterized by such methods and results as are described at the beginning of this chapter in connection with the Pennsylvania coal bootleggers. This was especially true during 1930-34 and part of 1935, when the Communist party, furiously active in the labor movement, proceeded on the seeming theory that America was ripe for a drastic revolution and the dictatorship of labor, presumably with Bill Foster or Earl Browder as dictator.

That the "Communist" leaders actually engaged in such daydreams was demonstrated by the articles in their official party organ, *The Communist*. Of course, it may be that in their secret minds Bill Foster and Earl Browder believed no such thing; that, in writing their "analyses" of America, they were but toeing, or trying to toe according to their lights, the "line" drawn by the inside group of the Kremlin-controlled Third International. But many of their momentarily or wontedly fanatic followers and underlings, like the people who "invaded" the bootleg-coal territory in 1932, actually expected the opportunity for a fundamental upheaval in America to knock any day; so, living in a fantastic period and imagining themselves to be tools of history, they were in a fearful rush to create the "apparatus for seizing power"—for such was the terminology they used back in 1931-33, possibly even later. The "apparatus" must include a strong labor movement; *ergo,* they went ahead to get themselves a labor movement.

The reactionary A.F. of L. and its unions stood in their way; so these "revolutionaries" proceeded to "bore from within" and play the devil with the organizations from without. It would take too much space to describe the methods they employed while leaning on the precept that, as in war and love, everything was fair in "revolution." Many unions were badly shaken by the Depression; and these "Communist organizers" had no great trouble wrecking, disrupting, and creating dissension in, hundreds of labor organizations the country over. They pulled wildcat strikes. They acted as scabs in strikes not called by them. . . . Offspring of America's basic disharmony and all its side-chaoses which I have discussed in connection with Cantrell, they were functionally—although superficially quite different—closely related to the San Francisco "gorillas" of 1910, to Job Harriman and the McNamaras. Having inhaled bits of *Das Kapital,* they uttered Marxist phrases, which were but props of their ignorance. Reclining on the great Marxist simplifications, many developed a smugness more repellent than that of the bourgeoisie they attacked, and an intellectual arrogance which was distinctly anti-democratic and un-American.

The Daily Worker was printed in special editions for various localities. It bristled with lies and exaggerations. Every "story" in it was "class-angled." Its columns were popguns used to assassinate the characters of non-"Communist" labor leaders. John L. Lewis, as already suggested, was one of their favorite targets. Their philosophy and strategy were to wreck, by any means, every organization that refused to turn "Communist" on their demand. A rank-and-file leader in Youngstown, Ohio, said to me in 1934, "If I were in charge of the Steel Trust and didn't want labor to organize I'd pay the Communist party agitators to stay permanently on the job and keep throwing monkey-wrenches into every union and every attempt to organize—just what they've been doing hereabouts the past couple of years."

The "Communists" maintained these tactics in the labor movement well into the third year of the New Deal, which, with its Section 7-a of the National Industrial Recovery Act, invited labor to organize; and in a great many places, directly or indirectly, they did all they could to sabotage mass unionization, for in their eyes the New Deal was counter-revolutionary and Franklin D. Roosevelt, with his General Hugh Johnson, was nothing but a fascist in disguise who wanted to herd the workers into A.F. of L. unions, where labor "skates" like William Green, Matthew Woll, and John Lewis would then hold them safely corralled.

In fact, the "Communists" continued this sabotage of the labor movement till the inner group of the Third International—out of motives connected largely with Russia's foreign policy and the developments in France, Spain, and in the Orient—decided that the United States should have a "United Front" instead of a "revolution"; and so early in 1936 the Communist party of the United States went to the support of John Lewis and the C.I.O. (of which more in the next section); then, in the same year, "helped" President Roosevelt to win his re-election; and in 1937 joined the fusion movement, which included the Republican party, to reëlect Fiorello La Guardia mayor of New York City![1] . . . Early in February, 1938, Earl Browder, as the top leader of the American Communist party, came out—in *The New Republic*—for saving "all the *capitalist world* from unparalleled reaction and catastrophe" (my italics).

As I write this, only God knows what some of its "lines" will be in the future. Possibly "revolution" and "dictatorship of the proletariat" again, or selling war bonds in the next war "to make the world safe for democracy" on the bland assumption that Russia is a democratic country. Or, conceivably, "united front" with the fascistic and sadistic elements of the country, for the "Communists" and fascist movements already are close in Germany and Italy.[2]

THE "COMMUNISTS" AND THE ARMY

Early in 1931 I happened to step into the Workers' Bookshop on East Thirteenth Street in New York and bought a tiny two-cent pamphlet on conditions in the United States Army. It was published by the Communist party organization and presumably circulated among the regular army soldiers. According to it, the conditions in the Army were terrible. The officers were generally brutes, sadists, etc. They beat, tortured, and taunted the enlisted men under their command. They engaged in orgies in luxurious quarters provided by the Government, while the plain soldiers were quartered in inadequate firetrap barracks and required to eat decayed meat and moldy bread. . . . There were pen-and-ink illustrations showing the horrors of army life.

I had served in the regular army all through the war and awhile after. I had come in close contact with a number of officers from General Charles Summerall down who were extraordinarily fine and decent human beings. I had never been abused by any of my superiors in rank, nor seen any other soldier sadistically mistreated. While in garrison I had been better fed than it probably was good for me, and had slept between sheets. . . .

"REVOLUTION" IN THE U. S. A.?

During 1931-35 I spent much time and energy arguing with "Communists" and their "fellow travelers" in different parts of the country, who either at-

---

[1] In Russia they have a fable: A fly sat all day on the horns of an ox harnessed to a plow. In the evening the fly met a second fly, who asked, "Well, what did you do today?" "Oh," replied the first fly, "we plowed all day."

[2] From *International Press Correspondence*, an official organ of the Communist International, for October 24, 1936: "In order to facilitate the fraternization of all Italians, the Communist Party of Italy *declares that it adopts as its own the fascist program of 1919 which is a program of freedom and is prepared to fight for it*." (p. 1305; italics in the original). Similar sentiments are expressed by the Communist Party of Germany (p. 1302).

From the same official organ, for May 1, 1933: "The establishment of an open fascist dictatorship, by destroying all the democratic illusions among the masses and liberating them from the influence of social-democracy, accelerates the rate of Germany's development towards proletarian revolution" (pp. 245-246).

tacked me because I opposed their wild talk about the imminent "revolution," or who tried to convert me to their ideas—(at the same time that some of the people on the Right, as wild and thoughtless as the "Communists," considered me a Communist).

I asked my antagonists, "But what·do you mean by 'revolution'?" Their replies included such words and phrases as "barricades," "street fighting," "workers seizing the factories," which were echoes from the Russian Revolution; and when that sounded silly even to their ears, they decided to skip the details, and they read to me such excerpts from William Z. Foster's book, *Toward Soviet America,* as where he drew the picture of how America would look after the "revolution" was accomplished and the dictatorship of the proletariat established along the lines of the Russian soviets; or where he told how the "capitalist" parties—Republican, Democratic, Progressive, Socialist, etc.—would be "liquidated" along with such other organizations as the chambers of commerce, employers' associations, Rotary clubs, American Legion, Y.M.C.A., the Masons, Odd Fellows, Elks, Knights of Columbus, and so on.

I called the "Communists'" attention to such, to me obvious, facts as that America of the 1930's was not Russia of 1917; that in America, even in these years of the Depression, we had 10,500,000 owner-occupied homes, with an average value of $4,778; 20,600,000 registered automobiles, exclusive of trucks; 39,000,000 deposits in savings accounts totaling over twenty-one billion dollars; over 115,000,000 insurance policies in force, their insurance exceeding one hundred billion dollars—etc. All of which, however, meant nothing to my adversaries.

I insisted that America, with its complex industrialism, was not feudalist-peasant Russia; that in America a successful revolutionary outbreak would mean civil war, for, no matter what Bill Foster said, the Democratic and Republican parties, like the Rotary clubs, the Amercian Legion, the Y.M.C.A., the Masons, Odd Fellows, Elks, Knights of Columbus, etc. would not want to be liquidated or dissolved, and would fight. I quoted to them Kirby Page, who, writing on "Can Communism Capture America?" in *The Christian Century* for October 9, 1935, thought that but a few months of such warfare "between somewhat equal fighting forces would create a holocaust through the nation never surpassed in all history. Supplied with numberless airplanes and vast quantities of poison gas, the red terror and the white terror would alternately scourge the land. Production and distribution would be thrown into utter chaos. Central power-houses could easily be crippled alike by revolutionaries and counterrevolutionaries. Continental pipe lines of oil and natural gas could be wrecked by a few blows on strategic valves. Railway tracks could be torn up within a few hours and transportation stopped at important terminals. The food supply of vast metropolitan communities could be shut off and entire populations would quickly face starvation."

From the same article by Kirby Page I read to them a quotation from Stuart Chase, who thought that if the above situation came about, "lethal epidemics, those great scourges which medical science has steadily been forcing back for a hundred years, will break their fetters overnight, and fall like avenging demons on a population weak with hunger and with thirst. . . . Violent revolutions are bitter medicine, but medicine, in handicraft societies ground down by feudalism. In societies pledged to the machine, they are a lethal poison, swift and terrible."

But this also meant nothing to the "Communists"—till it was decided for them to take a different "line" and abandon "revolution."

SOME AMERICAN FUNDAMENTALS

During the writing of this volume I read *The Long Road*, a little book by the engineer-educator, Arthur E. Morgan, published in 1936 by the National Home Library at twenty-five cents the copy and very much worth reading by anyone interested in America. Included in it is a report of a luncheon conversation between Morgan and H. G. Wells, which occurred in 1935 in the presence of three members of the President's Cabinet.

Wells said that America must speedily decide between individualism and socialism. Morgan disagreed with him, maintaining that America had room for, and liked to use, different kinds of social organizations. Wells then repeated, "No, no, America must choose between socialism and individualism"; and returning to England, he declared that America had no philosophy of government; America was "just drifting"—to which Morgan, than who there is, in many respects, no more American American in America, comments as follows:

"In my opinion America has a philosophy of government—a philosophy which is skeptical of abstract theory, and of abstract reasoning, a preference for trying out life in various ways, and for guiding our policies by the results. This philosophy represents a certain modesty and humility in the American mind. We do not presume to answer the riddle of the social universe all at once. We are willing to feel our way tentatively in the faint morning twilight of human society, and to decide our course a few steps at a time. This is the American philosophy of government, which has stubbornly resisted efforts to overthrow it, whether those efforts come from the extreme left, from communists who would destroy it for a certain kind of regimentation, or from the extreme right, as represented by certain businessmen's associations or by certain fascist newspapers."

With which I fully agree, except that in speaking of what Morgan calls the American "philosophy of government" I would say that America has an *instinct* for government that guides her, which is basically and generally sound—*democratic, equalitarian, progressive*—though often at cross-purposes within itself. Basically and generally, it has no quarrel with the ideal of Communism, which is essentially the ideal of equality; but, in the long run it has no regard for anyone or any movement that tries, as the "Communists" have tried with their Marxist blueprint during the Depression, to tie it to some definite plan of political or any other procedure of action.

I think that, for quite a while, and for a complexity of reasons at least some of which I hope are implicit in these numerous pages, America—with the best of luck, considering the world of which she is a part—will be essentially much the same country she was during 1928-38, much as I partly and most imperfectly describe her here: a country in the grip of her fundamental incongruity, with severe and sudden socio-economic-political ups and downs, which will throw up all manner of strange, unsound, ultimately futile people and movements; dynamic, over-dynamic; naïve, confused, self-conscious, bewildered, uneasy within herself and in the world; democratic, violent, chaotic, ignorant of herself; subtle and obvious, torn by inner contradictions, but not fatally so; pragmatic, experimental, wasteful, elemental, splendid in spots and now and then as a whole; a continent full of misery and promise, fooling the would-be prophets, analysts, and diagnosticians of her trends and ills; swinging from Right to Left, back to Right, back to Left, pendulum-like; now (seemingly) standing still, then going ahead, progressing with a furious gradualness and hesitancy; springing one revolution after another in various phases of her life, but none of which, nor all together, will be *the* Revolution, the opening of the door to utopia; pursuing her "Dream," as partly stated by those great, inspired somnambulists, the authors of the Declaration of Independence; trying to work herself out of her basic incongruity, but apt here and there, now and then, to sink deeper into it for a time. America, in short, will remain at once the creation and the victim of her people, who are more or less as I describe them between these covers—day-to-day creatures tending to veer simultaneously in various directions, essentially good, in many respects the best people under the sun, but still involved in the uncertain process of human evolution— somnambulists hard to awaken because their "Dream," occasionally invaded by nightmares, is a powerful and lovely thing.

America is a process—long—endless.

My "Side"

I HAVE IN ME, I THINK, A SORT OF PEASANT RESISTANCE TO INFLUENCES OF ALL sorts. I tend to hold off forces plotting to change me or steer and swerve me this way or that before I am ready to turn myself. Some people who think they know me (and probably they do) accuse me of perverseness in this respect. There is no doubt, however, that because I happened more or less to develop as a writer during the Depression I am a different writer from what I would have been had there been no Depression, or had I started writing, say, ten years earlier. I think that the play of the Depression upon my mind and emotions definitely strengthened in me a natural bent toward the social, economic, political, and cultural subjects and treatment of my material.

In the autumn of 1931, as already told, I finished my first autobiographical book, *Laughing in the Jungle,* much as I had planned it late in 1928 and early 1929, before I had become involved in the Cantrell story and the rest of the material that eventually resulted in *Dynamite.* When I finished it I was uneasy; it was not quite the book I had wanted to write, though I felt that some of the things in it were not bad. But I did not know how to change it; my publishers seemed to think it was all right, and so it got into print. . . .

Soon after, I received a letter from the editor of the New York *Sun's* book page, which included a department called (God knows why) "The Bear Garden," to which writers were asked to contribute letters on the trends of the times. Would I contribute a letter? I did, and the editor entitled it "No More Laughter":

To the Editor of the Bear Garden: In 1923, when Prosperity had just begun and I was 24, Mr. Mencken published the third volume of *Prejudices.* The leading and longest essay in the book was "On Being an American," a vigorous, lusty, humorous piece, wherein the author announced that he was a happy man—happier than he could be anywhere else under the sun—because the United States was so amusing a scene, a "circus," which kept him laughing most of the time.

"Here," to quote him, ". . . the daily panorama of human existence, of private and communal folly—the unending procession of government extortions and chicaneries, of commercial brigandages and throat-slittings, of theological buffooneries, of æsthetic ribaldries, of legal swindles and harlotries, of miscellaneous rogueries, villainies, imbecilities, grotesqueries and extravagances—is so inordinately gross and preposterous, so perfectly brought up to the highest conceivable amperage, so steadily enriched with an almost fabulous daring and originality that only the man who was born with a petrified diaphragm can fail to laugh himself to sleep every night and to wake up every morning with all the eager, unflagging expectation of a Sunday school superintendent touring the Paris peep-shows."

I remember that the essay amused me hugely and greatly enhanced my natural tendency to laugh. I recall, too, that in the West at least, where I lived then, it was widely read and discussed, and there was much laughing. No end of college

magazines adopted some pale imitation of the Menckenian attitude of amusement.
There was a flood of smart-aleck novels making fun of somebody or something.
The *American Mercury* was primarily an amusing magazine; it was a great success. Young writers everywhere vied with one another to "crash" the *Mercury* with
a smart, funny piece. Not a few imitations of the green-covered magazine came
into existence during the middle twenties.

For five or six years this laughing went on. America was a fantastic, preposterous
scene. A circus. Let us laugh! Those lacking a sense of humor exiled themselves
to Paris.

Then the Crash of 1929; the end of Prosperity. Less laughter. Then the tragic
year of 1931. Still less laughter. Now we are facing "the worst winter." Europe
is in chaos. America is tied into a knot. Racketeering is the only booming industry.
Millions are hungry. In Detroit a person dies of starvation every seven and a half
hours. And now there is no laughter, unless it is hysterical. What was amusing
in 1923 is no longer funny in 1931. Lately I reread "On Being an American" and
I don't believe I got more than two chuckles out of it. It seemed unconvincing.

Everybody, it appears to me, is getting serious. Even *The American Mercury* is
full of statistics. Young novelists are no longer thinking of writing smart, witty
novels. They are working on labor novels.

One of the most significant magazine articles printed during the last year—I
think generally recognized as such—was Stuart Chase's "The Luxury of Integrity"
in *Harper's*, perhaps our most serious and most successful magazine of its class. In
that article Mr. Chase pointed out that nowadays but few can afford to be decent
and honorable.

Laughter is no longer pleasant and smart laughter in the United States. There
probably won't be any more pleasantly cynical laughter for some time. We are
living in a serious, tragic period. . . . There is much serious work ahead for everybody. There is much bewilderment; men and women don't know what to lay their
hands to. Many are beginning to think in terms of conflict.

When I wrote the above, I did not know my immediate directions as a
writer, except the general direction of telling the truth as I saw it. Menckenism
was finished; now Marxism was beginning to fill the intellectual air. Its recent
converts yelled, "There are two sides! You must choose. Come over here on
the Left; you must be a Marxist! It's the only thing to be. Revolution! Revolution!" The empty fury of this movement caused me to stand further aside from
it than I might have stood otherwise. Also, back in 1931-32, as I looked at these
very vocal people in New York, some of whom had just deserted the forces of the
"bedroom rebellion" in Greenwich Village, my scepticism deepened.

Then I went to Europe—to Yugoslavia, which in many vital respects resembled Tsarist Russia. *There,* at the time, with Soviet Russia still four years
removed from the 1936-38 "purges," did appear to be two sides, clear and terrible. Also, just before I returned to the United States, Hitler came into power
in Germany. I visited Italy under Mussolini. . . . And in *The Native's Return*
I chose my side so far as Yugoslavia and most of Europe were concerned.

In regard to America, however, I was on my return essentially where I had been before my trip. My year abroad had convinced me that America *was* different—was not Russia of 1917, was not Yugoslavia of 1933. It was America involved in conditions many of which were peculiarly her own. As I have said, I was deeply glad to be back. . . . By and by I decided that my "side" was to keep America different.——

The Workers

Life is a place where you dig in the ditch to get enough money to buy food to provide enough strength to dig in the ditch.

—LUTHER LANGSTON.

The laborer is worthy of his hire.

—*New Testament, Luke*: x. 7.

By some it is assumed that labor is available only in connection with capital—that nobody labors unless somebody else owning capital, somehow, by the use of it, induces him to do it. . . . But another class of reasoners . . . hold that labor is prior to, and independent of capital; that, in fact, capital is the fruit of labor, and could never have existed if labor had not first existed without capital.

I hold that if the Almighty had ever made a set of men that should do all the eating and none of the work, He would have made them with mouths only and no hands; and if He had ever made another class that He intended should do all the work and no eating, He would have made them with hands only and no mouths.

—ABRAHAM LINCOLN, *Mud-sill Theory of Labor,* 1859.

I Witness the Earliest Beginnings
of a New Labor Movement: 1934

WHATEVER MAY BE SAID—FROM THE DIFFERENT VIEWPOINTS—OF THE VARIOUS parts, phases and specific performances of the New Deal, one thing cannot be taken away from it—it snapped America out of its deep, deadly three-year socio-economic-political-spiritual paralysis. During 1930-32, as I have said, only the "Communists" had seemed to be alive and active. Now, by midsummer of 1933, the country was looking up again, watching the Blue Eagle trying to fly. It was none too graceful a bird, but it flew low and high, screeching loudly and flapping its wings with great effort.

One of the Blue Eagle's longest and most conspicuous tail feathers was Section 7-a of the National Industrial Recovery Act, which encouraged—urged —the workers in all industries to organize. The Roosevelt administration with its original "Brain Trust," which included several extremely naïve liberals and quasi-radicals, seemed to be eager for the rapid development of a great mass labor movement, which might help it become effective: that is, insure its (and the Democratic party's) political future and police industry, compelling it to be a responsible social agency living up to the provisions of the NIRA, some of which provisions it hoped might be extended into the post-emergency period or even made permanent.

The Blue Eagle increased—for a while—the wages and number of jobs, shortened the workday, and improved the conditions of labor generally. Stunned with surprise by this abrupt apparent dawning of a new period, the workers rubbed their eyes. They still had not quite recovered from the effects of the past three years. Was this possible? Was it not, as the Reds said it was, all a trick to corral labor and control it? . . . This smiling face of the new President, so unlike Hoover's! . . . By and by, however, deciding that the new President (who seemed too good to be true, but there he was!) really wished them to organize, millions of workers became eager or ready to join the unions; and the winter of 1933-34 and the ensuing spring, when I traveled around the country, witnessed a great and vital confusion among the laboring masses. The elements of this confusion, as I saw it, were as follows:

(1) The workers' own bewilderment as individuals and as a class. Their individualism, whose fabric had been torn during the previous three years, still hung on. They were acquainted with some of the local unions, which were near-rackets. They remembered sell-outs in the past. Some had moments of suspicion about Roosevelt, who they heard was a rich man. And so, at the same time that they wanted to, they did not want to, join any union.

(2) The "Communists," as already told, were still active in the field of organized labor—here and there, indeed, more so than ever before. They

warned that the NIRA was incipient fascism. Workers, beware! This genial, smiling President was but a screen for the forces of reaction. He was the Kerensky of America! And spreading this propaganda, they "bored from within" in the established unions, causing dissension and ill feeling, which made many of the existing organizations unattractive to the unorganized men and women; and they tried—often not in vain—to sabotage every effort at organization which was not "Communist"-controlled.

But the most important element of this confusion was (3) the American Federation of Labor, then the dominant labor organization. I have an analysis of the A.F. of L. as it stood in 1934 in the last chapter of the revised edition of *Dynamite*. Here it is sufficient to say that the mass organization of American labor, such as the New Deal desired early in its career, was possible only on industrial lines; that the A.F. of L., an affiliation preponderantly of unions formed and conducted on craft lines, was intrinsically and generally opposed to industrial organization; and that the majority of A.F. of L. officials, but especially the executive council presided over by William Green, did not desire (in fact, feared) mass organization of any sort: for, though not particularly perspicacious, they knew that *they* could control and run as they saw fit only a small movement such as the A.F. of L. which, to be exact, was no longer a movement but a static outfit existing to protect the special interests of its members, no matter at whose expense or to whose detriment. Of the A.F. of L. unions only the United Mine Workers of America, an industrial organization, whose president was John L. Lewis, took full advantage of Section 7-a. Some of the semi-industrial garment amalgamations and the textile unions took partial advantage of it.

Under the encouragement of the New Deal, no end of new local unions, big and small, came into existence in various industries. Their leaders were for the most part inexperienced, ignorant, naïve. They wanted to get into the A.F. of L., and the A.F. of L. reluctantly received them, labelling them independent "federal unions." It took them not because it wanted their membership, but (I mean this literally) to keep them from developing and becoming part of some rival national organization which might spring up sometime in the future. For two or three years, aided by the "Communists," the A.F. of L. was extremely successful in this gigantic sabotage of a potential mass labor movement. It defeated the naïve New Dealers' dream for it and rendered enormous aid to the forces of reaction in their effort to destroy the New Deal as a whole.

Nevertheless, the workers of America livened up greatly during 1934, and—due chiefly to improved economic conditions—that year and part of 1935 were punctuated by numerous and bitter capital-labor struggles, particularly in Toledo, Ohio, in Minneapolis, and in Seattle and San Francisco. The last two cities were scenes of brief general strikes, and a general strike had been threatened in Toledo. . . . There were rumblings in the auto, rubber, and steel industries. Particularly in steel.

In June, 1934, I was living in a little white house on a mountain-side near the village of Woodstock, in Vermont, revising *Dynamite*, which Viking Press wanted to bring out in a new edition as soon as possible: for the extremely explosive capital-labor situation made the book timely. One day I was interrupted by a long-distance telephone call from New York. It was Freda Kirchwey, then managing editor of *The Nation*. I *must* go to Pittsburgh at once and cover the steel situation. Freda was quite excited, as I was myself, having been reading the New York papers regularly during the past two weeks.

During those two weeks large sections of the American people of all classes had stood on their toes, tense with hope or apprehension or both, watching—through the poorly focused telescope of the daily press reports—the on-rush of developments in the threatened strike of the Amalgamated Association of Iron, Steel, and Tin Workers, with its more than two hundred lodges or local unions in the various steel-producing centers in the United States. For days toward the middle of June, but especially on the day when Freda Kirchwey called me, it looked—through the aforesaid telescope—as though a general strike in the country's basic industry was inevitable at midnight of June 15th, or soon thereafter; and numerous persons everywhere believed that it probably would be one of the bitterest, bloodiest, most consequential class-war battles ever fought in America.

Freda's call came in mid-afternoon. At four o'clock I was in my car, then drove all night and till noon the next day, when I arrived in Pittsburgh: without stopping except to fill my tank and to eat—about six hundred and fifty miles in twenty hours. I was tired, but it was another twenty-four hours before I had a decent sleep.

The special, so-called "strike" convention of the Amalgamated Association called for June 14th was considered so important that on the 13th some of the country's foremost newspapermen rushed to Pittsburgh to cover the situation, and simultaneously there arrived also a flock of excited mediators, conciliators, observers, spies, and other such factotums sent out by federal offices in Washington and by the governments of the various steel states, notably Pennsylvania. The Pittsburgher Hotel, where I stopped, was teeming with these people. Many of them—including Cornelia Bryce Pinchot, wife of the then Governor of Pennsylvania, whom I met on this occasion—believed that a strike was wellnigh certain within two days, and, once called, was likely to become the spark for a bloody social revolution, or the next thing to it. With the fierce strike of Toledo the previous month still fresh in everybody's mind, they expected labor, employed and unemployed, all over the United States to rise against capitalism, unemployment, company unionism, the New Deal, the President, and what not.

Yet twenty-four hours later, or five or six hours after I arrived in Pittsburgh, the strike idea completely fizzled out . . . and thereby hangs an immensely interesting and significant tale, worth telling in this book, I think, in some detail, because it so clearly mirrors the entire labor situation in the United

States at the time, which was a sort of prologue to the inception, slightly over a year later, of John L. Lewis' Committee for Industrial Organization—the C.I.O.

To begin at the beginning, the Amalgamated Association of Iron, Steel, and Tin Workers was one of the oldest bodies affiliated with the A.F. of L. It had come into existence in 1887, when a group of highly skilled metal workers seceded from the old Sons of Vulcan. Before the New Deal it never was anything more than a collection of fraternal benefit lodges of the "aristocracy of labor" in the steel, iron, and tin (mostly tin) industries, and a convenient stepping-stone for its so-called executive officers who had ambitions (and most of them had) for political and economic self-advancement. One president of the A.A. left his office to become secretary of the American Tin Plate Company, then United States Consul at Birmingham, England, and finally a business man in Pittsburgh; another became inspector of immigration in New York; a third, a Republican Congressman; a fourth, a Republican city councilman in Pittsburgh; a fifth, secretary of the steel manufacturers' association on the Pacific Coast.

Since about 1895 no one could possibly have accused the outfit of being a labor movement. Its central office was nearly always on closer terms with the managers of most of the mills than with their workers. It never made any effort to organize the industry. Several of the local lodges, composed exclusively or mainly of highly skilled wrought-iron and sheet-metal men, were recognized by otherwise anti-union bosses and had wage-and-hour contracts with them. The organization played a semi-strike-breaking rôle in the great steel strike of 1919.

Its president in 1934 and for some while before was a fattish, drooling, loose-lipped, watery-eyed old codger in his late seventies, M. J. Tighe, familiarly known as "Old Mike" or "Grandmother" Tighe. He was with the organization from its birth. A typical old-time trade-union bureaucrat, he was profoundly ignorant of the forces operating in the world or in the country in the 1930's; was narrow, fussy, old-womanish, but deeply experienced in the official trickeries and "practical trade-union politics" perfected by leaders of A.F. of L. affiliates. In his official duties Tighe was ably assisted by the secretary-treasurer, Louis (Shorty) Leonard, a round, compact little fellow, somewhat younger than the president but also an old-timer in the outfit, with a loud Fourth of July voice and an inexhaustible supply of labor blah-blah; to me fully as objectionable, both as a person and as a labor-union official, as Tighe. Ed Miller and Tom Gillis, the two vice-presidents, were essentially of the same type. All these men drew salaries ("and expenses") they could not conceivably have hoped to receive in any other racket except by some fluke, and they naturally thought a great deal of their positions and wanted to keep them.

For fourteen years the A.A. had been on the toboggan. By the middle of 1933 its membership had fallen to 4,700, of whom fewer than three thousand were paying their dues. Then the New Deal came, with its Section 7-a in the NIRA, which gave the nearly half a million steel, iron, and tin workers in New York, Pennsylvania, Ohio, West Virginia, Indiana, Michigan, Maryland, Alabama, Kentucky, California, and elsewhere a sudden and powerful impulse to unionization. Tens of thousands of workers, full of old Hoover-era jitters and new Roosevelt-inspired hope, were asking, "Which union can I join?" "Communist" organizers were in the field with their Steel and Metal Workers' Industrial Union. Two or three thousand men joined that organization. At the same time, the Iron and Steel Institute, under the direction of Arthur Young (getting $40,000 a year for his work), started its big push for company unions. Sincere, if none too intelligent, would-be leaders of non-"Communist" but radical or progressive independent unionization movements appeared among the steel people. And there were lively stirrings in several lodges of the A.A. The leaders of these locals appealed for advice and help to the central office of the A.A. in Pittsburgh. They wrote letters and went to the office in person. They telephoned "Old Mike" and wired "Shorty" Leonard. But the "executive officers" did nothing for three months, until some of the lodge presidents threatened to start organizing what possibly might turn out to be a new union movement in the steel industry.

Then, in September, 1933, largely to stop the growing "Communist" and other independent movements, "Grandmother" and "Shorty" decided—possibly, as the "Communists" maintained, on the urging of Iron and Steel Institute agents—to send out three dozen "organizers," most of whom were unemployed old-time trade unionists, friends of the central office, with no experience as organizers. These men received considerable salaries (and expenses), although in most cases their sole qualification was that they wrote a legible hand; but that was enough, for all that they had to do was to fill out union cards for the thousands of men who eagerly stood in line to be signed up.

The only aggressive organizer for the A.A. was Cornelia Bryce Pinchot, who had no official connection with the union. She was a naïve rich woman with red hair and an overabundance of nervous energy who got more thrill out of labor agitation and strike picketing than out of bridge and society and had, besides strong political ambitions for her husband and herself, a few vague notions that something was wrong with our social system. She attracted vast crowds of steel workers and their wives and spoke with a furious incoherence at scores of meetings in Pennsylvania, Ohio, and West Virginia, urging the men to sign up and get behind the NIRA and the President. But the A.A. "executives," apparently, were anything but enthusiastic about the help the lady was trying to give the organization. They sent no one to her mass-meetings to sign up the men. The old fogies in the central office were beside themselves with fear of what was happening to their hitherto nice, quiet old outfit, and soon after starting the organizing "campaign" they began to do everything in their power to prevent or restrict its success.

But, despite all this, in less than two months the A.A. had more than 125 new lodges, many of them called by such names as the Blue Eagle Lodge, Recovery Lodge, President Roosevelt Lodge and Nira (or Arin) Lodge, and its membership was increased from 4,700 to anywhere from 60,000 to 100,000. In June, 1934, nobody knew what the new total was. The central office made no real effort to find out. The officials in that office knew that, whatever it was, the number was too high for the good of the organization as they wanted it to continue.

In short, the old, dying A.A. suddenly bulged out into a vast organization, a great, virile new body full of raw, undisciplined, undirected strength and spirit, with but a few sick old cells here and there, and, alas, with the same old head, the same senile "executive" officers, utterly lacking in real brains, in knowledge of what was going on in the country, in honesty and social vision. Suddenly the big, healthy body and the small, hollow head were at violent cross-purposes. But for some time the body did not realize that. It merely felt very strong and very uncomfortable, and anxious to be doing something.

Toward the end of 1933 the situation began to clarify itself a bit. Several men of the new element and a few older but more or less progressive fellows who had helped to bring in the new ones began to feel that there were two factions in the organizations, sharply opposed one to the other. They started to refer to themselves as the Young Boys, and to the old-timers in power and the old craft lodges, which supported the central office, as the Old Boys. The Young Boys were, for the most part, the presidents of the newly formed industrial lodges and the newly elected district chairmen, who—to the great annoyance of the central office—gradually began to act as spokesmen for the new element in its differences with the Old Boys—differences which rapidly increased both in frequency and bitterness. Unlike the leaders of the Old Boys, they were actual steel workers employed in mills, unless lately discharged for rank-and-file union activities; none of them received any salary from their lodge treasuries, and some of them covered even their expenses on union business out of their own pockets; some of them were still in their early and middle twenties, small-town boys, "little men," with scant education and less natural ability or experience as labor-union leaders and politicians.

For months these new leaders and would-be leaders talked among themselves, and plotted against the Old Boys and against one another, for there was a good deal of suspicion and jealousy among them. They hardly knew one another, and several wanted to be the big leader. But as time passed they became united on one point—action. The entire rank-and-file element, growing conscious of its overwhelming numerical strength in the A.A., wanted action. "Boys, let's do somethin'!" Thousands of workers on signing up with the A.A. lodges paid no initiation fees or dues, promising to pay when the union started to do something for them. Having been fooled before, they did not trust the A.A. or the rank-and-file leaders.

The matter of union recognition by the steel companies was on everybody's mind. Lodge presidents asked the A.A.'s central office what they could do.

"Old Mike" and "Shorty" stalled; they did not know. So some of the lodge leaders took the matter into their own hands. They visited the Pittsburgh NRA office. No result. They wrote letters to Washington. No answer, or they received printed material on what a wonderful thing the NRA was for labor. A few went to Washington and called on the A.F. of L. and National Labor Board, not once, but four, five times. They talked with Senator Wagner and other New Dealers and demanded elections in the mills. The National Labor Board stalled, promised them action, but for a month, two months, nothing happened. The gentlemen in the A.F. of L. urged patience. The boys tried to see the Secretary of Labor, "Ma" Perkins, as they called her, who some months before had been in the steel region and had seemed interested in the steel people, but most of them got only as far as her assistant, Ed McGrady. No result anywhere, no satisfaction. Washington was full of fuss and fury which had no relation to the steel workers of America. Bill Spang of Duquesne, one of the lodge leaders who journeyed several times to Washington, finally came to the conclusion that Roosevelt, evidently, had not meant what he signed in the NIRA and in all probability was afraid of the iron-and-steel gang. Bill made a report to that effect to his lodge and the leaders of other rank-and-file lodges. NRA, he said, meant "National Run Around" for the workers, and Washington was "a labor college where a working stiff like me can get an education like he can get nowhere else—believe me!"

The rank-and-file boys, like workers in many other industries throughout the land, rapidly developed a strike mood. In this mood, in mid-April, the rank-and-file delegates, still lacking a real leader, assembled with the Old Boys in the annual convention of the A.A. in the Elks' Hall in Pittsburgh. They had a clear two-thirds majority over the Old Boys, and Tighe and Leonard were at their wits' end. The Young Boys shouted, "Action! Action!" The Old Boys, trying to wear them down, stretched the convention by various parliamentary tricks, with which the new men had no acquaintance, to more than two weeks. To no avail. "Action!" There was a bar in the Elks' Hall and there was some drinking, which made the Young Boys even stronger for action. The end of it all was that they passed a resolution with a program, which included the call for a national steel strike in the middle of June if the bosses refused to grant the union's demand for recognition and collective bargaining before then. No strike plan was outlined for the eventuality that the bosses would not recognize the union. The Young Boys invented no way to make the Old Boys in the central office prepare the organization for the big walk-out. They merely appointed a committee of ten to get busy about the matter as soon as possible.

Tired from the long sessions both in the hall and at the bar, the committee did not meet till May twentieth. After much squabbling among themselves, they formed a "strike committee of five" and demanded of the executive officers that one of the committee be allowed to take a desk in the central office and work on strike preparations. Tighe, Leonard, and their colleagues, having, in the face of the Young Boys' now patent ineptitude, regained their composure, said, "Nothing doing!" Then the whole committee of ten, duly appointed in the convention, asked the executive officers for a conference on the morning of May twenty-sixth. When on that day the committee arrived at the A.A.'s central office, only the janitor was there to receive them. This made the Young Boys "pretty sore" and they began to call the old-timers Yellow Dogs, while the latter, in turn, started to refer to the rank and filers as Greenhorn Goats.

At this point a young student from the University of Pittsburgh, Harold Ruttenberg, who had grown up in steel-mill towns and was interested in labor, got next to the sore and bewildered Greenhorn Goats and commenced to act as their publicity man and "brain trust." On his suggestion a group of them journeyed to Washington to ask for an interview with the President. They meant to inform him that they were about to call a strike to help him fetch the steel trust to book, and ask him to accept their aid—the aid of the workers in the steel industry—and meet the issue squarely. "We will shut down the mills," they wished to say to Mr. Roosevelt, "until the steel magnates sign before you their acceptance of the law and actually begin collective bargaining with our unions." They did not expect to get any results. The real idea was to get publicity for the strike. But though they did not get to the President, they were received by everyone else of any importance in the NRA, scared a lot of people, caused much discomfort in the White House and the A.F. of L. Building, engaged in a hot exchange of insults with General Johnson, and before leaving the capital signed a sizzling open letter to the President, written by young Harold Ruttenberg, which landed them on the front pages of all important papers in the country. They said, in effect, that they were going back home to call the strike.

The Iron and Steel Institute announced it would never recognize the A.A. or any other outside union. Meanwhile, William Green called Tighe to Washington, and the Old Boy, by now quite sure of his ground again, smiled as broadly as his old face permitted, talked with General Johnson and other big people there, and let the Greenhorn Goats do what they liked. Then—very probably with the full approval of the A.F. of L. panjandrums, who were in touch with the National Labor Board, Miss Perkins, and the White House—he announced that he would reconvene the delegates of the last annual convention and let them decide what the organization would do in the matter of the threatened strike.

And on June fourteenth, when the A.A. convention met again two floors above the Elks' barroom in Pittsburgh, large sections of the American people, as I have said, raised themselves high on their toes and glued their eyes closer to the poorly focused telescope of daily press reports. They expected hell to break loose within a couple of days. They did not know (neither did I) that the whole thing was practically cut and dried, and that, save for an unlikely slip-up, the boys would not call the strike.

When the delegates reconvened, most of the Greenhorn Goats were for calling the walkout, if for no other reason than that they could see no other way out. But many of them, when on the way to the convention, had already begun to develop serious misgivings about such an action. Most of the mills were armed. Because of this the men's wives had begged them not to call the strike. And with times so hard, how many workers would really walk out at their call? It probably was true, as it was generally said, that the bosses would welcome a strike at this time; it would give them an opportunity to beat down the workers' spirit during a slack in production. All these and similar considerations were heavy on the Young Boys' minds. On the other hand, they figured, if they did not strike they would get nothing.

At the opening of the convention the most aggressive of the strike-minded Greenhorns had in their hands copies of two resolutions, both written by young Ruttenberg—one calling the strike and setting up the strike machinery, the other calling upon the A.F. of L. for financial and moral support. But the Yellow Dogs running the convention from the platform gave them no chance to present them. Parliamentary trickery was utilized to the utmost. They killed time on the rules of procedure. Who was to be admitted besides the delegates? Resolutions. Amendments. Amendments to amendments. Which confused the inexperienced boys, made them feel like "a bunch of damn' fools." Then serious difficulties with roll call. More resolutions. Amendments. Amendments to amendments.

Finally, at eleven-thirty, they adjourned till three-thirty to "fix up the roll call," but actually, of course, to stretch the convention, to give William Green time to come to Pittsburgh. At three-thirty a squabble over credentials. Pointless, time-wasting resolutions. Delegations were asked to report whether or not the bosses had recognized their respective unions. A Slovak priest, one of the few "guests" in the hall, made a long speech urging the boys, with several of whom he had some influence, to postpone the strike. Then it was announced that word had been received from Washington that William Green, the great leader of organized labor in America, blah, blah . . . was coming to Pittsburgh to address the convention to-morrow, and meantime his brotherly appeal to the boys was to keep their shirts on. Convention adjourned.

Confused, their spirit down, uncertain what would be the best or most sensible thing to do, some of the Young Boys proceeded to get drunk, much to the glee of "Grandmother" Tighe, a teetotaler who generally frowns upon hard liquor. I do not mean to say that any considerable number of the delegates got drunk, but several of those who did were leaders, and the fact that they incapacitated themselves for leadership the next day tended further to demoralize those who stayed sober. Only a few newspapermen knew of this, and they were kind enough not to tell about it. I mention it because it is so important—so human: for the labor movement is at the mercy not only of the quality of its top-leaders but the human weaknesses of its members.

By the time Bill Green arrived, the strike idea was practically dead. Then he dug the grave for it; the boys themselves, half-consciously, half-unconsciously, buried it. From the Old Boys' and Bill Green's viewpoint it all worked to perfection, just as they had hoped it would when plotting the whole show, perhaps as long as a week before. Bill Green stepped before the boys as a "fellow-worker," a "miner," though he had not seen the inside of a pit for thirty-five years, and begged them to be calm and not allow their judgment to give way to their feelings. But many had no judgment or feelings, except bewilderment, in the matter. Several of them had katzenjammers; a few were in their cups during Green's speech and throughout the rest of the day. He proposed a peace plan which he was sure President Roosevelt would accept and support. Blah, blah, blah. . . . When Green finished, Shorty Leonard and the other Yellow Dogs leaped to their feet and led the applause. The convention promptly accepted Green's proposition and "postponed" the strike. Telegrams were sent to the locals telling the workers, tens of thousands of whom were ready to strike at midnight, to stay put.

Shorty Leonard whispered a joyous remark to Old Mike, who grinned cynically, and a few hours later one of the other Old Boys remarked, "Now we got 'em where we want 'em. Now we'll teach 'em discipline."

Immediately after the conclusion of the convention I spoke to one of the more intelligent of the young militants. He said, "I feel like Carnera must of felt last night." Others, even among the sober ones, told me they didn't know exactly what had happened. "Things were done so fast." I overheard a conversation of two Young Boys. One said, "The strike is only postponed, ain't it?" "Yeah, I guess." "Have we, I mean the Young Boys, any authority left to call the strike if—in case—" "Damn' if I know. Don't think we have." "Well, I guess we sold ourselves out." A third young fellow, a little drunk, who stood by listening, said, "Nuts!" and walked off.

Bewilderment, bewilderment. I had a feeling, in that dismal hall, that I was witnessing the whole essential tragedy of American labor. On the platform, surrounded by reporters, Old Mike drooled away: "We're not Communists . . . no, not Communists. We're trade unionists. I'm a highest type of trade unionist. . . . Strike? Haw-haw! There ain't gonna be no strike. All over! We ain't a strike organization. . . . I'm tired, boys, nothin' else to say, nothin' to say, boys. Haven't had a bite all day, now it's midnight. Good-night, boys."

The sense of tragedy deepened in me during the ensuing few days as I motored through the steel towns in Pennsylvania, Ohio, and West Virginia, and talked with "leaders" and ordinary members of A.A. lodges. Bewilderment. None knew what had really happened in Pittsburgh.

Not that I favored the strike. The idea for it at the time was, in fact, palpably wild. But what Green and Tighe did seemed to me one of the vilest things I had ever witnessed. They took advantage of the men's personal weaknesses, their inexperience and ineptitude, to kill their spirit.

But, somehow, the tragic and sordid incident was not in vain. At close range, watching it, was Philip Murray, a vice-president of the United Mine Workers, a shrewd man representing John L. Lewis, who was already thinking

of the C.I.O. Two years later Murray was chairman of the Steel Workers
Organizing Committee, a branch of the C.I.O. Actively engaged in the sorry
affair, though not officially connected with any movement, was the young
student of the University of Pittsburgh I have mentioned, Harold Ruttenberg,
who in 1936 became the research director of the S.W.O.C. Watching the incident in his capactiy as a mediator for the State of Pennsylvania was Clinton
Golden, who two years later become director-organizer of S.W.O.C. Present
in Pittsburgh at the moment, acting as secretary to Cornelia Pinchot, was a
young man named Ralph Hetzel, who, as I write this, is a confidential assistant
of John L. Lewis in Washington.

It does not quite belong here, at least not on the face of it, but I seem unable
to refrain from quoting at the end of this chapter an entry in my Diary:

June 17, 1934, in Pittsburgh.—This morning I walked about with a young fellow
named Fred K. He is a steel worker from a near-by town; was a delegate to the
unfortunate "strike" convention of his union, just ended. One of the Young Boys,
he was rather mixed up and disgusted about things. He cursed Tighe. . . . Then
we passed a haberdashery store. He interrupted himself in the middle of a sentence
and stopped to look into the display window. "Nice pair of pants, ain't it?" he
said, referring to a pair of white flannel trousers with dark stripes, marked $4.85.
I said, "Yes, pretty nice."—"Gee! I think I'll go buy 'em." We went into the
store. He bought the pants, deriving a great satisfaction out of the purchase. He
asked me twice if I liked them. I said I did, and remembered that not a few
delegates to this workers' convention had worn such "ice cream" pants, which
somehow removed them a good distance from the status of the proletariat. . . .
Fred K. and I went out and walked around awhile longer. He was very happy.
I asked him something else pertaining to his union. "Huh?" he said. "What did
you say?"

Those trousers, or the fact that he could buy them, compensated this young
worker and would-be labor leader for all sorts of things he did not like in his
life. The fact that he could and did buy them, and would wear them, took
the edge off any bitterness he might have in him. What the actual wearing of
them will do to his "class-consciousness" would sadden Karl Marx. . . .

The Cunning of Desperate Men: 1934

THE DAY AFTER THE CLOSING OF THE "STRIKE" CONVENTION IN PITTSBURGH, ON A Saturday, Harold Ruttenberg asked me if I would not like to come with him to a big steel workers' picnic in Canton, just over the state line in Ohio. I went.

The picnic was held in a vast park beside a lake on the outskirts of the town. It was given by the Sixth District of the Amalgamated Association of Iron, Steel, and Tin Workers, which included lodges in Canton, Youngstown, and the lesser steel towns thereabouts. Several thousand workers were there, mostly steel men with their families and girl friends. It was an all-day affair. Most of the folks had baskets of food with them, and beer, soda pop, hot dogs, sandwiches, and ice cream were to be had at the big pavilion near the shooting-galleries.

There were all sorts of "doings." Some of the younger people had a good time in and on the lake, diving, swimming, rowing. The children had their games, the merry-go-round, and other amusement devices. Some of the youngsters shouted hilariously and dashed about. Most of them, perhaps, looked healthy enough; not a few, however, were all too obviously working-class children growing up during a great economic crisis in dismal, musty dwellings along cinder-strewn streets and alleyways. They were thin and old-looking; and malnutrition was the reason.

Women of all ages, wearing cheap clothes, sat on the grass in small groups, chatting, or just sitting in silence, keeping an eye on the kids. Some of them no doubt were younger than they looked. Lots of them had bad teeth; for years they had had no money for dental attention. A few of them, here and there, talked among themselves of what had happened in Pittsburgh the day before. No strike, thank God! They were relieved by the sudden turn of events. They approved the decision of the delegates to the "strike" convention not to strike. They did not know that that decision had not been made by the delegates. Anyhow, they were glad, these steel workers' wives, that the men were not going to strike rightaway. Times were so hard, and some of the men were just beginning to work again a little after years of almost steady idleness. And had a strike been started, some of the men would surely have been killed or wounded, for a number of the mills had armed for battle. What good would that have done?

"Of course," I overheard a woman say, "it would be different if we, I mean the men, could pull a real strike, a *real* one—all the steel and iron and tin workers organized in one union—all quitting at the same time, then just staying home till they got what they wanted, and none of 'em going near the mills to be shot at. But as things are now, the workers are all split up. Here are these A.A. lodges of Young Boys and Old Boys that don't get along: like cats and dogs. There's the Communist union. All kinds of unions, none of 'em pullin' together. And then those company unions——"

"Those company unions," put in a second woman, quickly, "they are bad; if it wasn't for them ——"

"They're bad, all right," said a third woman, listlessly, "but what can you do?"

The men, especially some of the younger men, the Young Boys, stood or sat about in small groups or around the tables in the pavilion, talking in snatches, smoking, munching sandwiches, drinking a bit, all plainly uncomfortable, bewildered, trying to appear indifferent. The shooting-galleries were not attracting many of them. I talked with a few. None really knew what had happened in Pittsburgh the previous day; what the labor movement or the NRA really was all about. I asked, "And what do you think of company unions?" "I'm against 'em," was the typical and prompt reply. "How about the other steel workers you know; do they feel the same as you?" I asked. The usual answer was, "Everybody I know is against company unions." The company unions were the only subject to which they reacted with spirit. In some instances the answer was a brusque, fierce laugh and a look which seemed to say, "You don't think we're saps enough to go for company unions, do you?"

In the afternoon, the speeches. None of the rank-and-file leaders spoke. None had any experience in talking to large crowds, and over the radio besides, for the speeches were broadcast. Moreover, as I have said before, all the rank-and-filers were confused; what could they say? . . . I did not hear all the speeches. The first one I listened to was by a former A.F. of L. union official now running for office in Canton; a thick, short man with a bull voice. He spoke of the grand and glorious American labor movement, its traditions, achievements: blah, blah . . . for ten minutes. Faint, scattered applause. No life in the audience. . . . Then the speaker embarked upon a long-winded attack on the company unions. Furiously and voluminously, he denounced the "steel barons," the "autocratic Steel and Iron Institute," for not recognizing the virtuous A.A. and for coercing the workers to join company unions. He described all the evils, from the workers' point of view, of company unionism. And at nearly every other sentence, the huge audience, now suddenly alive, vehemently applauded. Many of those who clapped probably realized that the speaker was a wind-bag, but passionately agreed with what he said about the company unions.

The next speaker was "Shorty" Leonard, whom I have mentioned earlier: a former Socialist party spellbinder gone A.F. of L. conservative. He "explained" what had happened at the "strike" convention, eulogized William Green, that great, that sterling leader of American labor: blah, blah . . . praised Franklin Roosevelt, the greatest President since Lincoln: blah, blah . . . To all this there was little or no applause. The workers and their women just stood and listened apathetically.

"Shorty" then tore into the subject of company unions and, using very much the same words as the previous speaker, denounced the "autocratic, un-American steel barons," the "ruthless, undemocratic, steel interests," who refused to grant the request of organized labor in their industry for recognition of the union and collective bargaining; who defied the President and Congress of the United States, and, by various methods, forced—"*forced,* my friends"— their employees to join company unions, thus viciously, purposefully, retarding the normal growth of "legitimate" labor organizations. He kept this up for fifteen minutes or longer, repeating himself three or four times; and on the average of once a minute, if not oftener, he was interrupted by loud, spontaneous applause.

It was evident that the workers really felt strongly about company unions, and that this feeling, which in the ensuing few days, while going around in the steel regions, I encountered elsewhere, was the result of bitter personal experiences or long, consistent anti-company union propaganda, or both; probably both.

Two days later, "Shorty" Leonard made essentially the same speech at the Hungry Club luncheon in Pittsburgh, attended largely by liberals and radicals of that city; and I was· told that he and other A.F. of L. labor officials in the Pennsylvania, West Virginia, and Ohio steel regions had been talking to that effect every chance they had had for months—blaming company unions for the A.F. of L. organization's failure to organize labor in. a big way, while simultaneously, as I have shown, subtly retarding, frustrating unorganized labor in its NRA-inspired urge toward organization.

In brief, the A.F. of L. union officials were utilizing, exploiting the workers' hate for company unions, stirring and intensifying it, focusing their thoughts and feelings on the company-union evil, exaggerating the power of company unionism, in order to keep them blind to the faults and shortcomings of the A.F. of L. organizations. This hate focused on the company unions made the A.F. of L. group safe. and free from criticism on the part of the workers, except the more intelligent ones, of course, who could not be blinded so easily. Were the A.F. of L. unions weak and ineffective? Yes. But why? Because they had to contend with that awful enemy of organized labor, that great evil, the company unions. Hence, if the A.F. of L. unions were not what they should be, it was not their fault, but the company unions', the bosses', the Steel and Iron Institute's. Also, by talking so furiously against company unions the A.F. of L. leaders made themselves appear friends of labor. Labor, ill-informed and bewildered, fearing and hating company unions, did not repudiate them. It allowed itself to be "led" by them. This talking so furiously against company unions kept labor from looking around for other leaders, from becoming a raw mass for a new movement, which, by and by, would displace the A.F. of L.

The Steel and Iron Institute released some figures pertaining to company unions. It claimed that over ninety per cent of steel, iron, and tin workers were in company unions or in favor of such organizations. As a matter of fact, the overwhelming majority, probably over ninety per cent, of workers in the steel regions that I visited in Pennsylvania, Ohio, and West Virginia, were fiercely anti-company union. There were company unions in nearly every town, but few workers who succeeded in overcoming their fear of not belonging to them joined them.

Until 1933 the company unions were comparatively unimportant in the workers' consideration. Then the A.F. of L. spellbinders, fellows like "Shorty" Leonard, commenced to harp on them and thus built them up in the workers' minds to such an extent that thousands of men joined them because they were afraid that if they did not they would—according to the A.F. of L. union leaders, whom they heard talk—lose their jobs or suffer some other calamity. Thus A.F. of L. officials acted as organizers for company unions!

Consciously? Deliberately? Intentionally? Yes, in all probability, consciously, deliberately, intentionally. As I have suggested, it was not to the advantage of the old A.F. of L. oligarchy to have their unions become big organizations. How could they keep out the thousands of workers who, NRA-inspired, wanted to come in? By impressing them with the importance and formidableness of company unionism, by scaring them, and driving them, fear-stricken, into the company unions.

Am I giving the A.F. of L. leaders credit for more brains than they were likely to have? I think not. They were not very intelligent men, but were desperate. They were fighting for their existence. The C.I.O. was not yet in existence, but they knew that sooner or later, probably sooner, something like it was bound to appear. And in such a situation even a normally dull or stupid person or group is apt to develop great cunning.

A.F. of L. Sabotage in Rubber: 1934-35

IN NO INDUSTRY WAS THE A.F. OF L.'S ATTITUDE TOWARD THE IDEA OF A NEW mass labor movement clearer than in rubber, whose capital—which I visited early in 1935—is the city of Akron, Ohio, home of the great Goodyear, Goodrich, General, India Rubber, and Firestone plants and of more than twenty lesser factories, together employing at peak production nearly forty thousand workers.

In the fall of 1933, when the fame of the NIRA had reached its height, the A.F. of L. rubber unions—to the distress of the executive council—had about forty thousand members, or approximately half of all the rubber workers in the country. Of these more than twenty-five thousand were in Akron and its suburbs. The others were in the various rubber works in Indianapolis, Detroit, Los Angeles, and elsewhere. The organizational and individual morale of the rubber workers was then higher than ever before. Both the morale and the union membership zigzagged downward in 1934. The main, indeed, almost the sole important reason for this condition was the A.F. of L., or, to be more specific, a man by the name of Coleman C. Claherty, the A.F. of L.'s official rubber "organizer" in Akron.

Claherty was a former sheet-metal worker who by playing the game had put himself in the good graces of Bill Green and the executive council in Washington. For many years he was the walking delegate of a union in Cleveland. For a while, too, he worked for John L. Lewis in the West Virginia coal fields. As smooth a specimen of labor "leader" as you would wish to meet, he was scholarly and extremely dignified in bearing, speech, and manner. Claiming personal friendship with the president of the A.F. of L., he had for a good while no serious difficulties in manipulating the rank-and-filers, who were as tragically inexperienced in unionism as their fellow would-be labor leaders in steel.

Claherty appeared in Akron late in 1933 as a personal emissary of Bill Green. His job ostensibly was to "advise" the leaders of the new unions; actually, he was there to "pack ice on the hot heads" of the militant rank-and-filers, some of whom erroneously considered themselves competent labor leaders because they had been members of miners' organizations in the West Virginia, Ohio, and western Pennsylvania coal fields, whence they had come to Akron after having been frozen out of employment in the declining bituminous industry. During the peak-production period of the late winter and early spring of 1934 the unions and thousands of union members as individuals clamored for action, wanted to organize the industry one hundred per cent, and mutinied against their vague and invisible shackles. A great many workers did not join because they feared the employers, who disapproved of unions. The thing to do was to force the companies to recognize the organizations. Then everybody would join. "Let's strike! Compel the bosses to recognize the union!" A general rubber strike in Akron appeared almost a certainty every few weeks, but Claherty—secretly engaging in inter- and intra-union intrigue and publicly preaching patience and faith in President Roosevelt, who was trying to save the country—prevented it each time.

In January, 1934, two hundred rank-and-file leaders, representing nearly every rubber plant and shop in this country and a number in Canada, assembled in a "rump" convention and attempted to form an international amalgamation of rubber unions along industrial lines, but Claherty cleverly smashed the convention and with it the effort to form a great rubber workers' amalgamation, and subsequently succeeded in having the leaders of this movement expelled from their respective unions.

In February, 1934, a strike threat at the India Rubber Company plant in a suburb of Akron brought union recognition and small pay increases. Toward the end of the winter other strike stirrings were put down by Claherty's promise to call a "legal" national convention to form an international union with a broad industrial base. Of course Claherty found all sorts of excuses for inaction.

Meanwhile the Young Boys in rubber, with the seeming approbation of Claherty, drew up a set of demands, which the unions approved, to be presented to the Rubber Manufacturers' Association. The manufacturers refused to receive the workers' delegation. This, on top of all the rest, made a strike imminent in mid-May, but Claherty managed to pack more ice on the hot heads till the fact that the slack season had arrived became apparent to everybody, and a general rubber strike in Akron was unthinkable.

None the less, eleven hundred workers of the General Company walked out spontaneously early in June of that year and maintained strong picket lines for six weeks despite the regional labor board's pleas for arbitration, which were seconded by Claherty and additional emissaries of Bill Green from Washington. The strikers gained a partial victory in spite of the slack season since the other unions vigorously supported the strike both with money and on the picket line.

Wherever possible, Claherty forced out the original rank-and-file leaders and put in their place as local leaders his own henchmen, whom he developed as he went along. In mid-spring the so-called United Rubber Workers' Council was set up, supposedly to create an alliance between the craft unions within the industry in Akron and the actual federal locals, which then comprised the majority of rubber workers in the city. Claherty's intention in this move, it later appeared, was just the opposite. He did not want the rank-and-filers to start something similar. He contrived to be made president of the council, which was composed of seven members only, one of whom was an honest-to-goodness industrial rubber worker. The other six represented crafts in rubber. The sop tossed to the big Akron rubber locals was two ex officio members on the council.

The workers' restlessness continued and grew. The plants speeded up production, until late in 1934, with improved machinery and methods, one worker did the work done by two in 1920 and, considering the rise in cost of living, for approximately the same pay that one received fourteen years before. Efficiency engineers swarmed about, instructing everybody how to work harder but not mentioning any increase in pay. (The average rubber wage was between $800 and $1,000 a year, although the company estimates were higher. Hourly rates ran between sixty cents and a dollar, but the long seasonal lay-offs, usually beginning in June, accelerating up to August, and continuing till January, made the annual wage extremely low. Also, some of the tasks in rubber production undermined the workers' health. Tire-builders, for instance, are good for about eight years, after which they are replaced by younger men. The use of sulphur to compound rubber fills the factories with stench and dust.) Claherty still preached patience.

In the autumn 1934, after the membership of the Goodrich local had dropped from eight to under four thousand, with corresponding declines in other unions, Claherty pressed a fight for elections through the National Labor Relations Board. These were granted for the Firestone and Goodrich locals in December. The Goodyear local, fearing to test its waning numerical strength against the company union, which was sixteen years old, made no request. The Firestone and Goodrich companies tied up the election in the federal courts: which Claherty knew they would do.

Then, three days before Christmas, Firestone laid off three hundred men in the battery department, which was the stronghold of the union. Indignation ran so high that a strike vote meeting was forced, but the motion for a strike was defeated by a slight majority. Since only six hundred men attended the meeting, the union suffered serious impairment of prestige. It goes without saying that the "czar," as the men were commencing to call Claherty, did his part to sabotage the strike. He was the chairman and gave the floor mainly to his attorney, who counseled no strike, more patience.

I do not say that there should have been a strike. What I am trying to do here is to show the A.F. of L.'s ruinous tactics. As in steel, they ruined the men's morale. They made the intelligent Young Boys, who were not completely demoralized, desperate. One of them said to me, "If we don't do something soon, demoralization will deepen and more men will leave the unions." . . . But, winning in its destructive aims, the A.F. of L. was actually losing. In some of the Young Boys it intensified the passion for broad industrial organization. It intensified their inner urge to invent and perfect the sitdown strike as a weapon in industrial warfare, which originated in Akron (and of which more later). It helped to prepare the ground for the C.I.O. and its great organizational success in 1936-37.

Detroit: 1934-35—Anything to Beat the Unions

JANUARY, 1935, WHEN I WAS IN DETROIT, WAS THE MOST AUSPICIOUS BEGINNING of a new year that the automobile industry had had since 1929. Two months before, the New York Automobile Show had been a vast success. Similar shows, with their attractive new models, had subsequently been very successful also in other large cities: for by then the New Deal had more or less "primed the pump" and there was a trickle of Prosperity. Orders were pouring into Detroit. Some of the departments of the Ford plants were working three shifts six days a week. Several General Motors plants operated in two shifts seven days a week. Employment was increasing. A number of Detroit boosters to whom I talked gave me glowing accounts of the sudden upswing in the automobile industry. Things were starting to hum again, no maybe about that. They all used the word "hum." And to my question about the labor situation they replied—most of them, it is true, with a touch of uneasiness—that there was nothing to worry about. Yes, all was quiet. . . . No, no, absolutely no danger of anything resembling real trouble for years, perhaps forever. Detroit was back on its feet.

Detroit had been one of the worst Depression-hit cities in the United States. Now, early in 1935, it still had fifty-two thousand families, or approximately a quarter of a million people, on various forms of relief, while there were somewhere between fifty and seventy-five thousand jobless persons in the city who, getting along in other ways, were not on relief. During the late autumn and early winter employment in some of the automobile plants had gone up as much as one hundred per cent, whereas the city's relief burden was decreased only about twenty per cent. The explanations of this discrepancy interested me.

For one thing, the companies had hired great numbers of girls and young women with no previous experience in the automobile industry; in many departments of the intricate but superbly organized production process no experience is necessary. These girls were given jobs in preference to experienced and physically better-equipped male workers. The companies' theory was that women and girls were not so apt to join unions or become otherwise troublesome as men. And many of these new automotive workers came not from families on relief but from a slightly higher economic level—again because such persons, not having been exposed to the extreme hardships and humiliations of the jobless, were less likely to respond to labor-union agitation than the ex-unemployed.

The automobile manufacturers' labor policy was this: The industry must

363

not be unionized, and to keep the unions from gaining foothold, we must take every precaution and spare no expense. Among the experienced automotive workers living in Detroit and the vicinity, only those were re-hired whom the plant employment managers personally knew to be "safe" or who could secure personal O. K.'s from prominent citizens in Detroit, such as well-known judges and commanders of American Legion posts. Workers known to be inclined, however slightly, toward unionism or radicalism were almost generally taboo in the production department, whether on relief or not. Those hired were watched by stool-pigeons, who in some plants went so far as to search in the men's overcoat pockets for possible union literature.

Apparently there was a great dearth of "safe" workers in Detroit. Beginning in mid-1934, with production increasing, it was necessary for the companies to bring in tens of thousands of people from outside, principally from the South, and put them to work in the busy plants. The companies had sent their labor agents to recruit so-called "hill-billies" from Kentucky, Tennessee, Louisiana and Alabama. These hill-billies were for the most part impoverished whites, "white trash" or a little better, from the rural regions. The majority of them were young fellows. They had had no close contact with modern industry or with labor unionism—this, of course, was their best qualification. Their number in Detroit was variously estimated as between fifteen and thirty thousand, with more of them coming weekly, not only in company-chartered buses but singly and in small groups on their own hook, for no one had a better chance of employment in Detroit at the time than a Southerner of unsophisticated mien. They were employed at simple, standardized tasks in production departments, for which very little or no training is necessary, at forty-five to fifty cents an hour, except in Ford's where the wages were slightly higher. These workers were happy to receive this pay and were much "safer" than local labor, poisoned by ideas of unionism.

The hill-billies, with their extremely low standard of living and lack of acquaintance with modern plumbing, were looked down upon by all but the most intelligent local workers, both native and foreign-born; they were despised also—indeed, mainly—because they took employment away from the old-time automotive workers. This, naturally, was agreeable to the geniuses running the Automobile Chamber of Commerce. In fact, it was exactly what they wanted. It split the workers still more. Any kind of solidarity between these newcomers and old-time Detroiters was out of the question in the immediate future. It took an American worker a long while to assimilate the union idea; and these unfortunate Southerners—though just now most of them considered themselves extremely fortunate—were nothing if not Americans.

It was all very, very clever—even if it cost Detroit a lot of money for relief. It certainly bewildered the Young Boys who, as the Young Boys in steel and rubber, dreamed of a labor movement. . . . Some of the individual workers, however, invented counter-tricks. To crash a job at a plant one old-time Detroiter I met practiced up on the Southern dialect and drawl, then presented himself at the factory gates, and was hired as soon as he opened his mouth. Another good way for a man to get a job in Detroit, I was told, was to look and act stupid.

Did the people of Detroit as a whole know about this importation of workers from the South? The newspapers never mentioned it. Naturally not. They were strongly in favor of the automobile industry remaining open shop. The same was true of important people in the city in general. Anything was justified that kept out the unions, which to them signified only trouble. They were willing to contribute to relief; they were willing to do almost anything to keep the industry from being "strangled to death by the unions." Of course, most of the big people when I asked them denied that the companies were importing outsiders wholesale. An important engineer of a great body plant, however, said to me: "The industry's been in the red for years. Now for the first time since the Depression began it looks as though a nice profit is probable. Can't you see the manufacturers' point of veiw? Can you blame them, things being as they are, if they take precautions—if they insure themselves against possible interference with production? True, some of the people brought into the city will be 'dumped,' as you say, into the lap of Detroit when high production ends in April or May, but what is more important to Detroit—the fact that the industry goes on humming uninterruptedly or the danger that the city will have ten or fifteen thousand more relief cases in May? Anyhow, I believe that both the city and the industry figure that they'll deal with that in May. No use crossing bridges till you come to them. That's the American way." He smiled. I suggested that it might be a bit cruel to bring in these people from the South, then dump them. "That may be true in some cases," was the answer, "but in a big thing like this and in serious times like the present you can't worry about that. The automobile industry is the most important industry in the country. The prosperity of other important industries depends on it."

The middle-class and lower-middle-class people were more or less aware of the importations of workers but were too full of troubles of their own to try to do anything about them. Petty landlords and realtors who rented their houses to the hill-billies complained that their tenants, unappreciative of modern appliances, were damaging their properties. The automobile workers, particularly the unemployed, felt the angriest about the importations, but were largely helpless against them. They had no organization through which to act, no power. Their anger was directed chiefly against the hill-billies.

There was then but one union in the automobile industry of any size, and this one of no great consequence—the Mechanics' Educational Society of America, an independent organization interested only in the "aristocracy" of automobile labor, the extremely well-paid tool-and-die men. It was part of the A.F. of L.

The A.F. of L. was pursuing the same tactics in the automobiles as in steel and rubber—only less energetically, for in Detroit and other motor towns there seemed no chance of any sort of great movement in the near future.

Yet some of the men who two years later became nationally known as leaders of the United Automobile Workers of America were already thinking hard what to do—how to do it.

Through 1934-35 I often had a strong feeling that a new labor movement built on industrial lines was bound to appear—in spite of and because of the A.F. of L.—in spite of and because of all the cunning that short-sighted employers applied to fighting unionism. It was only a matter of time.

Harry Bridges of San Francisco

BEFORE THE C.I.O. SUDDENLY BULGED INTO THE AMERICAN LABOR PICTURE, THE
Depression produced but one important rank-and-file leader—Harry
Bridges of the San Francisco waterfront. I met him in California in the spring,
1936, and then again in New York in the fall of that year. As I write this, his
future in America is problematical, for certain very powerful groups on the
Pacific Coast, in Washington, and elsewhere want him deported to his native
Australia on the ground that he is a Communist. But, regardless of what one
may think of his broader politics or of his specific acts, no picture of the labor
situation in the United States during the 1930's that did not include him would
be complete.

I might say at the outset that to me his personality and his career so far in
the United States are a bewildering amalgam of things that I consider admirable
or fortunate and of others that are questionable or even dangerous from the
viewpoint of basic America, and that tend to make his personality and function as a whole a puzzle and a question mark.

Bridges' father was a well-to-do real estate man of Melbourne, Australia. His
mother was an immigrant from Ireland. He was born in 1900 and christened
Alfred Renton Bridges, but twenty-odd years later, while he sailed on American ships, his fellow sailors renamed him Harry, which fits him better. As a
lad he did well in school and his father tried to turn him to real estate by
starting him in his early teens as a rent collector. But young Bridges was a
sensitive boy, reacting intensely to the poverty he observed on his rent-collecting
tours, and it soon became apparent he was not fitted for the real estate business.

His father was a conservative; through two of his uncles, however, who were
members of the Australian Labor party, he early developed—in conjunction
with his observations of social evils—radical ideas and feelings. At the same
time he craved adventure and desired to see the world, and became a sailor
before he was twenty. A tall, thin, high-strung but well-controlled young man,
he sailed mostly on American vessels for a number of years and was in two
shipwrecks. All through his journeyings he read a great deal.

Early in the 1920's he was in San Francisco, working on the docks and
interesting himself in waterfront union affairs. In the "shape-up"—the line
of dock-wallopers waiting daily at the piers for work—he listened to the men
complaining about their lot. Every once in a while his thin, sharp face would
go into a smirk and he would say, "Of course!" in a way that meant: "What
else can you expect under the circumstances, of which your own inadequacies
are a part?" Although naturally superior, he was one of these men, many of
whom drank excessively and fought and wasted themselves because they were
alone in the world and, living a formless, rhythmless life, considered themselves
(and, to a great extent, probably correctly) nothing but bums and toughs.

Bridges himself was a moderate drinker, but he spent much time in the diverse waterfront dives with the men, mostly to say "Of course!" when they "belly-ached." When he elaborated on that remark, he was often harsh and dogmatic in his pronouncements. Uttered by some one else in that cocksure tone of voice, his words would have provoked resentment and caused fists to fly; Bridges, however, could say anything he wished to the men. They knew he was honest; they sensed his intelligence. He could also see a joke and take part in plain, rough fun. He was a good worker, respected as such by his fellows and by the bosses. Early in the 1930's, just before his name flashed in the headlines all over America, he was one of the best winch-drivers in San Francisco, a member of the "star" gang of the American-Hawaiian Steamship Company.

Many waterfront unions, all A.F. of L. outfits, were out-and-out rackets, dominated by "gorillas" and grafters. *"Of course!"* The longshoremen's union did not amount to anything throughout the 1920's. *"Of course!"* Socially, humanly, the entire Embarcadero stank to high heaven. *"Of course!"* The Depression made things worse and worse. *"Of course!"* To be a longshoreman was not even equivalent to being a slave, for as a longshoreman you worked like a beast for twenty-four, thirty-six hours at a stretch, then you were in a state that you had to get drunk to go to sleep, whereupon you starved for two weeks or a month before you got another job. *"Of course!"* . . .

During the 1920's Bridges made two futile starts to build the longshore unions into a decent outfit. Once he failed because a union official absconded with the funds. In 1932 he tried again, and he and his rank-and-file group gained control of the organization. Within a year he had an almost model waterfront union, well-administered, democratically conducted. Bridges advised the men; they decided in open meeting, usually his way—and swore by him. By subtle indirect methods, he taught them how to live decent, effective, disciplined lives as individuals; how to be good unionists. He induced the men to read and study. He lent a hand wherever it was needed. As a union official he would take no more in pay than a longshoreman could earn on the docks.

By 1934 the union, which was a lodge of the International Longshoremen's Association, was a power. It made demands: higher wages, better hours, steadier work, abolition of the companies' "slave market," and the recognition of the union's own hiring-hall. Bridges was the organization's spokesman. The employers, following their usual habits, tried to buy him and were amazed when he could not be bribed. There came the strike, which then—under Bridges' masterful manipulation of the situation became a general strike, in which he acted as chairman of the strike committee. During the strike two men were killed and over a hundred wounded by the police under orders (*via* the Mayor and the chief of police of San Francisco) of panicky, ignorant, or brutal employers. The strike ended seemingly but, thanks to Bridges, not really in the workers' defeat.

Under his consistently shrewd leadership, the longshore union staged a "strategic retreat," agreeing to submit their demands to government arbitration. But week after week, as the arbitration dragged on, the shipowners and other waterfront employers lost ground; and the union's "retreat" was actually a great step ahead—the final National Longshore Award granted the men, essentially, all their demands.

The whole spirit of the waterfront changed. Competition for jobs at pierheads gave way to coöperation and solidarity. The longshore union membership increased from below two thousand to over four thousand, and the hiring halls distributed the work so evenly and fairly that all at once there were no unemployed longshoremen and the average wage was raised from about $20 to $37 a week, with opportunities to make, under greatly improved working conditions, as much as $200 a month. As one of the longshoremen put it to me, "We experienced the unaccustomed luxury of being men."

This stimulated labor in other crafts in San Francisco, and in many places it organized one hundred per cent; after which these and some of the old unions up and down the Coast under the leadership of Bridges and his associates formed the Maritime Federation of the Pacific Coast, which swiftly became a great and growing power. The federation spread to Canada and Hawaii, and its idea—that of industrial as opposed to craft organization for *all* sea and shoreside workers—commenced to excite the men in the Gulf ports. Committees called on federation officials for aid in setting up locals, and the organization spread to warehouse men, bargemen, and other workers on the Sacramento and San Joaquin rivers, while its prestige penetrated even to the agricultural areas. Rank-and-file leaders of rural migratory labor hit upon the notion that, since many agricultural products were shipped by sea and rivers, the agricultural workers' union should also be affiliated with the Maritime Federation. They looked forward to the time when organized maritime workers would refuse to handle or transport agricultural products not grown or harvested by organized field or orchard labor.

Nervous before, employers now—early in 1935—experienced panic, and their first thought naturally was: This man Bridges and his federation must be stopped! But how? Not a few people concerned with sea-shipping had interests also in river ports and boats and in vast ranch corporations; but while some of them unquestionably were nice enough fellows personally, few had overmuch intelligence or any long-range imagination. Functionally, in the business world, most of them were extreme individualists and opportunists, socially unconscious go-getters, lacking any sense of responsibility. Many engaged in cutthroat competition among themselves, distracting one another. They hated Bridges, but could not agree on any sort of plan by which they could get at him.

Meanwhile, under Bridges' direction, the I.L.A. union had developed subtly aggressive dock tactics, designed partly to keep the employers groggy and confused, but mainly to continue improving the men's job conditions. Bridges and other officials of the union believed in giving a fair day's work for a fair wage (they were satisfied that the wages now were good), and soldiering on the job was discouraged by them. On the other hand, they did not want men to over-work or work under unnecessarily dangerous conditions. So they instituted a system whereby every dock gang elected from among themselves a so-called gang or dock steward to look after their interests and act as their spokesman on the job. These stewards, always wanting something or protesting against this or that, became a great annoyance to the bosses. Some of their demands and protests were "unreasonable" from the employers' point of view, and as irresponsible from the viewpoint of the shipping industry as the employers were irresponsible socially. There were endless disputes, some resulting in "job action" on the part of workers or quick strikes ("quickies") localized to one dock. Suddenly, in the midst of unloading a ship, the longshore gang would walk off, causing the stubborn employer sailing delay, considerable additional expense, and general irritation.

The federal arbitrator ruled that while workers were obliged under the 1934 agreement to obey the employers, they could quit their jobs at any time, and that "quickies" were not breaches of the Award. Required by the Award to employ only union men, the employer called the union hiring-hall for another gang, which came promptly enough, but as likely as not pulled another "quicky" an hour later; and so on, till the employer yielded to, say, a demand that the slingload be made two or three thousand instead of four thousand pounds. There were also, during 1935, numerous outbursts of violence and fre-quent questions as to whether or not the ship to be unloaded was "hot," that is, had been loaded with cargo in another port by non-union labor or was manned by scabs. These fights were bitterest on docks operated by companies with strong banking and agricultural ties—the Matson Company, the American-Hawaiian Lines, and the Dollar Steamship Company—which were particularly antagonistic to the "Bridges union."

But the prestige of Maritime Federation and Bridges only increased. The newspapers called Bridges a Red, a Communist, an agent of Moscow, a sub-versive alien who ought to be deported, but the men only laughed at these appellations: "What do we care what he is! He's good for us, ain't he? He helped us to help ourselves. Our wages were raised, we work shorter hours; now we can marry, have a home, and raise kids. In the old days, if a long-shoreman married and had kids, his daughters likely or not became street-walkers; now they go to the university in Berkeley."

In November, 1935, the big companies, led by Matson and Dollar officials, determined to have a "showdown" and managed to create a loose united front among the employers, who promptly disagreed as to procedure. One faction was for cracking down on the I.L.A. union with vigilante terror and, if neces-sary, the National Guard. Another group felt such tactics would be unwise; there was too much sympathy with the men among the public. Finally, getting nowhere locally, they decided that this should not be merely a Coast fight but a national one.

On December 9th there met in the San Francisco office of the Waterfront Employers' Association representatives of all important shipping interests in the United States, but no definite decision was made then. Their conferences were transferred to New York and Washington. The United States Department of Justice was requested to investigate the waterfront unions, and newspapers in all big port cities began to harp on the communistic and subversive character of some of the seamen's and longshoremen's leaders. In these efforts the employers had the eager coöperation of numerous conservative A.F. of L. officials.

On December 31st Louis Stark reported from Washington in the New York *Times* that "employers on the Pacific Coast virtually have completed a coastwise vigilante organization to protect their interests in the event that they find themselves unable to obtain redress from the government should the international unions continue to be unable to discipline their Pacific Coast local unions. . . . The Pacific Coast owners are said to be in constant contact with the Atlantic operators . . . and well-informed sources indicate the employers are ready for a showdown."

On January 7, 1936, the representatives of all the important shipping interests reconvened in San Francisco and decided, at a date to be set later, to (1) repudiate publicly all agreements with the unions on the Coast on account of their "Communistic, irresponsible leadership," (2) deal with workers only as individuals, and (3) give this action at first a peaceful appearance by laying up for a while some of the ships, ostensibly because operation was financially impossible. In fine, the plan was to make the action a kind of semi-lockout.

On January 22nd shippers, importers, and exporters were notified that the long-planned semi-lockout would begin on January 26th. They were warned to clear up their business. But the Maritime Federation got wind of this and promptly exposed the plan. It called on the federal government to prevent "civil war" on the Pacific Coast waterfronts and charged that a nation-wide conspiracy existed among "waterfront employers, shippers, and allied financial interests to wipe out the Pacific Coast maritime unions," which, the statement said, "are run by their members, not by 'Communists.' It is a peculiarity of Pacific Coast maritime unions that officials must submit every action of the slightest importance to a majority vote of the membership. And that is precisely what the owners object to. They do not like democracy. They profess to admire Atlantic Coast maritime unions, where the members have absolutely nothing to say as to the functions of their own organizations. Obviously, this is the core of the whole matter: it is democracy the shipowners dislike; it is autocracy they desire. Because they do not like democracy they call it communism in an effort to obscure the real issue.

"Owners do not run the ships at a loss if they pay decent wages. Under mail-contract subsidies alone, shipowners received approximately $28,850,000 in 1935. This is more than the combined annual wages, subsistence, maintenance, and repair cost of the operation of all American-flag vessels on ocean mail routes, these costs amounting to $28,460,000 a year, according to the operators' own estimates."

This exposé, executed in the best Bridges manner, received considerable publicity in the liberal newspapers on the Coast; and the public's, but especially organized labor's, reaction to the planned lockout was against the employers. The plan was thus frustrated. The owners were outsmarted again.

It was early in April, 1936, and, enroute to Southern California, I stopped off in San Francisco and looked up Bridges. I had made an appointment with him three days earlier by long-distance from Sacramento.

In response to my knock Bridges opened the door in the thin partition that separated his dingy, windowless, four-by-six office from the rest of the vast and teeming I.L.A. headquarters on Clay Street, a stone's throw from the Embarcadero. "Sorry," he said quickly, "I've no time. I shouldn't be here now. I waited for you only because I promised you I'd be here and didn't know where to call you to cancel the appointment." Nonetheless, sliding into the rickety chair at his small roll-top desk, he invited me to sit down; then we talked rapidly for ten, fifteen minutes.

A slight, lanky fellow, with a narrow, longish head, receding dark hair, a good straight brow, an aggressive hook nose, and a tense-lipped mouth, he wears cheap clothes and is indifferent about his appearance.

The San Francisco headlines that morning told of a "plot" on the part of a member of the conservative element in the marine unions to kill one of the left-wing leaders, and Bridges—probably the hardest-working man in San Francisco—evidently was under great mental and nervous strain. His telephone rang every few minutes, and in the middle of our interview a man came in from the outer office to inform him that a worker had just been found slugged unconscious on a dock.

Bridges' replies to my questions were swift, brief, evasive; later I learned that on first meeting he is that way with everybody. Talking, he makes quick, irrelevant gestures with his hands, like a soda-jerker away from his counter. He looks anything but a longshoreman or labor leader. At first he does not strike one as a leader of any kind. He does not look at one directly, but takes short, sudden squints from under his brows. These squints gradually lengthen into glances, which then spread into a shrewd, scrutinizing look. Talk spurts out of him in a low, tensely controlled cockney voice.

For a minute or two I wondered: Can this man possibly be a strong leader? Then I could not help feeling that behind that jittery exterior, in that seemingly frail person, was a lot of deliberate power. He excited all my interest and I did my best to persuade him to explain himself, either then or later, in terms of his background and the influences that have played on his life. I said I would be in San Francisco again in a few days: would he have more time then and be willing to talk about himself? "No, no—sorry—it isn't only that I'm busy. I prefer not to be publicized as an individual. My personal background and life are unimportant. The movement is important, the situation; just now I don't want to talk about anything. Whatever I'd say might be twisted by our enemies and used to the detriment of the union."

His words were implied war talk. His philosophy, which vitalized his manner and attitude, was combative. He seemed impatient, and there was about him a suggestion of the conspirator who appeared to be struggling within himself to retain his none too certain energies till he could use them most advantageously to his purposes—whatever they were.

Having heard of efforts to get him deported as an "alien Red plotting to Sovietize industry and overthrow the government of the United States by force and violence," I asked him about his status as an immigrant. He said he was not worried about that: he had taken out his first papers and expected to get the full citizenship in due course.

We parted; Bridges hurried off somewhere.

A few days later, when an engagement required me to return to San Francisco, the *Santa Rosa* affair flared up, and I was given an opportunity to observe Bridges and his movement in action.

Throughout the early spring of 1936 the East Coast had witnessed numerous rank-and-file "quickies" or small outlaw strikes, which naturally had the sympathy of Bridges and the Maritime Federation of the Pacific, for they were directed mainly against the absolutist A.F. of L. semi-racketeers who were the officials of various seamen's and longshoremen's unions.

Early in April, Bridges' organization received word from New York that the Grace Line passenger-and-freight ship, the *Santa Rosa*, had left for Los Angeles and San Francisco in a "hot" condition. It seemed that the ship had been picketed in New York as "unfair to organized labor" and that she had signed on some scabs, whom the A.F. of L. seamen's union officials had supplied with union books just before sailing. This was all the information that the Bridges group had. They suspected a plot, although heretofore the Grace Line had had a comparatively good record, from their angle. They had been hearing rumors of "tricks" about to be played on the Bridges movement. The *Santa Rosa* was tensely awaited by the men. When she arrived, the Maritime Federation of the Pacific had a picket line at the pier. Everybody believed she was "hot." Crowds of men who were not authorized pickets came to the pier. The company called the hiring-hall for stevedores. The gangs came but as "good union men" refused to go through the crowd, which by then had begun to consider itself the picket line. Meanwhile Bridges and other leaders of the Maritime Federation officials were trying to find out the facts about the ship's temperature, but were not allowed aboard. A few of the crew came off, and one or two of them confirmed the report that there had been some irregularity in signing up the men in New York.

The Federation officials, including Bridges, held a conference and, deciding that their information was too slender to justify creating an issue in the already tense situation, called off the pickets and told the gangs to go and work the ship. But meanwhile—in fact, almost immediately after the gangs stopped at the Federation's picket line—the Waterfront Employers, as though prepared beforehand, issued an announcement suspending all relations with "Bridges' union" and ordering employers all along the front to (1) call for no more gangs from the hiring-hall, (2) summon back men then employed on uncompleted jobs, and (3) employ in the future only those registered longshoremen eligible to work under the Award who reported directly to the job.

A lockout, but badly messed up from the start. The union immediately denied that the men refused to work the ship. The hiring-hall again sent the gangs and was willing to send more. In fact, more gangs were sent, but the Grace Line superintendent turned them away. In brief, the owners found themselves fighting mad in a ring empty of opponents—a ridiculous situation which "drew the berry" from four thousand organized longshoremen and tens of thousands of their sympathizers in and outside the labor movement up and down the Coast. In their excitement and embarrassment the pugnacious organizers of the lockout forgot they were fighting Communism and said they were the sworn enemies of the union hiring hall. Then they discovered that was a "bum issue." The public at large was not against the hiring-hall. It was good for the longshoremen, good for San Francisco. Longshoremen were fanatically in love with it. Expressions of solidarity on the issue came from up and down the Coast, even from conservative labor officials who hated Bridges no less than the employers hated him. So, still more confused, the employers' leaders claimed they had been misunderstood: the hiring hall was not the issue. "We are opposed to its abolition," read one of their sudden statements. "We likewise are opposed to any change of the provisions of the Arbitration Award. We insist that every provision of the Award be strictly observed."

In short, there was no issue. Then they recalled that Bridges was a Red, a tool of Moscow, and blamed the situation on him. He had ordered out the Maritime Federation picket line. Which was not true, for Bridges never ordered anyone to do anything. All decisions in the Maritime Federation as well as in the I.L.A. local were made by the membership *en masse* or by elected committees. So the men laughed still more.

Meantime the lockout was an actuality. The *Santa Rosa* was not worked. The same was true of the majority of other ships in port when the lockout began. Scores of San Francisco-bound vessels were diverted to San Pedro and Portland, and, according to various estimates, the great port within the Golden Gate lost between a quarter of a million and a million dollars a day in wages and wharfage fees; for eight days, while Mayor Rossi issued frantic statements, the Embarcadero was quiet as a graveyard.

It was all a deep mess. The newspapers and the general public were bewildered. The whole situation resembled nothing more than confusion. The shipowners and other industrialists affected by the serious situation were beside themselves. They raged. Bridges, the dirty alien so-and-so, had outsmarted them again! And he could not be bribed (which of course was what really made him a dirty so-and-so)! They bombarded Secretary of Labor Perkins and Colonel MacCormack, the Commissioner of Immigration, with hysterical telegrams, demanding to have Bridges deported on the grounds that he was a Communist. Few owners were able to look at their predicament objectively and honestly, and see that it was due in considerable part to their own stupidity, which was a matter not only of this fantastic *Santa Rosa* incident, but pretty much of the entire history of capital-labor struggles in San Francisco, on the Coast, in the United States. Perhaps none could see that Bridges was as much a phenomenon of the capital-labor situation they had had a big hand in creating as he was a product of Marxist philosophy or of his background in the Australian Labor party.

For eight days, as I say, the San Francisco waterfront was paralyzed. The owners were mentally and emotionally paralyzed by their hate of Bridges, by the hurt to their egos, which were shot through with ignorance and confused fascistic, un-American tendencies. Bridges and the men maintained a distant, amused attitude, suggesting that the next move was up to the other side. On the ninth or tenth day the union hiring-hall began to receive calls for men again and the great port began to get slowly, self-consciously back to normal operations. The immediate results of the *Santa Rosa* incident were that the owners and the city, including the waterfront workers, had lost a good deal of money and that the prestige of Bridges' leadership had gone up many notches, making him potentially one of the most important figures on the Coast; while the employers felt groggy, sore, and foolish, wondering what they could do next to get rid of that so-and-so.

In the autumn, 1936, nearly all seaports and several lake harbors of the United States were totally tied up or seriously affected by a rank-and-file seamen's and longshoremen's general strike, which was directed as much against the selfish, autocratic A.F. of L. leadership of the old maritime unions as against the employers who supported (and had actively helped to corrupt) that leadership. The strike lasted over three months, costing the country as a whole hundreds of millions of dollars in trade turnover and wages.

In New York at the time, I had some contact with the shipowners and other waterfront employers, both as an organization and as individuals. They all fumed against Harry Bridges. The goddamn so-and-so! He had started this whole pernicious, communistic rank-and-file movement! They gathered in meetings, not to exchange views as to what might be done to end the strike or anything of that sort, but to curse and abuse Bridges while drinking cocktails and highballs. By and large, they had no idea of what the labor situation was, what had brought it about, except that they were. completely blameless in the matter. They were practically unaware of the fact that a new labor movement was painfully making its way into the life of the country, except that John L. Lewis, too, was a so-and-so, a fit sidekick for Franklin Roosevelt. . . . And the strike dragged on.

Then Bridges came East. His decision to come was evidently a sudden one, influenced by immediate developments in the maritime strike situation, and there was no advance publicity of his arrival. His first meeting, called on the shortest possible notice, was in the Olympic Arena at Philadelphia, where some fifteen hundred striking seamen, longshoremen, and sympathizers with the maritime strike gave him a rousing welcome. He explained why the Western sea and alongshore unions had levied a ten per cent assessment for their Eastern fellow strikers. "We on the West Coast," he said, "have a selfish interest in helping you win your strike against the shipowners. If the employers beat one union they beat all. We have learned that lesson." He described what unity had accomplished on the West Coast. "We longshore-men used to work for miserable wages. We were hired at the same degrading 'shape up' on the docks that you have here, or at company hiring halls. We had the speed-up you have here. Only twenty-two hundred men worked on the San Francisco docks in the days of the speed-up. Now forty-eight hundred men are needed to do the work and wages average thirty-seven dollars a week. Men are hired at union hiring-halls in rotation." This was exciting stuff to Philadelphia dock-wallopers, many of whom were jobless while others worked from thirty to forty hours at a stretch without rest. Exciting to them also was Bridges' statement that his union's hiring-hall in San Francisco was considering a plan to hire by radio. "Instead of coming to the hall for his job, the longshoreman would tune in at a certain hour every morning to get the radio call, telling him where to report for work. When no ship came in he could pull up the covers and go to sleep again."

Next day, Bridges was in New York most of the day. He called on his superior officer, President Joseph P. Ryan of the International Longshoremen's Association, who was also president of the New York City Central Trades and Labor Council and to whom he had previously addressed an open letter accusing him and most of the local I.L.A. union officials on the Atlantic Coast of virtual strike-breaking because Eastern longshoremen were handling "hot-ship" cargoes to the detriment of the seamen's strike. He was anything but welcome. Joe Ryan, in fact, hit the ceiling and, according to newspaper reports, called Bridges a "punk"; told him he had no business coming East, and auto-cratically discharged him as an organizer of the I.L.A.—obviously because Bridges had succeeded in organizing the most effective alongshore union in the country and was intent on making all other maritime unions as effective.

That same afternoon Bridges flew to Boston and in the evening addressed the marine and alongshore workers at a mass meeting in the Franklin Union Institute, also called on very short notice. The Boston *Post* reported the next morning that "a police stenographer present took the text of Bridges' speech [which was essentially what he had said in Philadelphia] but there was nothing un-American in the text that called for criticism." He talked Americanism, called for democracy in the labor movement as opposed to Ryanism and the increasing anti-labor tendencies of the A.F. of L., and encouraged the Boston longshoremen to turn their backs on the I.L.A. misleaders in the East and back the seamen's strike by refusing to handle "hot ships." He told them not to care if the old A.F. of L. autocrats called the strike outlaw, for it was they (the autocrats) who, keeping themselves in power illegally, were really outlaws. According to the Boston *Post*, the men "split the rafters with cheers for Bridges and other rank-and-file union leaders."

In New York sixteen thousand maritime workers and other rank-and-file unionists and their sympathizers came to hear him in Madison Square Garden. They paid a quarter apiece, which was enough to cover the rent and other expenses of the meeting. The rally was inadequately advertised and poorly handled by an inexperienced committee and a worse chairman, but none the less was very successful. The meeting was at least an hour too long but when Bridges, the last speaker, was finally introduced the sixteen thousand leaned forward not to miss a word.

Telling the story of what had been accomplished on the Coast, he made a profound immediate impression. Here was a man who wanted his fellow men to be men, not slaves or bums or hoodlums. . . . Less than a year afterward he became the head of the C.I.O. movement on the Pacific Coast.

But——

There are important *buts* in the story of Harry Bridges. As I write this, although there are rumors to that effect, I don't know whether he is, or ever was, a member of the Communist party on the Pacific Coast, either under his own name or under a *nom de guerre*. I don't doubt, however, that much of his inspiration, which helped him to do some of the things he has achieved, came not so much out of an understanding or love of basic America as out of Marxism, Leninism, Stalinism, the Soviet Union, and the Australian labor movement: which mean mostly violent conflict. Nor do I doubt that, throughout his career as a labor leader, his closest advisers have been members of the inner group of the Communist party on the Coast, whose middle name— like Bridges'—is Conflict. Therein lies the most important *but* regarding Bridges, which is apt to annul in the long run all the immediate results of his activity in 1933-36, which I approve. In view of what I have already said about the Communist movement in America, I scarcely need to elaborate on this to any great extent. Besides, I touch on this point, directly or indirectly, later in this book.

Here I want to say only this—that his Marxism—Leninism—Stalinism and his connection with the Communist movement, which is one thing today and another thing tomorrow, depending on the decisions of the Comintern in Moscow, will tend increasingly to complicate Bridges' position and embarrass and harm the C.I.O. movement, and is apt to overwhelm him eventually. His Stalinism has already—in 1937—caused him to take part in vicious persecution of so-called "Trotskyists" in San Francisco, and perhaps to neglect important matters in the trade union movement for which he, as the C.I.O. head on the Coast, must be held responsible.

His Stalinism—which is liable to be something entirely different (God knows what) in 1939 than it was in 1937—will, if he sticks to it, tend also to diminish his chances of developing into an American who will know that, while some struggle of course is inevitable, what is needed in America is less class consciousness and class war, and more social consciousness and social action. His Marxism-Leninism-Stalinism will handicap him in other ways. It will, in all probability, operate to make him more and more combative, rather than statesmanlike. It will make it difficult for him to realize that such democracy as he promulgates in his longshore unions on the Coast is scarcely embryonic; it does not yet include any developed sense of responsibility toward or for the industry. It will make it impossible for him to understand fully, and to appreciate deeply the importance of, the mood which pervades, I believe, the accurate content of the following letter which I received in mid-January, 1938, from a young and observant friend of mine, who is a middle-class professional man in San Francisco:

. . . The average San Franciscan is becoming fed up on unions and union tactics. There are pickets in every other block. They yell and scream, "Unfair!" etc. We don't even listen any more. To many people pickets are part of the scene, as are lamp-posts and water-hydrants. We are all so used to them. If we notice them, we often feel that the picketing is probably unjustified, anyhow. After all, when a janitor gets drunk over the holidays (as did the janitor in the building where I have my office) and lets his boilers go out and is subsequently fired, it is ridiculous that elevator operators should insist on a walkout and inconvenience thousands of people because he got drunk and laid down on the job and got his just deserts for it. How the devil can a standard of efficiency be maintained in anything when the union not only allows such things but actually condones them? . . .

This sort of thing can't last—even people with labor sympathies get tired of the continual unrest. I guess what most of us are chiefly interested in is to make a living in peace, not in the midst of war. I know that you have considerable regard for Bridges, but ceaseless unrest gets on our nerves; we want peace . . . and it is no wonder to me that more and more of the white-collar class is turning to fascism, although they don't really like that idea, either. Some feel: anything is preferable to this endless bellowing on the sidewalks, this labor violence and threat of violence. . . .

Not that I fully sympathize with every detail or the entire mood of this letter, but there is much in it worth pondering, especially, I think, for Harry Bridges. The same is true of the following lines which I quote from a letter written to me by another friend, who was for years pro-Bridges, and who lives in San Pedro, California, but makes frequent visits to San Francisco, which he loves:

. . . The long labor battle has lessened the charm of San Francisco. The streets are no longer as clean as they used to be; parts of the town are almost grimy. Prices are shocking; living is expensive for poor and middle-class people. . . . Of course I don't blame Bridges solely for this; he's just a part of the whole mess of things. I wish, however, that somebody would ask him if he realizes what is happening to our 'Frisco, which was once one of the swellest cities in the world. Not that all the charm of the place is gone; much of it is still left; in some way, 'Frisco is still one of the most pleasant towns—but people *do* tend to be cynical and "boxed-in" where they once were gay and hospitable. I've begun to notice this during the last year or so [1937-38]. . . . I wish somebody would ask Bridges where he thinks his communist ideas are taking him—and us, if we will let him. I think I am off him. . . .

It may be that his "communist ideas" make Bridges incapable of understanding, emotionally and intellectually, the situation suggested in these two letters. It may be that his Marxism causes him to dismiss middle-class opinion and reactions with contempt. If so, and if he cannot go beyond his "communist ideas," his future in America is not very bright. All his virtues as a labor leader, which he demonstrated in immediate results during 1933-36, will eventually be negated—and the number of important people in the C.I.O. who, I am informed as I write this, already regret that he was made the C.I.O. head on the Pacific Coast will increase, along with the efforts on the part of reactionary employers to have him deported.

Marxist tactics and attitudes can be effective in America only to a very limited extent. Mere combativeness has no long-range future; it works only now and then, for a while. And Americans generally don't like the conspiratorial manner in their public figures; they want the intentions and purposes of their leaders out in the open. Bridges' reticence about himself is irritating in a country where, through the press and the radio, the people are accustomed, as they should be in a democracy, to having the "low-down" on their leaders. Americans want to know one as a person, not only what one does after one does it. This is one of their democratic means of participating in government.

I have referred to Bridges' speech in Madison Square Garden in New York late in 1937. He made a good immediate impression, but when one thought about it, the speech was full of evasions, puzzles, deft little efforts to obscure himself as a person and leader. He persistently avoids public revelation of himself. Why? Why is ignorance of his makeup desirable? He does as little as possible to clear up his status. He neither affirms nor denies that he is a Communist. He is a force, but nonetheless an enigma. One can attempt to analyze him, but all manner of queries occur, which are not found answered or even suggested in all the mass of material printed about him. The radicals laud him; the conservatives are equally emphatic in denouncing him. All on what bases? . . . John L. Lewis, as I shall tell, gives one a feeling of intellectual vagueness because he is genuinely uncertain as to the future, and is reluctant to turn seer. Bridges gives the impression that he knows but is withholding his confidence.

Much emphasis has been given to Bridges' honesty. He cannot be bribed by corruptionist employers. Such honesty is rare, is commendable, but it is not enough. His intellectual honesty lies within a more uncertain light. Is he a thoroughgoing Stalinist "Communist," whatever that may be from time to time? Or is he only a sort of semi-Stalinist, a "fellow-traveler"? If he is one or the other, his intellectual, as well as emotional, honesty is circumscribed; that is, he will not look or see outside his convictions, which have already been formed. In the long run, democracy has no use for rigid, previously-formed convictions, which are shut to suggestion, or adaptation to the variable peculiarities of the American scene. Democracy wants fluid minds.

Cherries Are Red in San Joaquin

From My Diary—Stockton, California, May 27, 1936.—MAY IS A RICH, EXCITING month in the San Joaquin Valley of California. Vast hay meadows and lucerne and alfalfa fields wave and ripple high and ripe in the breeze. Asparagus and beets need hoeing. There are onions, peas, potatoes, carrots. And cherries are red and must be picked in a hurry.

Migratory workers come to the valley from all sides, on foot and in battered, sputtering flivvers; and for a month from eight to nine thousand of them, mostly men, toil seven days a week. San Joaquin in May has work for nearly everybody who wants it, but wages are meager, ranging from seventeen to thirty cents an hour. You work hard under the hot bright sun and, lest you faint, you must eat solid food at least once a day; and that costs money. Evenings, unless you are a Spartan or very old, you crave, if not a girl who charges two bits, a glass of beer, and you drink two or three glasses against your better judgment. Thus you spend from day to day everything you earn, just to keep going. Then, with the last days of May, the rush is over, and through most of June only about three thousand temporary workers are needed in the valley; the chances are that you move on, with five thousand others, as poor as you were in April.

San Joaquin has many small farms owned and run by little people, most of whom are nice enough folk as husbands or wives or as parents or neighbors, and probably in other ways, but apt to be hard with migratory workers. The idea of paying the hands as little as possible and working them as hard as possible is in the air. Besides, caught in competition with the big corporation farms and ranches, the little people are "up against it," and some cannot very well pay more than twenty-five cents an hour.

The big farms dominate—indirectly, but firmly—the valley's labor policy. They are owned by the big people in San Francisco and elsewhere, who are also in banking and shipping. Very often the land is leased, sometimes to Japanese; but in many instances the owners manage their farms, even if they happen to be big ones. Most operators, however, whether owners or lessees, turn the important work over to labor contractors or bosses. These contractors are Mexicans and Japanese, sprinkled with Americans and Italian-Americans, who, by and large, work on a shoestring. Petty would-be capitalists without money, trading in the energy and ability of others, they are bent of course on making as high a profit as possible. They have no labor camps or money for camps. Every morning between four-thirty and five-thirty they go into Stockton, the valley's principal city, and pick up a truckload of men, jamming as many as sixty or seventy into one truck. The trucks bring the men, ten, twenty, forty miles to the job, where they work an average of nine hours, and then are hauled back to town. They are paid only for actual time at work.

381

A few owner-operators have camps, but these are usually poor, showerless, unsanitary. Some bunk and board the men and profit in the process. One man with whom I spoke went out on a farm at two bits an hour and had to pay a dollar a day for board. He worked an hour in this field, two hours in that orchard, but received wages only for actual labor time—nothing for going from field to orchard—and on quitting collected $1.40 for three days' work. But his net earning was only forty cents, for he had paid an employment agent a dollar for the job!

In cherries, which is probably the most important business in May, the following system is generally in effect: The owner engages a labor contractor to pick and pack the crop. He furnishes ladders, buckets, and packing-boxes. He pays the contractor from thirty-five to forty-five cents a bucket for picking. The contractor goes to the so-called "Skidway" or "slave market" at Market and Center Streets in Stockton, hires the pickers at from twenty to thirty cents a bucket, and although his sole expense is that of running a truck or bus into town, makes from ten to fifteen cents on each bucket. The packing is a different process but is handled similarly.

At four-forty-five A.M. streets around the Skidway in Stockton are jammed with men—Mexicans, Filipinos, Italians and other immigrants, Americans from Oklahoma and Arkansas and probably every other state in the Union. Last night some of them looked like bums. They drank. Some drank on the curb pints of wine charged with "dynamite." Their life is generally low. Bums. Some slept in fifteen-cent flop houses or in the open, or spent the night in two-bit brothels. "Why not? What else is there to this life?" But now, quarter to five, with the rich California sun well up in the blue sky, none look like bums. They are sober. Workers. Thousands of them waiting to be bought off the curb for a day.

Huge trucks with trailers pull in. They are after men for beets. Two bits an hour. No, no more! Smaller trucks for cherry-pickers. Two bits a bucket. No, no more! One truck offers twenty-seven and a half cents a bucket. There is a rush. Fifty men climb aboard. The contractor needs only twenty. He picks his crew. The others climb down.

Most trucks and buses have no trouble filling up. But here is a guy—that is what the men call him—in checked overalls, a white man, an American, who calls out coaxingly to the dense crowd on the curb. "Royal Anns," he says. "Good pickin', no kiddin'." He looks around, waiting. "Some guys made four bucks apiece yesterday." "Yeah, them and who else?" retort two or three workers from the crowd. Others laugh. "Christ! I wouldn't horse you," says the boss. "Oh no!" the men roar. They "know" the guy. They "know" several other guys, but this guy especially, and some of the fellows tell him from the curb what they think of him and what he did to a gang of cherry-pickers a week ago. "Make it thirty-five cents and pay in advance!" He whines. He has two trucks to fill, wants sixty pickers. A woman in white pants who looks shyly at the men drives the other truck. She and the guy are working together.

She is the sex appeal in the racket. Her pants are tight, and her arms bare, and her blouse is thin and low in front, showing part of her loose breasts. "Come on, boys!" she cries, "pickin' is real good where we're goin' today, near Lodi." But there is something decent in her, and she is genuinely embarrassed before all these men—Mexicans, Negroes, Filipinos, Slavs, Italians, and Americans, young and old—some of whom wince and smile sheepishly before her. She is a dame: what wouldn't a man do for a dame? And so, hungry in more ways than one, a few of them jump on her truck. The guy wants more and gives her a quick, sharp look. "Come on, boys!" she cries again and gives a gay little jump on the running-board so her breasts bounce in her blouse. By five-thirty the guy fills both trucks at two bits an hour, and he and the woman drive off with their loads.

A worker still on the curb says, "Christ! we'll never stick!"—"The hell we won't!" says another worker. "This is their last trick. They gotta use women to get us."—"We gotta organize," says a third man. "Organize, organize—" The word goes around.

There is talk of organizing on the Skidway every morning. In the fields there is talk. Then, evenings, in the beer-joints, in pool halls, in flop houses, on the curb. The "stiffs" and "bums," as they call themselves, discuss what happened in Salinas, in Watsonville, in Santa Maria, where the Fruit and Vegetable Workers' Union won some demands in the lettuce and celery fields. They discuss the vigilante terror in Imperial Valley and the bloody riots in the fields at Venice and Dominguez Junction, near Los Angeles. There are arguments. Some one always says, "But you can't organize us! We're here today, there tomorrow. Bums. Tramps. Who'll organize us? The A.F. of L.? They don't want us!"—"The Reds want us."—"We don't want the Reds."—"We don't want no politics." "You don't, don't you? I guess you don't want more than two bits an hour, either, do you? And you want to work twelve hours and get paid for nine, do you? And you want to ride in trucks twenty, thirty, forty miles each way to the job and back, and have the guts jolted outa you, do you?"—"Oh, nuts! We don't want the A.F. of L.; we don't want the Reds, even if they want us. We just want to organize."

There is talk of Paul Scharrenberg, the A.F. of L. officer in charge of "organization" in agricultural fields for twenty years. "He did a swell job for the bosses. He didn't organize a single local."—"The hay-balers organized a coupla months ago, got a charter in Stockton, but the big shots in the A.F. of L. told 'em not to take in any field workers."—"Those hay-bailin' stiffs better take us in, because if they ever pull the pin on a job over chow or wages, you'll see what'll happen. A thousand stiffs will walk all over 'em and take their goddam jobs."—"They don't want us. They are A.F. of L."—"The top guys don't want us, sure, but we gotta talk to the stiffs, the rank and file. They'll take us in all right—if not right away, by and by."—"Aw, hell, we're just talkin'!"—"Sure, we're talkin', but stiffs like us never talked before like we talk now; not since the I.W.W. Stiffs like us are talkin' like this all over California, and there's close to three hundred thousand of us. That's a lot of stiffs, especially when most of 'em· are· talkin' the same thing. And what are we sayin'? Organize. We ain't got nothin' to lose and lots to gain. Look at those dock-wallopers in Frisco! Bridges . . ."

It is six-thirty, then seven-thirty; men are still talking on the Skidway; others are talking in the fields. At eight o'clock jobs begin to appear on the boards of employment agencies. Six men to hoe potatoes, seventeen and a half cents an hour. One hay hand, thirty dollars and board. You pay a dollar for the job.

John L. Lewis' Push to Power

IN THE MIDSUMMER OF 1936 I WAS STAYING WITH COLONEL MACCORMICK IN Washington, where, in his pleasantly air-conditioned office in the Department of Labor Building, I studied the alien and other immigration problems; and evenings we went somewhere for dinner and talked. The Colonel was an acute observer of people and events and wonderfully articulate and frank. One night I asked him if he knew John Lewis and, if so, what he thought of him.

"Yes, I know Lewis," he said, "and I like him. You should meet him. He is the only man who still stands out of that NRA mess." The Colonel telephoned to Lewis and arranged that we lunch together the next day.

The restaurant was a large, popular place in the center of Washington, frequented by the better-paid Government employees. When I got there a few minutes to one, the place was crowded and noisy. Was Mr. John L. Lewis there yet? I had to raise my voice for the headwaiter to understand me. "Mr. Lewis of the Miners?" he asked, eagerly. I nodded. "No, sir, not yet," he said then, and, taking me to the farthest table from the entrance, promised to bring him over when he came.

I watched the door over the guests' heads. Promptly at one Lewis—a big man in loose, dark, conservative summer garb—entered and followed the bustling headwaiter across the long room. A six-footer, broad, very broad, almost abnormally deep-chested, he seemed bigger than he actually is; and as he strode up the narrow aisle between two rows of tables nearly everybody looked up, many craned their necks and trailed him with their eyes, and the volume of noise and talk in the great room suddenly and noticeably diminished. Waiters paused in their hurry and stared at him. "There's Lewis!" I heard a voice exclaim in an excited whisper several tables away.

This occurred, perhaps, partly because the date was August 4th, when the executive council of the American Federation of Labor was meeting in the Gold Room of the Hamilton Hotel to decide whether or not it should suspend the unions forming the C.I.O.; and, as their leader, Lewis was in the headlines in Washington, as he was everywhere else in the country. But he had been one of the most discussed, looked-at, and sought-after men in the capital for months before that. Government officials from the President down, members of Congress, journalists, and private persons had been obliged to realize that Lewis was important not merely as an extremely astute and aggressive labor leader, but also, indeed especially, as a man of vast personal capacity and power and probably high political aspirations who—with the creation of a mass labor movement as his central and immediate purpose—was to be reckoned with as an all-around national figure.

"Big" is one of the first words that tumble into any description of the exterior of John L. Lewis. He weighs in the vicinity of 230 pounds, but, although in his late fifties as I write this, he has little excess flesh anywhere about him. At that age most men begin to slip into the shady side of middle-age; Lewis seems to have just reached his prime. His great body is a marvelously fit and efficient organism, all its parts working, clicking, integrated. Coming, as he told me at a later meeting, of a "long line of stalwart progenitors who bequeathed me a rugged constitution," and following "fairly rational habits," he does not know from experience what illness is and takes no exercise beyond walking and an occasional wide gesture as he talks. He watches his diet. Lunching with me, he had a lettuce-tomato-and-cottage-cheese salad.

He has been likened to a steam-roller and described as "thick" and "burly," but I think a trifle carelessly. "Tough," "ruthless," "domineering," "pugnacious," and "Napoleonic," also much used in journalistic efforts to characterize him, are better; while to "solid," "dominating," "formidable-looking," "vital," and "potent" not even his daughter and private secretary, Kathryn Lewis, a former Bryn Mawr student, who just then was disturbed by the other adjectives, could object. As a youth, working in an Illinois coal-mine, Lewis is said to have laid out an unruly mule with a piece of mine-prop timber, and he still carries a hard blow in his huge fist and is more agile than many a man half his age, as witness the quick, decisive outcome of his historic encounter at the 1935 A.F. of L. convention in Atlantic City with President William Hutcheson of the Carpenters, who is no pigmy or softy—which encounter, incidentally, was really the beginning of the C.I.O.

Lewis' head is the most impressive affair I have ever seen on top of a man's neck. No photograph, drawing, or painting of him that has come to my notice renders it entire justice. Alongside it, the average male head is something faint and inane. Lewis' head is round, massive, not unhandsome; newspaper men love to describe it as "leonine." Set on a short neck, it is harmonious with the rest of the body. The thick mane of dark, long, wavy hair is starting to gray. The wide, medium-high forehead is crossed by two deep, uneven lines immediately above the tremendous dark eyebrows, which, also turning ashen, curve shaggily upward. The wide-apart, lively blue eyes are capable of long-continued, deliberate calm as well as fierce, abrupt fire, probably no less deliberate. The not overlarge, firm-lipped mouth usually holds a ten-cent cigar. The clean-scraped jowls bespeak his fighting proclivities, as does the medium-sized, well-shaped, big-nostriled, and aggressive nose.

The whole face, with its firm, leathery skin and deep lines, which are no mere wrinkles, but what writers of Western yarns used to call "crags," is well-nigh symmetrical. It is a large, round, attractive face—when he wants it to be attractive. It can register every important human emotion, but seems most effective in wrath, scorn, contempt and bulldog tenacity; he has had more practice in that than in the softer, more pleasant, expressions. The face holds just a hint of incongruity. Above the nose it is the face of a philosopher, a brooder; below, that of a fighter, a man of action. The two are not fused or integrated. The fighter dominates the brooder.

Lewis' manner is seldom simply human. It is generally reserved, deliberate, official. I am told, however, that when it is simply human it is also simply superb. That occurs when he sits down with a few intimate friends—he has not many—and tells vivid tales of miners he has known. Which, I think, indicates where his human base is.

He likes to avoid clever people who are merely clever and has little traffic with cynics and the so-called sophisticates.

His voice, effective on the radio, is dramatic, with a remote rumble in the most ordinary talk, as though it were under rigid control lest it break into a roar—which it sometimes almost does, anyhow, even during lunch-time conversation, causing people at other tables to turn around. Very much the actor, he is closer to being an orator than a talker or speaker. His sentences often swing and roll redundantly, and surge and pound upon your ears with a sort of rough, elemental rhythm, as they did in parts of his first important nation-wide radio address, in the summer of 1936, for example:

"I salute the members of my own union as they listen tonight in every mining community on this continent. From the Warrior River in the southland up through the great Appalachian range to the island of Cape Breton, they listen. Across our parched midwestern plains to the slopes of the Rockies and the Cascades, and to the far province of Saskatchewan, they are at attention. To them, whose servant I am, I express my pride in their courage and loyalty. They are the household troops of the great movement for industrial democracy, and from their collective sentiment and crystallized power I derive my strength."

He seems to strive—unnecessarily—to impress. Often he is somewhat grandiose, ponderous, pompous, pontifical, bombastic; and one speculates: are the bombast and pomposity there to conceal self-doubt or some feeling of inferiority? Or are they the attributes of a demagogue? The answer is that that possibly was the case, in part, originally, but that, perhaps to a considerable extent, these characteristics also were, early in his career, just a phase of the manner of a typical union-hall spellbinder; now they hang on as a habit, a bit of personal atavism. Since the creation of the C.I.O., in his day-to-day function, he has probably been entirely free of self-doubt and feelings of inferiority or inadequacy. Headed for the future, he is cluttered up—as who isn't, more or less?—with his own past.

Every now and then, as he talks to one (seldom altogether frankly), his whole complex, powerful make-up seems to vibrate and blaze with ambition. For what? Those claiming to know him best agree that he is not interested in money. His wants are those of a middle-class man of modest, naturally disciplined desires and appetites, and he has passed up opportunities for great wealth. Does he want great power? No doubt. However, I think not mere power for power's sake. His ambition is no new thing. He has long wanted to become a national figure, for he doubtless is an exceptionally endowed man,

perhaps potentially even a superior man, a self-made man with great capacity
for growth and needing wide fields for his function. He has often been crassly
opportunistic in promoting his cause and brutal and unfair (at least from their
angle) to his opponents within the labor movement; but basically, as his friends
and daughter insist, he *is* a sort of idealist—not very clear in his idealism and,
American-like, maybe a little ashamed of it but at the same time seeking opportunities to practice it. Basically, he is of labor, a son of a miner who was blacklisted for union activity, a product of labor; and he is for labor and wants to
serve it, believing that by serving it he can best serve the country. Basically, he
is a patriot, conscious of labor's ability under his leadership to make a contribution to America's progress. However, he is also a great egoist. He wants to
stand out. These are the important elements of his ambition.

In many respects an exceptional man, yes; but also a deeply ordinary one.
He is pleased when *Fortune* gives him a long and respectful write-up and
dictates an appreciative letter to the editors in which he refers to himself—over
his famous signature that is a perfect diagram of all the bombast in his character—as "my humble self" and thus exposes himself to comments by the clever,
anonymous young men who write the articles in that most unordinary magazine. Only a very ordinary man would do such a thing. And he has a chauffeur in whipcords to drive him about in the twelve-cylinder automobile his
union bought for him: which is what every ordinary man in America would
like to have. When Lewis goes to the White House to see the President or to
the Capitol, there ride in that shiny car—vicariously—the four hundred thousand United Mine Workers of America, most of them ordinary men, common
Americans of old or recent-immigrant stock or naturalized citizens, full of the
instinct and impulse to improve themselves, to get on, to acquire the material
symbols of well-being, power, and progress that are the chief contemporary
elements of the American "Dream." That fine machine and the snappy cap
on the chauffeur's head are ordinary symbols, generally craved in America,
though rarely attained, and which, incidentally, are apt to be an important
source of Lewis' power in this country.

In a very real sense of that much misused phrase, he is a man of the people.
An ex-miner, he has risen "out of the bowels of the earth" to great prominence
by force of sheer character and ability, coupled with modern ballyhoo. Or we
can say that he erupted out of the great laboring masses and for this reason is
—in addition to what I have suggested in the paragraph immediately above—
naturally and intimately representative of the "hosts of labor" (his phrase),
who form a growing mass of the American nation and, amid great inner
wriggling and squirming, are beginning to realize that they are doomed to
remain workers. He is, moreover, a born, an instinctive leader, an unequaled
labor politician, a superb showman, adept at creating dramatic incidents and
at uttering picturesque, impressive phrases which result in publicity favorable
to him. He is thoroughly American in terms of current America. About the
time that I first saw him, Sinclair Lewis said in an interview printed in the

Daily Worker that "Cousin John [they are no relation] is going places," while
Dorothy Thompson speculated about him as "a man of destiny," and *Fortune*
announced he was "a looming force."

John Lewis was born in 1880 in an Iowa coal town called Lucas. His parents,
to quote his words to me, "were most superior persons, possessed of many
stern virtues." His father, who was of a long line of miners in Wales, joined
the Knights of Labor soon after he arrived in this country and became active
in that then great but—because of its romantic vagueness—already doomed
organization. The operators controlling the coal fields in that part of Iowa
blacklisted the elder Lewis as an agitator, and the family—which included six
sons, all miners—moved to a coal town in southern Illinois called Panama.

The oldest of the Lewis boys, John went to work in the mines at twelve and
his formal education, of course, was extremely scant. He was physically solid
and powerful, but inclined to be moody, restless, a rover. For ten years he
roamed the West, working in the mines, quitting, moving on, working again,
moving on, digging out buried miners or their crushed bodies, occasionally
picking up a book, newspaper, or magazine; looking for himself. Now he prefers to avoid discussion of "my years of irresponsibility," and even his family
and closest friends appear to know little about that period of his life. I think
that he himself considers it biographically unimportant. His daughter tells
me that every now and then, in one connection or another, he mentions having
been or done something or seen some one somewhere in Utah, Colorado, or
Wyoming back in 1898 or 1902, which is news to everybody.

In his mid-twenties John Lewis returned to the Illinois coal fields. Those
were the great, exciting days of John Mitchell's leadership of the United Mine
Workers of America, just before Mitchell began to drink heavily, decline in
prestige, and hasten his death, and young Lewis settled in the town of Panama,
where his brothers already controlled the local union.

In 1908 John married Myrta Edith Bell, a local school-teacher near his own
age, who was a country doctor's daughter, a quiet, serious, intelligent young
woman. Her sympathies were with the miners. She was interested in the
union and enhanced John's own bent that way. A natural orator, he began to
get up in union meetings and speak. Mrs. Lewis is said to have helped him
polish his early talks and made him rehearse them before her. But the theory,
which has crept into print, that she "made him" is, of course, an exaggeration,
as are most such rumors about prominent men. There can, however, be no
question that his wife has been a most beneficent and important factor in his
development. She was familiar with good books, the classics, which he read
and re-read with avidity after their marriage, and still reads. She doubtless had
also a subtle and generally refining influence upon him, of which neither of
them was aware.

Following his marriage, Lewis' progress in the labor movement was rapid.
In 1910 we find him lobbying for a workers' compensation act in Springfield,

the Illinois state capital, where he was so effective that he caught the shrewd eye of Sam Gompers. In 1911 he attended the convention of the United Mine Workers in Indianapolis. In 1912 he became an organizer for the A.F. of L., in which capacity he enjoyed the confidence of Gompers, traveled through many parts of America for four years, and learned a great deal. In 1916 he was made chief statistician of the U.M.W. and in that position did important work which was instrumental that year in increasing the miners' daily wages. In 1917 he became vice-president, and two years later president of the U.M.W.

Immediately on his assumption of the presidency he found himself leading, and under Government pressure suddenly terminating, a popular country-wide strike involving three hundred thousand men, which brought him some prestige among the more realistic sub-leaders of the U.M.W., as well as in the organization as a whole, but also set off a raft of enemies within the union, who, with diverse motives, started to fight him openly and secretly, helping mine operators and the generally critical conditions in the coal industry to make his life one continuous battle.

As Lewis now sees these men, some were motivated by personal ambitions. He gave me to understand that many of the older officers opposed him because they considered him a youthful interloper, and made common cause against him. Others, he suggested to me, came out against him, or worked surreptitiously to undermine his authority, at the instigation of coal operators or local politicians in the major parties; still others because he insisted on temperate conduct and sobriety; and some because they honestly differed with him on policy. Whatever their motives, for ten, fifteen years, they continued to accuse him of treason, of selling out the union, of graft, tyranny, strong-arm methods, and what not. Some hired private detectives to "get something on 'im," but none of their charges or suspicions were ever proved. Conversely, proof exists that they were unjust, although surface appearances occasionally substantiated their accusations.

Rival movements were started to ruin Lewis, even at the risk of ruining or seriously harming the U.M.W.; and one of these—the United Progressive Miners—became a serious problem in his life. The Illinois coal fields were a scene of veritable warfare for years, in which dynamite and gunfire were employed and hundreds of men, belonging to both sides, as well as mine officials and bosses, were killed or wounded, and millions of dollars' worth of property—bridges, railroad tracks, mine shafts, breakers, office buildings, and private homes—was destroyed. For years Lewis' life was in constant danger.

Lewis fought these men and movements with every means at his command, including some that may not seem wholly admirable, and, I think, earned the adjective "ruthless." He cried "Moscow!" and resorted to ordinary Red-baiting to dispose of honest opponents who differed with him on policy. In their struggle with rival organizations, local U.M.W. unionists doubtless employed violence, which he could have prevented or stopped. And he made himself virtual dictator of the U.M.W.

But in retrospect he appears more or less justified in nearly everything he has done—at least from his angle. What was his angle? By 1920 his whole life was tied up with the U.M.W., as Gompers' was with the A.F. of L. He belonged in it, to it, and in the American labor movement as a whole. His entire background was Labor. And as a natural leader, incontestably superior to others who aspired to high positions in the union, he could function in it, as he grew older, only as its head. Seeing the man today, it is impossible to imagine him in a subordinate position. He fought to stay in power. But he fought not only to enable himself to function as a superior man, a natural leader, but also for the sake of the U.M.W. as an organization and the "hosts of labor" in the mines generally. In fact, the latter purpose very likely was uppermost in his conscious mind. He believed—and, as it now seems, correctly —that he was the only man who could take the union over the hard bumps that the immediate future had in store for it; for Lewis saw after the war that King Coal was lurching into a great crisis, and that the U.M.W. needed strong, intelligent leadership capable of assuming responsibilities pertaining not only to labor, but for the industry as a whole.

He won.

By 1935 he was more or less a hero to the overwhelming majority of the U.M.W. membership. All his opponents were beaten. Some were dead or broken men. Not a few now recognize that he probably had been right most or part of the way, even in fighting them as he did; or else that recent events and developments, such as the NRA, which neither he nor anyone else had foreseen, have conspired to make his course appear right. Some of those who had honestly differed with him on policy offered to return to the movement and put themselves at his disposal, and he accepted them and gave them important positions, proving himself both big and shrewd: for some of them were men of long experience in labor activities. Of these the best known is John Brophy, an idealistic mine-labor leader and devout Catholic, whom Lewis fought savagely and drove out of the union in 1929, and who in 1936 became executive director of the Committee for Industrial Organization in Washington and then helped to bring back into the movement a number of Lewis' other old enemies who had "come around."

Lewis is not especially proud of his past. In 1937 he said, "I live for today and tomorrow. I will only say this: It takes every man some time to find himself in this world, to decide what he wants to do with his life. It took me longer than most people."

In 1930 the United Mine Workers were in a critical state as an organization apart from the intra-union struggles. Coal had been in a bad way long before the crash of 1929; the Depression laid it still lower; and although the union had "won" strikes during the 1920's and Lewis, by various cunning methods, had forced the operators into agreements seemingly very advantageous to the workers, there was little work, men became willing to mine coal for less than the union scale, and in the Harding-Coolidge-Hoover period the membership had declined by half from the 1919 peak of nearly four hundred thousand. The union treasury was low and by the beginning of the current decade Lewis himself was weary.

Then, almost in the nick of time, along came the New Deal, and Lewis and his assistants helped to write and push through Congress Section 7-a of the NIRA; whereupon he took full and brilliant advantage of it and organized, organized, organized, till by 1934 the U.M.W. had a greater membership and more money in the treasury than ever before. Lewis, in fact, as I have suggested in a previous chapter, was the one big labor leader who took entire advantage of the NRA period—and this, mark well, not only to restore his union in morale and numerical and financial strength, and himself to such prestige within the union that he is today by general consent its supreme leader, but also to make himself into a front-rank national figure. He had his eyes shrewdly on the future.

Lewis told me that if fate bid him to go again through a struggle such as he waged during the 1920's and early '30's he would hesitate to take it up. What gray hair he has he blames on those years. But that fight was invaluable to him. It had drilled and strengthened him in his natural realistic approach to things, sharpened his intelligence, and made him keenly opportunistic. In the 1920-32 period he had not missed—could not afford to miss—a chance to advance his cause. Constantly "on the spot," he had been required to know everything bearing on his and the U.M.W. problems better than anyone else, and had burned barrels of midnight oil, studying the coal business inside and out, in all its phases, till, when he appeared at a wage or arbitration conference or a government commission, he knew as much about the smallest details of the various companies' business as, or more than, their owners. He acquired the habit of thoroughness and developed an almost phenomenal memory. Even when the U.M.W. was financially low, he had never spared expense for research and reliable information. When he needed outside help, he had hired the best talent—for a while Charles Evans Hughes, who later became Chief Justice of the United States Supreme Court, was on the legal staff of the U.M.W. And so, when the Blue Eagle soared over the American scene and the coal code was being framed, Lewis made a terrific impression with his exact knowledge of coal economics and the social problems involved in the coal industry, as well as the circumstances of the individual companies, bituminous and anthracite, their production and financial problems, down to the business connections and managerial blunders of their officers and directors, and the names of their principal stockholders. Edward F. McGrady, then Assistant Secretary of Labor, with whom I discussed him, said to me that at the coal-code hearings Lewis was nothing short of amazing. He put to shame several operators, then heaped scorn on them, telling them and the world (for newspaper men were present) that they did not know their own businesses. In this he was aided by his lieutenant, Phil Murray, a vice-president of the U.M.W.

and an extremely able man, whose head is also crammed with inside information about the coal industry. Not a few operators had had a deep, if grudging, respect for Lewis before the NRA; others developed it now.

During the coal-code hearings there were memorable scenes which made Lewis into front-page news and a vivid labor hero. Perhaps the most sensational of these was when he denounced Patrick Hurley—a one-time mine-worker, later Hoover's Secretary of War, now boasting of his union card but selling his legal talent to corporations.

General Hugh Johnson became one of Lewis' warm admirers. Edward McGrady, who in those days spent much time with both of them, told me a story which, I think, throws a significant light on Lewis. One day they had been working on the coal code from early forenoon till late evening, when, tired and hungry, Johnson, Lewis, and McGrady were leaving the conference-room together and a passer-by, who knew all three intimately, remarked, laughingly, "You look like a trio of Napoleons after Waterloo!" At which Johnson and Lewis instantly perked up and, exchanging some words, discovered they were both old and passionate students of Napoleon, each owning a rare collection of Napoleonana. Suddenly forgetting their weariness and hunger, they became involved in a discussion of the battle of Waterloo, sat down, and in the next several hours used up a couple of large scratch-pads drawing maps with positions of the opposing armies, arguing why Bonaparte had lost and how he could have won. The next morning, before the coal-code hearings were resumed, Johnson presented Lewis with a rare Napoleonana item for his library. . . .

In addition to developing his memory, his capacity for work, and the habit of thoroughness, Lewis had learned from bitter experience during those years of stress in the U.M.W. two other, even more important, lessons. By the end of the last decade he realized that he had made, as he told me, "plenty of mistakes," but that "my greatest error was to believe too long that the innate fairness and sense of honor of the leaders of finance and industry would cause them to work voluntarily with labor for the solution of our great economic questions and problems of industrial relations." Simultaneously he had become convinced that his union, even with the best of leadership he or anyone else could give it, would· never be safe or really strong while the overwhelming majority—thirty-five out of thirty-eight millions—of American wage-earners were unorganized; and that that applied to· nearly every other great union in this country.

How to organize the unorganized? Through the A.F. of L. as it stood? Hardly—for craft unions, ruled over by reactionary dodos, predominated in the old Federation, while, with modern industry being what it was, the bulk of unorganized labor could be formed only into vast *industrial* unions, such as the U.M.W., which contained not only actual miners but *all* workers in and around the mines. None the less, as members of the executive council and delegates to A.F. of L. conventions, Lewis and a few other industrial-union leaders tried to bring the Federation around to their views. Speaking to me of this, he said, "Reading your labor articles in *Harpers* and *The Nation* in recent years, I have noticed your impatience with the A.F. of L., but, believe me, you, who were outside, were not half so impatient as I was, inside." The Federation as a whole and most of its member unions not only failed to take advantage of Section 7-a, but—as I have shown in this book—sabotaged or suppressed all important rank-and-file or spontaneous organization movements in 1933 and 1934, especially those in steel and rubber. The one exception was the Bridges movement on the Coast. This outraged Lewis, and doubtless he saw already at the beginning of the New Deal's second year that, to retain their recent gains, he and the U.M.W. would in all probability have to assume the leadership for industrial organization—and this, at least in the beginning, *outside* of the A.F. of L.

Being closest to coal, steel was of course the first industry to be tackled; and Pennsylvania being the center of the steel industry, Lewis—with great foresight (he practically admitted this move to me)—concentrated in 1934 on helping to elect George Earle, a New Deal Democrat, Governor of that state and Tom Kennedy, secretary-treasurer of the U.M.W., Lieutenant-Governor, so that, when the time came, the government of Pennsylvania would not help the industrialists to beat down the workers' organizing campaign as it did in 1919. This was a master stroke. In a speech at Homestead in the summer of 1936 Lieutenant-Governor Kennedy advised steel workers that in case of trouble the state would not allow any law officers "to interfere with the rights of the worker," and, moreover, that the men were assured of relief if mills closed down!

Knowing the personnel of the executive council and the whole A.F. of L. set-up as few men know them, John Lewis, I think, largely foresaw as far back as 1934 how things would turn out; and during 1935-'36 he handled his side of the rapidly developing situation with the sure touch of an experienced labor politician. At the Atlantic City convention in 1935 he put up a terrific fight for industrial unionism, knowing in advance he would be defeated, and during the debate knocked down the most vociferous champion of craft unionism, Hutcheson, who had called him an offensive name. This was big news throughout the country, causing intelligent workers to talk of the industrial *versus* the craft idea. The Lewis group then formed the C.I.O. and, in the spring of 1936, the Labor Non-partisan League. Lewis dramatically resigned from the executive council of the A.F. of L. and thereupon, from the outside, deftly maneuvered poor, little-minded Bill Green and his "colleagues" into splitting the American labor movement over the issue in such a manner the responsibility for the split was not on his but on their shoulders.

Early in 1936, too, Lewis and his group were behind the creation of the subsequently famous Civil Service subcommittee of the United States Senate, which, under the chairmanship of "Young Bob" La Follette began to investigate employers' terror methods in labor disputes, spreading authentic stories of professional "finks," "labor rats," and spies, strike-breakers and *agents provocateur*, and their relations with big corporations over the pages of many important papers in the country, exposing whole industries engaged in the manufacture and selling of weapons used in beating down labor. This was a masterful move, for it partly disarmed the terroristically inclined management of many an industry.

To return to my first meeting with Lewis, in the Washington restaurant in the midsummer of 1936—I said, "You must be very busy these days, Mr. Lewis."

"Yes," he smiled, "twenty-four hours a day is not enough. But every once in a while I sort of jerk myself up and wonder if I am not taking myself too seriously."

I said, "What do you mean?"

"Here we all are," Lewis continued, "you and I and the next fellow, everybody in this country, working, struggling, striving, scheming, pushing, joining hands in this effort and that, creating and releasing new forces: but what are our objectives—the objectives of our civilization?" He implied that collectively we were at sea without destination or compass; that some of us, perhaps, had some notion of what we were after from day to day, possibly year to year, but as for the long-range or ultimate aims of our civilization we were all rather blind, though apparently headed somewhere at a great rate.

I wondered: did he know I was interested in this question? Did he bring it up for that reason? Subsequently Edward McGrady, who has known Lewis for twenty years, told me that, "like every other sincere and honest labor leader, John broods a good deal, wondering where he is headed." Now here he sat opposite me, hunched over the edge of the little table, a sad, serious, curiously soft and, at the same time, intensely dramatic expression on his face. Was he acting? Maybe not; certainly not *merely* acting. As a public man he doubtless acted a little most of the time, had to act, but that expression was also genuine; it belonged on that face.

"Well," I said, "what *should* be our objectives—the objectives of our civilization? I mean: what should be the ideals and values of serious, sincere leaders in the various phases of our national life who are vitally concerned with the future of America? This is a big question, but blame yourself for it. I had no intention of asking it; you brought it up."

Lewis looked at me, silent; then his vast shoulders heaved in a slow shrug of deep puzzlement, his eyes opened big, and the front of his mouth filled with his tongue, which I did not know then was a sign he wished to change the subject.

I tried to make him search out his mind on the question by stating what I thought should be the general, long-range or ultimate objectives of a civilization: to afford people full opportunity to function according to their creative powers, abilities, instincts, and urges, as against the widespread ruin and waste of mankind that seemed to be among the outstanding results of the processes of "civilization" as we now had it.

Nodding, Lewis appeared to agree with this; but as he continued to be silent, I—still hoping that, since he touched upon it, he would have some ideas on the subject—went on something like this:

"Nowadays, Mr. Lewis, we are producing marvelous machines and erecting fine buildings; on the other hand, the masses of people—at least in the industrial sections—are becoming more and more hectic, jittery, unhappy, unhuman. By unhuman I mean unimaginative, individually or personally uncreative: for essentially, I think, we are human only to the extent of our imagination and creativeness. . . . The miner who still digs coal with his own hands is, in this respect, despite the dangers accompanying his job, comparatively well-off. He must use his wits, his imagination. He wrestles with nature and takes risks. He sees the fruit of his toil; he can touch it. He realizes that coal, for instance, if he happens to be a coal-miner, is important. He knows, too, that mining has a long and noble history. All of which gives him a kind of human satisfaction, an occasional good feeling about himself, apart from the wages he makes. In short, he more or less functions as a man. . . . But in this, I am afraid, he is almost exceptional among modern industrial workers, most of whom do not function as men or women while in their jobs; do not function imaginatively and creatively. Many are mere appendages to machines and do not see or know what they are doing. Most are in wrong jobs, working not to be doing something, but to be earning a few dollars; while millions have no jobs at all. But whether jobless or in work, their imaginative-creative or human powers or potentialities are not developed, are not being used; so those powers and potentialities fade, shrivel, wane, and die in them: which is to say, I think, that they—countless men and women caught in this so-called industrial civilization, as it now stands—die as human beings. They die, but are not buried. They walk around in various states of ruin, hollowness, and lopsidedness, mere shadows of themselves, or rather of what they could have been·if their human qualities and potentialities had been developed, encouraged, and used. Recent psychiatric researches indicate that between twenty and thirty per cent of persons employed in our industries and offices, from executives and superintendents down to laborers and janitors, or between ten and fifteen million grown-up persons, are 'daffy,' disbalanced in one way or another, afflicted with all manner of mental aberrations, roaming on the borderline between sanity and insanity. You have probably seen Charlie Chaplin in his film *Modern Times*. . . . Do you see what I mean, Mr. Lewis?"

"I follow you," he answered, then fell silent again.

"The problem," I said, "is how to stop this ruinous process and lay the base-pattern for a new, a real civilization."

Lewis nodded thoughtfully and said nothing.

I tried another tack: "I hear people say—in New York City and on Long Island, where I was recently, and elsewhere—that you're 'dangerous' and

'ambitious.' Now, I know that in the last fifteen years you passed up opportunities to become a great coal magnate, but I don't doubt that you *are* ambitious, in another way. You are endowed with certain qualities and abilities
which are vitalized by certain drives and compulsions within you, and you
cannot help seeking opportunities to function in line with those qualities and
abilities. But, seeking them, following your inner compulsions, you *do* seem
'dangerous' to some people. What do you suppose: why? What are you after?
If you do not see your ultimate objectives, or—for understandable reasons—
do not wish to discuss them in terms of the politics of your movement, what
are your more or less immediate aims? Wherein lies your 'dangerousness'—
and to whom? to what?"

The sad, brooding expression had suddenly and completely left Lewis' face
and he was a hard, practical man. "I can conceive," he replied, "that I may
look 'dangerous' to some people," and repeating my question "Why?" he
shrugged his shoulders and lifted his hands, giving me freedom to make my
own guess.

"As for long-range objectives," he continued, the expression on his face
sharply rebuking the philosopher and brooder of a minute before, "any consideration of them would necessarily be only an academic question, a matter
of speculation, which would not get us anywhere. There is, I think, little
point in blueprinting the future. Things happen out of their turn, unfore-
seen. . . . There are also reasons why I should not try to speculate about the
distant future." He knew I might write about him, partly on the basis of this
interview. "I really would prefer not to be quoted with particularity. After all,
the value to your readers of what you write will be the picture your eyes see
when you gaze in my direction."

"What you think and say," I countered, "is part of the picture."

"Have it your way," he smiled.

We talked for nearly three hours while waiters, as the restaurant emptied,
hung around our table to hear what Lewis was saying.

I asked him what he meant by the phrase "industrial democracy" which he
frequently used.

Lewis answered, in effect, that as things now stood big industrial employers
were so effectively organized and so single-minded in their profit-seeking that
in their relationship with labor, to say nothing with the public as a whole,
they were nothing short of dictatorial. Except in purely personal relationships
here and there between workers and bosses, there was in this country, which
boasted of democracy, little or no democracy in industry. Every mine, mill,
shop, office, or factory where labor was unorganized was a miniature dictatorship, and as such a subdivision of the super-dictatorship of finance capital,
which was in the hands of what President Roosevelt called "economic royal-
ists," who were totally undemocratic, un-American—indeed, *anti*-democratic,
anti-American—in their character, function, and political influence. With their
great economic power they threatened the very spirit and political pattern of

America. Under them, the country was in danger of actual fascism. In fact, fascism was a near-certainty in no far future unless the power of our economic dictators was speedily curbed by the establishment of democracy in industry. How? The initial step, which alone might do much to curb their power, was to win simultaneously the right for workers to organize, organize them, and establish the practice of collective bargaining. Labor must, first of all, make itself articulate through organization and win for itself the status of meeting the employers as their socio-economic equals in industry. "Now," to quote him directly, "comparatively small and few labor groups have that status and it is not safe for them as long as the great masses of labor lack it. We, the United Mine Workers, and the other unions now forming the C.I.O., are joined in this effort to achieve a mass labor movement with the collective bargaining status, as you know, not wholly unselfishly; in fact, very selfishly. On the other hand, now that, thanks to the NRA, we have a little extra strength, we also want to make a contribution to democracy in this country."

"Collective bargaining?" I said, doubtfully. "The collective bargainer aims to get something for labor out of the economic process; he is not responsible for seeing that it works. Is that enough? Will it stop at that? If not, what next?"

His reply to this was, in substance, that industrial democracy, like democracy in every other phase of a people's life, was something dynamic—a *process*. Once started, it went on from one objective to another. Collective bargaining, once won, would lead to other developments. Unions and individual workers would almost inevitably begin to assume responsibility in, to, and for industry. Sceptical as to this inevitability, I tried vainly to make Lewis elaborate.

"All right," I said—"industrial democracy: organization, collective bargaining, a process going from objective to objective; but, Mr. Lewis"—my mind was full of *buts*—"what do *you,* as the leader of this dynamic idea, want or expect in terms of social order or civilization? Industrial organization and collective bargaining are only the means, not the end or aim. To frame my question another way, if labor develops great organized power, what will it do—or what do you *hope* it will do?"

This returned us close to the question of long-range objectives, and for an instant he looked as though he would shake his head, unwilling to reply; then he said, "Recently a business man of my acquaintance asked me a similar question. 'If labor develops great power,' he said, 'can you guarantee it will not ruin the country?' I answered him, 'No one can guarantee the future; but I am certain that if labor does develop great power it cannot possibly make a worse mess of things than did big business in the last two decades, to go no further back in our history.'" He fell silent.

That probably disposed of the business man, but it was not exactly a positive answer so far as I was concerned, nor in keeping with Lewis' character as it appeared to me. He was evasive. So I said, "Very well. Let us not try to blueprint the future in detail, nor discuss involved political ideas and procedures; but is there not something in the average worker and in labor as a class to give us a positive faith in organized-labor power?"

This brought us closer to earth. Lewis opened up again, and I gathered that the basis of his faith in the future and in the masses of people, but particularly in the laboring masses, was the fact that nearly every normal person had in him an impulse, however confused it might seem at times, to improve himself and his circumstances and the conditions of others. That impulse was the propelling force behind democracy. It was, of course, especially strong in many people on the lower economic levels whom poverty and industrial labor have not yet dehumanized and unspirited. It must be organized, crystallized, made articulate. The average worker needed opportunity to get started on the way to self-improvement. That opportunity existed for him now only in organization, in labor unions. We had come to a pass in the United States where the once-a-worker-always-a-worker idea was becoming obvious. . . . Millions of American families had an income of less than a thousand dollars a year, while the minimum for a decent American standard of living was $2,500. Here, in these two figures, was the immediate problem that must be tackled. It was an economic problem. Industry, said Lewis, could well afford to pay wages so that every family's income would be $2,500 or more a year. Industry would not do so of its own accord. It must be *made* to do so. "And," he added, "our job here in the C.I.O., as I see it, is to contribute something toward making it do so. . . ."

After a pause he continued, "You ask me what I want or expect. Speaking very generally, I want to see created social sluices or chutes through which the benefits of civilization will come down to every man, woman, and child in this country according to their needs. Let me illustrate what I mean. Along comes a new invention which makes production cheaper, more efficient. As things now stand, the masses do not benefit from the blessings of that new invention. Only a few profit by it. The invention now throws people out of work; working-hours are not lowered, nor wages raised. I want to see a change so that everybody will benefit from it." Lewis believes that if he does something to bring about that change he will have made his contribution to democracy.

"But, Mr. Lewis," I went on with misgivings, "suppose American labor does develop great power—will there not be danger of a kind of labor fascism in this country? And I do not ask this because John Frey"—head of the Metal Trades department in the A.F. of L. and a member of the executive council—"recently called you a Mussolini; I am worried quite apart from you, or even in spite of you. . . . You say your idea and movement are dynamic. So is life generally, so is history; yet here are Hitler and Mussolini who, at least for a while, have stopped the march of history in their respective countries and created a furious sort of stagnation; in fact, a regress into history. You talk of collective bargaining and industrial democracy; there is a wide gap between the two. The latter may be defined as the operation of economic units in the

interests of all; the former may be little more than irresponsible pressure, a
sort of tyranny-by-force-of-numbers for the sake of wages and other mainly
material gains on the part of workers, or their representatives, regardless of the
other problems of a real civilizaiton, which, you will grant, is not a matter only,
or even primarily, of wages. . . . Is it not possible that a labor movement such
as yours might be satisfied too long with mere collective bargaining, or get
stuck in that status too long; for our American working-class is made up of
individuals who, true enough, have the impulse to self-improvement, but that
impulse, I think, is limited in all sorts of ways. The workers are partly corrupted by the go-getting psychology of our business class, mainly materialistic
in its values, and, like people in other classes and groups, badly confused and
full of fears, to say nothing of the widespread 'daffiness' I mentioned awhile
ago (which, of course, is not restricted to industrial and office workers, but is
probably even more serious among the farmers and the idle rich). In other
words, though I do not like to say so, I believe that not a few individual workers, in common with Americans of other classes, carry in them unprogressive,
unliberal, undemocratic tendencies; and, if I am correct, will not those tendencies when organized—organized, naturally, with their other tendencies—be
dangerous, unless something is done to remove or reduce them simultaneously
with the organization of a great labor movement and the bringing about of
collective bargaining? . . . You will probably agree that, unlike labor in some
of the European countries, where workers have been exposed to half a century or more of education along social, economic *and cultural* lines, our
American workers—like our labor leaders and like Americans generally—are
for the most part illiterate and unoriented so far as politics, economics, culture, and social responsibility go. Don't you think that your job as leader-
organizer of the new labor movement is not merely to organize but also—
and, perhaps, especially—to teach?"

Lewis replied slowly, "I think I know *some* of the things a powerful labor
will do. The virtue of some of them will be questioned by many who enjoy
special privileges." He paused. " 'Labor fascism'?" He paused again. "Naturally,
I cannot bond the purity of motive or the administrative rectitude of the labor
movement of the future. Serious mistakes may be made every step of the way.
We are not perfect; not by a long shot. Labor has its shortcomings. All sorts
of things may occur. It is all a process. . . . To the last part of your question
my answer is: workers' education is, of course, a great need, but then, every
real and sincere labor organizer is also, and inevitably, a teacher."

He added that in the campaign for the organization of steel labor which
had begun in July of that year his own function, so far, has been mainly educational, but he admitted that that education, for the time being, was limited
to the value of organization to workers in terms of concrete and immediate
material advantages. He evidently had not yet given much thought to the
rest of the education that workers needed, but appeared to believe that workers' education was also a process, one thing leading to another. He implied

that labor might gradually develop the impulse to self-education along with a consciousness of responsibility to and for industry, civilization, and order.

No Marxist, Lewis shuns the term *class struggle*, but is for the "have nots" waging organized, not mere guerilla, warfare simultaneously on the industrial and political fronts against the "haves" who function so that the former cannot improve their lot. This war, he seems to believe, is essentially not unlike military war. He is a student of war—specializing, as I have suggested, in Napoleonic campaigns—and in discussing labor movements, campaigns, and battles of the past, he often breaks into military phraseology. He told me, for example, that the trouble with the old I.W.W. organization, in his opinion, was that "it never attempted to consolidate or perpetuate its gains. It continually bled itself white by the vigor of its struggles and was always vulnerable from the rear." I gathered that one of his efforts would be to make the C.I.O. unlike the I.W.W. in this respect, as well as in some others.

No Marxist, as I say, Lewis is not against capitalism *in toto*; he wants it controlled, not abolished. He intends, as he told me, to have a law which will provide for the licensing by the federal government of every corporation. Capital now is wild, irresponsible, unsocial; he means to "subdue" it. He wants an organized labor that will be in position to put pressure upon Congress and the President for anything it wants, "within reason"; and by its strength and importance cause the Supreme Court to think long before it gives a decision unfavorable to labor's interests. Lewis believes this sort of pressure to be democracy.

Beyond that, as I have shown, he has no objectives, but has a hunch he is on the right track, linked to the processes of progress. To an interviewer before me he had said that his thinking was "American, unhampered by dependence on the requirements of any philosophy." He has a general direction and is pushing on through the murk, not knowing what is ahead, except maybe a little more light. The politician in him, who is ambitious both egoistically and idealistically, sees in the murk not far ahead of him the outline of a building that seems to be the White House, wherein is the switch, he thinks, for more light to dispel the murk. At odd moments he broods about the future, but normally dislikes to discuss it. The practical man in him, always in control of the leader and public figure, insists that to talk of the problems and situations that may confront America two, five, ten, twenty years hence is "idle speculation, mere imagining." In this, as in many other respects, he is, although the son of an immigrant, a one-hundred-per cent American, functioning in America.

He is a big man, vaguely tremendous, a compound of all sorts of qualities and several tendencies, right and left and center. I believe he has no real notion of the possibilities of human life on this continent, but, brooding, he wonders where he is headed and if he is not taking himself too seriously. There is no doubt that he possesses a great capacity for growth. He has a sense of responsibility and, as I have said, *is* an idealist, but is also a fiercely ambitious man of action. His values are mainly quantitative, rather than qualitative; material, rather than spiritual. His æsthetic sense is not highly developed; ugly things do not disturb him. His past, with which, as I have said, he is heavily cluttered, was a matter of struggle for personal power, for better wages and hours: for material aims. He has been more or less conditioned by that struggle. He does not know, not *really*, that the economic question is actually but incidental to the general human problem; that the economic question must be solved mainly, not for itself, but in order that we may then be free and able to begin tackling other, more fundamental, more serious predicaments in which we find ourselves.

This chapter is not an attempt to give a complete picture of Lewis or a diagram of all the motives and forces behind the C.I.O. It is, for the most part, but a suggestion of how he and the C.I.O. appeared to me personally in 1936. The few ensuing chapters of this section will suggest some other things about him and his organization; only suggest, for the essential story of the C.I.O. is more or less in the air as this book nears completion. Besides, during the writing of this volume about a dozen books, good and bad, dealing with the C.I.O. have been published, which the reader is free to peruse if he is eager for details and analyses from various angles. More such books are certain to appear during 1938 and later. Here I want to quote a few notes from my Diary as I wrote them after my two meetings with Lewis in 1936. The second meeting occurred, also in Washington, early in October.

THE DANGEROUSNESS OF LEWIS

August 7, 1936.— . . . I think that Lewis *is* on the right track, and I am generally for him, but—*but* ——

He is also a dangerous man—and this not so much from the viewpoint of the capitalists and the idle rich who now stupidly hate him, as from the viewpoint of those who, like myself, believing that he is on the right track and linked to progress, now support him and the C.I.O. . . . I believe he is apt to create a great labor organization which, operating on the industrial and political fronts, will ultimately force up wages and lower working hours as far as they will go without ruining the industries within the frame of capitalism; will keep industries from over-expansion and spread out purchasing power; and will thus probably lengthen the business cycle and shorten the periods of depressions when they come. But I fear that, being the sort of man he is, that is about all he will do. He is against fascism—fascism run by capital—but, without wanting to, he is liable to become the leader of a kind of labor fascism whose principal long-run function and achievement will be that of saving capitalism from itself and pushing the American people deeper into a life based on, and revolving mostly around, narrow materialist and quantitative concepts.

Lewis [as already said] has a great capacity for growth, and, judging by my talks with him, it is possible that as a man and a leader he will grow mentally along with acquisition of power and responsibility, but my hunch is not to bank too much on that. I think that liberal and progressive writers and editors who of late have suddenly discovered that Lewis is a sort of Lenin and Lincoln rolled into one man should not cheer and praise and "yes" him indiscriminately as the white hope of the American working-class and of America. The big C.I.O. push is on, and hereafter, I think, it will be wise for liberal and progressive journals and writers, as well as his colleagues within the C.I.O. and the officials of the C.I.O. unions, to contemplate Lewis critically, with the idea that the big man, no matter how right he may be momentarily, perhaps needs in the long run to be saved from himself, if he is to help save America. . . .

LEWIS AND ROOSEVELT

October. 4, 1936.— . . . I asked him [Lewis] what he thought of Earle and Roosevelt, and for a while he was reluctant to say anything. I sensed he was not sold on either man, at least not completely. I said, "But for your support Earle might not have been elected Governor of Pennsylvania in '34. Now you're supporting Roosevelt. Neither of them is exactly a proletarian." Finally he suggested that he was not placing all his bets, if any, on such men as Earle and Roosevelt. I pressed him to come to a point, and he said, "Roosevelt only serves to hold the fences *until*—" I did not ask him until when; it was obvious that he meant until labor under his leadership was able to take them over.

I had a feeling, too, that Lewis does not like Roosevelt personally. This, if it is so, is not surprising. I have never met Roosevelt, but I can well imagine that the two men are very different and far apart in their mental and emotional processes. Of course this may mean that in all likelihood Roosevelt does not like Lewis, either. For the time being, they are using one another. Roosevelt is holding the fences for Lewis, who is momentarily helping him to be reëlected so that he can hold the fences. . . . I understand that the United Mine Workers and other C.I.O. unions have given vast sums for Roosevelt's campaign, but Lewis will not be surprised if after election Roosevelt's passion for labor cools all of a sudden.

LEWIS, C.I.O., AND THE "COMMUNISTS"

October 7, 1936.—Lewis, I think, has dipped into *Das Kapital*, but believes, as he says, that Marxism, which "grew out of conditions in Europe and may have had applications there," has no place in America. Back in 1928-30 he fought the "Communists" who were trying to take over his U.M.W. unions with every means at his command. He called them "Com'yoonists" and he denounced the Soviet Government and the Third International. . . . Now, as head of the C.I.O., however, Lewis is not anti-Marxian, but merely *un*-Marxian, apparently believing that Marxists have, in the very nature of things, no chance in the United States, and hence it would be pointless to fight them. He says he is willing to work with anybody who is willing to work with him.

I don't know how wise he is in this. Time will show.

The Sitdown and the Swift Growth
of the C.I.O.

S IMULTANEOUSLY WITH THE SUDDEN AND DRAMATIC APPEARANCE OF THE C.I.O. ON
the American scene a new word—*sitdown*—came into general usage in the
United States. It described a powerful new weapon invented by rubber workers
in·Akron, Ohio, for use by them in their struggle for better working conditions.
At first the word was hyphenated—*sit-down*—, but by and by numerous newspapers reporting the use of the weapon printed it without the hyphen. The
workers themselves did not give a hoot how anyone wrote it. Nor were the
managers and superintendents of the great rubber factories interested in its
spelling. When one of them remarked to me late in the spring 1936, "We
wish to hell we'd never heard it," he expressed the sentiment of them all. I
decided to spell it *sitdown*, for it impressed me as a definite word, which might
soon be as important as *walkout, lockout, speedup, stretchout, sellout,* and other
such expressions born of one of the basic, most dangerous realities of the times—
the economic conflict between capital and labor, between the haves and the
have-nots.

The word, I was sure, would eventually get into dictionaries, and I was
curious how the successors of Sam Johnson and Noah Webster would define
it. I have no standing as a lexicologist, but I attempted a definition in my
Diary:

October 22, 1936.— . . . SITDOWN, *n.* Act of quitting work in one or a few
departments of a delicately organized mass-production factory with the aim of
stopping operations in the entire or most of the plant; specif., such an act done by
mutual agreement ·by workers in one or a few departments of such a factory as
a means of enforcing compliance with demands made on their employers; sudden
strike by workers in one or a few departments of such a factory, decided upon
and called by themselves while on the job, usually without the sanction of any
recognized labor-union leader or official and, as a rule, of short duration, the
strikers and the rest of the workers remaining idle (sitting down) by their machines or belt conveyors pending the compliance with their (the strikers') demands.
See STAY-IN and QUICKY.

Which was not wholly adequate and was meant to be tentative, for the full
significance and the application of the word were as yet not clearly established.
In spite of the fact that *sit* was the base of its· construction, it was an extremely
dynamic, active, and pregnant word—in the fall of 1936 still busy acquiring
new shadings of meaning and giving birth to synonyms.

Although my standing as an etymologist is no greater than it is as a lexicologist, this chapter is intended to be, in part, an etymological study; so let me

proceed with the history of the word—the circumstances of its origin, so far as known, and its development during 1936-37.

During the 1920's and later much was written, in America and in Europe, about the rapid "robotization" of labor in mass-production industries. Various alleged students of the worker "on the belt" concluded that he was rapidly ceasing to be a normal human being; he was helpless, docile, machine-like. I, myself, inclined to that view, which, to an extent, was true. But much written and said on the subject was exaggerated. As Charlie Chaplin suggested in *Modern Times*, all the manhood was not stamped and squeezed out of the industrial workers—and most certainly not out of the rubber worker in Akron.

The rubber worker in Akron may be a hillbilly from West Virginia, or a mountaineer from Tennessee or North Carolina, or a husky Negro from Georgia or Alabama, or a Pole, a Croatian, a Lithuanian, an Italian, a Hungarian, or a native Ohio or Pennsylvania farm boy, or a young man with high-school education born right in Akron. During the boom years, 1910 to 1929, when his productivity increased three hundred per cent, he made, besides millions and millions of automobile tires and mountains of other rubber goods, one hundred and twenty millionaires.

With the 1929 Crash thousands of rubber workers left Akron for their native hills of West Virginia and the states further south; some of the foreign born returned to their old countries or moved elsewhere in the United States; other thousands went into the queues in front of relief offices. But tens of thousands stayed. Those who retained their jobs lived in fear of losing them. When the New Deal came along, the accumulated discontent found an expression in unionization, which, as I have shown, was obstructed and inhibited by the A.F. of L. in every way possible. During the middle NRA period, however, an aggressive and intelligent rank-and-file movement developed which ultimately overcame the A.F. of L. "organizers," forced them out of Akron, and took over the United Rubber Workers of America, which soon became one of the healthiest unions in the country and an important member of the C.I.O.

The rank-and-file movement in Akron really got under way in a curious and peculiarly American way. The story goes to the effect that one Sunday afternoon a couple of baseball teams composed of workers employed in two big rubber factories suddenly refused to play a scheduled game because they discovered that the umpire—to whom some of them objected, incidentally, also as a person and an umpire—was not a union man. The players just *sat down* literally, some on the grass, others on the benches beneath the grandstand, while the crowd, consisting mainly of workingmen—partly "for the hell of it" and partly in seriousness—yelled for an umpire who was a union member, cheered the NIRA, and generally raised a merry din, till the non-union umpire withdrew and a union man called the game. It is said that the expression "sitdown" was first used in the discussions that followed that game.

Not long afterward a petty dispute over a point in working conditions developed between the workers and the superintendent of a department in one of the great rubber factories. The superintendent would not yield and, annoyed, made an indiscreet remark which angered the workers in question; about a dozen in all. They had been on the verge of dropping their demand or complaint, whatever it was; now, remembering the sitdown at the ball game, one of them blurted out, "Aw, to hell with 'im, let's sit down!" And they sat down.

In a few minutes several other departments of the extremely complex and delicately organized production process in the factory, which employed seven thousand men, were in a mess. What had happened? The question was asked all over the plant. The answer quickly spread through the place: There was a sitdown in such-and-such a department! A sitdown? Yeah, a sitdown; don't you know what a sitdown is, you dope? Like what happened at the ball game the other Sunday!

Hundreds of workers who did not know what the sitdown was about but who belonged more or less to the rank-and-file element experienced a thrill. A sitdown in the plant! Well, what do you know! In no time the most important departments of the factory were at a standstill. Thousands of workers sat down. Some because they wanted to, more because everything stopped anyhow.

And sitting by their machines, caldrons, boilers, and work benches, they talked. Some realized *for the first time how important they were in the process of rubber production*. Twelve men had practically stopped the works! Almost any dozen or score of them could do it! In some departments six could do it! The active rank-and-filers, scattered through the various sections of the plant, took the initiative in saying, "We've got to stick with 'em!" And they stuck with them, union and non-union men alike. Most of them were non-union. Some probably were vaguely afraid not to stick. Some were bewildered. Others amused. There was much laughter through the works. Oh boy, oh boy! Just like at the ball game, no kiddin'. There the crowd had stuck with the players and they got an umpire who was a member of a labor union. Here everybody stuck with the twelve guys who first sat down, and the factory management was beside itself. Superintendents, foremen, and straw bosses were dashing about. They looked funny, these corporals, sergeants, and shavetails of industry. Telephones were ringing all over the plant. This sudden suspension of production was costing the company many hundreds of dollars every minute. . . . In less than an hour the dispute which had led to the sitdown was settled— full victory for the men!

Walking out of the factory gates that evening, the men laughed. They told the night shift about it. The thing got into the Akron newspapers. It was in the Cleveland papers. There was no little talk about the affair, most of it perhaps, to the effect that the sitdown was a good joke on the factory management. The rank-and-file leaders, some of whom were more or less leftist, others mainly inspired by the New Deal and its Section 7-a, did their best to keep the talk going. They reiterated that, as had been demonstrated by the sitdown on the baseball diamond and the sitdown in the factory, workers could get somewhere only collectively, by sticking and working together. The thing to do was to join the unions. Many did join and new federal unions were organized.

Some of the leftist rank-and-filers, free-lance agitators without authority from any union, whom the employers called "trouble-makers," began to encourage sitdowns. Working in various departments in the several Akron rubber plants, they subtly organized sitdowns when disputes arose. As a result, there were scores of sitdowns, some lasting only an hour or even less, others several hours or most of the day, running into the next shift; and a few stretching over two, three, four, or more days, thus becoming "stay-ins."

Some sitdowns tied up production only in parts of a given factory, others paralyzed the whole plant. When the sitdowns became longer, the men sitting in their working places took to whiling away the time by playing cards or checkers, telling yarns, singing, or reading. Some of them simply stretched on the benches or on the floor and went to sleep. When a sitdown ran into the next shift, the incoming workers relieved the old shift and did the same thing —sat, talked, sang, played cards or checkers, and slept on the floor—till the dispute that had produced the sitdown was settled; or else they gave their dinner pails to the sitters-down and went home—which made the sitdown a stay-in.

Of course, like the original sitdown, several sitdowns—perhaps a majority of them—in the Akron rubber plants occurred without encouragement from any rank-and-file organizer. They were sudden, spontaneous affairs, springing out of immediate conditions in a department.

Nearly all the sitdowns were effective, winning the demands of the men who started them. So far as I know, during 1935-36 only one or two fizzled out. The men in other departments almost invariably backed the initiators of the sitdown. Why? Let me give a list of the virtues and advantages of the sitdown as a method of labor aggression from the point of view not so much of the rank-and-file organizer or radical agitator as of the average workingman in a mass-production industry like rubber.

1. The sitdown is the opposite of sabotage, to which many workers are opposed. It destroys nothing. Before shutting down a department in a rubber plant, for instance, the men take the compounded rubber from the mills, or they finish building or curing the tires then being built or cured, so that nothing is needlessly ruined. Taking the same precautions during the sitdown as they do during production, the men do not smoke in departments where benzine is used. There is no drinking. This discipline—of which more in a moment—is instinctive.

2. To say, as did a New York *Times* reporter, writing from Akron in January 1936, that the sitdown "resembles the old Oriental practice of passive resistance" is a bit far-fetched, but it probably is a sort of development of the old I.W.W. "folded-arm" strike and of "striking on the job"; only it is better than the latter, which required men to pretend they were working, and to

accomplish as little as possible without being discharged, which was more fatiguing than to work according to one's capacity, as well as contrary to the natural inclinations of many of the workers.

3. The sitdown is the reverse of the ordinary strike. When a sitdown is called, a man does not walk out; he stays in, implying that he is willing to work if——

4. Workers' wives generally object to regular strikes, which often are long, sometimes violent and dangerous, and as likely as not end in sellouts and defeat. Sitdowns are quick, short, and free of violence. There are no strike-breakers in the majority of instances; the factory management. does not dare to get tough and try to drive the sitting men out and replace them with other workers, for such violence would turn the public against the employers and the police, and might result in damage to costly machinery. In a sitdown there are no picket-lines outside the factories, where police and company guards have great advantage when a fight starts. The sitdown action occurs. wholly inside the plant, where the workers, who know every detail of the interior, have obvious advantages. The sitters-down organize their own "police squads," arming them—in rubber—with crowbars normally used to pry open molds in which tires are cured. These worker cops patrol the belt, watch for possible scabs, and stand guard near the doors. In a few instances where. city police and company cops entered a factory, they were bewildered, frightened, and driven out by the "sitting" workers with no difficulty whatever.

5. Most workers distrust—if not consciously, then unconsciously—union officials and strike leaders and committees, even when they themselves have elected them. The beauty of the sitdown or the stay-in is that there are no leaders or officials to distrust. There can be no sellout. Such standard procedure as strike sanction is hopelessly obsolete when workers drop their tools, stop their machines, and sit down beside them. The initiative, conduct, and control of the sitdown come directly from the men involved.

6. The fact that the sitdown gives the worker in mass-production industries a vital sense of importance cannot be overemphasized. Two sitdowns which completely tied up plants employing close to ten thousand men were started by half a dozen men each. Imagine the feeling of power those men experienced! And the thousands of workers who sat down in their support shared that feeling in varying degrees, depending on their individual power of imagination. One husky gum-miner said to me, "Now we don't feel like taking the sass off any snot-nose college-boy foreman." Another man said, "Now we know our labor is more important than the money of the stockholders, than the gambling in Wall Street, than the doings of the managers and foremen." One man's grievance, if the majority of his fellow-workers in his department agreed that it was a just grievance, could tie up the whole plant. He became a strike leader; the other members of the working force in his department became members of the strike committee. *They* assumed full responsibility in the matter: formed their own patrols, they kept the machines from being pointlessly destroyed, and

they met with the management and dictated their terms. *They* turned their individual self-control and restraint into group self-discipline—which probably was the best aspect of the sitdown. *They* settled the dispute, not some outsider.

7. Work in most of the departments of a rubber factory or any other kind of mass-production factory is drudgery of the worst sort—mechanical and uncreative, insistent and requiring no imagination; and any interruption is welcomed by workers, even if only subconsciously. The conscious part of their mind may worry about the loss of pay; their subconscious, however, does not care a whit about that. The sitdown is dramatic, thrilling.

8. All these factors were important in the early sitdowns. In addition, in Akron there was toward the end of 1936, when I became seriously interested in the phenomenon, the three-year-old tradition that when a sitdown began anywhere along the line of production everybody else was to sit down, too. And while I am explaining the men's solidarity in sitdowns, I must not forget also that the average worker in a mass-production plant is full of grievances and complaints, some of them hardly realized, and any vent of them is welcomed.

9. The sitdown is a purely democratic action, as democracy is understood in America within the capitalist system. It is pressure action. It is a bit anarchic, which also helps to make it truly American. It is pragmatism: anything is more or less all right that works, or that you "get away with."

10. The sitdown is a social affair. Sitting workers talk. They get acquainted. And they like that. In a regular strike it is impossible to bring together under one roof more than one or two thousand people, and these only for a meeting, where they do not talk with one another but listen to speakers. A sitdown holds under the same roof up to ten or twelve thousand idle men, free to talk among themselves, man to man. "Why, my God, man," one Goodyear gumminer told me in November 1936, "during the sitdowns last spring I found out that the guy who works next to me is the same as I am, even if I was born in West Virginia and he is from Poland. His grievances are the same. Why shouldn't we stick?"

Of course the sitdown and stay-in were not purely American inventions and weapons. So far as I am aware, the first European stay-in—that is, since the sporadic and anarchic "revolutionary occupations" of factories by Italian workers between 1919 and 1922, which were partly the pretext for Mussolini taking power—occurred in a coal mine in my native Carniola in July, 1934, which was followed by one in a coal mine in Poland a few months later. Both succeeded in winning the demands of the men. But the first brief sitdowns are said to have occurred, and were so called, in Akron's rubber mills nearly a year before that. They all ended in prompt victory for the workers. Only a few of them were extended into short stay-ins, which also succeeded. In the United States before 1937 the majority of sitdowns were in Akron, although many occurred in other industries; in Europe, stay-ins—which of course began with sitdowns—became one of the central realities in the socio-political life of at least one country, France.

The sitdown situation in Akron reached a kind of climax in February 1936 with the sitdowns and stay-ins in two of the big rubber factories which resulted in a prolonged and bitter strike that closed two of the plants for weeks. These events were extensively reported in European labor papers, especially in those that circulate among rubber workers; and it is believed that these reports at least partly inspired the great sitdown on March 22, 1936, in the Semperit rubber works at Cracow, Poland, which led to a bloody strike—six killed and twenty wounded—that received wide publicity in Europe, particularly in France. The Akron dispute of that winter ended in a kind of agreement between the management and the newly organized United Rubber Workers of America, but sitdowns continued. As the rank-and-filers put it, "They put teeth into the agreement." During the spring—or, to be exact, between March 27 and June 13—there were nineteen known sitdowns in the Goodyear plant alone; how many others that never received notice, no one knows. These frequent sitdowns in the American rubber capital continued to interest the European labor press; and it is not to be wondered at, perhaps, that among the first workers in France to greet the Front Populaire with sitdowns and stay-ins late in May 1936 were the men in the French plant of the Goodrich Company at Colombes, in the Seine district, and that one of the toughest nuts the Blum government had to crack in June was the stay-in at the Michelin rubber works.

I do not mean to suggest that the sitdown and the stay-in were purely the inventions of the Akron rubber workers of the early 1930's which were then picked up by European labor, but rather that they were mutually, or shall I say instinctively or *elementally*, invented by industrial workers who were confronted by more or less the same problems.

I have mentioned the Italian "revolutionary occupations" of factories just before Mussolini. But similar things had occurred in various parts of the world, including America, before that; only there was as yet no name for them. Sitdowns, as we would now call them, happened during the construction of Brooklyn Bridge. At the dawn of the twentieth century French railroaders stopped their trains for fifteen minutes every day for several days till certain demands were granted, and incidentally caused Aristide Briand, who was unable to stop these sitdowns, to be laughed out of the premiership. Some while later the Argentine railroad men invented a method, which was close to the sitdown. They "worked" strictly according to rules, which prevented operation of the roads, as no railroad anywhere in the world, I am told, can be operated if all rules are obeyed literally. According to Arthur Keep, editor of *The Railroad Telegrapher*, who gave me most of the rest of the information contained in this paragraph, American railroad men have long "indulged" in sitdowns, the most recent of which occurred on March 1, 1920. At one minute past midnight on that date the Shore Line road between Toledo and Detroit posted a bulletin abolishing the eight-hour day and other rights granted during the war-time Federal control, whereupon all engineers, firemen, conductors, and other trainmen refused to work while staying on the job until the notice was withdrawn. In the late 1900's the I.W.W. invented the already mentioned "folded-arms" strike, which was practically the modern sitdown; and the anti-capital method known as "striking-on-the-job," which I describe in *Dynamite*. In 1906 three thousand I.W.W.'s closed down eight General Electric plants in various parts of the country, but this action received very little notice because just then the country was in the grip of a great coal strike. Something very close to a stay-in occurred in the Amoskeag textile mills at Manchester, New Hampshire, during a labor difficulty in 1922. . . . It cannot be denied, however, that the Akron rubber workers have developed and improved the sitdown and put it on the socio-economic map of the United States.

In Akron in 1936 a week seldom passed without one or more sitdowns. The local newspapers noticed only the more serious ones, those which developed, or threatened to develop, into stay-ins and close-downs. A typical one took place on November 17, when I was in Akron, in the huge Goodyear No. 1 plant. After an inconclusive argument with the management over an adjustment in wage rates, ninety-eight workers in one of the departments sat down, stopping the work of seven thousand men for a day and a half, at the end of which period the company promised speedy action on the adjustment.

Officials of rubber companies, with whom I talked, were frantic in their attempts to stop the sitdowns. They blamed them on "trouble-makers" and the union movement in general. They tried to terrorize union sympathizers. The Goodyear management, for instance, assigned two non-union inspectors to a department with instructions to disqualify tires produced by known union men. After pelting them with milk bottles for a while, the men sat down and refused to work till the inspectors were removed. The company officials rushed in forty factory guards with clubs, but a sixty-five-year-old union gum-miner met the army at the entrance and told them to "beat it." They went—and the non-union inspectors were replaced.

Akron sitdowns were provoked by various other causes. In the early autumn of 1936 S. H. Dalrymple, president of the United Rubber Workers of America, was beaten by thugs employed by a rubber factory, whereupon the factory workers sat down in protest, forcing the company to close for a day. When work was resumed the next night, a K.K.K. fiery cross blazed up within view of the plant. This caused the men to sit down again—and to despatch a squad of "huskies" to extinguish the cross.

In the automobile industry the earliest known sitdowns, called "quick strikes," occurred in the Auto-Lite plant at Toledo soon after the bloody 1934 strike. The idea is said to have come from Akron, for the rank-and-filers of the two towns were in close contact. Most of these sitdowns were settled quickly and in favor of the workers.

In 1936 sitdowns were also frequent in and around Detroit, most of them in unorganized plants or unorganized departments of partially organized plants. Ordinarily, although many of them were well executed, they were not planned in advance. Some "just happened." Even where the workers were organized, the sitdowns had an element of spontaneity; they seemed an instinctive revolt against some particularly vexing condition—too much speedup, too low wages, or the like. They were usually organized on the job or during lunch and represented the crystallization of weeks or months of dissatisfaction. A noteworthy fact was that most sitdowns in the automobile industry occurred in body plants, where the nature of the work—painting, polishing, sandpapering, heavy lifting, and so on—was more disagreeable or arduous than in other shops, and the wages were lower.

During the first three weeks of November, 1936, sitdowns were pulled almost daily in different departments of the Briggs Manufacturing Company, where conditions of work were particularly poor and irregular. Two or three groups of welders sat down on different occasions for more wages and promptly received raises. The trim division sat down one night around midnight demanding a ten-cents-an-hour boost. Then other departments joined in asking raises, till about fifteen hundred workers were involved; increases ranging from five to thirty cents an hour were granted.

In the partially organized Fisher Body plant at Atlanta, Georgia, union members staged a sitdown to force the management to meet their committee to negotiate an adjustment in wages. They would not resume work till the committee went into the office.

In mid-October, 1936, the Chrysler plant in Detroit was the scene of an interesting sitdown staged by the metal finishers in protest against the speedup. The company pacified them by eliminating seven "jobs" per hour and adding four men to each of the two production lines in the department. Late in '36 similar sitdowns occurred also in Packard, Hudson, Dodge, and General Motors plants.

In the Hudson plant a rather amusing and significant thing happened on the hood line. One day, by placing the hoods closer together on the line, the management increased production from 140 to 160 an hour. The men figured that the increase of twenty was one-seventh of normal production and, amid laughter, skipped every seventh hood, which immediately messed up production ahead of them. The hood-line superintendent raged at first, then, helpless, went back to 140. This sort of partial sitdown—similar things occurred in other plants—was called a "skippy." When I was in Detroit, I heard a rumor that successful skippies have been pulled even in the Ford plant.

Sitdowns were most effective in mass-production industries using the conveyor system, but they took place also in other industries. The great 1936 seamen's strike, which I have mentioned in connection with Harry Bridges, began—at least on the East Coast—with sitdowns on scores of ships, which extended into stay-ins, which in turn developed into a big strike.

In Hollywood a group of girl extras sat down because casting directors were hiring Santa Barbara and Pasadena society girls at "scab wages." They were supported by such well-known players as Jack Benny, George Burns, and Gracie Allen, and directors found themselves forced to restrict their hiring to legitimate extras.

On December 1, 1936, there was a sitdown at the Libby-Owens-Ford glass factory in Ottawa, Illinois. A few days before that a long stay-in began at the Midland Steel Products Company in Detroit, which affected production in the Plymouth, Chrysler, and Ford plants.

It was obvious to me that the sitdown and the stay-in were most significant as extremely practical devices adopted by labor to promote unionization. Both the United Rubber Workers of America and the United Automobile Workers of America doubtless owed their growth in the latter half of 1936 partly to them. Two or three years before, the rubber rank-and-file organizers had brought many a federal union into existence or to numerical strength with the aid of sitdowns, which, as I have hinted, were more eloquent arguments for organization and collective action than any speech by the best labor leader. The federal unions, as already told, were subsequently for the most part destroyed by A.F. of L. "organizers" sent to Akron for that purpose, and in September, 1935, when the newly formed United Rubber Workers held its constitutional convention, there were only about three thousand organized rubber workers in America out of a possible one hundred thousand. The strikes in February, 1936, however, and the numerous successful sitdowns and stay-ins during the spring shot that number up to thirty thousand by June. In November I was told in Akron that nearly every serious sitdown boosted the membership by as much as five hundred. Organizers signed up men while they "sat" . . . and at this writing, early in 1938, U.R.W. are over seventy-five thousand strong.

Through the late autumn, 1936, sitdowns played a major role in the organization of automobile workers. Here is a report and analysis of an organized "organizational sitdown" on November 13th at the Fisher Body Plant No. 1 in Flint, Michigan, given to me by an organizer:

There was no organization in the plant. Flint is a General Motors center, once well organized but organization has disintegrated. This, plus the fact that the town is thoroughly controlled by G. M. and full of stool-pigeons, has made it particularly difficult to organize. Organization was carried on quietly through home meetings, personal contact, and contact with the key men in the plant, but with no real success.

On the 13th five men who had been working actively though quietly for the union were discharged. They found their cards "pulled" when they came to work. These men were in the body-building department, employing about seven hundred.

The most active union man, not among the five dismissed, had been prepared for this and had other workers interested in organizing posted at strategic places along the line.

One man questioned a foreman about the five discharged men. There was an exchange of words. Then the foreman took the worker by the arm, saying if he didn't like it he could leave, too. The above-mentioned leader, seeing this, stopped the foreman, told him if anybody went everybody would go, gave the signal to his key men, and within one minute all work ceased.

A committee went to the management, demanded the return of the five men, refused to accept promises that they would be returned on Monday, insisted they be reëmployed before they themselves would resume work. The management had some difficulty in locating all the men, and the division was "down" four and a half hours before they were finally returned.

The leader of the sitdown, an excellent strategist, dramatized the incident to the utmost, using it not only as an instrument to protect workers against discrimination but as an organizational weapon. In the manager's presence he took a vote of the men on whether or not they would resume work before the men were returned. The vote not to resume work was unanimous. After the five men had been located, he asked each of them to stand on a bench and testify in the presence of all that the union was responsible for getting their jobs back.

This sitdown cracked Flint wide open. That night and the next day five hundred workers joined the union. Since then they have been signing up at the rate of one hundred and fifty a day.

At about the same time the unionized workers in the Bendix plant at South Bend, Indiana, started a sitdown to overcome the threat of a company union. The sitdown became national news. It overcame the threat.

For reasons suggested or implicit in this chapter many of the rank-and-file automobile and rubber workers, as well as many of the organizers in the field and some of the people in the offices of the rubber and automobile unions, thought the world of the sitdown when I asked them about it. The top leadership of these unions, however, like the responsible leaders of the C.I.O., seemed to view it with misgivings. Some did not know what to think of the "damned thing," as an Akron leader called it. None went so far as to fight it, but to some of them it looked like "dangerous business" in the long run even if now it helped to organize unions. They at once liked and feared it. Some feared it, perhaps, because it deprived the regular labor official of much of his authority; others because the sitdown was too spontaneous and seemingly haphazard. Too anarchic. It threatened to play the devil with the collective-bargaining idea.

John Brophy, director of the C.I.O., sent me early in December, 1936, no doubt with the approval of John Lewis, the following careful, politic statement with permission to quote it as his view in an article on the sitdown I was writing for *The Nation*:

We do not condemn sitdown strikes *per se*. We consider that various kinds of labor activity will be used to promote organization of workers and establish collective bargaining. Sitdown strikes, under some of these conditions, may be a very necessary and useful weapon. In the formative and promotional stage of unionism in a certain type of industry, the sitdown strike has real value. After the workers are organized and labor relations are regularized through collective bargaining, then we do urge that the means provided within the wage contract for adjusting grievances be used by the workers. It is only in those instances when there is a failure of the workers to exercise the means for adjustment provided in the agreement that we disapprove of sitdown strikes. Sitdown strikes, in my opinion, occur when the employer fails to meet in full the requirements of collective bargaining.

It seemed to me that the leaders of the C.I.O. and its member unions had not yet clearly thought out, in all their aspects, either the importance or the possibilities of the sitdown. Fearing it, some of them were trying not to destroy it but to dull it. There was a C.I.O. representative in Akron who gave interviews about "disciplining" workers who had a tendency to use sitdowns.

To me, all this looked a little silly: for, going around the country and watching the sitdown develop, I saw that it was an elemental thing, a manifestation of the modern industrial worker's rebellion against the existing economic system's plot to turn him into a machine less important than the actual machine he operated. The weapon *was* dangerous, but I felt it was bound to be used. It was not only that some of the leftist rank-and-file leaders found it conducive to organization, but that the workers found it *exciting*.

During the autumn of 1936 I met several important, though at the time as yet little known, C.I.O. leaders in Washington, Pittsburgh, Akron, and Detroit. I watched the development of the sitdown as a weapon and as part of the organizational technique. In September and October I observed that the C.I.O. drive was largely halted as a favor to President Roosevelt, who was pro-labor, so as not to complicate his campaign for reëlection. By mid-November the C.I.O. push was on again, and I heard that steel workers were signing up at the rate of only two thousand a day because the Steel Workers Organizing Committee, under the leadership of Lewis' friend, Phil Murray, did not have enough organizers and clerical assistants to sign them up faster! A steel strike was almost a certainty. A considerable element among the auto workers was wild for "action," which meant strikes. Rubber seemed tensed to a point where it might snap. The seamen's strike was on. Harry Bridges came East. There were riots and killings in connection with the agricultural labor troubles in California. The Newspaper Guild, headed by Heywood Broun, was intensely active. There were stirrings among other white-collar workers. The entire country was on the verge of tremendously important events, the immediate center of which appeared almost certain to be the sitdown strike. I felt that the C.I.O. leadership would be compelled to accept it as a weapon and a method. . . .

By the end of November I developed within myself something very closely akin to a neurosis about the situation. I could think of almost nothing else. I lived in New York, and during the day I rushed out every hour to get the latest editions of the various newspapers. Evenings, though terribly tired, I could not go to sleep. I had to wait till the next day's *Times* and *Herald Tribune* came out at eleven-thirty o'clock, then read them till one or two in the morning. This intense consciousness of the situation, coupled with near-certainty of imminent developments (especially since I was thinking of starting to write this book), was such a strain that early in December I seemed on the border of a breakdown. I was compelled to "get away from it all" for a while . . . and sailed for Guatemala on the S.S. *Musa*, whose master was my friend, Captain George H. Grant, who between tours of duty on the bridge writes books on his sea experiences. Under George's kind supervision, I slept for two days solid, then sat in the sun——

Part of January 1937 I spent in the ancient ruined city of Antigua, which I more or less describe in *The House in Antigua*. I became absorbed in its story, which to me was a sort of journey in time, and which is bound to make anyone who studies it a bit philosophical. Occasionally I listened on the radio for news broadcasts from the United States, where there was evidently great excitement. The auto strike had begun! Sitdown! Was steel to be next? Rubber? Detroit seemed beside itself. The whole country was in jitters. The C.I.O. push was really on in a big way. The seamen's strike continued. John Lewis was started toward becoming the most important personality in the land. Industrialists were reacting with fascistic tendencies. . . . But, no doubt partly because of the influence upon me of Antigua, which is a most quieting town, I was not excited. The events in Detroit *were* important, to be sure. The sitdown was everything I had expected it to become. The C.I.O., apparently, continued to grow by leaps and bounds—too fast. All of which was important. But not all-important, not ultimately decisive in America, or in any phase of America's life. All this was eventually to find its place in the story or picture of the country as a whole. My geographical distance from the United States, my not seeing the sensational headlines, and —most important of all—my journey-in-time *via* Antigua helped me to have and hold a perspective on these events in America and on America as a whole. Once in a while it is good to see things, especially important things, from afar.

When I returned from Guatemala in late February, America was still in an uproar. Headlines screeched at me. Hundreds of sitdown strikes were going on. In three months the C.I.O. had gained over a million new members. Labor was on the march! Such brilliant political careers as that of Governor Murphy of Michigan were at stake. And President Roosevelt had sprung on the country his sensational proposal for a drastic reform of the Supreme Court. The intellectual world of New York was all excited. I met people who saw fascism lurking behind the current events. Labor was going too far, too fast, employing improper, dangerous methods and weapons. The sitdown was dangerous.

Were not Communists manipulating it? Occupying factories! That was what had helped to bring on fascism in Italy! . . . But, somehow, I was not terribly upset by all this. I managed more or less to maintain the perspective on current events that I had acquired at Antigua.

By the end of the spring the "sitdown epidemic" showed two results. One was very definite: the C.I.O. had gone over three million in membership. This success, plus other factors in the general economic-political situation, had prompted the United States Steel Corporation to yield to the C.I.O., which then quickly organized most of the steel labor and procured agreements with several hundred independent steel companies.

But even more important, it seemed to me, was the second, not so tangible, result of the "sitdown epidemic." Out of it had sprung the idea that *the job, perhaps, belonged to the worker as much as the machine at which he worked belonged to the employer.*

Just where this idea first appeared would be difficult to determine. The possibility is that it occurred simultaneously, or almost so, to people in various places. At any rate, by the end of the spring of 1937 the idea was suddenly in the air. Hundreds of thousands, and probably millions, of American workers, had the feeling that they had a *right* to their jobs. The employers, of course, protested against the sitdown. They called on the authorities to do something about it. The authorities did nothing, really: first, because they could not do anything; second, because they were not terribly interested in doing anything. For a good while Secretary of Labor Perkins insisted, perhaps with the approval of the President, that there was no question as to the legality of the sitdown. The House of Representatives refused to investigate the situation, while the dean of a great law school—Leon Green, of Northwestern—wrote an article for *The New Republic* upholding the sitdown.

In the fall of 1937, the three hundred thousand United Automobile Workers, in convention assembled officially, declared that the sitdown was a definite part of their tactical equipment. Unofficially this was true of not a few other C.I.O. unions.

All through the last half of 1937 I felt that the idea born of the sitdown, that the worker has a right to his job which was similar to the employer's property rights, was one of the most important additions to the makeup of the American mind. As I write this early in 1938, there is not much being said about it, but I am fairly certain that it—with the thoughts and feelings it awakened—is destined to play a big rôle in the future of America. I briefly return to this point in a later chapter, which deals with Walter Locke, of Dayton, Ohio.

What the C.I.O. REALLY Is

URING THE LATE SPRING AND EARLY SUMMER OF 1937 THE SO-CALLED LITTLE Steel strike was, aside from the now historical Supreme Court reform debate, perhaps the most important event in America. It is not my intention here to describe it in detail, for the story of it is available elsewhere. As a beginning, in fact, I shall merely say that it was one of the nastiest, most acrimonious capital-labor battles in the history of the United States. Several workers were killed; scores were wounded. It involved the largest independent steel companies (that is, companies not controlled by the United States Steel Corporation), which continued anti-union and were willing to pursue that policy at all costs to themselves and the country; tens of thousands of workers; about a dozen communities, large and small; and the emotions of the entire country. It cost the country at large upward of a quarter of a billion dollars in general economic turnover. It brought into the limelight Tom Girdler, head of the Republic Steel Corporation, one of the companies involved, as an example of a potential fascist leader of the United States. It caused John Lewis to utter words in public whose wisdom was immediately questioned. And it prompted President Roosevelt to declare suddenly toward the middle of the strike that the country's attitude toward the complex mess was: a plague on both your houses! The remark was, perhaps, politically necessary from the viewpoint of the diverse legislative irons the Administration had then in the fire; or it may be that Mr. Roosevelt had need of venting his own momentary feeling about the bitter situation that had abruptly developed in connection or simultaneously with the Little Steel strike. Whatever its immediate motive and purpose, the remark was, in the long run, not the wisest thing to say. In the long run, Americans as a nation have no such attitude.

Yet, at the time the President uttered it, it echoed true and appropriate in millions of craniums the country over. And it echoed truest and most appropriate in the emptiest of craniums—those in which the "thinking" about capital-labor struggles, unhampered by knowledge or understanding, swings freely around or concerns itself solely with issues, incidents, and personalities of the moment. Especially around incidents and personalities. People get upset or enthusiastic about John Lewis or Tom Girdler, the Chicago Memorial Day massacre or the strikers' tactics which momentarily obstruct mail delivery in an Ohio steel town. They know nothing else nor can know anything else, at least not at the moment. They are mostly emotional; their feelings run hot and cold at the conflicting reports of complex situations. Presently they cannot make head or tail of anything—their feelings cannot run hot and cold indefinitely—so, to the devil with the whole business! They do not really think, merely react. Lacking any idea of the capital-labor problem as a *whole*, they see a strike or some other event as an isolated thing. They do not know that the capital-labor problem, with its strikes, outbursts of violence, threats, and rumblings, is an important phase of the American Process, which, albeit seldom if ever clearly visualized by the majority of people, has now for two hundred years been, fumblingly but consistently, working for more and more democracy in all departments of our national life—for more and more social, economic, and political liberty and equality—in short, for the gradual abolition of the country's basic incongruity.

What I call the American Process began quite definitely in the second quarter of the eighteenth century. Its first climax, the Revolutionary War, led to the writing of the Declaration of Independence, the Constitution, and the Constitution's postscript—the Bill of Rights; to the birth of a new nation and the establishment of political equality and the freedom of assembly, speech, press, and religion. Its second climax was the Civil War, resulting in the abolition of inequalities between Northern and Southern commerce and the establishment of theoretical equality, in certain respects and functions, for the Negro with the white man. Early in the twentieth century, the question of women's political equality with men came up, and was theoretically settled with the Nineteenth Amendment, letting time put it into practical effect. And almost ever since the first climax in American history there has been going on the sporadic-seeming but really constant, the seldom articulated but always strongly instinctive struggle of labor for democracy in the shop and factory, which have been from the start—and, for the most part, are still as this volume nears completion—palpably undemocratic, absolutist, or (to use a popular word) fascist institutions, with the employer the sole authority, having power which he most often exercises for his own immediate profit. His power extends not only through the shop or factory but also, by virtue of his economic standing, into politics, education, religion, and most other important public processes and institutions which might be used to improve conditions in industry and to improve generally the quality, tone, and color of civilization.

For decades labor's struggle was essentially, in *the immediate sense*, for nothing else, nothing more concrete than the acceptance by the public and its representatives in government of the concept that workers were not a mere commodity but men, women, and children and as such, in America, entitled to the right to claim as their due anything that was claimed by any other human element in the land. By and large, this struggle was partly won after many battles with the absolutist, undemocratic powers controlling and running the industries and, to a great extent, the government. And the victory demanded many martyrs. However, it was won not by labor alone or by the working class as a whole but by comparatively small, aggressive labor movements. These sprang out of conditions of glaring inequality, out of the basic incongruity of the country, and were never backed by a majority of workers as such. But (and this is important) they had seldom if ever the immediate but always the eventual support of a majority of the politically active American people who, consciously or otherwise, were addicted to democracy as a principle and a way of life, individually and nationally; who, consciously or otherwise, were for abolishing the national incongruity.

The first state law recognizing the workers' right to organize and strike was passed in this country in 1836. It was enacted not only because an aggressive small group of workers wanted it but because those workers received the approbation of a majority of the politically active democratic citizens in the state. Since that first victory, the militancy and effectiveness of American labor movements and their leaders have grown, with occasional seeming lapses, by leaps and bounds, reaching a new high along with the early New Deal, which encouraged organization; while, during 1936-'37, with the C.I.O. under the leadership of John Lewis rapidly becoming one of the most potent factors in America's national life, it has been clear that we are approaching—how rapidly it is as yet difficult to say—the third climax in the American Process. This climax may not be as distinct as were the first two, but, *unless America becomes a country much different from what she started out to be,* it will ultimately lead to the extension of the now still, in the main, only theoretically accepted idea that labor is a human element to the establishment of actual democracy or equality in industry—*and this either as between capital and labor in some well-defined partnership or through the abolition of capitalism as we now know it.*

The above fundamentals appear to me as prerequisite to any sound thinking about the labor situation as it began to develop in this country during the great Depression. Without them, a serious person, who can never quite assume the neat "plague on both your houses!" impartiality, is bound sooner or later to end in deep confusion, as did a liberal and progressive friend of mine in Cleveland whom I visited soon after the Little Steel strike collapsed. Quoting Shakespeare, the President did not quite speak for him. "But almost," my friend told me.

"You know," he went on, "this strike began on a sudden. The C.I.O. top leaders themselves, as I heard soon after it had started, didn't expect or want it when it broke out—weren't ready for it. The strike was a spontaneous movement that grew out of workers' grievances, and I was all for the men as against Tom Girdler—whom I know personally, by the way. He is a very competent man when it comes to making steel, but a tough guy, if there ever was one, with whom fighting is practically a habit. . . . I watched the strike from its beginning, not only in Cleveland but, as far as I could, in Youngstown, Canton, Johnstown, and other Little Steel towns. The C.I.O. leadership took hold of it and probably did its best in what it considered a bad situation not of its own making; but, although I make no claim to being an expert in strike tactics, its very best didn't seem any good to me. The C.I.O. leaders' moves looked to me like one blunder after another.

"They announced the strike's aim was to get contracts with the Little Steel companies, such as labor had with Big Steel and many small firms. Of course, John Lewis and Philip Murray meant that, once they sat down with the employers in conference, they would be in position to bring up the men's grievances. The trouble was that *contract* is too abstract a word to have any clear or vital meaning for the average steelworker who has not yet been educated in collective-bargaining terminology but is hot and bothered about concrete grievances; and, when nothing was said about them by the top leaders, he soon lost interest in the fight and, in most cases, became ready to return to work. This was blunder number one, of which Girdler & Co. took quick advantage.

"I did not approve—naturally—of the unions' interference with mail delivery in some of the strike towns, but, though unquestionably a serious blunder, which gave the reactionary press a chance to raise a big howl, I thought it was due to bad judgment of local leaders, who were young, inexperienced, excited, eager to show their power.

"The next big blunder, in Ohio, was that the steel leaders trusted Governor Davey. When he ordered out the National Guard, which I knew—without being on the inside—was done with the intention of ending the strike, the unions sent delegations to the station to welcome the soldiers, under the delusion that they came to take over their picket lines. Dumb! . . . It's not easy to sympathize with a loser but it's downright hard to sympathize with a cause losing to fellows like Girdler, Weir, and Davey through its own blunders— even though there may be all sorts of extenuations for those blunders. And, when your sympathies go weak, you're inclined to believe all sorts of things about the loser and his friends and relations and say, 'Oh, hell!'

"When, during the strike, the Cleveland police captured a couple of cars filled with obvious plug-uglies, who were armed and carried C.I.O. buttons or cards on them, most Clevelanders turned against the strikers. I, myself, had an 'Oh, hell!' moment; and when it developed that the gangsters had apparently been hired by the A.F. of L. forces opposed to the C.I.O., with orders to get themselves arrested and photographed in order to discredit the C.I.O., I experienced, along with a pain in the neck, a dizzy sensation where my brains are supposed to be. Well, if such things went on, labor pulling dirty tricks on labor, what could you think? I couldn't spend my time investigating such incidents. Whom to believe? How could I be sure the C.I.O. hadn't really hired and equipped the gangsters, intending to blame them on the A.F. of L.? You certainly couldn't find much fault with anyone for saying the equivalent of 'a plague on both your houses!'

"My sympathies are naturally with the underdog and the 'have nots.' I am, somehow, for fair play. Everybody ought to have a chance in life, including the fellow who perhaps doesn't deserve it. The industrial-democracy idea is swell. John Lewis, Phillip Murray, and Sidney Hillman may be wonderful men who know what it is all about. But, frankly, when Roosevelt made his crack I had to exert all the something-or-other in me to curb an impulse to applaud, figuratively speaking: for during the steel strike all manner of other damned things kept happening as part of the Cleveland labor situation.

"Like numerous other shops or factories in town, the place where I work got all tied up in a knot because of a jurisdictional dispute between two A.F. of L. unions, aggravated by a C.I.O. threat to come in and organize the workers not qualified to become members of either of the disputing unions. Disgusting! Instead of trying to figure out how to get together and do something to increase labor's constructive effectiveness in the country, they work up a three-cornered fight.

"Then the A.F. of L. union painters drove through the city nights, splattering tar on newly painted houses—newly painted, mind you, not by hired non-union painters but by house owners themselves with their own hands. And most of these victims of union vandalism were workers, some non-union, others belonging to the A.F. of L. and still others to the C.I.O., while a few were unemployed, who could not possibly have hired painters. The newspapers made much of this, and the city, including naturally pro-labor people like me, as well as many workingmen, perhaps a majority of them, got dizzier and dizzier trying to figure out what was what and why.

"Finally, the other day, I got to talking with a cab driver. What did he think of all these strikes, the C.I.O., and so on? He said, 'Not much; to hell with 'em all!' He told me of his own union, which, he hastened to remark, was no union but a racket, part of the A.F. of L. The same men ran the taxi company and the union. As union officials, they forced themselves (in the capacity of employers) to maintain a closed shop. As employers, they paid the drivers nine dollars or eleven dollars a week. As union officials, they made the drivers pay dues, which they stuck into their pockets. If a cab driver kicked about this setup, he got kicked out on his ear. . . . What can the average man think of a situation like that when he hears of it?

"One more thing. A liberal, progressive, whatever you want to call me, I am for gradual progress, so we can see what we are doing as we go along, and I am against violent revolution or a quick change such as the Communists have in mind, though just now they seem publicly to pretend otherwise . . . and what I want to know is: why does John Lewis, why does the C.I.O., tolerate the Communists in this new labor movement and thereby enable Tom Girdler to call it communistic? It seems dumb to me, which, as I say, makes it difficult for me to keep my pro-labor sympathies steady. . . ."

The previous week, visiting Johnstown, Pittsburgh, Youngstown, Akron, and lesser industrial cities, I had met a number of liberals, progressives, and decent, well-meaning New Deal Democrats who had not expressed themselves as thoroughly as had my above quoted Cleveland friend but whose natural pro-labor sympathies were as unsteady and confused as his. In every case, this unsteadiness and confusion seemed to date from the Little Steel strike and were due mainly to their knowing only a few local facts without perceiving the truth of the situation as a whole or understanding the fundamentals of the capital-labor problem, without being aware of America's basic incongruity. Almost everything that perturbed my Cleveland friend was factually, in the local Cleveland sense, exactly as he told me; yet he was basically and typically nearly all wrong. The truth of the things that disturbed him was really something on this order:

1. THE STRIKE

When I discussed the Little Steel strike with the Steel Workers' Organizing Committee officials in Pittsburgh, they were unaware of having committed any serious blunders in that strike. True, they had not wanted the walkout; the sentiment for it had developed more or less out of the working conditions, and there was nothing to do but to make the best of an unplanned, spontaneous, unadvantageous development. In demanding contracts, instead of airing the workers' numerous grievances, which were different in every mill, the S.W.O.C. and C.I.O. leaders had done only what had hitherto proven highly successful in their drive to unionize the steel industry.

As for Governor Davey, he had promised the C.I.O. representatives in Columbus to use the National Guard impartially, to prevent violence; then he betrayed them and broke the strike. But, as one S.W.O.C. official was quick to point out to me, this had another side. Davey had, thereby, stuck out his political neck, which they would chop off when his term of office expired in 1938.

As for Tom Girdler and the Republic Steel Corporation, their victory over the C.I.O. was mostly a matter of sensational headlines. The strike cost the company millions of dollars in profits and settled nothing, for a new strike was an eventual certainty. Also, it anything but enhanced Girdler's standing in the corporation. Many of the Republic stockholders, feeling they were losing money, turned against Girdler on the ground that he was too unyielding, too violently anti-union, and habitually pugnacious.

2. THE LEADERS

Most of the top leaders in the C.I.O. unions, as I write this, are either very competent old-time unionists, of whom S.W.O.C.'s Murray is the outstanding example, or able but inexperienced new men, such as Martin of the U.A.W. Many local or district leaders, however, are young, new, inexperienced, not over-intelligent, nor too well balanced. Many are motivated by petty personal aspirations that have scant relation to the great cause of labor. That is inevitable. The C.I.O. is one of the biggest things ever conceived in this country. Because of the great need it suddenly filled, it grew too fast during 1936-'37. All sorts of people got into it, inevitably. They took over all sorts of jobs and functions. Many who do not belong in responsible positions doubtless will gradually be eliminated from them; some perhaps not for some time. Meanwhile their ill-considered actions are not to be ascribed to the C.I.O. movement as a whole.

3. THE A.F. OF L.

During 1937 many cities—for one, Cleveland, which had a corrupt, top-heavy, and not incompetent A.F. of L. organization—were scenes of unutterably dirty struggles between the old A.F. of L. and the new C.I.O. In Cleveland, A.F. of L. officials, by direct orders from bitter, aging William Green, were hiring themselves out to factory managements as virtual strikebreakers and organizers of company unions, with the aim of halting the great, long-delayed tide of labor organization, while A.F. of L. unions—many of which, by virtue of the A.F. of L. philosophy, were never democratic or equalitarian but always discriminatory and shot through with semi-gangsterism—are sinking closer and closer to the status of rackets.

But in 1937 it became clear to me that Bill Green & Co. could not be long with us. Entire state federations and city labor councils were getting ready to toss their aged misleaders into oblivion, for increasing numbers of A.F. of L. workers saw no sense in fighting, or indeed were sympathetic with, the C.I.O., which they realized was bound sooner or later to take over the old organization.

4. THE "COMMUNISTS"

John Lewis, as pointed out in a previous chapter, is no Communist. Nor "Communist." He has the personal respect or admiration of such men as Myron C. Taylor and Thomas W. Lamont. In a way, as I say, he is Labor personified; socially and personally, however, he is more at home in the ornate lobby of the high-toned Mayflower Hotel in Washington than he would be in the home of the average coal miner in Luzerne County, Pennsylvania: which is all right with the coal miner. The same month (January, 1938), that he publicly threatened the capitalist system with the possibility of a "communal" social order, he remarked to a great financier, "What can we do to stop that fellow"—President Roosevelt—"disquieting the country?" or words to that effect.

Nor, of course (let me emphasize) is the C.I.O. a communistic or radical outfit. It is a mass trade-union movement. In its early stages, as Ben Stolberg has pointed out, it was bound now and then to appear "radical," especially to people who lack understanding of such things or are generally superficial.[1] As a trade-union movement, it was naturally and properly open from the beginning to all workers regardless of their politics, race, or creed.

When the C.I.O. was started, a considerable number (say, a few thousand) of "Communists"—that is, members of the Communist party, with records of such doings as I have described to have been typical of their activities during

---

[1] In the middle 1880's the A.F. of L., when it was first launched as a national organization, was considered "radical." Ill-informed people discussed it in the same breath with the Anarchists and the Haymarket bombing.

1930-35—and a few more or less real Communists, who were all-around admirable people, were scattered along the various labor fronts. Under their new banner, Lewis and the rest of the C.I.O. were unwilling to engage in Red-baiting, for it might only confuse things still more than they already were confused. If fought, the "Communists" might well do the C.I.O. great harm. They had had much experience in union-wrecking in the past. They were aggressive, energetic, articulate, vocal, and capable of being fanatic. Their potential nuisance value was considerable. Besides, why fight them? Their new party "line" having just then been decided for them, they were eager to go into a "united front," let bygones be bygones, and coöperate with everybody. So it was best to take them in, get along with them, and use them; for some of them, figured Lewis, knew a good deal about the labor situation. He felt that not a few would soon cease being "Communists"; the rest, if necessary, he could get rid of at any time he wished. Whether or not he was right in this was heatedly debated late in 1937 and early in 1938 in various circles interested in the American industrial-social scene. This debate will doubtless continue when this book appears, and long after.

During 1937 I watched the "Communist" situation in connection with the C.I.O. rather carefully. Many "Communists" were naturally eliminated from responsible positions. A considerable number of them did shed, as Lewis had expected, their Communism, such as it was, and were thinking how they might serve, and advance themselves in, the C.I.O. movement, which was full of opportunities for up-and-coming young men. Some of those who remained members of the Communist party, which now stood for "united front" and against "revolution," were often to the right of non-"Communist" C.I.O. leaders or organizers, whom they endeavored to keep from doing anything drastic which might disrupt the "united front." They were the so-called "Stalinists," and as such fought the "Trotskyists," who considered themselves the real revolutionary Communists, but whose number was scarcely sufficient to provide steady sport for the "Stalinists." This was true of most of the C.I.O. unions and the majority of the localities where the C.I.O. figured prominently.

The general American public's knowledge of the C.I.O.'s connection with the Communist party was based—at least until Ben Stolberg wrote his series of articles in the Scripps-Howard newspapers early in 1938 under the general title of *Inside the C.I.O.*—mainly on the fact that every once in a while General Secretary Earl Browder of the party sent out press releases, which were printed in important newspapers, boasting of how much his organization was doing to keep the C.I.O. going. But Browder's statements were partly intended to impress the heads of the Third International in Moscow. Incidentally, he acted as a stooge for Bill Green and Tom Girdler, who paraphrased his boasts to suit their momentary fascistic, undemocratic purposes; while the fascistic, undemocratic effusions of Bill Green and Tom Girdler, in turn, helped to give a little substance to Browder's verbal efforts to save the United States from fascism. In this respect, the collaboration between the "Communists" and fascists was perfect.

The membership of every C.I.O. union includes "Communists." Most of the C.I.O. organizations, however, are completely free of any "Communist" influence to which anyone should object. The few "Communists" in their ranks are, in many cases, good for them; they seem to have a tendency to liven them up. The central C.I.O. organization is almost entirely free of "Communist" influence. In fact, it includes potent anti-Communists.

One great C.I.O. union, however, namely the United Automobile Workers was—through most of 1937 and the early weeks of 1938—torn by fierce inner struggle between the "Communists," who wanted to control it, and the non-"Communists," headed by President Homer Martin, who did control it. In this the "Communists" employed destructive tactics very similar to those they had used in the labor movement a few years before. Most of the scores of unauthorized sitdowns and strikes in the auto industry during 1937, which were in violation of contracts and did the C.I.O. cause great harm, were organized and led by "Communists," under the general direction of the Communist party headquarters in New York, with the direct aim of discrediting the Martin regime.

John L. Lewis' own union, the United Mine Workers, bars known "Communists" or Communists from membership. Personally, I think this is a wrong policy. If there are "Communists" or Communists among the miners, they ought to be admitted to the unions and dealt with democratically within the organization. They may, conceivably, have something to contribute. But an even more important consideration is this: if you bar one group today, you may bar another tomorrow, and eventually you may be thrown out yourself.

I am told that what I have just said may look all right on paper, but it is not so pleasant when "Red fanatics under the influence of the conniving Communist party leadership" rise in local-union meetings and eloquently denounce as "sellouts" and "stool-pigeons" all who disagree with them. How would I cope with such people? My answer (which I know may be too pat and too general) is that the rest of the membership must develop democratic means to deal with such fanatics and would-be character assassins. They need to be analyzed, opposed, and exposed. I understand that now—in 1937-38—when "Communists" unjustly assail inexperienced local-union leaders, the latter often are helpless. They are unable to deal with character defamation, and the "Communists" "get away with it" and "mess up the unions." To this I would say that that inability on the part of local-union leaders is something they need to correct in themselves.

There is a so-called "Communist situation" in the labor movement on the Pacific Coast, which I have touched upon in the chapter on Harry Bridges, and which complicates things considerably for the C.I.O. and for the onlookers who are trying to see them straight and clearly. But, unless one is ready to condemn Bridges and everything he has done, the "Communist situation" on the Coast is not entirely villainous. I am told that (as I write this early in 1938) the "guts" of the new labor movement in Los Angeles, where there has been no labor movement since the McNamara fiasco in 1911, are three young "Communists," whose "Communism" belongs in quotation marks because for the time they are not really Communists in any feasible sense of the word, nor revolutionists. They are merely under the influence of the Communist party of the United States, which momentarily, following its "line," is not really Communist, not revolutionary. They give me misgivings only on the score that a "line," which originated outside the labor movement, and which may be changed any moment, rules their actions, and that generally I want the labor movement to be free of control of any political party. On this score, the Los Angeles "Communistic" labor leaders, like Harry Bridges and like all other leaders and would-be leaders of labor, are to be watched and discussed critically—however, not at any point with fear-motivated fascistic passion, but calmly, deliberately, accurately, in democratic public debate, as a matter of precaution and all-around clarification.

My guess is that in the long run the "Communists" in the C.I.O. and the labor movement generally will not be very important. Momentarily (in 1938, as I write this) they are slightly more important in other respects, namely, in being the projectors into America of certain phases of the current Old World insanity: to be touched upon later in this book.

So far as I know, the best way to avoid fascistic passion in connection with the "Communists" in the new American labor movement, is to bear in mind what the C.I.O. really is; that, with all the faults of its leaders and in spite (as well as because) of the nasty and complex situations and incidents that every now and then develop along with it, the C.I.O., to repeat, is clearly an expression and manifestation of the American laboring masses' urge—as yet ill understood in their own minds—for democracy and equality, as against absolutism or fascism, in the shop and factory and for more democracy, more liberty, less absolutism generally in the life of the American people.

In the C.I.O., in contrast to the A.F. of L., white and black men belong to the same unions. Many A.F. of L. organizations discriminate (unofficially, of course) also against non-Irish immigrants, non-Catholics, and even against American-born citizens with Polish, Slovak, Croatian, Lithuanian, Finnish, or other "foreign" names, while in the C.I.O. many local-union and district leaders are immigrants or immigrants' American-born sons, quite regardless of their names. The C.I.O. has no Jim Crowism or alien-baiting, and this is a victory for equality that is of paramount importance to all America. The C.I.O. may well become an important factor in the delicate and vital process of integration of our heterogeneous population, which I touch upon earlier in this book.

As one of the biggest things yet conceived and attempted in the United States (and as I have suggested in the chapter on John Lewis), the C.I.O. is of course pregnant with dangers to itself, labor generally, and the country. But, as far as it has gone up to the early months of 1938, it undoubtedly is on the right track. It must be watched locally but also—and especially—as a whole. Its "Communist" faction must be allowed to be, but—in common with all other political factions—not allowed to control. The C.I.O. must be studied, criticized. But it ought to have the steady general support of intelligent, democratic Americans who do not want America to become anything different basically from what she started out to be. The C.I.O. deserves such support, if not for every detail of its movement, certainly for what it is fundamentally— a logical development of the American Process, a part of America's approach to the next climax in that Process. Such support will steady its direction and measurably decrease and temper its inherent dangers to itself and the country.

Talk with a C.I.O. Employer

E ARLY ONE FORENOON IN MID-AUTUMN, 1937, I SAT IN THE OFFICE OF A FRIEND
of mine who is an important man in the C.I.O. campaign to unionize the
steel industry, on the thirty-sixth floor of the Grant Building in Pittsburgh,
which is part of the elegant headquarters of the Steel Workers' Organizing
Committee. The day before, a strike had begun in one of the smaller local
mills, whose general manager refused to deal with "those communistic, irresponsible unions run by John L. Lewis." This phrase, when I quoted it to
him from a front-page story in the Pittsburgh newspaper I had brought with
me, amused my friend. The man, he said, was parroting Tom Girdler and
Bill Green, both of whom knew better. In the first place, the C.I.O. was a
trade-union movement, and how could a trade-union movement be communistic? The traditional meaning of "trade unionism" was unionism aiming to
advance the cause of labor within the frame of capitalism; wasn't it? In the
second place, "irresponsible" about what? Contracts? Agreements?

"Listen," said my C.I.O. friend, "there are scores of steel industrialists in
and around Pittsburgh who have signed up with the S.W.O.C. in the last
seven months and are glad of it, and have a high regard for the C.I.O. and
John Lewis and Phil Murray. A few even actively help us in our work. Eight
months ago they had arsenals in their mill yards, ready to fight us; now they
stand ready to render us favors and services such as we could not get in any
other way for love or money. In fact, I am expecting a call from one of them,
who has lately helped us get next to the top men of several companies, which
led to the signing of agreements, and who just now is trying to arrange for us
a contact with this fellow who calls us communistic and irresponsible, whom
he has known personally for many years. That's what he is to call me about.
His name is Richard Paynter—top man in the National Steel, Iron, and Tin
Company at Coalburg, eight miles from here."[1]

My friend answered the telephone: "Yes, Dick. . . . Fine. . . . Uh-huh.
. . . I see. . . . O. K.," and so on for several minutes. The contact had evidently been arranged. Then: "By the way, Dick, there is a writer here in my
office"—telling him my name and some of the things I had written—"who is
interested in the whole situation and would like to talk with you. Could
you . . . ?"

Mr. Paynter and I met that afternoon in the air-conditioned Continental Bar
of the William Penn Hotel, and we talked for an hour and a half. He is a
medium-sized, wiry man with a handsome, square-jawed face; maybe fifty,
possibly a few years younger, and obviously very competent. He has a quick
eye, a firm handclasp, an agreeable smile, a warm manner, a ready word or

[1] At his request, the names of this man, his company, and the town are disguised.

remark. Neither frank nor cagy, he lets one draw him out. He dresses conservatively but well, smokes one cigarette after the other, and drinks canned beer of a local brew. The waiter, who knows him, brought him the can and an opener, and Mr. Paynter poured the beer himself into his glass. His company makes beer cans. He evidently doesn't miss a trick.

A successful man. His salary is written well up in five figures. He lives in one of the suburbs, midway between Pittsburgh and Coalburg. His oldest son is an assistant superintendent in the mill with him; apparently a chip off the old block. A younger boy is at the Phillips Academy in Andover. Mr. Paynter is personally a contented man. He owns a $40,000 home and loves Mrs. Paynter. He reads the Pittsburgh *Post-Gazette*, the New York *Times*, the various trade journals pertaining to steel, iron, tin, and related industries, and *Time, Fortune,* and *Reader's Digest.* The last named he reads in bed evenings or if he wakes up during the night. When very tired or annoyed about something, he likes to read Omar Khayyám; the verses soothe him.

But most of these personal details about him I learned toward the end of our talk, the significant parts of which went something like this:

ADAMIC: I understand, Mr. Paynter, that you practically grew up in the steel industry and that you received your early training as a steel man under Tom Girdler.

PAYNTER: That's right.

A.: I am told that in the 1919 steel strike you were, if I may put it bluntly, in charge of a strong-arm force in the mill where you were then an assistant superintendent, and that you did your bit in breaking that strike.

P. (*smiling*): That, roughly, is correct.

A.: How do you explain that?

P.: What do you mean?

A.: I mean, how do you justify your 1919 position in relation to labor?

P. (*considering the question a trifle silly*): I don't justify it. Nor explain it. Nor apologize for it. Nor regret it, if that's what you mean. That was the thing to do in those days. Everybody ——

A.: I see. I understand too, Mr. Paynter, that a year ago, or even more recently, you had—shall I say?—an arsenal in the yard of your mill at Coalburg, prepared to give battle to the C.I.O., perhaps much in the way you fought the 1919 strike.

P. (*smiling*): "Arsenal" is a big word; apart from that, yes, together with the steel industry as a whole, we were ready to resist unionization.

A.: You were prepared to fight it out.

P.: Put it that way if you like.

A.: Then, what are you doing now, chumming around with these C.I.O. Reds [*smiling*]—these "Communists," as your former superior, Mr. Girdler, calls them? What do you mean helping the C.I.O. agitators, as I am told you are, to organize the steel industry—calling their office, and so on?

P. (*chuckling, pouring beer*): We got converted, Mr. Adamic.

A.: How? Why? By whom? When?

P. (*laughing*): There's nothing you don't want to know, is there?

A.: Well, anyhow, what started you on this new path?

P.: One day early last spring, a man came to my office—a C.I.O. organizer from the S.W.O.C. office; nice fellow, with a clean-cut, intelligent face, neatly dressed, and so on. He told me right off who he was and what he wanted to talk about. I asked him to sit down, and he began to sell me the idea of us letting the C.I.O. start a union in our plant. He implied it would be to our advantage. Talking very calmly, persuasively, he proceeded to tell me—quite accurately, by the way—all the petty troubles and pains-in-the-neck we'd had in the mill the past few weeks, which in the long run, he hastened to point out to me, amounted to a lot of trouble and expense, which, he further lost no time in emphasizing, were bound to increase as the years went by, regardless of how good a personnel manager we had. Why? Because, he said, in shops where the union was fought and men belonged to it secretly all sorts of damned things happened all the time, which led to fear, nervousness, and jitters among the men, to secret sabotage and loafing on the job, and so on. What he was saying was, to an extent, undoubtedly true, and he proceeded to tell me, too, that if we let the union come in, it would take care of most of our petty labor difficulties. The union, he said, would form a grievance committee consisting of workers in the mill; all the union men in the shop would be required, and others allowed, to take their grievances to the committee, which would assemble all the kicks and complaints and what-nots, then take them up with us—the management—once every so often, say, once a week; and many, perhaps most, of the grievances would be smoothed out by the committee itself without bothering us with them. He made a good argument, and, well, to make a long story short, we thought things over, our superintendents and I; we sounded out our biggest stockholders; our directors gave me a free hand; and by and by we said "O.K.," and the C.I.O. came in. We signed an agreement for a year, the union was formed, about half the men joined, a grievance committee was organized, and, sure enough, the thing began to work out—in an imperfect sort of way, to be sure, but we *do* have fewer petty difficulties with the men, the plant, somehow, does seem generally a better place to work in, and——

A. (*interrupting*): Excuse me, Mr. Paynter—before you go any further, tell me, was the fact that a C.I.O. organizer came to talk to you *really* the reason why you said "O.K." to the C.I.O.?

P. (*his eyes flashing amusement*): No-o-o, of course, not really. . . . We were, naturally, surprised when we read in the papers, early in March about the agreement between Mr. Myron Taylor, of the United States Steel Corporation, and Mr. John Lewis. But I don't mind telling you we were also relieved. Business was picking up beautifully, and we didn't want a strike, which might disrupt production. . . . We are, if I may say so, a successful concern, but not a big one; employing between three and four thousand men all told. We are completely independent of the United States Steel Corporation, but we have been having pleasant relations with it ever since I know; I am personally acquainted with many of its officials, and our policy has always been: What is good for the Corporation is good enough for us. We have always followed its lead. Their labor policy was, traditionally, our labor policy.

A.: Was there any other reason that led you to sign up with the C.I.O.?

P.: Ye-e-e-es, I suppose there was. . . . Our plant at Coalburg is our only plant, and Coalburg is primarily a coal town, with all the mines closed-shop. All the miners are members of the United Mine Workers, whose president, as you know, is Mr. John Lewis, who, we know from long ago, is a most able man, practical and resourceful, a realist, not afraid of a fight. Last year, when the C.I.O. began to look like a serious business, we realized that by using his miners as pickets, while Mr. Earle was Governor of Pennsylvania [*smiling*], Lewis could close us down and keep us closed, which meant that, since we had no other plant to which we might transfer our important orders, we would be up against it if it came to a showdown. Together with the United States Steel Corporation and the rest of the industry, we could have put up an effective fight and won; and we might have given the C.I.O. a damned good fight and licked it even single-handed, in that we would not sign a contract—but that would have been a case of an irresistible force and an immovable body. Lewis and the C.I.O. would have been licked, but they would have ruined our business. After the battle there would have been very little, if anything, left of the good old National Steel, Iron, and Tin Company. So to fight Lewis—to fight the C.I.O.—was not the constructive thing to do; and after the United States Steel entered in agreement with the C.I.O., when the C.I.O. man came to us, we said "O.K." and we're not sorry.

A.: Why aren't you sorry?

P. (*pondering*): Well, we signed an agreement with the S.W.O.C., which provides that we allow the union to organize and any worker to join who wants to, and the union can employ no coercive method to make any worker join who is disinclined to do so. So far, I think, approximately 60 per cent have joined. The rest are holding off from the union out of a variety of motives. Some are individualists who don't believe in unions, others have had unpleasant experiences in unions in other industries or believe that the C.I.O. is communistic, and still others imagine that we, the "bosses," don't really want a union, don't really want them to join; but most of them don't sign up simply because they see no sense of paying union dues when they get all the benefits that the union claims to have won, anyhow. The agreement further provides for certain desirable working conditions, which were in effect before we entered into it, and for certain seniority privileges of workers. The plant remains open shop; we remain, for the most part, free to hire and fire. Thus far both we and the union—which is still under the general supervision of the S.W.O.C. people, who are fine, able fellows—have been careful to live up both to the letter and the spirit of the agreement. As a matter of fact, on our part, we have done things for the union we have not been required to do. We have given it a building in the millyard, which the union men use as a sort of clubhouse and for committee meetings and collecting of union dues on pay day. The most important thing is the grievance committee, which consists of nine union workers appointed by the S.W.O.C. officers and confirmed by the union membership in the plant. Later on, when the union is better organized, the men will elect their own committees, without direction or suggestion from S.W.O.C. or any superior organization. We, the management, had no hand in the formation of this first grievance committee.

A.: How does it function?

P.: Imperfectly, as I say—it's new; it must be given time. We think that it's liable to be a good thing all around. It seems to act as a sort of collective vent, at least for the union members; in a way, for the whole plant. The men bring their grievances to committee members, then argue about them, then the first thing they know, in many instances, the grievances disappear. One trouble with the thing, so far as we are concerned, is that the men comprising the committee, while granting they probably are as good as we could have, are new, green, inexperienced fellows, apt to get excited about nothing at all. As yet they can't quite handle authority and responsibility. They get "tough" with us over little matters. There seldom is a "grievance meeting" between the committee and the management that something doesn't happen to cause one or all of us on the management side to come near flying off the handle. It is hard, but we try to control our tempers, mend our old pugnacious habits, and be patient. We keep on telling ourselves that the thing—in principle, anyhow—is O.K. and is liable to get better right along. Two of the three men on the grievance committee who are most apt to raise their voices unnecessarily at the grievance meetings are, we feel, open to bribery; that is, we could buy them off, if we wanted to—but, then, why should we? Why should we corrupt the thing?

A.: But, then, why not? Employers have been known to corrupt union officials.

P.: Yes; but maybe that was one of the serious troubles with industry heretofore—and still is. We industrialists, it seems to me, need an entirely new education, a new way of looking at things.

A.: Of course, I imagine that your troubles, as you see them, with the grievance committee are rather slight, over petty matters and differences. But suppose that sometime in the future you come face to face with more serious problems or demands, what will you do then? Won't you probably be tempted to buy off the officials of the new union?

P. (*smiling*): We'll try not to be. Much will depend on how the C.I.O. goes and conducts itself as a whole; what sort of people get at the head of its unions, as it continues to grow, and how successful we are in acquiring a new education, which—at my age, for instance—is no easy matter.

A.: But suppose—just suppose—that sometime in the future, possibly not very far off, when the C.I.O. is much stronger than it is already, you are presented with a demand for a closed shop and the check-off. What will you do if, or when, that comes?

P.: If it comes in the near future, we will oppose it with every means at our command.

A.: Why?

P.: Because, with things being as they are, closed shop and check-off will not be constructive; will make conditions in the plant impossible. The men are not yet—and, in my opinion, cannot be for some time—sufficiently trained or educated in exercising responsibility, authority, and the necessary self-discipline in a complicated industry like steel. Mind you, as people go, steel workers are good men, but they will have to become much better in every respect—as workers, as human beings—before anything like a closed shop is possible and still keep the industry constructive, progressive, and healthy.

A.: It may be, too, that there is room for improvement among employers.

P.: Oh, no doubt! I've been saying that what we need is to be entirely re-educated so far as our relations with the workers are concerned. . . . But let me say this to you, which I think will cover my attitude to this entire question in a general way: I, for one, am willing to go with the men and this union on the road that seems to lie dimly ahead of the C.I.O. as far as it is constructive.

A.: Meaning what?

P.: Meaning that I want steel to be made efficiently; that I want the country to be prosperous and progressive, industrially and otherwise; that, working, I want to be able to make a little money; that I want the industrial set-up to be such as to permit new ability to come in and be rewarded. Although, as you know, I am practically a C.I.O. organizer, I am glad that, after the Little Steel strike started, Girdler beat the C.I.O. and told a few things to the Administration in Washington. Had the C.I.O. won that strike, it would have been too much of a good thing for it. Even as it is, it's growing too fast.

A.: Then, why do you become, as you say, practically a C.I.O. organizer?

P.: Oh, for the hell of it.

A.: Come, come, Mr. Paynter.

P. (*smiling*): It's an inconsistency on my part. My position, I admit, is not entirely clear. But, in a way, I am on the spot among the independents who, following Girdler rather than the United States Steel Corporation, have not yet signed up with the C.I.O. They kid and criticize me; I have to defend myself—and, believing offense to be the best defense, I go after them when they refuse to deal with the S.W.O.C. people. . . .

My Friend Bob Weaver Suggests—

A S I AM WRITING THESE CHAPTERS, PAINFULLY CONSCIOUS THAT THEY PROBABLY are not very adequate, the socio-economic-industrial situation in America shows no sign of beginning to crystallize itself. Everything is more or less in a chaos. The so-called business "recession," which began in the autumn 1937, is blamed for increasing unemployment. The number of jobless is said to be over ten million. New Deal spokesmen storm against "monopolies" and the "Sixty Families," who are said to control the wealth of America. . . . John Lewis continues to be vaguely tremendous. Most other men whose personalities and functions touch upon the situation are tremendously vague. Those who are trying seriously to perceive things broadly, honestly, and in detail, and are steering clear of simplifications, snap judgments and neat intellectual solutions of problems, are confused: naturally so. They (as I) are but commencing to see the country's basic incongruity and its effects on everything in America, including the problem of progress. Some people are trying hard, and successfully, not to think. They swing uncomfortably and miserably between the pat, short-cut programs of the fascist and Communist totalitarian world movements. A few employers find themselves in such positions as "Mr. Paynter" in the chapter immediately before this one. They are confronted by enormous difficulties within themselves, within labor, within industry, and within the country as a whole.

Many employers, including some of the most important ones, are fascist-minded. This is due in part to their entire background as industrialists in a highly competitive system. They have been autocrats all their lives, issuing orders and seeing them obeyed, liquidating opposition to their interests, banishing to the Siberia of unemployment all who displeased them or whom they did not need. To a very great extent and in a very real sense, industry was war; industrialists were generals in that war, and they just naturally acted autocratically. Things being fundamentally what they were, they had to act that way; it never occurred to them that things could be changed fundamentally, so that they could act differently. They were too busy, too deeply involved in their inhuman, dehumanizing business, to think of anything like that. Now seemingly out of nowhere, but really out of the background and essential nature of America as a whole, there suddenly comes—in the midst of other troubles—the idea for a change, the idea of democracy in industry; and many of them react to it desperately, fascistically.

The more intelligent of them perceive the basic incongruity of the country; they admit that to have the country politically democratic and economically absolutist is all wrong, making everything more or less "cockeyed"; but their idea to abolish the incongruity is to do away with political democracy, instead of economic absolutism, and make the country entirely absolutist.

This is their idea . . . but it also is not their idea: for they are not entirely absolutist, not really. Even Tom Girdler—in an article in the January, 1938, *Fortune* magazine—insists that he is not and provides argument to prove it. Most of the fascist-minded employers are also Americans; that is, at least partly addicted or committed to democracy. Then, too, there is this: most great industries are geared for mass production, which calls for mass distribution of products, which calls for democracy and freedom of the broadest kind.[1] And so industrialists, financiers, and business men simultaneously are and are not fascist-minded, and are more or less confused and miserable as Americans, as employers, and as human beings. They seem increasingly conscious of the dehumanized state of their businesses; of the social irresponsibility of their corporations; of the great difficulties ahead of them and the country . . . and many of them, victims of the whole complex situation, their instincts at cross-purposes, are ready for anything and nothing. They are afraid, and not at all the big, confident men they strive to appear. They are afraid of Lewis; of the C.I.O.; of democracy in industry. They are so used to having things done autocratically that they cannot see how anything will ever be done, should anything resembling democracy really come into the shop. The workers—why, they are fit only to take orders and execute them. That they should eventually have something to say in the shop is absurd. And yet—and yet— Employers are disturbed when John Lewis declares, as he did late in 1937: "The time has come in this country for the workers to do some thinking, because whoever has been doing the thinking in the country has not done enough of it." . . .

Employers are beginning to think, or at least are trying to. There is my friend Robert A. Weaver, of Cleveland.

[1] A few days after writing this paragraph I came, in a book review in the New York *Times*, upon the following quotation from Miriam Beard's *History of the Business Man* published early in 1938 by The Macmillan Co.:

"American industries are founded, far more than European, upon catering to ever-rising needs of millions of people. They would not thrive upon producing a few elegant cars, like the German and Italian motor industries, or the sale of champagne to Party heroes. Nor would armament programs, the chief prop of such European regimes, be sufficient in America, where heavy industries could rapidly fill all possible needs and then would come to a halt, unable to sell enough abroad to keep themselves running. . . . The tremendous national machine of American economy must be fed by mass orders, which depend in turn upon mass-prosperity and, to a very much greater degree than in even a European democracy, upon free speech and good spirits. As fascism in Europe has worked out, the atmosphere of fear created by censorship has ruined many branches of business, the publishing and newspaper trades, the theatrical and cinema fields; in Europe this may not entail such serious disorganizations of economy, but in America terrible prostration would result if the people were afraid to dine out, speak out and run around in cars to talk to their friends."

Then, on January 20, 1938, Tom Girdler, who but a few months before was the outstanding would-be fascist leader, said this in a speech at Lehigh University: "Government spokesmen say they want to abolish poverty and increase the purchasing power of the mass of the people. Industry wants the same thing. Industry is absolutely dependent for its life in this country upon the mass consumption of goods. Anything that will increase mass purchasing will help the farmer, labor and business in general. How long do you think the automobile industry or the steel industry would survive if they had to depend upon the purchases of a few wealthy people?"

I first met Bob in 1934 at Kenyon College in Gambier, Ohio, of which he is an alumnus and a trustee. A native of Bradford, Pennsylvania, he was then in his mid-forties; a compact, energetic man with a pleasant, eager personality and manner; president of the Ferro Enamel Corporation, which controls most of the enamel business in the United States and Canada. We got into a discussion about the Depression and the capital-labor problem the first time we met, then carried it on intermittently through 1935-37. We met whenever I went to Cleveland and often when he came to New York. A conservative, he was anti-Roosevelt in 1936, and had been generally anti-New Deal before the election. We argued endlessly. Bob was always full of questions and ideas pertaining to the social-economic-political scene in America. He seemed to like to talk with me because I often disagreed with him. I liked him as a person and he interested me as a seeker after ideas.

By the end of 1937 his ideas evolved to something as follows—quoting freely what he said to me on our last encounter before this writing:

"I believe we can properly, if negatively, describe the capital-labor problem very simply by declaring that everybody concerned with the problem is wrong. The manufacturer considers labor a commodity, something like pig iron, yet at the same time really likes and admires most of his employees whom he happens to know as human beings. He is wrong in his commodity idea, but in extenuation of his error, this may be said: the idea is not really his; he has inherited it. It's an old fallacy that has been floating around now for a century. . . . On the other hand, the workers are wrong in submitting to the kind of leadership they have been receiving for years from, or through, their unions. They have done nothing toward the elimination of the racketeers who brought so much discredit on unions, and they have also been perfectly willing to grab all the extra money they could get even though it was at the expense of their fellow workers. In this they were as bad as the industrialists. Take the building trades unions, for example, and see what they have done with their greed for higher wages. They have simply increased tremendously the rents for their fellow workers and at the same time pushed the building cost so high that they have all but eliminated jobs for themselves. Labor at no time seems to have had any conception of the idea of *real wages*.[2]

"Both parties, capital and labor, have developed a spirit of conflict and have shown no willingness or ability to consider their mutual problem. Each side, instead of studying the problem and coöperating to solve it, has depended on the politicians to give it—now one, then the other—some advantage by supporting partisan laws. On the one hand, the employer has tried to benefit

[2] The academic definition of "real wages" is usually "the relationship between money wages and the index of the cost of living." To Bob Weaver "real wages" are practically synonymous with "barter wages." . . . "In other words," he says, "if your wages are increased this year ten percent and the cost of living also goes up ten percent, your real wages have not been increased at all, because you can still only buy the same things you could before the raise. On the other hand, of course, if you have your wages reduced and simultaneously the cost of living goes down, your real wages have not been reduced. . . ."

by the use of injunctions and, on the other, the unions tried to have wages and hours and working conditions changed by law. Between the two of them, they have played into the politicians' hands and brought about a situation which in the long run is ruinous to both and to the country as a whole.

"That—roughly—is the problem as I see it . . . and my plan for solving it is simply for both groups to declare a truce for a period of five years, with each group in the meantime trying to do a real job in decreasing costs and increasing real wages.

"The plan would start with a conference of representatives of the ten industries employing most labor, plus responsible union heads, government representatives, and the heads of the great economic-research organizations. Dr. Moulton of Brookings has done some splendid work showing how real wages can be advanced. There is another first-class research group in Pittsburgh which recently declared in favor of the unionization of steel mills. . . . This conference should agree to stay in session, with suitable adjournments, until a plan could be evolved which would be satisfactory for trial to both parties. They should consider the annual wage possibilities. This might be intelligently tied to the cost of living.

"This plan could be made acceptable to the industrialists by starting it, if absolutely necessary, with a real reduction in hourly rates but a guaranteed annual wage at least as great as the average in that industry for the last ten years. To induce labor to accept this, it is quite possible that the manufacturer could be made to set aside a certain substantial percentage of his profits to be divided with the workers. It is my impression that most workingmen are not interested in a high hourly wage, but in a regular annual wage that they can count on.

"As another beginning, in such a conference manufacturers might well offer to withdraw their opposition to unions if the unions on their part would become more democratic and would allow responsible leadership an opportunity to function. The unions should also arrange to have their finances checked in the same way that corporations' finances are checked. It might be also suggested to unions that they employ expert economists to advise them on projects submitted to or by the other side.

"In my opinion America is a business country, and this not only because of the rich resources which it contains, but because of the opportunity it offers every citizen which has made it the kind of a country it is. Practically all the friends I have who are heading big companies are men who originally came from comparatively poor surroundings. And I think a poll of laboringmen would show that they do not want taken from them the opportunity of rising to high places in industry.

"If we start on the premise that this is a business country and has produced the best kind of living for the greatest number of people in the world because it is a business country, then I think we can assume that anything that hurts business hurts everybody. The interests of capital and labor are mutual. In our particular company I am working for the company just like any of the laboring-men. I get a larger salary because I have a more responsible job. If I don't do a good job, I'll probably lose my job. So, if our interests are mutual, there is every reason in the world why we should sit down together to work out our mutual problems rather than fight with each other.

"The big study by a long-term conference that I suggest should be made in order to see how everybody could get more out of his job.

"There is nothing new in this idea, except my suggestion that the two groups stay in conference until some plan is evolved."

I give Bob Weaver's idea as indicative of the trend of thought on the part of the more or less progressive yet conservative business men and industrialists, of whom, I think, there are not a few. It is, of course, afflicted with several weaknesses, the chief of which is a manifestation of Bob's lack of knowledge of the essential nature of Big Business, which I have sketched in the section on the Depression. Bob apparently does not realize that Big Business would have to be induced to join in such a conference and stick with it till some plan is evolved. Induced by whom or what, and how? By the Government? By organized labor? By its own fear of economic collapse?

Moreover, is not the industrial situation intrinsically too dynamic, too tied up with every other life-throb of the country, to be put under a five-year truce, during which all manner of "chiselers" would take advantage of labor's promise not to fight for advantages? Who would police the "chiselers"?

There are other misgivings. Bob sent an outline of his idea to G. A. Drew, of United Investment Counsel, Boston, who appears to have an exceptionally interesting mind, which, more than merely aware of Marx, looks at socioeconomic problems from the viewpoint of business; and who, in a letter to Bob, raised this objection:

"I am inclined to think . . . that if a plan such as you outline were put into effect and the labor-leaders accepted some adjustment in wage rates, they would be accused of having 'sold out' by the ignorant and more numerous element. In other words, it would probably split the labor ranks in any one company or industry between the more intelligent minority and the larger group who are unable to see beyond their own noses."

In the same letter to Bob, Mr. Drew says several other highly interesting things which I want to quote in this book, whose general scheme and character aim, I think, more toward stimulating thought about the various phases of American life than to insist that I am one-hundred-per-cent right and everyone else who disagrees with me is completely wrong:

. . . You [Bob] remark that "the manufacturer considers labor a commodity." Well, shorn of its social aspect, it *is* a commodity. Marx says it is different because its "use value" is itself a source of value, but he is after something different. Except to the extent that better paid labor may decrease total costs because it is more efficient or for some similar intangible reason, the individual manufacturer is driven to buy his labor as he buys any commodity; *i.e.,* as cheaply as possible. If not, he must take a smaller profit or a larger loss, the latter being something that the theorist seldom thinks of.

Those who are as pro-labor as Mr. Adamic, for example, never seem to refer to a business as making anything but a profit—and a huge one at that. But as we know, there are thousands of small enterprises with what are undoubtedly underpaid employees, but whose owners are struggling to keep their own heads above water and to keep the whole enterprise afloat. Neither, of course, is Big Business at all immune from the red ink.

However, my point is that when the employer goes farther than the purchase of labor as a commodity, he must be moved by social concern or humanitarian feelings, which are directly at war with his normal desire to keep costs at the lowest point compatible with greatest operating efficiency.

I don't think there is any doubt but what the average management today does feel a far greater social responsibility for steadiness of employment and maintenance of wages than was the case twenty-five or thirty years ago. But I regard that as a normal evolution in a society that is more complex, more sensitive, and expanding at a less rapid rate. Labor has not forced the change upon capital, although it may have accelerated the process. In fact, from the standpoint I must adopt, General Motors, for instance, is already more of a social institution than it is a profit-making enterprise, although for Mr. Adamic the statement would undoubtedly be reversed.

On the whole, I think that capital has come further in understanding the viewpoint of labor than labor has in understanding the problems of capital. Granted that there are still plenty of unfair employers, there are, I think, fewer of them, whereas it seems to me that the unions—as representatives of labor—are more unreasoning and irresponsible than they were some years ago.

Of course, it is obvious, as you say, that what is needed is a greater mutual understanding of their problem, but the willingness to achieve that must, I think, come from within and it cannot be forced upon either side. . . .

My feeling is that a lot can be accomplished by the education of labor in individual companies so that the men will understand just what may be reasonably expected. I think that a profit-sharing system is highly desirable, but obviously, this is something where the system has got to be different in individual cases. But, the point is that it should show the worker exactly what is happening in a simple form. I see no reason why in most cases, for instance, simple monthly figures could not be posted somewhere showing them the sales, the cost of doing business and the amount left over to be divided among them and reserves, or whatever might be decided upon under the particular plan.

As Mr. Adamic has shown in some of his books, notably in *Dynamite,* one of the major difficulties is that in many companies—particularly in those where the management is far removed from the employees—, the worker just does not give a damn about the business he works for, and has no compunctions about resorting to sabotage if he feels he has a grievance. Where that spirit exists, no progress is going to be made, and for that reason I think that the employee must be made to feel something at least of the spirit of enterprise and partnership. Obviously, he is going to get that only if he in some way shares in the profits so that when the business does well, he is better off personally.

It goes without saying, of course, that management has got to do its best to keep employment as steady and as large as possible without undue sacrifice of efficiency. . . . I think you are right that as far as the more intelligent workingman is concerned at least, he is more interested in a regular annual income than in a high hourly wage. It is a long uphill climb; however, I do think progress is being made. But, as indicated above, I believe it must continue more as the result of a "regeneration from within" on both sides rather than by the laying down of arbitrary plans by the Government or any other authority. Things of that sort cannot be forced, and my only concrete suggestion is that business should take workers more into its confidence in order to make their relations more of a partnership and less of a conflict.

I don't feel that anything I have said here is very satisfactory, because it is just one of those subjects that you can talk on endlessly and simply keep going around in circles. I'd feel on much firmer ground if you asked me what I thought about the stock market.

A CORPORATION REPORTS TO ITS JOBHOLDERS

Early in March, 1938, I noticed in the daily press that Lewis H. Brown, president of Johns-Manville Corporation, New York City, "reported to its 11,200 jobholders for 1937," thus "marking a new departure in corporate reporting practice." His report began: "It has long been the custom for business firms to issue annual reports to their stockholders. I propose this year to make a report to the jobholders, the persons whose time and labor invested in Johns-Manville make it possible to manufacture and distribute and sell our products."

The report pointed out that of the $64,161,722 received from customers in 1937, $20,311,813 was spent for materials and $3,988,330 was paid to railroads and trucking concerns for transporting goods and paid for cancelled sales, leaving $39,861,579 as the actual amount Johns-Manville received for the value it added by manufacturing raw materials into finished products and for handling certain products manufactured by other companies. Of this sum, 51 percent or $20,354,000 was turned over to the company's jobholders in wages and salaries, $4,562,500, or 11½ percent was paid to stockholders as their "wages" in the form of dividends, $2,077,000, or 5 percent was paid out in taxes, $2,179,000, or 6 percent in depreciation and depletion, $603,000 or 1½ percent for research, $889,-343, or 2 percent, was put aside for new plants and additional working capital, while $9,196,736, or 23 percent went for "all other expenses," including repairs and maintenance, advertising, etc.

The report mentioned that in back of every employee there was an investment of $4,561 in buildings, machinery, tools, and other property, totalling $51,281,512; and it concluded that "it is the chief concern of the managers to try to plan for the best possible, uninterrupted annual wage or salary for both jobholders and stockholders. Then neither of them will be laid off. Your company managers know that both stockholders and jobholders are dependent upon each other, and that neither could profit without the support and cooperation of the other."

SAM LEWISOHN'S CALL FOR MORE DEMOCRACY

Highly indicative, too, of the intellectual trends among industrialists during 1937-38 was the keynote address by Sam A. Lewisohn, who has large interests in mining and banking, before the Personnel Research Federation's conference on labor relations in December, 1937. "It is commonplace," he said, "to stress the natural physical assets of America and it has also become commonplace to stress the enormous human energy and resourcefulness that has made possible the exploitation of our physical resources. But there is one resource that has been too little exploited and indeed almost forgotten. That resource is our democratic spirit. With all the surface bitterness that runs through our life, this democratic spirit unites us. There is a jaunty good nature—a camaraderie—that is imbedded in the nature of all of us, from taxicab driver to investment banker. . . . The outstanding genius of this country is that we have liquidated the caste system which underlies the social fabric of all Europe and Asia." Lewisohn urged democratic attitudes and understanding in industry. "I hope no executive here will get the idea that this policy of democratic understanding is some impractical ideal advanced by gushy social workers. A diplomatic, democratic attitude on the part of an executive has become a real business asset. An industrial executive just can't afford to be without it if he is going to be a success in the position that he occupies.—In industry the democratic non-class attitude pays. It is good business."

Someone once said that there was more democracy in the relationship between the average American industrialist and the average American worker than in the relationship between the average Soviet commissar and the average Russian muzhik. That is probably true, as is what Lewisohn said about America's democratic spirit. To many of his employees, Bob Weaver, for instance, is merely "Bob," as they are to him merely "Jim" or "Slim" or "Dick" or "Shorty." This sort of thing is prevalent throughout the United States, and more of it would, of course, be marvelous. However, it seems to me that the minds of Messrs. Weaver, Drew and Lewisohn have not yet begun to consider the essential structure and nature of big business, which are the same in 1938 as they were in 1930, and which, as I have tried to analyze them, are impersonal, inhuman, socially unintelligent and irresponsible, not conducive to democracy; indeed, the opposite. Mr. Knudsen, of General Motors, is a very democratic man, and yet—and in spite of Mr. Drew's statement that that great firm is more a social institution than a profit-making enterprise—late in 1937, General Motors suddenly and arbitrarily laid off 30,000 workers because orders had fallen off.

The problem is not so much how to enhance the personal democracy of Mr. Knudsen and his fellow managers, but how to overhaul the whole industrial system so that, American-like, the relations between workers and employers will be naturally, inevitably democratic, based upon a mutual sense of security.

Notes on the Difficult Task Facing the C.I.O.

WITH THE C.I.O. LAUNCHED, AND LABOR FORCES AT LEAST PARTLY AWARE of their importance, organized labor will in all probability play a central rôle in the drama of American life for some time to come, even should the movement as a whole suffer some set-backs (which is likely) during the years immediately after the publication of this book. I think (or hope) that, by and large, it will play a good rôle; it is conceivable, however, or even very possible, as already suggested, that the rôle will be a bad one, and probable that it will be not so good as could reasonably be expected. And this, I have no doubt, will—in the long run—depend greatly upon what sort of educational movement will develop within and in connection with the unions, which in turn will depend a good deal upon the top leaders of the C.I.O.

At the time I saw John Lewis in 1936 he was not very deeply interested in workers' education apart from organization, which he said had a certain intrinsic educational value. Speaking with other C.I.O. union leaders during 1936-37, I felt that, outside the preponderantly Jewish garment workers' unions whose headquarters are in New York and whose interest in education already is a matter of decades, none had any real idea of the new labor movements' educational needs. One reason for this was their preoccupation with the immediate problems of organization, administration, and tactics. Another, more serious, reason was that most of them personally were not very well educated men in any sense of the word, nor naturally brilliant or imaginative. Many local and district union leaders whom I met were but slightly above average; some not even that, but merely more aggressive, ambitious, and articulate than the majority of union members. Some impressed me as potentially not unlike the general run of A.F. of L. "skates" who for decades had deliberately opposed any kind of workers' education or cultural activity on, from their point of view, the sound theory that unions whose memberships were intellectually and spiritually dead were easier to handle.

One may be justified in saying that John Lewis himself, while in the A.F. of L., never manifested any considerable interest in workers' education. The United Mine Workers, under his presidency since 1920, have within their ranks even at this late date no educational movement worth mentioning. Their unions are almost solely economic in purpose and function, with wellnigh no cultural content. The only education that Lewis believed in was to the effect that workers needed the union, that the union was good for the workers, and that the union was most effective under his leadership. *The United Mine Workers' Journal,* published under his supervision, was always (still is) a mediocre paper, devoted to the idea stated in the sentence immediately preceding. There is no doubt that in this respect at least Lewis was a very ordinary laborite: he did not believe in workers' education in any real sense of the word. Indeed, it may be said that, in common with most A.F. of L. leaders, he feared it. Education led to all sorts of disconcerting developments in an individual as well as in a group; it was apt to precipitate all manner of trouble in a vast organization like the U.M.W., which, Lewis probably figured, might complicate his problems as top leader. There may be much extenuation of this attitude on the part of the pre-C.I.O. Lewis, and one can understand his desire or inclination to hang on to it in the C.I.O. . . . but it is impossible to sympathize with it.

Just now—1937-38—John Lewis finds himself as a leader and public figure in an anomalous rôle in America. He is preaching and, as I have suggested, really working within his lights for what he calls industrial democracy; yet the C.I.O. is anything but a democratic movement. He dominates it (not entirely but largely) by methods which are not far from dictatorial. His heavy and competent hand draws all the important lines of the C.I.O. policy. This may be inevitable for the time being, while this new mass labor movement is in the formative stage; and as its initiator Lewis is perhaps entitled to the biggest say-so. But, in view of his background, in view of the fact that for nearly twenty years he has been virtually the fighting dictator of the U.M.W., and in view of the probability that dictatorship is in his nature, and domi- nance his medium of expression, it is extremely urgent that he does not continue too long as the sole and indispensable big boss and policy-maker of the C.I.O. and of the great labor organization developing under its auspices.

For reasons which I hope I need not enumerate, it is vastly important that this new mass labor movement which now—in 1937-38—centers around the potent, dramatic personality of Lewis, develops (the sooner, the better) into a truly democratic movement. If it does not develop into a democratic move- ment within itself, the now vital slogan of "industrial democracy" will presently lose its meaning and the C.I.O. unions are apt to become anything but the bright hope of America. And I think that it can develop into a democratic movement only with the aid of a proper vital and integral education whose ulti- mate aim or ideal is democracy.

Preparing to write this chapter, I opened the January, 1938, number of The Social Frontier, the always interesting "journal of educational criticism and reconstruction," as it describes itself, which is the organ of the John Dewey Society for the Study of Education and Culture and other educational groups; and I came upon an article on "Workers' Education—C.I.O. Model" by Mark Starr, educational director of the International Ladies' Garment Workers' Union, which, under the leadership of David Dubinsky, is prob- able one of the most progressive, effective, and generally respected labor or- ganizations in America.

Four thousand recruits [begins the article] of the Amalgamated Workers in

Cincinnati taking a solemn mass obligation to appropriate music by a labor choir; a union carnival in Tennessee featuring a spitting contest with union-labor tobacco as ammunition; taxi-drivers on the graveyard shift studying public speaking at three A.M.; four hundred members of the International Ladies' Garment Workers staging a pageant on the union's history in the St. Louis Municipal Auditorium; steel workers studying trade-union problems in morning and evening classes at Aliquippa, Pa., where previously it was a problem to be a trade unionist and keep alive; "canned" speeches of nationally known leaders for use over local radio stations; unions setting aside per-capita funds for education; a tremendous increase in workers' education literature, ranging from *Mother Goose Goes Union* to pamphlets on union methods; a whole host of new local papers, mimeographed and printed; labor history in photo-illustrated magazines such as the Maritime Federation's *Men and Ships*; unions running their own health centers, sport leagues, songfests, bands and radio programs and branching out in many new ways of publicity—this is workers' education, new in its extent and variety, spreading through the United States. During the present year (1937-38), there will be, at a conservative estimate, over one hundred thousand workers meeting in weekly study classes and recreational groups.

Which, albeit somewhat whimsical, appears much more impressive and flattering to the C.I.O. as a whole than it actually is. Most of the more or less important educational doings enumerated are conducted not so much by the C.I.O. or its new unions as by the International Ladies' Garment Workers, the Amalgamated Clothing Workers, and the American Federation of Hosiery Workers—especially the first two, which have a long pre-C.I.O. record in educational and generally cultural activities. There is some, but comparatively very little, educational work going on in the steel, rubber, and auto organizations; what there is of it is barely scratching the surface of the problem. It is mostly organizational and recreational, but it is not enough by a long, long way.

It is perfectly all right, I suppose, to stage spitting contests with union tobacco juice, and, of course, necessary to have courses in trade-union problems, by which is usually meant organization, union administration, shop grievances, company unions, collective bargaining, strike tactics, and so on. It is all very fine to be doing all the other things Mr. Starr suggests and it is encouraging to note that the automobile unions bought two hundred thousand copies of Upton Sinclair's pamphlet, *The Flivver King,* for use in the campaign to organize the Ford industry. . . . But the problem of the education that ought to be tackled by organized labor goes infinitely deeper and farther than these organizational-educational and mainly recreational doings can possibly reach.

America as a whole has almost no actual understanding of the worker, either as worker or as human being. This is partly the fault of newspapers, speakers, labor leaders themselves. Too often the presentation of, or the reference to, real and definite and immediate problems of the workingman are obscured or confused by referring to them as problems of "Labor," which of course is an inclusive abstraction, and which greatly lessens the punch, the drama, or truth of such a presentation, and spreads the facts over so wide an area that there is little to see or feel. Thus the misery of the worker, pressing and vital, is submerged in mass misery. The worker himself tends to the abstraction and finds no little comfort in knowing that there are others in the same boat. It is, in part, an extenuating device, and makes him willing to endure much more, to feel little individual responsibility toward the problem of which he is a part, and to wait for some Moses like Lewis to appear and lead him out of his plight. Although he is aware of the fact that others are in the same boat, the realization arouses little or no solidarity in him. His stint at the factory finished for the day, he leaves that mostly behind him. When he suffers, he suffers as an individual. He may feel an emotional kinship with other sufferers, but at the same time he tends to see them impersonally in terms of wage rates and "30,000 LAID OFF BY GENERAL MOTORS." The situation becomes a headline. . . . In other words, John Jones, the lathe-hand, faced with certain problems, does not see the thousands or millions of other John Joneses whose problems are similar to his own; he only gets a vague emotional notion that "labor" is so-so or in a bad way, that there is a slump or a slight rise in work or a depression. As I have said earlier here, it took the American worker a long time after the 1929 crash to realize that he was not entirely and personally responsible for his failure to get work during the Depression. This was because he had only a meager conception of his position in the whole scheme of things in America. Later on this manifested itself in another way. He joined a union, not because it would generally improve the situation *for everybody*, including himself, but because he finally realized that as an individual he was pathetically helpless, and that "in union there is strength," and he thus availed himself of that strength, *for himself*. There was (is) in him little knowledge of the relationship that bound (binds) him to other workers and the entire vast and wonderful setup of America.

I know, or have known, hundreds of unskilled workers, particularly in the smaller industries, whose apathy and resignation are something appalling. Where no union has appeared to rouse them, most of them remain basically indifferent to the conditions they have to endure. Because certain conditions exist, they see no possibility of having them altered. There is a dead fatalism. The novelty factories of New York are a notorious example. The exploitation is outrageous, but the workers merely grumble. When unionization is suggested, they oppose it: it might lose them their jobs! Yet they hate their jobs. That hate expresses itself in subversive talk, sabotage, defeatism.

The American workers' greatest obstacle is not the employers' opposition to the improvement of their situation, but their ignorance of their position, their rights in industry, in American life.

Most American workers have little or no conception of jobs outside their fields. They are unaware of the interdependence of the workers' functions, and so ignorant of their importance, the indispensability of their work. Many tend to deprecate their functions, if not orally, then to themselves and perform listlessly, as workers, as human beings . . . and the general public, as uninformed as they are concerning what makes the wheels go round, tends to agree with them. All the public sees is the solitary worker going home in the evening, begrimed, spiritless with fatigue.

In America all too many people, including (and especially) workers, believe that really to be something one must be at least an insurance agent. Not to be obliged to work with one's hands for wages is the life-ideal of millions of workers who have no pride in their jobs: which I think is socially and individually unsound. Men are oppressed by feelings of inferiority because they are workers; and resultantly many are not half the men and citizens they could be. Of course this is all tied up with the workers' lack of security which is part of the entire industrial chaos; and if, or when, the labor movement succeeds in introducing a touch of security into industry, some of the workers' inferiority feelings will naturally vanish, but not all, nor possibly most or the worst. Therein is a great task for adult education which, so far as I can see, can be effectively undertaken only by a great labor movement with an intelligent, subtle, far-seeing, patriotic, *socially conscious* leadership. Most workers have no strong sense of belonging anywhere. They are disoriented, ignorant of their position; many, as I have said, are in consequence neurotic, disbalanced, or "cracked" persons: which, of course, has consequences in turn. They need to be helped to get a feeling of belonging, of having a place, in the socio-economic scheme of the country; of being important.

I shall not presume here to outline the technique of such education. As yet almost nothing has been thought on the subject; generally, it has not been recognized as a problem. It is a problem for many minds. I incline to think, however, that the core of the technique of this adult education, if it is ever started, will have to be indirection impregnated in life-situations; it will have to be addressed to the public as a whole, as suggested in the chapter "What the C.I.O. REALLY Is," which, of course, also needs urgently to be educated about the place of the workers in the scheme of America. Some of the obvious ways to get at this problem are, perhaps, to publish, in newspapers and magazines and books, well-done dramatic and factual and fictional stories about *workers* (not about "Labor") in industries; to give dramatic lectures and radio broadcasts on the same subject delivered by effective speakers; to go in for dramatic presentations in some such way as indicated by the International Ladies' Garment Workers' Labor Stage, whose *Pins and Needles* was a Broadway hit in the winter of 1937-38; to present industrial labor—its truth, its drama, and its immense importance in the life of the entire country—in striking, artistic posters on roadside billboards. For this purpose the labor movement will have to develop its own talent and to attract to itself competent people in the educational, literary, artistic, theatrical, radio, advertising, publicity, and other fields. People in these fields would find it advantageous to go into the labor movement, which offers vast opportunities for work and function, for service to labor and the country.

Much of labor education should, of course, be direct, specific and special. Unions—many of which have large sums of money at their disposal—should start labor schools and substantially help to support the few labor schools already in existence.

Of the existing labor schools of which I am aware, perhaps the most interesting, though (for financial and other reasons) woefully inadequate, is the Highlander Folk School at Monteagle, in the mountains of Tennessee, founded and headed by a young Southern ex-minister named Myles Horton, whom I know. Its story is, I think, worth telling in some detail.

During the late 1920's the Rev. Horton watched the people of his locality leave their mountain homes in response to the industrial agents' stories of mill villages and towns, and return in a few months or a year broken in health and spirit. Some never returned, but stayed "below." He visited them and discovered exploitation of the worst kind. He found ex-members of his mountain congregation who but a short time before had been, as he puts it, "bright-eyed girls and freedom-loving outdoor men" and were now doomed to spend the rest of their lives coughing up lint. A few of the younger folk were eager to understand what was happening to them and their region. He knew some farmer boys and girls back in the hills who also realized something was wrong in the world and wanted to know what that was. So in November, 1932, on a mountain farm within five hours' drive of several industrial centers, Myles Horton started a school, calling it The Highlander Folk School.

"At first," as he now tells, "the school was only a large farmhouse and an idea. There were about half a dozen of us, all from the neighborhood; and it was hard to tell who was student and who teacher. We just talked, exchanging experiences and views. It was two months before any students came from beyond the immediate vicinity. During that time we cut wood and worked on the farm. The first outside student was the son of an Alabama coal miner. There was no curriculum. One evening, while visiting a neighbor, we started to discuss psychology. The farmer, his wife, and the boy from Alabama wanted to continue the discussion, so we met at the school the following evening and held our first class. I had had a little psychology in college and had been reading up on it. Soon we had a class of twenty-five, including farmers, miners, college graduates, and mill folk. Our ages ranged from eighteen to eighty. No classes were started that were not asked for or that did not grow out of some life situation with which we, or some of us, were familiar. A class in cultural geography followed the neighbors' interest in some snapshots I had taken in Europe. Stories of a miners' strike brought back by those who had visited the coal camp at Wilder, Tennessee, raised questions that led to a class in economics. . . ."

With the school developed, its program now consists of residence courses, extension work, and community activities. Workers who show promise of becoming active in the labor movement as organizers or local leaders are selected as resident students. Their number is between one and two dozen. Most of them are from the mills and sharecropper families. Not a few are graduates of such colleges as Vassar, Williams, and Smith who are interested in workers' education and want to find a place for themselves in the labor movement. The definite courses given are economics, labor history, and tactics, workers' problems, public speaking, dramatics, and journalism. In each class an effort is made to stay within the experience of the students. Horton does probably most of the teaching; he is assisted by such former students of other schools as I have mentioned, by the more articulate Southern labor leaders and organizers who come there for a few weeks at a time, and now and then— unwittingly—by the industrialists. In 1934 an agent of a near-by coal company tried to dynamite the school because the students and teachers had taken part in a United Mine Workers' strike. For two weeks the residents of the school and its neighbors guarded the place night and day: "which," Horton told me, "was of course very educational."

The H.F.S. extension program is carried on throughout the year in connection with unions and farmers' organizations in the various communities. The teachers and students take part in organization campaigns and in strikes, then lead discussions dealing with what had happened. The more systematic work is done through study groups set up by the extension director and by former students. Most of the new students are recruited through the extension work.

The community activities, also year-round, are of a cultural as well as of a labor-educational nature. Piano lessons are provided for anyone in the community. As many as twenty children and young people have been taking music lessons at one time. Old and young take part in dramatics and folk dancing. A few adults attend regular morning classes during residence courses. Special lectures are given at night so that a larger number from the community can attend.

As I write, the school has six more or less full-time teachers, who receive no regular salary. Most of the food is raised on the school's farm or is given by the neighbors in payment for tuition. The annual cash budget is less than five thousands dollars, which the school gets in small donations from interested unions and private persons.

Up to 1938 the results of the H.F.S. have been small in any concrete or easily demonstrable sense. I do not believe that Myles Horton or anyone else connected with it has as yet any well-rounded-out idea of what the problem of labor education in the United States as a whole actually is. I do think, however, that this little school in Tennessee, which seems to me so very American in origin and in its history so far, holds an interesting suggestion at least as to the immediate and surface phases of workers' education.

But, as already suggested, here I am mainly interested in the broader and deeper phases of the vast educational job that I think confronts the C.I.O. leadership.

Industrial democracy—

This phrase is used ponderously, pontifically by John Lewis, glibly and frequently by his lieutenants and C.I.O.'s publicity men. One cannot object to their using it. But I wonder how much thought they have really given to the idea it promulgates. I wonder if they realize, even dimly, that democracy— "of all the forms of government," Henry Sumner Maine has said, "the most difficult"—is less a system or instrument of power than *a state of social consciousness* (as distinct from *class* consciousness), which everybody in industry will more or less have to possess, or strive for within himself and his group, if we are to attain a regime of industrial democracy, or even an encouraging semblance thereof; and that such a state of *social* consciousness can become a reality in an individual or in a group only through the slow process of education, which will have to have an intense awareness of the great difficulties of democracy.

Industrial democracy—

What do they—Lewis and his fellow leaders—*feel* when they use this phrase? I know the difficulties of defining "democracy," and I do not expect anyone to define it; but whereto do their thoughts tend when they use the phrase? Toward the revolutionary-Socialist idea of Daniel De Leon? De Leon wanted the workers, the producers, those actually working in industries, in all capacities, to own the machinery of production. He wanted the industries, including agriculture, organized into huge units, industrial principalities, within which the workers, technicians, managers, and social engineers, all members of a single union, would run things democratically, elect their bosses in free election, then submit to their authority; and over all of them, over the whole country, there would be a central government for everything: not only for industry, but for all important phases of life. De Leon's aim was not merely that workers and technicians, those actually taking part in production, should own the industries as such, control the capital in them, and get more material return for their daily effort, but that through the control of the economy of the country they would have power to develop the ability and a program for creating a new moral and spiritual civilization, a new culture, and there would be stability and a controlled organic development of things: progress for the benefit of the masses. . . . Do John Lewis' thoughts tend that way? I doubt it. Then, what?

A friend who is looking over my shoulder as I write these pages does not believe that the C.I.O. leaders see industrial democracy, as they use the phrase, as a means or instrument of power. Democracy, he says, is not an instrument, but a frame within which instruments are freely used. "What Lewis & Co. want to do," he goes on, "is to implant industrial democracy in democracy. In other words, the part wants to become the whole, the lesser the greater, the shard a vase. I think this is Lewis' ultimate vision. But the vision is a form of astigmatism. He has his eyes off the real center of things: that is, off real democracy. . . . There are two things which will have a tremendous influence on the C.I.O.'s development and its place in America. The first is a desire for power on the part of its leaders. The second: these leaders, pulled by the unformed, haphazard passions of aroused but uninformed workers, may not know where to stop, or will not want to stop anywhere, for they will have behind them, pushing them still further on, the forces they set in motion. A labor movement, conscious of its power, may start almost anything, bring almost anything into existence. Lewis must be conscious of this. And thus it follows that the C.I.O. sees democracy less as an instrument of power, less as a means, than as an end. If one studies the C.I.O., a revolution in the direction of Socialism (and a bloodless one at the beginning) becomes, perhaps not probable or even possible, but conceivable. Don't forget that hundreds of thousands of workers are tasting power for the first time; it tastes good; it is being flavored for them by the propagandists, most of whom are irresponsible people; and, as you say, the working class is not made up, any more than is any other class, of well-balanced, informed individuals. So what? So, if the C.I.O. becomes successfully revolutionary, we are then liable to have here the same or a similar situation we now see in Russia. Dictatorship; struggle for power within the dictatorship; sabotage. Then blood will flow. . . . Therefore, even if we admit what I say only as something barely conceivable, it is intensely important that we know what lies behind the mask of Lewis' personality and power to date, whether he really conceives of industrial democracy as an instrument or as an end. As you say, he is the policy-maker of the C.I.O. Does he know that the C.I.O. he has created is not a sure vehicle of progress but a pile of dynamite? . . ."

In saying the above, my friend does not consider that the C.I.O., as it goes on, will be checked by all manner of obstacles, by other great forces operating in America; none the less what he says contains noteworthy thoughts. I would say that the C.I.O., as it stands, is both a vehicle of progress and a pile of dynamite; and that John Lewis and his fellow leaders realize this none too clearly—and some of them, perhaps, not at all.

They—John Lewis & Co.—talk and act as though they are aware of the basic incongruity of America (which I mention so often in this book because it is really its theme). They talk and act as though they want to abolish that incongruity by abolishing industrial absolutism or economic royalism, to use the phrase popularized by President Roosevelt in his periodic political forays on the would-be but hesitant napoleons and hitlers and mussolinis of America, and to replace it with industrial democracy. But are they aware of the difficulties of democracy? Or do they, or some of them, employ the phrase "industrial democracy" only with an empty vigor, having nothing else in mind but a few cents more per hour and an hour or two less in the workday?

Do they know that democracy is a comparatively new idea in the world?—that in America, which in certain ways is perhaps the most democratic country on earth, it is scarcely more than an ideal even in politics?—that, as yet, very little thought has been given to the subject of democracy?—that much of the education now dispensed in American schools, colleges, and universities is, in the way it works out in individual lives, not particularly friendly to the democratic idea and ideals?—that democracy cannot be attained merely by destroying the people and institutions that seem to stand in its way?—that the slogan "the remedy for the ills of democracy is more democracy" is not really as true as it sounds?

Anent this last question I want to quote from an article by Joseph Dana Miller on democracy which appeared years ago in the *International Journal of Ethics* (London):

. . . Those who are perplexed or disappointed at the results of democracy should realize that the course of development through which civilizations and peoples must pass is analogous to that which confronts the infant learning to walk. Democracy will stumble and lean upon rotten pillars long before it learns to walk alone. Like the Israelites, it will return every now and then to its idols, and set up brazen images of demagogues before which it will prostrate itself, so that the very friends of democracy will despair of its future.

The ills of democracy, then, are not to be remedied by more democracy. For they are inherent in democracy. The methods by which it seeks to express itself will be found to be halting, inarticulate, stammering. . . .

. . . Perhaps democracy is a lesson to be learned—learned through suffering and travail—reached through long and tortuous journeying. Maybe it is not something that springs full-armed and perfected like Minerva from the head of Jupiter. Maybe the cure for the ills of democracy is not only more democracy, but more knowledge and more love.

Why not recognize that democracy grows only as public opinion grows in intelligence and toleration? Public opinion as a governing force was born hardly more than a hundred years ago. Its advent was heralded in France by the ferment of revolution, in America by the Declaration of Independence, in England by the Reform Bills. . . .

Industrial democracy in America will grow only as American public opinion, including (and perhaps especially) the opinion of industry and labor, will grow in intelligence. But the initial requisite of intelligent public opinion is *consciousness,* of which there is very little in the world. As is true of people almost generally, American workers, including most of the union leaders, are not very conscious of the world in which they live, from either the social or any other viewpoint. I believe that the picture in "Mr. Paynter's" steel mill at "Coalburg, Pennsylvania," which he drew for me, is fairly accurate; it shows a profound need for education—for consciousness—for responsibility. And Mr. Drew's views of labor cannot be dismissed, either, on the grounds that he is an investment counselor and his standpoint is pro-capital. I think that both in "Paynter's" and in Drew's words, as well as in some of the things that Bob Weaver has to say, the workers and their leaders should find much to ponder. Labor (like capital, of course, and like the public) has a long way to go in the matter of social relations.

John Lewis' statement to me, to the effect that labor's responsibility in, to, and for industry will come well-nigh inevitably as a result of such beginnings in the process of industrial democracy as organization and collective bargaining is to be seriously questioned. Many A.F. of L. unions have bargained col-lectively now for decades; they or their leaders or members still have no re-sponsibility in, to, and for the industries. Indeed, one does not have to be a union-hater to say that the A.F. of L. unions have certainly had a hand in putting some of the industries, notably building, on the rocks. They had (still have) no glimmering of any consciousness pertaining to industry that is anything more than narrow class, group, or (one might say) racket con-sciousness, whose chief characteristics are inner fear and outward arrogance, which is the manner of the average A.F. of L. walking delegate. In fact, mere organization and collective bargaining, which are a matter of conflict, dispute, and wrangling of all sorts, are very apt to preclude the development of any-thing but group or class consciousness, which has almost no relation to social consciousness, which alone can inevitably result in responsibility.

Here my friend says to me, "What you have just written is, I imagine, a fairly good description of collective bargaining. As it stands now [in 1938] the C.I.O.'s big idea is collective bargaining. The C.I.O. is an instrument for wresting privileges for its members; and the more they get the better. The object is immediate benefits. And of course the employers are on the other side of the fence. Both are determined either to get hold of or to retain some-thing. . . . They have no real common meeting-ground, no long-range ob-jective which would give them, capital and labor, some kind of perspective and yardstick. Their collective-bargaining meetings are dead ends, till the next one comes along, which is only a repetition of the preceding one. Thus, essen-tially, all of it is mere wrangling. There is nothing really creative, positive. Neither side has any values outside of themselves or their positions which might remove the fence between them, lift their encounters above mere squab-bles. There is no give-and-take, but mere force and yielding to force; mere taking advantage of one another's weaknesses—in other words, essentially a negative business. No ideal, to speak of, plays a rôle in this sort of thing, even if some of the labor leaders are idealists. If they are idealists, they exist as such in a vacuum, in which they stand dedicated to the ideals of one definite group. Are these ideals, however, of any great validity if in the fight to realize them questionable methods are used upon their opponents, at their expense? To me, one of the most amazing aspects of this situation lies in the persistence of both capital and labor in maintaining a rigid line of demarcation. Both admit, or almost so, that one cannot exist without the other, yet seldom is this realized practically to any great extent. The attitude of suspicion, on both sides, stands in the way of the harmony that should prevail, if for no other reason, for efficiency. There is no serious effort to realize *mutually* that workers and employers are integral factors of the whole process of enterprise, which includes other factors. This will sound silly to Marxists; but I think that such an effort is essential before idealists, as such, both among labor and among the industrialists, will begin to function effectively. But in such an effort the emphasis ought to be on realizing that labor and capital are but parts of something vastly greater than both of them together—of a civilization dedicated to the principles of democracy; and that they can function harmoniously and idealistically only in the midst of a citizenry, which includes them, and which is articulate and consciously moving toward democracy and increasing social consciousness; a citizenry able, willing, and eager to contribute, rather than shouting, 'Gimme!' . . ."

Question: which comes first—democracy or social consciousness? I am not sure. As I say, so little has been thought on this subject. Perhaps the two come and work together. Or even are one and the same thing. One cannot go without the other. Industrial democracy perhaps is no more than an approach to a state of social consciousness. After all, industry is but a part of our lives. And is not, perhaps, a state of social consciousness primarily a well-rounded-out conception of our position as human beings and our duties and responsibilities attendant upon it? In a way, is it not an awareness of the relationship that binds or should bind all people? I think that if it is not that, all we have is *class* consciousness, which means surface fuss and fury—struggle, which only leads to more and more intense class consciousness, and so on. After all, what is the common denominator among mankind? Is it not a desire for happiness, for function? How to attain them? . . . Fumbling about in the difficult subject of this chapter, I ask questions, to which, I know, there can be no definite answers. . . .

I say: after all, industry is but a part of our lives. But this is superficial. The question involves more than industry in our lives. Industry is *one* form of function. John Lewis has invaded the political field and evidently wants to go further in that field. No objection to that *per se*; but what is in his mind? Is his aim to make that one form of function, industry, the basis of government in America? I am asking this question because Lewis, as the C.I.O. leader, with his tremendous vagueness which I have mentioned, is the center of the nebulousness of the subject I am discussing here. Here I am trying to examine that nebulousness, which is an extremely hard thing to do (causing me to be nebulous myself). With his C.I.O., Lewis looms immense on the American scene, and out of him rumbles a phrase, an abstraction—*industrial democracy*—and that is all. No attempt at explanation. A mask.

The C.I.O., as I have told, is essentially good. But what is behind the mask of its leader? Ignorance? Design? Either is dangerous. Mere opportunism? . . .

Industrial democracy—

Is not social consciousness immeasurably more than *industrial* democracy, whatever Lewis may mean by the latter phrase beyond collective bargaining? To me, social consciousness means that people generally will not tolerate the raising of the price of food and clothing merely as a matter of greater profit for somebody; that the better-to-do will not be at ease within themselves while others live in slums and firetrap dwellings; that kids will have a chance to develop sound lives; that men will not have to, will not be allowed to, stand themselves up in the "slave market" or bread lines; that business competitors will not be obliged to cut each other's throats; that the Smiths will not look down on the Joneses because the latter have no car or radio; that man will assume a responsibility toward his fellow man. I know I say this inadequately; but, briefly, I mean that people will have a chance to be human, sociable, generous, good, because it is expedient (if only that) to be human, sociable, generous, and good. Social consciousness means a humanity concerned for the welfare of all its members.

Social consciousness—democracy—

Democracy is something not full-fledged and final. Social consciousness, the awareness of one's obligation to his fellow men, is itself democracy. And it is the trying to place this awareness into dynamic operation that determines how much democracy there is. *Laissez-faire* has long been one of the tenets of democracy, but wrongly so. It is passive, negative; at least as it develops in practice. If it were true and right, then most of our concepts of civilization are wrong. *Laissez-faire* is more like nature, than civilization; and nature, by and large, is brutal, taking no account of the weak and momentarily disabled. Followed or practiced rigorously (as it was in America before 1929, and still is), it is a demoralizing, destructive creed. As Dr. Charles A. Beard has suggested, it is not in line with the traditions of the American frontier period, when human and social attitudes were, in many respects, deeply communal. Those defending it may call themselves the Liberty League; however, it is not liberty they defend, but license; not civilization, but the jungle. If we practice it in a big way, then, in what respect are we superior to the so-called lower animals? However naïve-seeming, this is a question that must be raised and made vivid in the public mind if we are to get anywhere out of the current chaotic attempts at civilization and democracy. Who or what can raise it, make it vivid, and keep it alive for any length of time if organized labor itself does not?

The *laissez-faire* mind is the brutal, arrogant mind, smug and complacent within the jungle-order it has created or appropriated for itself. It seems vital in spots, but in the long run it makes for stagnation. In democracy—as I

vaguely conceive it, but as it will be made somewhat clearer toward the end
of this book, especially in connection with Walter Locke of Dayton, Ohio—
brutality and arrogance are out of place. Where they exist there can be no real
democracy. And (as made patent in "Mr. Paynter's" account of the situation
in his mill) they are hard for an individual or a group to fight in himself or
in itself. But, if we are to have democracy, or if we are to progress democratically and toward democracy, they must be fought; and we must help
one another to fight them. I have described the negative side of the shipowners' minds during the 1936-37 maritime strike which expressed itself in a
paralyzing, arrogant hatred of Harry Bridges, which helped to prolong the
strike and to add to the total economic losses to the country; but let me say
here what I did not say in the chapter on Bridges—namely, that Bridges, with
his class consciousness, his class arrogance, was in an ultimate and very concrete sense partly responsible for that state of mind among the shipowners.
Bridges' class consciousness and arrogance unquestionably enhanced the class
consciousness and arrogance among the employers. It intensified the materials
and motives of struggle and hatred. It helped to make inevitable more bitter
conflicts, more hatred, more arrogance, etc. It established and more clearly
defined the line of demarcation within the whole; it set the parts off in battle,
and understanding and harmony were vitiated by acrimony. John Lewis and
Phil Murray are a good deal better in this respect, but they, too, as most other
leaders (in fact, as most of us) are anything but free of arrogance, which encourages the arrogance on the other end. There is entirely too much snarling
and snorting. The question to be raised and pondered all around is: What can
this sort of thing lead to in the long run if not to mutually damaging or even
destructive warring, to economic paralysis and generally an unsound, increasingly undesirable situation? Labor needs to raise and ponder this problem
within itself, and to raise it and cause it to be pondered by the country.

I am more or less aware of other factors in what we call the public mind
and in the minds of workers and industrialists which are dangerous to democracy or/and social consciousness and to civilization on America's traditional
lines. These should be dealt with—and, as far as I see, they can be dealt with
only by education such as I am vaguely suggesting here ought to be started
on broad lines by the labor movement, and addressed to the country as a
whole. My feeling is that in the long run the labor movement will get nowhere
in any desirable direction unless it involves the minds and emotions of a considerable proportion of the American people of all classes into its purposes and
aims as it goes along.

In my native country there is a proverb which occurs also in the folklore of
other nations: Offer a fellow your thumb and he will reach for your hand.
This is one of the things industrialists are afraid of, and with some reason.
Not a few, I think, would willingly give in to the C.I.O. if they could feel half
sure that the worker through his new unions, which might develop great

power, would know where to stop in his demands. And this has worked conversely. Industrialists have been taking advantage of the little fellow's passivity and confusion, and have been grinding him further down. How to overcome this two-edged tendency, which now can lead only to conflict? I think it is a matter of education in social consciousness, education for democracy.

A man's relation to his work constitutes another vital question. Work in most cases in America is not regarded as the end in itself, an expression and epitome of oneself. The ambitious stick to humble jobs as a necessary drudgery before they can go into "something better." The immediate job is a means to get on, something to be put behind them at the first opportunity. While holding that job, many hate it. A few rise; most of them, lacking in qualities to push them ahead and thus suffering frustration, are lucky if they keep their petty job; and if they keep it, they do so with a sort of sick, sour, resigned air. In neither case is the work a source of happiness. One finds in it a point from which to watch for opportunity; the other, the few dollars on which to exist. Both are "putting in time," nothing else. They "put in" thus about one-third of their lives. And here, if we stop to think, we glimpse a horrible fact; perhaps I need not elaborate on it to any great extent. I shall merely ask a few questions, which I think should begin to perturb the top leaders of America's new labor movement. What is the influence of this fact on human beings involved in this process? If they feel they are only "putting in time," going through the motions so that they may exist, is this feeling or attitude not bound to affect them in things outside the job? Does not all life then begin to seem like a matter of "putting in time"? . . .

The problem, as I see it, is how to make the worker take pride in his task, his immediate job. I think no one will quarrel with me if I say that human beings ought to live creatively. And is not the question, then, how to make a job creative? I know that, so far as our present thought on the matter can suggest to us, it is almost impossible to make the work on the belt line creative, but somehow it will have to be done, or the modern industrial process will continue to erode the human spirit till this erosion overwhelms progress.

Perhaps I can offer a suggestion by telling of a Slovenian-immigrant worker I know in Cleveland. He came to America about thirty years ago and in that time worked mostly in a great nail factory, an operator of several machines spitting out nails. In that time, too, he had remodeled for himself in his spare time almost single-handedly two houses, hammering in thousands of nails . . . and, making and using these nails, on coming home from work evenings, he spoke of the machines at which he worked in the shop as though they were living things. He gave them names, endowed them with personalities, and told his wife and sons if they caused him trouble; or if, after misbehaving for a while, they again performed satisfactorily. He kept them oiled and clean, and developed a real affection for them. His wife and boys became solicitous of their condition and welfare. When he did not mention it himself, they asked him how they acted, as though they were old friends of the family's, which they, in fact, were. In the course of years he invented a few gadgets which kept the machines from going out of order and increased the production of nails. He did this not because he loved the company that employed him or wanted to impress the boss above him and get a raise, but because he admired and liked the machines. Even if they got out of order, they were marvelously efficient producers of nails. And nails, as he intimately realized re-building his houses, were important. He kept going the machines that made the nails, so *he* was important. He reached this idea less by an intellectual process than emotionally. The walls of the house in which he lived were held together by those nails, which held together also the walls in thousands of other houses throughout the country. Passing some dwelling, it often occurred to him that the nails in it had probably come from the factory where he worked, and had possibly been made by the admirable machines in his charge. In short, he achieved by himself a rather clear idea of the process of which he was a part, and with it attained a dignity and balance within himself. He knew and felt he was doing good and had a definite place in the scheme of things. This vitalized him; in fact, it is no exaggeration to say that he was an inspired worker. He enjoyed watching the nails pour out of his machines, for those nails were going into houses for people to live in all over America. He was happy on the job and thus never had the least desire to become an insurance agent or grocer or undertaker. Content to be a nail-maker, he was a fine, solid man and citizen.

This man realized by himself that he had an important place in the scheme of things. Most American workers in highly mechanized industries, however, need to be helped toward that realization. To help them, is a task of education that is the duty of the labor movement.

I am trying, as I write, to think of the problem of workers' education from various angles. In 1936 I saw one of the best motion pictures ever made, "Mr. Deeds Goes to Town," and I want to refer to it here to illustrate a point. Deeds was being twitted by professional poets for writing verse for greeting cards. For answer he let off some steam, which included words to this effect: "And, anyhow, it's the best I can do." He had what few people have in America today—a realistic understanding of his abilities and just how far he could go with them. He was content to function in his sphere, however limited it was, because he felt he was doing the best he could; and in this he was a most exceptional American. Millions of American workers are waiting, hoping, pining, wailing for "the break." While they might be good mechanics if they put their minds to it (and some doubtless are already), they are not satisfied with that, but must go on dreaming of the insurance office or the store, for which in all probability they have no aptitude. They are unhappy and do not understand themselves. They merely want to quit being factory workers. Why? Because it is part of the American atmosphere that the man on the belt or in any shop or factory is a "flop." He is unlike the hero of the "success story."

He wants to be like that hero, so he does his best to get "into something else," but often—in fact, usually—fails; which makes him miserable, distorts him as a human being, for he tries again and again (at least in his mind), and never settles down anywhere where he might eventually belong. Yet most workers, I think, long to settle down and would settle down in the job they hold if they did not imagine their neighbors talking among themselves in this way: "Joe Doaks sure is a stick-in-the-mud, ain't he? Wonder what's wrong with him to be satisfied working where he is now. I guess there just ain't no push to the guy." If Joe Doaks, at the end, does decide to stay on his factory job, he does so with rather a guilty conscience. He may be perfectly suited to the job, be happy in it at times when he permits himself to be entirely himself; however, unless the whole country is involved in an education which will change this psychology, he will never find a deep satisfaction in it because it is not what the neighbors expect from "a man of his caliber." I wager that there are hundreds of thousands of ex-workers today sitting in swivel chairs who would really be far happier running a lathe or pounding out stampings, and would, therefore, be better citizens and democrats: for their secret dissatisfactions cause them to be full of neurotic and fear-driven reactionary, fascistic, and snobbish tendencies. . . . This problem can be dealt with, I feel, only by such country-wide education, or awakening, as I suggest the labor movement should undertake.

Another urgent problem to be dealt with by labor education is that of leisure: for if the labor movement succeeds in its aim to shorten the hours of labor, its seriousness will increase. I know how time hangs on the hands of several workers of my acquaintance. They are miserable, they feel out of place even in their own homes, they take to drink, they drive their cars about in circles. Many would be far better off working longer hours regardless of pay.

But before I conclude these notes on the great task facing the C.I.O. (let me italicize that they are only *notes*), I want to return briefly to the problem of democracy within the labor unions.

What sort of person is the average union member? Let us name him John Smith. He has most of the tendencies of the average American citizen in all walks of life who joins an organization, no matter for what reason. One of these is to sit back and let the leaders and a few exceptional members do the work. He calls the head of his union, or even John Lewis or Phil Murray if he happens to meet him, by his first name and kids himself he is "on the inside" of the whole movement. Actually he is not a very conscious and responsible fellow. He inclines to think that if he strikes and pickets or sits-down occasionally, his duties as a union man are fulfilled. Beyond that he contributes little or nothing. He gets in the habit of abiding by the decisions of the leaders. He tends, not only to become "labor," anonymous under the blanket label or abstraction, but a nonentity. This is the *general* situation in the A.F. of L.

unions, which are, essentially, little fascist islands, not deeply different from the Labor Front outfits in Hitler's Germany. In fact, President Green of the A.F. of L. is a sort of labor Hitler; he orders purges, puts into office his men to displace those opposing what he stands for, and so on.

And the C.I.O. is pregnant with the same dangers. The problem centers on John Smith, union member. He needs to be educated, made and kept alive. He needs to be, not only a worker and unionist, but a man, a character, a functioning democrat, a person by himself, an individual, conscious and responsible. And, above all, he must *want* to be this kind of man. But the desire for this, if it is to be at all effective, cannot be entirely stimulated from without. Outside forces can, at best, only awaken him, rouse him from his torpor. Once he has been provoked into exercising his faculties, further initiative will have to spring directly from him, from the basic, essential man. However, he must be provoked, or helped to provoke himself into that state, to begin with. If he is not, the C.I.O. movement is apt to become a training ground for people who will fit into any sort of totalitarian scheme of things in the future. . . . I think it is true that the dangers of fascism or totalitarianism stem not only from the Right but from the Left, as well.

The educational task of the American labor movement is, in short, a stupendous one, but I feel that unless it undertakes it before long, the labor movement will really get nowhere in any desirable direction, such as toward democracy, without engaging into its aims, issues, and purposes the minds and emotions of not only a majority of wage-earners but a majority of the American people as it goes along—without taking steps to change certain phases of the American atmosphere which I have suggested.

Random Portraits and Snapshots

Men and women and the earth and all upon it are simply to be taken as they are, and the investigation of their past and present and future shall be unintermitted and shall be done with perfect candor.

—WHITMAN, Preface of 1855 edition of *Leaves of Grass*

Robinson Jeffers

IN THE SUMMER OF 1928 MY FRIEND CAREY MCWILLIAMS AND I DROVE FROM LOS Angeles to San Francisco and stopped enroute at Carmel-by-the-Sea to visit the poet Robinson Jeffers. Both Carey and I had been reading his curiously impressive—beautiful and terrible—poetry for several years, and were keen to see him. Carey had written him we were coming.

After the visit, up till that time one of my most interesting experiences, I looked up people in California who knew him, and I exchanged a few letters with his wife Una; then wrote my impressions of the man, which some time later appeared in a little pamphlet issued in a few hundred copies by the University of Washington Book Store at Seattle, and which I want to reprint here with a few slight changes, because Jeffers is definitely part of my America and generally noteworthy.

AS I SAW HIM IN 1928

Seeing him for the first time, one is not readily at ease in his presence because evidently the man is himself uncomfortable. This seems to have been the experience of nearly everyone I know who has met him. He glances at one reticently, shrinking with a sort of alarm. He looks about as though seeking a way of escape or of getting rid of the intruder. His manner is intense with restraint, which one is apt to mistake for nervousness. His hand-grip is reluctant and, while firm, lacking in friendly warmth. He is like Lawrence of Arabia in his dislike of being touched, and never shakes hands voluntarily with anyone.

His mesmeric eyes, which are the color of the Pacific along the Monterey shore on a sunless day, meet your own, but just for an instant at a time; then he lowers the sensitive eyelids as though resenting your natural curiosity to know the thoughts and feelings beyond them, or perhaps fearing to fascinate you too much with their metallic strangeness, of which he must be aware. One eye seems slightly out of focus, at times even different in color, and you wonder if the singular gaze of the two eyes is the result of a physical deformity or the manifestation of some mental or emotional condition of his inmost being. Sitting silently in a company of people in his house, while the charming Una Jeffers entertains them, he keeps his eyes lowered most of the time; and even when he talks with one, part of him appears to be "away" some place, in an aloof detachment, which, however, cannot be taken for a personal affront, for under this manner one glimpses in him a desire for friendliness, which is thus disconcertingly held in abeyance.

He smiles, but the quality of his smile, too, is illusive. You wonder: does he smile because that is the thing to do? Before his wife takes charge of the visitors, he is painfully ill at ease and gives the impression that he is unsociable. He is that; but one of his best friends assures me that at the bottom of his unsociability is his extremely self-conscious sensitiveness and shyness which verge upon morbidity. To those who during the summer months pass through his gate he is polite and seems even to want to be nice to them after they are settled down in his living-room and Una is conducting the conversation, but evidently he is determined that none will affect him aside from wasting his time. He has written: "I am quits with the people."

He is uninterested in what anyone thinks of him, his verse, or anything else. He almost never talks of his work. "If I bring it into light," he explains, "it leaves me." He accepts no invitations and he and Una extend few. He never goes out of his way to meet anyone. One of his best friends, Dr. Lyman Stookey—of whom more anon—he has seen but once in seventeen years, and of his other friends he would think just as much if they came near him once in a decade. Yet there is no trace of malice or spite in him. He just does not care for such things.

He never speaks ill of people or imputes mean motives. Indeed, he seldom speaks of anyone. A number of very fine people I know consider him the most completely and consistently courteous person within their ken. He never argues with anyone about anything if he can avoid it. He is extremely reserved. Usually his attention in conversation disarms the visitors' pique at his silence. Notwithstanding the things he has written about the "apes that walk like herons" and "brainfuls of perplexed passions," he appears to have a strong feeling for essential human dignity and never violates his own or others'. He writes few letters and reads fewer criticisms of his poetry.

His voice comes in low, restrained tones which for a time make it difficult to understand him. He uses the fewest words possible. Most questions and remarks he answers in monosyllables, some wordlessly with a barely perceptible shrug or a Mona Lisa smile, which you are free to interpret as you like or can.

Every phase of his personality seems to be under powerful, palpably conscious and voluntary, control. Before you are with him long, you know that he is an extraordinary character. His face is thin, a poet's face, not quite of this age and place, medieval, with strength impressed all over it: pale-brown, weather-beaten, masculine, clean shaven, with a straight slim nose and sensitive nostrils, a well-formed mouth with lips of moderate thickness, a firm chin, a high smooth forehead rising from straight eyebrows, and medium-sized, handsome ears. His hair is brown, beginning to gray at the temples. There appears to be just a suggestion of asymmetry. All his senses obviously are very acute.

The occasional smile enlivens the face but little; which is also true of his gaze. Somehow, both the smile and the eyes seem to insist with their singularity that the observer consider them by themselves, individually, apart from the face; it is they that do most to make his outward personality enigmatic, fascinating.

His physique harmonizes with the cut of the face. The slender body is above medium height, hard, sinewy, agile. My first glimpse of him was as he vaulted a fence just as Carey and I entered the young forest of cypress-trees and eucalypti he is planting on his estate. As I saw later, he had turned on the hydrant to water the seedlings and was making a dash around the building to beat the current to the nozzle of the hose on the other end of the grounds. The leap, performed with grace and a minimum of movement, testified to the fine control he has over his body. He is forty-two. He is a good swimmer, summer and winter, and hikes considerably along the Monterey coast and in the hills in back of Point Lobos. He likes to toss a ball, wrestle, jump, and race with his two young sons, who are twins twelve years of age. He has no taste for competitive sport and abhors the killing of animals and birds.

He wears shirts open at the throat, army breeches and leggings; in cool weather, a leather jerkin over the shirt. He disdains fine raiment and luxurious motors. He eats sparingly, and only the simplest food. A man of the out-of-doors, an athlete. His excellent physical condition may be partly due to his low pulse—forty in the morning, sixty in the afternoon. There is a cool aura about his person, which, however, does not cause shivers; rather, it endows him with an odd dignity I have never seen in anyone else.

The work of a poet, like the work of any other man, is largely conditioned by the circumstances of his life. George Jean Nathan said that "if Walt Whitman had owned an extra pair of pants he would have been a royalist." Possibly so; it is safe to say that Whitman could not have written *Leaves of Grass* had he not come of workman parentage, had he not at an early age had to shift for himself, and had he not had that American world of seemingly boundless possibilities to do it in. Moreover, Whitman was ignorant of science, of philosophy, and of the fine arts. "A morning-glory at my window satisfies me more than the metaphysics of books"—and therein lay both his great strength and his weakness as a poet and an artist.

Robinson Jeffers, on the other hand, was born into the home of a well-known Christian divine, William Hamilton Jeffers, LL.D., of Pittsburgh, who was also a scholar in languages, especially Latin, Greek, Hebrew and Arabic, with a comfortable fortune and frequent opportunities for travel. The future poet was reared on the marrow of the classics and spent most of his boyhood and early manhood traveling with his father, who was also his teacher, over Europe and the Near East. Abroad, he also studied at the University of Zürich; in the United States, at the University of Western Pennsylvania, the University of Southern California, Occidental College in Los Angeles, and the University of Washington in Seattle. He reads and speaks French and German well and reads Latin and Greek fluently. He has delved into Western and Oriental systems of thought; and in the realm of science, on one hand, he has dipped into psychology, biology and bacteriology, and, on the other, reached into astronomical immensities.

In Jeffers' early life some incidents are of interest. At the age of eight, on his father's country estate "Twin Hollows" in Pennsylvania, the boy experienced the triumph of teaching himself to swim, no mean accomplishment for one so young. His father was somewhat of a moralist and disciplinarian, and between the ages of eight and eleven young John (the poet's original given name) expended most of his best energy in vain rebellions against compulsory studiousness under parental authority. He was allowed only an occasional ramble in the country. At the age of twelve he found himself in a Swiss boarding-school, where he had relative freedom, lakes to swim in, and mountains to climb, preferably alone. His teachers called him "the little Spartan."

At fourteen he came upon a copy of Rossetti's poems which he read and re-read till the book was worn out. He developed a vigorously self-conscious interest in poetry. A while later he read Swinburne. The Bible was his steady diet throughout boyhood. At fifteen an Englishwoman in Zürich lent him *Also Sprach Zarathustra.* Years later, in Los Angeles, a fellow-student, Una Call, who later became his wife, gave him Arthur Symons' essay, "Wordsworth and Shelley." Plutarch's *Lives* he read through several times while yet in his teens. In his twenties he studied Freud and Jung, but mostly at second hand. While in medical school he was deeply interested in bacteriology.

The general ideas that have played vital rôles in his thought processes are the theory of evolution which he got from his father in childhood; the mechanistic, anti-spiritual point of view which, during the three years in medical school, intruded itself with great force upon his innate mysticism; and, finally, fatalism (perhaps a heritage from his Calvinist and Celtic ancestry) reinforced by scientific determinism.

His father, his wife, and his twin sons are the only people who have deeply entered into his intimate life as purely human influences. Dr. Lyman Stookey, formerly a professor of bacteriology at the University of Southern California, now a practicing pathologist in Los Angeles, is perhaps his closest personal friend. "Jeff," as the doctor calls him, was his best student and, as such, lived in his house for nearly two years. It took Dr. Stookey a year to overcome Jeffers' shyness so that he would talk with him freely, and then it was sheer joy to sit with him in a room, smoking and talking. "Jeff is hyper-sensitive and shy, rather than unsociable," insists Dr. Stookey. "And he is the most thoroughly fine man I know." Besides bacteriology, Dr. Stookey taught him wrestling, and one year Jeffers won the heavyweight wrestling championship of the University.

Jeffers' fellow-students considered him odd. He had little to say and seemed absorbed in himself. Now and then he would drift along with them, drink, sow wild oats, kill time, but never for long. He was fond of swimming and going on solitary trips, afoot or on horseback, into Southern California mountains.

In his mid-twenties he came into a small legacy which, considering his modest wants, made him economically free. Some time later he married one of the most beautiful and generally adored young women on the Coast, who was eagerly and intelligently interested in the development of his talents.

To write of Robinson Jeffers the man and the artist with any pretension to thoroughness without writing also of Una Jeffers is impossible. I have no doubt that some day she will be an important factor in all serious considerations of her poet-husband's life and work; at this time, one must be content to deal with her very briefly.

Swinburne remarked about William Blake's wife that she "deserves remembrance as about the most perfect wife on record"; and it seems to me that something to the same effect can be said of Una Jeffers, though, of course, Catherine Blake, who was an uneducated peasant woman, and the lady at Carmel-by-the-Sea can—in relation to their husbands as poets and artists—hardly be compared on any particular point.

Robin, as Una Jeffers calls him, says himself: " 'She gave me eyes, she gave me ears' "—quoting a line from Wordsworth's poem about his sister Dorothy —"and arranged my life."

Jeffers had in his make-up certain traits which, lacking Una, might have kept him from attaining a high place in American poetry. He is disinclined to try to change things; indeed, people who have known him best in his student years and later say he used to be entirely a fatalist and an introvert. Occupied with his thoughts, and being, besides, economically independent, he felt little inclined to bother about publishing for other people's reading. Una Jeffers, on the other hand, possesses great driving force and the energy of concentrated effort.

Before his marriage, Jeffers had never done a moment's labor with his hands. Subsequently, under Una's subtle urging, his most satisfying hours were spent doing stone work and digging on his five acres, planting trees and tending them. The famous Hawk Tower was largely her idea; and for five years he spent hours every day rolling or carrying granite boulders up from the beach two or three hundred yards away, mixing mortar, erecting one of the strangest buildings in America. It is built to last. The walls at the base are nearly six feet in width, thick enough to hide, on one side, a narrow stairway that winds up to the upper stories. In Carmel, Jeffers is famous chiefly for the five years he has "wasted" building a tower a contractor could put up in a week. People used to stop along the sea road that winds past the place, to watch the seemingly harmless lunatic manipulate rocks with his primitive pulley, such as the old Egyptians are said to have used. Some one made up a story of the feeling of timelessness around Jeffers' tower-building. It seems that one day at sunset a traveler came along and paused to watch Robin at his work. The next day he went to China and lived there for three years. Returning to Carmel late in the fourth year, the man again went walking on the shore road one day at sunset-time and, coming to Jeffers' place, he saw Robin in precisely the same attitude rolling up stones from the beach. . . .

The building of the tower, although originally Una's idea, is characteristic of Jeffers. He is one of the serenest, most deliberate and self-sufficient persons alive. He is bored only if molested too much by people.

As a poet and artist, he unquestionably has grown greatly since settling in Carmel in 1914. One can scarcely believe that the John Robinson Jeffers who in 1913 published a third-rate story in the *Smart Set* has become crystallized into the Robinson Jeffers who wrote *Tamar, Roan Stallion, The Women at Point Sur,* and *Cawdor.* The coast and hills of the Monterey country no doubt have contributed generously to his development. He has become a part of the place, and the place of him, so that now it would be difficult to imagine him anywhere else. It is one of the most weirdly beautiful regions in America, and Jeffers and his tower fit into it perfectly.

His days are arranged for him so that he spends the hours until one in the afternoon in his study or in the turret of the tower at his writing. He likes best to have a routine of carefully planned tasks so that the little things need not be thought over. He devotes most of his afternoons to the two thousand young trees he has planted. Watching him work in the grove, one thinks of Giles Winterborne in Thomas Hardy's *The Woodlanders:*

. . . He had a marvelous power of making trees grow . . . a sort of sympathy between him and them . . . so that the roots took hold of the soil in a few days. Winterborne's fingers were endowed with a gentle conjuror's touch in spreading the roots of each little tree, resulting in a sort of caress under which the delicate fibres all laid themselves out in their proper directions for growth. He put most of these roots toward the southwest: for he said in forty years' time, when some great gale is blowing from that quarter, the trees will require the strongest holdfast on that side to stand against it and not fall. . . .

Evenings he reads to his family. Between him and his sons exists an extraordinarily close relationship. He has an infinite patience and will explain and re-explain matters to them, and they are mutually utterly devoted. In the last two years he has read to them all of W. H. Hudson, ten Waverly novels, ten Hardy, three Dostoievski, besides many travel books and other volumes, such as Lawrence's *Revolt in the Desert,* Doughty's *Arabia Deserta,* and even Cellini's Autobiography. He reads verse exquisitely, in a sort of monotone, with due weight given to accent and rhythms.

Once in a fortnight or so he takes his family for a long tramp back in the Monterey hills and redwood canyons. He is fond of examining stones and geological formations closely; also trees and plants, water courses, animals and their tracks, and old abandoned human habitations and enterprises which, in that peculiar region, one is apt to encounter at every turn. He is saturating himself with the Indian and old Spanish lore of the country. He goes practically never beyond the limits of Monterey County. If he appears in the business section of Carmel, it is an event. He dislikes to have people eye and follow him. Occasionally he goes to the Lick Observatory where his brother is engaged in astronomical work, in which he is much interested. In fifteen years he went to San Francisco once, in 1917, to be examined for military service.

Since his marriage, he has developed a profound interest in natural objects and scenery, in which Una Jeffers revels. No doubt, she has influenced him in that direction. Also, she has an acute instinct for seizing dramatic moments of human clashes and reactions, from which he as a writer profits considerably. She is to him simultaneously wife and mother and manager of his talents. She not only gave him eyes and ears and arranged his life, but, to go much deeper into the problem of his personality, she has—consciously or unconsciously—counteracted his intense introversion (of which more in a moment) and saved him from its fatal consequences to him as an artist.

Jeffers cares more for form than for color. He loves wet weather, low-hanging skies, and fog rolling up from the sea. Storms—"storm's kind, kind violence"—exhilarate him immensely. In the most inclement weather he often goes to the turret of his tower, to feel and absorb the furies of wind and sea. Both the tower and the family's house are built upon solid granite against which the waves beat, and the rhythm of the ocean ceaselessly reverberates through them. He distrusts a blazing sun, believes that the beneficial effects of sunshine are overestimated, and points to the hardy races of Northern Europe who live in dark countries. He observes the barometer closely and seldom goes to bed without going outdoors, about midnight, to walk around the place, marking the rising and setting of constellations, feel the direction of the wind, and notice the tide at ebb or flow.

He says that his inability to kill animals or birds is a matter of self-indulgence, not principle. Life is one of the cheapest and most abundant commodities on earth and in itself far from sacred to him: but he hates to inflict pain (although in his poetry he preaches pain). Una Jeffers tells me that he never picks a flower wantonly, or prunes a tree or roots up a weed if he can avoid it. She believes that life is more honored by him than he realizes. In his everyday life he is perhaps the gentlest person living.

He reads considerably, but never goes far out of his way to obtain a book. He prefers Hardy, George Moore, and Yeats to most other modern writers. Of the Americans, he reads with interest Edgar Lee Masters and Eugene O'Neill. D. H. Lawrence's *The Rainbow* and Dostoievski's *Crime and Punishment* he considers two of the finest novels written in recent times. He is on the mailing lists of several scientific journals printed in America and abroad. They are his newspapers. He is deeply interested in biology and psychology. He has a distaste for the theater and a dread of orchestral music, which he calls "noise"; but he enjoys the ancient English and Gaelic ballads which his wife frequently plays on her little reed organ in the tower.

He follows the more or less extraordinary ventures of civilization in and outside the United States with an aloof, disinterested eye. An extreme individualist, he has a deep aversion to group projects and thinks that America is mad on the subject of group activity. He watches all movements toward freedom; in general, dislikes laws, restrictions and bonds for people; but, on the other hand, does not feel hopeful of any utopias to be secured through new systems. In a letter he wrote: "Some of you think that you can save society. I think it is impossible, and that you [radicals, social uplifters, etc.] only hasten the process of decadence. Of course as a matter of right and justice I sympathize with radicalism; and in any case I don't oppose it; from an abstract point of view there is no reason that I know of for propping and prolonging the period of decadence. Perhaps the more rapid it is, the more rapid comes the new start." He insists that western civilization is on the chute.

But in spite of his hopelessness, his "terribleness," "tragic terror" and "vast despair," of which much has been written, and in spite of such complaints as may be found in his own writings, notably in the startling and lovely poem called "An Artist," he is a happy man, as happiness goes. In his philosophy, he recognizes that every personal story ends more or less in tragedy; comedy is an unfinished story. The impersonal or universal story never finishes at all and is neither merry nor sad, though to Jeffers it appears intensely in earnest. I am assured that he is quite ridiculously content with his personal environment. He says: "I should be glad to live like this for several centuries: but good and evil are very cunningly balanced in the most favored lives, and I should not consider myself ill-used if I was to die tomorrow, though it would be very annoying." In a letter to his publisher, Horace Liveright, who had asked him for biographical data, he wrote: "According to Laurence Sterne, the only things of consequence that a man can do are to plant a tree, get a child, build a house, write a book. I have just finished a book and have built a house and gotten two children, and planted two thousand trees—but none of these is biographical material."

A curious, extraordinary man, this Jeffers: living in a curious place on the western edge of America, with sharp rocks sticking out of the sea all along the shore and twisted trees stretching their arms landward: writing strange verse of excessive intensity and terribleness in terms of a mad philosophy that is the result of his profound personal introversion and great knowledge of facts and theories pertaining to the universe of man. His idea of our civilization's fatal introversion, which is an important although very obscure factor in his poetry, no doubt is an expansion of the self-consciousness of his own mind's introverted condition. His terribleness, perhaps, is but the mirror of the violent effort of his own strong personality to save itself from being self-devoured.

As to the form in Jeffers's poetry, in a note that I have before me he says: "I want it rhythmic and not rhymed, moulded more closely to the subject than older English poetry is but as formed as alcaics if that were possible too. The event is of course a compromise but I like to avoid arbitrary form and capricious lack or disruption of form. My feeling is for the number of beats to the line. There is a quantitative element too in which the unstressed syllables have part. The rhythm comes from many sources—physics, biology, beat of blood, the tidal environments of life, desire for singing emphasis that prose does not have."

Much has been written about the symbolism that underlies Jeffers's forbidden themes. The official explanation of this element in his poetry follows:

"In *Tamar* a little and vaguely, in *The Tower Beyond Tragedy* and *The Women at Point Sur* consciously and definitely, incest is symbolized racial introversion—man regarding man exclusively—founding his values, desires, his picture of the universe, all on his own humanity. With the thickening of civilization, science reforms the picture of the universe and makes it inhuman but the values and desires are ever more fixed inward. People living in cities hardly look at or think of anything but each other and each other's amusements and works. Barclay in *The Women at Point Sur* was finding and identifying himself and the world (emotionally conceived as God) until seduced by desire of disciples and incestuous love, *i.e.,* by letting himself be turned back on humanity. His tragedy grew from that impurity. For those who want little and have much strength can afford to be impure: but not those who want all and have little strength."

Many critics and most ordinary readers complain of obscurity in his longer poems; others arrive at opposite opinions about them; and a few well-meaning people even tremble for his family and neighbors, expecting any day to hear that the terrible poet has gone on a rampage of rape and murder. So it may be well to quote at some length from a rather revealing letter that Jeffers wrote to James Rorty, another poet, some time after the appearance of *The Women at Point Sur*:

You were right evidently about the need of an explanation. I have just read ————'s article, and if he, a first rate critic and a poet and a good friend of my work, quite misunderstands the book, it is very likely that no one else will understand it at present.

. . . a couple of letters ago I spoke of the morality—perhaps I said old-fashioned morality—implied in *Point Sur*. *Tamar* seemed to my later thought to have a tendency to romanticize unmoral freedom, and it was evident a good many people took it that way. That way lies destruction of course, often for the individual but always for the social organism, and one of the later intentions of this *Point Sur* was to indicate the destruction, and strip everything but its natural ugliness from the unmorality. Barclay incited people to "be your desires . . . flame . . . enter freedom." The remnant of his sanity—if that was the image of himself that he met on the hilltop—asks him whether it was for love of mankind that he is "pouring poison into the little vessels." He is forced to admit that if the motive seems love, the act is an act of hatred.

Another intention, this time a primary one, was to show in action the danger of that *Roan Stallion* idea of "breaking out of humanity," misinterpreted in the mind of a fool or a lunatic. . . . It is not anti-social, because it has nothing to do with society; but just as Ibsen, in *The Wild Duck*, made a warning against his own idea in the hands of a fool so *Point Sur* was meant to be a warning; but at the same time a reassertion.

*   *   *

For the rest of the book was meant to be:

(1) An attempt to uncenter the human mind from itself. There is no health for the individual whose attention is taken up with his own mind and processes; equally there is no health for the society that is always introverted on its own members, as ours become more and more, the interest engaged inward in love and hatred, companionship and competition. These are necessary of course, but as they absorb all the interest they become fatal. All past cultures have died of introversion at last, and so will this one, but the individual can be free of the net, in his mind. It is a matter of "transvaluing values," to use the phrase of somebody that local people accuse me quite falsely of deriving from.—I have often used incest as a symbol to express these introversions, and used it too often.

(2) The book was meant to be a tragedy, that is an exhibition of essential elements by the burning away through pain and ruin of inertia and the unessential.

(3) A valid study in psychology; the study valid, the psychology morbid, sketching the growth of a whole system of emotional delusions from a "private impurity" that was quite hidden from consciousness until insanity brought it to the surface.

(4) Therefore a partial and fragmentary study of the origin of religions; which have been necessary to society in the past, and I think remain necessary whether we like it or not, yet they derive from a "private impurity" of some kind in their originators.

(5) A satire on human self-importance; referring back to (1).

(6) A judgment of the tendencies of our civilization, which has very evidently turned the corner down hill. "Powers increase and power perishes." Our literature, as I said in answer to the *New Masses* questionnaire, is not especially decadent (because in general it is not especially anything); but our civilization has begun to be.

There were more intentions, but these are the chief ones that can readily be said in prose. Too many intentions. I believe they all carry over to an intelligent reader, as results though not as intentions, but no doubt I was asking him to hold too many things in mind at once. I had concentrated my energies for a long time on perceptions and expression, and forgot that the reader could not concentrate so long, nor so intensely, nor from the same detached and inclusive viewpoint.

"Too many intentions," is correct. Perhaps they are so obscure because so many. I doubt if very many people will detect all of them even with the aid of his explanation; and a reader would be justified, from his own viewpoint, in imagining that the poet discovered the intentions after completing the book. After writing the letter to Rorty, Jeffers remarked that the explanations were "very unsatisfactory after all; the book must stand by itself for much more than this rationalization." Doubtless it does. Chesterton says somewhere: "Great poets are obscure for two opposite reasons: now because they are talking about something too large for anyone to understand and now, again, because they are talking about something too small for anyone to see."

Jeffers has made an impression on America's literary consciousness. In San Francisco, after Carey and I had visited the poet at Carmel, Albert Bender, an elderly gentleman prominent in the cultural life of the Coast, congratulated us on our good fortune. "Some day," he said, "your visit with Robinson Jeffers will mean to you what the hour that I as a young man once spent with Walt Whitman in Camden, New Jersey, meant to me."

His poetry impresses, rather than appeals to, one. "I am greatly impressed by its power," said Havelock Ellis of *Roan Stallion*. Too often Jeffers impresses by the exasperation that his obscurity evokes in one. I read all his verse as soon as it appears and freely admit that the most magnificent passages in American poetry are his—as for example, the part in his last book where Cawdor describes the flight of the caged bird's spirit. I prefer, however, the shorter pieces to the more ambitious poems. "An Artist," for instance, is superb; inspired, as he remarks in the privately printed booklet in which it originally appeared, by some paragraphs about the independence of the artist in Oscar Wilde's essay on *The Soul of Man Under Socialism*, with which he felt "a certain (not more than emotional) sympathy," and was written "to carry that independence to its logical conclusion."

Jeffers' attitude is that of the artist-aristocrat, withdrawn, aloof, intensely serious, looking down from his tower. The human breed is degenerating (no doubt about it and no way to stop the process) and, viewing it in the mirror of his own mind, his cosmic consciousness, and in relation to the universe, he finds it offensive. America is a "perishing Republic" and will have "centuries of increasing decadence." There is a limited sort of salvation only for the individual. One can crawl into his cave or climb into his tower and stay there. A heron a-wing "over the black ebb" is dearer to him than the "many pieces of humanity . . . gathering shellfish" and dropping "paper and other filth" on his beach, heedless of the sign warning them against it which he has stuck by the road that winds through his place. Indeed, "humanity is needless."

The man comes of pre-Revolutionary stock, but he says that America and civilization are beyond redemption. He warns his young boys to be moderate in their "love of man" and goes on singing of Points Lobos and Sur, of his own hopelessness and violence, of which I spoke; of the elements in their most dramatic moods, of Time and Space. He can hardly be spoken of as an American poet. He is Jeffers, who lives in America, and cannot be discussed in terms of anything or anyone else. It may be said that he stems from the Greeks —Aeschylus, Euripides, Sophocles—but he goes beyond them in style and form as well as in the dreadfulness of his themes.

Critics—"local people," he calls them—eager to do justice to Jeffers's significance as a poet, try to establish a kinship between his work and Whitman's. Their eagerness is justified, but wild. Whitman's and Jeffers' statures as poets may stand comparisons; aside from their sizes, however, they are as unlike as day and night. S. S. Albers has made this abundantly clear in his *Bibliography of the Works of Robinson Jeffers,* wherein he—himself a poet— says also this about Jeffers' poetry:

Whatever other fault may be found with R. J.'s poetry, it can not, in any sense of the word, be called *derivative*. It is the articulate voice of an individual creator; it is the work of the first Jeffers, the second nobody else. It is concerned with the basic forces of nature, as expressed in the race's human relations and their attendant emotions, love, hate, fear, joy, grief, courage, cowardice, jealousy, desire, hope; and in the race's inhuman surroundings, the earth, the sea, the sky, the trees, the stones. These form the basis of major poetry, and it is these that Jeffers uses, turning them about and re-creating them as his genius dictates. The beauty and power of the poems is not something external, superimposed, artificially stimulated by a fetching pattern of sound rhymingly repeated. Rather, it is intrinsic, deriving from the very thought-content of the poems, an intellectual beauty, beautiful as truth is beautiful,— the suiting of diction to clarity and purity of thought,—that precise treatment of a subject that makes the reader feel he has come on the ultimate expression.

A LETTER FROM HIM AND OUR SECOND MEETING

Following my departure from California for New York, Jeffers and his poetry continued to interest me. I read at least parts of his books as they came out: *Dear Judas, Thurso's Landing, Give Your Heart to the Hawks, Solstice,* and *Such Counsels You Gave to Me.* Now and then Una and I exchanged notes and brief letters. She seemed to have liked my pamphlet on Robin. I sent them my books as they were published . . . and in the spring, 1935, I received this letter:

TOR HOUSE, CARMEL, CALIFORNIA,
May 17, 1935

DEAR ADAMIC:

I am ashamed not to have written sooner. I read *Grandsons* soon after it came, with pleasure and deep interest—I that am almost as incapable of reading a novel as of writing a letter. It seems to me an excellent diagnosis of the recent American state of mind. Of course, as you know and say, this restlessness, aimlessness and unrest are present in Europe too. I think they are necessary results of the present state of civilization—not necessary in any particular person, but in people in general. The individual can conquer them, can make roots and find aims for himself; but I do not think society can, except by letting itself be worked into a quasi-religious intoxication, like Nazism or communism, in which the pleasure of persecution plays a great part, and which I think is worse than that aimless unrest; and they are temporary passages to Caesarism. (It seems to me that Russia has made the passage already.) I like none of these, though I believe we are to taste them if we live long enough.

It seems to me that in a degenerating society the individual has got to isolate himself morally to a certain extent or else degenerate too. He *can* keep his own morals; he cannot save society's, not even though he himself should happen to be Caesar, like Marcus Aurelius (who did all his civic duty and more, but remained isolated in his philosophy, apart from decaying Rome).

It is no use our turning to the factory-workers, as Tolstoy did to the peasant and Rousseau to the primitive, for what the factory-workers want is exactly what the middle-classes want, and if they got it they would have all the middle-class fatuities; only more so, because they would have less incentive and more security.

They might be self-satisfied Peter Gales, instead of searching, tormented ones. [Peter Gale is the central character of *Grandsons*.] . . .

Sincerely,

ROBINSON JEFFERS

I was pressed with work just then, and continued to be so through the rest of 1935, and did not answer Jeffers. When I came to California in the spring, 1936, I meant to call on the Jefferses after my last lecture engagement in that state, but then I heard that they had just gone upon an extended visit to Mabel Dodge Luhan at Taos, in New Mexico.

Finally, in midsummer, 1937, almost exactly nine years after I had first met them, they all—Robin and Una and their two sons, now twenty-one— came to New York. They were *en route* to Ireland. Jeffers' publisher, Bennett Cerf, of Random House, gave a dinner for them at his apartment, and Stella and I had been invited. It was frightfully hot all evening, but Jeffers appeared surprisingly at ease. Like Una, he had not changed much physically during the nine years, but seemed quite different otherwise. He was almost free and natural in manner, and spoke a good deal, giving full answers to questions, offering remarks of his own, and being generally very sociable.

Referring to his letter to me apropos of *Grandsons*, I said something to the effect that things indubitably were in a bad way in the world—that the developments in Russia during 1936-37 forced me to go a long way even toward agreeing with what he had written about "Cæsarism" in that country—and that I had read with profound interest his poem in the November 9, 1936, *Pacific Weekly,* entitled "Sinverguenza"—

> They snarl over Spain like cur-dogs over a bone, then look at each other and shamelessly
> Lie out of the sides of their mouths.
> Brag, threat and lie, these are diplomacy; wolf-fierce, cobra-deadly and monkeyshameless,
> These are the masters of powerful nations.
> I wonder is it any satisfaction to Spaniards to see that their blood is only
> The first drops of a forming rain-storm.

—but that I did not believe the situation was hopeless and the utter collapse of civilization as we knew it inevitable or even likely. Conditions the world over, not excluding America, *were* rotten, insane, and terribly dangerous— palpably so; but did he not think that within or underneath these forces of insanity and destruction, which might be loosed upon us at any moment, there were also forces of the opposite kind, working less obviously than the others, but there nevertheless—especially in the United States?

Jeffers nodded, saying that was possible, or even probable.

The story of *Grandsons*, I said, revolved about the tormented, jittery, idealistic intellectual Peter Gale and his racketeer brother Andy, and their proletarian cousin Jack who believed in class struggle, and their sister Margaret who was an ignorant social climber, and Jack's wife Mildred who was hellbent for revolution, and the sheriff who killed Jack; but in the story was also

Jack's and Mildred's son, Peter's nephew, Anthony, a calm-faced little boy who seemed intent upon asking questions and finding out what the fuss and fury were all about. I added that I had meant Anthony, with his calm face, to be symbolical of the good, the positive forces stirring in the world amid chaos which in all probability had more to do with the future than the mad, destructive forces.

Jeffers nodded again, but I do not know whether in agreement or merely in understanding.

As for the "forming rainstorm" of which the Spanish blood was the first drops, I agreed that, to all appearances, it was coming, but could not we— America—stay out of it?

Jeffers was doubtful.

I wanted to quote to him Emerson: "Things refuse to be mismanaged long. . . . Though no check to a new evil appear, the checks exist and will appear."

To escape the heat of the evening, Bennet Cerf took us all to the top of the Empire State Building. There we spent perhaps an hour in a cool high wind, in which it was difficult to talk.

Next day I re-read some of Jeffers' poetry, then wrote in my Diary:

. . . Doubtless an interesting man. He is the introvert struggling against introversion in himself by writing symbolically—and magnificently—about the introversion of human society, which *is* introvert, all right, and seriously so, but I think not quite as thoroughly and hopelessly so as he wishes to suggest or indicate. Man spends a good deal of time and some of his best talent "going into himself" and thereby complicating himself no end, but he is also reaching out, sometimes simultaneously with "going into himself"—much as Jeffers is, who is reaching out through his individual personal complexity; only less self-consciously so, more matter-of-factly. Jeffers' poetry is his victory over his introversion. Some other men more or less win over it in other forms. And humanity as a whole never thoroughly succumbs to introversion. There are times when it seems entirely introvert, and there is "decadence," insane violence, social incest; and it may be that this is one of those periods—certainly it seems so in parts of Europe. But my feeling is that while this "decadence" is here, there is also the opposite—certainly in America, where unquestionably much is "perishing," to use Jeffers' word, but where also much is coming up.

Jeffers is a great word artist and he is vastly important in that he goes on pointing out the horrors and dangers of introversion, personal and social; as an introvert erupting out of his introversion he is deeply representative of vast mobs of introverts and, as such, worthy of the closest study. He is magnificent poetically, which is strange—for philosophically, with all his "terribleness," he is more the self-conscious worm under a lowering heel about to crush him, than, say, a raindrop, which does not resign itself to despair even if it happens to fall on a rotting carcass and sinks therein. It stays there awhile, becomes involved in the whole process of decomposition, then rises again, ready for another cycle of adventure. . . . Basically, I think, Jeffers is a case of "arrested vision." He sees things as a series of goings-on, which he calls "decadence," and does not see them as a whole, as a process, as life which is death which is life, and so on.

Mary Austin

I HAVE ALREADY REFERRED TO MY SEEING MARY AUSTIN DURING THE EARLY
1930's when she came to New York on her semiannual visits. She usually
invited me to lunch with her at the National Arts Club, or I took her out
somewhere if I had the necessary extra money. Parties were usually given for
her when she came, and she had me invited to them.

Just then she was writing her autobiography, which was published late in
1932 under the title of *Earth Horizon*, and she discussed with me her problems
in connection with it. She had me go to the New York Public Library and
verify for her data about which she was uncertain. Her material was exceedingly rich and for that reason replete with difficulties, which kept popping
out as she wrote the book. There were such problems as this: She knew
the Herbert Hoovers very well and liked "Herbie," who, she had no doubt,
was essentially a good and able man. She respected him as an administrator,
although as President in that particular period he was an obvious failure.
She thought he might make a very excellent President the next term, when
he might repair the damage done by the Depression during his present term,
but of course he had no chance of reëlection. He was, she said, really a very
sad case; a minor tragedy. She believed she understood him thoroughly, but
felt she could not explain him in print, certainly not at this time, for her
explanations rested on very personal matters, and she felt she ought not exploit the fact that this man whom she knew so well was the President of
the United States. Yet, she added, he was a most significant man apart from
his present office. He had become tired of merely making money and gone
into public service with the sincere desire to do good; the trouble was that
he had brought into the White House the character he had developed in his
business and personal life—which was not a bad character in itself, but full
of dangerous inhibitions and cross-purposes. . . . She was undecided on this
point for some time; finally, Hoover appeared in *Earth Horizon* minus all
his really significant aspects.

Her views upon autobiography as a form or way of writing interested me.
She had most definite opinions on some of the recent autobiographies. There
were, for instance, Hamlin Garland's and Theodore Dreiser's. "Such a lot of
unimportant obscenity in Dreiser's, and too much boot-licking in Hamlin
Garland's." She had read Gertrude Atherton's and felt that it was "too revealing in unimportant matters and not revealing enough in the really significant
phases." Perhaps the basic trouble with autobiographers, she said, was that
they were old when they sat down to write their books; were no longer vitally
connected with the times and thus unable to imagine what in their generation
remained significant for the present generation and what might be significant
for future generations. And on occasion she told me that she discussed her
autobiography with me because I was of a later generation than she, and

477

helped her, whether I knew it or not, to decide what was significant in her material for the present and possibly for the future. Also, she said, I had the additional virtue of being foreign-born, which gave me a certain detachment.

One day I remarked to her that I was inclined to think that the thing to do was to write autobiographically right along. "Yes," said Mary Austin, "but what will guide you? How will you know that what seemed interesting to you yesterday will be at all interesting, not to say significant, a year, a decade, or a century later?"

"The thing to do," I said, "is to write the truth as one feels and sees it—or, anyhow, write truthwardly and as well as one can—and at the same time reveal oneself sufficiently as one writes so that the reader a year, a decade, or a century hence will be able to see what sort of person the writer was when he wrote and why he saw things as he recorded them, and thereby will arrive at truth of his own in his own peculiar, significant way."

She nodded.

I told her my drama-is-truth idea, which is stated in the March 24, 1928, entry in my Diary, quoted in the preface to this book. The theory interested her, appealed to her. "But what is drama?" she asked. I said, "The interaction, the interplay of all the factors in a situation or event, or in the world, for that matter."

Thinking aloud, she raised objections to my definition of drama. "Is farce drama?"

"No," I said. "In farce there is no real interaction or interplay of factors; things happen, merely happen, irrelevantly, illogically, without connection or sequence. We will not argue, I think, that this is true of farce on the stage, where things are made to happen by a certain kind of mind—the farcical mind. Things happen in real life which look farcical, irrelevant, illogical, and which are and remain farcical as long as we don't see or understand all the factors in the event or situation. When we do see the whole, what was farce becomes elements in a drama."

Mary Austin listened attentively and, talking, I was clarifying my own ideas on the subject.

"In other words," I continued, "drama exists, I think, only in relation to the person contemplating a given situation or event, or a country or a period or the world. He must see all the factors in the event, situation, or period, or at least there must be something in him which makes him want to see all the factors; and he must have a sense of discrimination, so he can more or less see them in their proper relation, in their effect upon one another, and in their totality. That is to say, he must be a fairly well organized person, with a mind at once specific and general, with a vision or idea or philosophy and a sense of sequence or logic. He must be free, or as free as possible. He must not be bound even to his vision or idea or philosophy, or to his sense of logic or sequence. He must be involved in the event or situation or period which he contemplates, or in the world; in short, in the whole drama of the thing; but at the same time he must see himself in that involvement—see himself as a factor in the drama. If one can write and is that sort of person, and has a few other virtues, one cannot help writing truthfully or truthwardly or dramatically (these words, in this connection, are almost synonymous); and if he writes that way, no matter at what period in his life, his writing is bound to be significant no matter when it is read, for he does become part of the drama of things, part of the push truthward." . . .

It was at once a very simple and extremely complex idea, and I did not explain it very well . . . but I think Mary Austin understood it. She urged me to write an essay on it. For a while I thought of doing that, but then decided that to formulate the idea minutely might be bad for it, at least so far as I was concerned. I did not want to imprison it into an essay and then become responsible for it as its jailer. I decided to let it hang loosely in the back of my mind, whence it might eventually more or less manifest itself in my work.

In this decision Mary Austin was a sort of indirect factor. Her interest in my idea stimulated me in that direction.

On the other hand, I am afraid I did not help her very much with *Earth Horizon*. She was too consciously concerned about posterity and her place in it. She was confused about her material, and in the long run I possibly added to that confusion. Much of the book, as it finally appeared, is glorious reading, especially its early parts; much of it, however, is also very rigid and incomplete. After sending the manuscript to her publishers, she wrote to me she was not very well pleased with it herself. "I had to cut out so much that I sort of got out of key and I am not at all sure that I have succeeded in any respect. . . ."

She wrote me a kind letter after the publication of *The Native's Return*. She was in her late sixties and not well. She urged Stella and me to come for an extended stay to Santa Fe. We wanted to go, but could not. Her letters became infrequent. We knew she was ill. Yet the news of her death in 1934 came as a blow.

My feeling for her had been one of affection, but also more than that—of deep respect. She was a strange, grand woman. I did not understand her in my mind, for she was full of contradictions. She was at once extremely fine and perilously near to being bombastic; now all sound common sense, then a vague folk-cultist. Much of her passion for the Indian and his lore and symbols seemed to me crackpot. She insisted *Abie's Irish Rose* was a great folk play. On an occasion when she discussed the Depression she told me to read all her books and I would find The Solution of the Economic Problem. She considered herself a prophetess and, in her books and out of them, played always with mystic, occult concepts. Once she said she would send me a fetish. But she forgot to; so, curious, writing a letter to her one day, I reminded her of it. She sent me a little foot of a furred animal (I never could determine what it was) and wrote me that this was the fetish; adding that a fetish "is a perfectly scientific method for releasing the subconscious forces. You fix upon it the idea that by handling, touching it, the proper release will be accomplished for you. Carry it on your person and when you have occasion to think of it finger it a little and remind yourself of what it is to do for you. It is probably the psychological source of the collecting habit. I am quite serious when I say that I have made great and profitable use of fetishes of various sorts. This one I am sending you is Mokiach, my Lord Puma, the great hunting fetish of the Keres tribe. It has been properly made with due attention to endowing it with all sorts of mystical powers." . . .

All this, however, did not obscure her other, entirely different characteristics and traits. When I met her I was always a little awed. There was about her a democratic majesty. She was not actually tall or heavy, yet appeared big. Carey McWilliams, who also had much contact with her, perhaps more than I, called her the "mother titaness"—an apt description. When she told (not asked) me to go look up something for her at the library, it was much in the manner in which the mother sends her little boy for an armload of firewood or for a cake of soap at the village store. Already on our second meeting I knew that she had adopted me. I was just starting to write and having a somewhat tough time. I needed help. She championed me in New York, where her formidable personality rather than her work commanded attention and respect. She sent me, as I have told, to Walter Lippmann on the *World*, practically ordering him to listen to me. Before I had published my first book she pulled me before Henry Seidel Canby in a way that all but said to him, "Now, Henry, you take notice of this young man who, besides coming from somewhere in Europe, also comes from my West." In all this her motives were at least partly motherly: generous, matter-of-fact, brusque, almost fierce. When I began to understand this in her, I was deeply touched. I don't know if she knew that I understood or not. Her immediate manner toward me was always a little reserved. But, in 1930, when she learned of Stella, she wanted to meet her, saying it was very important that I married the right kind of girl. She approved of Stella; in fact, adopted her, too, though we did not clearly realize all this till some time after her death, when we recalled things she had said or written to us.

In the depth of her being, Mary Austin was a tragic and heroic woman. Early in the 1930's she wrote an anonymous autobiographical article entitled "Woman Alone." Her personal life was most unhappy. That unhappiness, almost indescribable, was with her all her life, but she somehow made it part of her amazing strength and her determination to lead a full and varied life, to be somebody, make herself felt in the world. Out of that unhappiness, too, came the need for a place in posterity. A seemingly plain Western housewife in the early 1900's, she made of herself—with her bold, original mind—into one of the most interesting American women writers of her time and a force in the awakening culture of the West. Out of her personal loneliness she reached out and mothered people like me.

I am profoundly grateful to have known her.

Harriet Monroe

HORACE GREGORY AND HIS WIFE, MARYA, BOTH POETS WHOM I HAD FIRST MET early in the 1930's, had been telling me of her; I had been reading *Poetry—A Magazine of Verse* off and on for years; and when, early in the spring of 1934, I came to Chicago, there was a note from her at my hotel: "Marya Gregory writes that you are, or soon will be, in this city. If this is true, . . . won't you call me up . . . and arrange to come over? If you can lunch with me some day in this neighborhood, I shall be much pleased. . . ."

I called her and went to the *Poetry* office at 232 East Erie Street, in an industrial section of Chicago, near one of the many canals that cross the great city; and there was a lively, talkative frail wisp of a gray-haired woman, weighing perhaps less than a hundred pounds, but charged with energy and enthusiasm. One wanted to tell her to be still for a minute and to cup her tiny head into one's hands and look long into the slightly wrinkled, excited, and appealing bird-like face. There was something to ponder there, and to understand.

The *Poetry* office was a tight, crowded place of two or three rooms. There were bookshelves crammed with little volumes—probably the largest collection of modern American poetry between book covers in existence: most of them autographed. The other walls were covered with inscribed photographs of modern American poets. Much of what had happened in American poetry since shortly before America's entrance in the war was to be ascribed to what had been thought, felt, and done within these walls.

Editor Harriet Monroe introduced me to her assistant, a tall young man named Morton Dauwen Zabel; and she talked on at a great rate, I hardly knew what about, for it took me some time to become accustomed to this amazingly young person who should really have been an old woman. She was seventy-three.

I came to the office slightly before twelve. Harriet Monroe said it was too early to lunch: what did I want to do for a while, say till one o'clock? Did I like Chicago? I did not know whether I did or not; I scarcely knew it. "Oh, well, then," said the editor of *Poetry*, "we'll go out and I'll show you the town."

Outside I waved to a passing cab. "What do you want a cab for?" she smiled. Disconcerted, I said, "I thought you—" She laughed. "Oh no, I prefer to walk if you are sure you care to walk." I said, "Of course. Forgive me." There was an awkward minute. I had assumed she was too old to walk any distance on hard pavement. But she quickly overcame my embarrassment.

We walked along a canal. It was a beautiful early-spring day, but a little cool and windy. Every once in a while I wanted to ask her if she was all right— she wore only a light coat—but I did not, for of course she was all right. She talked in her lively way, gratifying my interest in the story of *Poetry*, which is a long and dramatic tale; but I need not recount it here, since it is available elsewhere, particularly in Harriet Monroe's autobiography, which she was writing just then. And every once in a while she would interrupt herself and explain some sight to me. "That's a striking house—don't you think it looks lovely from here? . . . Of course much of Chicago is terribly ugly; no excuse for it; but it's vital, and beauty will probably come next." Her voice was sheer pleasure to listen to; her English was American, with the rhythm one hears only in the Middle West.

We left the canal and walked in a street lined with warehouses on both sides. Trucks, loading and unloading, were parked all along. The drivers stood about singly and in groups. Some were in the seats of their trucks eating lunch. Many of the warehouse men were eating, too, or resting, stretched on the pavement or the loading-platforms. "There is something splendid about these men—their movements as they work, their postures as they stand, their positions as they lie down or recline against a wall, as that fellow over there. See him?" She saw and heard everything.

Having just finished his lunch and closed his lunch-pail, a workman let out a mighty belch the moment Harriet Monroe and I passed him; in fact, we not only heard the belch, but practically felt it. "And that's all right, too," said Harriet Monroe; "the most wonderful belch I have ever heard. Now why should a belch sound all right here and terrible in a salon?" . . .

She walked rapidly and talked on of *Poetry* and poetry. Weren't Horace and Marya Gregory a fine pair? She had known them when they were still at Madison. Was Marya well? Weren't their children wonderful? . . . Had I seen Robinson Jeffers lately? . . . Did I know Carl Sandburg and Edgar Lee Masters? T. S. Eliot? Edwin Rolfe? William C. Williams? She mentioned others, many of whose names were unfamiliar to me. They all figured in the story of *Poetry*, which had been the core of her life for the past twenty-five years.

We walked well over an hour: four or five miles, all through the Loop, on Michigan Avenue, the main part of which she considered "almost beautiful." She was not the least out of breath. I forgot her age and was aware only of her intense consciousness and her ubiquitous spirit. In her talk she flitted all over the earth. She seemed at home everywhere. Five years before, she said, she had been to Dalmatia; it was too bad I had not written *The Native's Return* before that; it would have helped her to get to know the people living on those stony ridges and along the sea. Next summer she was planning to go with some friends to China. . . . Now, here were Ivan Mestrovich's monuments to the American Indian. No, she had never met him; but wasn't it strange that a Yugoslav from Dalmatia should create those monuments? Yes, she rather liked them, though she had not at first.

A man greeted her on Michigan Avenue, "Why, hello, Harriet!" He was a middle-aged, solid-looking citizen, and stopped to talk with her for a minute. She introduced us. When we moved on, she told me he was a business man who had been giving a hundred dollars a year to *Poetry* for nearly twenty years.

During lunch she asked me about Carniola. Didn't I exaggerate its charm just a little? Was literature really so important in the life of the Slovenian people? Poetry? . . . I told her of Oton Zupanchich, somewhat in the way I tell of him in the chapter "On Being of Two Worlds." . . . Did I think poetry could ever become as deep a factor in the life of the American people as it was in the life of Carniola? If some one had asked me this two hours earlier I would probably have said, "Impossible!" Now, having met her, I was not so sure. "Sometimes I hope," she said, "that our best poetry will be heard over the radio; that poets themselves—the Carl Sandburgs, the Vachel Lindsays, the Edna Millays of the not too distant future will write a poem this week and go on the air with it the next."

We walked back to her office, which was a distance of two or three more miles. She regretted I did not know more people in Chicago; the city was really full of extraordinarily fine men and women; and it was too bad I was rushing right on. I had an engagement at St. Paul the following evening. But when I returned to Chicago, I must let her know in advance and she would arrange a party. Perhaps I would give a little talk on poetry in Slovenia. I promised I would.

I said good-by to her in front of the *Poetry* office. She hurried inside. I hailed the first taxi I saw, not only because I was in a hurry to get to an appointment in the Loop, but because I was tired.

This was the only time I saw Harriet Monroe. I had a charming letter from her some time later. I was in Chicago about a year subsequently and had written her ahead, but she was not there just then. She was probably traveling somewhere or living away from Chicago, writing her life.

Late in the summer 1936 I read a little notice somewhere—I think in the *Saturday Review of Literature*—that Harriet Monroe was going to Buenos Aires to attend the celebration of an Argentine poetry club. I thought to myself: she would!

A few weeks later I opened the October *Poetry*, which was the twenty-fourth anniversary issue of the magazine. There was an editorial, signed "H.M.," written just before her departure for Latin America. She was looking ahead: "We shall put on a drive for more subscribers, more guarantors—more enthusiastic support, not only for the magazine, but for the art. We shall remind the people, as we did with quite a din twenty-four years ago, of the meager and lackadaisical support given to the finest of the fine arts, the art most powerful for making the story of our deeds immortal by telling it to the next age. We shall insist again, as many times in our history, that great poetry is not a creation *in vacuo*, but antiphonal between a poet and his audience, that it is not enough to sing—the song must be heard." She went on to say that it was her hope and belief the best poets would eventually be "literally heard over the radio." Until then, however, the poet would depend on the printing-press. "What a printing may mean to a struggling poet in the way of spiritual food and refreshment, hundreds of letters in our files would show. It is that realization which has impelled me to continue the effort to finance and run *Poetry* all these twenty-four years. How much longer it will be my special province and pleasure only the fates can tell."

Late in September I read in the press that Harriet Monroe died in the town of Arequipa, Peru. She had been in her seventy-sixth year, and I suppose the altitude of several thousand feet was just a little too much for her. It took the Andes to stop her heart.

Man from New England

I CANNOT MENTION THE NAME OF THE RATHER LARGE WESTERN CITY WHERE I MET Mr. Spragg, for he still lives there; it is his town; and if I mentioned it, some people there might identify him, although Spragg, of course, is not his name. I wrote to him that I wished to put him in this book; in reply he gave his consent, but indicated he did not want to be "found out"—yet.

I lectured in this city one evening early in 1936, and the next morning the telephone rang in my hotel room. "My name's Spragg," said a pleasant male voice. "I heard you talk last night and wish to see you if you have a little time." I asked him to come over.

He was a tall, strong, handsome man, forty-eight, as I learned later, but younger-looking—: one of the most agreeable personalities I had ever come upon. I liked him at once. He stayed with me till it was time for me to catch my train.

"I was very much interested in what you said last night," he began. ". . . Most of us have not yet begun to live; we don't know how. We go through all sorts of motions, vague and emphatic. Some of us lead well-fed, respectable lives and become outwardly smug and conservative. We pretend that our social life is satisfying. But it isn't. Nothing is, really. Everything we are or do is more or less empty. You've read Sinclair Lewis' *Babbitt*, of course. It's true as a superficial picture. I've read it three times, and I don't like it. It's not really true. The truth is much deeper, sadder; also, in a way, more hopeful. . . . Does what I am saying mean anything to you?"

"Yes, it does," I said, "or I think it does." I asked him if he would care to tell me something about himself.

He told me he was first vice-president in charge of the credit department of the biggest local bank . . . and he was writing a book, which was the real reason for his calling on me this morning. The book was a novel. He had been working on it, off and on, for years; thinking it out rather than actually writing it. He had been at it four or five years, but had only about a hundred pages of it written. He did not say so, but evidently he was in no hurry to finish it; was, perhaps, a little uncertain about it. He told me the story in outline:

"It is the tale of a man born in 1888, the year of the Great Blizzard. He lives the first twelve years of his life in a small and old, highly cultured community just outside of Boston. His father and mother are the best sort of New England people. They are well-to-do, cultivated, persons of taste. Their home is an old and spacious Colonial house. Its walls are decorated with original paintings, etchings, and the best of prints. There is a library containing autographed first editions of Emerson, who had been a visitor in the house. New books and art exhibitions in Boston and New York are events carefully noted in this home, which is also the gathering-place for people of achievement in various fields, but particularly in the arts.

"Then, suddenly, when the boy—the central character of the story—is twelve, his father loses his fortune and the entire family moves West, where the father has a connection and goes into business. The atmosphere of this Western city where they settle is different from that in the small town outside of Boston. Here life is generally crude; there is little culture, little art; Boston and Cambridge and New York are far off . . . and the boy, instead of going to Harvard or Williams, enters the rather inadequate state university and prepares himself for a business career. He goes into banking and is very successful; marries and has children; lives in a so-called fine house; is respected and considered a 'leading citizen'; but things are not what they seem to be or what he pretends to think they are. . . . I shall not attempt to sketch the details of the story. . . . Throughout his thirties he is secretly questioning everything, but, involved in his tasks and duties, in his family and position, he gets nowhere within himself. Outwardly he is like everybody else on his economic and social level. No one knows what is going on inside of him. Not even he himself, clearly.

"When he is forty, business takes him East. He goes to Boston, to New York. He walks through the Harvard Yard, through the town of his boyhood. He sees the house of his birth, now inhabited by some one else. He visits several art galleries in New York and Boston, all but forgetting the business purpose of his trip.

"In one of these galleries he sees a picture that does something to him. He cannot get it off his mind. For some reason, he doesn't know why, it is the finest thing he has ever seen. He starts to return West, thinking that perhaps he will forget it; but in Chicago he turns around, goes back to New York and buys the painting, takes it back West with him, and thereafter the story revolves around his inner life under the influence of the painting. . . ."

The story was, of course, autobiographical. Mr. Spragg asked me how one got a book published. I told him. Then, hesitantly, would I be so good as to read some of the chapters when he finally got them into shape? . . .

Months later I received Chapter One, which seemed to me—and to Stella, the only person to whom I showed it—a masterful fictional study of a blizzard, in which the hero of the story is born. The man was an artist. . . . But this is all I can tell of him. As I write this, he is still working on his novel. He does not know how long it may take him to complete it.

Americans Drinking

YOUNG MAN FROM PHILLY

MIND IF I SIT BY YOU?" HE ASKED.

"Oh no," I said, picking up my hat and the afternoon newspapers from the seat beside me.

We were at the Pennsylvania Station, due to leave in eight or ten minutes. "Train's pretty full, ain't it?" he remarked further.

"Yes," I agreed.

He was a young man, in his late twenties or very early thirties; tall, strong, sunburnt, not handsome nor the opposite, typically American, in the sense that you could not expect him to be a native of any other place under the sun; rather well-dressed and just a trifle drunk. He lifted his suitcase onto the rack above me, and placed a paper bag containing a dozen or more bottles of beer in the space between us.

"Hot, ain't it?" he said, removing his hat and putting it on top of the suitcase, while wiping the sweat off his face and neck with a handkerchief.

"Pretty warm," I said.

"I see you got your coat off, so I guess you ain't gonna mind if I take mine off, too. Put on a clean shirt this morning—that's a old gag; you heard it before."

His hands suggested he might be a mechanic of some sort.

"Say, wanna bottle beer?" he said.

"No, thanks."

"Aw, come on, have one."

"Not right now, thanks. I just had lunch."

"O.K. When you feel like havin' some, here they are. I'm goin' to Philly. Where you goin'?"

"Washington."

"Must be a scorcher in Washington," he said. "I tell you: you better have a bottle now while they're cold. I just got 'em, right off the ice. There's no use bein' thirsty when you ride on a train to Philly on a hot day like this."

He took a bottle-opener from his pants pocket, reached for a bottle, snapped the top off it, and drank it a little more than half down. "Boy, is this good!"—wiping his mouth with the back of his hand. "Sure you don' wanna try a bottle while it's cold?"

"No, thanks, not right now."

"O.K. Don' do nothin' you don' wanna do. This is a free country. Help yourself when you wannit."

"O.K."

"That's all right. But, say, I'm a dope. Maybe you wanna be left alone and read the papers, and don' wanna talk."

487

"Yes. I thought I'd read the papers."

"O.K., go ahead. Don' mind me. I get that way sometime, too, when I don' wanna talk. Only help yourself when you think you wanna drink. Savvy? I guess they'll stay cold awhile."

I read the papers for a few minutes. He finished his first bottle of beer and put the empty on the floor under the seat.

Then he called the Western Union boy who was passing through the car. Taking the pencil and blank pad (as I watched him from the corner of my eye), he hesitated for a moment, as though he scarcely knew to whom he wanted to telegraph, but finally he wrote out two messages in a big awkward script, and gave the boy a dollar and told him to keep the change. The boy saluted, saying, "Thank you, sir!" and he said, "O.K., kid!"

"You know," he turned to me, forgetting I wanted to read the papers, "I didn' have to wire anybody; they all know I'm comin'; but I like to send telegrams when I get on a train like this. What the hell: if I get a kick out of sendin' wires, why not!"

I echoed, "Why not!"

"That's what I say. Let me tell you somethin'. I work on a big yacht—assistant engineer—and my boss—I mean the guy who owns the yacht—he sends a coupla dozen telegrams wherever we stop, and when we're at sea, all kindsa radiograms. Of course, he's a big-shot—George Sommerwell, big Wall Street guy. Ever hear of 'im?"

"No."

"Well, anyhow, he's this boss o' mine, and I suppose he's gotta send lotsa telegrams and radio messages, but maybe not so many like he does send. I got a hunch he sends so many because he likes the idea—makes 'im important, savvy?—gives him a kick, so why shouldn' he? He's got plenty of dough. But, then, why shouldn't I send a coupla telegrams once in a while?"

"No reason at all."

"You tell 'em! I'm as good as he is. This is a free country and one guy's good as the next. And, what's more, I'm from Philly, born right in Philly, where we got the Liberty Bell, even if it's cracked. I say, to hell with 'em all but six; save 'em for pall-bearers! That's a old gag, too; maybe you heard it."

The train started.

"O.K., let 'er go, Knute!" he said. "Bound for Philly! Say, ain't you ready for a drinka beer yet?"

"No, not yet, thanks."

"O.K. Here it is, when you wannit; yours for the takin', and I'll even open the bottle for you. That fair enough?"

"Fair enough," I said.

"O.K." He opened his second bottle and emptied it with only a gasp between the top and bottom. "Boy!"

A pause. Then: "This is great, ain't it, ridin' on a train through a tunnel that goes under a river a mile wide, and drinkin' beer. This is a great country, no maybe about it. Ain't it?"

"It certainly is."

"You betcha! But, speakin' of this boss o' mine, that owns the yacht, let me tell you somethin'. Only don' misunderstand me; he's O.K., and I'm not kickin'; I just wanna tell you somethin'. Last Febr'ary we was in Miami, a swell town in winter; and layin' there I saw 'im, this boss o' mine, lose fifty bucks playin' four-bit pieces in a slot-machine. Down from Nova Scotia this week, we stopped in Boston, an' what does he do there but order the steward to buy a hundred bucks' worth of roses and flowers of all kinds, and spread 'em around all over the goddamn' yacht. Now, flowers is all right; I like to look at 'em myself, but a hundred bucks for flowers—oh boy! I had to laugh at myself when I got to thinkin' that I get a hundred a month and the steward gets only fifty, an' I wondered what the boss'd say if we asked 'im for a raise. He'd say prob'ly we was tryin' to take the pants offa 'im. But then, on the other hand, as I told you, I'm not kickin'. Why should I? Why should he pay us more than he's gotta? I bet if I was him, and he was me, I'd pay 'im no more than he pays me. Why should I? Neither would you or nobody else, if you was in his place. And if I was nuts about some jane I had on the yacht, I'd prob'ly buy a hundred bucks' worth of roses in Boston. Why shouldn't I? See what I mean?"

"I think I do."

"Say, how about a drink?"

"Just have one yourself," I said. "Drinking doesn't go well with me on a hot day."

"O.K. I just want you to feel that here it is, and plenty of it. Maybe you don' like beer. That's your privilege. This is a free country. *I* like beer"—opening his third bottle as we approached Newark—"and I can drink thirty bottles a day 'tout battin' an eye. If I can get all the beer I want when I wannit, my boss can have his yacht. What the hell! But, jeez, I guess you wanna read your papers. Holy mac! I talk a lot, don' I? But don' mind me."

"That's all right; I can read the papers later." I was beginning to like him.

"Don' mind me. I useta read papers, but don' any more. On the yacht, I lissen on the radio and get all the news. But things sure are screwed up—no kiddin'—ain't they? Hitler, Mussolini, and Spain, and what's-his-name in Roossia—oh yeah, Stalin bumpin' 'em off right-'n'-left. Boy! Europe, I guess, *is* in one hell of a fix! What's it say in the paper today. Will there be war?"

"Hard to say."

" 'S a matter of fact, let me tell you: I don' give a damn either way so long's they don' drag us in. And if they do, what the hell! we'll lick any of 'em, or all of 'em put together. But say, I guess they're havin' a pretty hot time in Washington, too, ain't they? Are you in politics?"

"No, I'm not."

"That's all a racket, politics. They fight like anything. What about? Who knows? Damn if I do. . . . What town is this? Oh yeah, New Brunswick. I used to have a girl here onct, but that's a long story. She worked in the Johnson factory, makin' tooth-brushes. Boy! did I have plenty o' tooth-brushes in

them days! Damnear married her, but I didn't. Then she took on another guy.
Say! how about a bottle now?"

"I don't know——"

"Come on, have one. What the hell! Pretty soon it'll all be warm and then
maybe you ain't gonna like it."

He opened two bottles, gave me one, and drank his down.

I drank a bit.

"This beer's gettin' a little warm already," he said. "I told you to have one
way back there. But it's O.K. by me; I can drink beer any temperature at all.
And speakin' of that dame, I almost married in New Brunswick, I'll tell you
somethin'. I'm goin' to Philly to visit my mother, and you know what she'll
say to me about four minutes after I get home? She'll say, 'Jimmy, why don'
you quit runnin' around, sailin' the sea, and why don' you settle down and
marry some nice girl?' She'll say that sure's you're alive, and I'll laugh at 'er
when she starts like that; and we'll have a swell time. She's wonderful, my old
lady. Nobody like 'er! I'll buy 'er a big buncha flowers, but not a hundred
bucks' worth, and maybe take 'er to a movie tonight if she wants to go. I
sent 'er a wire, though I sent 'er a radiogram from the yacht yesterday afternoon that I was comin', and she'll say I waste money for telegrams. 'Jimmy,
you're extravagant,' she'll say. 'But why the hell not?' I'll say, and she'll say
not to say why-the-hell—and, oh boy! ain't we gonna have fun! But she does
wanna get me married off to some dame; has two or three of 'em picked out
for me, but why should I settle down? Drink your beer, why don' you; or is
it too warm for you? . . ."

He drank another bottle and offered one to the conductor, who smilingly
declined it.

Then, to me: "See that girl in the third seat on the left?"

"Yes."

"She turned round little while ago, and I bet she thinks she's a looker, and,
if you come down to it, she ain't bad to see . . . but lissen, let me tell you
somethin'. I was in Japan last year, on this yacht, and me and the second officer
went to a geisha garden— Ever heard of geisha girls?"

"Yes."

"Boy! they're a knockout, them geishas! Beautiful and refined," he whistled.
"Nothin' cheap or low about 'em, and what they don' know about givin' a man
a good time is nobody's business. But all wonderful and refined. Boy! wouldn'
I like to be drinkin' beer with one of 'em again some day—even if Jap beer
ain't so hot!"

He opened his sixth or seventh bottle; I had ceased counting.

"Well, another hour and we'll be in Philly. And, you know, Philly ain't a
bad town, though I prob'ly wouldn' live there on a bet. It's kinda slow and
quiet, but O.K. otherwise. Full o' nice people. My mother wouldn' live any-
wheres else. Matter of taste. Live anywhere you like, do anything you like;
this is a free country. . . . Jeez! I'm sorry this beer got all warm on us."

"That's all right; I really don't care for beer very much."

"Sure, it's a matter of taste. Say, did you hear the one about ——"

Then, while emptying another three or four bottles, he told me stories till we got to Philadelphia. At Broad Street station, he put on his coat and hat, and said:

"Well, s'long, Washington!"

I said, "So long, Philly!"

"Glad to of met you"—pulling down his suitcase.

"Same here."

"Don't take any wooden nickels!"

"O.K.," I said.

"And don' believe anythin' you read in the papers. S'long!"

MAN WHO RETURNED FROM EUROPE

One evening in mid-August, 1937, a local friend of mine and I sat talking of nothing in particular in a corner of the Hotel Hollenden bar-room in Cleveland. All of a sudden a slight, middle-aged man in a loose Palm Beach suit with his Panama pushed 'way back on his head and evidently a few drinks too many under his belt, came over to us from the bar in a sociable, wide-open mood, which made him appear a very attractive individual. Neither my friend nor I had, of course, ever seen him before. He said, "Gentlemen, will you empty your glasses and have a drink or two on me?"

He introduced himself. Let me call him Mr. White of Middleton, Ohio, though that was neither his name nor his town, which was about a hundred miles from Cleveland. Later, when I asked him, he told us he was the manufacturer of a nationally advertised product used in most homes in the United States. Still later I found him listed in *Who's Who*.

We ordered; whereupon, for several minutes, our new friend talked rapidly in an incoherent, mildly-drunk fashion. I gathered that he had arrived in Cleveland that afternoon. The day before he had arrived with his two sons, Lee and Bill, in New York from a five-week trip in Europe. "And just now," he went on, his talk becoming clearer, "I'm stranded in Cleveland—though I shouldn't say 'stranded,' because you can't really be stranded in Cleveland, now can you? At least I can't. But let me tell you how all this happened. I'm a Yale man; and both my sons are in Yale. Lee will be a senior this year, and Bill, who is two years Lee's junior, will be a sophomore. Anyhow, I took them to Europe; or, to be exact, they took me, which is a long story. They're great fellows. . . . Yesterday we returned, as I told you—or did I tell you? . . . Well, be as it may, we got back on the *Queen Mary*—some boat! I had to hurry home on urgent business, while Lee and Bill wanted to stay in New York for a few days. They know a couple of girls in Rye, which is a town near New York, so why not? Well, anyhow, I asked the boys to wire home to Middleton so Bert, our chauffeur, would meet me at the station in Cleveland on my arrival at four-seventeen, but Lee and Bill apparently forgot, or else one thought that the other had wired; and so, when I arrived here at four-seventeen—no

Bert. I telephoned to Middleton and Bert started out for me right away, but as luck would have it, and life being one damned thing after another, anyhow, somewhere on the other side of Akron he broke down and at seven o'clock he called me here at the Hollenden, where I told him he would find me. A part broke, and they had to go for it to Akron, but had a hard time getting it because the agency and all the accessory and parts stores were closed by then . . . and so here it's ten-thirty, or whatever the time is, and I'm still waiting for Bert. . . .

"But 'stranded,' as I say, is the wrong word. I know all sorts of people in Cleveland—business and personal friends, whom I could have called up, but didn't because I didn't know when Bert might turn up; I had told him I would be here at the Hollenden till he came. Besides, I didn't want to get mixed up in a lot of company. I must get home soon as possible. Business.——"

He paused. The waiter brought the drinks. "Well," said Mr. White, "here is to the good old U.S.A.!" We drank. I asked him how he had found Europe.

"Europe," he said—"well, sir, let me tell you. All three of us, my two sons and I, came back strong with the idea: not only three cheers, but three times three times three cheers for the U.S.A. I am going to talk before the Business Men's Luncheon Club of Middleton, and that is going to be my message, sir, and my theme song, as it were. . . . Europe has it all over us in certain ways; they have things over there which we don't even dream of—culture, art, and so forth and so on; but they have also Hitler and Mussolini and Stalin and this bloody business in Spain which my boy Lee thinks is the prelude to the next world war.

"We were in Germany for a week or eight days, and the atmosphere there is such that—well, the idea is, three times three times three cheers for the good old U.S.A.! We went through a factory in Hamburg, which turns out a product similar to ours, and my boy Lee, who knows German and had talked with several men, said afterwards that if he were one of these workers he'd blow up the damned place. The men were scared to say anything to him, although they knew he was a foreigner. German factories are like prisons. Everybody is watched, even, and especially, after work, and the men didn't look good to me. Cowed; no spirit. . . .

"We were in Turin, Milan, and Naples, and the poverty in some of the back streets is something awful. . . .

"The only countries where I think I could stay for any length of time are Czechoslovakia, France, and England; perhaps also in the Scandinavian countries, which I hear are all right in some ways—we didn't visit them this time."

"Were you in Russia?" I asked.

"Yes," replied Mr. White, "but only for three days, in Moscow. We flew there from Prague. Everybody was afraid to have anything to do with us— even at the hotel where we stopped. We were foreigners. I talked to a man connected with the American Embassy, or tried to talk with him. He had no idea what was going on, or didn't want to tell me. I don't know what to think of Russia. My boy Lee is all mixed up about it, too, though a couple of years ago he was sort of sympathetic to what they seemed to be trying to do there."

"But how about this country?" said my friend. "This country is no paradise, either."

"Who said it was?" returned Mr. White. "Did I say it was? . . . All I said is what my sons and I think: three times three times three cheers for U.S.A. We mean comparatively——"

"All right," I said, "but what about President Roosevelt and his proposal to change the Supreme Court and now his appointment of Senator Black, who is supposed to be a former K.K.K.? What do you think of that?"

"I voted for Landon in 1936," said Mr. White, "and I didn't and don't like the idea of packing the Supreme Court, nor do I like the appointment of Senator Black, though I don't know all about it because I've been away and haven't been reading the papers regular, except the Paris *Herald*. I talked to a Chicago man on the train coming from New York, and he was all against Roosevelt; but I told him that even if the President was all wrong, which maybe he wasn't, it was all right, because this was America—goddam it! In America things were done in the open, mistakes were made in the open; so what?—as my son Bill would say, so what? The Supreme Court idea was debated in the open, and it was a pretty good debate, too. The President got licked, but I think the debate was good for the country. It probably won't do the President any harm. It showed that even if a fellow gets every state but Maine and Vermont he can't do everything he wants to do his own way. If Roosevelt made a mistake with Black, that's his hard luck more than the country's; unless he's learned a lesson."

"But how about the C.I.O. and the sitdowns?" I asked.

"All right," said Mr. White, "what about the C.I.O. and the sitdowns? You two gentlemen may be business men, I don't know; I didn't ask you and you didn't tell me what you are, which is all right. I told you what I do for a living, and it may be that as a manufacturer I'd prefer not to have the C.I.O. and sit-down strikes; it would be simpler and easier; but now here they are—they are a force—a reality—they must be met and dealt with."

"How?"

"How? By bringing our problems out in the open and keeping them in the open; by compromising and getting along somehow as free citizens of the same country.——"

A bell-hop brought a man to our table. It was Mr. White's chauffeur.

"Hello, Bert, you son-of-a-gun!" said Mr. White.

"Hello, Mr. White," said Bert. "Welcome back."

They shook hands and talked about the car awhile. Bert was entirely at ease before his employer. "Well," said Mr. White, "I guess we'll have to turn this one in and get a new car." He said good-by to my friend and me, repeating "three times three times three cheers for the U.S.A.!" and went out with the smiling chauffeur, who was amused by his boss' slight inebriation.

Honey John

M YLES HORTON—WHOM I HAVE MENTIONED BEFORE THIS AS THE FOUNDER AND head of the interesting Highlander Folk School—and I were going about in the Cumberland Mountains (in Fentress County, Tennessee, I believe), and we overheard a conversation about a certain Honey John's daughter going off to a teachers' college as if anyone going off to college from those parts was unusual. The name "Honey John" interested Myles and me. We asked where Honey John lived and were told to follow the hollow road until we came to a mail-box with "Honey John" on it and we would be at the corner of his patch.

We did as instructed and found the fence around the patch, which we followed until we came to a dilapidated gate in front of a one-room cabin. A half-dozen small boys and girls and a baby or two watched us from the grassless and littered front yard as we approached the place.

Myles called out "Hello!" two or three times, as is the custom in the mountains, and by-and-by a youngish-looking woman came to the door and stood without saying a word, waiting for one of us to open the conversation. Myles said, "Does Honey John live here?" She was pleasant-enough looking as she answered with the one word, "Yes." Myles asked, "Is he at home?" She gave a quick shake of her head, answering, "No." Myles said, "Where is he?" And she directed us across the fenced-in patch and into the woods, and told us to listen for a saw or an ax.

In ten or fifteen minutes we found Honey John cutting cross-ties. He stopped when we came up, to cool off and take a chew of tobacco. It was a hot day, and he seemed glad to have some one to talk with. Myles and I sat down on one log, Honey John on another, facing us; then Myles got to talking with him.

Myles asked him about his name, and Honey John said he was one of a large family of boys whose father had kept bees, and since he was the only one to take up his father's part-time occupation, he was consequently called Honey John. The name had become so popular, he said, that he seldom used his last name, which he told us, but which I forget. Most of his neighbors knew him only as Honey John.

Honey John spoke with pride of his daughter who was going off to college to learn to be a teacher. Myles asked him how many children he had. He answered, "Four or five." Like myself (who kept quiet), Myles was puzzled; we had counted at least half a dozen in the yard in front of the cabin. When Myles mentioned what was in his mind, Honey John explained that the children we had seen were his wife's, not his.

Myles and I, naturally, assumed that both Honey John and his wife had been married before, but when Myles phrased a question referring to that point,

Honey John explained that he had been married before, sure enough, but that his wife had not. Still more puzzled, Myles and I looked at one another; whereupon Myles, who knows how to talk with the mountaineers, played for time by talking about other things, thinking the matter which interested us might clarify itself indirectly. But it did not.

Finally, Myles cautiously approached the subject again. No, said Honey John, the woman we had seen in his cabin had never been married before, but the kids were hers. He. said that he knew the fathers of some of them, but was not sure about the others. Honey John told these facts very calmly and matter-of-factly, without any show of interest in the matter. He chewed his tobacco and spat. When Myles asked him if he did not object to raising half a dozen kids accumulated by his wife before their marriage, he hit his cud of tobacco a lick or two, and drawled, "It's as fair for one as 'tis for t'other, somebody's got to take care of my stray younguns. It equals up."

Girl on the Road

IT WAS NEAR SEVEN O'CLOCK ON A MID-NOVEMBER MORNING, COLD AND WINDY under a bleak Ohio sky, and—New York-bound—I was driving out of Cleveland, where I had spent the previous evening with pleasant friends, dining at their home, and spending the rest of the night at a comfortable hotel. I had had my breakfast and was warm in the new overcoat and gloves I had bought in Detroit a few days before. There was a heater in the car, and when the wind occasionally lurched into me with great force and threatened to swerve me off the road, I almost enjoyed the sensation I experienced.

For two or three miles, approaching the village of Chagrin Falls, not far from Cleveland, I met or passed no car, and none passed me. Then, just ahead, as I swung around a turn, I noticed a little figure—woman or girl—moving across the top of a slight rise in the road. Stumbling and staggering under the wind's impact, she carried a suitcase; and, wondering what she was doing out so early on such a morning, I assumed she must be going some place close by. I decided to offer her the lift she evidently sought, and I slowed down going up the incline.

She turned about and beckoned to me with a feeble, despairing gesture of her arm, then stumbled—seemingly over her own feet, as the wind pushed her—and fell on the suitcase, which hit the pavement simultaneously with her knees. This occurred when I was perhaps fifty feet from her, and I had to shift into second to enable the car to pull upgrade against the strong wind. By the time I had stopped she had scrambled up again, and was about to pick up the suitcase when, abruptly, it blew open, and the wind scooped out most of its contents and flung them against the fence and amid the cornstalks of the field along the highway.

I hurriedly stepped out of the automobile and ran to her, and was confronted at closest proximity by a girl who was but little more than a skin-enveloped skeleton. Her cheap clothing was threadbare, wrinkled, ripped in several places. Her thin, sharp face was blue from the cold and wind, except where it was black and yellow around two considerable scars, one on her left cheek and the other above her right eye. Her whole body, and every part of it separately, quaked and twitched in short, swift jerks.

The palms and the under sides of the fingers of her black cloth gloves were worn through from carrying the suitcase. Her shoes were broken. Her cheap silk stockings, with several holes and runs, afforded scarcely any covering. The wind whipped against her, and I knew that underneath her frayed garments she was also all blue and bruised and scratched, for, an instant before I reached her and put a hand on her shoulder lest the wind take her off, her light coat and skirt had billowed about her and, flying up, revealed her skinny legs midway above her knees.

She seemed small, the size of a girl of twelve or thirteen. Later she told me the last time she weighed herself, days ago, she had tipped the scales at eighty-four, but now she probably was even less than eighty. Her normal weight was a hundred and six or seven. Her teeth chattered so it was a wonder they did not shatter one another. Her lower lip was covered with little cuts and congealed blood, as though the teeth had been hacking at it for a long time.

"Get in the car!" I yelled, feeling as though I myself would begin to tremble at any moment. The wind pushed the words back into my mouth. As she did not move, I pulled her toward the autombile. She was at once limp and rigid.

Just then a car rushed toward us and I yanked the girl out of the way. She dragged the open suitcase along with her.

Except for a small package tied with a faded red ribbon which evidently was too heavy to be blown out, the suitcase was empty. The girl clutched its handle frenziedly. But immediately the car whizzed by us, a sudden convulsion in her, which originated perhaps in the cold center of her bones, caused her to loose her grip on it, and the suitcase began to slither across the road. Unable to talk through her chattering teeth, she let out a shrill, pathetic whimper, and I quickly stepped on the suitcase, halting its progress ditchward.

I stooped over to close it, but the girl emitted another piercing whimper. An indescribable misery in her eyes, she pointed at her things snapping in the wind on the wire fence and the cornstalks on the other side of the road, which I had seen a moment before but since momentarily forgotten.

"All right," I shouted, "I'll get them. You go inside!"

But she was frantic about her things and the suitcase, and I felt compelled to seize her and carry her into the car: which gave me one of the worst sensations of my life. The whole horror of her wretched, cold-pierced being engulfed me. There was no strength left in it. A wisp of her stringy hair, which stuck out from under her tiny, battered summer hat, touched my face, and it was all I could do not to drop her. My sensation was a mixture of revulsion and pity and shame—shame at the revulsion that pulsed through me; but I could not help feeling as I did.

My car was a coupé, and I managed to get her in and at least into the semblance of a sitting position. She whimpered and made faint half-gestures while shaking as violently as she had shaken outside.

The motor and the heater were going, but I had left the car open, and now it was as cold inside as out; so I wrapped the girl in my old autumn topcoat and the raincoat which I had with me on the ledge above the seat. Then I closed the car and proceeded to gather up her things. I was terribly awkward crawling through the wire fence . . . and for a moment I wondered if all this were not really a nightmare. There was that girl in my car; here was I collecting her soiled, torn garments from the barbed-wire fence and the cornstalks. . . .

I spent probably five minutes in the field, making sure I did not leave anything. Besides the pitifully cheap, bedraggled, and torn underthings, I found also a frayed garter, a red belt, and a large photograph of a sailor in the United States navy with a rather flashy young lady, who I guessed was identical with the girl in my car, though she no longer resembled her. I crawled back to the road and hastily jammed everything I had found into the suitcase. Then, closing it as well as I could, I put it on the ledge inside the coupé, and got in myself and shut the door.

Trying to get as close to the heater as possible, the girl had, meantime, slid from the seat, and, all tangled in my coats, she half sat and half squatted on the floor, her head between her knees. She looked up and wanted to say something, but was still unable to talk, though she appeared to shake less and her teeth no longer rat-tat-tatted so violently.

I said, "I picked up everything I saw."

She let out a weak sound I could not make out over the whir of the heater; it probably was "Thank you."

Now, of a sudden, I was deeply confused. What was I going to do with her? Where was she going? Of course, I might find that out eventually when, or if, she became able to speak, but ——

Several *buts* occurred to me. My gasoline gauge indicated only two or three more gallons in the tank, and I would have to stop soon to have it refilled: but what would the gas-station attendant say when he saw the battered, wasted girl in my car? He might telephone the police; the thing might get into the newspapers, and who knew what reporters—say, in Warren or Youngstown, which were the next big towns on my route—would do with my explanation of how I had found her on the road.

And there was this: while she doubtless was cold and, to all appearances, in a dreadful condition, the whole thing might conceivably be a trap. I had heard of female racketeers on state lines exploiting the Mann Act by all manner of tricks to extort money from solitary male motorists. In a few hours, on the other side of Youngstown, I would be crossing the Ohio-Pennsylvania line; then she was apt to give me trouble.

But at the same time I felt a twinge of shame. In all probability, the girl was in actual distress. Those cuts and black and yellowing marks on her face were real. Were she a Mann Act racketeer, she very likely would be nearer the state line than this. And she would not be operating on so unpleasant a morning. Even now she might be in danger of pneumonia or some other equally serious illness. Certainly she was cold and near exhaustion; the thing to do was to act on the assumption she was in trouble.

"Shouldn't I take you to a hospital or a doctor?" I inquired.

She looked up, to stare at me. I repeated my question twice, whereupon she wagged her head desperately in the negative.

"You're probably ill," I said.

She shook her head again.

Huddling against the heater, she was also close to the gear-shift and emergency brake. I asked her to get back on the seat, and, with a faint " 'Scuse me," she complied as quickly as she could. I helped her to raise herself, then put my coats around her again, and I drove on. She scarcely shook any more and her teeth clicked only intermittently. Vaguely uneasy, I glanced at her every half-minute or so. I inquired how she was, but she could not talk yet.

She tried to place her feet upon the heater, but her leg muscles lacked strength to keep them there. They plunked down immediately she lifted them.

I said, "You'll have some breakfast at the first eating-place we come to."

She whimpered and struggled to say something, but I could not understand her. She got an arm out from under the topcoat and attempted some signs and gestures, but just then some cars came, and I was obliged to keep my eyes on the road and could not watch her. Presently, however, she managed to say, "Gotta cigarette?"

I had no cigarettes, said I was sorry, and asked her again how she was.

"Oh," she said, "this is . . . wunnerful." She spoke with difficulty.

"You needn't talk," I said; "take it easy. Besides, I can hardly hear you; the heater makes so much noise."

She closed her eyes and evidently fell asleep.

In Chagrin Falls I looked for an eating-place, but saw none except one, which, however, was not yet open. So I went on, assuming the girl's destination, if she had one, was some distance in the direction I was going. I doubtless would come to a restaurant or "diner" before long.

After about ten minutes' sleep, my passenger awoke with a start and a cry, and stared at me. The brief slumber had helped her to recover her speech and the partial control of her limbs. She moved and kicked her legs a little. The blueness of her face faded to pallor, and she looked slightly less a skeleton.

"Sure you ain't gotta cigarette?" she asked. Her faint voice rasped a trifle.

I said: "No. I'm sorry. I don't smoke."

"Gee! funny you don't smoke. Nearly all the guys that pick me up smoke."

I came to a stretch of straight road with no other car in view, and I looked at her a long moment.

"I must be a sight!" she cried, self-consciously, half ashamed, half defiant. She reached for the mirror over the windshield and manipulated it so she could see herself. "I look awful, don't I? How old do you suppose I am?"

I said, "About twenty-two," though she could have been taken for a good deal older.

"That's right, twenty-two," she echoed, eagerly. "But, gee, I do look a mess! He oughta see me now, the son-of-a-bee! 'Scuse me; but I only said bee!"

"You needn't apologize. I don't care."

"You don't care if I say bee or—you know what?"

"No," I said.

"Say, I bet you think I'm bad."

"No, I don't think anything at all," I said, "except that—apparently—you've had a strong dose of hard luck."

"Oh boy! did I!" she cried. Her voice was getting stronger.

"Just take it easy," I repeated. "You'd probably better not talk. Try to get warm."

She seemed not to be listening. "I'd give a million for a Lucky, Camel, Bull Durham, anythin'. Out West I smoked lotsa Bull Durham. Truck-drivers roll 'eir own."

"We'll get some cigarettes, too, the first chance. There don't seem to be any towns on this stretch."

"Gotta needle?"

"No."

"Gee! you ain't got nothin', have you?"

"I'm sorry."

"You're 'scused. But don't mind me. I'm just talkin'; I don't mean nothin'. You ain't mad, are you? I was fresh."

"I don't care."

"You're funny; you don't care about nothin'. But you sure gotta swell car, no kiddin'. Chevvy, ain't it? How much you got on the speedometer?" She bent over to read the mileage figure, and bumped her head on the steering-wheel.

"Careful," I cautioned.

"One bump more or less don't matter. Say, you ain't even got four thousand. Gee! almos' a bran'-new car. Sure you ain't gotta needle 'n' thread? . . . Lotsa guys got needles 'n' thread with 'em—sewin'-kits—but, oh yeah, this ain't no truck. 'Scuse me." She made a stab at laughing. "Truck-drivers carry needles, all kinds, big 'n' small. They use the big ones to sew up canvas; the small ones to stitch rips in their pants or shirts. Las' few weeks I sewed up lotsa truck-drivers' shirts. Well, coupla, anyhow. Now I'd like to sew myself up a little. I'm all torn everywhere."

She would talk for a few minutes, then close her eyes and be perfectly still for five or ten minutes, sleeping; whereupon she would suddenly start and stare at me bug-eyed, then again resume talking as though there were in her an hysterical necessity to talk, almost as if to reassure herself that she could talk and there was someone to listen to her. "You know what?" she said, "I'm tough. You wouldn't think so, lookin' at me, but I am, and how! Tough's my middle name."

"I guess you *are* tough," I agreed.

"Oh boy, am I! Me 'n' Popeye the Sailor! You like Popeye? . . . My fav'rite movie star, only I don't like spinach. But say, where's my suitcase? . . . Oh yeah. 'Scuse me. I saw you put it there, but forgot. 'Scuse me. I'm all groggy yet, I guess, and don't know the half-a what's goin' on. I feel like I been on a long drunk. But what I really am is punch-drunk."

She went on, but I missed entire stretches of her talk. Then, raising her feeble voice: "You know, 'twas white of you to pick up all that stuffa mine all over that field. Did you find a pitcher, me with a guy?"

"Yes, it's in the suitcase—you and the sailor."

"That's who I mean when I say 'the son-of-a-bee,' and you know what I mean when I say *bee*. He was my husband—still is, matter of fack." She paused, as though waiting for me to say something; then, as I kept silent, "Say, don't you wanna hear my story?"

"I don't know if it's interesting," I said.

This remark seemed to worry her. "It's interestin', all right. Lotsa guys that pick me up want to know my story."

"All I want to know," I said, "is where you're going, if you want to tell me."

"You're polite, no kiddin'. Think it's a secret? I'm goin' to Baltimore. Where you goin'?"

"New York. But I can take you as far as Harrisburg. A route from there goes to Baltimore."

"Harrisburg—how far's that from here?"

"Well over two hundred miles. I'm planning to stop there overnight."

"Will you take me far's you go today?"

"Yes." By now I was certain she was no Mann Act racketeer, and also, I had lost my feeling of shame in relation to her.

She fell asleep again.

I took this opportunity to stop at a gasoline station, where I half covered her face with a sleeve of my topcoat, so the attendant, who came out hurriedly, could not see it. He barely noticed her. I told him to fill the tank; he sold cigarettes, and I bought a package and a box of matches. He told me there were roadside eating-places ahead, but it was early, not quite eight, and they might not be open yet. Some, he said, were even closed altogether till spring.

I drove on.

When the girl awoke, I gave her the cigarettes and matches. She took them eagerly, but, her fingers numbed and weak, she had difficulty in opening the package. I offered to stop the car and open it for her, but she said, "Ne'r mind, I'll open it myself. I'm tough. I guess I slept some, didn't I? . . . Lookit, sun's comin' out!"

Finally she opened the package, lighted her cigarette, and smoked ravenously. "Ummm!" She inhaled deeply and held the smoke in her lungs, then exhaled slowly. "Believe it or not, my first cigarette in two days, and, boy! there was times in my life when I useta smoke two packs a day. It drives me nuts when I can't get a smoke. I bet you think I'm bad."

"No," I said. "Why should I?"

"Because the way I talk and look. Matter of fack, I'm not bad; I'm just no good, if you know what I mean. But you saved my life with this pack, no kiddin'. Mind if I have 'nother right away?"

"Go ahead; they're yours. Smoke all you want."

But instead of lighting another cigarette she passed out again for another five or ten minutes. I took the smoking stub of her first cigarette out of her hand.

The sun broke through the mist and the wind had subsided considerably. I felt warm, and opened the window on my side about halfway down, leaving the heater on.

Suddenly she screamed and awakened, to stare at me. "Did I yell?" she asked then.

"Yes," I said.

"I guess I slept and musta been dreamin' or somethin'. Or I got the jitters. Say, I had a cigarette, didn't I? I smell it. Oh yeah, I forgot. Where's the package?" She found it and smoked another cigarette. "You know, this country right 'round here is pretty, no kiddin'; a little like where I was born and raised. Know where I was born? . . . Near Carbondale, Pee-ay—little burg called Simpson, but no relation to Mrs. Simpson. Say, what do you think of 'er? I mean Mrs. Simpson."

"I don't know what to think."

"I guess it'd be pretty swell for 'er if she married the king, don't you think?"

"I guess."

"She'd be the Queen of England then, wouldn't she?"

"I suppose so."

"*I* say it'd be swell . . . Anyhow, I was born in this town called Simpson, just a mining town—coal—all grimy 'n' black—you wouldna wanna live there—but the country 'round it is nice. There's a lake near Simpson, Crystal Lake, where I used to go as a kid with my old man. He's dead ——"

Listening to her, I saw none too soon a car that came speeding toward us in the middle of the road, and the girl screamed, seizing my right arm. Luckily, I was not going very fast and had no trouble getting out of the roadhog's way. I rebuked her for grabbing my arm; then I noticed she trembled all over, and for a minute she was unable to talk.

At last she said: "I'm sorry . . . gee! I'm sorry, honest. Don't be mad. Was a dumb thing to do, to grab your arm like I did when you drive, but I got scared 'cause I was in a accident in Missouri, drivin' with a guy that give me a lift. That's where I got these cuts on my face. I ain't gonna do it again, honest; I ain't gonna grab your arm again. You ain't gonna ditch me now somewhere, are you?"—panic in her voice.

"No, no," I said, annoyed at myself for having rebuked her.

"Gonna take me all the way to Harrisburg like you said you would?"

"Yes."

"Honest—cross your heart?"

"Yes. Forget the whole thing."

"And you'll treat me to breakfast?"

"Soon as we come to a town."

"You don't have to treat me, you know."

"I know."

"Are you rich?"

"No, but I can buy you a breakfast."

"O. K., it's up to you. I didn't ask you to buy me breakfast, did I?"

"No."

"Say I *didn't*."

"You didn't."

"No, I didn't, by God! I got my pride, too."

A pause; then, suddenly, irrelevantly, she broke into song—*I can't give you anything but love, baby*—but her voice cracked on the high note and she gave it up, taking another long pull at her cigarette. "You're a life-saver, all right. I may be down, but I ain't out, am I?"

"Of course not."

"I'll get back on my feet. What's the next big town?"

"Warren, Ohio."

"Maybe we can get somethin' to eat there. How far's Warren?"

"Fifteen, twenty miles."

"You had breakfast yet?"

"Yes. When did you eat last?"

"Day before yesterday morning in Toledo. My stomach thinks my throat's cut."

She threw away the cigarette end, made another attempt at *I can't give you anything but love, baby*; and, failing, fell asleep once more, and slept all the way to Warren.

In Warren, I parked near the least pretentious of the restaurants—the sign over it was merely "EATS." I shook the girl, but she gave no sign of awakening.

It was half past nine, and it had taken me all that time to get here from Cleveland, while but for my passenger I could easily have been beyond Youngstown. I had wired my friend in Harrisburg to expect me shortly after one, and asked him to wait for lunch for me; but at this rate of speed, with this girl in my car, talking to me, I would be doing well if I got there for dinner.

I shook her again . . . several times . . . finally she stirred, then jumped and screamed, so that a frumpy middle-aged female passer-by stopped and peered into my car to see what was going on. Seeing the girl's scarred face, the woman motioned to a man, evidently her husband, and bid him interest himself in us.

"What's the trouble here?" he demanded.

"She screamed," said the woman, also coming closer.

"What'd she scream for?" asked the man, looking at me, then at the girl, who, drugged by sleep, stared at me.

"I don't know," I replied. "I picked her up this side of Cleveland. She's been in an accident; she was cold; then she fell asleep here; and now I woke her up and she screamed. I imagine she's scared, nervous, and exhausted."

A small crowd gathered around the car.

The girl regained her wits and snapped at the man who was questioning me: "What's it to you? None of your business, you old son-of-a-bee!"

The woman outside gasped audibly.

"I said *bee*," said the girl. "I didn't say nothin' else. Can I help it if you think somethin' worse?"

"Get a policeman!" said the woman. "Let 'im check up on 'em."

"You're all a buncha buttinskies," said the girl. "What's it to you? He"—meaning me—"told you the truth. He picked me up on the road. I was freezin' to death."

A policeman appeared and put a foot on the running-board and his elbows on the window on my side of the car. Fortunately, he was an intelligent man, and, asking me several questions and examining my driver's license and owner's certificate, presently indicated he believed my story.

"Who are you?" he asked the girl, then.

"Mrs. Wally Simpson!" she said, and laughed a bit.

"Quit your kidding," I said to her, "and answer the officer's questions."

"All right," she said, " 'Scuse me 'n' don' get sore at me, will you? Officer, my name is Hazel Leyton—L-e-y-t-o-n—Mrs. Leyton—and I'm on the bum—it's a long story—I was in a accident 'n' he picked me up, just like he says; now he wants to buy me breakfast 'n' he promised to take me far's Harrisburg. Everythin's just like he told you. I'm goin' to Baltimore, where somebody's gonna help me get a job 'n' set myself on my feet again."

The officer looked at her, then at me, then back at her. "You're pretty well bunged up, though."

"Yeah, but what's it to you? I can take it, don' worry about me; I'm tough."

The policeman grunted and turned to the crowd, "All right, move on! Leave 'em alone! There's nothin' to it." To a bystander who was in shirt sleeves and wore an apron, he remarked: "Let 'er get somethin' to eat, Nick, then let 'em get t'hell outa town. She's a tramp; he a damfool for pickin' 'er up. No use havin' 'spenses here with 'em."

Immediately on parking I had drawn a dollar bill out of my pocket; now I proffered it to my passenger, suggesting she go into the restaurant and breakfast. "I'll stay here in the car," I said, "and read the paper," which I had bought in Cleveland.

"You come with me!" she cried, panicky.

"I've had breakfast."

"Come 'n' have a cup of coffee, why don' you?" desperately.

"You go in yourself," I insisted, feeling mean and simultaneously trying to understand her panic.

"You'll drive off without me."

"I won't do anything of the sort."

"How do I know?"

"I'm telling you."

"You wanna get rid of me, 'n' I don't blame you. You're ashamed of me, 'n' I don't blame you; I pretty near got you in dutch; but—" Her voice broke with a threat of tears.

"All right, all right," I said, "I'll go in with you. I'm not ashamed of you," wondering how close I was to lying. "What put that into your head?"

"I wouldn't blame you if you was," she said. "But you're a white guy, no kiddin', and I believe you wouldna drove off without me, because you wouldna want to take my suitcase, if not because of anythin' else."

There was a lump in my midriff.

Going out of the car, the girl said, "Mind if I take your coat out and keep it 'round me?"

"No; go ahead."

The be-aproned proprietor of the dingy little eating-joint, a Pole or Slovak, asked no questions, and acted with an assumed matter-of-factness; showed Hazel to the washroom, then took her order—orange juice, cereal, bacon and eggs, rolls and jam, and coffee. She asked him whether he had a needle and some black thread, and he answered his wife had all that upstairs; and he went up and came back with a threaded needle; whereupon, while waiting for her food, Hazel stitched some of the worst tears in her outer garments.

I tried to read the paper, but Hazel, smoking, kept interrupting me with her condemnations of the "buttinskies" and with questions concerning the latest news about the king and Mrs. Simpson. She began to fascinate me, and I asked her, "Why did you say to the policeman that you were Mrs. Wally Simpson?"

"I don't know. I just said it. I bet he thought I was nuts. Say, I heard you tell the cop you was a writer, when he was askin' you. Are you for a fack, or was you just stringin' 'im?"

"I'm a writer."

"And you're goin' 'round the country for a magazine, writin' things up, like you told 'im? Gee, I wish I was a writer. I bet I could write a hot story. What do you write?"

"Books and things."

"I guess you must be pretty smart. But you know what? 'bout the time I graduated from grammar school I wrote a pome 'bout miners. My father was still alive then. Then he was killed in a cave-in." Pause. "He was a Austrian, but born in this country; his father came over long time ago. My mother was Welsh or somethin', but born here, too, 'n' she was all right long's my father was alive; then she cracked up or somethin' 'n' became no good— kinda crazy—married 'nother guy, who was a son-of-a-bee 'n' treated me awful. I was her only kid, and I lived with 'er 'n' the stepfather for six years, till I was fifteen; then I run away. She 'n' her new husband moved, 'n' I dunno where they're at now. Charming family, eh what, Edward darling? But I guess that's wrong; I read somewhere, or somebody told me, that Wally calls the king Davie. Ain't that wunnerful!"

She gulped the orange juice, then ate the rest of the meal. I warned her not to eat so fast, nor so much; it might harm her, since she had not eaten for two days; but she repeated she was tough and said food never harmed her except when she had none. She asked for a second cup of coffee and smoked two cigarettes. "You ever been on the bum?"

"A long time ago," I said, "after the war for a while."

"Been in the war? . . . Lotsa guys that pick me up was in it. How old was you when you was on the bum?"

"About twenty-one," I said.

"But was you as low-down on the bum as I am?"

"Hard to say. For one thing, I wasn't hurt in an accident."

"But you was broke and missed meals and spent nights outdoors?"

I nodded.

"Gee! now here you are, buyin' me breakfast, wearin' good clothes, money in your pocket, and a swell car by the curb outside. Just goes to show I can do the same. Gee! I'll get off the bum sure's anythin'."

Hazel finished her coffee, I paid the check, and the proprietor said "Good luck" to her.

"Same to you," returned Hazel.

Outside it was sunny and warm, and she exclaimed, "Ain'tit wunnerful!" In the car we decided we did not need the heater any more. Hazel stayed wrapped in my topcoat.

I drove off and she fell asleep. Every once in a while her head and the upper part of her body swung toward me and the steering-wheel, and I pushed her back without waking her.

In Youngstown, while she slept, I wired my friend in Harrisburg I might not arrive till late afternoon or early evening. . . .

Hazel slept on.

She awakened with a start, but did not scream; and she looked at me. "Hi, there!"

"Hi, yourself!" I said. "How do you feel?"

"With my fingers," she replied, and laughed, adding: "Don't mind me; I'm silly. I guess I feel better than I have for long time." She lighted a cigarette and took a few puffs in silence, looking out of the window. Then: "Where are we, anyhow?"

"In Pennsylvania, going toward Butler. The last place we went through was New Castle."

She sang again, *I can't give you anything but love, baby ——*"

"You like that song, don't you?" I said.

"What song? Was I singin'?"

"Yes, *I can't give you anything but love, baby.*"

"Oh yeah, I 'member. Yeah, I like it"—confused. "Say, how much further to what-chuma-call-it—Harrisburg?"

"Six or seven hours, possibly longer."

"Then I'll be 't'out a home again."

"I've been thinking about you," I said, ". . . and when I let you out in Harrisburg I'll give you a little money, so you can ——"

"Say," sharply, "you're sorry for me."

"No, no," I said.

"You are, too!"

"I'm not. I guess I shouldn't have mentioned it now, but I thought you were worrying how you were to spend the night, and so on." I recalled my friend in Herzegovina.

"You think I'm bad!"

"No, no; I don't think anything. It makes no difference to me if you're 'bad' or 'good.'"

"What d' you wanna give me money for?" She looked at me suspiciously. "I don' mean nothin' by that song, get me? I just sing it ——"

"You're crazy," I said. "Don't let it worry you what I think. You see, I'm a writer and having you in the car gives me an idea for a story."

"About me?"

"Yes, or about a girl like you. I don't know yet how I'll write it. I have only a rough idea. But when, and if, I write it, there'll probably be a chance of selling it to some magazine; and if I sell it ——"

"How much will you get for it?"

"I don't know. In fact, I'm not sure I'll sell it; but if I do, I'm liable to get very little, quite a bit, or a great deal, depending on what magazine will take it."

"How much do you want to give me?"

I told her.

"Honest?" she cried. "Gee! S'pose you don't sell it?"

"I'll put you in a book."

She was silent for a half-minute, pondering all this. Then: "But what can you write about me? You don't know my story, 'n' you even said you didn' wanna hear it 'cause maybe it wasn't interestin'—that's what you said, 'member?"

"Yes; but I've learned a great deal about you, none the less."

"What?"

"The sort of person you are."

"What sort of person am I?"—quickly.

"A little run down and 'groggy' or 'punch drunk' just now, as you put it yourself, but O.K., tough, proud—all I need to know."

"You don't know any facks."

It was futile to argue with her, and I regretted having told her I would write about her. I blamed my friend in Herzegovina. What I should have done was to have kept silent till I let her out in Harrisburg, then have given her the money, and driven on.

"I told you 'bout my father," she went on, "he got buried in a mine accident, 'n' a little 'bout my mother . . . but you dunno what I did after I run away when I was fifteen.

"In a town called Port Jervis, in New York State near the Pee-ay border, a old lady took me in 'er home when I told 'er I was hungry. She had little store near the bus depot, sellin' candy 'n' cigarettes, pop, pies 'n' cake, newspapers 'n' magazines, 'n' she lived in backa the store. She wanted to know where was I from, who was my parents, but I wouldn' tell 'er. I only said I run away 'n' never want to go back, 'n' I cried. So she told me to stay, 'n' told the neighbors 'n' people that knowed 'er I was 'er niece from Hawley—that's a town in Pee-ay.

"She got to love me like I was 'er daughter, 'n' made me swear I was never to tell a soul we was no relation. My name was Hazel Culick, but after I come to Port Jervis I was Hazel Schugg—Schugg was the old lady's name—'n' I helped in the store; then, when she—I mean the old lady—took sick, I looked after 'er 'n' the store. I was there little more 'n two years, till she died. Gee! I felt terrible when she died. . . . She had nobody else in the world 'n' left me the store, 'n' I run it by myself 'n' lived alone in the backroom for six months. Then I got married to a Greyhound bus-driver that got nuts about me 'n' me about 'im. I was goin' on eighteen.

"Gee! he was wunnerful, 'n' we was awful happy"—her voice breaking a little. "He never found out the old lady was not my aunt; wasn't even interested in my family, he was so crazy about me. He was from Passaic, 'n' his name was Joe Sigafoos. He was on the Scranton-New York run, 'n' he was home every third night 'n' up to lunchtime the next day. Joe was in the war 'n' been gassed, so one day he come home with a cold 'n' fever, 'n' in three days he was dead. We wasn't married even a year. Gee! was terrible! I cried like I was goin' outa my nut.

"When I got over it a little, so I didn't cry all the time, I sold the store, got four hundred dollars for it, 'n' I went to New York on a bus 'n' was so miserable I got to talkin' with the driver, who knowed Joe. In fack, Joe 'n' this driver was friends. Then, to keep from bein' blue all the time, I went in for a good time in a big way; got some swell clothes at Gimbel's 'n' even bought a coupla things at Saks Fifth Avenue; 'n' I run around with bus-drivers, but I wasn't really bad—just wild 'n' crazy—just wasn't good—because I couldn't think of Joe 't'out bawlin' my head off when I was alone, because I loved 'im so. . . .

"I got a job as check-girl at Charles'—the night club, you know. I worked there coupla years, savin' my money. I went out with guys, to shows, to prize fights and races, to Lindy's for supper, and to the beach in summertime, that's all—honest. You believe me?"

"Yes, sure," I said.

"Is the story interestin'?"

"Yes."

"What did I tell you? But wait, best part's still to come. . . . I was savin' my money like I told you, thinkin' maybe some day another right guy'll come along; 'n' then one day I met this gob—Willis Leyton—who's in the pitcher you picked up in Ohio. Gee! he was good-lookin', big 'n' strong, 'n' he looked to be a wunnerful guy right through. I had a friend once, 'n' she married a sailor, 'n' he quit the navy after he married 'er 'n' went in business in Brooklyn, 'n' they was happy like nobody's business. Gee! they was happy; 'n' would you believe it, she got so respec'able she wouldn' see me any more. I knowed other gobs before that was O.K. So I thought this gob o' mine was, too, 'n' I said O.K. and we went to Hoboken and got married.

"This was last summer. I took a month off for honeymoon, he was on leave, 'n' we was both crazy to go drivin'; so we bought a new Plymouth— with my money. I loved 'im, gee! I was nuts about 'im, 'n' I didn' think there was anythin' fishy when he said we oughta buy the car in his name because he was a United States sailor 'n' sailors don't have to pay any sales tax. We saved forty dollars that way, 'n' I said O.K. Then we drove 'round for ten days, far up as Vermont and through upstate New York; 'n' we had that pitcher taken, 'n' had a wunnerful time. Gee! he was swell, no kiddin', 'n' I think he really loved me, but, like a lotta guys, he was also a heel inside.

"One morning I woke up in a tourist house near Troy, New York, 'n' there was no husband. He was gone with the car 'n' all the money 'cept three dollars and seventy-four cents he left in my purse. Big-hearted guy, eh what, Davie? . . . I'm just foolin'—Davie: that's what Wally Simpson calls the king. . . .

"Findin' myself alone like this, jilted 'n' robbed, this was worse'n the time my first husband died. Gee! I hated the son-of-a-bee, you know what I mean; but I was hurt, too, 'n' don't think I wasn't. I can't tell you what I went through. Gee! it hurt—maybe, bein' a writer, you can 'magine it. I guess writers can 'magine most anythin', that's why they're writers. I guess that's why you didn't care if I tell my story or not; you could 'magine it. . . .

"My first idea was to go to New London, Connecticut, where his ship was—a submarine—'n' make trouble for 'im. Then I changed my mind. I said to my- self, I loved the guy; all right; now I never wanna see 'im again, or have anythin' to do with 'im. . . . I bet he wonders what's become of me—why I never made no trouble for 'im. Let 'im wonder. But I forgived 'im, long ago. . . .

"I was pretty sicka the whole thing, sicka New York, 'n' I didn't wanna go near anybody I knowed. I was afraid the girls and guys at Charles' 'd kid me: where was my gob? So I was through with 'em, too. I had fifty dollars left in postal-savings; I took that out 'n' got a room in a hotel on Madison Square, where nobody I know ever comes, 'n' I got drunk and stayed stiff

for a week, all by myself, till the manager turned me over to the police . . .
'n' the police turned me over to a outfit for wayward girls. Can you 'magine?

"All I had in the world was a few dollars 'n' what was in this suitcase 'n'
on my back . . . 'n' bingo! just like that, I decided to go to California. I always
heard-a California—Los Angeles—Hollywood—what a swell place it was;
so I slipped out of this house for wayward girls, where they tried to be nice
to me, but I hated it, 'n' I got a bus through Holland Tunnel to Jersey City,
then began to hitch—California, here I come! . . .

"That was middle-a September 'n' still warm—gee! it was wunnerful, with
the leaves beginnin' to turn red in the country, 'n' I had no trouble gettin'
picked up. I was good-lookin', if I say so myself, 'n' I wore good clothes; 'n'
guys slammed on the brakes soon's they saw me.

"The first guy took me to Phillipsburg, New Jersey, where I quit 'im because
he got fresh, you know what I mean. The next lift got me far's Altoona, Pee-ay,
and I slept there in a hotel. I had little over five dollars left.

"Then . . . Cleveland . . . Chi . . . Kansas . . . Iowa . . . Colorado . . .
New Mexico . . . Arizona——"

For a while after passing through Butler, Pennsylvania, I understood only
a word or sentence now and then. She mumbled faintly, intermittently, like a
child falling asleep; then was silent. . . .

She awoke suddenly, eighty miles later.

"Where was I?" she asked.

I laughed. "You were just getting to Arizona."

"I musta fallen asleep for coupla minutes."

"You slept over two hours," I said.

"You wouldna kid me?"

"We're nearing Altoona."

"What do you know about that! I thought I just dozed off for a minute
or two while I was tellin' you about my travels."

We both laughed.

"I'm hungry," I said. "How about you?"

"Gonna treat me again?"

I nodded.

"I didn't ask you to, you know."

"No, you didn't ask me."

"I'm ready to eat, though, any time. Say, lookit that barn!" she cried,
suddenly.

I looked where she was pointing at a group of farm buildings a stone-
throw from the road, of which a large newly-painted barn was the most striking—a veritable edifice.

"Ain'tit a beaut!" she exclaimed. "I seen lotsa barns in my travels—thousands of 'em; in fack, I'm a expert on barns, 'n' when I say a barn is beautiful, that barn is beautiful."

I drew up at a roadside "diner," and we had lunch. The man behind the counter eyed us awhile, then evidently decided we were none of his business.

Hazel picked up the narrative where she had left off:

". . . New Mexico . . . Arizona . . . This is one big country, let *me* tell you. *Big*—B-I-G—and how! It took me three weeks to get to Arizona, 'n' what I don't know about U.S.A.'s nobody's business. Wunnerful country!"

Her power of expression seemed to collapse. "I mean the land is wunnerful, 'cept where it was ruined by what-chuma-call-it—erosion 'n' windstorms. Even Arizona, what's mostly sand, is beautiful like anythin'. Such colors you see nowhere like in Arizona, Colorado, 'n' New Mexico. . . .

"People, that's 'nother story. . . . Guys that pick you up this side of Mississippi are mostly heels, you know what I mean, though you find some pretty good eggs 'mongst 'em, too. When they do you a favor, mosta 'em wanna get somethin' back; you know what I mean; you wasn't born yesterday. . . .

"Out West, you find heels, too; mosta 'em, though, are square-shooters, wunnerful guys, any way you take 'em. In Colorado 'n' New Mexico 'n' Arizona, they shoved money in my pocket when I wasn't lookin' or put it in my hand when they couldn' take me no further. One guy put a five-dollar bill in a chewin'-gum wrapper 'n' give it to me, pretendin' it was gum. 'Nother guy in Davenport, Iowa, 'n' one in Denver, took me to a hotel 'n' asked how much was the room, paid 'n' went away. I never saw either offum again.

"Out in Arizona a woman picked me up. She had a ranch somewhere; I guess was about fifty, but healthy, all brown 'n' hard 'n' beautiful; 'n' at a place called Flagstaff she got me a bag-a san'wiches 'n' oranges, 'n' put a silver dollar in the bag when I wasn't lookin'—first silver dollar I ever had. I wished she was my mother. She was worried 'bout me, 'n' said I was liable to have hard time gettin' to California, because Los Angeles cops was all over the desert, turnin' back people that had no money, 'n' beatin' 'em up, because California was fulla unemployed 'n' hobos 'n' good-f'r-nothin's that come there 'bout this time of the year when it starts gettin' cold other places.

"In Flagstaff, I got picked up by a old what they call desert rat, maybe fifty, maybe more, 'n' he wanted to marry me 'n' make me his 'pardner'—that's what he said, his 'pardner.' He said he was lonely on the desert but had plentya money 'n' gold, 'n' would build us a house. I was tempted like anythin' to take 'im on, but then, like a fool, I don't know what made me say I was married 'n' was goin' to L.A. to meet my husband. I coulda kick myself, because he wouldof asked no questions—that's how those guys are out West when they're lonely 'n' gettin' on in years—no questions asked—'n' nobody wouldof ever knowed I was married to the gob, 'n' I coulda been all fixed by now, 'n' maybe I coulda learned to love 'im, I mean the old guy.

"He was sad like anythin' when I told 'im I was married, 'n' he took me far's Williams, Arizona, 'n' put me up at the little hotel there 'n' said good-by. I coulda cried when he was gone, gee! I was a dope.

"Next day I had a awful time gettin' a lift. Everybody said no use tryin' to cross the line to California—the L.A. bulls was sure to get me. They was all over, the bulls; some of 'em operatin' right in Arizona, even if it was against the law. Gee! I was scared 'n' wished the old desert rat would come back, so I could tell 'im I wasn't married 'n' was willin' to take 'im on. . . . .

"By-'n'-by, though, a truck-driver took a chance on me 'n' said he'll smuggle me over the line to Bakersfield, California, which was where he was goin', if I didn' mind lyin' under a pile-a empty gunny sacks in backa the truck mosta the way, because he didn't know where the bulls was liable to stop 'im 'n' ask 'im if he had any hitchers or bums.

"I let 'im bury me under the sacks, 'n', gee! it was hot 'n' the sacks stunk . . . but we was only a little way past a town called Ash Fork, still in Arizona, when a coupla guys stopped us—they was in civvies 'n' drivin' a car with a Arizona license plate—'n' searched the truck 'n' found me under the sacks. I guess they was Arizona guys hired by L.A. cops to keep the likesa me outa California. One of 'em kicked me, slapped me more times 'n' I could count, pulled my hair, got fresh, 'n' threw me on the sand beside the road like a sack of potatoes or somethin'. The truck-driver called 'em a coupla son-of-a-bees, you know what I mean; 'n' swung on 'em, so then the two of 'em beat 'im up somethin' awful, but he could take it. They called me bad names; boy! what they called me—'n' him, too, the truck-driver—'n' they told 'im not to go to California, even if he had business there, because they was gonna notify the bulls ahead, 'n' they'll beat 'im up again, because he was tryin' to smuggle in people like me. So he turned around, the poor guy, all beat up 'n' black 'n' blue in the face, 'n' ast me to come with 'im if I wanted to.

" 'Course I wanted to; what wouldof I been doin' there in the middle of the desert? He was mad like a hornet—not at me, though, but at the bulls and L.A. 'This useta be a free country,' he said. 'Look at it now!' . . .

"On t'other hand, though, when I cooled off and thought 'bout it, I couldn' blame L.A. for not wantin' the likesa me if the town and the whole state was, like everybody said, all full with all kindsa hard-luck people. Only they shouldnof beat me up, or the truck driver, or anybody else. Gee! I was sore, because that was first time anybody hit me since I run away from Simpson, Pee-ay, where my stepfather used to thrash me once in a while. Later, though, when I had time to think, it come to me that maybe they didn't like to beat me up, but did it so's to scare others, because they prob'ly figured I was gonna meet others 'n' tell 'em what to 'spect if they tried to get to California.

"Well, anyhow, we went back to Williams; 'n' would you believe it, this truck-driver—he was just a kid, 'bout twenty-four—made me take a dollar from 'im 'cause I was broke. He was a good egg, wasn't he, to be so kind after he got beat up because-a me. I coulda cried, no kiddin'. . . ."

We finished lunch and drove on. I felt a deep satisfaction in having picked her up—she obviously was a "good egg" herself.

She fell asleep again . . . awakened in Newport and talked to me the rest of the way to Harrisburg:

". . . In Williams, I met a lady from Baltimore; she was there on a ranch near town for her health, 'n' she got interested in me, 'n' I told 'er some-a the things I'm tellin' you, 'n' she thought I oughta go back East. There was more opportunities in the East, she said, 'n' I was liable to get on my feet quicker than in the West. I didn' wanna go back to New York, so she give me a note to a frienda hers that has a rest'rant in Baltimore 'n' maybe would give me a job. . . .

"Gee! I didn't know what to do 'n' wished that desert rat 'd come along again, but he didn't, though I hung around Williams for coupla days. I felt like a little girl, a little child, no kiddin'. I was so scared I shook inside.

". . . I took a lift from a guy with a California license plate who was goin' to Albuquerque, New Mexico, 'n' said he was a comyoonist—a red—'n' he tried to make me one, too. He gave me stuff to read 'n' said I was a victim of the capitalist system, 'n' there was lotsa other girls—millions of 'em— in the same fix like I was in, 'n' those bulls that beat me up was servants of the capitalist system. . . . Boy! he had everythin' figured out down to a *t* 'n' what he didn' all tell me's nobody's business, no kiddin', but I couldn' unnerstand much 'cause it was all so new to me, 'n' deep's anythin'; 'n' besides, I didn' like the guy, though it's meana me to say so, because he did give me the lift 'n' didn't bother me at all, you know what I mean, 'n' bought me san'wiches. He said he was a artist.

"But I could follow this guy when we talked about Mrs. Simpson. She was liable to become queen, but don't let that worry me, he said—I was as good as she was 'n' maybe a damsite better. Under the capitalist system it was all a toss-up if a girl became Mrs. Simpson or got on the bum like me; 'n' let me tell you, I been thinkin' 'bout that ever since, 'n' it's true, it's true, though I dunno how come. It's a toss-up, all right; mattera luck, mattera gettin' a break, the right kinda schoolin' 'n' upbringin': that's what it is. What do you think?"

I said there was something to what she was saying.

"You tell 'em!" she said. "That's why I told the cop in what-chuma-call-it-town I was Wally Simpson. I *couldof* been her if I had the breaks she had. . . . But never mind; I wanna tell you the rest of the facks about my travels— are they interestin'?"

"Very," I said.

"See? What did I tell you, 'n' you wasn't sure if my story was interestin'!" she reproached me.

"I didn't want to seem to pry—to pump you," I explained.

"But how was you gonna write 'bout me if you didn't know the facks?"

"I could imagine many details."

"You couldnof 'magined things like I told you."

"Not exactly, but similar things."

"Gee! you're a funny guy. Don' mind me sayin' this, though. Everybody's funny."

Pause.

"Anyhow," she went on, "now you know the facks. . . . In Albuquerque I got a truck with a Kansas license plate. He was a fresh guy, but I told 'im where I stand, so he apologized 'n' was O.K. after that; 'n' we drove all afternoon 'n' night because he had to be in Wichita, Kansas, a certain time 'n' he was late. He wasn't a bad guy, though, married 'n' had kids, 'n' he told me to watch 'im so he don't fall asleep at the wheel, 'n' I fed 'im wakies——"

"Wakies?"

"Yeah, don't you know—wakies—that's pills, some kinda dope, truck-drivers take so they don't fall asleep. They pick up people like me so they got some-body to watch 'em 'n' feed 'em those pills—one every half-hour or so. Gee! it's no cinch to drive a truck on long hauls, let me tell you.

"Anyhow, in the mornin' we got to a little place called Raton, near the Raton Pass on the Colorado line, and the guy told me he can't take me no further. Gee! I tried to tell 'im I wasn't Mann Act, but he wasn't takin' no chances—so long!—'n' pulled out.

"That happened to me numbera times—guys ditched me just before crossin' from one state to 'nother, 'n' you can't blame 'em. There's girls playin' the Mann Act all over, 'n' what I don't know 'bout that game's nobody's business. Guys told me of other guys that got played suckers, 'n' you know what?—big truckin' companies have standin' orders no driver can take a girl over any state line. . . . You took me over the Ohio-Pee-ay line. Wasn't you worried?"

"Just for a minute," I confessed. "Then I decided you were all right."

"What made you decide I was all right?"

"I just had a feeling."

My saying this pleased her.

"I go on hunches, too, only mine offen are all cockeyed. . . .

"Anyhow, in Raton, a man 'n' his wife picked me up, 'n' took me only over the Pass, to Trinidad, Colorado; 'n' there I caught 'nother truck all the way to Kansas City. The guy was like you, wasn't afraida me, 'n' took me over the Colorado-Kansas line. I popped a wakie in his mouth every so offen 'n' kept 'im awake.

"He let me off on the Missouri side of Kansas City, 'n' there a fellah with a Illinois license plate stopped for me—the worst heel I met durin' my travels, 'n' I didn' tell you much 'bout the other heels, because I just as soon forget 'bout 'em. Well, this one was no good, had a dirty mind, 'n' so on, you know what I mean, 'n' was a little drunk 'n' jittery; 'n' after ridin' with 'im maybe half a hour I closed my eyes, thinkin' how I'll get 'im to let me off, when—bang, alla sudden, we hit somethin', I never found out what. My head went bang in the windshield 'n' the next thing I knowed I was in a police-station back in Kansas City, bleedin' outa these two cuts on my face.

"What happened I guess was the guy crashed maybe in a telegraph pole, but didn' hurt himself or damage his car so much he couldn' use it. I was hurt, unconscious; so he drove on a ways, then dumped me in a ditch behind a pile-a brush with my suitcase. He was scared I'd sue 'im. Then a traffic cop found me 'n' phoned for a police ambulance.

"Gee! was I in a mess! I wanted to die. I was good-lookin' once, if I say so myself; now these two gashes on my face! The doctor at the emergency station went through the motions of doctorin' me up, but that's all; then said there's nothin' the matter with me, though I had cuts and bruises all over, which I got maybe when the guy dumped me in the ditch. The idea was, I was no good, anyhow, just a little tramp or somethin' worse.

"Anyhow, I was out in the world again 'n' now guys was afraida me. I looked awful, like somethin' the cat dragged home, all black 'n' blue 'n' cut up; 'n' my dress 'n' coat was torn. I dunno, but I think I walked least a hundred miles a-tween Kansas City 'n' Cleveland the last ten days. The rest I made in short hitches, 'n' many of 'em that give me a lift got ridda me soon's they could, once they seen me up close. I looked worse every day. I didn' eat. The last time I ate before meetin' you was in Toledo; a truck-driver treated me.

"Then it got cold, gee! alla-sudden, 'specially on the stretch a-tween Toledo 'n' Cleveland. This was the only clothes I have, 'n' I shook 'n' my weight was fallin' down to nothin'. I seen leaves fall offa the trees 'n' I couldof cried; I wasn' even 's good as them leaves. . . .

"But it's partly my fault, though I can't help it. I'm not stuck up 'xactly, but I hate to crawl 'n' beg 'n' ask for handouts. I know that lotsa folks in Cleveland, if I knocked on their doors, maybe wouldof let me in 'n' feed me, 'n' let me get warm, but I couldn' bring myself to knock. It's one thing to bum rides, even when you look like the pitchera everythin' nobody wants to see, and it's somethin' else to crash in people's homes where they're happy— man 'n' wife 'n' children 'n' carpets on the floor 'n' things in the icebox— Say, do you think many people are really happy?"

"I guess some are," I said, "or they think they are, which is about the same thing."

"Are you?"

"I suppose."

"You married?"

"Yes."

"Where's your wife?"

"In New York."

"Gee! I bet you're happy——"

Late in the afternoon we approached Harrisburg.

"What river is this?" she asked.

"Susquehanna," I said.

"Oh yeah; beautiful ain't'it?"

"Yes. . . . But listen here," I went on. "I'm quite sure I'll sell the story about you or I'll put you in a book, so I'll give you double the amount I said I would give you."

"Charity business!"

"No, no. What you told me is worth to me every cent I want to give you.

Consider it a business proposition. You're going to Baltimore and see if you can get a job with the letter the lady gave you in Arizona?"

"Yeah."

"All right," I said. "Maybe you'll get fixed up in Baltimore, maybe not. I'll give you the money and my address. Eventually, if you feel like it, write to me and I'll tell you whether or not I sold the story. If you wish, consider this money a loan, which you can pay back sometime in the future if I don't sell the story, and which is annulled if I do sell it."

She was biting her lip.

"And," I continued, "I suggest you spend the night in Harrisburg and have a bath and a good night's sleep. I'm staying at some friends' house, but I'll take you to a hotel if you like. Also, it's just four-thirty, the stores are still open, and you should buy yourself some clothes, shoes, a hat, whatever else you need. Then in the morning take a bus to Baltimore. I'll come for you at the hotel about eight o'clock."

She burst out crying, and I felt like the devil, but let her cry awhile; then I chided her about saying she was tough, and she dried her eyes.

Next morning I took her to the bus depot. She had some new clothes and looked much better than she had the day before. She talked a good deal and said she had enjoyed a good breakfast. I had bought a newspaper: what was the latest about Mrs. Simpson? . . .

"How do I look?" she asked.

"Fine."

"Well, I feel like I was turnin' over a new leaf," she said. "Maybe meetin' you yesterday means I'm gonna be in for a little good luck from now on, for a change. Say you hope so," she said, almost desperately.

"I hope so very much."

"Gee!" Then, after a moment: "Too bad these darn cuts on my face will leave scars."

"Maybe they won't," I said.

Before going into the bus, she kissed me quickly; then said, "You don't mind, do you?"

"Don't be silly," I said.

"Tell your wife I kissed you, and tell 'er I kissed you in a way she wouldn' mind if she knew how I kissed you."

"All right. Good-by."

"Good-by!"

She waved to me from the bus.

I have not yet heard from her. Perhaps she lost my address and forgot my name. Or probably I did not break her spell of "hard luck" as she hoped I might have done. Or . . . God knows.

Woman Who Loved America

IN 1935 I HAD THE HABIT OF INVOLVING PEOPLE I KNEW OR MET FOR THE FIRST time into conversation in such a way that I could—without much risk of being considered crazy—ask them if they loved their country, and why. Most answers were very unsatisfactory. "Well," I asked then, "what is the first thing that comes to your mind when you say 'of course I love my country'?"

One evening, in New York, I met the mother of a friend of mine. She was over seventy, a large, quiet woman, who had just come East from Oregon, where she had lived nearly all her life and now resided with her married daughter in Portland. As a girl and young and middle-aged woman she had lived on the land, on her husband's farm, and brought up a family. Now her numerous children, a few of them well-to-do, were scattered all over the country, and part of each year she traveled, visiting them and her grandchildren.

I asked her my usual question, and she said, slowly:

"Yes, I love my country. . . . The first thing that comes to my mind when I say that is the place where I spent my happiest years—on our farm in Oregon. We had a big house, which by the time I was thirty was full of children. My mother was with us, helping me with housekeeping. She was a wonderful woman; had come West from Ohio as a girl of nineteen with her father in a covered wagon. . . . I remember especially one day, though I suppose it was not very different from many others. I was cooking—we always had plenty to eat; everybody was healthy. It was late spring. My husband and the men were out working. It was noontime. The table was set, and I went out to ring the bell that hung from the big bough of the apple tree in front of the house. I stepped out of the house and walked to the bell-rope, then stopped and looked over the valley. It was beautiful. One of my children came to me from behind the house and touched my skirt and asked if he could ring the bell, and I said he could. He rang it . . . the most wonderful sound, although it was a very ordinary bell: it was wonderful to me . . . and there was that beautiful clear day, full of sun, with a few white clouds; and there was the wheat . . . wheat for miles around, almost ripe for reaping, waving in the little wind . . . Oh, I am sorry, I can't describe it——"

Letters from My Friend in Hollywood

WHEN I WAS IN CALIFORNIA IN 1936 OUR MUTUAL FRIEND, CAREY MCWILLIAMS, introduced me to Ross Wills of Hollywood. Wills and I spent a couple of evenings together and became friends. I have not seen him since then, but we have exchanged dozens of letters. In one of them he wrote me about his boyhood and youth, which he spent in a little Missouri town of perhaps a thousand people, located in the heart of the Mid-West: twenty miles north of Kansas City and thirty-five south of St. Joseph. "Ancestors of mine helped settle the place, which was founded in the 1840's; and soon afterward a flour mill, around which the town grew, was built there on the banks of the Little Platte River. I was born on a farm just a mile from this town . . . and lived in it from my sixth to my seventeenth year.

"What a town it was then! It is not the same now—since the War, there has been a 'rock road' strung from K.C. to St. Joe and far beyond either, and the town has become only a bus-stop between those places. Once, though, it was an entity, complete within itself; at that time a journey to K.C. was a big event, prepared for for some time, and it got into the weekly *Democrat-Herald*. If you drove a horse and buggy (I was born in 1900, remember), it took several hours; now, in a car, about thirty minutes. And St. Joe was so far away that I never went there but once—and that was when I was sixteen, to see a girl. There was—still is—one railroad, the renowned 'O.K.' train, but it took almost as much time to get anywhere as did a nice fast team and buggy.

"Of all my life this is the part I remember the most vividly, treasure by far the most, and which, no doubt, has had the deepest impression on me. It was, indeed, a *country* town, but amazingly alive, vital. It was a bit rough, a bit crude, and in the early 1900's still had a lot of the pioneer atmosphere about it. There was a heartiness in the people one hardly finds in any similar community today, for now there are almost no isolated towns of its sort. As an illustration of its 'roughness' when I was a kid I remember when the Younger Brothers, famous outlaws, passed through the town once, stopping for a drink at Pete Bowen's saloon, and then riding on. And the James boys were there or thereabouts many times. Indeed, one of my proudest memories is of Frank James, Jesse's brother. Jesse was killed a year or so before I was born, but Frank lived to be an old man. Frank's home was a farm about fifteen miles from my town. He raised stock and attended live-stock auctions in the vicinity. We kids used to attend them, too, just to gape at Frank James, perhaps not expecting him to draw a six-shooter, exactly, but at least to say something, tell some yarn about his past. But he never would; indeed, he abruptly quit being an outlaw and settled down to be a highly respected citizen. Although small in stature, with his white hair and goatee, he was a distinguished-looking man. He had excellent manners, but was quiet, silent, deliberate, and rarely said a word. One characteristic thrilled us kids; we never noticed him when he was not standing or sitting with his back to the wall—a habit from the old days, when he couldn't let anyone get behind him.

"Mentioning Pete Bowen's saloon reminds me of a low-down racket us kids used to practice. Every Saturday the farmers from all around would come to town. Saturday nights the farmer boys would drive behind Pete's, hitch their horse-and-buggies or just horses; then they would buy a week's supply of hootch and cache it in their saddle bags or buggies. They would do this before getting drunk and forgetting about it. Us kids would hide behind a shed and watch them, and when they had cached their booze we would steal it and pour it out, although often keeping a bottle or two to drink ourselves!— and then take the bottles back into the saloon and sell them to Pete—we got five cents each for empty quart whisky-bottles, two cents each for empty pints, and one cent each for empty beer bottles. We thought nothing of emptying whole cases of beer to resell the bottles to Pete. We made extra money by scouring the alleys and gutters, collecting bottles to sell.

"It may be wondered why we didn't sell the full bottles to adults at a discount. But I can't recall why—unless it was because there was no fun in that, and it was somehow amusing to empty the contents and take the bottles in and dispose of them right under the eyes of the original purchasers. It was a stunt, 'lots of fun,' just as were the sensational stunts we pulled on Hallowe'en —such as with block and tackle hauling old man Reynolds' cow halfway up a telegraph pole and leaving her there to bawl the whole town awake . . . or soaping the railroad tracks beyond the water-tank, so that the 'O.K.,' after watering up, couldn't make traction to reach the 'dee-po,' and the brakeman and fireman had to get out and shovel sand, while us kids lay in the ditch and held our sides.

". . . Every Easter Sunday we took our first swim of the year. It would always be cold; sometimes we even had to break a sheet of ice over the water. But it was a ritual, and everyone had to do it. . . . Spring meant getting doped with sulphur and molasses for 'our blood'; somehow, we survived that, as we survived wearing hideous little bags of 'asafoetida' (or however you spell it) about our necks in winter, to 'ward off' colds and other diseases. But, really, we were hardly ever sick—regardless of the season. Life was one terrific round of activities, 'fun,' and we didn't have time to get more than a cold, and we laughed at that. . . . And the long summers, and bare feet plopping contentedly in the warm dust of the roads, or going 'cross the cool grass of the woods, and wearing 'overhalls' and shirt, and maybe a straw hat, but no more than that. . . . And building rafts and boats and going down the river, taking provisions, or a rifle and getting rabbits, and poles and getting fish to eat, and 'exploring.' . . . Summer—persimmons and watermelons put in springs to get cold; and autumn—life quickening and the woods turning such rapturous colors, and we gathering black walnuts and getting the stain on our hands that would never come off. And going coon-hunting and 'possum-hunting at night, with the hounds baying far away and the familiar woods becoming at night thrilling hallways of awful mystery. . . . Then fall and going back to school and football, and then winter and snow and ice and sleds and skates, and going to country dances in farmers' barns and laughing and dancing the night away while some old fiddlers sawed off 'Turkey in the Straw' or 'White Oaks,' and then the weary but happy people breaking up and saying good-by at four or six a.m., and going home in sleighs with the bells jingling over the lonely country roads, or in big horse-drawn sleds, and the telephone wires humming their cold, monotonous, but somehow charming, tone, echoing messages from some fairyland far away; and you thinking how you liked people and how nice they were, really. . . .

"You can talk about democracy. This was *it*. It was a kind of 'communism,' or 'socialism.' Why, I remember the quilting-bees of the women, the corn-husking parties, the threshing parties, when farmers helped each other in turn voluntarily. And among the kids, it never mattered at all how rich or how poor one's old man was; the leader, in so far as we had one—and we didn't really have any conscious 'leaders'—was likely as not the son of the meanest man in town. Our activities were whole-hearted and fancy-free, and utterly and absolutely without direction by any 'play director' or any such person— we would not have understood what one meant, and if we did we would have laughed at him, or ridiculed him to death, and played tricks on him until he would have given up. We did just what the seasons permitted us to do. The absolute freedom we had amazes me now, to think of it. . . . Much of that life and activity were startlingly like Mark Twain's classic kids'. Hannibal was his home, you know, and the source of his material—and that town is not very far from mine. It was more or less a 'Southern' town, with a plentiful quantity of old Civil War soldiers, all Confederates. . . . Come to think of it, I wouldn't have been born in any other time—for I saw, when I was old enough to gain impressions, an era passing out and a new one coming in, and felt them and, in a sense, lived them. . . .

"The town is really no more, now. The buildings are still there and the population is about the same, but 'progress,' symbolized by the 'rock road' that came in in the 1920's, when I, thank God, was away from there, has converted it into a sort of hybrid. The business people are much less prosperous, for the farmers can hop into their cars and dash to K.C. to trade, and also find their entertainment there. But when the town was 'far away,' by itself, it had personality, individuality; it lived, glowed, was *vulgar* with life; people found and made their own entertainment, and I can testify it was infinitely more satisfying than all the movies made since Adam; it made for a life in which one *participated* in its activities and fun and tragedies, and did not merely observe. You were *in* life, because you were alive, and it bubbled up all around you, and it was rich. . . . The big flour mill, once prosperous and rather widely known in that particular part of the country, and around which the town grew, is gone now. It burned down several years ago, and hasn't been replaced. And it is somehow appropriate. Even the river, once deep and wide and flowing, has almost dried up, and, curiously, *since* the mill has disappeared. I was back there in September, and how strange it all seemed, and how sad it made me. Many of the fellows with whom I grew up are still living there, have families; they retain the charm, the vitality that they absorbed into their bones with their active, rich, and wonderful youth; but, somehow, it all seems wasted. They seem now to be only existing, a little baffled. They speak wistfully of 'getting out,' of 'going to California.' But they sense that there is no place to go, that great change has come over everything; and at best that it is a process of transition, a pause, a time of confusion in the entire world . . . and that wherever they went they could find just a change of scene. . . ."

At seventeen, on America's entry into the war, Ross joined the navy, because he thought there would be more excitement in the navy than in the army; there was so much talk about German submarines and the probability that the United States would not send a large army to France, and he wanted action. He was a tall, handsome youth, as one can well imagine looking at him twenty years later. Throughout his 'teens, in his home town, he had studied music and now played well several band instruments. When this was discovered at the training station in Great Lakes, where he was stationed in the spring, 1917, action was initiated to have him transferred to the band, just then being taken over by John Philip Sousa. But before this transfer was effected, Marshal Joffre of France came over on his famous mission to secure America's immediate active participation in the Allied cause; and when he visited Chicago, Seaman Ross Wills, because of his neat appearance, was selected to be a member of the great French soldier's guard of honor. The ceremonies of welcoming Joffre to the metropolis of the Middle West were elaborate, lasting all day. It was cold and it rained. The guard of honor got soaked to the skin; then the boys sat in a cold, draughty hall, where the marshal spoke. There were endless speeches and the bands, including Sousa's, played the French and American anthems. A lovely Frenchwoman, tightly wrapped in the tricolor, sang the "Marseillaise."

That was the last music Ross ever heard.

By evening—due in part, no doubt, to exposure, which reduced their resistance—several members of the guard of honor were seriously ill. A few lost consciousness on the train returning them to Great Lakes. Spinal meningitis. Ross found himself in hospital, within an inch of death. Most of the others died. In time Ross recovered, but he had lost his hearing. He has not heard a sound since that day of Joffre's visit to Chicago.

After the war, he "bummed around" for several years, going to college, working in banks, on farms, for a mining company . . . then, I don't know how, he became a scenario reader and writer in Hollywood. When I met him, he had been for years in one of the larger studios and had to his credit a number of original screen plays.

Aside from what may be gathered from his letters, which I shall quote, this is approximately all I know about Ross—except that, an intensely alive and vital man, he partly overcame his serious disability by developing, somehow, what may be called a sixth sense, or a new instinct. He drove me in his car through the traffic of Hollywood and Sunset Boulevards and downtown Los Angeles, and "heard" the bell of a speeding ambulance which required him to stop at a crossing. Conversing, he talked to me, while what I wanted to say to him I wrote on a pad of paper; but usually all that was necessary for me to scribble down was a word or not even that. He does not read lips, but he read the expression on my face; sometimes he seemed to divine what I was going to say as soon as I had the thought formed. He is extremely well informed, which does not surprise me. He has a great many friends who keep in touch with him; he corresponds with numerous people in various parts of the country; both as part of his job and in his spare time, he reads a vast lot of books, magazines, and newspapers; and—perhaps most important—he has the ability to draw the essence, the truth, or drama of a situation or event or personality out of the atmosphere about it. From the first he seemed sound or interesting to me on most things we discussed; subsequently, writing to me his long letters, he swiftly became an important part of my America. He is not always consistent, is often contradictory. His mind is not always logical, nor firmly attached to any philosophy; it is avid, quick, observant, sensitive, instinctive, almost unintellectual; progressive, idealistic, realistic; not given to simplifications or formulas, nor afraid of being called confused; honest, independent, forthright, shrewd, sometimes erring—elemental, American. In his letters, he now says one thing; then, seemingly and oftentimes actually, almost the exact opposite—and usually is right both times, especially when he generalizes about the ways and moods of the American people.

I wrote to him for permission to quote a few of his letters and he promptly gave it to me, adding, "I'll probably get drummed out of Hollywood, if not tarred and feathered, when your book comes out—but what if I do! . . ."

AFTER THE ROOSEVELT LANDSLIDE

"Hollywood, November 5, 1936

". . . There are so many features attaching to this election wherein one can find all sorts of 'breathless significance.' But the main thing is the obvious fact that the mass of the people are far more to the left than they are to the right, so far as we can use those terms in America; and that they remain quite indifferent, and actually hostile, to the majority of the practicing would-be leaders. About eighty-five per cent of the press supported Landon and opposed Roosevelt; if this is not a strikingly significant feature I don't know what one is. How far, how unutterably far away from the mass of people our newspapers have gone! In every state in the Union (excepting the South, of course) the largest and most powerful press, for months, kept up the most ruthless gun-fire on F.D.R., and built up Landon, with every ounce of propaganda at their not unskilled command. And yet the people, not only did not succumb, but came back stronger than ever to flout the press.

"The people, one may well be justified in suspecting, are much farther along than their leaders. And if there is room for despair in America, it is in bad taste, not to say false, to direct it generally and solely at the people. Failure, now, not merely to hold every advantage gained, but to press on to more and more advantages, can't be laid in the laps of the people—it can mostly be attributed to F.D.R. & Co. If ever a man got a mandate to go on, he did. But it will be absurd, of course, to assume that the people want him to begin right away by sending the army to blow up Wall Street, and having the government take over next week all the basic industries. . . . I cannot interpret the election in anything like that spirit. I think F.D.R. was dead right, that he knew exactly what he was talking about, when he said a year or so ago to Upton Sinclair, 'Mr. Sinclair, I can't possibly go any faster than the people will let me!'

"It is surely plain that the people do not want to go too far nor too fast. I am convinced that if F.D.R. tried a real, complete socialization of some important industry, that the people would get panicky. I think the only important industry which they would agree to being substantially 'socialized' just now would be the munitions industry, and, conceivably, the railroads, and next the power industry.

"I am frank to admit—and may be foolish—that I believe F.D.R. has done, when you consider *everything*, a pretty good job during his first term. His prosperity-through-scarcity trick was a terrible one of itself; but in the long run it may have a profound good influence on preparing the people not merely to see, but eventually to act on, the essential problem of distribution. The NRA hurt the little business men, and the AAA was full of serious holes; but the Securities Exchange Act is good, and even the Social Security Act, pitiful as it is, nevertheless is that necessary step forward.

"There has been so much criticism that F.D.R. 'hasn't gone far enough.' True. But we have already seen that he has the Supreme Court to deal with, and he has always had to face the possibility—in his first term—of making the people panicky with fear of going too far or too fast. He could not have foretold what little effect upon the people the massed attack upon him and his 'communistic experiments' would have. He knows now.

"F.D.R., after all, has had before him the lesson of Italy, and much more immediately the lesson of Germany. A premature, and much too sudden and extreme move to the left, and you lay the way open for some rabble-rouser to turn a great mass of people against you and wreck and nullify even the few points gained. For instance, a Huey Long in the position of the obscure and colorless Lemke, might have made a different result in the election: for as sound as we demonstrated ourselves to be in this last election, our political character is full of holes, through which cheap or dangerous demagogues can crawl to power. . . .

"Moreover, in casting up the ledger, no leader was ever faced with precisely the problems confronting Roosevelt; his acts, therefore, *had* to be in the nature of experiments whether or not he or we liked it, though we have indicated we liked it. And I think he has kept at least fairly well his promise to shift his line completely when he discovers that one will not work out. As for me, I think it is a good plan to follow just now; it is rather in line with our traditions, though, of course, a time may soon come when it won't be the thing at all.

"I admit that I have never been able to think kindly of an armed uprising in the United States. In Spain or Russia, yes. But we are so violent a people that such a business would cause a wreckage here that would make Spain's and Russia's look like the mere destruction of a decayed outhouse. I am favorable toward 'most any compromise, in regard to the nation at large, that would tend to prevent armed insurrection or a civil war.

"Some of my more extremist friends are inclined to think me just an ol' mossback, a 'conservative liberal.' Labels mean nothing. But I think that I am far more in harmony with the traditions of the American people at large, than are they, when I say that if socialism is what is to be desired in this country (and I don't know that it is) we are more likely to get it through the ballot-box than we are through an armed uprising, and Roosevelt is the most fortunate intermediary we could have had to carry the nation along the line of social progress, with the least possible damage to our marvelous industrial institutions.

"I am afraid the powerfully religious element in the Communist Party has distorted much of the progressive thinking in this country, and twisted it out of line with American traditions; they have, in the past, shown a terrific urge to destroy everything with the capitalist 'taint'—so that even a great and efficient industry, so long as it has been used to increase the profits of the owners, comes under the range of their all-inclusive fire. Of course, the Communists, lately, have greatly toned down in their childish silliness, and got away from the preposterous ideology of the Third International of as recently as a year ago. However, the damage they did before they woke up and got wise to things, has not been wholly made up for. Their shortsightedness and misrepresentation still obtain, as I know from personal experience, and as I shall illustrate in a minute. . . .

"America, I am certain, remains in a most peculiarly fortunate position. And that position has been made so much surer through Roosevelt's sensational reëlection. Our good fortune is that we have not even approached the utter collapse with which countries in Europe have been faced; so that we can afford to experiment, and even to make serious mistakes, and still remain relatively secure. For the extremists to sneer loftily that '*that* isn't anything' is merely for them to prefer an attitude to the reality—the 'Cæsar or nothing' philosophy, a philosophy which has wrecked far more ideals than it has ever built. . . .

"I have said the situation is surer now. Roosevelt was elected by the masses of the people. Now he can go ahead; and if he isn't mostly fake, if the developments during his first term were not mostly accidental, he will go ahead—in the direction suggested by the New Deal so far. . . .

"Meantime, never mind Roosevelt. We must think. I am anxious to see a movement begun for the starting of a new and sound political party. A sort of 'Commonwealth Party,' to give it a name. It should be set up under a broad, progressive standard, and should begin to work among the people, encouraging them not merely to hold present gains, but to press on for more and more, and to exert pressure upon the government *continually*, consciously. For if the people do not keep watch on F.D.R. he is not unlikely to wiggle and wabble and get nowhere at all. The people, therefore, cannot just sit back and leave it all to F.D.R.; if failure lay mostly in his hands, yet a good share of it would lie in theirs.

"There has been, and still is, much talk about the so-called Farmer-Labor Party. I can predict right now that the idea for such a party will—and should—fold up. It starts out with a strong prejudice against it, since its loudest promoters have been the Communists. It makes no difference if the people are or are not fair to the Communists, the prejudice against them is real, and they (the people), as a whole, will have no truck with the Communist Party or its connections in the long run. They—instinctively—cheer the U.S.S.R.'s rising line of production, for that is something up their own alley. But they don't like the smell of Russian politics and won't have anything to do with it. Not for nothing did Roosevelt forthrightly denounce all Communistic support—he knew his people. . . .

"But even without the Communist overtones, the Farmer-Labor Party is preposterous. The name itself is ludicrous, uniting as it does perhaps the two most hostile elements of our citizenry. . . . Look over the election returns and you will see that F.D.R. had his closest battles in the strictly rural sections, everywhere; it was the industrial centers, full of 'laborers,' that really went hog-wild for him. Farmers have always instinctively regarded themselves as several cuts above 'laborers'; they are, anyhow, always potential employers of labor. They are the most bedrock conservative element in the American political circus. I should know something of them. . . . Invariably, they are scared to death of any *real* changes, since they have property at stake; and often, those who are mortgaged to the hilt to the bankers are the most conservative and reactionary. The most forward-looking farmers I ever knew were the richer ones, those who owned their land outright, made money, took life reasonably easy, and were liberal, sometimes amazingly. (I used to know a rich farmer in Missouri who read Marx, Fourier, Rousseau, but mostly Marx!) The poorer the farmer the more tory he is; the poorer he grows, the more reactionary he becomes. Whereas Labor, having comparatively no property stake, and although inclined by tradition to be conservative rather than radical, is more easily propagandized; and unlike the farmer, the poorer the laborer becomes the more likely he is to turn to the left. Conversely, as the farmer tends to grow more liberal-minded as he prospers, the laborer tends to grow more reactionary as he prospers. I have not observed any extreme alterations of this general rule.

"Why the propagandists do not see the absurdity of such a party, but seriously yelp about it, baffles me. Certainly their propaganda gets precisely nowhere. No group of 'farmers' would ever unite with a group of 'laborers'—except to sell them out when the gravy was in sight, and probably vice versa!

"What is wanted, then, is a new party, under a new name, which does not classify its members along the old idiotic 'class line' so sedulously propounded by the intellectuals of the Communist Party, who learned about America at large by growing up in New York and Brooklyn. Lord! Not a one of them but is ignorant as could be of the country at large.

"The best name I have seen so far is 'Commonwealth.' Under some such banner all types and classes of people could unite without having to leap over the class-line barrier. American people have no peasant traditions, no liking or instinct for thinking of themselves as 'farmers' or 'laborers' or 'workers.' And it is not snobbishness which would act to prevent a professional man, say, from subjecting his economic personality to a 'Farmer-Labor' Party. Not even the average laborer, that is, an auto mechanic or a loom-worker, likes to think of himself here as a mere 'laborer.' Where, in Europe, he has bowed and said 'Yes, master,' here he continues to say what he has always said: 'Oh yeah?' Where in Europe an aristocrat could kick him off the sidewalk with impunity, here the same dude would get his block knocked off.

"The European importation of the class-conscious ideology, and its disproportioned super-imposition upon the American situation politically, has been one of the worst mistakes the leftist groups have made; and that move has done vast damage in the way of preventing the formation of a powerful, united, progressive party. We, therefore, instead of being able to get going from scratch, have to blast out of the way the hurdles erected in our path by the extremists, the impatient Europeanists.

"The American people are the most violent, changeable, unpredictable, unmanageable, least sheep-like people in modern history. If we seem sheep-like occasionally, the fact remains that it is only for a time. We take such an extreme law as Prohibition, and violate hell out of it, and then as everybody is agreed that we are just a great flock of sheep, and will be burdened forever with the law, we rise up suddenly, and almost unaccountably, and do away with it. . . . To undertake to get a substantial proportion of such a rebellious, unclassifiable, untamable, people to submit to a political party named and ideologized under some such term as 'Labor' or 'Farmer-Labor' or 'Workers' or 'Toilers' Party might be done as a lark, but not seriously. The psychology of those trying to promote such a party is akin to the doings of a Don Quixote. They are tilting at windmills in a land that actually does not exist!

(I am talking, you understand, about a political party, and not at all about labor or employed groups organizing for practical economic purposes.)

"The smart thing to do, obviously, would be for the more intelligent leaders of the leftist groups to get together and sink their individual personalities completely under one broadly liberal banner, such as the 'Commonwealth' or one equally unclass-conscious, and seriously to promote those numerous important ideals that they already, at bottom, agree upon. They would be quite surprised at the great swarm and the varieties and 'classes' of people who would unite with them. This is hardly as naïve as the old hope of some visionaries that all the churches would destroy their sectarian boundaries and come under one banner, for the reason that religion has never in the modern world been a critical, or almost a life-and-death issue, whereas the social and economic problem is very much so indeed. . . .

"Speaking of the Communist brethren, and their flair for misrepresentation, my own trivial experience, to which I have referred, was this: The other day I picked up a *Sunday Worker*, and on the movie page read a Hollywood feature by one Louis Norden. It was about the war pictures that the producers are preparing to make. As his prize exhibit, Norden named 'The Siege of Alcazar' to be written by Knickerbocker of the Hearst press. He properly pointed out that it could hardly be less than derogatory to the Loyalists, a pro-Franco thing, and should be protested by all liberals, churches, leftist groups, etc. He went on to name a dozen or more other pictures in project, which, he demonstrated, should also be denounced and opposed. Among these, as one of the worst, by inference, he named a certain picture which is to start at Metro in a month or so—and which story, an original, happened to have been written by myself.

"Obviously, I knew much more about that picture than Prof. Norden did. And having designed it myself, I knew it was, far from being a pro-war or even a war-mongering picture, a deliberate and studied *anti*-war picture, as definitely anti-war as any picture could possibly be. Moreover, it even used the World War as a background, wherein the taking of sides is out of the question. But I was not alone in this wholesale lambasting. Among other war pictures which he indexed, but which are emphatically anti-war, was that notorious 'militarist' Erich Remarque's 'Road Back,' author of that infamous 'war-mongering' book, *All Quiet!*

"This seems to be the case of a fanatic determined to put over his gag even if he has to misrepresent. Here we have a would-be rabble-rouser calling for boycotts against a lot of pictures without discrimination. They all deal with war, therefore— The trouble seems to lie in some weird conviction on the writer's part that the producers are a set of vicious, fascist-minded men cunningly contriving schemes to make our people warlike and to put over a Hitler. Such an assumption is simply naïve at best, and at worst it is vicious itself. The producers are simply men engaged in watching the public temper and catering to it with entertainment it will support. The great majority of our people are definitely against war, and the producers would no more try to shove pro-war or war-mongering pictures down their throats than they would cut their own. I can assure you that the great majority of pictures contemplated, which deal with war, are emphatically anti-war. All this the writer would have learned with a little inquiry—but perhaps he didn't want to know the facts, perhaps he even suspected he wouldn't have a case 'ag'in' Hollywood' if he got them.

"Of course, this incident is trivial, and the *Sunday Worker* hardly rivals the N. Y. *Times* in power or circulation. But it is significant of the shallowness and misrepresentation which the professional leftists engage in; that vicious process in which propaganda takes the place of the truth. How, in the face of such instances, trivial though they may be, can one trust such fellows? Really, the leftists had better wake up and give encouragement where it is due, rather than lump everything into one and lambaste it."

THE "COMMUNISTS"[1]

"May 26, 1937

". . . In vain these days does one search the magazines and the columns of the regular, professional interpreters of events for a clear, sound voice. Perhaps, though, such is the uproar going on that we wouldn't recognize any that even now may be saying plenty worth listening to.

"I don't really mind the uproar so much. In a sense it is healthy, and I cannot but feel a little grateful toward a land wherein proponents of all varieties of opinions and ideas can go to it in a knock-down-and-drag-out fashion, and will not land in jail because of it. Still, there is such a thing as getting out of hand, and I would feel a bit more comfortable and assured over the future if there were one tolerant, but authoritative voice, grinding no axes whatever, but cautioning toward serenity and keeping our sense of humor, being heard in the land, even if not listened to religiously. A sort of super-informed Will Rogers, or half a dozen of them. With all his faults, his lamentable characteristic of being primarily and almost wholly an opportunist rather than a careful, thinking leader, Roosevelt seems momentarily to stand best in this rôle. And he is such a one only by accident, and will cease to have much meaning when his term is over. He may fold up even earlier.

"I already am firmly decided that I am definitely opposed to turning the country over to the Reds and their 'liberal' sympathizers and sidekicks. As I have written to you before, I am not an enemy of Communism, by any means, but I do not like the cut of the present Red gentry's jib. The country now is being held in a kind of political escrow, and when I think of it, it always strikes me as indeed a very lucky thing for us. We don't want fascism, and if anything on earth is obvious it is that the American people are not prepared, or anywhere near prepared, for too strong a dose of socialism or

[1] This title is mine; Ross Wills, usually, does not write of "Communists" in quotation marks.— L. A.

nationalization all at once. Our very feeble steps leftward give ample warning of the mess we would get into if the country were handed over bodily to any exclusive group. Here, if anywhere on earth, the educational method—education by a little experience at a time, I mean—is the only one that can possibly work, if there is to be anything left to work upon.

"I am sure that I have paid diligent and careful attention to what has been going on these past few years, and in particular to the persons who have made it go on. I have one key to go on—that this or that organization, whatever its ideals, rules, and regulations, etc., means exactly nothing; it is the *men* who make up, who control or direct, the organization who are important, and who make the organization what it is. Applying this rule to the Communist Party in the United States, and having applied it long with prejudice *in their favor* (instinctively often, out of an instinctive support for the under dog), I come at last to the unavoidable conclusion that not only am I no longer for them, I am against them—that is, I am against not Communism, but the Browders, the Fosters, *et al.,* as prospective powers in These States. . . .

"To go into my reasons, I would have to dig into such subjects as religion, passion, psychology, and the works in general. Suffice it to say that these men, and their enemies as well—the so-called 'Trotskyites'—have proved themselves far beyond the hilt to be not fit leaders of a people, but grim and ugly fanatics, without humor, without tolerance, without—in plain words—alert, sound intelligence. They are nothing more nor less, when scraped of paint, than throw-backs to the Crusaders, religiously impassioned hotheads and god-screamers. I am rather annoyed with them because I went along with them for a time, and allowed them to step me up, too, aflame with indignation over inequalities and injustices; but when I came to see that they were not fit men to lead a people into a 'promised land,' that the land they would get to would be one as vicious, at bottom, as the one they destroyed, I said nuts, and do now.[2]

"Well, I want to make one prediction: That John L. Lewis is going to pay through the nose for his acceptance of the Communist Party's support. . . . Really, the Partysans have been so arrogant and bumptious with their down-right falsehoods, misrepresentations (observe, merely, on the intellectual front,

---

[2] As I am finishing this book, Brooks Atkinson, drama critic of the New York *Times,* in its issue of February 27, 1938, discusses a current play on Broadway, *Wine of Choice,* by S. N. Behrman, in which a character called Ryder, who is a liberal, says to Chris, a parlor Communist (as quoted by Mr. Atkinson): "You are locked deep in the cold fastnesses of theory; on that surface nothing can take hold, nothing can take root, nothing can flower—neither love nor friendship nor affection. I see how people like you can condemn to death their best friends, because equally well you can condemn yourselves to lovelessness, to abnegation, to death. . . .

"It is you who are sentimental. Your sentimentality is the most perverted of all because it ignores the most powerful impulse in all people—to be free, to choose. It ignores their imaginations, their best instincts. . . . We affirm their capacity to comprehend and their right to their errors. On that affirmation I shall fight you. I shall devote my life to fighting you. . . . Against you I shall struggle to keep alive a world in which choice will still be possible—without dictation."—L. A.

how maliciously they treat John Dewey), and actual celebration of their errors, which they refuse to acknowledge—I say they have just about merited the angry uprising against them by the 'patriot' societies and the Catholic Church.

"You know as well as I do, that any half-witted organization would never have tried the European technic, and certainly not as stupidly as this gang did, in the United States; they would never have gone off quixotically lashing at various institutions in the United States in the manner these birds have done—sneering one day and 'united-fronting' the next. Americans may be sappy enough, but not quite such fools as to fall for such brazen two-faced wooing. They go on committing their silly boners, and regarding them as the sacred spittle of Lenin.

"The Partysans are really getting power, through the C.I.O. Anyone who thinks they won't demand payment for their 'help' later is just simple. I, for one, do not like the idea of such fanatics in power over anything in any sense at all. One plugs along, rooting for John Lewis, at the same time that one suspects that everything is not going to be so pretty when judgment day comes up. I do not give two hoots what happens to American business (apart from industrial institutions and production system as such) but I know that I am absolutely unwilling to have it taken over by these boys, if the cost is that my intellectual freedom is going to be dictated by them.

"What worries me, is that there is not a determined rebellion against this dangerous business going on now—a rebellion by the aforesaid liberals and intellectuals in concert. They seem to be stymied, afraid to speak up, for fear of 'encouraging Fascism,' of being called red-baiters. Ah, how neatly the Communist International has got 'em sewed up! All it amounts to, in sum, is that a dictatorship of a real sort is in actual power over men's minds, and that all over the globe liberals and intellectuals who hate Fascism as emphatically as the Communist Party does hesitate to speak plainly because they have to buck this mountain of bunky propaganda the party has built up everywhere. And so discrediting passes as sober judgment, misrepresentation as the truth. Let a liberal venture a mild doubt—and they are after him in gangster fashion. A kind of political gangsterism, but still that is what holds nearly all Europe in a vice, and one shouldn't be surprised that this business has reached considerable power here. Not being one who regards Russia as the Fatherland, I gravely doubt that the sacrifice of intellectual freedom in America at the risk of danger to Russia is worth it. And, anyhow, I do not believe Russia would collapse! If, indeed, it is ever necessary to sacrifice intellectual freedom and self-respect for the attainment of any ideal—however lovely it sounds— then that ideal is a fraud and not worth it. . . .

"Here, let me pause to have a look-around. Am I, then, quite blind to the actual good the Communists have done, or am I perhaps narrowly prejudiced from some variety of backward '100 per cent American' standpoint? Do I merely lampoon the Communists all over the place, and yet say nothing of the shenanigans of our reactionaries who are certainly more dangerous to whatever democracy we have left than all the radical outfits ever heard of? . . . But why belabor the obvious? I have nothing whatever in common with the reactionaries, and I do have something in common with the Communists. To wit: a common, broad recognition with them of certain serious shortcomings, and a common, broad recognition with them that 'something must be done about it.' In a nutshell, here is my whole case summed up: For the work of the Communists in the field, such as aiding and supporting the dispossessed, the disinherited, for defending those unjustly used, and for going about and instructing oppressed working people in their rights and encouraging them to organize and fight for every right they are entitled to under the law—when they do this quite apart from any ideology, they have my real respect. (And, incidentally, in the same measure, do the hundred and one other organizations or individuals of no connection with the Communists who have done and do the same thing!) But—not merely my departure from, but my opposition to, the Communists comes in right here: That the Communists, in exchange for such aid and support arrogantly attempt to exact as the outrageous price for it, the complete subjection of their beneficiaries to the political and ideological control of the Communists exclusively. I am against them here, just as I would be against *any other* minority group which tried the same trick. It is just crooked, no less. I am just as suspicious of a 'good' minority, and as opposed to its lust for power over the majority, as I am of a 'bad' one. Neither has any resemblance to democracy; the one is, or would be, as ruthless and absolute a dictator as the other. Isn't Stalin, or his sidekick Yezhov, as ruthless as Hitler?

"Yet, it has been this damnable practice which has tended, in my opinion, to cast grave doubts even upon the quality of whatever good the Communists have done. The good will and generosity of a Samaritan is measured, surely, in exact proportion as he demands or expects nothing in return for his deed. And yet the Communists, succoring the man in distress, seem to say: 'Now we have succored you and given you help, and in return we expect you to take up our cross and follow us, and obey us and fight our battles and support our ideals.' . . . Now, just how far away is this business from the very essence of the old Tammany system?

"All along the line, in fields other than labor or economics, the Communists have played, more or less, this same amazing trick. They have arrogantly assumed divine control over the arts, literature, and what not. In literature, they tried to set up a cabal of grand-high-moguls whose practice it was in unison to denounce every novel, poem, or play produced that was not, in their particular view, 'social conscious,' and to exalt to the skies every piece of tosh, no matter how feeble it might be, that came under their patented label of 'proletarian'! The results, of course, have been wildly hilarious in many respects.

"But—talk about 'red-baiting' by the reactionaries. Why, these fellows have been past masters in baiting every 'unbeliever' all over the place. They rose up, anyhow, with a chip on their shoulder, daring anyone to touch it. And they have been like an angry animal, snarling and snapping at sympathizer as well as foe. From the first they have been ruthlessly, savagely intolerant of even the mildest cautions by liberals, whirling upon them in return with the epithet of 'Trotskyite'; it used to be 'social Fascist.' And so, if now, in the complete inversion of their tactics from sardonic sneers at democracy as a 'fraud,' to frantic pleas to 'save democracy'—if now they are having such a tough time luring the liberals that they once screamed at, into their 'united front' to 'save all humanity,' they had better go and look in the mirror to see who is responsible.

"The conclusion I reach is this: Some of the work of individual Communists, some of the work of the Browders and Fosters, has been useful and important, as work purely. But in the end it is part and parcel of a very narrow and highly doubtful ethic as a whole; and above all it stands for a body of doctrine that is essentially strange to and at variance with the traditions of America, and it never can possibly gain support from a substantial majority. The Communist Party can never be anything but a small minority here, at best, and as such its net effect seems to be to disrupt, to distort, and actually to check the rise and spread of a broad, united, liberal and democratic movement uncontaminated by wholly unnecessary class-struggling and quite out of place and erratically visionary internationalism. The Communist Party may be the answer to Russia, may be the answer to Spain, it may be the answer even to Germany where it was born—but it certainly is not the answer to America."

ON HOLLYWOOD

"August 16, 1937

". . . The whole question of the quality of the motion pictures, which you raised in your last letter, always comes smack against an immovable rock: That they are what they are because the public, for whom they are made, is what it is. And the makers of the pictures, above all the most competent and successful of them, are first and last simply business men who have never made the naïve mistake of assuming that they were also, or even incidentally, artists. The movies are first, last, and all the time a *business*, an *industry*, and they have about as much to do with art as the banking or the textile industry, both of which cater directly to the general public, also.

"Generally speaking, Hollywood is simply no place for an artist. It has produced possibly two original artists, as artists strictly—Chaplin and Disney; and Chaplin, though he produces his own pictures, stands out as a screen character, and Disney works in a highly unique medium.

"The director or anyone else highly placed who begins thinking of the movies as an art, and of himself as an artist, is in the process of losing contact with his bread and butter, precisely and in the same way as would a banker who began mooning about some scheme to hitch sculpture up with banking.

"As for creative brains in Hollywood—where are the creative brains in banking, in the oil business, in textiles? Precisely! As for the Hollywood writers, God help us! The largest bunch of intellectual grease monkeys and thimble-riggers ever assembled on one spot in the history of the globe. Few of them ever read a book of their own volition, fewer still have any idea beyond that of a high school sophomore as to what is going on in the world. Even the highest paid of them are like the reporter on the *Daily News* who was approached by an organizer for the Newspaper Guild when it first began to sound out Los Angeles. The reporter was asked to join. He sat listening, growing more and more excited. Finally, he could not contain himself and blurted out: 'S-a-y! That thing is almost like a union, ain't it?'

"It is the solemn truth that many 'big' writers positively refuse to read books of vital social, political, or economic nature, or become closely familiar with such problems, for fear it will somehow injure their effectiveness as movie writers. And hence their salaries. Attempts by the few intelligent ones among them to get them simply to recognize themselves as workers, hired people, run up against smart-alecky opposition by such charming Great Individualists as Rupert Hughes, a sort of Dr. Johnson of Hollywood. They fail to see through such fellows, which is not the Hugheses' fault, but is due to the indifferent stupidity, and the intellectual and moral cowardice, on the more intelligent side, of the writers themselves.

"How do I reach such conclusions? When the writers themselves, in private, let down their hair, they disclose themselves with monotonous invariability as disappointed playwrights, as novelists who couldn't even write their own names, or as soreheaded ex-newspapermen still nursing grudges because their editors had too much sense to make them foreign correspondents.

"If, in the movies, you want to find intelligent conversationalists, and meet people whose vision is considerably beyond the movie lots, who are alert to what is going on everywhere in various fields, then you will have to go, with a few exceptions, to the technicians, to the departmental heads, to the story and scenario editors, the cameramen, the engineers, etc. Among these you will find an occasional preposterous crackpot, a 'relative,' perhaps, but they are not the rule by any means. It is these who are the informed people, and who have in proportion infinitely more brains than the more widely advertised and celebrated writers.

"Surface cleverness, facility at repartee and snappy chatter—these are the marks of the characteristic or average Hollywood movie writers. The physical shyness, the air of quietness, of humility, of inner profundity that not uncommonly mark the real literary artist—these are so rare in Hollywood as to be amazing. For every Claudine West or Robert Riskin, exclusively movie writers who know their trade and take it seriously and conduct it ably, or for every Donald Ogden Stewart or Dorothy Parker, not only first-rate movie writers, but people with literary accomplishments behind them, and, more than that, alert, highly informed people vitally concerned with social and economic problems—for these few and perhaps half a dozen more, you have the five hundred or more who are, in greater or lesser degree, hacks. That is to say, at least 99 per cent of the movies have to come from the overwhelming majority of these hacks, who are so helpless, on the whole, that they can write only in gangs of four to eight on a picture, and then the producer, or producer and director in combination, have to wet-nurse them through the job.

"This *average* Hollywood writer is the most scandalously overpaid person in any business on earth. That, indeed, has been one reason why it has been so hard to organize them into a guild, or union—the inner panic in the breasts of so many that any meddling with the murder they were getting away with might be disastrous; they might be 'found out.' They had and have many legitimate grievances quite unrelated to the salary matter, but they have been content to suffer various indignities at the hands of producers rather than risk any monkeying with salary levels. The leaders of the Guild movement have had to go to extraordinary lengths—to ridicule, to wheedle, flatter, cajole, and even occasionally threaten—to get it going and hold it together. The leaders' patience has been beyond belief, and one fears that if the present leaders should resign the whole movement would collapse. It is curious and significant that the present leaders and moving spirits of the Guild are among the very best writers, and highest paid, and in the most secure positions in the studios.

"It is, of course, the most logical and necessary thing that the movie writers should be organized. As much so as that mechanics or carpenters should be organized; and, conversely, just as it is most logical that genuine literary artists should not.

"Your typical Hollywood writers, then, have virtually nothing in common with literary workers—those, I mean, who are more or less intent upon contributing something to an understanding of mankind and the world it inhabits. They more closely resemble pulp writers, true-confession writers, confectors of radio plays, and that ilk, in so far as they resemble writers at all. On the whole they resemble tool-makers, loom-workers, gardeners, carpenters, woodworkers, plumbers, and those of such skilled trades, much more than they resemble writers at all. Just as the workers at these respectable trades work under the direction of master mechanics, or architects, or such superiors, so do the average Hollywood writers. For they lack originality and can do little except by direction from above. And if we ever had Socialism, or a system in which every man got exactly what he deserved or earned, there is no doubt that the average screen writer's salary would be somewhere near that of the skilled plumber, rather than several times that of a Supreme Court Justice, or often even the President.

"The extreme paucity of any originality or creative brains among this gentry is indicated by the extreme rarity of acceptable original stories produced by them. They feed, and feed richly, upon the ideas of other and better men and women. Here is, typically enough, how this goes: A real literary artist spends a year, say—no unusual length of time—producing a sincere and able novel. Being a typical instance, it will not be a best seller, or anything like it, but the critics will praise it. Now the author will feel very lucky if his royalties reach as high as $6,000 in a year. Along come the movies, desperately seeking material, which they cannot obtain from their own writers. They see a movie possibility in the author's novel, and they buy it. Since the novel is not widely popular, there is no publicity for the movies to buy, and they naturally get it as cheaply as they can. Say the movies pay $10,000 for this novel for the movie rights, and that is a fairly average sum. Of this sum a portion must go to the agent and perhaps—though not in all cases—a part to the publisher. Let us be generous and say that the author winds up with $7,500, so that his total profit from the novel, including royalties, is about $13,500 for his year's hard work. A fair enough reward, it seems.

"Now this novel is turned over to the movie writers. And not, typically, to one writer, but to anywhere from four to eight men and women on the staff. But let us not be extreme, and say that only four writers are employed on this novel, converting it into a screen play. And let us be quite modest and say they work on it for eight weeks, at an average salary of $750 per week each. I assure you that two months is a very short time, indeed; and that six months is very common, and a year on a movie story not uncommon at all. But we'll cut the time to eight weeks, so as to avoid extremes. Figure it up yourself: The converting of the novel into a screen play will have cost the studio, in salaries alone, a total of $24,000, or a total of $6,000 for each writer for only two months work. What we have, then, is the enlightening spectacle of each movie writer making nearly half as much in two months as the author of the novel made in an entire year. Moreover, the author had to work on speculation, on a gamble, whereas the movie writers were regularly paid weekly. And the author has created and contributed every basic or important idea that has gone into the eventual screen play. Remember—this novel was purchased for its *ideas*, particularly, and in such cases they are almost certain to be followed pretty closely. Publicity value does not figure much in such a deal; studios often buy notorious plays or books largely for their high publicity value, and in such instances pay enormous prices—but they're so rare they make the headlines.

"One can hardly avoid concluding that there is something wrong here. It would seem that by far the larger proportion of the profits should go to the essential creator of the work, but actually it goes to the steam-fitters and grease monkeys who tinker with the original vehicle and by their allegedly mysterious arts 'transform' it into a screen play. And even here, at least half the time, the actual screen-authors will have been the producer and director orally telling the screen writers how to write the screen play!

"Compared to the writers, the story and scenario and film editors, the skilled artisans, the technicians, the engineers, the cutters, etc., are shockingly under-rated and under-paid. Yet it is these, and the cameramen, who are able to clothe even the feeblest ideas, which not even a gum-chewer would read in a pulp magazine, with such skill and charm that even intelligent people can sit through them without being driven mad enough to shoot the manager and burn down the theater."

"October 15, 1937

". . . You want to know what really happened out here in connection with Vittorio Mussolini. Well, in the first place, Mr. Hal Roach, who made the original arrangement with Vittorio, is perhaps not the Statesman Mr. Roach thought he was. Mr. Roach is personally a man of the highest probity and integrity, a man who has well merited the respect that is given him both as a gentleman and as a producer. As a producer, he is by far the most successful producer of comedies, and especially slap-stick, in the history of the movies. Indeed, where other comedy producers have risen and fallen by the wayside, Mr. Roach has consistently forged ahead until he is now the dominant figure in the strictly comedy field. And deservedly so. The man who has given the world those hilarious comics, Laurel and Hardy, alone, is entitled to all the admiration in the book.

"But it seems, or so they say, that Mr. Roach was not satisfied with being the most successful comedy producer in town; he also got the itch to perform a statesman-like deed in a naughty world. A laudable enough ambition and one that the world could stand a lot more of, to tell the truth. Those who say that Mr. Roach was only thinking of the rich commercial possibilities of his tie-up with the son of Il Duce, are wrong—as though all a Hollywood producer ever thinks of is money! And there was the ingenious reason given by some vulgarians, that Mr. Roach was really bringing Vittorio here to supplant one of the inclined-to-desert members of his famous comedy team; they were equally absurd, although Vittorio's dead-pan was commented upon speculatively by some of the local experts who lament the passing from the screen of Buster Keaton.

"The more serious observers insist that the association was due to Mr. Roach's desire, as they call it, to Aid International Harmony, and, these smart boys add, there in the background, with International Harmony all slicked up prettily, would be Mr. Roach modestly taking the bows. Moreover, this yarn has it, Mr. Roach was not only thinking of the honors and hooraws from the public, indeed, from the world, but it would be one for Hollywood to digest, it would knock the Mayers and Zukors and Warners for a row of swastikas, and all these men who were used to mingling with the politically *élite*, and entertaining visiting ambassadors and senators and governors with casual familiarity, would have one to keep them quiet for a while. So Mr. Roach leaps right over the heads of mere governors and such, and forms a united front with the son of one of the most famous and powerful rulers in history. . . .

"So, with fitting fanfare, Mr. Roach brings Vittorio over from Italy to learn how to make movies in a two-weeks visit to Hollywood—which was an excellent tribute to Vittorio's intelligence, seeing that many men have been in the movie business for twenty years and haven't yet learned how to make movies. Anyhow, with flash-bulbs popping and headlines screaming, Mr. Roach escorted Mussolini Junior across America in characteristic movie publicity style. But this was all to the good for, say the cynics, Mr. Roach, like all movie moguls, knows the value of publicity when it walks right up and smacks you in the eye, and he knows, too, they point out, that in some cases even sensational publicity is smart—for eventually the critical aspects of it die away, and there is Ye Great Producer sitting snugly on a nestful of golden eggs hatched out under the bright glare of publicity. . . .

"Only—something went wrong. Came the dawn, as the movies used to have it, and with it the appearance of the villain, lurking in ambush waiting to snatch Our Nell out of the hands of the Hero and do her damage. That villain was the Hollywood Anti-Nazi League, a 'contemptible little outfit,' some of the trade-papers called it, leaping to Mr. Roach's defense; a 'worrisome little group of loud-mouths and stink-bombers,' and 'nobody need pay any attention to them' except that all their bellering was liable to 'destroy the international market' for Hollywood's pictures. Considerably before Mr. Roach reached the Movie Capital with Vittorio, this 'ridiculous' outfit had been kicking up a dust everywhere. Its emissaries had been going through the studios and meeting and talking with the employees—and the employers, of evenings, at the Trocadero and the Bali, and putting down a spiel. The Writers and the Actors Guilds, the various unions, were 'visited' and the case laid down. To wit: this coming to Hollywood of a scion of Il Duce, and particularly under the aegis of one of its most important and respected producers, was a serious encroachment of Fascism into the industry; the time to stop it was now, before it got going. Embarrass Mr. Roach? Possibly. Perhaps Mr. Roach did not understand the temper of the American people on the issue of Fascism, but that couldn't be helped; Mr. Roach had been cautioned, anyhow.

"But Mr. Roach stuck to his guns, or Mussolini. Perhaps he was encouraged by a few of the more reactionary trade papers, which had leapt to his support. Then it was that the League went to town. With the unions, guilds, etc., already primed, the moment Vittorio touched Hollywood soil, a smashing barrage was laid down. Public meetings were held everywhere, not only by movie groups but by political and anti-Fascist organizations of all kinds; and space was bought in the trade-papers and one or two local dailies. The high point of these attacks was the public reprinting of sections of Vittorio's book, which he published in Italy last year, telling of his enjoyment of his career as a flyer for Italy in Papa's conquest of Ethiopia. They quoted his 'rare pleasure' in dropping bombs upon the humble huts of the blacks and seeing their bodies blown heavenward with the debris. Cuts from the advertisements were mailed to all important functionaries.

"In short, the League got the whole city up in arms—you'd have thought, from the effects, that General Balbo was hovering, just over the Tehachapis with a hundred fighting planes, ready to swoop over and bomb Hollywood into abject surrender. . . . In every studio, important stars, who had been won over, sent word to the moguls that if Vittorio walked on the lot, even to visit, they would quit the set and damn the cost.

"The next step was obvious enough. Word went out to Mr. Roach that he would have to cut loose from young Mussolini, kit and caboodle; this tieup was risking the welfare of the industry; boycotts from labor everywhere were likely; it might even bring on a disastrous strike of studio employees; and, anyhow, it would serve as a powerful motive to spur ahead the already growing union sentiment in the industry. And this last was probably as effective a bludgeon as any of them. For unionism is growing out here, and the producers are fighting to stop it, but just now it is a losing fight. . . .

"So that is what happened to Vittorio. The heat on him was even extended socially to a really cruel degree. Previously arranged parties were hurriedly canceled as soon as the party-throwers could be 'got to' by the League, or when the guests sent word they would not attend any gathering Vittorio attended. Famous stars openly and publicly snubbed him; in their eyes, they said, he was a killer, a bomber of helpless women and children. Really, the snub to Vittorio was one of the most complete and overwhelming ever heard of in These States!

"No need to dwell on the significance of this. Nobody here hates Hal Roach, he is as much respected as ever. It just goes down as a boner, and no one in his right mind thinks he was maliciously trying to promote Fascism; at worst it is regarded as a blundering attempt at 'statesmanship,' or a coup to flabbergast rival producers. The whole episode will quickly be forgotten. But Hollywood will for a long time remember, and be impressed with, the extraordinary power and effectiveness of the Hollywood Anti-Nazi League. Of all the organizations remotely like it that I know about, it is by far the most competently and intelligently conducted. Unproselyting, it wisely does not essay to drive out one political gospel so that it can put over its own. It stands simply as a bulwark against any encroachments upon the democratic ideal by patently anti-American ideologies. Thus, the people can and do give it their respect. And thus, the really powerful anti-Nazi, anti-Fascist sentiment out here can be traced directly to the work of this League."

RADICALISM IN HOLLYWOOD

"October 25, 1937

". . . There is altogether too much loose talk about the current radical tendencies of the picture people. To come to the point as quickly as I can, they are *not* turning 'red' or revolutionary in any real sense of those terms; but there has spread to Hollywood the infection which is more or less sweeping all America and awaking the common people to the necessity of organizing and fighting for that which they have been entitled to under the long-existing setup, but which they have lacked not merely through so-called capitalist aggression, but through their own lack of organization.

"Just as in the C.I.O. you find some of the loudest 'haters' of Communism and deniers of radicalism, so among the most active and effective of Hollywood's liberals. I remember when, a couple of years ago, the Anti-Nazi League was formed there was a long and dreadful row among its founders over the momentous question whether to call it a 'non-Communist, non-Fascist' organization. It was only after many meetings, involving dirty words, face-slappings, hair-pullings, and indignant resignations and so on, that the League finally was launched without the 'non-Communist' label. And the majority of the members of that organization are distinctly not Communists by several hundred miles, even though Communists are surely in it. Actually the League as a whole is opposed to either Fascism or Communism, and is 'for American democracy.' That they waste no time hating Communism, and devote their time to forestalling Nazism-Fascism, is due to the simple fact that Communism has never been the slightest menace to Hollywood, whereas the same thing cannot be said of the other. . . .

"As to our Marxists, then, I gravely doubt if there are more than a dozen serious Marxists, profound students of Marxism, amongst all the thousands of Hollywood people. There are probably a couple of hundred fashionable 'Marxists,' *i.e.,* people who spout some phase of Marxism but have never read Marx, and if they have do not understand him. I do not joke, but so many of our 'Marxists'—particularly those who get from two to three thousand a week and swim in private pools surrounded by beautiful houris—are only being what they think is 'mentally up-to-date'; they are the 'moderns,' of that vast phony class who just couldn't *bear* being behind-the-times, and so give lip-service to causes with which they would be quite out of sympathy if they understood them. They have never studied the cause, whatever it is; they just adopt it, and by their alert, surface facility at poll-parroting popular slogans fool many people into believing they are the goods. And you know as well as I, that whenever such people come into direct contact with the particular issue when it is 'on the barricades,' you will likely as not find them cavorting on the other side! No, no, our 'Marxists' of this particular species, and I assure you they are in the great majority, are not conjuring up any dire plots to overthrow the government, or even, God forbid!, the movies. They are, flatly, not a menace. They are really just creatures of a superficial environment, mental and physical, who never, never realize what they do think until brought face to face with grim reality—and, also, with so many of them their lives are so comfortable and protected that Grim Reality hardly ever comes near their door, and so they can often live an entire lifetime under a 'many-colored cloake to goe inbisible.'

"One of Hollywood's leading and best known 'Communists' is—well, let me call him Mr. X. He is one of the four or five cleverest, most competent film writers. He gets three thousand a week, and is outwardly a gay dog with a cynical, suave manner. Inside of him, though, he is bitter; he hates Hollywood and the producers and, because of his dependence on the picture industry (for he 'needs' most of the money he receives), is not overfond of himself. He finds a curious satisfaction in posing as a red, in uttering Marxist phrases and ideas while holding a long-stemmed cocktail or champagne goblet at some large Hollywood party; in writing out a check for a thousand dollars and handing it to the Communist Party; in asking big-shot producers to contribute also to the same cause and watching the wry expressions on their faces. He invents fantastic arguments why they, who are capitalists, should contribute to the Communist Party. Of course he can afford to indulge in this sort of fun; he is so good a movie writer no one would think of firing him. To illustrate what sort of fellow X is: Not long ago he sat with a girl at the Trocadero; she said something that rubbed him the wrong way; he rose, walked out sans his hat, got into a cab and said, 'San Francisco,' which city, as you know, is something less than five hundred miles from Hollywood. The cab-driver looked at him; X flashed a roll of bills at him and repeated his order to take him to San Francisco. . . . He was gone for ten days, holding up production on a picture, costing the studio tens of thousands of dollars a day. The studio, keeping things quiet, hired private detectives to find him; they failed. Under a *nom de plume*, he spent a week with a few cases of his favorite Scotch in a San Francisco hotel. When he returned, his secretary exclaimed, 'Why, Mr. X! Where have you been?' He chucked her under the chin, passed off a wisecrack, and went to work on the story where he had left off ten days before; and the studio executives and everybody else acted as though nothing had happened. . . . That girl at the Trocadero had said something to him (God knows what) that he could not overcome by writing out a check to the Communist Party! . . .

"So, if anyone comes breathlessly telling you that Hollywood has gone radical in a big way, and the reds are just about to take over the movies and run them by a Soviet, just tell them with equal solemnity that you have just learned that Leon Trotsky has been elected mayor of Hutchinson, Kansas.

"Hollywood, indeed, could stand for a great deal more radicalism than it has, and profit by it; at least, it might increase the mental activity of the place. But our so-called radicalism is nothing more or less, I repeat, than neuroticism and—more important—a local aspect of the nationwide move toward unionism, and which, far from being a really aggressive move toward actual power, is basically a *defensive* gesture. Nothing positive about it. The Depression has disclosed serious holes in our economic structure and shown that it is full of pitfalls for the average man, dangerous to our democratic institutions and liberties; and the upsurge of unionism and organization, or so it seems to me, is primarily a defensive measure against complete collapse. Hollywood is just a part of that drama; no more."

"January 5, 1938

". . . If you write anything about Hollywood in your book,[3] just remember to think of it simply as the very epitome of that great American institution, the Circus. It is a circus under a permanent tent, with something for everybody. It is the direct and legitimate inheritor of the tradition of Barnum. Hollywood is authentic, as the circus is; it is necessary, it is legitimate. It is not America at all, and it is *all* America. It is Bangor, Maine, in intimate embrace with San Diego, California. It is an entertainment factory for the millions.

"Few writers or observers who come out here to look us over ever reflect upon this basic and pertinent fact. They fail to see Hollywood in proper perspective. So, because it is not like the Stage, not like Sculpture, not like Literature, they go away doling out cynical wise-cracks that are as meaningless as the smart-cracks in the pictures themselves. And many of the big-name authors who condescend to work in pictures come pig-headed and big-headed, all set to impress their own individual personalities upon the movie public—and invariably they come a cropper. Egotistically they want to 'reform' the American people and their tastes through the movies. But it is not the producers, here, who are 'stupid,' or the writers or directors. It is these wise guys who are stupid. For the fact simply is, for better or worse, the American movie public—or any other that I ever heard of—does not want to be 'reformed' by its movies—it wants to be *entertained*, just as you and I want and expect to be entertained when we go to the circus, and not given some pompous lectures on dull subjects or grave instruction in certain arty 'rhythms.'

"I have told you before that the typical Hollywood writer is a very dumb cluck in the matter of awareness of social and political forces and important ideas generally. But, in cold fact, a keen awareness and understanding of such things would be a real handicap, rather than an asset, to him—just as they would be to a trapeze artist or a tight-wire walker in the circus. The general run of successful writers are smart, facile, quick-maneuvering fellows, always prepared and ready to drop one idea midway of working it out to pounce on another, according as they are directed; they are immediately responsive to sudden and complete changes of lines of thought. Could a scientist, a deep thinker, a serious or profound artist, pursue such a course without going mad? Obviously not! Hence, any profundity, any genuine depth of thought, or complexity, is a severe handicap to a movie writer.

"It is my guess—though I have no statistics to prove it—that most of the successful Hollywood writers are ex-newspapermen, men who have been trained to produce sensations daily, and to meet dead-lines. Newspapermen understand picture-writing rapidly, and they shift easily into it. It is natural enough. A movie is a series of sensations more or less cleverly arranged and designed to

[3] I had meant to write a chapter of my own on Hollywood, where I have been a number of times; then decided to use my friend's letters, instead.—L. A.

keep an average audience continually entertained for a period of one to two hours. Whereas a novel, on the other hand, for comparison, may deal with but a single sensation, and the whole of it be given over to explaining or clarifying that single 'sensation' or phenomenon. Newspapermen are trained 'sensationalists,' for one thing, and they are used to taking orders and counter-orders without quibble. I should say, then, that the newspaperman has it all over the novelist or other professional in adaptability to movie writing; and I am certain men of that profession greatly outnumber those of any other in the business.

"Of course, the really important people in Hollywood, though it sends many writers and directors and stars into a frenzy to admit it, are the Mayers, the Zanucks, the Selznicks, the Warners. You may say what you like of most producers, and whether as business men or as 'civilized' human beings, the worst of it will be true. But I am talking only of the really important ones, and of them only as business men. These are the men who do their level best to make the best pictures that the public will support, always aware of the fact that you cannot compel a public to embrace a round of calculus when it is just struggling to comprehend simple arithmetic. These are the men who, in the most wasteful, extravagant business on earth, amidst the most vicious, cut-throat, knifing competition, year after year keep in the van. The men who know how to exact from their writers, casts, directors, etc., the relative degree of excellence and kind of entertainment that their customers will consistently accept. The men who know that, just as it would be idiotic to turn over a newspaper to a flock of 'oppressed' reporters to write whatever stories they liked, so would it be insane to turn over a studio to the individual egos of a lot of whining writers who have sold their alleged creative ability for the movie gold and yet still lust to strut in solitary magnificence as 'artists.'

"You are compelled, whether it is gratifying or not, to admit, for example, that there is not a smarter or abler man in any other field than Zanuck in his. And that, in the matter of running a huge studio, of holding it together year after year, relatively unaffected by panic and decline, while nearly all others go bankrupt or have to be 'reorganized,' Louis B. Mayer, whatever one may think of his politics or other extraneous matters, is one of the ablest men in the entire country. In his studio he is better than all his writers, actors, and directors combined; they are there for the simple reason that he is there, and they stay there, if they have anything, for many years profitably, because he is there.

"We have enough competent leadership in Hollywood; the trouble is actually a paucity of creative brains. Some producers, indeed, are more or less compelled to surround themselves absolutely and entirely with sycophants and boot-lickers, men who are only rubber-stamps, and can mechanically carry out at least the orders of the producers. Others, more gifted, know how to select competent employees and then let them go to it, but always with a check-rein on their more soul-soaring flights—in this category Mayer probably is the best.

"I know all this somehow looks 'unfair,' that it is easy to praise such moguls, and that there surely are unappreciated men of great ability who do not get a chance. Of course! But I am not trying to exhaust the subject, only to give you some conclusions, as unbiased as I can, drawn from more than a decade of intimate observation.

"One respects such men. As showmen, they have got it over even Barnum. And as one respects them in their business, strictly, so, in a measure, are the obscure but facile smart-guys who are able to turn out acceptable movie entertainment for the millions, the writers, entitled to respect. Not, however, as one gives it to the Hemingways, the Cathers, *et al*. And to be fair, perhaps most of the old heads do not consider themselves as 'important' in the sense that literary artists are. Mainly, as people, they are a decent enough outfit, as amusing and charming as so many newspapermen would be, with few delusions about their importance to humanity. It is the occasional popinjay who goes on a strut, who gives the idea pompously that he is important, that he is doing something of profound or permanent worth to humanity, who gives the impression that most of his fellows have an exaggerated ego. On the whole the Hollywood writers are genial cynics who draw high pay, that they know they don't really earn, and which they squander in ways most amusing to them. But they know this, too—that they will *all* pass away and never be remembered even with a brass nameplate thrown into an old box somewhere—remembered no more than the obscure men who staff newspapers, live and die, or get fired, and pass on to complete oblivion. The only ones who will be remembered at all are the Mayers and Zanucks and a few directors—much as one remembers Barnum—and maybe a very few actors and actresses, as one recalls Jenny Lind in association with Barnum. And Chaplin and Disney. . . .[4]

"But, perhaps, even these are but a part of the circus, the passing show, and in the end only Hollywood will be remembered. But it remains important. To the great majority of the people, entertainment is at least as important as worship, and justly so. And if the former becomes more 'worshiped' than the latter, possibly that is a reflection upon the latter's character or method of presentation, but hardly upon the more popular entertainment itself. The people, then, who provide this entertainment, do a very useful service and are entitled to at least as much respect as is given to bankers or surgeons or engineers."

ATTENTION: MR. SIDNEY HOWARD

"February 15, 1938

"I have just read an earnest plea by Sidney Howard that more important literary artists and dramatists should sign up with the movies. Obviously Mr. Howard is misguided here, owing perhaps to the fact that he is himself a rare exception—a competent dramatist and a first-rate movie writer.

[4] In a later letter touching on the same subject Ross Wills said: "The other day I asked Monta Bell, the well-known director, who or what would be remembered as products of Hollywood. He replied: 'You can count them on the fingers of this hand. They are Garbo; D. W. Griffith (don't forget him, for he started all this); Chaplin; Disney, and the newsreels. All the rest you can toss in the ocean!' . . ." Mr. Bell's permission to quote him here was secured.—L. A.

"As a matter of fact, the more important the novelist or dramatist, the farther he should keep away from Hollywood. If Mr. Howard had pleaded for more successful pulp writers, or newspaper serial inventors, or even radio play confectors, he would have performed a service for Hollywood. For Hollywood needs more of these to supplant the altogether too many movie writers it now has who can barely write their own names. Such writers as the above can at least invent or appear to invent simple ideas, and they have a knack of finding favor with the masses, as important writers rarely do.

"The serious or important author, as I have tried to suggest to you before, has nothing in common with the movies. Indeed, they are enemies, and attempts to bring them together invariably have pathetic results, and usually for the author. The end of each is exactly opposite. Where the earnest author is primarily after artistic accomplishment, the movies are after dough, first, last, and all the time.

"Dough is the big idea in Hollywood—it is what makes all Hollywood shove, push, cut friends' throats, knife them, kick them in the face, chisel, and generally behave like hogs at a trough. This lamentable state of affairs is not due to the alleged 'stupidity' of the producers. On the contrary. There are plenty of numbskull producers, but—at the risk of repeating what I wrote to you a few weeks ago—they are not among the important ones; these are very, very smart, indeed. In the movies, the producer is a vastly smarter man than the most important writer. The producer is honest and sensible enough to recognize the movies as a business, whose object is to make money, which can be done only by making a product that appeals to the largest number of customers. Thus, where the producer seeks the largest common denominator—the largest possible audience, the sincere artist seeks the smallest common denominator, or smallest audience, seeks it, of course, because he has to, owing to the relatively small fraction of literate humanity.

"The serious author should think deeply before quitting his comparatively free, unbounded horizons wherein he has been able to disport himself more or less as he pleased. For when he comes into the movies, he moves into an alien world, he moves into a kind of rich, luxurious prison wherein he must feed upon the food that is given him, and conduct himself as he is ordered to by his rude and realistic gaolers, the smart business men who run the movies.

"And he should reflect upon the problem of censorship. I do not mean the censorship that is generally yelped about. A great deal of shrewd, but dishonest bawling goes up from Hollywood about censorship. They howl about the unctuous little boards of church-members and moral guardians which, in absolute control of the pictures in many cities, states, and countries, maltreat their works of art and hold over their heads a threatening ax that warns them never to be original. Now, most of this bawling against the censor boards is bunk; it is an alibi. For the fact is that it is rare that these censor boards, whatever their narrow and doubtful motives, cut or keep anything out of the pictures that injures them, or that could not better be eliminated, anyhow!

"It is not *this* censorship that should bother the serious author, and which is important. The real censorship that should give him pause, and that holds the movies in a vise, is the censorship of the *public taste*. It is not a censorship which dictates what can *not* be put on the screen; it is that infinitely more exacting, more ruthless and dominating censorship which dictates what shall, indeed what *must*, be put on the screen. So—if the serious writer is willing to give up his moon rocket for a popgun, or lower his sights a hundred miles——

"Hollywood people do not have much respect for 'important' writers, who come out here to work. The cynical Hollywoodians snicker at them behind their backs, knowing they are either naïve or have temporarily swallowed their principles for greed. The naïve ones afford the most amusement to the old settlers. Now and then the producers go on a prestige hunt; that is, they get a yen to add some big name in the literary world to their pictures, so that they can enjoy the distinction of having such an important and respected figure as their hired man. So they go after the Big Writer, who may hardly ever have seen a movie, and they honey him and pump him up until they actually make him think that his coming to Hollywood will virtually revolutionize the place. This poor soul never suspects that the producer who is luring him actually has no respect at all for his brains, and has no intention of using them—for the simple reason that the producer knows ten times more about movie writing than the Big One can ever learn. So he falls, he is brought to Hollywood with a lot of pomp, and installed in a gorgeous office. He is given some paper, a typewriter, a beautiful secretary—and then he is given the studio 'white elephant' and put to work on it. The studio 'white elephant' is always some mistaken purchase of a past era, which the studio never had any intention of filming, and has less now. But it is a kind of baby-rattle to keep the Big Name Writer occupied whilst half a dozen obscure studio hacks, in a grimy little office at the opposite end of the lot, put together the great masterpiece that the Big Name Writer knows nothing about, but which his distinguished name, bought and paid for with plenty of cash, will eventually grace as author.

"It is a classic gag, and the old settlers richly enjoy it. From the first they watch it work out with glee, eagerly anticipating the always uproarious climax that occurs when the Great Literary Artist awakes from his heroic dream and begins to howl and bawl about his outraged virtue.

"On the other hand, there is the Big Author who more or less swallows his principles, and sells his prestige for as much as he can get in order to relieve a financial crisis, or even to get enough money quickly to enable him to live comfortably in Europe or the South Seas while he writes his next book. Hollywood understands him, for he is patently out for the dough, and so is Hollywood. But the Hollywoodians understand him, too, rather better than he understands himself. And so they keep a skeptical eye peeled on him. If he proves to be the rare one who knows how to *use* Hollywood, and never lets it hold him longer than two months out of any year, while he devotes the major part of his time and interest to writing respectable books, then Hollywood bows down to him in profound respect—for that rare soul has guts. Nine times out of ten, however, his guts turn to water, alas! When he first comes out here, he lurks about in hiding, rarely being seen publicly, for he is secretly ashamed, and knows that Hollywood holds him in contempt, at least as large as his contempt for Hollywood. And he doesn't want to mingle with these 'cattle'; he will, he has assured himself, grab as much movie dough as he can, as quickly as he can, and as quietly, and leave the dirty place flat and forever.

"But that fifteen hundred a week begins to come in, and it is very pleasant. Gradually he begins to get around, but to salve his artistic conscience and preserve it in its cold storage he adopts the attitude of sneering at his superiors and berating Hollywood. You begin to find him of evenings at a corner table in the dim light at the Trocadero or the Bali with some sympathetic little female pal. Watch him and he will look about frequently with a worried, frightened look on his face. If you pause for a drink and a chat with him, his talk will be punctuated with venomous excoriations of certain producers and violent epigrams calculated to dynamite all Hollywood off the map. If you are untutored, you're impressed by these observations of the Big Author—but if you're an old settler, you know that these outbursts are simply a little automatic that he draws in a panic to threaten away an increasingly persistent vision. It is 'that novel' that he should have written, or should be writing even now, crying out desperately to save it from that horrid specter of a smiling, cunning, wicked producer-villain holding out a large bag of gold.

"A year later you will see this Battling Nelson of the arts lolling back in his Rolls, as he proceeds to a meeting of the inner council of that eminent writers' company union, the Screen Playwrights, whose basic principles are (*a*) the exaltation of the screen writer as an important, individual artist on a level with Eugene O'Neill, and (*b*) the promotion of the idea that the producers are a lot of kindly, fatherly Santy Clauses whose sole purpose in producing movies at all is to enhance the artistic importance and the financial prosperity of the screen writers.

"One could make up an appalling list of writers in Hollywood who once showed much promise or talent, or even accomplishment, as novelists and dramatists, but who, confronted with that amusing party-game question: What would you rather have, money or artistic distinction? answered it definitely.

"One of the most embarrassing defects of modern civilization is the unhappy fact that there are so many talented poor who are anxious to exchange their honor for wealth, and so many envious rich who are anxious to exchange their wealth for honor."

The Long Road

Here is action untied from strings necessarily blind to particulars and details magnificently moving in vast masses. . . .

The Americans of all nations at any time upon the earth have probably the fullest poetical nature. The United States themselves are essentially the greatest poem. In the history of the earth hitherto the largest and most stirring appear tame and orderly to their ampler largeness and stir. Here at last is something in the doings of man that corresponds with the broadcast doings of the day and night. . . .

WHITMAN, Preface to 1855 edition of *Leaves of Grass.*

"Hello, Phil!"

During my stay in Yugoslavia in 1932-33 I met three or four provincial governors, the mayors of several cities, and four or five Ministers of the Belgrade government. I did not tell of my experiences with these politicos in *The Native's Return*, but—for a purpose to be presently apparent—I want to recount a few of them here.

One of the Ministers was a fellow named Ivan Pucelj, who held the portfolio of *socialna politika* (which cannot be adequately translated into English), with jurisdiction over state hospitals, poor farms, asylums, national sanitation, social security, unemployed relief, and the like. He was a Slovenian; in fact, a native of a town near my mother's home village. Upon my arrival in Belgrade in January, 1933, he sent a message to my hotel: I should come right over for a chat. I went; and, entering the ministry's courtyard, I had difficulty moving through the scores of peasants and workers and other people, some of whom were wearing vast sheep-cloaks, while others were less adequately clad against the near-zero weather. The same was true of the corridors downstairs. These people were delegations seeking—or, to use the equivalents of the terms used in Yugoslavia, "pleading" or "begging" for—some "privilege" or other from the government. In the Minister's anteroom I came upon a number of men and women; but the secretary, who had evidently been awaiting me, requested me to go inside right away. I said I had plenty of time and would like to wait my turn. "Oh no," cried the flustered, obsequious secretary. "Pay no attention to these people; some have been waiting for days; they can wait awhile longer. The *gospod* Minister has directed me to bring you to him the moment you arrive." Thinking I would remain only a few minutes, I went in; but the Minister kept me close to two hours. He was a genial, expansive man and talked at a great rate. As a young man he had been in America for a year, and thought he knew a great deal about it and insisted on giving me the benefit of his knowledge. Partly because I was conscious of the delegations and individuals standing in the cold outside and waiting to see him, I suggested every few minutes that I leave and twice I even rose, but, crying, "Oh, no, no!" he detained me. I said, "But *gospod* Minister, all those people waiting for you, you haven't time to talk with me." He laughed heartily. "I take time! *Zakaj sem pa minister?* What am I Minister for? Let them wait, they have plenty of time." His insensitiveness to the people in the anteroom and in the cold and windy courtyard appalled me.

The next day I was invited to call on the Minister of Education, Dr. Radenko Stankovich, who, after the assassination of King Alexander, became one of the regents. Here I waited about two minutes before I was received; and, waiting, witnessed the following incident. An old woman, clad in black garments pitifully inadequate for midwinter, with a drawn, sad face, entered the anteroom, smiling apprehensively. When the secretary saw her, he stepped to her and said, sharply, "Are you here again!" The pathos of the woman was indescribable. She fumbled about her with a trembling hand, starting to say, "But, *gospodiné,* I beg you—" Interrupting her, the secretary talked to her sternly, cut her off again as she tried to say something, and finally pushed her out of the room. A few of the men, who doubtless had been waiting for several days to see the Minister, smiled as though they had witnessed this scene before. . . . Two or three hours later I found the woman standing forlornly in the street outside the building and, stopping to talk with her, learned she had been a village teacher somewhere in Slavonia for thirty-odd years. She had been retired now for several years, but of late months she had failed to receive her retirement pay, which amounted to something like four dollars a month—all she had to live on; so she had taken her last few dinars and come to Belgrade four days ago to see what was the matter. She had seen numerous minor officials in the Ministry of Education, none of whom were interested in her retirement pay; so this morning she had tried to see the Minister himself for the third time, in vain. . . .

But before talking with her, I had seen the Minister. He was a hale, hearty man, wearing a suit evidently tailored in London. He also had been in America, knew English, had connections in Yale, had read my book *Laughing in the Jungle,* and his remarks about my becoming an American writer were palpably meant to be most flattering. He was the foremost physician in the country and had come into politics through having diagnosed and successfully treated a stomach ailment of King Alexander's. I asked him about the latter matter, and Dr. Stankovich answered His Majesty's health was satisfactory. Then he rang, summoning a flunky, who entered obsequiously, and continued to bow and scrape while the Minister ordered him to serve us Turkish coffee. Leaving, the flunky did not turn about and walk out in the wake of his nose; he backed out, while his body, frozen into a servile bow, suggested a half-opened pocket knife. He did the same after bringing us the coffee.

The Minister did nearly all the talking; he spoke of America, the Depression in America, how America could solve her economic problem. He knew Professor Irving Fisher and had high regard for his political and economic ideas. The few times I tried to correct some view of his about America, he stopped me by raising his hand—a request not to interrupt him. This for two hours. . . .

The previous summer Stella and I had spent awhile in Rogashka Slatina. In the restaurant where we usually took lunch, our table was next that of a Minister's wife, who was a haughty and generally objectionable dame. Nothing seemed to suit her, and the headwaiter, who always personally attended her, was a pitiable sight as he stood beside her. He bowed and fussed and fidgeted, and he yessed her and smiled to her, while the general expression of his face seemed to say, "Oh yes, yes, Lady of High Station, I *am* but a species of vermin and my ultimate happiness would be to perish beneath your heel. But since that would require the great effort on your part of stepping on me, will you not grant me the lesser honor of spitting into my face?" . . . The woman and the waiter together were a depressing picture.

While at Rogashka Slatina, I witnessed, too, the visit of the provincial governor; there was no end of bowing to him and calling him "Your Excellency." . . .

All these and similar scenes, incidents, and experiences stood out in my mind with great vividness when, early in 1935, I visited Madison, Wisconsin.

I had met Philip F. La Follette at a party in New York early the previous December. He had then just been elected Governor of Wisconsin for the second time, after having been out of office for two years, and had come East to relax from the strenuous campaign he had gone through. A slight, agile man, he was in his late thirties, and, except for his graying hair, very boyish-looking. He was like a college lad out for a good time and was not inclined to discuss Wisconsin, the La Follette Idea, The Situation, or anything of that nature. "Besides," he said, "I think one must *see* Wisconsin to understand what it's all about. Why don't you come out and let me show you things? Come to the Inauguration, next month."

I could not go to the Inauguration, but, happening to be in the Middle West a few weeks after Phil's induction into office, I wired him I would come on Sunday. His return telegram invited me to come to his office at the Capitol about nine o'clock. My train arrived in Madison at five or six in the morning and I went to a hotel. At about a quarter to nine I decided to walk over to the Capitol; and as I stepped into the elevator which was to take me down, there was Phil.

After we had exchanged greetings and our pleasure at meeting before the appointed time, Phil explained he had been visiting a sick friend of his, who lived in the hotel. Leaving the elevator, we walked through the lobby. Two or three men sat about, reading the Sunday papers. One glanced up, nodded to Phil, went on reading. Phil returned the nod.

Near the exit stood a bellhop, a boy in his late 'teens. As we passed him he said, casually, "Hello, Phil."

Phil said, "Hello, Fred," and we went out to Phil's car, which was parked down the street.

Driving with him to the Capitol, I found myself in a curious emotional-intellectual stew, which subsequently I analyzed in my Diary in this self-amused fashion:

The immigrant, the Yugoslav or European in me, was startled and impressed by the utter matter-of-factness and naturalness of the bellhop's "Hello, Phil" and Phil's equally natural response to the greeting. For an instant I was not sure who had spoken first, then I realized the bellhop had, but probably only because Phil had been busy talking to me. Otherwise Phil might just as likely have greeted the bellhop first.

On the other hand, the American in me who, like most Americans, tended to take things in America for granted, said: "What are you impressed about? This is how it ought to be."

"Yes," agreed the Yugoslav in me, "but in Yugoslavia, for instance—don't you remember how appalled you were by Pucelj and by what you observed in Stankovich's office?"

"Yes," said the American in me, "but there's no point to getting excited about that bellhop's greeting Phil as he did. It was natural. The boy is an American. Phil is Phil. This is America. What the hell!"

"Yes," said the Yugoslav, "but Phil *is* the governor ——"

Between the Yugoslav and the American in me was the free-lance, sociologically inclined student of the American scene who, since my return from abroad, rather enjoyed comparing the New World with the Old and trying to see things objectively, and who now saw the incident in the hotel lobby as follows:

"Phil, to be sure, *is* the governor of Wisconsin, but he is also Phil; everybody calls him that. When he gets in the papers, the headlines read PHIL DOES SO-AND-SO. He is governor of the state partly because he is his father's son, but also because he is the sort of fellow people, including bellhops, naturally and casually call Phil, which is what the people of Wisconsin like to do, they being the sort of people they are; and which is perfectly all right with Phil, who, in fact, likes to be just Phil—he knows that among other things it is part of his political capital, as it was part of Coolidge's to be Cal to a lot of people. Anyhow, Phil is just Phil, not 'His Excellency' or anything like that; in short, an American in Wisconsin. His father before him was just Bob or Old Bob to a lot of people. His older brother, now a United States Senator, is just Bob, too, or Young Bob. . . . That bellhop's *un*conscious attitude toward Phil is: you're the governor, I'm a bellhop—so what? And Phil, also *un*consciously, returns the compliment: you're a bellhop, I'm the governor—so *what*? And Wisconsin's and, to an extent, America's attitude toward this situation between the governor and the bellhop is essentially and unconsciously—so what?"

The American in me: "So—nothing!"

The Yugoslav: "I wouldn't say that."

The student-sociologist: "That unconscious 'So what?' flung all over the scene is the most marvelous aspect of the whole matter. It is the core of one of the differences between America and Europe. It helps to make America America. But most Americans are inclined to be too matter-of-fact about their country. Even Phil here doesn't realize how really wonderful it is that he is just Phil and not 'His Excellency' or something like that. But, on the other hand, that is part of the wonderfulness of it."

The American in me: "I refuse to be impressed by this 'Hello, Phil!' business. Why compare America with Europe, especially with the unfortunate, backward aspects of Europe? Wouldn't it be better to measure America by herself, against herself, against our American ideals? After all, we have had advantages here which Europe never had. There is a good deal of this 'Hello,

Phil!' democracy, especially in politics, but there is not enough democracy in our industry, and I bet you that, if we looked around a bit, we would find rich women and waiters in America who are as bad as those we saw in Rogashka Slatina. Let us get excited by our lacks, rather than by our virtues."

"But you don't understand," said the Yugoslav in me. "Comparisons are good, instructive—inevitable."

The trying-to-be objective student of America: "You are probably both right. It is, of course, very important that America becomes more conscious of her lacks and faults than of her virtues; on the other hand, it is desirable right now, when there is so much talk of the dangers of Fascism in this country, that America does realize in what ways she differs from Europe, where Fascism already is an actuality. It is important for America to know what her inner resources are, as compared with the inner resources of Europe. . . ."

The next couple of days I spent considerable time in or near the Executive Office in the Capitol, and the difference between what went on there and what I had observed in Yugoslavia *was* profound. Delegations of peasants, of course, were not shivering in the courtyard or the corridors. There were no peasants. Some of the people might have been farmers or business men; one could not tell from their looks. Those who entered the office were promptly, courteously attended to. If somebody came and Phil could not see him rightaway because he was busy inside with some one else, he came out for a minute to say hello and asked the person to wait awhile; and of course the person, who might have been a farmer, did not bow and scrape and tremble when Phil appeared. On the contrary, he remained wholly at ease; his manner was that of every day. As likely as not he called him Phil. And if anything, it was Phil whose manner had a touch of eagerness to be nice and agreeable; which I later noticed also in his brother Bob, and even in their sister Fola, who was not in politics. The explanation for this was that "Old Bob" and Mrs. La Follette had raised the boys for political life, with the idea that a politician or officeholder was a public servant and should act and behave as one conscious of this fundamental obligation, without sacrificing his human dignity. That idea had been part of the atmosphere in which the La Follette children had grown up. And, watching Phil on the occasion of that first visit of mine to Madison, I recalled Whitman's lines to the effect that in America it was the President who took off his hat to the people, not they to him.

The "Europeanists" (as Ross Wills calls them) in New York—among them Ben Stolberg and Louis Fischer, whom I had seen shortly before leaving for the Middle West—were vociferous in insisting that "basically" and "essentially" America was like Europe. Nobody could make me believe that. True, thanks to "Old Bob," Wisconsin was perhaps one of the finest states in the Union, politically and humanly; but fundamentally Wisconsin was not so drastically different from other states, from Illinois, or Michigan or Pennsylvania or Minnesota. . . . America *was* different. Madison, Wisconsin, was not Belgrade.

While I was in Yugoslavia, and for a year and a half after returning to America, I had disliked Pucelj, Stankovich, *et al.,* and abhorred the whole official attitude on the part of the politicians and bureaucrats toward the public; now, however, in Madison, I suddenly and vividly realized that I had—almost—been unjust to Pucelj and Stankovich. They were not personally to blame for what I had seen in their Ministries. They were simply part of the European order of things in which the government, the state, and *ipso facto* those in charge of the government or the state, were more important than the people. They were *above* the people. In Europe, it almost seemed that the people existed for the state, not the government for the people.[1] That, no doubt, was due to the whole monarachic tradition, to the "divine right" on the part of the rulers, to the fact that the officials administering the affairs of the countries had always been appointed by some one *above*, not elected by the mass of people or elevated from below. So, naturally, the Puceljs and the Stankoviches, both put into their jobs by an absolutist, "divine right" king, behaved as they did. So, too, and naturally, their secretaries behaved as they did. The people did not like it exactly, but by and large they put up with it. It was part of their tradition to put up with it. I recalled Yovan Vukomanovitch, my peasant friend in Herzegovina whom I describe earlier in this book, and felt that he, too, despite all his pride and dignity as a man, had fidgeted and trembled and rolled his little cap in his hand as he faced the magistrate.

In the intellectual circles of New York there was then—in 1934-35—endless talk about the "revolution" and Fascism, and the American situation was being interpreted—dogmatically—in the light of *Das Kapital*. Louis Fischer, freshly back from Russia and the Continent, discerned Fascist tendencies in "the American ruling class and the middle classes." I did not dismiss Marx as one who had nothing to teach us; on the contrary, his rigidly economic theories, as I saw them, were exceedingly bright flashlights by which one might study important phases of America; but there were things in the United States of which Marx had been almost wholly ignorant—certainly of which many of his current followers in and around Union Square were not even dimly cognizant.

If pondered, that "Hello, Phil" became as important, almost, as the business cycle. The utterance had come out of a historic development in American life. Because of the country's basic incongruity, American politics were generally a rather stenchy business; but when that was said, this fact remained—that the people of America had been electing and ejecting their governors and legislators now for a hundred and fifty years; had been elevating them from below and kicking them down, and had been leading a life for most of that time which was the freest, most democratic ever lived upon this earth by any people. That fact went deep into America. When the President lifted his hat to the people, or when Phil La Follette was a bit too eager to shake the hand of

---

[1] During the writing of this book, the Reich Press Chief declared, "In Germany the individual does not exist; he is only an aspect of the state."

a Wisconsin farmer, of course there was a political (even if, in the case of Phil, unconscious) motive behind it, which might seem superficial. But there was nothing superficial about the attitude toward him of the people who came to see him. It was not merely psychological with them, but downright *physio-logical*. Those backs simply could *not* bend to Phil, just as millions of European backs *did* bend in front of the European governors almost reflexly.

If a crisis arose in the American economic setup which touched the people, the American politician—whether Phil or Roosevelt—had to do something about it sooner or later; the sooner the better for him. If he failed to, as was the case with Hoover, he was finished. But, as Ross Wills suggests, he must watch himself that he did not attempt to do too much, too fast. If he did that, he was finished also. The American people were at once radical and conservative. They were progressive. They were pragmatists. If the system did not work, they were for "fixing" it a little, for changing it here and there; the politicians had to get busy; and changing it here and there, they played the devil with the theories about the system that had been built up around it.

This, of course, is a simplification of the American temper and the American way, but it is, I think, essentially true. There are, I know, other tendencies in the American people, but I believe that this "Hello, Phil" thing, manifesting itself variously and not as obviously everywhere as it does in Wisconsin, is in the long run dominant.

My consciousness of it is, perhaps, the most important element of such steady feeling as I have about America.

The Wisconsin Idea

WHILE I WAS IN MADISON, I TOOK THE OPPORTUNITY TO GO A BIT INTO THE current state of the so-called Wisconsin Idea, which had developed in that state in the first three decades of the twentieth century around the personality of the elder Robert M. La Follette, and which in that period had greatly influenced the American socio-political scene and—with the aid of James Bryce, who discussed it lengthily in his book *The American Commonwealth*—had become world-famous. It had greatly interested me, however, for at least a dozen years before I visited Wisconsin. During the war, I had not been very aware of old Bob La Follette's opposition to the United States' entry into it; if I had been, I would probably have disapproved of him at the time (I was only seventeen), for I believed Imperial Germany had to be defeated; but I voted for him for President in 1924. Studying at long range the Wisconsin Idea and Old Bob's record (including the war record) in the Senate, I had decided by then that he was a great man.

The Wisconsin Idea continued to interest me after the old Senator's death in 1925, when there was much speculation in the country as to what would become of it. His sons were young men: Bob in his early thirties, Phil in his late twenties, both as yet untried in public life. Much depended upon them, for the Progressive cause and movement were so intimately tied up with the La Follette name that "the boys"—as many in Wisconsin refer to them—were bound to affect them. In the ensuing decade both Bob and Phil had been tested and had shown themselves to be La Follettes in the tradition created by their illustrious father, equipped in their characters, personalities, and minds to serve and perpetuate the idea. The Senator—to say nothing of his wife, whose rôle in the affairs of Wisconsin and in building up the prestige of the La Follette name was second in importance only to his own—doubtless had seen to that in the boys' formative years.

In 1934, Bob and Phil had taken a leading part in an important step of the so-called La Follette Progressives in their state. They broke away from the Republican Party, within which Old Bob had so shrewdly developed his policies and program, and formed a third party, which obviously was meant to be a possible nucleus of an eventual national third party, for its preliminary platform was national in scope, containing planks in favor of government manufacture and sale of arms and munitions, public ownership of utilities, national control of the country's banking business, a job for everyone able to work, financial and old-age security through state and national legislation creating unemployment insurance, sickness and accident insurance, legislation guaranteeing workers the right to organize as they choose, a tax on corporate dividends, immediate payment of the soldiers' bonus, adequate legislation to secure the tenure of land for those who own it through moratorium laws, abolition of

speculation and profiteering in food, and establishment of coöperative market-
ing to reduce the spread between prices received by the farmers and those paid
by the consumers, and a reaffirmation of faith in the democratic form of
government and the right of free speech. There were also planks against the
sales tax, the exemption of securities and governmental salaries from taxation,
and the destruction of goods and wealth while the people were in need.

This was not a strictly La Follette platform, for Bob and Phil are no
"bosses." It was an expression of the politico-social sentiment of various progressive elements, led by such other men as Congressman Thomas R. Amlie,
who was probably a good deal to the left of Bob and Phil, and possibly as
important a factor in the crystallization of the movement to break away from
the "party of wealth and talent" as were "the boys."

In the fall 1934, which was a period of deep confusion involving the Republicans, the conservative Democrats, the New Deal, and the split motives of the
Roosevelt Administration, the new Progressive Party experienced the great victory of reëlecting Bob to the Senate and Phil to the governorship and returning
or newly sending several Progressives, including Amlie, to the House of Representatives; and so, when I came to Madison a few months later, I found all
sorts of Progressives ready, even eager, to talk about the future of their party
and Idea. The following is a composite and, for brevity's sake, much simplified
report of the various ideas, guesses, hopes, fears, and misgivings that were
expressed to me:

"Progressivism, we believe, has a big future in this country. The idea of
progress is a powerful factor in the American mind. Progress is a good American word. It is our national middle name. It has more vital meaning in the
United States than anywhere else in the world. Progress, change; the two go
together and are instinctively recognized by Americans. They used to fire
American imagination in the past. They are part of our tradition. They will fire
American imagination again. If we are wrong in this, it is just too bad—not
only for us, but for the country.

"Our program, our ideology? We refer you to our platform. Our political
method? Democracy. Opportunism along the lines of the Wisconsin Idea. We'll
try to take the masses just as far as we feel fairly sure they'll be willing to go
from time to time. If our socio-economic order continues for any length of
time in its present state, the people will soon be willing to go a long way
toward a new social order to be built on the American pattern, which is a matter of our past and our present; or toward a considerable revision of the old
order. We are realists. We believe in practical politics. In action. The Wisconsin
Idea always led to action. Democracy is dynamic, active; it must be, or it is not
democracy. In our thinking and our tactics, we consider the people, their mentality, the fact they are Americans, which means they are great optimists and
inclined to consider and deal with their problems only from moment to
moment, as they arise and develop, and not before. We don't think much of
Al Smith since 1928, but back in 1931 he said something which is very true:

'The American people never carry an umbrella. They prepare to walk in eternal sunshine.' That is how we are. That is the American way, whether it is good or bad is immaterial. It is our way; we are Americans. It was the way of Jefferson, Lincoln, and Old Bob.

"But there is also this—the American mind is being stirred today as it has never been stirred before. The people's social and economic conditions are critical and growing worse in many sections. There is no 'sunshine'; the people are thinking of picking up an 'umbrella' somewhere, somehow. Their personal problems are becoming more acute daily. They are being forced to think, to seek an explanation for their plight. They are hearing all sorts of explanations. They listen to Franklin Roosevelt and Father Coughlin. There is Huey Long [who was still alive then and going strong]. There was EPIC. There was Technocracy. There is Townsend with his plan. There is Utopia, Inc. There are the Socialists and Communists and the radical writers and lecturers. There will be other persons and movements, many of them pretty crazy, unlinked to the American past, not geared to our current material and psychological realities, and most of them have no future by themselves. They pop up and go. Some leave no trace. Others do. They become—they will become—factors in the awakening of the American mind, in the intensification of the American wrath, if this Depression continues or becomes worse, or if sometime soon a new depression follows the recovery from the present one, which is likely. When the time comes for progressive political action, the people will have become disillusioned with the crackpots and will be ready for us, for our Idea. And we hope to be ready for them. We have the real thing. Of course everybody else thinks the same of their plan but we can prove the efficacy of ours. The Wisconsin Idea has been tried. It is pretty well in effect here in Wisconsin. It is the logical continuation of the best basic American traditions.

"No, we have no immediate national plans. Ideologically and programmatically we are closest to the Farmer-Labor Party of Minnesota. There are groups in other states which can become the core of a new political state organization. They will be useful. For the time being, we probably shall not participate in any immediate effort to start a third party upon a country-wide basis. It is too early for that. We can't be sure there will ever be a third party. But if a new national party does arise, the chances are nine to one it will be ours. The vitality of the word 'Progressive' and the magic of the La Follette name are important.

"Significant things are happening the country over. The New Deal is crazy in many respects, and scandalously uneconomic and erratic, and irresponsibly experimental. It does not follow things through. It is sound"—with a smile—"only (or, let us say, mostly) in so far as it has borrowed from the Wisconsin Idea: and it has borrowed heavily. . . . But for the first time in the history of America the federal government is supporting millions of citizens. The government is engaging in vast public-works projects. It can't possibly stop. The old order has cracked. The South is being loosened up and wakened by the advent of cheap power and other forces. The solidness of the South may not last much beyond 1936, and the political changes there are extremely likely to be in our favor.

"We figure that within the next few years organized labor will succeed in freeing itself from the strangle-hold of its present corrupt and intellectually bankrupt bureaucracy. That, too, will be in our favor, as it already is here in Wisconsin, where we have the higher type of labor leader.

"Nationally, we support what good we think there is in the New Deal. We believe that Roosevelt will be reëlected. He wants to be, and it seems that nothing short of death can stop him. The probability, indeed, is that he will get a tremendous majority; he is an immensely clever man, and not a bad man. We know we haven't a chance in 1936, except in Wisconsin. We'll support Roosevelt for the Presidency. His victory will possibly be not only with a huge majority, but an elemental landslide, which will bury a good part of what is still left of the Republican Party. It is quite possible that in 1937 there will be eighty-five[1] Democrats in the United States Senate. In short, the Republican Party will practically cease to exist. The Democratic majority will be so great that it will be unwieldy and embarrassing. Roosevelt will go farther and farther to the right. Inevitably so. Since he is not really against the fundamental reason for the way things are, things will drive him that way.

"In consequence, his prestige will have diminished by 1940. Then—God knows. Five years is too far ahead in this country nowadays for any close figuring as to what will happen. All that we addicted to the Wisconsin Idea can do is to be around when, or if, the political realignment begins, and be ready to serve as a nucleus for progressives now in the old parties. We may conceivably have a chance in 1940. Possibly in 1944. Or ——"

At this point, talking with a prominent La Follette Progressive, I mentioned Charles A. Beard's powerful article on "National Politics and War," which had just then appeared in *Scribner's* (February, 1935), and in which he hinted that such developments as outlined above up to about 1939 are very probable, but argued that by 1940 Roosevelt, faced by terrible domestic problems and a split in his own party, torn by conflicting emotions and unable to develop a "strong" domestic policy, might adopt a "strong" foreign policy, and thus cause the country to "stumble" into war, beyond which "lies the Shadowy Shape of Things to Come."

"Of course," said this La Follette Progressive with an uneasy smile, "much is liable to happen between now and 1940 that will play the very devil with our expectations. A new war *is* possible, even probable."

A non-Progressive political observer, with whom I talked, stressed the La Follettes' opportunism. "They are progressives, all right; in fact, too much so for my taste; but I think they are not married to the label 'Progressive.' They can never become Republicans again, but, should the organization of the Progressive Party on a national basis prove to be too problematical a matter (which

[1] This guess, made by one of Phil LaFollette's close friends, missed by nine.

is likely), they might easily become Democrats and become a part, possibly the leaders, of the left-wing element in the Democratic Party. They are ambitious, you know, especially Phil, which is not saying anything against him or them; part of their ambition is to extend the Wisconsin Idea to the nation. . . ."

A TALK WITH PHIL

As already suggested, when I visited him, Phil had been but a few weeks in office in his second term as governor of Wisconsin, and he was confronted by a difficult immediate situation. There were, of course, the pressing problems of unemployment, taxation, and security for the farmer. There was the old question of public utilities. There was the immediate necessity of doing something about the school system, which had been badly crippled by lower appropriations during the conservative Democratic régime. There was the plank in the Progressive Party's platform, on which Phil had been elected, for virtually outlawing company unions in Wisconsin; and "no La Follette ever broke a platform pledge."

Phil, I gathered, had very definite ideas on all these matters and several others coming up for consideration, but the Progressive victory had not included the Legislature—both houses were controlled by conservative anti-La Follette Democrats and Republicans. The senate, in fact, was preponderantly anti-La Follette. And a fight between the young governor and the lawmakers was just around the corner. Phil was at his desk in the Capitol fourteen hours a day, overworked but in a calm, cheerful mood, perhaps rather deliberately so, curbing his energy, ambition, impatience, and fighting proclivities.

Unlike other Progressives in Madison, he was not inclined to discuss 1936, '40, or '44, or anything else as remote and, at the same time, as specific as that. He was, as a matter of fact, not especially eager to talk about anything in particular. "There's been much too much talking in recent years about everything," he said—to quote him perhaps a bit freely.

He continued: "The country's been flooded with words and speeches, ballyhoo and blah, ideas and resolutions, theories and writings of all sorts, which for the most part have not clarified but only confused matters. Most of them have been no more related to the practical, urgent problems we face than is the metaphysical issue of how many spirits can dance on the point of a needle. . . . Understand, I am not an anti-theorist; I am not against ideas. I do my share of theorizing. Theory, of course, is necessary, but theories, discussion, resolutions are empty, futile, provocative of wasteful dissension if they do not soon lead to practical, constructive action. The important, the practical thing about the Wisconsin Idea has been—and still is—that it produced the Progressive movement, which has been—and is—dedicated to action, to doing things for the people, making for progress, not on some distant tomorrow, but now, as soon as humanly possible; or perhaps I should say that the Wisconsin Idea and the Progressive movement developed almost simultaneously, one because of the other. It is no accident that nearly every forward-looking, concrete achievement in American public affairs during the past thirty years has had its origin in action in Wisconsin. . . ."

He said he wished I had been in Madison for the Inauguration. As was their custom, people from all over the state had come—farmers, workers, business and professional men and their wives and children—to shake hands and wish him and Isen, his wife, a happy new year. They had moved through the Executive Mansion all day: simple, solid, good Americans of all racial and national strains that make up the population of Wisconsin. "And I wish," said Phil, "I could leave my desk for a day or two and drive with you through the state, and stop in homes, in farmhouses, whether the people living in them are Progressives or not, and talk with the men and their wives and their sons and daughters while sitting with them in their kitchens, eating a piece of pie and drinking a cup of coffee. . . . When one knows the people of Wisconsin, there is very little need of talking."

But, prodded, he spoke of things in general. Everything depended upon recovery, and the present effort for recovery on the part of the federal government was a race between time and the translation of federal plans into action. Too much delay might even bring on collapse of the national effort for recovery, which might throw back upon states or sectional groups of states the burden of maintaining civilization.

Some time before, John Strachey, the English Communist author and lecturer, had declared in New York that he had interviewed Phil, and that Phil's remarks to him had led him to the conclusion that Phil was a Fascist—a potential American Fascist leader. I mentioned this to Phil and said: "I think that not a few people in New York were disturbed by Strachey's idea of you. What do you say about it?"

Phil smiled. "The trouble with these fellows from abroad is that they come here and look at America with eyes accustomed to pictures in the European pattern. They come to Wisconsin because some one in the East has told them about us here in the Middle West, and they visit me. They inquire about the peasantry in Wisconsin, and I tell them we have in this state a lot of farmers, whom we don't call peasants, and who, I think, *are* different from the peasants in Europe. Well, in what way are they different? I explain that our farmers in Wisconsin own the land, some quite a bit of it, others less; and own pretty good homes and implements and farm machinery, trucks and flivvers, and so on. Whereupon my visitors from afar, experiencing a flash of insight, smile, and I'm told that these farmers are kulaks of course.

"I am made speechless by this; so the next question is about the workers, the class-conscious proletariat. I say that we have some workers in Wisconsin —not many, though—who describe themselves as class-conscious proletarians, in the European sense. The overwhelming majority of them, however, are just workers, citizens, members of unions, but not especially class-conscious or anything like that. In fact, I venture to say, they are not class-conscious at all. Most of them are Progressives. We get along fine. They're fine people. I know hundreds of them. . . . No, I say to my European visitors, most of our workers are not class-conscious in your sense, but like our farmers, who are in danger of losing their land and homes, and our teachers, whose salaries have been reduced, and our small-business and professional people, whose income has dribbled away, they are sharply conscious of the fact that they are being robbed by the operation of the system under which we live; and I add that I see no reason why I should try to make them class-conscious. The idea of classes has no vital tradition in our American past, and in my opinion any effort to make them class-conscious would only confuse them, delay the whole thing, produce endless dissension among many who now have nothing against each other; for we Americans, I insist, *are* different from the Europeans."

"I agree," I said, interrupting him, in order to save him the effort of arguing with me. Phil went on:

"We in the North here skipped feudalism entirely, while Europe still has a terrible psychological hangover from it. For hundreds of years we were the freest people the sun ever shone upon. The frontier has influenced our minds, our manner in personal intercourse, our political methods. We are a democratic people if there ever was one. But there *is*, as I say, this sharp consciousness on the part of multitudes of our people that they are being ruined by the existing economic setup, and I for one believe that to organize this consciousness is basically what we need as a start to bring about changes in our social-economic structure which will be in line with our American experience and tradition.

"I usually say all this to my brilliant visitors from abroad, and they, with their eyes used to gazing upon things and figures in the Old World pattern, swiftly decide that I am a Fascist. Fascism of some sort probably is not impossible in this country, but, if I have any authority to say so, it will not develop out of the Wisconsin Idea and the Progressive movement. . . ."

A pause.

"Of course," Phil continued, "we are not Socialists. We Progressives don't agree with certain things in the Socialist program at all. But that, I maintain, does not make us Fascists, if by Fascist one means something akin to what they have in Italy or Germany. The Socialists want collective ownership of all the means of production and distribution. If the idea were carried into action, our farmers (a farm is a 'means of production') would be deprived of the ownership of their farms and homes. They would become employees of the government. . . . We Progressives believe in the right of men and women to own their homes, their farms, and their places of employment. What we believe to be the curse of our present system is the greed of corporate and absentee owners. Our aim is to restore to those who work on the farm and in the city the ownership that has been wrung from them by the exploitation of private monopoly.

"In those great utilities of common necessity which cannot function efficiently except in centralized organizations we recognize the necessity of public ownership. Progressives believe that municipalities and other units of government should be encouraged to own and operate these utilities.

"We recognize the basic law of the margin of diminishing returns in size. Organizations, whether publicly or privately owned and operated, can be so large that their very size works against their efficiency and satisfactory operation.

"There is no alternative to conscious distribution of income. To this end the Socialists and Communists advocate complete nationalization. Reactionaries advocate 'everybody for himself and the devil take the hindmost,' relying solely on the lure of private profit to entice investment in capital enterprises to diffuse the unexpendable income now received by the holders of great fortunes.

"The purely private investment of capital was effective while frontiers still beckoned for development. But it becomes a failure when the great enterprises demanding investment are in the realm of housing, slum-clearance, education, and other phases of life here at home. Purely private capital will invest horizontally, but it will not invest perpendicularly. It will raise the standard of living on frontiers, but not at home.

"Nationalization of all property breaks down with the unmanageable task of administration. It is not theory that fails, but the definite limitation of the capacity of the human brain. We are a vast country, very complicated.

"The purely private investment of capital has failed. That failure has produced untold misery and suffering in this land of abundance. We Progressives hold that the alternative is not nationalization of all property or adherence to private monopoly. It is rather the assumption by government of the distribution of national income; or, in other words, the clear recognition of a new social obligation of property.

"The methods by which that distribution of the national income can be accomplished are not by any means limited to a single measure. There are the income tax, the inheritance tax, public ownership of necessary utilities such as light, heat, power, certain phases of transportation, central banks. But the basic law that Progressives recognize must be obeyed is the limitation of the capacity of human beings to administer units, whether privately or publicly owned, that are too large.

"It is one thing for the government to assume the function of distribution of income to support purchasing power and quite another to assume the administrative responsibility for millions of farms, every corner grocery store, and hundreds of thousands of factories."

How, I asked him, would or could all this change be brought about? He was not ready to particularize. I asked him if he did not think any action in the direction of socialization would straightway collide with the Constitution, or rather with those who consider the federal and state constitutions static instruments designed to perpetuate the existing social order.

In reply, Phil proceeded to give me his views of the Constitution as a factor in the matter, which in the main were a restatement of what he had declared in his brief inaugural address a few weeks before. "The constitutions of this

State and of the United States, which I swore to uphold on taking office, are to me living documents. They embody the principle of American government. To preserve that principle is the supreme duty of our time. It is essential that we recognize the fact that this American principle of popular government, and the constitutions conceived to secure it, were not designed to sustain any particular economic system. The assumption made at one time that under the Constitution we were committed to the perpetuation of Negro slavery was the tragic error which produced the Civil War.

"Our paramount task is to maintain the kind of government which had its birth on this continent, which it took a Revolutionary War to establish, a Civil War to preserve, and a century and a half of day-to-day work on the part of countless men and women to put into operation as a functioning instrument—an instrument for realizing the great human end for which it was designed, the material and spiritual well-being of our people.

"The founders of this country made their intentions clear, 'to establish justice, insure domestic tranquillity, promote the general welfare, and secure the blessings of liberty to ourselves and our posterity.' These, to my mind, are the chief concepts of our fundamental law, and it is our privilege today to give vitality—through action—to these concepts. It is our duty to apply them to the conditions of our time, and so prove loyal, in the truest sense, to our traditions. . . . This is the challenge of our times."

YOUNG BOB

I met Bob in Washington, shortly after visiting Madison. I sat for a couple of hours in his office in the Senate Building, talking. He was in many respects unlike Phil, who had a quick, avid, dramatic, dynamic, almost over-dynamic, personality. Bob was slower, more cautious, less impatient, but, as I had been told by people in Madison who knew both, equally effective in the long run. He was two years older than Phil, but had been seriously ill in his early youth. He graduated from high school and had two years at the University of Wisconsin. Before becoming a Senator he served for six years as Old Bob's secretary, where he had close contact with all manner of people in Washington, including such outstanding men as Justice Brandeis, an old friend of the LaFollette family.

When the old Senator died, Bob was just thirty; he ran and was elected, and has been a Senator ever since, while Phil has stayed in Madison, refusing to take important appointments from the New Deal Administration which might have taken him from the capital of the Wisconsin Idea. Bob and Phil are close personally and politically. They quite naturally start from the same premise and consult each other on matters of major policy, but maintain complete independence of action so far as their separate responsibilities in office are concerned. This close friendship is most fortunate; one's qualities effectively supplement the other's.

Thanks to a combination of circumstances, not the least of which is his own character and inner balance, Bob became during the Depression, while still in his thirties, one of the outstanding men in American politics. As I write, he is forty-two, apparently in excellent health, and with a future—very likely—as promising as his record in the Senate, which so far has been full of sound and courageous presagement.

His record during the Depression shows him to be a statesman. In an article in *Forum* Oswald Garrison Villard summarized it as follows:

In 1928, a year and a half before the crash, he introduced a resolution calling for an investigation of the possibility of collecting and interpreting statistics on unemployment; of the organization and extension of public employment agencies, unemployment insurance, and the planning of a public-works program for the stabilization of employment. He said that fifteen times in the last 110 years there had been serious depressions and the time had come when Congress must act. Had it done so, the government would have been in a splendid position in which to deal with what actually took place. When the crash came, Bob acted at once, opposing the refunding of $160,000,000 of income taxes in December, 1929, on the correct ground that the government would need every cent of it for the relief of the unemployed. A year later he was again declaring: "The relief of human suffering in this emergency should take precedence over the consideration of the interests of the wealthy income tax payers."

By February 10, 1931, he was demanding federal aid for the States and introduced the first bill so to provide. The resultant La Follette-Costigan relief bill was defeated on February 16, 1932, because, incredible as it now seems, it called for federal grants to States of the beggarly sum of $375,000,000. Another bill sponsored by these two men and Senator Wagner called for $500,000,000. This bill became the basis of the federal emergency relief act that passed the Senate May 9, 1933. His public-works record is similarly remarkable; he horrified everybody by introducing a bill on December 22, 1931, to appropriate $5,500,000,000 for a public-works program. An outraged Senate voted it down by 56 to 12. Less than two years later he voted for the national industrial recovery bill, which appropriated $3,300,000,000 for public works and was carried by an overwhelming vote. Side by side with these constructive measures, he has steadfastly insisted that the wealth of the nation must be redistributed to bring about an economic revival and, hereafter, economic safety.

Franklin Roosevelt, when elected President in 1932, had no definite ideas as to what to do about the Depression. His program was one almost solely of good intentions. On taking office, he and the "Brain Trust" hastily took over the LaFollette and generally Progressive program—which is one reason why I am writing in this book more of the LaFollettes than of Roosevelt, though of course I am not uncognizant of the latter's importance as a brilliant political personality, who momentarily overshadows Bob and Phil, the Wisconsin Idea, and the memory of Old Bob.

In 1935 Young Bob made it clear to me that as a Senator he would continue to work toward making the federal government into a definite, permanent, and consistent social apparatus which will not tyrannize over private industry or over the life of any citizen, but act as a watchful stabilizer of the country's socio-economic life by helping to distribute wealth that accumulated in places where it is not socially useful. The country (to repeat what Phil had said to me) was too huge and complex to be administered in every detail from a vast central office in Washington, but the government, said Bob in effect, would have to be in the position to take money where it was not needed, or where it was even socially or humanly detrimental, and put it without delay where a breakdown in economic health threatened. . . . Which, incidentally, perhaps is the gist of the LaFollette political aims of the 1930's. . . .

During 1936-38 Bob—with Senator Elbert D. Thomas of Utah—did superb work conducting the hearings of the subcommittee of the Committee on Education and Labor of the United States Senate, which I have mentioned elsewhere in this volume. He exposed to public view some of the worst sadist-Fascist tendencies in this country, and I feel that every American citizen should read the transcripts of those hearings, which are easily procurable for little money from the United States Printing Office in Washington.

Early in 1938, Bob became a vigorous leader of forces which are against America's becoming involved in "the next world war"—of which more in the final chapter of this volume.

I do not know if Phil and Bob will continue as leaders of the Progressive Party and try to make it into a direct national force, or if they will go Democrat and try to function as influential progressives within the Democratic Party. At this writing it seems to me that the creation of a third party which might have a chance of achieving power in 1940—either under the LaFollette label of "Progressive" or under some such other name as "Commonwealth," suggested by my friend Ross Wills—is out of the question. How this situation might change by 1944 I do not know.

Nor do I know how seriously Phil and Bob are thinking of the Presidency. I merely know of people who are trying to "groom" them for it. As Progressives in the sense defined in this chapter, they are opportunists, which is as dangerous sometimes as it is wise at other times; and it may be that opportunity and history-on-the-make will rap on their door and they will try to convert Progressivism from an influence, which it is now, into a definite force. If they do that, and succeed, they and Progressivism will probably be in all manner of dangers. Progressivism, perhaps, is better, safer, as an influence than a definite force exercising power.

In a sense, Progressivism unquestionably *is* the American way. Its roots *are* in the basic makeup of human America. It is part of the "lift" that I feel occasionally in the freedom and vastness of America. In spite of this, however, Progressivism *is* in danger of becoming mostly a word, among the leaders, especially if they get into power. It is a bit like John Lewis' "industrial democracy," with which I had such difficulties in the chapter entitled "Notes on the Great Task Facing the C.I.O." Phil speaks of "consciousness," but, as I understand him, only of consciousness directed against evil economic conditions. He wants to organize it, use it. For what? Economic security. Neither Phil nor Bob, so far as I am aware, go beyond that, are concerned about the human conditions which go deeper than economics. They are interested in the University of Wisconsin, which has many good features, and in schools generally; but I doubt if they are concerned, even privately, or as a matter of their minds' background, about education which, if democracy is to have security and be something positive, must go on all the time, in and out of school.

Of course the Wisconsin Idea is more or less successful in Wisconsin. It has really got into a lot of people there, but not all. Perhaps only into those who naturally have vision. How about those who lack it? How would it work nationally? The country *is* democratic, but none too positively so. As it is, democracy works, for the most part negatively: against these conditions and against that bunch of grafters, and so on. The Progressive movement in Wisconsin, as it was revealed to me, is mostly negative in its immediate program. Its opportunism is a matter of waiting. It will step in when the country is so sick of existing conditions that it will accept almost anything. The emphasis is on a negative basis. The American people will take to Progressivism not because they see it as the best way, but because at the moment they see in it a promise of possible immediate solution of something or other, just as they saw it in the smiling personality of Franklin Roosevelt. They would also accept it with the same enthusiasm; then—what? . . .

The Wisconsin Idea is good as a beginning, also as a basis for future developments, and, to repeat, I am for it; but an idea must grow, develop, change, or by-and-by it becomes static, merely defensive. Old Bob created the Wisconsin Idea; Young Bob and Phil have guarded it and kept it alive, which is a lot, but not enough. They have not noticeably added to it. . . . From our leaders we must demand almost the impossible.

Jack Raper: Cleveland's Wasp of Virtue

DURING THE PERIOD COVERED IN THIS BOOK, AND PARTICULARLY SINCE 1934, I FREquently visited Ohio. It is one of my favorite states. Much of such steadiness of feeling as I possess about America is linked to Ohio—to people I know there, but especially to two men, both journalists: my friends John W. ("Jack") Raper of the Cleveland *Press* and Walter Locke of the Dayton *Daily News*.

Their stories are a pleasure to write. In this chapter, I want to tell Raper's; in the following one, Locke's.

Jack Raper is of old Virginia stock that came to Ohio about the year 1800. He was born at McArthur, in Vinton County, a town he describes as "pure hick." His father was a country newspaper man, and Jack became a reporter when he was still in his 'teens. As a youth he worked briefly on numerous papers in Ohio and also in Chicago, Buffalo, and Albany.

Back in the mid-'90's, between newspaper jobs, Raper—then about twentyfive—worked for the famous minstrel and monologist, Lew Dockstader, whose buffoonery, old-timers will recall, was punctuated by shrewd observations and comments on current local, national, and world events, trends, and personalities. Officially Jack was the great vaudevillian's "press representative," but he also wrote or suggested many of his most popular songs and monologues, and was responsible for some of his sharpest and funniest "wise cracks." Indeed, Dockstader used Jack's stuff to the end of his career.

When he got married, Jack gave up this job; it required him to travel too much and lead too hectic a life; and late in the '90's he became a reporter on the Cleveland *Press*, a Scripps paper. He was (still is) an excellent and ardent newsman, and his stories were well-written: terse, clear, and brief. His interviews with stuffed shirts and bunk-shooters, like his reports of their speeches, were sharp with wasp-like stings. He wrote as he talked; his work with Dockstader had taught him to time and place his stings so they were most effective.

He was naturally independent. The Scripps organization encouraged him to be so.

Having been connected with the theater while on Dockstader's staff, Jack became, in addition to his reportorial duties, the *Press's* dramatic critic. Once his sole comment upon a performance of *Resurrection*, with Eugenie Blair in the leading rôle, was "Burn a rag." This crack enraged the producer and the star, closed the show, and then went, among guffaws, throughout the show world, where the phrase is to this day used as a comment on stenchy performances. This sort of criticism caused the organized local theater managers to boycott the *Press*, which lost over a hundred thousand dollars a year for two years in theatrical advertising. But Jack Raper kept his job—thanks mainly to the fact that old man Scripps was interested less in immediate profits than in developing newspapers which would be increasingly appreciated for their honesty, independence, and courage; however, in great part also to his respect for Jack's competence and integrity, sense of rightness, balance, and justice and his general character, which included a subtle charm, compelled respect and inspired confidence in the idea (inherent in his daily work and conduct) that his method would prove wise and productive in the long run.

Jack is a small, wiry, extremely lean fellow, alert and agile, with a wasp waist even at sixty-eight, which is his age as I write this; and it is a commonplace that, by way of compensation, physically slight men often develop the knack of defending themselves and of attacking with fiery tongue and barbed word. This, in all probability, is at least a part of the explanation of Jack's mental and verbal waspishness.

But waspishness is by no means his central characteristic. His other, more important, qualities are not so easily defined and explained. He has a fierce attachment to the principles and the practice of truth, honesty, liberty, democracy, fair play, common sense, and common human decency, which he considers civilized man's highest and basic virtues. This attachment to these virtues comes, no doubt, from his background in Virginia and the Ohio frontier; from the old, the basic, the essential America, now often obscured, here and there, by buncombe, hypocrisy, and attempts at violations of personal and civil liberties, which set Jack off into a finely controlled and well-directed fury, as do abuse of power by those in high positions, stupidity, and cowardice on the part of those who occupy positions which demand of them that they should be wise and courageous, and he holds up to the public eye all manifestations of pomp, bombast, chicanery, charlatanry, and demagoguery, whenever he spots them.

One of his colleagues on the *Press*—Elrick Davis, book critic—calls him the Wasp of Virtue, which is as apt a short characterization of Jack as one could wish for. But one must hasten to add that there is in him no trace of righteousness, no suggestion of any sort of holier-than-thou attitude, nor the least touch of puritanism or vindictiveness. He has little, if any, interest in small virtues, in what is generally known as morality. He never manifests the least impatience with the stupid, the poor of spirit, the "lowly mean," the common thieves, the plain murderers, pimps, prostitutes, highjackers, and gangsters, all of whom he considers not one-thousandth as dangerous and offensive as the cunning, dishonest, big-shot politicians or the church-going "banksters" who, behind their respectable fronts, are really thieves and corruptionists.

One day in the summer of 1900, Editor Rickey of the *Press*, an old-time Scripps man, said to Raper, "Say, Jack," or words to this effect, "why don't you write down some of these things you're saying around here—these comments on things—and let's put them in a column. Make it a daily trick if you can. Just as you talk. . . . What should you call it? I don't know; call it 'most anything."

Jack started the column and called it "Most Anything." He was thirty then. It is still "Most Anything"—one of the first columns in the country, now in its thirty-eighth year. He has been running it all this time, writing it himself, six days a week, never missing a day, except for his annual vacation periods and for another two months in 1906, when he made a one-man investigation of the state prison in Columbus and wrote an *exposé* of its evils which led to drastic state-wide penal reforms.

He is the dean of American columnists, but practically unknown outside of Ohio. The *Who's Who in America* is oblivious of him. He has never sought national recognition, and is more than content to function only locally.

In 1907 Burr Gongwer, one of Cleveland's political bosses, made a public statement which was pure "bull"—ideal meat for Jack. He copied the juiciest part of it for his column: what could he say about it? He asked the staff artist to draw him a bull in silhouette, which he then printed alongside the quotation, and made no verbal comment at all. The bull was an immediate hit, Gongwer himself "got a kick out of it," and Jack has been using him ever since, with pungent and steady effectiveness. During political campaigns he uses him daily. On some days the column is a veritable bullpen. And in the course of decades the bull has entered the service of numerous other columnists, scattered through the country, most of whom have written to Jack for his permission to use him— although the beast, of course, is not copyrighted.

"Most Anything" is not at all what the present generation of New Yorkers, for instance, brought up on *The New Yorker*, would call "clever" or "brilliant" or "subtle." It is simple, direct, and shrewd, a bit old-fashioned and not at all profound, its humor closer to Artemus Ward and Josh Billings than to Frank Sullivan, Walter Winchell, and Robert Benchley. It is made up mostly of little squibs of between two and ten lines—many of which are purely local (Cleveland and Ohio), so that the average transient who happens to pick up the *Press* in his hotel lobby or at the depot, and casually glances at the column, finds much of it meaningless or a little flat. A brief item such as this—

Assistant Safety Director John R. Flynn, says Director Ness, was ill advised when he appointed Frank J. Cadek, Jr., a rookie policeman. But not any more ill advised than the official who appointed John R. Flynn assistant safety director.

has scant significance for a stranger, but is of immediate interest to Clevelanders; while something like this—

A Democratic candidate for Attorney-General of Ohio is going around the state telling voters that Martin Davey has saved the taxpayers $30,000,000 a year. When? In the years he wasn't governor?

gets chuckles which are not pure mirth all over town, as does this—

Fifty persons turned out in the 12th Ward Thursday night to hear Councilman Herman Finkle. It beats all what a grip that man has on the people.

Jack's most important paragraphs concern politics, the police, the judiciary, the banking fraternity, the big-shots generally who thrive on sham, cover, and corruption, and the organizations and institutions which they control and use for reactionary purposes; and logically enough "Most Anything" is the first thing that many of the so-called important people in Cleveland turn to at eleven A.M., when the first edition of the paper comes out. Each laughs at the cuts Jack takes at the others, but he is constantly and uneasily aware of the possibility of his being himself the next victim of Jack's devastating comment. Each enjoys Jack's quotations from his rivals' or colleagues' speeches, decorated with the bull, but shudders at the thought that next week the bull may be the comment on something he himself will have said or done; for in the last three decades many a figure has departed from Cleveland's and Ohio's political, business, and religious life, his public flesh punctured by Jack's stings and his ears filled with the roar of Jack's bull, and this roar all but drowned out by the laughter of tens of thousands of people.

And if Jack is somewhat of a wasp, he is also a bit of an elephant. He never forgets—and makes sure that the public's memory remains as good as his own. When, through the passage of time, the town would forget its injuries or the state, the asininities of its officials, he returns to them, taking good care that he does not become a bore. Two or three lines a week for a month are enough to revitalize the people's memory of some scandal that happened two months ago and has not lost its current significance. After that two or three lines every four or six months are sufficient to keep the matter alive. Of course these reminders are worded differently each time and are used only when the subject is again immediately pertinent.

Back in the 1900's, or even more recently, when "Most Anything" was still a young column and its author not as firmly established in the minds and hearts of the people of Cleveland as I shall show he is now, frequent and desperate efforts were made by powerful groups and individuals to get Jack off the *Press* and out of Cleveland and Ohio. But, as already suggested, the Scripps policy of honesty and independence in journalism protected him.

"Most Anything" was a popular column from the start. Its popularity gradually increased. At first it was read because it was something new in Cleveland, then it naturally "grew" on the readers. Jack went in for homespun wisdom (which at once appeals to him and amuses him), and he invented an old rustic named "Josh Wise" and put his picture on top of the column alongside some such saws or commonplaces as these:

Th' average man has t' steal his hours uv pleasure either from his work er his sleep.

Th' man th't can afford t' pay his fare is th' one th't has the least trouble getting a pass.

You never hear a woman braggin' th't she's self-made.

A man c'n make a lot o' fatal mistakes an' still live.

I oncet knowed a man th't didn't pay any attention t' th' complimentary things th't wuz said about him. He wuz deaf.

A mother with a sunny disposition tans no children.

Many a man reaches his second childhood without havin' enjoyed his first.

Th' snow on our own sidewalk never seems t' be much uv a nuisance.

Some men are so unlucky th't if they sat down on a haystack they would find a needle.

Jack Raper is essentially a small-town fellow, a shrewd, cracker-barrel philosopher, and has always kept his feet close to the grass roots, which explains much of his popularity and lastingness. On every Monday, for over twenty years now, he has been running a feature in his column called "All the News from Hicksville." Using the place names of his boyhood, he burlesques a rural correspondent's notes in a country newspaper. Yet burlesque is not quite the word. He takes stings at the follies, the pretensions, the fake urbanism of small towns. But he is also kindly and tolerant. Through the feature runs a sort of sophisticated naïveté. It reads as simple as it is shrewd and accurate. And Cleveland, like the rural areas around it, loves it. Most of the city's citizens of Anglo-Saxon origin still have small-town backgrounds, while many of the immigrants and their American-born children find the American small town extremely amusing.

But the column itself is not half of Jack Raper's function in Cleveland.

With "Most Anything" increasingly successful, Jack Raper became in great demand as a speaker. In 1914 he probably made fifty talks, long and short; while since 1920 he has been averaging between two and three hundred a year, often speaking twice, three times a day. And this before all sorts of audiences, ranging from a dozen to several thousand: old-stock Americans, immigrants, and second-generation folk; women's, service, luncheon, and dinner clubs, labor unions, fraternal societies, teachers' conventions, parent-and-teachers' conferences, and gatherings of high-school students. Preferring to talk to the latter, he never charges them anything, while for well-to-do clubs his fees are all the traffic can bear—and then he often tells them things they would rather not hear.

He is at his best before audiences of high-school students. Although now four times the average high-school age, he becomes one of them; seems to understand them better than anyone else, and they him. He talks to them as his equals upon any of several subjects: the newspaper game as he knows it, the Constitution, the city government, the general mess of things, and themselves and their future in this "cockeyed world"—and he is usually a little funny and mildly cynical. He never preaches; only urges them by indirect suggestion to think for themselves and to question everything, including what their teachers tell them, but especially the motives of people in high places and of those "on the make." He is a born teacher, and the young enjoy him. Sometimes their meetings with him last two, three hours. They ply him with questions, which he answers if he can; if he cannot, unlike most adults, he says he does not know, which but enhances their regard for him. In the last twenty years or so he has talked to hundreds of thousands of students who are now in their thirties or late twenties: citizens of Cleveland, devoted readers of "Most Anything," but not agreeing with him or with everything he writes—which he does not want them to, anyhow.

As he walks in downtown Cleveland, it is "Hello, Jack! How are you, you old ——?" or "Good morning, Mr. Raper!" every half a block or so. He doesn't know the names of many of these greeters. Sometimes it takes him a half-hour to walk two or three blocks; people stop to talk with him. Not infrequently, as he stands on the curb to cross the street at the change of lights, some one touches his sleeve and says, "You don't know me, Mr. Raper, but while going to Lincoln High I was a member of the Journalism class, and one afternoon—in 1921 I guess it was—you came and spoke to us. Of course you probably don't remember." Youngsters come to his office in the *Press* building, or telephone to him and say, "Mr. Raper, you talked to the Lakewood High current-events group when my oldest brother, Bill Cramer—of course, you don't remember him—was president of it, in 1930. Now I am on the program committee, Mr. Raper, and we would like to have you come and speak to us next Wednesday at two-thirty." Jack looks at his calendar, which is always full of engagements for weeks ahead, and says, "Wednesday, two-thirty—O.K.; but I may be a few minutes late, because I'm talking to a luncheon bunch here downtown"—making a dour face—"and may not be able to get away in time."

Jack is somewhat of an actor in the Lew Dockstader tradition, a bit of a clown; and frequently, appearing before groups of high-school students, he burlesques some inflated old judge, cheap politician, or business Babbitt, and speaks to them solemnly, emptily, platitudinously on the subject "Youth—the Hope of the Future," which the kids receive with gales of laughter—as they do the speech of the solemn, empty, platitudinous, inflated old judge, cheap politician, or business Babbitt, whoever he may be, when he actually comes to address them a month or two later. Jack is a sly old dog. After the judge's, politician's or Babbitt's speech, youngsters come to his office and he and they have a grand time talking about it.

Whenever in Cleveland, I drop in at the *Press* office, where I know a few other members of the staff, and nearly every time the bench outside Jack's office is full of youngsters seeking advice on all manner of problems, while he talks with one of them inside. If I want to say hello to him, I must wait—the kids were there before me and they come first, anyhow. He has all the time in the world for them. In his column he is tough, bitter, perfectly ruthless, cynical in his attitude toward the adults, a wasp, a human porcupine; with children or very young persons he is all gentleness. He listens sympathetically to their troubles and not only advises them, but often spends time, energy, and money to solve their problems. Many tell him things they would not tell their parents. . . . There is a theory in the *Press* office that the youngsters keep him young in his late sixties; also that, through contact with them, he—a born

and incorrigible idealist—momentarily gets over the peeve of his disillusionment which became part of his make-up early in his life as he watched the
essentials of civilization in America being kicked around by vulgarity, sham,
speed, greed, coercion, brutal force, and corruption.

At any rate, he knows, or has known, intimately thousands of youngsters.
They are his friends and many remain his friends after they get jobs and marry
and beget children and join clubs. They read his column and often call him
up and "give him hell" or bits of information about the secret exploits of this
or that political or business crook or faker, with whom they come in contact.
During election campaigns he is swamped with information concerning methods used in various great mills and offices to force employees to vote for
reactionary candidates, and he publishes it.

In the course of three and a half decades, Jack has created for himself a great
following that is at once intensely personal and more than personal. It is
held together by mutual attachment to the principles of which he is the high
priest in the great community. He and his friends and constant readers, whose
total is perhaps a quarter of a million, and half of whom, perhaps, are so-
called "foreigners" with such names as Ambrozich, Sczymanski or Hatjas,
form the bulwark of democracy and traditional Americanism in the north-
eastern corner of Ohio. Together they carry on the tradition of Jack's late
great friend Tom Johnson, and are generally responsible for the fact that
Cleveland usually votes overwhelmingly progressive or liberal—even when
the liberal or progressive candidate (as was the case with the elder La Follette,
in 1924) has no chance of winning. They are to be largely credited, too, for the
fact that Cleveland's own government is—in spite (or I should say *because*) of
Jack's constant columnar bellyaching—far from being the worst in the United
States.

Jack is somewhat of a political perfectionist. There is but one living politician
in Cleveland—in fact, in the whole of Ohio—of whom he fully approves. He
is Robert Crosser who, like Jack, is not known to the country at large and
lacks all desire for fame, but has been an extremely able independent-Demo-
cratic member of Congress now for twenty-odd years, representing the Twenty-
first Ohio district, which is a section of Cleveland inhabited largely by Polish,
Slovak, Hungarian, Bohemian, and Lithuanian families, who always reëlect
him. Bob Crosser hates ordinary political publicity and buncombe, has no
campaign fund, no support from the Democratic machine, no machine of his
own, no campaign manager, and makes no regular campaign speeches, but
delivers, instead, an occasional brief talk in some Polish or Slovak hall on
liberty, democracy, social justice, progress, and other such essentials of what
he calls Americanism, and gives a party for his Hunky supporters in his
house, where—personally a dry, but politically a wet—he serves coffee and
doughnuts! He is Jack's best friend in Cleveland, and Jack supports him in
"Most Anything" and takes the stump for him every time he runs. Between

the two of them, they probably keep electioneering on the highest plane of anyone in America.

Jack often opposes candidates' the *Press* supports.

Jack Raper is an old member of the City Club of Cleveland, one of the most important and interesting organizations of its kind in America. It has a membership of some sixteen hundred, mostly business and professional men, and every Saturday after lunch they have a forum, usually with some well-known speaker, whose talk, as well as the ensuing discussion, is broadcast locally. The club's avowed objective is the free exchange of thought and the expression of views and opinions upon any question. But most of the members are conservative.

Soon after he joined, Jack became a sort of center of a group of liberal- and progressive-minded members whose interest was in the various things relating to government; and, lunching there daily, they usually gathered around a table seating ten or twelve. One day, just after the war, a club member who was a florist sent bunches of flowers to the dining-room, among them a bunch of red roses to the table wontedly occupied by Jack's bunch. When the group was seated, some one jokingly exclaimed, "At last your true colors! This is the Soviet Table!" None of them, including Jack, knew then exactly what a Soviet was, but they knew they had been called a terribly bad name, and that pleased them. Like a lot of bad boys, they stuck it onto themselves and, now numbering several hundred, are known as The Soviet Table to this day. They have a huge main table for twenty or more in the center of which are their two insignias—the hammer-and-sickle and the bull Jack has made famous. Around the main Soviet Table are smaller Soviet tables. And that the club is, as I say, an important and interesting organization is due in large part to this Soviet Table, which includes all species of socio-political thinkers and would-be thinkers, an assortment of crackpots, and a few more or less good-humored conservatives and reactionaries, who have "sneaked in," so the theory goes, "to bore from within"; which is instrumental in bringing to Cleveland every third or fourth Saturday some liberal, progressive, or radical speaker, who is then heard all over Cleveland and for about two hundred miles around; which is the watch-dog, the consciousness, of the city; and which, in 1924, became the brains and soul of a temporary political machine that carried Cleveland for La Follette.

There are people in Cleveland to whom Jack is a "Red," a "Bolshevik," but to Jack the bull, which is of iron, is a truer emblem of the Soviet Table than the hammer-and-sickle. He lunches there daily and talks and listens and picks up many an item for "Most Anything," which he writes after lunch.

Once a year or so the iron bull is moved from the Soviet Table to the speakers' table and Jack delivers a long address before the entire membership and their guests and over the radio, to which perhaps a half million people listen—even if it takes, as it usually does, two hours. This annual speech is

a stinging review and criticism, from the Soviet Table's viewpoint, of the
political, social, and economic situation in Cleveland, with glimpses of the
rest of Ohio and the United States. He spends weeks preparing himself for
this feat, but his delivery makes it seem an impromptu oration.

In 1935 his title was "The Soviet Table, or, The Rise of Civilization in
Cleveland," and his address seemed to be a résumé of the recent history of
the Table and a reply to some of the attacks upon it, but actually it was a
fierce onslaught, interspersed with sharp, double-edged phrases and funny
"wise-cracks," upon the politico-economic bosses of the town, especially on
two local financiers (since dead), brothers and bachelors, who, while well
known for their pure and exemplary personal lives, often employed questionable methods and were mainly to blame for Cleveland's acute bank crisis in
1933. When he came to them, he said, "You may remember that Pete Witt"—
another prominent member of the Soviet Table—"once presented to the city
a certain politician as an unkissed icicle. May I now present to you the two unkissed cherubs? There they sit in the Tower, the wonderful Tower reaching
up into the clouds—the highest thing in Cleveland, except the pile of defaulted
bonds they built; that wonderful tower in whose top there burns a powerful
light, its bright rays going far across the boundaries of the city, far out into
the country. There in the Tower top it burns, night after night, in memory
of the unknown bondholder. And there they sit, the unkissed cherubs, symbols
of the sublimity of virginity in masculinity. Pure in their private lives. But
it can hardly be said that in their financial relations with the public they
practiced continence."

Sitting at the big Soviet Table or in his cubbyhole office, Jack knows
everything that happens—some things before they happen: and, foreseeing
them, he occasionally prevents the worst of them from happening . . . and
then, as likely as not, tells no one anything about it for years afterward,
if ever. One day he was recounting to me in detail Cleveland's great bank
crisis of 1933 and, to bring out a point, hesitantly mentioned something he
had done in connection with it. Sensing one of his secrets, I pumped him and
learned that when the crisis hit the city he had feared the governor would
appoint as conservators certain local politicians who hovered over the scene
like vultures, getting ready to steal such of the banks' resources that had as
yet not evaporated: and that, in his fear, he had jumped on a train for Washington one Saturday afternoon, looked up a member of the new "Brain
Trust" who happened to know him and his position in Cleveland, and spent
most of Sunday with Secretary of Treasury Woodin, who as a result of their
talk then applied pressure on the Ohio governor to appoint as conservators
two outside banking experts, whose financial abilities and disregard of local
political and business reputation were mainly responsible for the fact that the
depositors have since recovered from the wreckage around eighty per cent
of their money. He told me that the said Brain-Truster, Mrs. Raper, and I
were the only people who knew this, and made me promise to keep it to my-

self. Later he gave me leave to mention the incident in this book, but only after I had threatened to break my promise if he would not release me from it.

The man has an acute sense of responsibility to his community and is profoundly—almost morbidly—modest. He appears not to want credit for anything he does. When I told him I would write him up, he looked confused and was reluctant to coöperate. "I know the value of publicity," he said, his face engulfed in a grimace, "but—oh, hell!" I had to enlist the aid of my other friends on the *Press* to get him to talk to me for the purpose of this chapter.

In one of our conversations I hinted that I thought he exercised considerable, if indirect, influence on the *Press* as a whole, its editorial policy and its reporting; but Jack shook his head and began to list for me the personal and journalistic virtues of Louis Seltzer, who, although still in his thirties, had then been editor of the paper for several years, and who never interfered with "Most Anything" and almost never showed him the letters that reactionaries occasionally wrote to the paper, deploring Jack's potent bull and his generally "unconstructive" criticism. There can be no doubt, however, that Jack has a great deal to do, if only indirectly, with the *Press's* being perhaps the most liberal, independent, and interesting of the Scripps-Howard newspapers, and that its staff includes a number of excellent journalists who are also grand fellows and are proud to work on it. Jack will probably squirm when he reads this, but I think that in a sense he is the living embodiment in Cleveland of the old Scripps tradition of journalistic independence and courage.

Jack's cynicism, to which I have referred, is a surface characteristic, the defense mechanism of an active idealist who was kicked in the face by all manner of evils, which were at least temporarily stronger than he was. The usual expression on his lean face, which is beginning to resemble an apple that has lasted till February, verges on disgust. He seems to have a perpetual pain in the neck. Deep inside him, however, Jack is not a cynic, but a hopeful, happy man, for, as I have tried to suggest, he functions rather marvelously, and—beneath his modesty—he knows it.

I want to repeat that he has made himself an integral—in tens of thousands of cases, the soundest—part of the lives of a majority of people in and around Cleveland. In a most vital sense, he is a source and the core of the great city's well-known political health. Jack is no genius; indeed, basically he is a rather ordinary human being—but, simply by functioning long, energetically, and consistently on the same spot as one who is firmly committed to the principles of Americans and common decency, he has had no little to do also with the fact that in all-around culture Cleveland is superior to other big American cities, including many which greatly surpass it in size and wealth.

Personally, I go to Cleveland as often as I can. I find it a charming and exciting town. The people are friendly, hospitable, direct, but also critical and discriminating. If you lecture there, after the talk you are apt to be asked more searching questions than in most other towns. If you are a writer and get "fan" letters, the best, the most critical and intelligent, are liable to come to you—thanks at least in part to Jack—from Cleveland and its vicinity.

Since the break of the century, in his simple and honest way, Jack has been working for genuine democracy, common sense, scepticism, mental and spiritual avidity, consciousness of America's basic discords and their attendant evils (though he probably would not put it that way), and a progressive political mood and urge; and thus has become as much an institution in Cleveland as is the Public Square or the Tom Johnson monument. All this time he has not been a power in Cleveland, but something much more—an influence. He is probably the most successful citizen of Cleveland. He has made himself a part of the city's democratic, progressive psychology and atmosphere, which he has helped to create.

Jack Raper's story holds, I think, a powerful suggestion.

For decades now, young newspapermen, especially those of more than average talent and general competence, have been giving up their jobs on papers in cities and towns west of the Hudson, which were "not big enough" for them, or "too dead," and have been coming to New York in droves. Some found work on the big Manhattan dailies, and some are now well-known editors, editorial and special writers, foreign or Washington correspondents, and sport, gossip, book, drama, and political columnists. A few, very few, developed into more or less serious, more or less successful free-lance writers of non-fiction books, novels, and magazine articles and stories; several into well-paid staff writers on mass-circulation periodicals; some into "Communists" and red journalists—their redness splotched with yellow; and some into assorted intellectuals, a more accurate label for whom would be "ineffectuals." A few became editors of "slick" and "pulp" magazines; many general hacks and ghost writers. Thousands took (if not immediately, then in the course of time) to publicity, public relations, radio, and advertising. Of other thousands there is no trace in any of the writing professions, and nobody cares a hoot what became of them.

The majority have, in the main, failed to realize the dreams, urges, and ambitions which had propelled them to New York. In one way or another the big town "got" them—no need of telling the gruesome details. On top of the journalistic ladder there was room for but a few Walter Lippmanns, Westbrook Peglers, Heywood Brouns, F. P. A.'s, Damon Runyons, and Odd McIntyres. The Floyd Dells, who seemed even for a while to be doing something worth while as novelists, were rare; and in most cases their fame, function, and following were spread so wide and thin over the vast continent and through the racing years that the impression they made was at best very slight. The work of many of them was doomed from the start not to outlive their persons.

The amount of talent that New York, with its lures, which are inherent in its size and power, magnetized to itself during the first third of this century (to go no further back), and perverted, soured, prostituted, and never used, is beyond estimating. And, of course, the process is still going on—although the Depression, perhaps, has slowed it down somewhat. Every day trains and buses bring to Manhattan young men and women from Cincinnati and Salt Lake City, Altoona and Asheville, Topeka and Denver, Keokuk and Kokomo: all bent upon jobs on the *Times* or the *Herald Tribune,* or on getting drunk and chummy with magazine and book publishers' editors who will then accept their manuscripts, which will make them well known, well off, and significant; but of whom, perhaps, not one in a hundred is destined to amount to any-thing—not even in terms of material success, to say nothing of making an im-pression, of bringing himself to mean something in the streams and lakes and puddles of life in America.

Of course there are reasons, all tied up with the American press and the country as a whole, why this process has been going on and continues. I need not enumerate them; every other first novel deals with them. But, by and large, the process was—and is—an evil one. It may be partly responsible for the deft writing of some of the news stories in the New York *Herald Tribune*; on the other hand, it doubtless is greatly to blame for the all-around shabbiness of most of the newspapers outside of New York City—to which fact may, in turn, be partly ascribed the shabby quality of life in many communities beyond Hoboken and their pathetic dependence for mental and spiritual stimulation upon Manhattan. The process ruins much good talent. And most of what it does not ruin it makes ineffective. It takes the young man from Topeka or Denver, where, with effort and struggle, he might possibly have become locally effective in some constructive long-range way, and turns him—even if he does achieve momentary favors from the bitch goddess in the shape of some sort of brief national fame and a country house in Connecticut—into a close approximation of nothing at all, so far as any lasting, concrete influence for good is concerned.

I do not mean to imply that almost any good reporter or rewrite man in almost any town in America can become the local Wasp of Virtue *à la* Jack Raper . . . but I do intend to suggest that it would be immeasurably better all around if talented young newspapermen in Cincinnati and Salt Lake City, Altoona and Topeka, Asheville and Denver, Keokuk and Kokomo would begin to realize that their chances of becoming Westbrook Peglers or of getting on the staff of *Fortune* magazine or the *Herald Tribune* in New York are terribly slim; that, even with the best of luck in New York, their fame and effectiveness will be too diffused or short-lived to be satisfying; and that, even with much less luck than attended Jack Raper's career, they may—with intelligence and passion, effort and struggle, and a steady viewpoint and purpose, indigenous to America—get somewhere right where they are.

Walter Locke of Dayton: A Free Editor

THE STORY OF WALTER LOCKE HOLDS THE SAME SUGGESTION AS DOES JACK RAPER'S, but, telling it in some detail, I shall not be guilty of repetition, because the man is a good deal unlike Raper. His personality, mind, and manner are different. His life has been more dramatic.

He is the editor of the Dayton *Daily News*, owned by the one-time governor of Ohio and the 1920 Democratic candidate for President, James M. Cox. Sixty-three (as I write) but younger-looking, Walter Locke is a hale, medium-sized, slow-moving, slow-talking, quiet-mannered, simple and direct self-taught and self-made man. His editorials—some of which appear also in the three other Cox papers: the Miami (Florida) *Daily News* and the Springfield (Ohio) *Daily News* and *Daily Sun*—are exercises in common sense and plain human decency, dealing with local, state, national and world affairs, and generally human problems, and frequently achieve depth, breadth, and high prose. His friend, Arthur E. Morgan, described him to me as "a man of natural wisdom who has grown up close to the soil . . . one of those somewhat universal persons characteristic of frontier days."

Locke was born in the mid-'seventies in the hills of West Virginia. His mother was half Pennsylvania Dutch and half Irish; his father, a mixture of English, German, and Scotch, with perhaps a dash of Swede. The family maintained, as he says, "a corn-pone living" from the timber till the forests began to fail. As a six- or seven-year-old boy, Walter piled the barrel staves his father split, the brush they grubbed for clearings, and the tanbark they skinned from the trees. In winter, he trapped when not attending a four-month backwoods school, where he learned most of McGuffey and not a little of the Bible by heart.

When Walter was nine, the Lockes moved to Nebraska. In West Virginia they had lived in seventeenth-century style, cooking over a log fire and wearing homespun. Their log house had consisted of but one room. In Nebraska in 1884 they hit the frontier, where buffalo chips were still fuel and people lived in sod houses. In the frontier village school at Roca, the boy found a small library, a hundred volumes or so—Dickens, Prescott, Alcott, Eggleston—what one would expect in the rather Puritan West of the mid-'eighties. He read them all the first year, then began again. Back in West Virginia he had left a raft of cousins and, writing letters to them, he discovered he liked to write.

By the time he was sixteen the village school—two departments, two teachers, giving the equivalent of eight grades of elementary and one year of high school—had no further use for him. He went to an adjoining county where his age was unknown, took a teacher's examination, and for two years taught a country school in a Bohemian neighborhood, similar to the one described in Willa Cather's novel, *My Ántoniá*. He likes to recall those two years. "They were," he says, "a cosmopolitan education. I developed a taste for 'Czesky' food. A little of my Bohemian vocabulary stays with me still."

After that he taught alone for two years in a small village school with seventy-five pupils of from four to twenty-one years of age, then was "principal" of a two-teacher village school near Lincoln and finally spent a year at a Seminole Indian mission school in what was then Indian Territory, now Oklahoma.

This last experience influenced his subsequent general outlook. "The Seminoles," he told me forty years later, "were a small nation occupying an area of perhaps a thousand square miles in a wooded and prairie country a little east of where Oklahoma City is now. They were divided by family, not by geography, into fourteen bands. Each band elected two lawmakers, who elected a governor. They maintained a small police force and lived what seemed to me then, and seems to me still, well-nigh an ideal existence. Their land was held in common. A family was allowed no more land than it would use. As a result, there was no dependence there and, save as the white man's influence was felt, no graft. That experience confirmed my predilections for the simple life, the simple society. The destruction by the United States government of those Indian nations is to me a tragedy like the striking down of Abyssinia by Mussolini. . . . Last fall"—1936—"I drove through that country for the first time after leaving it. Its beautiful rolling prairies and trees had been transformed into a hideous forest of oil derricks. The 'free and independent' Indians I knew, such as were left, were at the white man's mercy, living by such jobs as they could get."

Afflicted in his early years with ailing eyes, Walter Locke was not able to read much, and he likes to describe himself as a "rather ignorant, illiterate man." But much of what he read was good. In his mid-twenties, expecting eventually to go totally blind, he began deliberately and systematically to memorize the best poetry available in English, and this practice became a habit, which is still with him—"by far the best habit I have ever acquired," he told me; "a refiner of feeling, a stimulator of imagination, and a training in the feel and use of words."

With this background and equipment he strayed, at twenty-eight, into journalism. The State Journal Company of Lincoln, Nebraska, employed him to edit a farmers' weekly it had been putting out for many years. Locke did not think much of the paper; it had a dull past, which might not be worth any attempt to overcome; so, after struggling with it for a few months, he recommended it be—and it was—discontinued. Whereupon he became editorial writer on *The State Journal*, a position he kept for twenty-four years, and in that time slowly and quietly made himself a powerful direct influence in Nebraska. Indirectly, his influence was national, for he became an important factor in the long and magnificent political career of George W. Norris.

The State Journal was traditionally a conservative-Republican paper; its business office was in static hands; but Locke happened to be working under a managing editor, Will Owen Jones, now dead, who though a conventional man, was a gentleman and not without liberal tendencies. Grinding out his editorials, Locke was testing events with reference to the democratic philosophy which came naturally to him by way of the obscurity of his origin and the primitiveness of his early life; and Jones let him "bootleg" his viewpoint and ideas into the editorial columns and acted as a buffer between him and the counting-room, which frequently agreed with the super-patriots in Lincoln and elsewhere in Nebraska that Locke was a dangerous radical, certainly no Republican, and as such should not be allowed to publish his views and notions in a reputable paper. His position was not a comfortable one; and why he stayed in it for nearly a quarter of a century can be explained partly by the fact that Locke is a slow, immensely patient, and personally charming man who gets along with almost everybody and inclines to make the best of a bad situation, and partly on the ground that he was not ineffective.

Every six years he helped to return Norris, who became one of his closest personal friends, to the United States Senate. He acted as a voice for the progressive, liberal, aggressively democratic element in Lincoln and in the rest of Nebraska. He fought the extortionate power of the railroads. In 1912 he led a small group which caused to be submitted to a vote of the people an amendment to the state constitution providing for the initiative and referendum. In 1914 he and his group used the referendum to kill a reactionary pork-barrel act authorizing a chain of armories across Nebraska. In 1913 and 1917 he was influential in providing for the non-partisan nomination and election of judges, regents of the university, and superintendents of public instruction; later, in introducing the non-partisan ballot for the nomination and election of state, county, school district, and municipal officers. He helped greatly in educating Nebraska to see the absurdities of the party circle on the ballot. He supported Senator Norris' idea for a unicameral legislature. He freely admitted the people made mistakes, and serious ones, but argued to this effect: Simplify the machinery of government, give the voters all the facts and opportunity for consideration, and in the long run they will make fewer blunders than the wisest benevolent dictators. Simplicity and more simplicity in government! The city of Lincoln owes him much for its present simple and reasonably efficient and decent municipal government.

In Lincoln, Locke acquired a band of friends—local lawyers, doctors and ministers, professors and students at the University of Nebraska, workers, and near-by farmers—most of whom thought and felt much as he did, and who— usually without Locke's knowledge—encouraged the occasionally perturbed Editor Jones to stand by his editorial-writer so he might continue to write as he wished. Free of intellectual egoism (one of the most important marks of a true democrat), he seldom wrote an important editorial without first discussing the matter with as many of his friends as possible; so that, when he wrote it, the editorial often was really a collective product. He was not a brilliant writer, in the sense that, say, Mencken was brilliant and Benjamin Stolberg still is; but he wrote well, clearly, simply—so simply that his style and expression got beyond the comprehension of the leading reactionary minds in Nebraska which had been made complex and foggy by their devious purposes, but went over with the majority of people whose background was similar to Locke's.

Among his university friends was John Andrew Rice, professor of classics—later of Rollins College, where he was, in 1933, the center of the famous "Rollins Row" and now is the head of the interesting experimental college at Black Mountain in North Carolina—who first introduced me to him and describes him as follows:

"Locke has a curious quiet way of sitting, which would lead you to believe that he was phlegmatic if you did not notice that his eyes have a strange teasing quality. This characteristic of his is particularly noticeable when he gets among students and generally young people, on whom he produces the effect of making them very anxious to explain what they mean. When they have done so, his observations have a calming quality about them. He knows how to say to young people the one thing they dislike most to hear: that it is going to take a long time. He never tells them not to be impatient, but by the way he deals with what they say shows them what patience does.

"His mouth, overhung by a strong nose, suggests with its lines resigned cynicism, an illusion which is immediately dispelled when he begins to speak. The mouth and eyes together tell you everything you need to know about a person. If there is conflict between them you may be sure that chaos runs deep. In Locke each is a kind of commentary on the other. When one seems harsh and uncompromising, the other has a way of reminding you of the good natured, tolerant affection that underlies everything he expresses. He is one of the few *real* believers in democracy I have ever known, and while he has and uses a very keen intellect, he knows that democracy can come only when based upon right feeling. He is, although it may sound trite to say so, the kind of man who can be found only in America."

In the middle 1920's Locke wrote several articles about Mid-Western affairs for *The New Republic*. They attracted attention. Among those who read them with particular interest was James M. Cox, who asked him—in 1926—if he would like to come to Dayton and take over the editorship of the *Daily News*.

"Cox," Locke told me ten years later, "is strong medicine. He is three men in one: journalist, politician (in the best sense), and business man, all three outstanding. I was reluctant to put myself in his shadow; he is a man who dominates by his sheer strength and superiority wherever he is. You remember the steel strike of 1919. The Pennsylvania government refused the strikers the right to meet. I had noticed in reports which reached us in Nebraska how on Sundays they used to march across the Ohio line to hold their meetings. Cox was governor of Ohio. It marked him, to me, as a tested liberal and democrat with a small *d*, and that had caused me to vote for him for President the next year. But could a man as vigorous as he give rope to an editor? We discussed this in our preliminary conversations, frankly. I said I had lost faith in the possibility of a vital, free editorial page. He disagreed. Why, then, I asked, were most publishers running their editorial columns empty, a sort of vestigial remain? He replied they couldn't get men of needed ability. I suggested the reason was we couldn't get publishers with the wisdom to see that good ability could not manifest itself unless it was free. I said he should study my work well, and unless he felt sure he would like my work as I liked to do it, we should stay apart: we'd be very unhappy together. Finally I took the chance and came over. During these ten years he must have felt a thousand times like wringing my neck, for naturally a man of his power of mind cannot always have been satisfied with the workings of my mind. But he has kept the faith. Never a finger has he laid on me. Of course, in turn, as any decent human being would do, I have taken every pain not to jeopardize him unnecessarily. As a matter of fact, he takes chances with his property on his own responsibility which I would not feel free to take on mine. A newspaper must be alive, of course, before it can be free. And freedom is at best a relative thing.

"The total of the situation is that I have been permitted, in making an editorial page, to be myself. I suspect that any person of fair capacity could make a worthy editorial page on those terms. I don't mean self-exploitation—the contrary should be true. I mean being oneself as the athlete is himself, working in the way natural and agreeable to him."

Cox, in discussing his editor, remarked to me, "He is a younger man now than when he came to Dayton ten years ago." Others who know him well agree with this statement. Locke himself believes it to be true. His explanation is that since coming to Dayton he has had all the opportunity he could take to function freely and naturally. Now he does not need to "bootleg" his ideas into print. He is a free man. Amid editorial-administrative duties, which take perhaps half his working day, he averages two thousand words a day seven days a week, with no more difficulty, he told me, "than eating my meals when mealtime comes. . . . I do not worry and wish for texts. The new day brings them."

Locke took the job as an experiment. The experiment has been a success. Cox is content. One Christmas he wrote Locke: "God was good to us when he dumped you on us," and every once in a while he sends clippings of some especially good editorial to his publisher friends in New York and elsewhere with some such remark as, "See what I picked up among the cornstalks." Of course he is quite sure Locke has no idea of ever quitting him for another job. Even the circulation manager—and circulation managers commonly think of editorial pages as their chief obstacle to success—considers Locke's editorial page an asset. It is widely read both in the Dayton *Daily News* and in the Cox papers at Springfield and Miami; and Locke spends a good part of his day reading the heap of letters that reach his desk in response to his editorial comments.

I asked him what he was trying to accomplish with his editorial page. "Subconsciously, I suppose," he replied, "I am trying to get everybody thinking as I think. Consciously, that isn't the idea. My highest aim, I make myself believe, is to give the people the materials to use in thinking for themselves. A great many people, including myself, are not sure of their thinking till they have followed the workings of other minds on the same subject; which I think is as it should be in a democratic country. That is the bottom reason why editorials are read at all, I suppose. I try in my columns to do an honest job of thinking myself—honest even if usually ignorant. Then, in the other columns, I like to print other points of view, including the letters of readers. I put Walter Lippmann and Dorothy Thompson on the page at times, usually taking no trouble to say why I think they are wrong. Sometimes people stop taking the paper, or threaten to, because I print or write in disagreement with them. It is an uphill job, getting a population to grant to others the freedom of opinion which they claim for themselves. Yet on the whole readers do not much punish an editor for honest, courageously expressed views, especially if they are backed by substantial evidence. My general attitude on social and political matters is wrong to a large majority of the more powerful people of the cities where they appear in print. You know how bitter the class line now stands, particularly on the part of the 'upper' class. Yet they do not punish me or the paper.

"Of course no backwoodsman like myself is ever a real 'radical.' . . . In practice, as far as we have developed it to date, the defense of democracy is largely a resistance to the predatory and parasitic in human nature which subjects us to the advances of special privilege and spoils. We had Alexander Hamilton's bankers, Calhoun's slave-drivers, Grant's land-grabbers, McKinley's tariff bloc, Hanna's monopolies, and Hoover's financial hierarchy, all perverting democracy, confusing it. They were called the conservatives, but to my mind the true conservative *in America* is the man who joins in keeping the ship of state free of such ever-encroaching barnacles. Our most revered leaders have been of this stamp: Jefferson, Jackson, Lincoln, to go no further. These were tory-hated 'radicals' in their times, but history gives them their right place as saving conservatives. My presidential votes from my beginning express, it still seems to me, that attitude: 1896 and 1900, Bryan; 1904, Theodore Roosevelt; 1908, Bryan; 1912 and 1916, Wilson; 1920, Cox; 1924, La Follette; 1928, Al Smith (not the present Al); 1932 and 1936, Roosevelt; 1940, Henry Wallace, Bob La Follette, LaGuardia——

"As an editor I have merely held to the line of equal opportunity, I suppose —to the primitive democracy of my West Virginia country or prairie frontier. But how seemingly 'radical' that course, the really constitutional course, has all my life seemed to intrenched privilege! I fought railroad dictatorship in Nebraska with direct primary and direct legislation. I have fought the tariff graft all my life. To myself, my course seems to have been strictly conservative at all points. That is a matter of judgment, of course. My Communist friends think I am reactionary. I have no Fascist friends, but if I had they would call me a red. Between the two, I feel myself where I think a West Virginia mountaineer ought to be."

As I write, it is eleven years since Locke has settled in Dayton; but, although *The State Journal* went promptly standpat when he left it, he is still one of the important people in Lincoln. His friends of eleven, twenty, thirty years ago are still his friends. Traveling between Washington and Nebraska, Senator Norris routes himself *via* Dayton and stops for a chat with him. When Locke occasionally returns to Lincoln for a visit, "the old bunch" would turn out bands in full regalia if he would let them. All he allows them to do is to organize a supper get-together, which usually lasts late into the night.

A genuinely modest man, Locke was no great help to me in writing this chapter, so I turned to a friend of his in Lincoln, who spread the word around that I wanted information about Walter, and for weeks I was swamped with letters from Nebraska describing Locke's personality, mind, and achievements before 1926. One of them wrote me, "The apples in Locke's barrel are as good on the bottom as on top. He is what he is in all places and at all times. To a painter he would not say, 'Add a little hair here, take out this wrinkle there'; but, as Cromwell, 'Paint me as I am, warts and all.' There is about him a refreshing forthrightness." A Daytonian, who has known Locke since 1927, characterized him to me in different words but to exactly the same effect.

Dayton—an important industrial city of nearly a quarter of a million, and the center of the famous Miami Valley which includes great stretches of fertile farm country and other, smaller, industrial towns—is unlike Lincoln, but as editor and citizen Locke has there the same general function he had in the Nebraska capital. He came to Dayton quietly and started at his job unsensationally, saying things on the editorial page that he thought needed to be said, simply, sanely, honestly, without fireworks. The only startling thing he did was to address an occasional letter to a couple of hundred leading people in town: what did they think of the Dayton schools?—or the police force?—or, was Dayton the "Middletown" of the Lynds' book?—and then he printed three or four pages of replies.

His editorials reflected a mellow philosophy built around such values or ideals as truth, decency, justice, liberty, democracy. Along with newspaper-readers in most other American cities and towns, the Daytonians had been in the habit of skipping the editorial page; now they gradually began to read it in the *News* and discuss the views of the new editor. Unaware of the understanding between him and Cox, a few took it upon themselves to talk to the "Governor," as the publisher is generally called in Dayton, urging him for Heaven's and Dayton's sakes to continue letting Locke write as he pleased, for they feared that certain elements in the city might rise and demand he be removed or curbed. However, while there were complaints, no one made any such demand —partly because Cox is generally known not to be a man to accept instructions on how to run his papers, and partly because the disturbing editorials were invariably well substantiated and clearly constructive, their spirit drawn from the stream of the best American traditions and reaching into the bases of America; and, even in attack, showing an understanding and tolerance that took away the sting after penetrating the skin.

The popularity of the editorial page increased steadily. It was regularly read—and even liked—by people whose interests were attacked by Locke, for he was so evidently without rancor and malice, so palpably idealistic and objective. When they met him, they liked him as a person. He became as well liked in Dayton as he was in Lincoln. Within a year he was a strong influence in the town and region, responsible for some of the best thinking in the Miami Valley. In 1930 he took a trip to Europe and Russia; when he returned, a spontaneous movement developed to give him a homecoming party, although in his reports to the paper from abroad he had praised much that he had seen in Russia which had disturbed not a few people in Dayton.

He and his page became a local institution.

The page is unique among editorial pages in the country. Most editors use no poetry; some use it as "fillers," instead of jokes; a few—the New York Times, for one—run a short poem at the bottom of the last column on the editorial page; while Locke, whose head holds an anthology of the greatest poems, places a bit of verse on the top of column one of the editorial page seven days a week . . . and a close observer of things in Dayton said it was amazing how many people read it.

This bit of verse is usually followed by about a thousand words of informal comment entitled "Trends of the Times," where one is apt to find a discussion of almost anything, but usually written with a philosophic, literary or naturalistic slant, sometimes combining all three. Through these pieces he seems to want to give the readers a perspective on time and the world.

Now and then he takes a day off and spends it on a piece of woodland near Dayton, where he has built himself two small log cabins (one for Mrs. Locke and himself, the other for guests), or at his farm in the southern Ohio hills; and next day, in place of "Trends of the Times," Dayton reads a dispatch from "Whistling Post, O."—all about the advent of spring or autumn at Whistling Post this year; the dandelion problem; the joy one experiences in bloodroot time; the way to eat pawpaws and the Ohio persimmons; what happened to three sycamores on the banks of the North Fork Creek that flows through Whistling Post; or the latest event in the life of a certain oak "full ten-stories high, healthy in every limb, not less than two hundred and fifty years old and yet young . . . [which] was well on its way to the mastery of its world when George Washington was still a carefree boy at Fredericksburg." . . . "Whistling Post" is one of the best liked Locke features. It is a strong, pleasant echo from his backwoods and pioneer background. When he first started it in Dayton, people wrote in asking the location of Whistling Post; they could not find it on any Ohio road map. Locke replied it was in a state of mind.

Every two or three months he fills his gasoline-tank and is off for several days, and the column usually occupied by "Trends" or "Whistling Post" becomes "Realm of the Road," with some such dispatch as the following he once sent from the backwoods birthplace of Abraham Lincoln:

Hodgenville, Ky.:—Hard by Hodgenville is the cabin where Abraham Lincoln was born. On Knob Creek, five miles away, is the farm where the boy Lincoln later lived and where his baby brother died. Over the rolling lands around Hodgenville, with their sprinkling of spruces and hickory and oak, Abraham Lincoln roved. The trails intersecting the pavement which now opens the once inaccessible region to the touring world were traversed by him. From these creeks the boy Lincoln slaked his thirst. On these valleys and hills he rested his eyes. To all America, Hodgenville means one thing. Who goes to Hodgenville goes seeing Lincoln, feeling Lincoln, thinking Lincoln.

Hodgenville, seat of Larue County, has a few more than a thousand people. Its business is built around a small square. The little courthouse and a sitting statue of Lincoln occupy one side of this square. Around the square most of the stores and the two little hotels are ranged. One can do all his trading in Hodgenville and not walk farther than he can throw a stone. This is a convenience the small town dweller has. The grocery store is around the corner from the general store. The barber shop is just across the street. There is no transportation to pay. There is no loneliness of the crowd. You know your neighbor's every step from the day of his birth to today. Everybody in Hodgenville lives, as Lincoln did, in the open view. The modern rush gets no farther in Hodgenville than the sign in the barber shop which says: "Positively no loafing on Saturday."

This is not Saturday and loafing is allowed. There is conversation touching every topic but one. This is Hodgenville, the most famous birthplace in America—the most famous but one, perhaps, in the world. One may listen at the loafing barber shop, trudge around the square, eavesdrop in the lobby of the hotel, attend the Hodgenville Rotary Club, visit with the ever alert and up-to-date gasoline station man; all matters are mentioned save the one which makes Hodgenville great. Of Lincoln, of whom the visitor exclusively thinks, Hodgenville has never a word.

If the seven cities where Homer was born were alive today they would be talking about everything but Homer himself. Men must live in their own personal right. The least man living is more important to himself than the greatest man dead. Hodgenville is talking about its jobs, the dent last week's cold snap made in its coal, the price of tobacco, the trend of politics, the chances of an early spring. Hodgenville, like any less famous place, wants to live its own life and does. To the world it means the Lincoln of long ago. To itself, it is its own friendly Kentucky present where the waiter confers so many biscuits you are about to burst and the porter puts more than a perfunctory heartiness into his "Be sure you-all come back some time."

The Lincoln eleven-log-high cabin stands on an elevation with a hollow below it and a ridge beyond. The other log houses in sight—the rest room and the place where Lincoln merchandise is sold and the tourist camp cabins not far away—are smoothly sawed and notched to make narrow, even daubing between. The Lincoln cabin was built in no such polished time. Its logs of oak were piled into the wall with a minimum of work. The red clay in the chinks, so shallow the notching is, is half as wide as the logs themselves. The ends of the logs were cut off as convenient and stand out unevenly. The rafters are logs run lengthwise of the roof. On them rest the board shingles or shakes, weighted down and held fast by cross timbers above, for Thomas Lincoln had no nails. When the wind blew hard the roof blew off.

The fireplace, familiar for its chimney seemingly half raised, is actually as it was when little Lincoln lived. It was chimney enough for those simple times. In an age when there were no matches and the fire must be kept alive for culinary ends from spring to fall they were not anxious for too much draft. A fire must smoulder there the summer through. Failure to keep it alive meant a trip to a neighbor's to borrow and bring home the hot coals from which to start a new blaze. How frequently in this cabin country of careless chimneys they have more fire than they want, the frequent chimneys standing gaunt, alone, their houses burned away from them, attest.

There is one window, closed by a wooden shutter, in the Lincoln cabin now. It was probably not there in Lincoln's day. It is a modern improvement, that window without glass. The loft where doubtless most of the family slept had no window, has no window still. Abraham Lincoln was born into a dwelling more primitive than the homes of most cows and chickens now.

Hovering over this irreducible minimum of a home, surrounding and covering and protecting it, rises a Grecian temple of glistening stone. Up the slope by which the Lincolns climbed by a footpath to their door rise now wide flights of steps. The visitor labors to the cabin level flight by flight. There is a resting seat for each stage. We make it easy to honor Lincoln now! About the cabin, exposed by the melting snow, is a scattering of grain put out for the birds. Lincoln of the great heart would have done something like that. We climb to the shining temple with its cut stone walls and carved inscriptions. We seek the cherished heart within the rich body without and find it: the crude cabin from which Abraham Lincoln of the overflowing heart emerged.

Here is cabin risen to culture. Here is culture confessing the simple, primitive humanity on which culture is founded and reared. Here is pride guarding against a fall by recognizing the humbleness from which it grew. Here is wealthy, machine-equipped America remembering that humble flesh and blood is prior and superior to its wealth and its machines.

Mocking birds and their melodies are as common about the Lincoln cabin as sparrows and their chirps in towns. Cardinals call from the shrubs down by the stream. The northward wave of spring is on its way. The grackles with their long tails show up on the Kentucky shore in the large flocks which left the farther north in the fall. The robins are here in force and the towhee calls where Lincoln used to hear. We speed southward and see a sign: "New Haven, Ky.: Speed limit twelve miles per hour."

We follow the traffic through New Haven at the current speed, some forty miles an hour. New times have made new ways—superimposed upon old signs, old rules. New temples over old huts. New speeds, new temples, new times—new Lincolns?

Locke's formal editorials are, as to both writing and content, amazingly and consistently good—amazingly even if one does not consider that, except for an occasional piece, they are written under pressure by one man day after day, two columns of them. They are unsensational; thoughtful, gently on-pushing, progressive, fair, never ranting or dogmatic, seldom even mildly sarcastic, clearly meant to produce less heat than light. There are usually three or four. The leader deals, as a rule, with some basic national or world question; often in reply to some pundit or public figure who has voiced a reactionary view or idea. In the last half of 1937, for instance, he took exception a number of times to Dorothy Thompson, whom the *News* prints regularly. One day she attacked President Roosevelt for favoring majority rule, which, she said with her customary vehemence, could be tyrannical rule. It could be mob rule. An inflamed majority, as we had seen during America's brief period in the war, was capable, she held forth, of brutal oppression of harmless, helpless minorities. Of the excesses of majorities we need ever to beware. A chief function of the Constitution, of laws and of courts was to hold majorities in their hours of excitement to rules of justice established in their hours of calm. . . . In his reply to her, entitled "Doleful Dorothy," Locke said:

As Dorothy Thompson scans the annals of our national life, she will discover, however, a certain other peril much more ubiquitous than that of a tyrannical majority. That is the peril of a tyrannical minority. Intrenched behind constitutions, laws and courts, established to protect minorities from aggression of tyrannical majorities, tyrannical minorities have from time to time ruled us with a hard hand. Beginning with the financial interests behind the skirts of Hamilton, proceeding with the slave-owning minority, then to the public utility and tariff-seeking minorities of the post-Civil War era and on to today, we have a tale of a nation almost constantly in trouble at the hands of too powerful minorities.

It is from this evil of overweening minorities the majority is fighting now to be free. Cannot the worried Dorothy Thompson possess her soul in patience till this is done? After that we can return to the much rarer problem of majority restraint.

Then there may be an editorial on something in Ohio—the proposal of Senator Donahey for a unicameral legislature, endorsing it, of course, for that would simplify the State government; or on the state's parole system, which allows a none too conscientious executive to release a convicted Cleveland banker while unmoneyed prisoners receive scant consideration.

The third and fourth pieces usually are "light stuff" about anything at all, unless some well-known person dies who has stood for, or typified, something in the country or the world; in which case Locke writes an estimate of the deceased in reference to the current American or world situation. Of Ed Howe he said, characteristically:

He wrote a book, "The Story of a Country Town." He edited a little newspaper in little Atchison. He was Atchison. For 40 years to say Atchison was to suggest Ed Howe. Twenty-five years ago he retired as active editor. He then printed sheets of comment of his own and scattered them about and Ed Howe remained Atchison till his death.

He was a little of Arthur Brisbane—a Miami neighbor of his—and something of Will Rogers and a touch of Mencken. He was all Ed Howe. He had a way of saying things that was uncommonly easy to read. The things he said were read by those who agreed with him because they agreed, and by those who disagreed with him because of the way they were said. They were more wholesome reading for those who disagreed than for those who agreed.

Why? Ed Howe was extreme in a direction contrary to current trends. He hated reform. If Ed Howe ever had a good word to say for any man or movement pressing for change we cannot remember the fact. In a generation absorbed in "progress" he was opposed to progress. Particularly did social "progress" invite his ire. Men's condition, Howe held, was the product of themselves. Men were rich or poor, happy or miserable by their own virtue or fault. Always he preached self dependence. The master was master because he had a master's strength. The slave was a slave because he had the weakness of a slave. Wait till the master became weak, the slave strong, and their places would be exchanged. The making of laws to protect men from their inefficiency or even to save them from tyranny was anathema to Ed Howe.

The times of Ed Howe ran always the other way. It was a generation of organization of the many weaker to protect themselves from the tyranny of the stronger few. The judgment of mankind is against Ed Howe. Something can be done by organization and government to improve the condition of men. But Ed Howe was not all wrong. Too much dependence can be placed on the protection of law and government. No society, in the end, can be better than the people comprising it. The most perfect government will have to await the most perfect people, the self dependent, energetic, courageous individual people whom Ed Howe forever promoted and preached. There will never be a time when a nation does not need its individualistic, albeit reactionary, Ed Howes.

Again and again Locke says indirectly: this is a big world, this is a big country; one needs only to travel to see how big it is. There is room for many kinds of people, for many viewpoints, attitudes, ideas, doings, what nots. Let them be, let them be free. All should be considered. Truth—not, to be sure, the ultimate truth, but workable truth, enough for direction—lies somewhere in the center of confusion. Let us, you and I, aim for that center, invite the people to look there and discern and understand; and the likelihood is that we will be all right in the long run.

Rather infrequently does Locke editorialize upon things in Dayton. One reason for this is that, with its city-manager system, the city is comparatively free from political vices, and is one of the best administered communities in America. It was so, to a great extent, before Locke came; it has, due to his presence, improved no little since his advent. Another reason, not unakin to the first, is that he is the clean, free, democratic, incorruptible moral-philosophical—and, simultaneously, practical—force in town and in the Miami Valley which everyone who wants to be or do something more or less important must consider. Only "force" is not really the word for Locke. He employs no pressure in the usual sense. He plays no politics as between himself and other men, only as between principles or ideas or common sense and men, including himself. And that which I incorrectly call "force" is not really Locke the man and editor, the high-minded individual who knows what is right and lays down the law, for he is never sure what is right or high-minded and has an innate disinclination to lay down any sort of law. He is not a boss. He is incapable of dogma. The "force" is the community spirit or interest, the social consciousness, which he, or rather what he stands for, keeps subtly, but naturally and effortlessly organized—except, again, that "organized" is not the word. As formerly in Lincoln, so now in Dayton, Locke has a large group of friends—local doctors, lawyers, engineers, workers, teachers and students in Antioch College (of which he is a trustee), and housewives and social workers—with whom he is wont to discuss issues, problems, and ideas as they reach his attention. There is no organization, only friendship and devotion to decency, fair play, liberty, democracy, common sense. This is the "force" the politicians and go-getters of Dayton must consider. When they get something up their sleeve, they usually come to Locke and tell him about it (and there is no use trying to lead Locke by his nose), or to one of his friends, who is asked to tell Locke. Never hasty, he listens, asks questions, then sleeps on what he has been told for a couple of nights, discusses the thing with "the governor," and calls up his friends, asks them to lunch, or they drop into his office or he goes to them, and together—representing all classes, several professions, and many viewpoints—they talk and form a judgment, which Locke or somebody else then conveys to the politicians or go-getters, who then have an opportunity to defend their side if the judgment is unfavorable to them, and so on, and so on, till the matter is put into effect as originally proposed, or is revised or dropped, sans daily editorial fireworks. If put into effect, the thing is then reported in the news columns and briefly and quietly commented upon, whereupon the public has its say . . . and so life goes on in Dayton.

Locke is one of the few non-engineer, non-technical, non-industrial members of Dayton's well-known Engineers Club, whose membership consists mainly of local and nearby industrialists and plant superintendents, engineers, chemists, and other technicians and production key men, most of whom are "conservative" (in the usual, not Lockean, sense) in politics and more or less "fascistic" in practice—that is, autocrats and dictators in their plants, used to giving orders and having them obeyed; at once children and fathers, victims and perpetrators of the country's basic incongruity; men who want results quickly when they want them, and who desire that what they say should go. In other words, fellows basically unlike Locke. Most are by nature against everything he stands for. Yet, although he is the same Walter Locke at the Club as he is in his office or anywhere else, he gets along with them. They like and respect him personally, and read his page. They argue with him. He is patient with them. His slow smile "gets" them. He asks questions which put them into uncomfortable positions, then helps them to get out of those positions. He takes his lunch at the Club, and sees one or a few of them every day. And he influences them, both in person and through his page. One indirect result of this is that, by and large, working conditions in Dayton and vicinity tend to compare rather favorably with working conditions elsewhere, both as to wages and hours and as to the general atmosphere in the shops.

Locke, like most liberals and progressives, is sometimes carelessly called a Red, a Bolshevik, a Communist, a follower of Marx. As already suggested, he is nothing like that at all. He is too intelligent to dismiss Marx entirely, but agrees with Henry Wallace, who has said, "Neither Socialism nor Communism meets the realities of human nature as I sense them. Both of them have an emotional dryness, a dogmatic thinness that repels me. They deal in the dry bones of the 'economic man' and I crave in addition the flesh and blood and spirit of the religious and artistic man." Communism and Fascism, Locke believes, are poor alternatives for America. He is partial to democracy, which he cannot define, and finds even hard to discuss, but which he feels intensely in his deeply American makeup.

He is probably the most democratic man I know.

He thinks that private property is an integral part of democracy—of democracy, that is, as far as we are capable of it at the present stage of human development, or will likely be capable of it for some time to come. He feels that America's economic problems will be more or less solved eventually, if they will be solved at all, on the basis and within the frame of private property. He holds that, in all probability, the United States will become a great and stable civilization only when the overwhelming majority of industrialists will own their industries, the overwhelming majority of farmers their farms, the overwhelming majority of dwellers their dwellings, and *the overwhelming majority of workers of all classes their jobs.*

He does not know how the United States will, or can, attain to such widespread ownership of industry, farms, dwellings, and jobs among its people. I am sure he would not tell if he knew; or if he told, he certainly would not be dogmatic about his idea, suggestion, or plan of procedure—for he knows and feels that the country *as a whole* must strive and grope, through stress and debate, toward a way of achieving such an end, or it will be no good, either at the start or in the long run. He thinks, however, that such an evolutionary spreading-out of ownership, however fantastic it might seem as a suggestion, would be far easier on the country at large and upon millions of individuals than any sort of "Marxian" or Hitler-Mussolinian revolution imaginable, and far more satisfactory in long-range results. Along with such spreading out of ownership there should be—as an additional standby of a broad-based democracy—a coöperative movement, both among farmers as consumers and producers and among others as producers. This movement should be primarily economic, politics being employed only as necessary to protect the process.

Locke believes that the country is beginning to grope in that direction. Throughout 1937, although he did not approve of it, he was no little interested in the sitdown strike, which appeared to him to have within its purpose and technique a hint of the idea that the job belonged to the worker—that it was his private property.

I sent Locke a draft of this chapter for factual corrections. The chapter ended with the above paragraph. Beneath it he wrote: "To give all my mind-twistings about the sitdown strike might take pages. . . . The democratic process, I believe, is a groping in the direction described in this chapter. The present readjustments in industry and in our economic, social, and political life generally are a too-long delayed broadening of the democratic base—by labor, by farmer organizations. The newly empowered are sure to abuse their power and use it crudely, as did the business elements against which they have lately been in revolt. The sitdown, as we saw it early in 1937, was an excess indulged in by labor as a recaption against the equal abuse of power by labor's employers. The excesses of both should cease as labor practices the responsibility of an equal, at the council table, with its employers. I tell my employer friends that they are in for many a bad hour in the years just ahead while labor learns the limits of power, but that it is like the lumberjacks going down to Bangor to get drunk—we dread it but it has to be done."

Arthur Morgan: Disciplined Pragmatist

IT IS NOT MY INTENTION TO IMPLY THAT I CONSIDER THE MEN I PORTRAY IN THESE final chapters to be some species of messiahs, but, rather, to suggest that— in what they are doing or trying to do: in their experiences, ideas, and functions—they represent certain positive characteristics and tendencies at the democratic bases of America which, in their various ways, are working under difficulties, but working, and perhaps much more effectively than might generally be granted, toward the loosening of the grip of the politico-economic incongruity upon the life of the country in favor of democracy. . . .

And so I come to Arthur E. Morgan, a most remarkable contemporary American whose story—for me—begins with his father, John D. Morgan.

John D. Morgan was the thirteenth of fourteen children born in a log cabin in the clay hills of southern Indiana. His father was a millwright who in later life moved to the Welsh Quaker settlement in Montgomery County in Pennsylvania. Eventually John became a surveyor . . . but before that happened, one day, when he was about seventeen years of age, he and one of his older brothers, whose name was Esquire, were splitting rails on the family homestead in Indiana. They were working on a specially knotty and crossgrained log, when of a sudden Esquire stopped driving in the wedge with his great maul, and said, "John, let's go to Minnesota."

Minnesota was then—in the middle of the nineteenth century—an unknown territory, but rumored to be full of riches: a kind of early Klondike. "All right," replied John. "When do we start?" Esquire said, "Let's start right soon." "All right," said John. "Next week." "Oh no," returned Esquire, his eyes flashing. "Let's go now." "All right, then," said John. "Tomorrow." "No, no," said Esquire. "Now." "All right," John acquiesced again. "We'll finish splitting this log, then go." Esquire said, "Never mind the log. Let's go right now." "All right," put in willing John. "Just let me knock this wedge out of the log." But Esquire urged him to let the wedge stay where it was. John agreed to that and they stepped into the house to pick up a few things, and then joining a covered-wagon caravan, went to Minnesota. . . .

Young John met a slight, intense, deeply puritanical girl, Anna Wiley, lately from Massachusetts, who at eighteen taught school on the raw frontier in Minnesota. He was a big, joyous, rather lazy (for that period), and bookish young man, but Anna married him, none the less; whereupon, temperamentally incompatible, they led a frictional life. As the railroads opened, they returned East for a while, and Arthur was born in Cincinnati in 1878. John became a surveyor and took his family back to bleak Minnesota, settling in St. Cloud, then a raw sawmill town, where Arthur spent a part of his early life, which was none too happy, mainly because of the essential divergence

595

in the parents' characters that were destined to blend painfully but effectively in him and, in the process, make him into a tense, nervous boy. From his father he inherited little joyousness, no humor or "laziness," but a love of books and a philosophical mind; from his mother, her puritanism, which included a fanatic industriousness, a moral integrity, indomitable perseverance, and a very exacting conscience. From the atmosphere of St. Cloud, which was a typical atmosphere of Western America, he imbibed the need of being a man of action and the urge to amount to something.

Arthur's mother—as portrayed in a little-known pamphlet, *Finding His World,* which is a compilation by his wife of notes on his beginnings—was a curiously hard woman. She permitted herself almost no tenderness toward her son. As a very young lad he overheard her remark of another boy: "How much he has improved in appearance! He used to be as homely as Arthur," who was a Lincolnesque lad, starved for affection and sometimes even as to physical nourishment. The family slept in the attic, to which they ascended by an outside ladder. When the mercury in winter often went down to forty below zero, snow drifted through cracks onto their beds. The boy seldom saw a piece of fruit, and to satisfy a natural need for the properties of an apple, plum, or peach he ate raw turnips and potatoes. His childhood and early boyhood were marked by serious illnesses, which aggravated his natural nervousness and seriously affected his eyesight.

Young Arthur, however, had in him a fierce power, which seemed to be augmented by every new disadvantage or handicap. He possessed an avid mind. Forty years later he let his wife quote him, "It was just torture for me not to be able to find out about things when I was young." His parents had no confidence in his ability and urged him not to dream of too high a future, but resign himself to some such humble occupation as that of a florist's helper. Partly on account of his health and awkward personality in his early youth, his father considered him unfit to be a surveyor or engineer.

When ten or eleven, Arthur earned enough money with vegetable gardening to keep himself in clothes. Going to high school, he worked for farmers. One autumn he attended school in the forenoons, then walked four miles to a farm where he worked in the afternoon and evening, slept in the hayloft, and in the morning footed it back to school. He was always building something.

Beyond three years in high school Arthur Morgan had no formal schooling. This is due in part to his poor health in boyhood, and in part to the fact that he became bitterly critical of educational methods while attending high school in St. Cloud. One was taught to read, write, do arithmetic, and memorize a few facts in geography, history, and the sciences, but was not helped or encouraged to learn how to think or seek further knowledge.

He himself read extensively already in his early 'teens; there was a library at St. Cloud, which included about a hundred worthwhile books. He read them all: Plato, Huxley, Gibbon, and other philosophers, scientists, and historians. For a while he thought that, while St. Cloud was of course a backward town culturally, Minneapolis, where he hoped to go soon, was a place where Platos and Huxleys were to be seen and heard in every square. Visiting Minneapolis, he was deeply disappointed, for the city was but a greater St. Cloud; while Chicago, which he visited during the 1893 exposition, was only a greater Minneapolis. He was unable to understand how people could be oblivious of or indifferent to the scientists and philosophers when their knowledge, wisdom, and experiences were so easily available in such wonderfully written books. Why did the volumes gather dust on library shelves? He blamed it on education and determined eventually to do something about it.

He read no novels; the Puritan in him considered them frivolous. But also, because of his poor eyes he sought to avoid the purely entertaining, and restricted himself to substantial books. He read biographies and deeply resented many, especially those by English writers who nearly always explained their subjects' success and fame on hereditary grounds. As Mrs. Morgan quotes him in *Finding His World*, he hated this "because I felt I had no worthwhile heredity, and yet I meant to be worthwhile."

When still in his 'teens, to build up his poor health and also because he saw no future in St. Cloud, he made a raft of logs and went down the Mississippi to make his way in the world. He was used to the great river, for he was a passionate explorer and had, already in his early 'teens, often floated on its current for five or ten miles or even farther, then walked back to St. Cloud. . . .

There followed years of roving in the West and working in the woods, in mines, on farms, in bakeshops, and teaching school, and reading, thinking, and doubting, revising his theology and attitudes, being lonely, going through the first stages of becoming a self-made man. In this period he wrote a diary, now quoted in part in *Finding His World*, which is a record of intense struggles both within him and between him and his environment. To quote a typical entry when he was twenty: "It seems to me that I am not becoming what I want to be, and am not achieving my object in life at all. But very little can be done along my desired lines until I can sleep well, and this sort of hard work may make me sleep. Oh, for a clear head, so that I could work hard with it." Three months later: "I do not know what to do. My health is poor, so that I cannot well do heavy work, my eyes are out of order and cannot stand continuous use. I have no trade, and see no way of using my education. This world seems to be the place for those who have good constitutions. I have tried my best to develop one, but thus far I have failed. I hardly see a place where I can fit and be useful, and at the same time improve my own condition." At twenty-two: "People often tell me I am foolish to bear with the tortures of sleeplessness when medicines would put an end to them. But I think I am right in not taking drugs. They usually tax the system dearly for the cures they make. When I find what laws of life I am disobeying and train myself to obedience to them, then, I trust, I shall gain a health which no drugs can give. Until then I shall try to bear with patience the reproaches of my system for not having found them. . . . When nature has a limited supply of material for making a man, she has different methods of using it. Sometimes she cuts him down to a small pattern, body and soul and makes him well, normal, and sound. But when she made me, she started out with a large, noble pattern, went bankrupt, and filled in with sawdust and straw."

In 1902, his health improved, and character so strengthened he was able to stand on his own feet in the presence of his doubting parents, Arthur Morgan returned to St. Cloud and, almost forcibly entering his father's business, rapidly established himself as a surveyor and became interested in drainage engineering, which was a profession then in its infancy in the West. He had no formal engineering education, but in less than five years, following his practical instincts and learning the technical tricks swiftly from trained engineers, he became the foremost man in the field. He drafted the drainage laws for Colorado, which then served as models for other states in the Southwest. By the time he was twenty-eight his drainage engineering practice increased to such an extent that he directed simultaneously thirty projects, employing numerous assistant engineers who were college graduates. In 1907, the United States government drew him into its services as supervising engineer, in which capacity he engaged for years in vast projects adding to his reputation as well as to his technical and general education. His diaries indicate that he studied constantly, and that almost nothing escaped his observant eyes and mind.

Early in the 1910's he returned to private engineering practice, and through most of that decade, in addition to other work, he served as chief engineer of the Miami Valley Flood Control, which was an intensely complicated politico-technical project, involving a vast area, the eccentricities of two or three rivers, and the divergent immediate and long-range interests of several cities, and which, executed in the typically sound and thorough Morgan manner, now stands as the best-known of his water-control jobs, though he planned and superintended the construction of seventy-five others scattered all over the country. In 1933 the President appointed him chairman of the board and chief engineer of the Tennessee Valley Authority. In the latter capacity he planned and supervised the building of vast dams.

But all during the period in which he rose to the top rank of American civil engineers, one of Arthur Morgan's chief and basic interests was education. The young college-educated engineers who entered his employ worried, distressed him. Most of them were decent enough fellows in immediate-personal respects and were competent as engineers. The majority had undeviating technical integrity; that is, they would not under any circumstances allow a steel girder to be a hair's breadth out of line, nor consent to the use of any defective material. But not a few were culturally, socially, and politically ignorant or dead. They were unable to discuss anything but shop, sports, and women. Many knew next to nothing about taking care of their health. Their education was one-sided. A depressing number had no civic pride or interest, no philosophy of life, no sense of proportion and social or human duty. No moral or artistic values. Apart from their profession, they had little character. Except in the matter of construction, they were irresponsible. The laborers who executed their plans and orders did not exist for them as human beings. If the contractor employed them at starvation wages, or quartered them in unsanitary houses, they remained oblivious of the conditions: it was none of their business. The aim of most of them was merely to make a living, to derive for themselves a happiness accrued from material advantages. They implicitly scorned Morgan's idea that to construct a bridge or a dam was a social event, along with the notion that the Italian and Slavic pick-and-shovel men were worthy of consideration. When, on the Miami Valley Flood Control job, he built at each dam, instead of the customary tar-paper or tent camp, a complete village equipped with a school, waterworks, sewers, electric illumination, a general store, individual family houses and a big bunk house for single men and a mess-hall in charge of a competent chef, his assistants had difficulty in understanding him till it was explained to them that labor was scarce (during the war) and it was best to treat it well. Morgan's own considerations in the matter were mainly human, based on the feeling that he had a certain responsibility toward the workers, while his college-trained men had to have those considerations translated into a "labor policy" tied to the profit motive.

The problem, as Morgan recognized it, was educational, cultural. Visiting colleges and universities, he discerned the basic fault; his early critical attitude toward education and the cultural situation in America continued and strengthened. In 1908 he visited one of the country's leading institutions of higher learning, then wrote in his diary: ". . . Took lunch with a number of faculty members, and then looked over the university buildings. Called on a faculty member. He took out a little tea-set and made the tea for us and then passed the cigars. Took supper with a number of faculty members. [This] is a beautiful place, the finest group of buildings I have ever seen. But there is a spirit about it that misses the meaning of life. I am glad that I did not go to school there. There is a tremendous advantage in some ways in not having been to college. The finest lot of men I saw that day were the Italian laborers working on the new buildings, and honestly, I would rather be one of those Italians than the professor who took supper with us. Most of the college men have been so busy studying that they have had no time to think or to be men. Introspection has reached a great development there."

ANTIOCH COLLEGE

I have mentioned that as a youth in St. Cloud Arthur Morgan had planned to do something about education. When he was still in his early thirties, but already a successful engineer, he began to save money with which he might eventually start a school or college of his own. Just before the outbreak of the World War he and Mrs. Morgan, who shared his ideas, acquired a tract of land in western Massachusetts, to be the site of the new school; and he

was thinking of quitting engineering for education very shortly, when he was
drawn into the Miami Valley Flood Control job, which occupied him for six
years. His headquarters were in Dayton.

Near by, in the village of Yellow Springs, was Antioch College, which had
once—under Horace Mann—been one of the most interesting schools in
America, but was now in the last stages of decline. Arthur Morgan was asked
to diagnose, and prescribe a cure for, the ailing institution; he expressed his
views on education . . . and, to make a long story short, he was urged, instead of starting a new school in the mountains of western Massachusetts,
to take over old Antioch and to transform it into his kind of school. In 1920
he assumed its presidency and in the ensuing thirteen years—at the end of
which period President Roosevelt appointed him chairman and chief engineer
of the TVA—he developed into one of the most creative and interesting
contemporary educators in the United States. He had always been one of
the hardest-working men imaginable, but these thirteen years were possibly
the busiest, most strenuous, of his life. Some one who knew him well at the
time tells me that throughout that period he never slept three successive nights
in the same bed. He was in Yellow Springs a few days a month, a day or two
at a time just long enough to impress his ideas and character on the place. He
traveled almost continuously, seeking teachers, getting students, collecting
funds (and refusing many a sum which might have tended to influence
Antioch unfavorably), and spreading—with the help of assistants—the Antioch
campus till it included twenty states of the Union: for an integral part of
the Morgan educational scheme was the so-called coöperative plan, under which
the students were at the college for five or ten weeks, then worked on jobs
in industries, stores, offices, etc., for a like period, which was no simple matter
and involved immense effort to get it started and then to keep it going.

The underlying purpose of Antioch was "to develop the entire personality
of the student in sound proportion, not allowing any fundamentally necessary
element of character to be neglected, nor permitting any element of education so to monopolize time and attention or to leave the student weak or one-
sided in qualities universally necessary for successful living." In carrying out
this plan, various distinct elements were gradually developed and organized into
a unified program. Some of these elements, as the plan now stands, are: (1)
A liberal college education, introducing the student to nearly all major fields
of human interest, including science, literature, and the social sciences, on
the theory that a well-balanced liberal education, combined with specialized
preparation in the field of the student's chief interest, will better prepare him
for a successful life than will a highly specialized training alone. (2) Academic
training for the special interest or the life work of the student, in the fields
for which the college is equipped, and preliminary training in such subjects
as law, medicine, nursing, chemistry, and architecture. (3) The aforementioned
"coöp" plan. (4) A plan of autonomous or self-directed study for students
beyond the sophomore year. (5) The personal interest and help of the faculty,

in conjunction with the "coöp" plan, in deciding upon a vocation and in meeting life problems. (6) An extensive health and physical education program with emphasis on intramural athletics.

To describe fully the Antioch setup, as developed under Morgan, and as it for the most part continues under the new president, Algo D. Henderson (a man rather unlike Morgan, but generally sympathetic to the setup), would take more pages in this book than I can allow for this chapter altogether; those who are not familiar with it, but wish to be, are free to write to the college for its several publications that explain it. It is not easily described adequately in print. To know it, one ought to spend a little time at Yellow Springs, then hunt up Morgan and have a long talk with him, and get in touch with a few hundred Antioch graduates: which are some of the things I did in 1937, after I had become interested in the Antioch ideas and the personality of Morgan.

The Antioch setup and its results, while not perfection, seemed to me, when I was there, extremely near to real education. The college was, essentially, still the place Morgan had created. The "Antioch spirit," of which I had heard, was no myth. The average student was as alive and conscious and interested as is only the exceptional student in the more conventional colleges, several of which I visited in 1934-37. Under the elaborate and heartening stimulus of the place, he believed in hard work and practical, vigorous effort, while his attitude was one of self-reliant adventure. The relations between the teachers and the student were close and mutually beneficial. His working in factories, stores, and offices between the periods of study, which often had direct reference to his experiences on the job, gave the student a sense of reality about the world for which he was preparing himself. Antioch had a real student government elected democratically, and an effective "honor system," under which students were trusted to act with straightforwardness and honesty in various relationships. This is of paramount importance, for, as Morgan has pointed out in one of his addresses, "our modern life is becoming far too complicated to be managed by surveillance, and unless the honor system can become established as a life habit, our social and economic structure will break down." A student-operated catering service placed sandwiches and other refreshments in the dormitories at night, with price lists and a box for money. Losses from dishonesty were slight.

I talked to students at Antioch who were enthusiastic about the place, but not in the surface, cheer-leader manner. They were not uncritical of various phases of the setup, or of the old or the new presidents, or of certain members of the faculty, or of one another, or the way the "coöp plan" was run, and felt free to speak their minds. They were eager to hear my impressions and were interested in my tentative misgivings.

One of these misgivings went something like this: The "coöp job" is the most unique part of the Antioch idea, and doubtless has many good phases, even within the limit of the fact that in nearly all cases the job is found for the student by the Personnel Division, which thus prevents him from experiencing the most serious reality in our industrial world, that of finding the job for himself. However, what really bothers me is that, when he goes to his job, which has been found for him by the college, the student is invited or urged, directly and indirectly, to adjust himself to various circumstances on the job, except when such adjustment would compromise his sense of morals: for the Personnel Division has had the devil of a time getting the job, which is not his only, but the students' who are to follow him, and the college as a whole might suffer if he should fail to adjust himself and get along. Adjustment, of course, is necessary nearly everywhere, most of the time; but I think that too much and too ready adjustment is bad; people should not compromise with, or yield to, their environment too readily. And what worries me is that the implicit or explicit demand of Antioch that the student get along on the job causes him to develop too apt a personal technique to get along, to put up with things that, from the viewpoint of social progress, he should not be putting up with. . . . When I mentioned it, this misgiving caused discussions throughout the college; and as I listened to and participated in them, the misgiving largely left me. Which was true of most other misgivings.

My contact, personal and by mail, with a large number of Antioch graduates was deeply satisfying. Most of them are still young men and women, and are not (or likely to become) "outstanding" or "successful" in the usual sense of these words; but they have something which seems to me profoundly important and desirable. They think clearly and dispassionately, which probably is a disqualification for the kind of leadership or positions which make one conspicuous; but they indubitably constitute a considerable part, in America, of that leaven which makes for a healthy, organic growth of society; and I believe that a college which is a source of such a leaven is performing the greatest possible service to democracy.

Antiochians, by and large, are conscious people, conscious of themselves and of the world, certainly more so than the great majority of graduates of other colleges. They are critical; at once radical and conservative. In back of their minds seems to hang an idea that in America one ought to be both: radical in the sense of going to the root of things, and conservative because the American civilization includes many tangible and intangible factors which are good and ought to be preserved. At the same time that I was prodding into the makeup of the Antiochians I happened to be in contact with a number of graduates of two great Eastern universities who seemed rather rabid on many important subjects. They saw no good in the New Deal or the Republican Party or the C.I.O. They shared, and were governed by, the current hates, prejudices, and blind loyalties. And it was relief to get with a group of Antioch men and women. In Washington, the active "New Dealers" among them could discuss the shortcomings of the Roosevelt Administration, and what should be done, after the New Deal "cracked up," to preserve the valuable progress achieved under it. Those who were ardent laborites could talk of the shortcomings of organized labor and what must be done to rid it of its present taint of petty dictatorship and racketeering. Those whose livelihood and substantial wealth is identified with big business could recognize the abuses of big business and were not only willing but eager to discuss the need for democracy in industry to preserve democracy and liberty in the country at large.

A great many Antiochians are in government service in Washington, and their influence—while as yet not very definite—operates within it.

MORGAN'S PHILOSOPHY

After visiting Antioch, I felt I must meet its creator. I found him in a tight, low-ceilinged room in his extremely modest dwelling in the TVA town of Norris, Tennessee. Spread upon a large bed, by which he sat, were papers, maps, blueprints. He was fifty-nine: a tall, sparse, tense, gray man, with a sharp-featured, at once naïve- and shrewd-seeming face, illumined by large, very honest eyes that appeared to look beyond me even when they were fixed upon my face as he talked. One of the most articulate men I have ever met, he talked rapidly in a firm, strong voice, in clean, simple English, expressing involved thoughts and describing complicated situations in a way that they became entirely clear to me, at the same time that I felt that Morgan himself was an immensely complicated man—and this partly because he realizes, intensely so, that the world is a huge complexity, with nothing very simple in it, which must be dissected, analyzed, and understood, and which it does no good to try to simplify.

We talked for a couple of hours, first in his house, then in his car while he drove me over the TVA domain around Norris; and I had a feeling that, if we had time, he could talk to me for years in that even clear way, never raising his voice, all his well-fashioned thoughts, theories, impressions, conclusions, and word pictures marching on the Long Road of his mind to a point not yet in sight; and I could listen to him all the while, fascinated. Here was an American talking; here was America, a part of America, talking, calmly, unhesitantly, with an authority stemming out of experience.

I had asked him if he was satisfied with what had been accomplished at Antioch, and he replied that, in a way, he was. What had happened at Antioch the past fifteen years had caused several other colleges to revise their methods, at least in part. It had become a point of influence for good. Within itself the college had developed a spirit of honest study, the attitude of free, critical inquiry, which led to intellectual moderation. Not a few Antiochians, partly as a result of the "coöp" program, showed growth in social and economic understanding. A considerable portion of them had attacked the problem of working out an inclusive philosophy and of developing inclusive purpose for their lives. . . . The process of the Antioch setup was long, halting, subject to interruptions, and, of course, it did not satisfy him in any final way. There

were all manner of difficulties. One was that a passion to achieve an integrated
philosophy was not characteristic of the academic or the general atmosphere
in Europe or America; the student's idea to prepare himself merely for making a living was too strongly prevalent to overcome in six years, which is the
length of the course at Antioch. Another difficulty was that the undertaking
at Antioch was not one of passing on a desirable temper and way of life directly
from those who have them to those who seek to attain them. If it were that, the
problem would be relatively simple. The project at Antioch was basically the
effort to work out together a purpose and way of living which as yet were
not fully achieved either by himself or anyone else who was or had been
connected with the college in a leading rôle. "I have heard," he had said in a
speech on this subject a year before I met him, "that perhaps half the physicians
specializing in tuberculosis have themselves suffered from the disease, and thus
have an intense desire to help overcome it. So the very origin of this element
of the Antioch program was a feeling of need, rather than of conscious possession of desired quality."

In the same address he had said: "Antioch, I think, is in advance of many
institutions in the desire to achieve a pattern of living as the finest fruit of
the educational process. The extent to which it is outstanding is a matter of
degree. As I return to Antioch from time to time I come to have a substantial
respect for the progress being made in this quest. The progress is not spectac-
ular, but it is real, definite, and considerable. As a result, Antioch is an institution of finer quality with each generation which passes on to the next its
growing inheritance. And the achievement of this purpose would, I believe, be
the greatest contribution Antioch could make to America."

I asked him if he would do it again, and he answered yes; only on a smaller
scale; Antioch was too big; it had taken him most of the thirteen years during
which he had been its active head just to get the money to keep it going.
Not that he planned to start another school; but if he did, he would begin,
as he had planned originally, with a half-dozen or a dozen students and increase that number gradually, but perhaps never beyond a few score, and try
to work out with them a way of life, a way of developing character.

Arthur Morgan is a pronounced individual, even an individualist, strongly
conscious of his background as well as of many of the problems of contemporary
America. With the aid of that consciousness he has developed an inclusive
and not at all simple philosophy, which he has more or less stated in his writings,[1] and which helps him in his endeavor to see America and the human

[1] The best known of these are perhaps his *Antioch Notes*, which he has been issuing for many
years as a monthly leaflet. They are read regularly by about 20,000 people. His appointment to
the chairmanship of the TVA was due in part to the fact that President Roosevelt had been
reading them throughout the late 1920's and early 1930's. Supreme Court Justice Brandeis considers them an American version of the *Spectator Papers* of Addison and Steele. A compendium
of them was issued in 1930 by the Antioch Press, Yellow Springs, Ohio, which also published
his book, *My World*, and many of his addresses in pamphlet form, as well as Mrs. Morgan's
Finding His World, from which I quote in this chapter. But, up to this writing, Morgan's
most important—also most concise—work is *The Long Road*, published by the National Home

problem generally, not in pieces or sections, which is how most people see them, but as a whole. Personally, I do not consider it a flawless philosophy, a key to human salvation; if for no other reason, because of the puritan in him it is devoid of humor, which I think is peculiarly necessary in the development of an American program. However, I go a long way with him.

His philosophy has few original elements; but the way he puts it makes it profoundly American. It wanders all over the lot, which is America and the human problem. It is full of learning and references to experience. And if it has a central emphasis, it is this—that the problem of human progress cannot be dealt with in a hurry, *via* sensational short-cuts, and through ballyhoo and newspaper headlines; that the road ahead is long and arduous and ill illumined, and what is needed is not dogma, not isms, not rigid ideologies or social programs, but character in men and women.

"When I use the word 'character,'" he says in *The Long Road*, "I have in mind three elements. First is purposefulness, or the pattern of desire—the vision of the life it would be well to lead, of the kind of a world which, so far as wisdom, judgment, and good will can determine, it would be well to live in.

"Second, I include good will and the skilled and disciplined drive of desire which presses toward the realization of aims and purposes. Great insight into what would constitute a good life for oneself and for society has value only as expressed in well-considered action, though under the term 'action' I should include the disciplined and carefully expressed thinking of the student, and the work of the artist, as well as the more obvious activity of the laborer or the businessman.

"Great vigor of action by itself, however, may have no more social value than the capricious force of a tornado, unless it is directed by a vision of what is desirable. A tornado may, by chance, break down harmful barriers as well as destroy values. The activity of Napoleon had some incidental value in breaking down what was obsolete in the structure of European government and society, and was not without constructive undertakings of importance, but it was largely capricious. What a pity his tremendous energy was not directed by a great vision of a good social order, and by the ethical controls which would have led him to use suitable means.

"The third factor is the ethical or moral quality, the habitual choice of means that are wholesome in their own effects. Even when the desired end is good and the disciplined energy great, it is important that the methods used shall be in themselves ethical or moral.

"My definition of ethical or moral action is as easy to state as it is difficult to apply. That is an ethical act which is good when judged by its total conse-

---

Library Foundation, Washington, D. C., first mentioned in the Depression section of this book. It has an understanding and stimulating preface by Dorothy Canfield Fisher. It is a running commentary on America, solid with specific illustrations to point out evidence in favor of his comment. Most of these illustrations are drawn from industrial, business, and engineering activities. One chapter is entitled "Tensile Strength of Steel and Men"; another, "Specifications for National Character."

quences—which is good for the future as well as for the present, for society as a whole as well as for ourselves. That action is unethical which, while its immediate or personal result may be good, displaces action which would result in greater good, or has later effects on others which are undesirable and which outweigh the good. In practice, 'good' and 'bad' must often be supplanted by the less absolute terms, 'better' and 'worse,' but that does not alter the argument. Our ability to judge the total effects of our acts is always limited and imperfect. It is increased by education and experience, by constant effort to use and refine such discrimination as we possess, and by the leadership of men of exceptional insight."

In *The Long Road*, he develops a picture of contemporary society, stressing industry and government, which has reached "such size and complexity that little further sound development . . . can be assured without a general and very marked strengthening of personal character"; and he warns and emphasizes that "unless such an improvement occurs, we shall have increasingly serious breakdowns both in government and in business, probably followed by harsh and arbitrary regimentation of our lives."

How can such improvement occur? "It is obvious that character is not acquired solely as the result of any sudden change of attitude or of loyalty. It is a product of gradual growth, with increasingly clear definition of aims, constant strengthening and refinement of motives, steady improvement of methods, and gradually developing decision and discipline of drives and energies. The infection of great leadership and the changing currents of public interest, however, may greatly accelerate the development, and once a great movement gets under way, as much may be gained in a year as usually in a decade or a century. It is probable, however, that a considerable period of relatively quiet and inconspicuous growth will be essential before there can be any sweeping change in our national character. As a rule, increase of genuine vigor and refinement of personality occurs primarily from the contagion of actual contact with the same qualities in others, though able persons enlarge upon and refine what they receive."

In short, what is needed is great leadership and an educational process whose core is a keen cognizance of this problem. I believe he thinks that what has been accomplished at Antioch is but a fumbling beginning in the right direction.

Arthur Morgan has a profound belief in democracy and liberty, and this on practical grounds. If anything, he is a pragmatist. "External control and regulation of intimate personal matters by law," such as we find now in certain European countries, "is generally arbitrary and relatively undiscriminating. In respect to many activities a normal, intelligent person can direct his own affairs with greater economy and discrimination than can be secured by legislation or other external regulation. Free men working together for common ends in the long run are more effective than men regimented by outward authority, whether that authority be economic, political, or spiritual." But, in order that free men may work toward common ends they must know that "in a society without arbitrary barriers the inmost action of every person affects society as a whole." In a free democracy, "no activity of a man, either in thought or in outward act, is wholly private in its consequences," and what we must come to, if we are to progress democratically within the framework of liberty, is the recognition of this fact.

The pragmatist in Morgan favors "a large element of personal freedom [also] because free men are in some degree creative. Since no persons are just alike, a man who originates his own action will give it some of the original quality of his own unique personality. Self-direction may interfere with the quick efficiency that uniformity of action sometimes achieves, but it adds variety and richness to life, and constantly introduces new elements of excellence. We cannot wholly dispense with imposed uniformity of conduct, such as our traffic rules, or as in the manufacture of uniform products like automobiles, but we do well to strive constantly to increase the range and the capacity for self-determination."

But because of this very fact that a large degree of personal liberty "is good—yes, essential—to a good social order . . . makes all the more necessary the development of social-mindedness. . . . The conflict between these two great facts, the interdependence of men in society and the practical value of self-determination and personal freedom, can be resolved only by personal character, which directs free action to social ends. . . ."

Very close to the center of Morgan's philosophy is his idea of diversity. It rests upon his deep sense of elbow room, which is a result of his background. He has been around and seen and studied many sections of America, and he emphasizes that "there is much room for choice and honest differences of taste and judgment" in the matter of "the type of social order men shall adopt." I have already referred to his conversation with H. G. Wells, who maintained that America must decide between individualism and socialism. "I hope," said Morgan, "that America is not going to make that decision. . . . America likes communism. In many respects we serve everybody alike regardless of his resources. Our fire departments are communistic. We serve everyone alike from public funds. Our public school system is communistic. There also we not only serve the public from public funds, regardless of relative financial contributions, but we compel children to take the schooling offered. Our highways are largely communistic. . . . We have state socialism in our country. Look at all the great municipal water supplies where government is in business. Our great irrigation systems are socialistic. . . . America also believes in democracy; we elect officers to represent us in government. . . . On the other hand, America is not afraid of other forms of social organization; America is not afraid of autocracy, of aristocracy. You have here a great university (the University of Chicago). Unless it is governed differently from most other great endowed universities, it is autocratically managed, and a little group of men who are its trustees choose their own successors. . . ." America, Morgan goes on, is not afraid of big business or of little business; she wants both. Here and there she tolerates even despotism and industrial feudalism.

Morgan approves of this diversity, as such . . . and here is where he seemingly comes in conflict with my objection, as expressed on many pages of this book, to America's basic incongruity. But only seemingly, superficially; not really or basically. He is, of course, not unaware of the dehumanized, irresponsible nature of corporate business, which I discuss in a Diary entry included in the "Depression" section of this volume, and which condition caused such havoc in America during the early 1930's in part because it had been functioning, not within the framework of the general government of the United States, but outside and above it, so that actually the government had functioned within the framework of dehumanized, irresponsible business; and I am sure that he is opposed to this situation as strongly as I am. He was for the early New Deal, which aimed to reverse matters by bringing the function of business within and under the general government. He, personally, is not in favor of *any* kind of diversity at all that happens to exist. Even if America is tolerant of despotism, autocracy, and industrial feudalism, that does not mean that he favors those social forms. He contributes to textile strikers in the South and to the movement that aims to abolish the sharecropping system. Not a Socialist himself, he makes no objection to his sons' being Socialists. He does what he can to influence America to cease being tolerant of industrial feudalism and agricultural tenancy; at the same time he holds that they can be effectively abolished not through any short-cut tricks, but only gradually, democratically, by an awakened citizenry, which has too strong a character, conscience, and social consciousness and responsibility to put up with such things.

Through his approval of diversity runs his passion for democracy, of which diversity in all fields is an integral part; and for freedom and for human character, as he defines it in *The Long Road*—which makes him as strongly anti-incongruity as I am. His emphasis is on character. He seems to say over and over again that, no matter what sort of system we adopt, the world cannot become a really better place to live in as long as we remain the sort of people we are.

He holds that under democracy and liberty, and with character, we can work our way future-ward, away from politico-economic incongruity, within and around the diverse existing economic and social institutions and setups; and that America will continue for some time part capitalistic, part socialistic, big business and little business, etc. America has room for such diversity and—within the large framework of government dedicated to democracy and liberty, under the leadership of men of character—can attain to harmony within it; in fact, with the aid of it. His vision of a harmonious America is like a forest he once visited. "There were trees one and two centuries old towering a hundred and fifty feet overhead; underneath them was another level of trees—ironwoods, sourwood, birches—growing half as high, and filling in the interstices where the sunlight was not being used by the larger trees. Then another order of trees—hawthorns, dogwood, and sassafras—filled in the unoccupied places in the more humble positions. Next below were viburnums and laurel, and beneath them blueberry bushes and smaller plants only a few feet high; and still underneath them came a whole class of flowers that get their sunshine and do their year's work early in the spring before the leaves on the trees are out, and while the sun can shine through. These included trillium, hepatica, Jack-in-the-pulpit, and anemones. Then down on the ground and on the tree trunks were mosses and lichens. . . ."

In fact, Morgan not only approves of diversity; if it did not exist in America, he would want to create it, on the theory that if a country, under the general setup of a government dedicated to democracy and freedom, includes many social forms, each may contribute out of its own peculiar talents and experiences to society as a whole.[2]

Arthur Morgan is significant to me as a product of the pioneer era, whose influences are still powerful—perhaps dominant—in America. His ideas are American, related to his background: at once pragmatic and idealistic, material and spiritual. He is unique in that he sees, or tries to see, America as a whole, with all its major or basic problems, and can articulate what he sees; and in that he, an individualist, has plumbed the depths of his being and come up with the realization that each person is individually responsible for the welfare of his community . . . but he is also a deeply representative man. His philosophy is, in the main, an extension of the communal attitude during the pioneer era, which I have mentioned once or twice before in this book, which included more freedom than civilized man ever before experienced, and which is still strong in the American people. "Under a régime of personal freedom," he says in *The Long Road*, "the first great principle of conduct is that a man's actions shall be determined by their probable total effect on society as a whole, and not on himself alone. . . ." Elsewhere in his little book he speaks of "social wisdom," which is primarily an individual's awareness of his duty to contribute to the welfare of his community, his business or industry or profession, according to his capacity. Basically, I suppose, his idea is the Golden Rule made dynamic, invested with vision and the urgency for action, which is the incentive and plan for a happier order of things. In *The Long Road* he shows how this idea can be applied to all the various departments of American life. He places the responsibility for the world in which the individual lives squarely on the latter's shoulders and gives his suggestions as to what he can do to fulfill that responsibility. If he is a person of character and purpose and ideals, he wants him to become, or to establish, what he calls a "center of influence." He

[2] This chapter was planned and partly written before the dispute within the Tennessee Valley Authority, early in March 1938, engulfed the United States and made Arthur E. Morgan one of the most controversial figures in the country. I do not intend here to go into that dispute or controversy; to deal with it fully would require a book by itself. This is an attempt to sketch the essential Morgan as I see him. I think, however, that his "diversity idea" is a key to his TVA difficulties.

wants to see created many such centers, which he also describes as "islands of brotherhood"—private homes, neighborhoods, schools, colleges, and informal groups and fellowships, within which "such qualities of character as I have described are dominant," and out of which will then "emerge men and women who will give the same qualities to the management of business and government. In fact, I see no other source of leadership than such centers of influence, which may be ever so humble and unseen, and yet be potent. If such centers are lacking, then we shall continue to bemoan the lack of great leadership. There is a saying that in times of stress 'the Lord will raise up a great leader.' But such a leader is not suddenly 'raised up.' He has been silently building up his life for probably twenty years or more."

Morgan, while against dogma and rigidity, is not nearly as naturally and inevitably democratic as his good and great friend Walter Locke; in fact, there is in him a bit of the prophet who gives the impression of talking from on high. I am told, however, that at Antioch, when the democratic majority of the college community registered protest against his natural puritanic prejudices and inclinations, he yielded gracefully. He can be Lincolnesque in tolerance and kindness. He is idealistic to the point of stubborness; in many respects, a non-compromiser, always a hater of deceit and sham and of mere personal ambition and opportunism; "a man to set your compass by," as one of his friends put it to me, but perhaps not always easy to get along with at close range.

How much Morgan has derived in his outlook and intellectual manner from his continuous self-education cannot be readily ascertained when it comes to particulars, but his philosophy is palpably gotten out of the incalculably rich store of the world's wisdom, which he has patiently sifted and fashioned to fit his own nature, and adapted to the peculiarities of American life. His own experience prepared him for this, and he was thereby made a highly conscious individual, capable of instinctive recognition of verities that have survived wars and time, and know no boundaries. His concept of social order is based on these fundamentals and on his pioneer background. My friend Cantrell may be said to have possessed the same general characteristics; but—due, perhaps, to somewhat different experiences (becoming a minister while Morgan became an engineer)—he found it necessary to tie his aspirations to the Socialist cause. Morgan was just a little more realistic, more elemental, incapable of being restricted by any ism. Both are fanatically truthful, honest men.

To determine the stature of a man like Morgan is difficult. But I feel he is a big man. He recognized a problem, went into it rather deeply, articulated it and made it into an issue as far as he could; and the probability is that his influence in the long run will not be trivial. He is deeply a product of America, which is a disturbing amalgam of practicality and vision. In Morgan these two qualities have more or less balanced. He places no faith in immediate results. Nor in mere size. He feels that good things must have humble beginnings, in little "islands of brotherhood." He is a pragmatist always, but his pragmatism is no blind, ignorant thing. It is disciplined, intelligent, tugged by vision.

American pragmatism is at times a ruthless procedure. The character that had gone into the making of various early enterprises, most of which were small, was largely suppressed in more modern times by the tremendous enterprises which came into being toward and after the start of the twentieth century. Personal character was blurred or drowned in them. The general business ethics, upon which trade could be conducted on large scale more expediently, absorbed, diffused it. The individual became more or less identified with his business concern and adopted its general—at times vaguely defined—code for his own, thus tending to obscure or render negligible his own more immediate human or personal qualities. This can, perhaps, be called a sublimation of his basic self. While I do not know whether Morgan has gone thus far in analyzing the situation pertaining to American character, his thinking is sound and challenging when he stresses the need of character in the individual; and when he translates his thought into action—as he did at Antioch—he appears to me, as I have suggested, one of the most noteworthy contemporary Americans.

Black Mountain: An Experiment in Education

EARLY IN THE AUTUMN 1935—TO GET AWAY FOR A WHILE FROM THE TEMPO, CON-
fusion, and exorbitance of New York—I drove South, where I had not
been for years and knew few people. I had no definite plans. I thought of places
to visit, but there was no "must" about any of them. One of these was Black
Mountain College in North Carolina, of which I had been hearing since it was
started by a group of teachers and students that, following a disagreement with
President Hamilton Holt, had broken away from Rollins College, in Winter
Park, Florida. Henry Allen Moe, of the Guggenheim Foundation, whom I had
happened to meet in the street in New York the day I left, had urged me to
drop in at the place; he knew the man at the head of it—Professor John A.
Rice—who was a fellow of the Foundation and, said Moe, an interesting man
"who seems to be doing something down there."

On my fifth day out, after a pleasant ramble through Virginia, I got to
Black Mountain, a tiny town wedged between the Blue Ridge and Great Craggy
ranges. Following a native's directions, I drove up a broad slope on the Blue
Ridge side, freshly splashed with autumn reds and yellows, till I reached a
great summer-hotel-like building which, I learned subsequently, the college
leased from the Southern Y.M.C.A., which during July and August used it as
a conference camp for its secretaries. Entering the vast barnlike lobby, I introduced myself to the first person I met, explaining I had heard of the place and
wished to know more about it.

I had thought to stay an hour or so, then go on to visit the TVA the next
day; but the first thing I knew I was established in a guest-room. I laid this to
Southern hospitality, though most of the people there seemed Northerners. I
had a few talks with teachers and students, supper in the college dining-room,
then more talks, including one with Rice which lasted till past midnight . . .
and, to shorten a long tale, instead of staying only overnight, I remained for
two and a half months; and I have been there a few times for shorter stays
since then.

To me, Black Mountain is one of the most fascinating places in America.
To tell its story adequately, one would have to turn it, assuming one could,
into a novel which in point of technique would suggest simultaneously Thomas
Mann's *Magic Mountain* and Vicki Baum's *Grand Hotel*, and in content and
effect would be unlike either.

My purpose here is to do little more than to suggest the story's outline up
to the fall of 1937, when I was there last before writing this chapter: for it is
different every time one sees it. I might also add—with a little emphasis—

that the ensuing sketch of it is presented as *I* see the place: for no two people see it alike even should they visit it together.

The inception of Black Mountain College was incredibly fine. And I am not thinking particularly of John Rice, who for years, while developing his philosophy of education, had openly criticized the American educational system and blasphemed the sacred cows grazing on the various campuses, and had then become successively the leader of the rebels at Rollins College[1] and the rector of the new college.

Nor have I specially in mind the several professors and instructors who stood by Rice after his dismissal from Rollins, thereby losing their jobs and making the fracas national news. I admire the courage of the whole group that left Rollins to launch a new college in the midst of the turbulent wake of the Bank Holiday. But my impulse is to toss an extra orchid at the fifteen boys and girls, average age twenty, including the president of the Rollins student body and the editor of the Rollins campus paper, who, indignant at President Holt's action, which in their view violated academic freedom and human decency, and having faith in Rice as a teacher and leader, quit their old college and joined the rebel professors in the seemingly impossible enterprise of starting a new college at a time when neither Rice nor any of his discharged colleagues had the least notion of where they were to start it or what they were to use for money. Unlike the dismissed teachers, these fifteen students were not compelled to leave their comfortable dormitories at Winter Park and go looking for a spot on which to pitch their tents. Indeed, in one or two cases, the rebel students forfeited Rollins scholarships; in several others they risked the displeasure of their parents; and in all cases they risked the probability of wasting at least a year in an undertaking nearly everyone said would fail. Without them, Rice and his associates could not have thought of starting a new school. And after the new college was announced, these students helped the teachers to raise the minimum sum necessary to rent the hotel-like building they chanced to find at Black Mountain and to buy the essential equipment for classes and the food needed by the group for a few months, and to get four more students and three additional instructors; so that when the college opened in September, 1933, the teaching staff numbered nine and the student body nineteen.

Students and teachers pooled their personal book collections and called the result the college library, and agreed to contribute manual labor voluntarily according to ability. That first year, the teachers drew out of the treasury only what they needed for clothes and incidentals, which averaged $7.27 per month per person. But even so, the college nearly collapsed twice for lack of money,

[1] The Rollins story is well known in the American academic world. Those unfamiliar with its details will find a ten-thousand-word report upon it in the November, 1933, *Bulletin* of the American Association of University Professors, which fully upholds Rice and his fellow rebels, and an almost equally long rebuttal to it in the December, 1933, *Bulletin* of Rollins College.

and was saved only by the joint resourcefulness and self-denial of both the faculty and the students.

The second year the number of teachers rose to eighteen, of students to thirty-two. In 1935, when I first visited the college, there were seventeen teachers and forty-eight students. As I write, the number is about the same. Such education as Black Mountain College holds up as desirable is possible only in a very small school. If all goes well, eventually the student body will number about one hundred and twenty-five and the faculty about thirty.

The Rollins rebels, when they decided to start a new college, were against many things in the prevalent system of education, but were unanimous on one objection—that college and university trustees or regents, presidents, and deans, most of whom were not teachers or scholars, but executives and disciplinarians, and sluices for influence from various non-educational sources, had the power to interfere with the teachers' function. The little group was determined to get back to the old American idea of "Mark Hopkins on one end of the log and the student on the other." And so Black Mountain College has no trustees, no president, no dean. There is but one person in the office, a typist, who is not also a teacher. As rector, Rice is the head of the college; his job, however, is not office work, but teaching. What office work there is is done by the registrar and the treasurer, who are also teachers before they are anything else. There is a so-called advisory council, which consists of friends of the college, including John Dewey, but has no legal authority. All important decisions are made by the board of fellows elected by the faculty which includes six teachers and the president of the student body, and is continually influenced by both the teaching staff and the student body as a whole. There is a real student government, whose officers meet periodically as equals with the whole faculty and the rector. Once a month or so the teachers and students gather in general meeting and air their problems. This setup has brought out unsuspected executive abilities. One teacher has turned out to be a competent treasurer, another an able registrar and office-manager.

Aside from the purely organizational problem, the majority of the original Black Mountain faculty had no clearly formed positive ideas in relation to the establishment of the college, and the questions of educational policy were left almost entirely to the leader, John Rice, whose head bristled with ideas, and who said at the start that he wanted a "new kind of college." That the educational policy was left largely to him was due also to the fact that all the fifteen rebel students had come along mainly out of their personal respect for him, because they liked what he taught and the way he taught it.

Since 1933 Rice's ideas of what is wrong with the prevalent educational system have largely receded into the background of his mind, and his positive ideas have grouped themselves into a philosophy of education of his own, which for adequate statement would require a book. He has promised to write it some day.[2] Here follow some of the things he said to me in 1935, as revised subsequently:

"... The job of a college is to bring young people to intellectual *and emotional* maturity; to intelligence, by which I mean a subtle balance between the intellect and the emotions; not merely to an arbitrarily selected amount of cramming. ... In great part I blame Hitlerism on German education, which always primarily concerned itself only with the intellect, with stuffing the head full of facts, and thus prepared for Hitler a nation of emotional infants ready to succumb to his obscene demagoguery. Many Nazis know a lot and are rightly called intellectuals, but most are incapable of decent adult feelings and reactions, which might have caused them to recoil from Hitler and to step out and fight his movement. We in America will have to realize and comprehend this condition; for, if our national life is to go on lurching toward a general crisis, we will be in similar danger, and for the same reason; our education has been powerfully influenced by Germany. Until the end of the last century a German Ph.D. was the ultimate goal of an American scholar. Now look at some of the people that come from our 'best' and largest universities. Their heads are crammed with facts, but what knowledge they possess is often barren . and does not include self-knowledge. Many of them are ailing children, sore with themselves and the world, ready to turn in a moment into 'infantile leftists' (calling themselves 'Communists') and even more infantile Fascists. There is scant essential difference between the two. I think it is significant that thousands of pre-1933 German Communists had, it seems, no difficulty whatever in becoming passionate Hitlerites in 1933. Emotionally immature, unformed, unstable people, no matter how well 'educated' intellectually, have no difficulty in swinging from one excitement or attachment to another, their 'ideologies' notwithstanding. ...

"... If we are to have equality and democracy between men and women, co-education is essential, not in the sense merely of having men and women in the same classroom, but in the sense of education in relation to each other. American civilization has been an experiment in co-education from the beginning. To separate men and women in colleges is to be guilty once more of stupidly copying Europe. ...

"... The constant admonition of a college should be not 'Be intellectual!' or 'Be muscular!' (in both cases the dividing line is the neck) but 'Be intelligent!' A college should take account of the *whole being* and be a sort of second womb from which young people are born to all-round human maturity. ...

"... I don't mean to suggest, of course, that none of our long-established colleges and large universities are any good. On the contrary. Speaking generally, however, there is not enough of what I call education going on in our great institutions, which is true, of course, also of England and other European countries besides Germany, which I have mentioned as a horrible example. ...

[2] An article by John A. Rice, "Fundamentalism and the Higher Learning," appeared in the May, 1937, *Harpers Magazine*.

The common expression 'to get' an education is significant. It lights up the entire fallacy of the prevailing system, for education can only be *experienced*; one 'gets' only information or 'facts'—and the 'facts' acquired in the average college have to do with the past and are mainly worthless to one destined to live in the future. To put the emphasis upon the teaching of 'facts,' the giving of mere information, is to train people in and for the past. Half the 'facts' at this moment being taught, say, in psychology classes are no longer facts, granting they ever were. We are beginning to see that history is merely restrained fiction. The so-called historian cannot go entirely wild, but he can do a pretty good job of it, when he sits down to write, for example, the history of the World War. It is not necessary to point out the part that guesswork, daydreaming, and wishful thinking play in the teaching of sociology and even economics, for that matter. There are some stubborn facts in the early stages of the physical sciences, in mathematics and biology, that must be learned. But once these stages are passed, you are in the realm of imagination, and often get lost because of the meager training the imagination has had. It is a commonplace that many scientists are, through long years of training in the factual world, unfitted for this leap into the world of the imagination. Worse yet, when they see how tenuous is their hold upon the factual world and feel themselves coming to the end of imagination, when unanswerable questions creep upon them in the dark, they pull the bedclothes about their heads and yell for God. They have been believers so long they must have something to believe in, even if that entails turning back to the middle ages. Nothing more ignominious has happened in our time than the scientists' betrayal of scepticism because of their whimpering fear of its consequences when straight, hard facts fail them. If truth were their goal, they could face the fierce, inviting light of the unknown, instead of groveling. . . . But surely, you will say, truth, education, not mere head-stuffing, is the goal of the humanities. I should like to think so, but, I am sorry to say that, if it is, it is a long way off, such a long way that the undergraduate in the average college seldom even gets a glimpse of it. . . . Take the queen of learning: professors of philosophy do not profess philosophy; they profess to be able to tell what philosophers have said and, sometimes, what they meant. If you are looking for a philosopher, stay away from departments of philosophy; you will get only reporters there. . . . Well, there is literature; but if you make an inspection of our colleges, you will find, for the most part, that the study of literature is concerned mainly with biography and antiquities; and where ideas are alleged to be the interest, the probability is that you will be served with stale classicism. There is no life in it; it is like turning over empty cans and poking about in the rubbish. . . . In a last desperate effort to find a trace of education that has some concern with living truth or ideas, with the oncoming future, you go to the departments of fine arts, music, dramatics; and all you discover there is the teachers weighed down with foolish hope and painful duty which incapacitate them for any sort of effective teaching. They hope some day to turn out a professional dauber, designer, fiddler, or actor who will become 'famous,' and they will be able to bask in his glory; meanwhile they are obliged to teach students 'to appreciate.' Every June the country is swamped with appreciators. Later you will find some of them in women's clubs, listening flatly, unimaginatively, uncritically to lectures and performances by all species of fools and charlatans; the rest, in a state of beneficent oblivion. . . . Everywhere the chief distinction of man, imagination, is neglected. . . .

". . . The question, then, is: how are you to train the imagination?—or, more important still: is it possible to train the imagination? An enormous question, but I think it can be answered. I believe that we here in Black Mountain—not I, as you know, but all of us, students and the faculty—have reached the threshold of the answer. We're trying, with increasing (though, off and on, faltering) success to teach method as against content. Our emphasis is on process as against results. To us, the way of handling facts is more important than facts themselves. Facts change, while the method of handling them—provided the method is life's own free, dynamic method which evidently works on the principle that nothing is permanent save change—remains the same; and so, if stability or order is what is wanted in this world (and I take it that it is), it can only be got by putting facts, results, the alleged content of life in the past in second place, and placing stress on the way of handling facts now and in the future, on the method, the process of life. . . . This is an awkward, involved way of stating it, for the thing is so new to us who are engaged in school education that even we here in Black Mountain have not found adequate verbal expression for it: but I hope you see what I mean. . . . What I am trying to articulate here, is as I say, new to us; but this idea of method, of process, of imagination as against 'facts,' static concepts, and concrete results is really not new. It is, indeed, very old. It has been for a long time a fierce little flame leaping out of the minds and *feelings* of a small section of humanity, the artists: by which, of course, I don't mean only painters, but artists of all kinds, including (in fact, especially) those who are not painters, sculptors, writers, musicians, or anything else of the sort, but who have the artistic approach or attitude to life as a whole and to everything in life; whose values are qualitative as opposed to quantitative; who are eternally modern and so distinguished from the non-moderns, not by what they know, but what they do with what they know; and to whom men, in their vague desperation in the face of the deep confusion of contemporary life, are at last, I think, slowly, shamefacedly beginning to turn. . . . The human race has tried out everyone else, priest, soldier, politician, technologist: but their working characteristic is generally not imagination, but lack of imagination. We must now turn to the 'queer' people, who have always been laughed at by the earthborn; who, indeed, *are* 'queer,' but only because they are divorced from the main processes of life and have little, if anything to do with life at it goes on, and must stay apart, in their garrets and ivory towers, because we don't want them, or act as though we don't want them. Actually, whether we know it or not, we *do* want them— we want artists, poets in the Greek sense of 'makers' or 'creators,' artists who are at the same time philosophers and scientists: and above all, teachers. We must go out and find them in their lonely places, where their desperate genius frets, sickens, and turns neurotic, and bring them into the center of life, and say to them, 'Here, look at this botch. Do something with it. Make something out of it. And don't be soft with us. Consider us your material. Use us. Don't let yourselves ever again be called 'gentle poets.' What we need is 'tough poets.' . . ."

(Now and then, here and there, during 1936-37, quoting and referring to this idea of Rice's, I encountered so much tendency to misunderstanding that I feel the need of a parenthetical note to emphasize his own explanation of it. Rice does not mean, of course, that educators should forthwith begin to agitate for the replacement of Franklin Roosevelt and Jim Farley by Thomas Benton and Ernest Hemingway; Bishop Manning by Robinson Jeffers; Henry Ford by Norman Bel Geddes; and the present chief of staff of the United States Army by Deems Taylor. Nor does he mean that we should promptly summon from their garrets and ivory towers the "queer" people to whom he refers. He knows that many of them are significant chiefly as symptoms of the ailments now afflicting humankind. He wants education to be so transformed—gradually: for he knows it cannot be done at once—that schools will turn out primarily, not potential political and financial schemers and go-getters to whom politics and finance are ends in themselves, not mere tinkerers, not mass-murderers, but *artists*. Not necessarily—in fact, preferably not—professional painters, sculptors, musicians, or writers of novels and poetry, but people who will have the artistic approach to life; whose values will be qualitative, not quantitative; who will be, to paraphrase and repeat his own words, ever modern and, as such, distinguished, from the non-moderns, not by what they will know, but what they will do with what they will know; and who will know and *feel* that, as Rice elaborates later, life is essentially not competitive, but calls for coöperation everywhere, and that, unless we want human affairs to go from bad to worse, men must cease spending most of their energy scheming how to harm one another, and begin looking toward a goal, toward something they wish to become and make of the world. . . . Rice would like to see the world swarm with people who are essentially, not stock brokers and mechanics and parrots, but artists; however, again, not mere Picassos and Vankas and Jefferses, but poets in the Greek sense, which he explains; who—unlike the artists nowadays, most of whom, because of the neglect they suffer, are neurotics— will go into the center of life, into politics, business, and professions, *and belong there*. He would like to see the world swarm with people who would function in the direction of turning the present incongruous world into a work of art.)

". . . At present," to resume quoting Rice, "artists, poets, 'makers,' 'creators'— have almost nothing to do with education in our colleges and universities. Here and there, however, we have professors and instructors who are potential artists or 'tough poets,' now unfunctioning, or largely so: though most of them don't realize they are what they are. These people must—somehow—be given a chance to develop, to function, to become working artists in the teaching world; to cease being passive recipients and handers-out of anything; to become productive, creative, always reaching out to mold and shape what seems to others intractable; to *use*, if they can, everything that comes within their orbit, including (and especially) people: to consider students, accumulated knowledge, etc., as materials out of which near perfection might be wrought.

". . . The method, the way of education, that I think—that I know—is needed, is the method, is the way of the poet, the philosopher-scientist-artist; and the reason we have not adopted it before is that we have foolishly, ignorantly believed life was essentially competitive: and we have pushed the poet aside because he knows competition for the senseless, wasteful thing it is. As long as we cling to this old idea, we shall continue to look toward one another and spend most of our energy scheming how to harm one another, instead of looking toward a goal, toward something that we want to become. The measure of your success, as long as you compete with men, is the distance between you and them. You are forever looking forward to the leaders and backward to the followers, and they are always men, usually no better than yourself. The measure of your success, if you are a poet, a philosopher-artist, a creator, is the distance between you and the thing you want to do, between you and the thing you want to create, between you and the person you want to become. You learn to follow ideas and ideals, which are always alive and headed for the future, instead of men, most of whom (nowadays, partly because of education) are largely dead creatures of the past; and you don't look back, except to find how other poets before you have created their goals, how they in their time have followed ideas, handled life, and looked into the future. . . . There is a technique to be learned, a grammar to the art of living. Logic as severe as it can be, must be learned, if for no other reason, to know its limitations. Dialectic must be learned; and no feelings spared, for you can't afford to be nice when truth is at stake. The hard, intractable facts of science must be learned, for truth has a habit of hiding in queer places. Man's responses to ideas in the past must be learned. These things are the pencil, the brush, the chisel. But these are not all. There are subtle means of communication that have been lost by mankind, as our nerve ends have been cauterized by schooling. These nerves must be re-sensitized. We must learn to move without fear, to be aware of everything around us, to *feel* as well as to see mentally our way into the future,—the poet is also the prophet. And we must become tough, awfully tough—tough poets, as I say—for this is a big, arduous job we have got to do, this job of making a decent humanity that is fit to live on the decent earth. . . . We teachers—we artists—must begin to get tough with the politicians, the militarists; with the cheap, ignorant schemers who blindly juggle with humanity and mar the face of the world. We must start to treat 'em rough. We must commence to bore into the pretense and sham of the world-savers— the world, as it is, isn't worth saving: it must be changed—and let the dust run out of their hollow innards, and say to the onlookers, 'See now, they're empty shirts!' But we mustn't expect to win every time. We'll get knocked about good and plenty. Nor must we expect to win in a generation. The job before us, that of remaking ourselves, is not only a big, an arduous one but a long one. Centuries. But we must begin. . . . And perhaps there will some day happen to us what has happened to men before, when after struggle and failure and struggle again a moment of magic came, and there was the picture or the book or the statue or the sound of a note, and they knew that it was good; not all that they dreamed and hoped it might be, but still, good. Perhaps this will happen to us who want to consider the world and humanity as material and remake them. Perhaps some day we will see a humanity to whom one can say, 'You're good. No doubt about it, you're good. But you're not so good as we'd hoped you'd be. It's up to you to make yourself better, and those who come after you still better. Then humanity will be on the way.' . . ."

The above, roughly and briefly, are John Rice's general ideas, the core of his philosophy, and, I think, a fairly good stab at an essential self-portrait. But a short sketch of his life and personality is necessary here, none the less.

As I write this early in 1938, Rice is just fifty. On initial impression, he does not seem a very formidable individual. He might be taken for a small-town doctor who has contempt for the rules of diet he prescribes for others. One notices his round, moon-faced head: full cheeks, a broad and high sloping brow under graying dark hair, a medium-sized nose, small mustache, wide-apart lively eyes behind spectacles, large regular ears, full lips, and double chin; then his big torso and bigger waist, his thick short neck, arms, and legs; and his carelessness in dress and geniality in manner, and his perennial pipe, from which he scatters ashes about him as he talks. After a while, however, his physical person yields in one's awareness to his extremely agile, energetic, intuitive, and experienced mind, which is full of Socratic tricks, capable of calculated subtlety and flashing directness, and endowed with great resources of wit, which is quite American and his own. His somewhat shapeless body returns fully to one's attention when laughter, which punctuates most of his discourses, shakes it inside and out in a vital rhythm. He loves to talk and laugh. When in a good, friendly mood, there is something Whitmanesque about him; except that Rice is enormously learned and intellectually brilliant, which the Old Gray Poet was not.

"Vital" enters into one's early attempts to characterize him, although, as one of his colleagues at Black Mountain once put it to me, he naturally "tends to the armchair rather than the saddle." Later, listening to his ideas, one begins to perceive that as a teacher he considers himself a man of action in a better and, in the long run, more important sense than that in which the title can be applied to any soldier, politician, or business hustler. In Rice's view, the two men who in the last two thousand years have influenced the Western world most actively and most profoundly were two teachers, Socrates and

Jesus. But he believes that they were not more effective than they were because one relied too much upon reason and the other on feeling; and that what this world needs is teachers in whom intellectuality and emotions will be blended or synchronized into all-round, balanced intelligence and sense of progress. He thinks that only a great teacher, but not necessarily one teaching in school, can be a truly great man.

Finally, attempting to put upon paper only the essential man, one remembers Rice's person mainly in connection with his laughter, retains "vital" and adds "dynamically intelligent . . . fanatically honest . . . almost recklessly courageous . . . optimistic . . . indifferent to his material interests . . . devoid of charlatanry in any field . . . passionately critical of education as generally practiced . . . immensely constructive . . . motivated by a deeply religious faith in humanity . . . essentially kind and good-natured, but capable of a fierce temper . . . an American: perhaps an unusual one, but an American, representative of a considerably widespread idealistic-optimistic mood: a pioneer, possible only in America." Rice is profoundly unlike Arthur Morgan. They are both on the Long Road, but as Morgan strides tensely, sternly, almost aloofly in the middle of it, scattering copies of *Antioch Notes*, but infrequently looking back whether anyone is following him, Rice is right in the mob, laughing, asking questions, stopping to argue, discussing the "mess of things," showing by his demeanor there is nothing to fear, going into the deep murk off the Road, wherein his voice explodes angrily as he tries to get people to stop grubbing in the muck and to look starward. Morgan tends to deal with the human problem in big, sweeping lines. He created Antioch as he built or constructed a dam—by working out the general idea, which was good, then putting other people to work on it. Rice wants to participate in all the details of the problem.

Born in Lynchburg, South Carolina, Rice is the son of a Methodist preacher, who, fiercely evangelical in his early life, came to be the leader of the "modern" movement in his church, and was in constant conflict with conservatism. John's mother—a profoundly lovely woman and character, as he remembers her—died when he was thirteen. Then he went to live with a couple of spinster aunts, neurotic, twisted persons, whom—or whose ways—he hated. While with them, he developed his fierce temper. When the old women were mean to him or nasty to anyone else, he let them know what he thought of them. His father remarried, and the stepmother, "an extraordinary woman who gracefully stood halfway between the Old South and the new world," became an important beneficent factor in the boy's life, which, meanwhile, came also under the strong influence of John Webb, one of the two headmasters of Webb School at Bellbuckle, Tennessee. "Although his name isn't well known," Rice told me, "John Webb was a great teacher, one of the greatest ever: a great man. He was one of the last of universal scholars in America. He taught the senior class everything that was taught them: Latin, Greek, English literature, mathematics, modern languages. By simply being what he was, he gave me the idea that teaching—pursuing ideas, working toward truth, wondering, talking in the give-and-take way—was the greatest, most thrilling and satisfying business in life. He taught all the time, especially when he was not holding class. We students followed him around; he talked *with* us, and the big question always was: what is it all about? He had a strong, kind face, a dry laugh, and his hand slowly patted his knee as he talked. He was a hero to me then, and remained heroic to the end of his days."

From Webb School, Rice went to Tulane University, in New Orleans; received a B.A. there in 1911, then went as a Rhodes Scholar to Oxford, Queens College, and got a B.A. there in 1914. He returned to Webb School as a teacher, but left in two years, after the aging John Webb had been forced to give up the headmastership; and he went to study at Chicago. During the war, he was in the intelligence service of the United States Army.

Rice's first university teaching job was at Nebraska, where he stayed eight years (and, as I have mentioned, became friends with Walter Locke, to whom he introduced me, ten or a dozen years later); and I have it from various sources that he showed pronounced signs of being a "trouble-maker" already there. He was vaguely uncomfortable and wont to make remarks about education and educators that enraged people, or provoked them to uproarious laughter. He thought of giving up teaching and becoming a writer, but decided, instead, to try a school in the East and went to Rutgers, where he got into hot water almost at once. So he took a Guggenheim fellowship, that had been awarded him some time before, and the year in London was one of the most important periods of his life. "I had time to think about things," he told me, "that had long bothered me. I got a perspective on them. I began to see what a mess my 'greatest business in life' really was." Returning from Europe, he went to Rollins because the job that Hamilton Holt offered him seemed the best among a lot of bad ones—bad from the viewpoint of, not a jobholder, but a teacher. However, Rollins turned out to be, in many respects, from Rice's point of view, no better than most colleges. He became more and more vocal in his criticism, and a "row" was inevitable.

By 1935, when he first talked to me, his criticism of education had rounded itself out into something like this: ". . . The center of control in American education has shifted in the past century, from those who really know or should know something about education, the teachers, to those who, in most cases, really know nothing about it, the trustees; and the result is irresponsibility.[3] . . . It is fairly easy, of course, to fix legal responsibility; but the other kind, ethical, moral, human, call it what you will, where does it rest in education? Sometimes within the board of trustees, sometimes within the institution, on the president or dean, or some more obscure official; sometimes, and worst

---

[3] On the subject of "responsibility" Rice is a near-fanatic. Once he said to me, "By responsibility I do not mean pliability, an over-nice attention to the wishes of others. Heretics are often the most responsible of mankind, and to mankind, insofar as they see what mankind and they themselves ought to become."

of all, outside, on some 'fixer.' Through these various sluices flow streams of influence from alumni, athletic and fraternal; from business interests, job-hunters, political manipulators, irate parents, and a thousand other hidden sources.

"But suppose you find a 'good' board, composed of those who attend to their business of conserving endowments and at long last dying and leaving something to the institution; even they will not—and, in the long run, can-not—confine themselves to this. Why? Because of the sort of people they are: for the most part 'successful' business men past middle age who are unwilling to relinquish the sacred right to hire and fire, who are accustomed to obedience from those over whom they hold this threat, and who are in league with the past. Their values are those inherent in the things and the methods by which they think they have become 'successful.' They are used to 'running' things. They *like* the sensation of 'running' things. So they 'run' the college or univer-sity; or, rather, they get some one to 'run' it for them, and he is responsible to *them*: not to any idea of education. Whom do they choose? Naturally some one who is not unlike themselves. They are practical men and proud of it and they choose a 'practical' man. They rarely elect a great scholar as president of a college or university, almost never a great teacher, for a great teacher is terribly unlike them. The poor fellow, as a rule, is not 'practical' at all. He is apt to be a little 'queer' or even disrespectful of 'successful,' 'practical' men. They make a choice that is a subtle flattery of themselves in electing some one who is ambitious and efficient—as if efficiency in business and education were the same thing—; one who is 'all things to all men,' in their sense of 'all.'"

(Here Rice is, of course, generalizing. He knows presidents whom he re-spects. He has high regard, for instance, for Frank P. Graham of the Univer-sity of North Carolina—"a miracle among state university presidents." . . . In this connection, too, I might mention the study made in 1937 by Dr. Earl J. McGrath, professor of education at the University of Buffalo, of twenty-five hundred trustees of large and small colleges throughout the United States. He concludes that "the control of higher education in America, both public and private, has been placed in the hands of a small group of the population, namely, financiers and business men. From two-thirds to three-fourths of the persons on these boards in recent decades have been selected from this group." How does such control affect academic freedom? Dr. McGrath has no definite answer, but he states "that instructors have been released most frequently in recent years because they expressed opinions which conflicted with business interests.") To resume quoting Rice:

"The president occupies an economic and social position inferior to the trustees', but considerably above the faculty's. His intellectual status is usually ambiguous. As a man, he knows himself to be ultimately a servant of those who have employed him and is uncomfortable. How can such a man be re-sponsible for education—for training men and women for the future? His roots are dead roots in a dead past.

"His principal assistants are the deans, who are, as a rule, nothing but office-managers—and the managerial mind is unproductive, uncreative. A dean's ideal of a college is one that runs smoothly. He looks upon men as machines, to be manipulated, and his idea of keeping a teacher up to his best is to apply salary grease. He is a top-sergeant disciplinarian. Too often the future of a good man rests in the hands of such a person, one who is the intellectual inferior of at least half the faculty. Can you hold *such* a man responsible for education?

"We come to the professors and instructors who, by various haphazard methods, are hired because they are supposed to know something about the technique of scholarship and teaching, but who are not permitted to assume an important or central responsibility, either individually or as faculties. They are under those who hire them, who 'run' the school. There are institutions where a professor, if he behaves, can finally get permanent tenure, but he isn't always safe even then. If he is not asked to resign, for whatever cause or whim of some non-teacher above him, there are always ways of pestering him and making his life miserable, such as increasing his teaching load, denying him adequate assistants, holding up his recommendations as to appointments, putting into his department appointees who understand it is part of their job to make him uncomfortable, refusing him promotion in salary and rank. . . . Important decisions affecting the professors as individuals and their functions as teachers are made by others. They have faculty meetings, to be sure; but go to any such meeting anywhere—the probability is nothing worth the attention of free men will be discussed. You will see the pitiable passion with which they debate the questions of hours, credits, cuts. They bring the full force of their manhood to bear upon trivialities. They know within themselves that they can roam at will only among minutiæ of no importance. And they get in the habit of considering only trivialities, and all life assumes a trivial aspect. If ever the occasion comes when they are given the chance to make an important decision, the habit of years and tradition stays with them and they bicker like peevish children. Usually, the 'practical-minded' administrative officer, knowing ahead of time how the faculty will behave, finds means of jamming through his proposals before they can get unlimbered. . . . And so we see that the teachers, such as they are, can't be held responsible for or to education, either. Many are not much to look at in their faculty meetings or in classrooms, some are clearly of the uncremated, but not a few have good stuff hidden in them. It could be developed. Faculties could become responsible bodies and really take charge of the business of education—but that never occurs to anyone. . . ."

At Black Mountain, as already suggested, the responsibility to education is entirely within the close-knit college community—in the hands of teachers and students.

The community at Black Mountain College is so close-knit that it has many characteristics of a huge family. Except for three or four faculty couples with small children occupying cottages in the immediate proximity, all members of the staff and all students live and do all their teaching and learning (save music and the dance), and all their studying, reading, and playing in the vast hotel-like structure I have mentioned. Everybody, including the families with little children, eat in a common mess-hall, connected with the main building by a roofed passageway. Except for a cook, his assistants, a furnace-man in the wintertime, and two persons who clean the main hall below, the stairs, corridors and lavatories, the college has no employees. All other chores are done by students and faculty without distinction, and altogether voluntarily. At meals students and teachers serve one another, though no one is detailed in advance to do anything specific. Food is brought to the tables, passed around, eaten; emptied dishes are taken to the kitchen and replenished, then the tables are cleared, some one gets the dessert, another tea and coffee; and all this is done in perfect order, without bickering, even with form. The students who pay less than the full fee, or those who pay nothing at all, are not expected to do anything around the college not done by the others; the chief reason for this being that it is bad for those who are served—it gives them a feeling of unsound superiority.

"In accepting students," Rice told me in 1935, "an effort is being made to obtain a cross-section of American life by economic, cultural, and geographic distribution. The common requirement for admission is the ability to live in and profit from living in such a community as ours"—to be further described hereinafter. "Basic requirement: intelligence—not necessarily of a high order, but certainly not too low. I don't mean intellect; to repeat, by intelligence I mean a subtle balance between emotion and intellect. Among the desiderata is a capacity for personal depression; a student ought to say to himself every once in a while, 'I'm no damn' good,' feel like the devil about himself, then get over it and try to be better; and, with that, achieve a sense of elation, which, from our experience here, is the process by which people make something of themselves. He ought to have also a capacity for indignation and get hot under the collar with fair regularity. Injustice, whatever he thinks of as injustice, must make him furious. And he must have a sense of order, a sense of form, and inwardly a love of truth—there is no hope for an essential liar.

"When a student enters, he or she finds that there are no required courses. Within the time of his stay in the college, however, he must, if he intends to graduate, submit to two tests of his knowledge: the first at the end of approximately two years, and the second about two years later, both depending upon his willingness and ability to work. How he is to obtain this knowledge is a matter for which he is mainly responsible. He may work on his own, under a tutor, or in classes. In general, the work of the student is at first in classes; later on, almost entirely individual.

"The range of knowledge at present is so nearly infinite that it is no longer possible to pick out a number of subjects and say of them, 'These one must know.' But before he can make an intelligent choice of the subject or subjects with which he is to deal, the student must make an exploration or reëxploration of the fields of knowledge in the junior division. This requirement is made of him in order to prevent his discovering his real interests as late as his third or fourth year, as often happens in college.

"The initiative in passing from the junior to the senior division, and from the latter to graduation, is always with the student, who must himself decide whether he is ready to make the move. Not that he is left, at this point or any other, to flounder about alone, for throughout his stay in the college, we are ready to give advice when it is requested. The first thing a student does during his first week, when he is not expected to register for any work but to spend the time planning what he is to do, is to choose some member of the faculty to be his adviser, a choice, however, that is not final.

"The senior division is a period of specialization, in a field or in cognate fields of knowledge. One of the requirements for entrance to this division is a carefully made plan of work to cover about two years. There is great flexibility in senior-division plans. Of the students graduating this year, for instance, one is specializing in writing, another in nineteenth century as a period of civilization, one in art, and three in English literature. When the student thinks he has completed his work in the senior division, he petitions the faculty for the right to graduate, accompanying his request with a statement of what he professes to know in his chosen field. If this statement is satisfactory, the faculty invites some competent person, not connected with the college, to examine him, to find out, not whether the student ought to graduate, but whether he really knows what he professes to know.

"In general, the effort of Black Mountain College is to produce individuals rather than individualists, in the belief that the individualist is bound to be a misfit in modern life, while, at the other extreme, the subordination of men and women to a uniform and consistent pattern of action will inevitably prevent the creation of a better society than we now have. The first step in the process is to make the student aware of himself and his capacities; in other words 'to know himself.'

"A beginning is often best made by persuading the student to submit himself to the discipline of one or more of the arts." (Of the reason for this, more in a minute.) "It is on this account that no classes are allowed to conflict in the schedule with elementary courses in music, dramatics, and the fine arts. It is not expected that many students will become artists; in fact, the college regards it as a sacred duty to discourage mere talent from thinking itself genius; but there is something of the artist in everyone, and the development of this talent, however small, carrying with it a severe discipline of its own, results in the student's becoming more and more sensitive to order in the world and within himself than he can ever possibly become through intellectual effort alone.

"But the individual, to be complete, must be aware of his relation to others.

Here the whole community becomes his teacher. Wood-chopping, road-mending, rolling the tennis courts, serving tea in the afternoon, and other tasks around the place done by groups composed of students and members of the faculty, help to rub off individualistic corners and give people training in assuming responsibility. They tend to involve the person into participation in the life and issues of the community as a whole. Last year the students of their own accord took over the running of the college farm, and during the summer some of them, by taking turns in staying on the place, got the crops ready for harvesting by the whole college this autumn; which was done, of course, without conflict with the academic schedule, and is a help to the college economically.

"There is—naturally—an element of fun in all these tasks for which the students and the faculty assume responsibility, but along with other things"—still to be mentioned—"they help to give the experiences that these students have while they are in college the quality of their experiences in later life. Attending to these tasks (which, incidentally, in a measure take the place of purely artificial sport activities one finds in most other schools), they have to overcome all sorts of very real difficulties within and outside themselves; which—again, in conjunction with their other experiences here—helps them toward maturity."

Also, performing the tasks for which they have assumed responsibility the Black Mountain students have a sense of participating in the vital day-to-day life of the place as a whole. They help the college, whose value to themselves and to the ideal of education most of them appreciate, to continue to exist. They feel they belong and function. They have what Rice calls a sense of being important.

In many colleges and universities—if one is to judge by academic processions, which come in this order: president and trustee, deans, faculty, and students—students are the least important. At Black Mountain, though he is never told so, the student cannot miss having the feeling that he is equally important with the rector and the rest of the staff. He has all the freedom and basic privileges anyone else has. He knows that the students who left Rollins in 1933 were as essential in starting the new college as were Rice and the other rebel professors; that without them the professors could not have begun the new college. He is as free to criticize the teachers as they are to criticize him, or to open his mouth about anything, any time, anywhere, and take the consequences. Some of the teachers are his friends. Several, including Rice, attend as students some of the classes he is taking. He knows they are learning just as he is. He is an integral part of the community simply because he is there and, no matter what he does, he influences it. Moments occur in which he is immensely significant. The place is so delicately organized (only "organized" is not the word), and is under such severe scrutiny on the part of the world about it, that he has it in his power to create a scandal and thereby severely damage it. Conversely, he has the power to prevent—however, only by persuasion—another student from creating such a scandal. Or he can do, or take part in doing, something which suddenly enhances the value of the place. . . . Rice knows the students have had as much to do with the making of the college as the faculty.

Anent this problem of the students' sense of importance, as it is working itself out at Black Mountain, Rice indicated to me his disagreement with psychologists like Adler who propound that everyone is trying to be superior. "I believe," he said, "that the average person is content when and where he 'fits,' where he functions in his unique way; for, in spite of the fact that we are largely unconscious of our uniqueness, we do not believe that anyone does a thing in quite the same way that we do it, especially when the thing done is our 'job.' If we are asked how we feel when we are doing something, we are likely to reply that we think we are doing our job better than anyone else could possibly do it; however, this is said, not while we are in action, but when we recall our action. When we are at it, the situation is this: we see the job to be done and our competition is not with someone else who is doing the same thing, but between our performance and our idea of what our performance might be. This is another way of saying that every man is an artist, a creator, when he really puts himself into a job, and it doesn't make any difference what that job is, screwing up a bolt, writing a novel, or collecting garbage, provided only that the man *feels* it is *his* job. One trouble with the world is that men and women are not doing *their* jobs, are not functioning in the thing in which they can function in a satisfactory way; that many of them are doing jobs which are for the most part assigned to them by chance, whether it be living a life of leisure on Long Island, running a subway train, or writing books. A former colleague of mine was really a designer and builder of houses, but chance made him a professor of Latin, and he was a miserable man and a poor teacher. Another was a salesman, but taught philosophy; still another a gardener, but taught history. There is a Senator in Washington who should not be a Senator, but perhaps a patrolman or some other such factotum of petty authority. The evil that man has perpetrated in American politics is incalculable; yet he is—or certainly was—basically a good man, who might have made an excellent traffic cop. . . . If the world is to become a decent place to live in, it must be made possible for everyone to find his own place, without acclaim or derision, without reference to any idea of success."[4]

The setup at Black Mountain makes it possible for a person, whether he be the son of a millionaire or a corner groceryman, to find out that he is not cut out to be a philosopher but to be a carpenter; not a writer, but a scientist; not a painter, but a labor-leader; not a chemist, but an editor. One of the efforts, in which practically the entire community participates, is to bring to each one's consciousness his uniqueness—and his uniqueness not only as a potential

[4] "Our educational system is suffering from an overdose of success stories. We must train pupils to become failures, since only a few will be considered successes—they will be failures in later life. One person in ten is neurotic, one in twenty-two is insane today, because we train for success."—*Dr. Mandel Sherman, psychiatrist at the University of Chicago.*

scientist, editor or plumber, but as a person who, by virtue of being a human being, is an artist, is creative.

This brings us close to the core of the Black Mountain setup.

"The village," Rice said to me in 1935, "is rapidly disappearing in America, but mankind needs the village. Only it must no longer be haphazard, a product of chance, but the best possible village that can be created, free of the old village meannesses, stupid cruelties, and obscurantism. And I think that we here in Black Mountain have stumbled onto the idea that the college—the college community—some such community as we have half-accidentally begun to develop here, or an improvement of it—must be this new village.

"In the past, the history of an individual has been that of his reaching out gradually in acquaintance and understanding of people. First came his awareness of his mother and his start in understanding humanity through her. Then there followed his adjustment to others in the family, all very gradual, for—fortunately—there were lots of them, and they represented, in little, what he would have to face later on. From some he could count upon the necessary human emollient, unreasonable affection; from others, guarded hostility. Old maid aunts and decrepit grandfathers were people he could begin cautiously to dislike, but with whom he had to get on. And he could count on the subtle thing, family feeling, to save him from disaster. He could escape no one; no one could escape him. He became adept in interpreting communication. The lifting of an eyebrow, the turn of a hand, every movement, every inflection of the voice, had its meaning. He was getting ready for the village.

"In the village, he met open hostility and criticism unsugared by unreasonable affection or family decency, but, being not without experience, he could give as good as he got. And, as in the family, nobody could get away from anybody. There they all were, in a tight little world (and here we are, at Black Mountain, in a tight little world). Individualism had a hard time in the village, but the right to individuality was recognized *per force*. This explains why, when you want to find characters, you go to the village.

"Much depended, however, upon the plane of existence in the village. Often it was pretty low, and the philosopher had a hard time coming into existence, and the artist never came. But even the bad village was better than nothing at all, which is what America now has; for even in the villages that remain, those of Sinclair Lewis' *Main Street*, the desire is to get to the city as quickly as possible—to escape—and hence the village lessons are not learned. The city is the home of loneliness. Most city-dwellers are lonely, however wide their acquaintance, and even when they have what they call friends, they uneasily know that these friendships are ephemeral and evanescent. They attempt to find in human relationships what can be found only in personal relationship. It is no accident that all the talk about 'human relationship' that one hears nowadays comes out of the city. Here starvation is manifest, nor is hunger satisfied, rather increased, by the attempt to water the family down to the thin gruel of human relationships. . . .

"What we now have all too generally in America is the carefully restricted family, each child the result, except in case of accidents, of many calculations. Conception is no longer an 'act of God,' to be deplored, perhaps, but in the end to be accepted. Now the stock exchange has its say (many children now alive in America owe their existence to a ten-point rise of A.T. & T.), as have the prospective mother's 'health' and the difference in price between a Ford and a Packard. In this small, deliberate family, the child—often an only child—does not meet with open indifference, criticism, or hostility. The tendency is for him to be treated always as the center of his small—but all he has—world. He is intensely intimate with one or two persons who 'share their every thought' with him and coddle and protect him. He has no privacy, no seclusion from curiosity that he might have occasionally had in a large family.

"Now also the village is for the most part omitted from experience. The step is from those one knows intimately to those one knows not at all. The immigrant into the world outside the home, in spite of the foretaste through public schooling, finds himself among strangers—and in the city among potential enemies. He then carries forward what he may have begun as a protective device against too much affectionate prying in the home and against the intrusions of a desiccated school-teacher, the building up of a superficial self to present to the world in lieu of reality. By the time he gets to college, this superficial self is often a work of art. His best thoughts and abilities have gone into its making. . . ."

To deal with this problem, the Black Mountain educational process includes or encourages what is called "group influence," which is not strictly peculiar to it—I find more than traces of it in Antioch and in other schools I visited during 1934-37—but which is probably more effective at Black Mountain than elsewhere because there it functions in conjunction with other influences, other factors in the process, which are carefully made to work toward producing people in whom intelligence will be a matter of subtle balance between emotions and intellect.

"Group influence" at Black Mountain is difficult to describe. It is essentially unconscious and it changes, as a factor in the process, right along. I described it in the April, 1936, issue of *Harpers Magazine* more or less as it had been the previous fall. When the magazine, which contained also a criticism of it (based on my article) by Bernard de Voto, appeared, it was already much changed. Mr. de Voto's article and mine affected it still further before the end of the term that year. It has been continually revised during the 1936-37 and 1937-38 school years. There are some things about it, however, that seem fairly permanent. It suggests psychoanalysis, but differs from it drastically. It implicitly disputes the modern psychologist's mechanistic concept of man, as a result of which people have come to regard themselves, not as entities, but as bundles of things that have been done to them and now cause them to do things they should not do. Black Mountain College is less interested in the students' high-school records and incidents in their past than in their potentialities as persons.

The new students come, in the main, unknown into an unknown world, which is also strangely and excitingly free. There are no rules at Black Mountain. This is their chance. If they have been fools before, they are free to be something different now. If they have built up for themselves a reputation of angelic virtue which has grown uncomfortable, they are no longer obliged to be angels. In September the place is like a grand week-end party. Everybody is glad to be there. The place is beautiful; the view of the Craggies superb. Everybody is "so free." Then the newcomer realizes the first implication of freedom: that if one does or says something, one must take the consequences. Back home, his superficial self was respected, even protected. Here there is no one to protect him. There is talk. Everything is more or less questioned, criticized. He is on his own. He realizes that he has taken advantage of the freedom of the place and said things about others. Now, suddenly, he doesn't like the place; its freedom was a sort of trap. But he gets over this. Consciousness of self begins, which is what is desired; Rice holds that without it nothing can be accomplished in the Black Mountain sort of education.

"Group influence" works from elevation to depression and up again. When the students achieve elevation from depression they think they have done it, and sit back and enjoy the peace of self-discovery. They swim in intelligence and desire to improve themselves. Then uncertainty steals upon them, and they sink again into dejection, which is accompanied by self-examination, self-criticism. Not that the process ends here. There are continuous waves. Or, to change the figure, one's thoughts about oneself are abrasive. One rubs down and down till one touches the thing which is one's real self.

This is experience—education—of the most acute sort. Students are partly prepared for it intellectually by being told on their arrival that they must expect to change; that if they do not change, then it is useless for them to have come; they can perfectly well remain what they are by returning home. Gradually, two things occur. One is that one's interest in others increases in both intensity and intelligence. The other is that one begins to like, almost enjoy, the process of being changed. That is explained as follows:

Men suffer most from unacknowledged self-contempt. The characteristic of children, on the contrary, is self-respect. Somewhere between the kindergarten and college self-respect has been destroyed or so repressed and twisted that it is no longer evident to its possessor. But a man must have self-respect or a similitude of it to present to society. The movement is then from without. He tries to act in such a way that he will be respected by others, and he becomes confused into thinking finally that this assumed self-respect he has pawned off on others is a reality. But underneath he knows or feels that it is all a lie. Behind the front he offers to the world he is a disorderly person, and afraid. He never knows when he walks into a room but that the enemy is waiting for him, ready to show him up for the liar he is. *And yet, unconsciously, he longs for this very thing to happen to him.* . . . He has constructed and elaborately decorated the superficial self that he is to present to society. It is as if he wore a carefully designed mask, to the making of which he has given his most tender care, and behind this lives the real man, growing increasingly chaotic, miserable, and unhappy, longing for his deliverer but ready to receive him as an enemy.

"The task of the college," holds Rice, "is to be his enemy-friend: the enemy of the superficial self, the friend of the real self. But the real one is often starved, emaciated. It must be fed back to life, while the superficial one must be allowed to recede and disappear."

Black Mountain has a diet for the poor "real self." There is good will. Most of the talk about people is free of malice or pettiness. There is desire to help. Except when the issue is slight, no one ever goes completely without a champion. Also, as already said, one belongs, functions, is "important" at Black Mountain, is a part of it. One, too, is constantly *invited* verbally and by implication, to be intelligent, to mature, which is slightly annoying but also rather flattering and pleasant. Candor, of which there is probably more on that mountainside than anywhere else in the United States, is discomfiting at times, yet it produces dramatic incidents which almost prove that truth *is* beauty. But the most important part of the diet for the "real self" is humor. Young students learn to laugh at themselves. Rice's own talent for laughter helps them in this. And so, in one way or another, they discover that, their past experiences and a great mass of literature to the contrary notwithstanding, humanity is basically a rather decent breed.

The original Black Mountain group began to develop this process back in 1933, mainly unconsciously and accidentally, when they abruptly found themselves in extremely tight quarters and had to get along *on a basis of freedom*, not only as students and teachers, but as persons endowed with various degrees of vitality. They had to rub the individualistic corners off one another's characters.

"Group influence" is one of the most important elements of Black Mountain education. It is stirring interest among psychologists, here and abroad, and among people studying human relations and kindred problems. What I tell of it here is a mere suggestion. To appreciate it fully one must experience it.

One immediate aim of "group influence" is that no student should be able to make a mistake in his or her marriage. It should make one a connoisseur of people. I think it already has made connoisseurs of several students. Some of those who have been there longest can also exchange complicated communications without saying a word. The lift of an eyebrow to them is a sentence. They are most definitely being "resensitized."

Another aim of "group influence," as it works in conjunction with other factors in the Black Mountain setup, is to give the student at least a hint of a technique of getting along constructively with people whose temperaments are unlike his own. Rice feels that there is an increase of personal incompatibility in all manner of enterprises and relationships in the world, and that this—unless dealt with by education—will play the very devil with human progress, for modern civilization is getting more and more complicated, which calls for more and more coöperativeness among people of divergent makeups and inclinations. For such coöperativeness a technique is needed. If we do not develop it, much of history will continue to be punctuated by such fateful antagonisms as those existing currently between Stalin and Trotsky, Franklin Roosevelt and Al Smith, Franklin Roosevelt and John Lewis, and Arthur Morgan and David Lilienthal.

Sex morals? One is free to do anything at Black Mountain, but the admonition always is "Be intelligent!" and on that basis nothing occurs that might create the possibility of a scandal to harm the college. The moral control pertaining to everything is within the group. It is not imposed on it. It comes partly from the fact that most people there, no matter how they may have resented certain phases of "group influences," develop a passionate devotion to the place.

Have people there *no* privacy? Students are two to a bedroom, but each person has a private study, on the door of which he can hang a "Don't disturb!" sign when alone in it. The sign is strictly respected. In this connection Rice said to me, "Americans should begin to learn to enjoy privacy, and for most of us this means we must be alone. Disciplined souls—Socrates, for one—have been able to cut themselves off from the crowd wherever they might be, but such self-discipline is rare; to most of us, only a goal. . . . There are times in one's life when one needs to muse and dream, to let experience be purified by reflection, and to allow the mind to wander wherever it will, through one's own thoughts or the thoughts of others. It is then that the stubble-field becomes a poem, an unnoticed fact of science, a discovery, a footnote on the entry in a diary, the beginning of a book. . . . Books, too, demand privacy, if you are to read alertly, to meet the author mind-to-mind, ready with laughter, applause, scorn, tears—but who can laugh or cry in a public library? There is nothing like laughing or crying when you are alone. . . . There are times when one must face oneself and have it out; for self-knowledge may begin in a crowd, but it must be completed in loneliness. Sometimes, too, in moments of deepest bitterness or joy, one has to shut the world out. . . ."

Age, position, reputation are no basis for respect at Black Mountain; respectworthy are only such virtues and values as intelligence, self-control, knowledge, decency, truth; and teachers, of course, are exposed to "group influence" no less than students. The result is a high proportion of effective, interesting teachers. Nowhere else do teachers work harder. In Black Mountain they are geared to the whole purpose of the place, which is most insistent. Some students doubtless are not what they could be as students; most of them, however, who have been there for some time want terribly to learn and know what they should be getting, and they must be satisfied. If they are not, they speak up; the unsatisfactory instructor is discussed—but again, there is no malice and little pettiness. The new teacher discovers the place really *is* a new kind of college. Facts, results are unimportant; process, method, imagination, are everything. Seeing how successful some of the others are in the classroom, he begins to suspect that their way may be right. In some cases, he resents that he has not been told what was expected of him. Later he realizes that he was not told anything because the idea is to let him develop, if possible, uniquely. He becomes a successful Black Mountain teacher when he becomes—with accompanying humility that adds to his dignity—more a student than a teacher. In 1935 Rice said to me, "I hope that eventually the faculty meetings will become our most important class."

I lack space to discuss all the Black Mountain teachers. I shall briefly describe the general methods of only three.

Rice is a natural-born teacher, perhaps one of the great teachers of all time. He insists, by word and example, that "a good teacher is always more a learner than a teacher, making the demand of everyone to be taught something. . . . A man who never asks himself any questions had better not try asking others. . . . A teacher must have something of humor, a deeply laid irony, and not be a cynic. In the center of his being he should be calm, quiet, *tough*. He must have in him the principle of growth; like a student, a sense of justice and a capacity for dejection. Teachers in a place where education is taken seriously should always bear in mind that they are the central problem, that we would provide the students with a liberal education if we merely let them watch us while we educated ourselves; also, that it is wrong for us to want others to be like ourselves; that we must want to attend to being the sort of people that others ought to be like."

While he teaches also Greek and Latin and writing (short stories, essays, poetry, etc.), Rice's most important class is "Plato," which has little to do with Plato and is attended by most of the senior division and several teachers. It should probably be called, as he described it to me, "Thought in Action." He starts it going with some such question as "How does individuality differ from individualism?" and then, by a deft Socratic handling of students, too complex to describe, galvanizes them—though not always—into a unit bent on arriving at some answer. Occasionally he succeeds in getting the class to forget his presence and in forgetting himself in the pursuit of an idea or definition, and together they achieve "complete anonymity, group thinking, coöperative intelligence—moments that can only be called mystical experiences, during which, when an impasse has been reached, the humblest intelligence in the room may suddenly offer the word that pushes the thing along. When we achieve such a moment one feels the joy of being a part instead of a whole. We are then in subjection, not one to the other, but to what can only be called truth."

In the autumn, 1937, I sat in his writing class, which he holds once a week, beginning at eight in the evening and lasting often till past midnight. Things *happened* in that class. A few of the stories and poems read there were definitely publishable; later I read others—written by persons of nineteen or twenty years of age—which suggested talent and even genius. Rice is, I think wisely, restraining them from trying to get published; and my feeling is that out of a group of a dozen he is almost bound to turn out two—possibly three— writers who are going to be noticed.

But as was the late John Webb's so Rice's most important teaching is out of class. He is at it all the time. "What is it all about?" Seldom in his office, he moves through the building, joins some group and gets them all talking of what is the matter with Black Mountain and why, or with education in general, or politics, let us say; or why is the average American town so unattractive . . . whereupon, as likely as not, the discussion spreads through the place, goes on at several tables during supper, and echoes of it occur next morning at breakfast. One day when I was there a student laughed at some stupidity that had been considered the opposite a century ago; then Rice quickly asked him and everybody else within the sound of his voice, "What are your grandchildren going to laugh at that you now consider sound and sacred?" For several minutes most of the people in the room were paralyzed with self-consciousness. Then the awful question reverberated through the place for days.

One of the Black Mountain people who knew Rice at Rollins tells me this story about him as teacher. When the Lynds' *Middletown* first came out, a teacher at Rollins required his sociology class to read, then write what they thought of it. Rice, who had read the book and considered it an important contribution to the study of the American scene, asked this teacher what results he had had with it. "Very poor," replied the sociologist. The book did not excite the students; one of them had said "Middletown is just like home," implying that therefore it was not interesting to him. The sociologist did not know what to do about it. With his permission, Rice then took some of the students, talked to them for a few days on values, reading to them from Plato and other Greek classics which touched on values and on the potentialities of human life; then asked them to read *Middletown* again. When they did, all four or five were furious that such a town as Middletown, which was most towns in America, should exist. . . .

Rice attends other teachers' classes as student; then, in his own classes or anywhere at all, he is constantly pointing out—not by special design, but just naturally—the interrelationship and interdependence of the subjects taught in the college, which has an almost normal curriculum, and integrating them in those who teach and study them. He aims to develop the idea and feeling that knowledge, truth, art, education, effort, action, experience, life are all of one piece, or at least that they can be synchronized. Rice teaches, of course, no socio-political-economic isms. I have witnessed masterful dissections by him of the class-consciousness of procapitalist and fascistically inclined students, and equally effective analyses by him of the class-consciousness of students who considered themselves Communists. He is anti-Fascist and anti-Communist (if Communism means violence and dictatorship); and he is for democracy. However, he does not talk about democracy, does not try to teach it directly, but endeavors to be, to live, to act democracy on the basis of values, virtues, and ideals which are particularly well expressed or implicit in the Greek classics, and which he does teach—however, again, not directly, and one could almost say, not really. He uses the classics and the Fifth Century, of which he is a passionate student, to light up immediate situations, conditions, problems, questions, or whatever it is that comes up in class or in the community, but seldom by direct reference to them. And "uses the classics etc.," is not quite correct, either. The Greek classics and the high moral-artistic values and ideals implied or directly dealt with in them are part of him as much as are his arms, because that is the sort of man he is, and he simply acts as he is. He believes in action in education. Things must *happen* in school.

"Any education of an American that leaves action out of account," he said to me in 1935, "is bound to be incomplete. The pioneer tradition is still strong within us, and the pioneer was first of all a man of action. He was, also, a man of forethought, but his forethought was limited to what we call being 'practical,' to the manipulation and management of things outside himself, among which he included his fellowman. He thought ahead about what he should do, not what he should become, through action. This is another way of saying that he was no philosopher. In fact, he was scornful of the philosopher; to him the philosopher was merely a man of reflection. This was all right for an old man, who was worn out by action and could no longer do anything; but for a young man,—well, he could only be called a loafer, and there is no place for the loafer in a new world. This explains why Americans are so incompetent and miserable when they have nothing to do, for to do nothing is an art, and no good American is going to allow any one to call him an artist and get away with it. It also explains, I think, why American undergraduates have such a deep distrust of intellection, why they will go to any lengths to avoid intellectual competition; any other kind of competition, yes; but say to them, 'Come on, boys, I'm going to find out how good a mind you've got,' and watch them scatter. If they could only move their muscles while they are learning! . . .

"But without reflection, no one can tell why he has done a thing. To turn away from reflection is to refuse to learn from the past, even one's own. Given action, one is confronted with the task of getting the student to broaden the basis of forethought so that he may learn to look forward to action that is to have as its object not only things and other people, but also himself, and, hardest of all, thought. It is lack of forethought of thought that makes American scientists so unhappy when their experiments give them unexpected results, that is, fail to give them the narrow results they had looked forward to. Their experiments might have a number of meanings, but they are unable to see them because they so want them to have only one, the one they need. To the lack of forethought that includes oneself is to be ascribed the American's singular ignorance of himself. If we can succeed in getting this far, there remains the task of getting the student to reflect upon what he has done. This kind of reflection should come later, for he has already become suspicious of the kind of reflection you will find in the universities of Europe, such as one finds, for instance, in Oxford, and imported into this country in a somewhat mutilated form. Americans have, some of them, succeeded in the, for them, difficult task of reflection upon the action of others; they have never reached the refinement of reflection upon the reflection of others.

"Later, when they have learned to reflect upon their own actions, they may be tentatively led to the other kinds of reflection. But the teacher—in America, at least—must always be ready to return to action as the basis of the thinking to be done.

"This then is the kind of man we should like to produce, one in whom there is a nice balance of forethought, action, and reflection. What is the best medium? The discipline of the humanities have been tried, and have been a failure; so has science, although the scientists don't yet know it (if science were made a free elective in this country, the registration in courses in science would drop fifty per cent at once). Now we are in the hands of the social scientists, who make brave promises. In history, sociology, psychology, economics, and the rest, there is plenty of action to be reflected upon; but it is *not the action of the student himself.* This is why they will prove as useless in the end as the others have already proved. As a beginning point they will not do, because they do not and cannot begin with the individual student as the actor, as the one who is doing the doing. This is why we at Black Mountain begin with art. The artist thinks about what he himself is going to do, does it himself, and then reflects upon the thing that he himself has done. Here is the concatenation that we want to use at the beginning, one in which each step involves the student inevitably, and one in which no step can be omitted without obvious injury to the rest. Observe, however, that I have said, 'in the beginning.' . . ."

Which brings me to Joseph Albers, formerly a member of the famous Bauhaus, in Dessau, Germany, now head of the art department at Black Mountain, whose importance in this college's setup is quite equal—in many respects superior—to Rice's.

One of the first acts of Hitler, after he came to power, was to close the Bauhaus, of which Rice had heard. When Black Mountain College was started, he sought an art teacher who might be able to put into effect his idea about the importance of art in general education. Quite by chance he heard of Albers, who, it seemed, was uncomfortable under Hitler and wanted to emigrate. Acting on a "hunch" that he was the man the new college needed, he cabled him to come, and Albers came . . . and, fitting perfectly as a teacher into the Black Mountain scheme, began to give courses in drawing, color, and so-called

Werklehre (work with materials and forms), supplementing them with exhibitions and discussions of old and modern art, of handicrafts and industrial products, of typographic and photographic work.

Albers is, as I write, fifty, but younger-seeming; a firm, confident personality, a good deal of the "tough poet," very German as a person; a self-made man as an artist, a natural teacher, and a great and original one (though rather unlike Rice). He is widely recognized as a leading artist, specializing in abstract paintings and drawings, and his work is annually exhibited in New York and elsewhere. He can go to a rubbish dump, pick up a dozen or more beer and vinegar bottles, cut the bottoms from them, and then, with the aid of a few wires, a piece of wood, etc., organize those bottoms into an extremely close and beautiful approximation of a stained-glass window. He can pick up almost any sort of junk and convert it into something lovely or striking.

An adequate description of his teaching technique, which is as simple as life but also as complex, would require a longer chapter than I can give here to Black Mountain as a whole; and the ensuing paragraphs are meant to be merely suggestive.

His courses, as he puts it himself, are "not for artists, but for people . . . life is more important than school, the student and the learning more important than the teacher and the teaching. More lasting than having heard and read is to have seen and experienced"—and to attend his classes is, very definitely, to *experience* art, not so much art as painting, sculpture, design, architecture or music, as art as a process.

"The result of the work of a school," he goes on, "is difficult to determine while the pupil is in school. The best proofs are the results in later life, not, for example, student exhibitions. Therefore to us the *act* of drawing is more important than the graphical product; a color correctly seen and understood is more important than a mediocre still-life." No mere college course, he says, can produce competent judges of art, and for the time being he is satisfied when a student sees "a connection between a modern picture and music by Bach, or a relationship between patterns of textiles and music, or if he is able to differentiate the form-character of a china pitcher from a glass pitcher; or to recognize the difference between an advertisement of 1925 and one of 1935; or when he finds out that in art we still can experience revelation and wonder." He endeavors, with no slight success, to make students see art as "neither a beauty shop nor imitation of nature, as more than embellishment and entertainment; as a spiritual documentation of life" . . . and that "real art is essential life and essential life is art."

His instructions in class are also corrective of the student as a person. For instance, if his motoric system is disbalanced so that he has a tendency to exaggerate the right-ward lines, the pupil is asked to practice deliberately drawing exaggerated lines to the left. This eventually balances him.

Possibly not more than two of his fifty-odd students during the first four or five years of Black Mountain's existence will become painters, but perhaps all will have a sense of form and order, an appreciation of lasting qualities, of life's essences and basic values which, he says, now lie lost for most people somewhere amid the so-called "facts" and "realities." His classes are among the largest and, with Rice's, the most exciting, emotionally and intellectually satisfying and important. Rice and other faculty members are among his students; and generally his influence upon the place and the development of the Black Mountain process and technique of education is very great. He was an important factor in the crystallization of Rice's ideas about teachers as artists.

Whenever I visit Black Mountain I go to Albers' *Werklehre* class. The work that he and his students do there looks ridiculous at first sight. They take, let us say, three green bottles, four red apples, a piece of yellow cloth, and a lady's slipper, or some such seemingly irrelevant or incongruous group of articles; then work with them, together and individually, trying to arrange them so that each thing enhances the form, line, texture, and color values of each of the others, and help to tie them all together into a well-proportioned, harmonious, effective picture. Watching it awhile, one realizes that this work is anything but ridiculous. It is, in fact, important training in seeing things, in discrimination, in taste, in acquiring a sense of form, line color, proportion, and in handling materials. It is also of indirect aid to the students in getting to know themselves and one another, for there are inner reasons why I want to place this bottle here and you there. It is action. Things *happen* in that class; things that can be seen, touched, changed, analyzed, reflected upon. Those students think, at the same time that their emotions, instincts and inclinations, which they did not even know that they had, come into play in coöperation with the mind. After one watches it several times, one realizes that it is really something extraordinary and very successful. After a few months of this sort of thing, when the student returns home to Scranton, Pennsylvania, he, as a rule, really sees his town for the first time—its incongruities, not only its architectural, but—if he is a successful Black Mountain student—also its social and spiritual incongruities and disharmonies. Thus art instruction, working jointly with other elements of the Black Mountain setup and process, is really indirect sociology—sociology grounded in artistic values, which are positive and eternally active in their objection to incongruity.

Albers' drawing classes are, as already suggested, not merely drawing. He realizes that student So-and-so is a timid young person, a victim of all sorts of fears, a product of modern social and family conditions and trends, doubtful about himself, not very comfortable in the college, as he would not be really comfortable anywhere; so Albers helps him in various subtle ways, which are part of his pedagogic technique, to overcome the feeling of terror with which this large blank sheet of white paper tacked on the drawing-board fills him, and to accept its challenge. He draws; he does something; things happen under his pencil, before his eyes; Albers watches him, helps him, and encourages him, jokes with him. . . . After a few months of this, when he begins to draw fairly well, this student sheds much of his timidity; he gradually becomes a new person. When he goes home for Christmas vacation, his people are startled by the change.

Once every so often there is an exhibition of all the drawings, and every member of the class—and anyone else who is interested—studies and analyzes them, not only as art work, but as work by persons who are interesting as such. Now here is a picture, and one of the questions is: what sort of person drew it? . . . Which all ties into the "group influence," one of whose results is that of making students connoisseurs of people and generally into acute, critical observers of anything that comes before their eyes and minds.

The average Black Mountain student does not become a "tough poet," in the sense defined by Rice—first, because he is not the material to be made into one, but only an average young person, to whom harm has probably been done in his early years; and, second, because the Black Mountain setup and process are not yet anywhere near perfect and fully effective, but only a highly interesting experiment in its first stages. In most cases, however, the student there becomes a seeing, feeling, conscious person, who sheds some of his fears, and whose personality and manner become touched by self-confidence. He acquires the means of developing his consciousness, perhaps the habit of forethought and reflection. His mind and emotions tend toward balance between them—toward intelligence, which will help him not to act as an infant at thirty or forty; to marry fairly sensibly, so that acute marital unhappiness will not pervert his political views; to recognize a stuffed shirt when he sees one; and to have the courage to become a plumber, if that is his natural vocational proclivity, instead of becoming a lawyer or business man and then, in his basic and often unconscious unhappiness as a human being, spend a hundred thousand of his, perhaps, ill-gotten dollars to get himself elected governor of his state, in which position he will then be, not a constructive, progressive factor, but a personification of what is wrong with the world.

Unlike the student of old too many schools where education is "handed out," and where he merely sits in class and remembers a few things and "gets by," the Black Mountain student becomes a participator, as distinct from a by-stander. He wants to go into things within the limits of his ability and general nature.

The intention of Black Mountain is to turn out graduates as keen intellectually as the best product of Robert Hutchins' proposed monasticism, but they must be something more. The outside examiners have generally praised the quality of work done by the students, the praise running from mild to enthusiastic.

I am told that in this educational process and setup the courses in music, which are in charge of teachers largely developed at Black Mountain, are important; but, unfortunately, knowing nothing about music, I am not competent to discuss them.

However, I think that I can mention briefly the dramatics, which also have an important function in the Black Mountain scheme. The course is in charge of William Robert ("Bob") Wunsch, a former highschool teacher in Louisville, Kentucky, who was at Rollins for a while and came with Rice to Black Mountain; still a young man, not as obviously brilliant as Rice or Albers, quiet mannered, but an almost unerring instinctive psychologist, and immensely valuable to "group influence." One of the hardest-working people there, he is passionately devoted to the Black Mountain idea, which is well-nigh a religion with him, and which he expounds, if one asks him about it, with a profound, utterly genuine humility that gives one the sense of being in the presence of one of at once the gentlest and most passionate men alive. He developed as a teacher largely in Black Mountain.

Under his direction, the students and the faculty present five or six plays annually, and, if I may judge by the two I saw, they are exceptionally well done. But to Bob Wunsch the play is *not* "the thing." Nor is his purpose in dramatics to develop actors, playwrights or imitative technicians, or to attain external artistic perfection and provide entertainment for spectators. What "the thing" is to him, he explained to me as follows: "We seem *really* to know only what we have experienced. Dramatics is the nearest thing to experience, and as such a good medium to knowledge, especially self-knowledge.

"You know about the so-called 'group influence' and why we believe it is vitally important that a student knows what sort of person he actually is, what kind of fictitious self he has built up around that actual self, and what the social group in which he moves thinks of those actual and fictitious selves. . . . Well, our dramatics is tied up with 'group influence.' Our method is to cast, for instance, an arrogant person in an arrogant rôle, in which his own arrogance stands out even more clearly than otherwise, so that not only the audience, which is the community, sees it, but he himself. We try to find rôles for boors, for the autocratically and over-egotistically inclined, for rich boys and girls whose main prop is their wealth, for persons who want to play gods, for ultra-individualists . . . so that the place sees them, and they see themselves, in all the glory of their outstanding characteristics: which almost invariably leads to corrective processes within those persons. Mainly in consequence of this method, the most unpleasant person we ever had here is now one of the most charming and well-liked individuals in the place.

"Of course, we put people in rôles which are the opposite of, or different from, their principal characteristics and circumstances. Thus a wealthy boy is induced to play the part of a poverty-ground tenant or worker; a poor girl the part of a miserable rich woman. We cast a young cynic in a rôle that helps him to know—and feel, for a while—what it means to fight and die for a cause. . . ."

I have said that Black Mountain is—to me—one of the most interesting places in America. It is, of course, not a world-shaking enterprise. It is important, perhaps, mainly as a suggestion; as something that happened—that could happen in America. It offers a glimpse of American possibilities. It is, as I write, a living emphasis on the old American democratic idea—that education is the hope of man, if he can manage to develop the right kind of education, which will make him into a conscious, steadily progressing, on-pushing, creative being, opposed to incongruities and disharmonies of all kinds. It is a criticism of education as generally practiced in the world. As such, it has become, in five brief years, what Arthur Morgan calls a "center of influence," and a strong one. Educators and teachers have heard of it, and Rice, Albers, and Wunsch are in constant demand as speakers; people want them to explain what they are trying to do. They go to colleges and schools, and talk. Their general ideas, variously revised, are gradually going into practice in not a few schools. Rice is a frequent visitor at the University of North Carolina, where the campus student newspaper urged late in 1937 to get him to come still more often. In this respect, Black Mountain has justified itself; also in that it has turned out a few students who, at least in partial consequence of their having been there, are admirable human beings, perhaps destined to be heard from. . . also in that it has beneficially touched a few score of others . . . and in that it has developed, or given function to, a few fine teachers.

But what its future is as a college, as an experiment, I don't know. As it may probably be gathered from this, even if all too sketchy, picture of it, it is an extremely tenuous place. Financially, it is in perpetual crisis; people who generally give money to schools and colleges have difficulty in understanding it. The "Fascistic" elements in the South attack it. Untrue rumors concerning it float about the country. Its setup is so personal and compact, involving or touching upon so many vital and explosive tendencies in human affairs, that every once in a while it goes through intense internal struggles which threaten to injure it. Within it are still people whose motives spring from the habit of competition among men rather than from ideals or a sense of values. Some of them are still unaware of what the place is all about. Rice, himself, is anything but perfect; at times he is too explosive—a hangover from his past, which was a matter of struggle. The place is terribly strenuous, especially for Rice. Sometimes, when I see him in the midst of its financial and internal difficulties, I marvel how he can endure it, why he does not pack up and go and never return.

Unlike the average dean's ideal in the typical conventional college, Rice's ideal is not to have a smoothly running place where everything is constantly under firm control, but a place where, within a regime of communal freedom, anything is liable to happen at any time.

So, as I say, I don't know its future. I feel, though, that its idea and experience are important; and for that reason I want to quote a few more things that Rice said to me in 1935, as I find them in my notes.

I said to Rice, "Albers just now probably is the strongest diffused influence on the place, but you are its center, its core, and inevitably so. Things revolve around you, and I see no one on the scene who would take your place in case you died next month. Are you developing—can you develop anyone to take your place? It seems to me that, for all its patent virtues, the structure of your vast idea as I see it here is extremely faint and brittle. Can you do—are you doing—anything about this?"

"The problem," answered Rice, "is how to rid ourselves of the necessity of leadership. The paradox lies in the fact that it can only be done through leadership. . . . Men must be taught, or somehow learn, to desire anonymity; to be willing, and to know how, to merge their individual intelligence with the intelligence of others, in order to produce the intelligence of the whole. We are trying to learn that in the Plato class; also, in our faculty meetings.

"It is clear to me that it is both undesirable and impossible for me to develop a leader to take my place, for, if the college is to continue under leadership, the leader must be different from me. If I try to train some one, I will be filling him with my ideas, and a man filled with the ideas of another is an empty man. Platonists and Christians are imitations, hence, poor sticks. The ideal pupil of Plato was Aristotle; and of Christ, Peter. They were quite unlike their teachers. . . . Even if I could train some one in my conception of method, in the process he would inevitably use my ideas, and they could not mean the same thing to him as they have meant to me. Discipleship is the graveyard of ideas. But, for reasons that will be clear to you, I really want disciples, however much I say I don't: but only disciples of a method which will forever free them from discipleship, the method of free inquiry. I believe this thing here is a good beginning; I know something about it, and am eager to tell what I know to those capable of following our example: but following it only in its most general outlines, if that. I want this idea of ours here to go on and develop beyond me, beyond what we are now. So the problem is, how to efface myself.

"I don't want loyalty. Loyalty to a man ('dear old Copey!') develops loyalty to a place, to an institution; and I don't want dead things—a boneyard. Loyalty to an institution is loyalty to something that is over with and done for. I want people to develop passion for ideas, which are never over with and done for.

"I am doing all I can to lessen my so-called importance to the college, and I think I am progressing. The first year I went away for a week and was called back by telegraph. Last year I could go away several times for longer periods, and they wired me to return but once. This fall, so far, I have been away twice, and was hardly missed. In fact, some desirable developments occurred *because* I was not here. . . . Last week I said in faculty meeting that we might as well face the evil of the one-man college. I hinted that if they wanted a one-man college, I don't want to be the man, nor remain here. I gave a brief exposition of what I am saying to you here and added I did not regard myself as committed to this college for the rest of my life, that in four or five years I might want to do something else. There was a moment of tense silence, but not panic, as there would have been two years ago.

"In our general meetings, we have developed a method of arriving at decisions without voting. We just discuss and postpone things, and discuss them some more, till we agree. So far, this method has worked out.

"This is all tenuous, I know. So much depends on the celerity with which I, the momentary so-called leader, can get the thing going. I have a good deal of support, and I am hopeful. I am convinced that this is the direction that humanity must take, if it is to survive. . . . The movement is from leadership to oligarchy, from oligarchy to democracy, and from within democracy to intelligent freedom of a self-disciplined humanity. I am trying here to skip oligarchy: but I know I have a job on my hands. . . .

" 'Tenuous' doubtless is the word that describes Black Mountain: tenuous, brittle, imponderable. We can promise no concrete results, what the world as it is may be willing to call results, under ten years at least. Perhaps no quantitative evaluation will ever be possible. This is an experiment in change. Every moment here is in part the past and the future. Here nothing stands still long enough to be measured. To give us support of any kind is an act of faith. . . .

"We need money—obviously. But just as obviously, remote though it may be, there is the danger of the wrong kind of money, and of too much money. I think I speak for most people here when I say that we don't want a penny from anyone who may want to dictate to us how to 'run' the place, or make any demands upon us other than an exact and detailed account of expenditures, and of our being polite to him if he will be considerate of us. . . . As for too much money, I think that a gift to us of five million dollars might ruin us. Greed might enter in. Trips to Europe might become necessities. Fords might not be good enough. And, worst of all, we could never tell whether a new member of the staff had been attracted by the idea or the money. . . . A moderate sum of money might, of course, do us no harm. We could get an adequate library (fifty thousand volumes, minimum); and disregard the financial status of applicants for entry as students. Now we are forced (I am ashamed to admit this) to prefer the boy or girl whose parents can pay the full tuition fee of $1,200 to the boy or girl who can pay less or nothing at all. We hope eventually to have, say, half the student body on full scholarships. . . . Then, too, if we had a moderate sum of *free* money, we could establish pensions and insurance, so that a permanent member of the staff could have the maximum security from financial worry now attainable. We could free students who are ready to leave but not sure of what they should do, from family pressure to 'get a job,' by allowing them to remain here, or, if the thing they have chosen does not work out, to return and make another start. We could build laboratories and buy pictures. I should like for every student and faculty member to have on loan in his study an original painting or piece of sculpture: for living with a work of art is different from seeing it in a museum. It gets into you. I should include in the collection some pictures and pieces of sculpture that connoisseurs agreed to be poor: for one must learn to differentiate good from bad as well as good from good. Also, if we had money, we would be able to have as guests for long periods writers, artists, composers, scientists, who would come here to work: for to see an artist, writer, scientist, or composer at work is to knock romantic nonsense out of one's head.

"In a word, I should like to build a kind of place in which salaries would be of no moment, but food, shelter, clothing, and other necessities were guaranteed to every member, so that I could prove my long-held conviction that the problem of humanity would then really become acute—that the removal of the element of economic interest from human affairs and motives would cause every other interest of humanity to assert itself; that the *real* class struggle would then begin—the struggle between people holding different tastes, with different sets of moral and artistic values."

(Here I want to interrupt Rice to say that Black Mountain differs from "ideal communities" in that they are set up for the sake of "happiness" whereas the job of Black Mountain College is to *get people ready to leave it*. The test within the ideal community is, "Am I happy?"; the test at Black Mountain is, "Am I ready to leave and take up my place in the world?"—a very important distinction.)

Rice: "Other dangers? . . . Two ogres stand at the gate, ready to come in at any time: complacency and dilettantism. We feel pretty good about ourselves, especially those who have taught elsewhere; and when visitors praise us we cheerfully agree. A quiet harbor is a pleasant place. But the moment we think we have arrived, we will be dead. Can we be sure that we will be treated as the dead should be? By no means. The deader an institution is, the more tenacious it is of existence.

"A time is apt to come, too, when the one man, teacher or student, who could put life into the place will be refused admission. He won't be 'our type' or may have bad manners, or be a conservative, or something the majority of us won't like. Heaven help us! . . . Dilettantism comes through a lack of seriousness; also, when there is too much teaching and not enough learning. There is no lack of seriousness now: but can we keep this up? I think we can: but who knows? . . . Our future depends, too, on the developments in this country, in the world. War? . . ." He raised his hands in a gesture of uncertainty.

"The Next War" and Fascism, and America

THERE IS MUCH IN AMERICA, ESPECIALLY IF ONE LOOKS CLOSELY, TO HELP ONE develop a steady feeling about the country and about oneself in it. I have tried to suggest some aspects that contribute to such steady feeling as I have about it and about myself. The Long Road, with all its turnings and difficulties, appeals to me. I think that some of the people trudging on it have the right idea about it. . . .

But I notice that I have said a number of times "such steady feeling as I have." Also, I remember that somewhere in the middle of this book, writing of the country's probable future, I thought that "for quite a while, and for a complexity of reasons at least some of which I hope are implicit in these numerous pages, America—with the best of luck, considering the world of which she is a part—will be essentially" such and such and such a place. The qualifying phrase: "with the best of luck, considering," etc., is pertinent.

I have been more or less at work on this book for many years. The actual writing of it, however, I began in July, 1937. As I am finishing it, it is March, 1938. And I must say that my feeling about America has wavered now and again in the face of certain developments. In the autumn, 1937, President Roosevelt made his startling speech indicating a possible change in the United States' traditional foreign policy. During this time, too, the "miniature world war" in Spain entered its second year, the events favoring a Franco victory. Japan invaded China, destroyed many of its leading cities, conquered immense stretches of its territories, murdered hundreds of thousands of its people. There was the *Panay* incident. Also, in the time I was writing this book, Mussolini visited Hitler. Early in February, 1938, there was a drastic shakeup in Germany, which seemingly enhanced Hitler's power, giving him a freer hand in the matter of "the next war." Almost simultaneously with that event in Germany, Stalin made a speech: war was a certainty, the Soviet Union must win to its active support the working classes of the bourgeois countries! Then, gangster fashion, Hitler held up the Vienna regime and grabbed Austria. Followed Cabinet crises in England. What next—Czechoslovakia? Danzig? *Drang nach Osten*. . . . The Soviet Union's Commissar of War Voroshilov made a statement signifying his country was prepared to use poison gases and deadly bacteria in the impending war, should its enemies use them. . . . An armament race is on. In 1938 more money is being spent on war preparations than ever before. As I write this, "the next war"—the second world war—appears inevitable.

In the United States, throughout the fall of 1937 and the ensuing winter, a debate has been going on: Isolation *vs.* Collective Security. On the President's request, Congress has appropriated over a billion dollars for an increase in our naval power. Will we go into the next war? Are we going to fight Japan and European Fascist powers? On the side of Russia? Where will England be?

At this moment, in March, 1938, it is difficult to be certain. . . . Confusion, uncertainty, a surging sea of doubt verging on panic engulfs a large portion of humanity; in the world at large nothing seems certain—only war, more brutality, more confusion.

What is America's position in this? Where will she be when or if hell breaks loose in Europe once more? Armed isolation? Aiding the democracies and Soviet Russia to beat the Fascist powers and Japan? . . . The debate goes on as I write, and in all likelihood will continue for some time after the date of this book's appearance. It goes on largely on the assumption that a European war before 1940, or soon after, is practically unavoidable. I enter the debate on that assumption. If it proves erroneous, I shall be glad. . . .

I was in the last World War. I know a little of what war means. Slaughter. Poverty. Suppression of democracy and freedom. Wealth blown up. Beauty destroyed. The earth scarred. Cities bombed. Epidemics. . . . Some one has figured it out that if America goes to war again, her bill for it will not be under forty billion dollars. Then, what? Inflation, depression, unemployment (unless the war does away with ten or fifteen million Americans), chaos, Fascism?

My friend Ross Wills, as I have mentioned, is an ex-service man, too; in a sense, a victim of the last war. In midwinter, 1938, as I was working on this last third of my book, I received a letter from him—not from Hollywood, however, but from a Veterans' Administration hospital in the West:

"Don't be alarmed by the above address. As a so-called war veteran, I have been drawing government compensation and insurance for many years. But in the annual physical examination last spring an inexperienced doctor sent an erroneous report about my ears to Washington. They clipped off my insurance entirely. I got the Legion to help me; now, to get the thing straightened out, I had to come here for two or three weeks, to be exhaustively reëxamined. . . .

"But this place here! A fine building in a lovely spot; in it, several hundred specimens of human war wreckage.

"I am in a room with a big, pleasant blond fellow with a bad heart; a bright-eyed little 'nut' with a cracked skull; and an Italian who was in the American army, with a machine-gun bullet in his spine. The nut, as he calls himself (his trouble, he says, is that he 'can't concentrate any more'), is a cheerful, charming cuss who spends his time plastering 'Keep Smiling' signs all over the room. The Italian, who is big, heavy, and about forty-three, lies on his back the live-long day and night, lamenting he was ever born. The nut blinks at me in disgust, glares at the Italian, and snorts 'No guts!'

"Good God, Louis! This is only *one* hospital, and they are all over America; all over the world, for that matter; full of men in wheel chairs or flat on their backs, or able only to hobble about on crutches. Twenty years! Two decades. . . . This is an institution. We all have to eat together, as in a prison, at big tables; eat what is set before us. We can't leave the ward between eight

A.M. and four P.M. Rules, regulations. No steel bars; but they are not needed. There are stronger bars than steel, invisible, of lead and gas and epidemic, strung across these men's cells twenty years ago; and they are in for life. . . . I am the youngest and healthiest man here, beyond a doubt, and I feel strange and self-conscious among all these old, gray human wrecks.

"The second day I am here I am walking up the corridor. I see a man rolling toward me in a wheel chair. He is gray and his body is somewhat distorted. His head hangs awkwardly to one side, though you can see he exerts powerful effort to hold it erect. His face is lined, tortured; but beneath the marks of twenty years of this life you can still discern the faint outlines of his youth, when he must have been handsome, alert, vital, even charming and dashing. He rolls up to me, stops, greets me respectfully. He has heard I am from Hollywood. (That seems to make me important to him.) Yes, I smile, I come from that den of iniquity. He nods and starts to say something. But suddenly he has a seizure. His legs lift violently up in the air and they begin to shake horribly. I stand there shocked and bewildered. But the man starts to curse furiously. He grabs his legs with his hands ferociously, and begins to struggle with them, to try to put them back down there where they belong. He fights them and fumes at them. His face is in a frenzy. And it is not the pain, either, for he is used to that. It is the goddamned outrageous indignity of it— no man's legs should behave in that preposterous and idiotic manner! Presently, he seizes one leg with both hands and struggles violently with it, whilst the other still waves and shakes dreadfully there in the air. Finally he gets the first leg conquered, then he conquers the other one. The seizure has passed —he has beat it! He looks up as though nothing had happened. He juts his head out at me and says belligerently, 'I was a major in the war!' and rolls triumphantly off down the hall.

"I go into the room and ask about the fellow, and I am informed that he is a little nuts. He was no major—just a private, who was badly shot up.

"But I still believe he was a major. It's like this: These poor devils were all virtually destroyed twenty years ago, but they had to go on living. They were cut down at twenty or so, just when their lives were starting, and before they had any chance to 'be important.' Now, there never was a man born who did not want to be important at some time in his life. But a helluva chance *they* had to be 'important,' lying around these hospitals for twenty years, waited on by nurses, having to be bathed like babies, and so on. So they've built up an imaginary world in which they once were 'important.' I haven't yet found a former private or, like me, a common seaman, in the whole place. They were all captains or colonels or majors or at least lieutenants or ensigns or sergeants—even though an inspection of their records would show that virtually all were privates, etc.; and they are all 'rich' or they've 'got pull' or something like that. Hell! When you can't live it, you've *got* to imagine it. And these guys have been imagining it so long that they now firmly believe it. And when they tell it to me I don't smile, I believe it, too. You don't pity them. Not at all. Twenty years makes a monkey out of pity. If you pitied one of them, he would probably hit you over the head with his crutch, as he should. And these men are no whit more insane than the normal man out in the world who, to escape from reality and, or, his failure in the world, concocts for himself a little sphere in which he forgets his twenty-dollar-a-week job, or finds refuge in drink or dope. . . .

"But I look around here at all these fellows, and I think of all the other hospitals—there is surely one in each state, at least, and several in some states. And I think how the war-mongers are bugling up another war—for 'democracy,' etc. I think of the agitators both radical and reactionary organizing and preparing public opinion to go out and 'make war upon the war-makers' and such piffle.

"And damned if I don't get a crazy notion like this—to go through all the hospitals all over the country and rouse these fellows—and we'll roar off to Washington in our wheelchairs and our beds with rollers on them, and we'll lay about us with our crutches and our braces and our urine-bottles and our bed-pans, and we will drive the war-mongers into the earth, and we'll blow up the munitions-plants and set fire to Roosevelt's 'Big Navy' plan, which is designed, it appears, to take the public's mind off the 'recession' and, mark you, with the blessings of the radical gang, notably the Communist Party.

"Oh, the sloganeers, the sloganeers! Oh, the tinpots and the frauds and the fake messiahs, the chiselers and mountebanks. I think how only a year ago it was the American League *Against* War and Fascism and now it has been slyly changed to American League *for* Peace and Democracy! And how only a year ago the Student Union went grimly and loudly on record as being opposed to any war the United States might engage in, except in case of actual invasion of our soil. And how, at the most recent meeting, under the leadership of the Communist Party, that stand was completely reversed.

"What lies, what falsehoods, what hysteria is all this! Why, these fellows are getting away with their stuff! They've impregnated us with a 'fear of Fascism' psychosis, until we're seeing Hitlers and Mussolinis under every bed. It is just crazy. There's no sense anywhere, nobody is doing much calm thinking. The idiots do not stop to think that even if we did combine with the 'other democracies' to 'stop the march of Fascism,' we would ourselves have to turn Fascist. Our government has a marvelous 'M-day' setup, all fixed so that when war comes, all our liberties and democracy go down the chutes, and are taken over and held in escrow by the government. We would have to turn Fascist; a democracy would be unwieldy, disruptive, and dangerous, opposed to a totalitarian enemy. And here's one little rub. How do we know that just the moment we 'won the war,' if we did, the Fascist setup would sweetly step aside—oh, yeah?

"But to me, the most utterly stupid and naïve policy ever heard of is this program the Communists are trying to promote—of a union of the 'three great democracies, in combination with Soviet Russia,' against 'fascism.' Of all the crazy plots, plans, schemes, ever designed by man for his own salvation, this is the most insane by far. This blather is getting serious and dangerous and those fools have got to be exposed before they get us into trouble. . . .

"They tell us we '*cain't* just shut ourselves up.' The devil we can't! If Europe is determined on suicide, let her go ahead. Now, just reflect: If we went into this 'war to save democracy' we would not only have to use our resources in men and material and food for ourselves—and that alone would call for an exorbitant demand upon ourselves—but we would also have to *provide for our allies,* and that would just about exhaust us. Where would we be at the end of it? Whereas, by 'shutting ourselves up' while Europe goes down with her madness, we have only to provide for ourselves under relatively ordinary conditions. . . . But, they say, if we don't get into it, this old meanie Fascism will conquer Europe and then it'll git us, too. They do not stop to think that while Europe was cutting its several throats, the United States, obviously warned, would be girding herself intelligently for defense, and doing it under comparatively comfortable circumstances. Even a Europe conquered by Fascism would scarcely be in shape, after the hell was over, there, to sail 3,000 miles and conquer a powerful, rich America. But my guess is that Fascism would not be Fascism when it did conquer Europe, if it did— that it would metamorphose into something else, and it probably would be relatively harmless to us—because it, too, would be exhausted. An exhausted Fascism *could not* threaten us, and Socialism would not. Those seem the only alternatives to the conclusion of a general European conflict. At any rate, I feel such observations are every whit as legitimate as the prophecies the tub-thumpers are making, and which are calculated to fling us into a bloody and disastrous war.

"But there must be one sound, highly developed nation left intact when this impending hell-on-earth has passed. It will be so awful, so terrible, there will be such a vital need of living men and efficient ones, technicians and engineers and experts, to lift up the stricken world again, and save it from starvation and utter ruin. We, America, could be—should be—that nation. That is our greater destiny, to stay entirely out of it, and keep to ourselves while war roars; and be ready, at the end of it, with all our energy and institutions kept intact, to lift the world to its feet, quickly, expeditiously. We are the logical nation to do that—we, almost alone, would have no designs of conquest upon any other weak and helpless nation. . . ."

Two weeks later, out of hospital and, as he said, "back again in the Hollywood salt-mines," he wrote me a second letter on the subject of the next war and Fascism, democracy and America, elaborating on the first:

"The insolence of the 'collective security' crowd! All set to unleash our country in the coming whoopla, as though they knew what it was all about; and they don't understand and don't want to understand this country. First they wanted us to 'save Spain,' still do, and now they're all hot for us to 'save China.'

"Now, even a nit-wit should realize that 'saving Spain' is not necessarily, or even likely, going to solve anything. What *is* the Spanish Loyalist government but a union of factions, only temporarily united in a mutual extremity. Once they are victorious (and of course we all want them to be), it seems almost foregone that another outbreak will occur between the strongest factions—a row over which shall inherit the victory, and which, alone, shall be blessed with the sacred right to 'glorify the blood of our illustrious dead.' Well, you can't fight a war without patriotism and it is after the war is over— in a revolution—that patriotism somehow turns into an ol' meanie and gets to be a horrible nuisance.

"And what would we save in 'saving China?' Only the world's largest poorhouse. Of course, our instincts rebel against the spectacle of the Japanese moving in upon a peaceful people and murdering them and robbing them of their country. But a pertinent fact remains: It was not as though Japan suddenly and unexpectedly 'snuck' up on China like an assassin in the dark! No— for China has known, for many decades, that Japan was a real menace and would certainly eventually move against her. But she slept on, shrugged it off, remained disunited, indifferent. But now that the Japanese have struck, she bawls to be saved. Of course, I like the Chinese, prefer them to the Japanese, and they have many virtues which Occidentals could acquire with profit, and I think they should be permitted to live as they damned please. But just the same: The Chinese have always snickered and hooted at the go-getters of the West, and gone on content to live on a sub-human level, and be enslaved to this or that native war lord. But come the inevitable drouth or flood or other disaster, and the Chinese forget to laugh, they bawl and howl to the West: Save us! Feed us! Clothe us! And the naïve, big-hearted and rich West, having the provisions, etc., because it has worked hard for them, always responds. Once China is 'saved,' fed and clothed again, she slops back into her old comfy, indifferent, snickering ways again. One wonders if there is any reason to believe if we, or anybody, now 'saved' China from Japan, she would turn over a new leaf, unite, install modern plumbing and machinery, etc., etc., and learn to take care of herself. One wonders, indeed, if the Chinese haven't been cunningly counting on the West saving her from Japan—expecting to bribe the West with loot in the form of trade concessions. And what does this make China in the end? Always an enormous poorhouse and slave-trap; would not the Chinese be exchanging their native war lords for Western commercial slave-masters, merely? . . .

"Anyhow, I keep bewilderedly wondering over and over just what it is that the 'collective security' boys are trying to *save*, anyhow! I am compelled, frequently, to come to this staggering conclusion—that they are bewitched by a mere *name*, and just want to save that—a name, a word spelled 'democracy.'

I can't see what good it will do to 'save' the same old thing we 'saved' in the last war—to bring blood and ruin for it and even worshiping it.

"Democracy is not universally a 'corpse'—I don't mean that; it is a good deal of a living reality in America—but it darned well likely will be a corpse here, too, if the guns are unleashed to 'save' it. And we certainly are talking through our hats when we think of saving Spain or China as saving democracy; for there has never been an ounce of it in either country. It seems very likely that the only successful government which can take over in Spain, after the war ends there, must be a most ruthless, dictatorial one, regardless of which side wins. Certainly it will be if Franco wins, and he will have relatively little factional trouble, at that. And if the Loyalists win, the only way the government can maintain 'peace' and 'order' will be to establish an equally, or even more, severe Stalin-type of dictatorship. Indeed, the Loyalists will surely have a harder time establishing peace and order than Franco would, just because Franco is relatively free from internal factionalism; and the Loyalists will, by so much, just *have* to establish an even harsher government, it seems to me, to maintain itself and keep order.

"And what if China were 'saved' by the Western powers, and Japan driven out by them? The Western powers would be very foolish if they did not exact some payment in return for their sacrifices for China; and it is hard to see them establishing, out of hand, an outright Socialism over there! One logically pictures them hogging vast trade concessions, and so enhancing their own capitalistic powers, and also enhancing that tradition in China. It is an absolute certainty that the Western powers would insist, as part of the price of 'saving' China, upon definite rights in directing and controlling China, in order to forestall any future crisis. Just to 'save' China, and not to make some guarantees against a future similar crisis, would be a horrible waste of men and resources. And obviously, the Western powers, the 'democracies,' would act in accord with their own ideas, and not China's, which had been proven so disastrous; they would have China over a barrel, have power over her, and they would use that power, too, not merely for China's own good but for theirs as well. Then, not even a real democracy could—or would—be set up in China by the Westerners. It could not be done successfully, by them, because there is no foundation to lay it upon; not a bit of real democratic tradition, for all the bush-wah about Sun Yat-Sen, who was a mere forerunner rather than a founder.

"Personally, I suspect that Japan is going to win a lot more in China than most of the experts seem to think. The only unity to speak of, that modern China has ever had, has developed only since the Japanese invasion. And that kind of unity is suspicious to me; it began far too late to send its roots deeply. It is only a temporary device, wrought by grim and bitter necessity, the old 'united front' last-resort, whose eventual victory, if it came, would produce the inevitable factional squabble, and so wind up in setting the country back on its heels again, as of yore.

"Perhaps I am in extreme minority, but I am one American, at least, who, despite his great preference for the Chinese to the Japanese, is able to contemplate with a startling calm the prospect of Japan conquering and grabbing all China, in so far as that prospective conquest may be a threat to America. Even though I do not approve, I can see the damned logic of it, the line of relative inevitability, and even 'necessity' in it. No doubt at all that the Japanese would enormously improve the living conditions of the Chinese masses, through the installation of modern machinery and sanitation, and so on. Of course they would enslave the masses, but the Chinese are used to that; the difference would be in the exchange of a filthy disease-ridden cell for a sanitary prison. As I say my sympathies are wholly with the Chinese, because I am fanatically prejudiced in favor of allowing anybody or any nation to live just as he or it chooses to, so long as he or it doesn't offend or encroach upon others. But if that nation values its ways of life so much, it is surely up to it to guard against obvious enemies.

"But if Japan conquers China—she will be a 'menace' to America! That one will take a great deal of convincing to raise my blood pressure one-half of one degree. In the first place that 'conquest,' even after it were officially acknowledged, would take many decades, beyond a doubt, to make certain. And meantime, one supposes, America would remain utterly idle, asleep, indifferent, against building up a powerful defense against the alleged threat? Nonsense. America may be many things, but it is not another China; it may bat around confusedly, but it never is really asleep. But is it altogether improbable that Japan's success in China would not appease her? Is it not possible, indeed, that she would be smart enough to realize that if she went off conquering America—and for what reason, pray?—other enemies, possibly Russia, would move in behind her back and hack away at China? One would think, to hear the owl-eyed thimble-wits who pass as authorities, spouting their hysterical war-college yells, that Japan's conquest of China would mean, *ipso facto,* Japan's domination of the entire world; and that, as well, the rest of the world would just sit back and fold its hands and tremble with terror. It never occurs to them that if Japan's conquest of China were a threat to America—and that is, as I say, doubtful—it is even more of a threat to Europe, and particularly Russia, which country is not precisely a Rumania in heft. Why, in the name of God, should Japan risk trying to conquer a powerful nation thousands of miles away by sea, when she has rich prospects much closer to home and much more easily and safely reached by air-fleets, etc.? And, then, too, one is supposed to assume idiotically that in event such a Japan assailed America, the latter would be without any allies! As though England and France, or even Germany, could contemplate a yellow conquest of the American continent!

"The truth is, all this gush is just propaganda, and it is shallow as a baby's sins, and as naïve and ignorant. It amazes me that Americans can sit and take this stuff about Japan's threats to Hawaii and Alaska, and get excited about it, and want to go right out and nip Japan before she gets going. But that is what the nit-witted propagandists want—to get the people het up, before they can think and see behind this piffle.

"Here I've been, seemingly, devoting myself to the very sins I rant against— ignoring America's problems and snorting around in Europe and Asia. But, really, the crux of the method is this: I am trying to get at a sound basis to show that there is absolutely no sense or use or plausibility in America involving herself in any foreign war. For my idea is that first we must do all we can to keep America out of war, *guard against that*; and then we must give our best attention toward correcting our internal difficulties. But one almost despairs—there is so much bilge being stuffed down the people's throats, and so very, very little sense. One fears there is no chance to get the people to pipe down and think and look into this thing.

"One fears, for look how completely even our most advanced liberal press has been permeated with propaganda. How even they have fallen for the line that our best causes are somehow sacred, sacrosanct, and never to be criticized. Criticism, the sympathetic pointing out of errors, even, is regarded with a fluttering of horror, and a warning to hush-hush! Take the C.I.O. Has any movement in modern American history ever been slavered over with more floor-touching humility and downright fetish-worship by our best liberal gazettes, than the C.I.O.? Why, the thing has been regarded as the Second Coming, and anybody raising a head to make an intelligent criticism has got himself jolly-well clouted and scorned by the same gazettes that have chided the Communists in the past for such very sectarian nonsense.

"Along comes a Ben Stolberg, a well-known pal of the C.I.O., and begins pointing out what, incidentally, everybody has more or less known for a long time, and what happens? My God! *The Nation* and *The New Republic* scream bloody murder, raging and ranting like fishwives; until one would think that Stolberg had dug up Papa Marx's bones and rushed to the Kremlin and flung them in Stalin's face. They whine and rant and tear their hair—because that ol' Bad Benny has 'gone and exposed our faults—though we ain't really got any—to the enemy, and now Mayor Hague will lead an army of cops against us and just wipe us right out.' Tch! Tch! It's too, too utterly utter!

"One wonders, indeed, how we are ever going to get down to the facts, when this fetich-worship permeates even our advanced liberal organs and paralyzes our best thinkers. They all seem to fear spooks; to tremble with superstitious terror at the prospect of delivering simple facts, as though by so doing the gobbeluns'll git 'um, and just walk right in and eat everything right up, and there won't be none a-tall no more. If there ever was a worthwhile and important 'cause' in more danger of being destroyed by its friends than by its enemies—indeed, it has prospered on its enemies—then it is the C.I.O. And Stolberg, with all his faults, has done some very acute and important pointing out in that respect, too! But when even our most advanced organs shrink from plain thinking and honest speaking, out of the dreadful fear that to reveal faults and errors in our best causes is to make them privy to the enemy and so give him aid and encouragement—well, one almost gives up. True, they take refuge in denying even that the faults or errors exist, which is even dumber.

"But—I can't help laughing. This very minute, as I am about to wind up, my eye lights on a piece in the afternoon paper. I quote:

San Francisco, February 4.—The great mistake and most tragic error of democratic Germans was not to take the Nazis seriously enough, according to Klaus Mann, son of Thomas Mann [etc.]. Klaus Mann, like his father and sister, an exile from Germany, declared: *'I hope the world, and particularly the democracies, will not repeat our mistake. . . .* [That line is the keynote, but he goes on incidentally:] There are,' Mann said, 'two Germanies: one, a part of Europe, belongs to the world; another, nationalistic, shut off by herself, selfish, aggrandized, a Germany that hates the rest of Europe.'

"The 'democratic Germans' makes one raise an eyebrow, and suspect that it is an evasion for the absurd 'democratic Germany.' The pay-off, though, is in that line *underscored*. In simple, it means just this: 'America! Look out, or you are liable to get a Hitler!' I don't know Klaus Mann, and he probably is all right in all sorts of ways; but it is this kind of gabble which has been doing real damage in America. It is calculated to arouse hysteria and result in fomenting 'cures' that are as dangerous as the alleged disease. How airily and easily so many otherwise intelligent people, Americans, forget that back of Stalin, an inevitable product, is a long line of ruthless Tsars; back of Mussolini, an ancient line of absolute monarchs; and back of Hitler, a storied and deep tradition of Fredericks, Bismarcks, and Kaisers. But where, in all our history, is our Bismarck, our mere Tsar Nicholas, or even our King Victor Emmanuel?

"We forget this enormous distinction and difference, and we set about concocting 'preventives'; we have them all lined up, so that when this gabble gets loud enough, and enough people get scared by it, why, we can run the 'preventive' right into the government—and muss everything all to hell and back! One way, as everybody knows, to get a disease, is to get a psychosis about it, and go around fearing and trembling that you are going to get it, or probably have got it already, only the darned doctors won't admit it. If this sort of thing keeps on, we are going to be, possibly, in the unhappy position of the man who is given a shot of salvarsan, when the sore was, after all, only a pimple—he goes needlessly through the sweats and horrors, but will never be quite the same again, mentally or physically. . . ."

I replied to my friend:

". . . Your analysis of the 'next war' situation is, I think, sound, at least emotionally and humanly so; and I am with you one hundred per cent for America's isolation as against her joining, or even remotely participating in, any 'collective security' scheme.

"In addition to what you say, there is something else that ought to cause the American people to think more than twice before the United States becomes involved in any sort of military adventure in Europe and Asia. In 1917, at least part of the motive of America going to war was idealistic; in 1919, that idealism was laughed at behind Woodrow Wilson's back in Versailles. Clemenceau, Orlando, and Lloyd George cynically made a fool of him, whereupon the 'irreconcilable' bloc in the United States Senate finished him. Since then the American idealism that played a rôle in the last war has been almost completely defeated. In the 'next war,' America's participation is liable to be even more tragic. Idealistically and morally, the leaders of the countries with which we are apt to be associated in the 'next war,' if we go into it, will be inferior even to the fellows Wilson bumped up against in 1919. This country won't be able to trust them. She won't be on the inside of their diverse 'games' and schemes. They will double-cross her at any point. There is in Europe, it seems to me, a profound decline of moral character. This not only in the countries that have gone Fascist, but also in the 'democracies.' No wonder. The best young men of the 1910's were killed in the first World War; in consequence now most of Europe is in the hands of shabby characters— gangsters and people capable of dealing with gangsters, yielding to them, compromising with them. America must not become involved with them.

"You know the story of my friend Cantrell. . . . Well, I believe that the dominant forces in Europe today, on the Right and the Left, are essentially the same in character as those that led to the McNamara disaster; only, of course, much greater, more terrible. I feel that in the end they will stalemate, defeat one another.

"The thing to do is to stay out of the 'next war' completely and at all cost. Isolation, as Elmer Davis points out in an interesting article in [the March, 1938] *Harpers*, will be no easy matter. In fact, it will be full of astounding difficulties, which are intrinsic in America's economic makeup. Incidentally, you ought to read that article. Elmer Davis is not pro-war, but he argues very convincingly that if a new world war breaks out and we stay neutral and refuse to sell anything to any of the belligerents in order to help us to remain neutral, our entire national economy will be so seriously dislocated by the sudden cessation of our foreign trade that we might have to become at least partly Fascist or Socialist, or a little of each, to prevent collapse. We isolationists must consider that. Elmer Davis says that we are almost bound to lose the next war, whether we go into it or not. I don't know about that, but we must ponder the problem deeply. I am not sure that you have fully thought it out. I haven't, either. Probably none of us can by himself. We must talk and write about it. The debate on it is in progress, but not enough of it. The best work on our side, so far, is being done by Charles A. Beard, John Dos Passos, Oswald Garrison Villard, and Alfred M. Bingham, among the publicists. Particularly by Beard; have you seen his reply, in *The New Republic* [February 9], to Earl Browder, who wrote a piece in favor of 'collective security'? Among political and labor leaders, the La Follettes, Lewis Schwellenbach, and Homer Martin are doing good work. John Lewis, when I last talked with him, was anti-war. We need to join these men and work with them; that is why I want to publish in my book your letters to me on the subject. Also, because we ex-service men of the last war should be speaking out on the matter.

"I think the most important phase of the problem is that isolation will plunge us into an economic crisis the moment war breaks out in Europe. What have we to say about that? Mere pacifism is no answer. In fact, mere pacifism is a silly thing. . . .

"I have a suggestion, which, I know, is perfectly fantastic and 'impracticable,' but no more so than the idea of America joining in the 'next war' and sending American soldiers to China and Europe, or of not doing anything in advance to cope with the consequences of isolation. If you don't think it is worth considering, you make a better suggestion. Mine is this: Our bill for the next war, if we go into it, is estimated to be sure about forty billion dollars. That is a lot of money. Why not simply decide right now, before hell breaks loose in the Old World, that we must spend it? Why not appropriate it right now, most of it to be used after the beginning of hostilities in the Old World? Let us appropriate two, three, five billions (how much ever may be needed) for defense, and begin spending that amount immediately: but only for defense. Then, when war begins, let us go in for public works, to be carefully planned ahead (not mere boondoggling) and for housing in a big way: say, to the extent of twenty, thirty, or thirty-five billion dollars, which we would blow up if we went to war.

"Personally, I think one of the best results of the New Deal is the Civilian Conservation Corps. The CCC boys have done some wonderful work, and their service has been fine for them as persons. The trouble is that they have not done enough; there have not been enough of them. Just now"—in March, 1938—"their number is only somewhere between two and three hundred thousand. There ought to be two or three *million* of them by the time Europe breaks loose with her next war. . . . H. H. Bennett, the CCC chief, lately remarked before the Senate Committee on Unemployment and Relief, that we have wasted our soil resources faster than any other known people in the history of the world. 'In this respect,' he said, 'we have been less wise than were the ancient Incas of Peru who on the slopes of the Andes constructed a terrace system of soil conservation which is still partly in use.' Government surveys have shown that soil erosion has affected some 300,000,000 acres of land. About 50,000,000 of these, which were once productive, have been ruined for further cultivation and virtually abandoned. Another 50,000,000 acres have been severely eroded, but have patches of better land to which farmers still cling. On still another 100,000,000 acres, all or most of the topsoil has been washed off, and here many thousands of farmers struggle for a meager living. Erosion is getting actively under way on still another vast area of more than 100,000,000 acres. These figures include the region stretching from the Texas

Panhandle to the Canadian border, of which about 70 percent is affected to some degree by wind and water erosion, and one-fourth is seriously affected. And this species of havoc is not confined to the Great Plains, but exists in large sections of the entire country, including the Appalachian region and even Florida. . . .

"We *must* do something about this. Let us do it instead of going in 'the next war.' Let us decide to go into this job in earnest, with the CCC, before 'the next war' begins. H. H. Bennett says that the United States has 200,000,000 gullies, most of which were not here a hundred years ago. Well, let us do something about those gullies. Let us construct dikes, field terraces, diversion waterways and stockwater reservoirs; let us resod worn-out fields for protection of permanent pastures, relocate fences, plant trees and shrubs (*billions* of them), lay out lines for contour cultivation and strip-cropping, and retire hopelessly depleted pastures and fields into permanent woodland and wild-life areas.

"We *must* do that even if there is no 'next war.' . . . To spend ten or twenty billions on conserving our soil, which is now going into the Gulf of Mexico, would be an extremely sound long-range investment. It would become part of our economic dynamics of the future. And let us get, as I say, a nationwide housing program going, so that when the smoke clears in Europe we will have five or ten million new homes for people to live in.

"This might not only take care of our isolation-created internal economic crisis, but might even start an era of high prosperity, which will give us some extra energy with which to lend a hand to Europe after——

"To repeat, I know that this is a crazy suggestion, completely 'impossible,' etc.; but we are living in a crazy, impossible period. Sometimes fire is fought with fire. If you don't like it, as I say, you think of a better one."

Ross Wills replied:

". . . Of course your idea is stark mad! But not half so mad as most of the brash political schemes being peddled by some of our more prominent reactionary and radical leaders and experts, whose chief anxiety seems to be that America may not be suckered into the universal lunacy that now convulses Europe. It is high time that the Toms-Dicks-and-Harrys and others of us who don't pretend to be 'experts,' but who will be the ones out in front facing the music while the 'experts' sit behind the scenes pulling the strings, put in *our* oar. 'Expertism' is the curse of Europe; there, individual 'experts,' or Great White Fathers, control the whole economic-political-social-cultural life of great nations. America is still something of a democracy. And if common American citizens like you and me sit back and leave it all up to our self-appointed 'experts,' and use our democratic processes only by proxy, then we will come out the same nine-hole as the European peoples—and darned well deserve our fate!

"So I don't hesitate to match your democratic impudence with some of my own. The obvious question about your idea—or any other—is: Who will pay for it? But that is eloquently answered by another question: *Who would produce the forty billions if we went to war?* The distinction is this: If we adopted an intelligent, defensive isolation policy, the American people would be the sole beneficiaries of the forty billions; but if we went into the war, our allies would surely benefit by at least half of it. If we were certain that lasting peace, justice, prosperity would ensue, no one would object to America's buying it for twenty billions; it would be the cheapest price ever paid for a good thing in human history. But Europe offers us no assurance whatever; on the contrary, the blood and wealth that America has already contributed toward holding Europe together have resulted only in the mess we see there now; and America has been repaid only with scorn by a pack of welchers.

"I am in sympathy with your 'crazy' idea. More than that, I want to expand on it. Let a part of this forty billions we would *have* to spend for a ruinous war be used to establish at once—say as soon as possible—coöperatives for the unemployed. Let us borrow Upton Sinclair's plan of Production for Use by the Unemployed. I know that you and I don't often jibe with Sinclair, but he has a real idea here, and I have never yet seen it convincingly refuted. And don't forget: he came within an eye-lash of being elected governor of California on that basic plan. . . . Thus, the idea is within range of being put over. Call it anything one likes: coöperatives on a great scale, or the adaptation of the Swedish system to America.

"Whatever its name, let the Government undertake to round up idle factories, farms, etc., recondition them and turn them over to coöperative groups of unemployed people. The Government must *not* run them, only oversee them, and take its repayment through a share in the produce until the project is out of debt. The coöps could and should be self-governing. Let the Government at the same time cut relief to the bone, so that malingerers will have to work or starve. Newcomers into the coöp could be made to prove that for six months they had been unable to find employment in private industry. All products made by the coöp would be for use, but any financial profit from sale of excess production should belong to the coöp as a whole, and could be used to establish an insurance or security fund, or for the purchase of heavy machinery or any other need that could not be supplied by another coöp.

"Visionary? Well, so are security and justice through war—a thousand times more so—and crazier! Is it 'visionary' to take the horrible tax-load of even peace times off the backs of the public? And it is not one-tenth as stupid as the idea that a socialization of our distribution economy will work permanently and satisfactorily. By now we know it will not. We have been using that makeshift scheme—a sort of robbing Peter to support Paul, and both of them justly resenting it—to tide us over our emergency during the Depression. But we cannot support that scheme much longer. It is the craziest visionary idea over heard of, yet one we *had* to take and use, and one that has been highly effective and useful in preventing wide starvation. The trouble with it is—too much control by Government. I am afraid of that, for the wrong men might get into the Government—they often do!

"Today, everybody is rebelling against this plan of socialization of distribution that we have had to use. It is becoming terribly oppressive. Our problem in no sense compares to Europe's, at bottom. Europe generally faces a production problem. Ours is a problem of distribution of wealth. Our production economy is quite efficient in private hands; but our system of distribution is way off plumb, and beginning to cause grave distress.

"Coöperatives for the unemployed would attend to that distributive problem, at least in its graver aspects. We already have some coöps, and a few of them are amazingly effective. But they remain scorned little brothers of our distorted economic system. The coöp plan must have the open recognition and the vigorous support of the Government and the people as a whole, at least to get started. Big business at present stands in the way of that. On the one hand, business rages at the taxation necessary to bear our huge relief load; on the other it opposes a system which would tremendously relieve that load and so greatly lower its taxes. What it fears, patently, is that the coöp plan would spread, and so eat up big business altogether. Bosh! If capitalism is a cat with nine lives, then I have no doubt it still has three or four lives left in America. Anyhow, it is past time we took to heart the unendurable situation of that 'one-third of the nation ill-fed, ill-clothed and ill-housed,' that Roosevelt had the laudable courage to speak out loud about.

"Unless the people as a whole soon get a decent deal, *they* are the force which will propel us into war. They will not continue to endure poverty, anxiety, suppression. War, to them, would come as a blessed relief, a catharsis. The fatal but irresistible appeal of so-called 'war prosperity'! Unless, therefore, a sound, comprehensive means is found to keep the vast majority of our dispossessed occupied profitably and contentedly, they will—to repeat—force the country into war, through desperation, as sure as shooting. And back of that ghastly but understandable impulse are the propaganda of our 'collective security' crowd and the reactionary blindness of big business. The two work hand in hand. The 'collective security' propaganda must be analyzed and shown up; big business must come to terms.

"Business must be made to see. The present reactionary policies of business, if persisted in, will force us into war. And that war will in all likelihood be far more disastrous than happy for business. War means a fascistic control of business by Government; the end of the next war, with its insane, bloody, high-falutin ideologies—may well mean the end of *all* private business. Business could make very good terms right now, and no doubt keep going indefinitely in a profitable way—if it will accept the plain facts which scream in its ear. Coöperation *with* the times in which we live may save it; war *upon* those times will kill it as sure as God made little onions.

"It comes to this: Shall we hold the millions in subjection, shall we risk their lives and the welfare of the nation, just to maintain big business for a few more years in its ancient, smug, self-same traditions that are decades behind the times? It is not a matter of liking or not liking, but of facing a blistering fact. The United States can survive, and do it well, without going to war, if we have the courage to face that fact and adjust ourselves to it. I am not 'rooting for socialism,' I am not 'attacking' business as such. I am yelping for a fair deal for the masses as a whole, and for a very selfish reason—even narrow, if you will, and not at all sentimental. I don't want America to get into another war. I am convinced that nothing but ruin would be at the end of it. I want to spend that forty billions that a war would cost us entirely to *save* ourselves and not to destroy us. I don't give a hoot, either, what they call the 'system' which would produce the vital adjustment necessary to spare us from universal disaster.

"I don't want to meet any more engineers like the one I met at the Veterans' hospital. I don't know whether I told you about him. . . . In 1917 he graduated *magna cum laude* in engineering from an important university, and promptly joined the Engineering Corps and went to France. I saw his picture as captain of his college football team—a big, broad-shouldered, alert, swell-looking guy . . . and now, twenty years later, when he walked into my room at the hospital, I saw him in the flesh. Only he didn't walk, really. He oozed along in a maddeningly slow, painful crawl on his feet, like a two-footed turtle. He was bent and bloated. His head, neck, legs, ankles and belly were enormously bloated. Plainly, he knew that he was repulsive. He made me think of Markham's famous poem *Man With a Hoe*.

"He had been struck in the belly by shrapnel. Infection had set in, and he never really recovered, for it had left him with loss of control over his bowels. A helpless invalid, he has lived in Vets hospitals since the War, never out of one longer than two months, always has to go back. . . .

"I looked at him as he approached me with that turtle slowness, and I instinctively shuddered: God damn' you, get the hell out of here! Get away from me! Scram! Of course, I didn't say that out loud. All of us are snivelling cowards. Instead, I said the usual nice thing . . . you know. . . .

"Sentimental—your aunt Emma! I just hate the waste of war, that's all. The senseless waste of brains, of intelligence, of the engineers, the artists, the doctors and technicians. A civilization that has, or *thinks* it has, to justify itself by periodically ripping the guts out of such people, or battering their senses loose with gun-butts, for a lot of high-falutin slogans—to hell with it! You bet it *is* time that the Toms-Dicks-and-Harrys, the Judys-and-Sues, and the me's and you's, who, after all, are the ones who get it in the neck, whilst the self-appointed 'experts' in ivory tower or on corner soap-box sound their cunning tunes—it is time we came out and laid down a few plans of our own. We just might get enough of us together to put a stop to *some*, at least, of this madness."

To Ross Wills, from me:

" . . . I sympathize, of course, with the reasons you give why America must not go into 'the next war.' My own reasons, in addition to those already stated or implied, I would put something like this:

"You have read most of *My America* [in manuscript], and you know my feeling and idea about the Long Road. It is the American way, and I want to see that Road kept open. I want to keep what lights there are along it burning, and I want to see more of them lighted.

"I want the C.I.O. to keep going.

"I want the problem of the 30,000,000 New Americans to be pondered and acted upon.

"I want Jack Raper to be able to print his black bull in the Cleveland *Press* any time he likes to, as long as he lives; and I want Walter Locke to continue a free democratic man and editor in every respect. I don't want criticism supplanted by slanderous name-calling, of which there is entirely too much in America already. I want the avenues of criticism kept open.

"I want more experimenting in education.

"As it now operates (and as you are well aware), democracy is, in a great many respects, a defensive, almost negative, way of conducting human affairs. Generally, I think, this is due to the fact that human development has not yet reached a very high level. In a more local or particular sense, the fault is that all too many Americans are mere bystanders, rather than participants-in-things. This may be due in part to our prevailing educational methods and the movies and commercialized sports, all of which ask us only to sit and keep our eyes open; the movies even don't care if we fall asleep in the seat. . . . Well, I want America to be roused from this merely defensive nature of her democracy, and have a chance to determine what she ought to do about it and then proceed to do it.

"I want America to have a chance to think and debate about the methods of progress most suited to her, and gradually—not *via* any short-cuts—to deal with her internal discords and incongruities, which are dislocating her life, throwing it out of focus.

"I want America to remain America.

"I want America eventually to become a work of art."

Index